THE
top10★
OF EVERYTHING
2002

THE
top10
OF EVERYTHING
2002

—— RUSSELL ASH ——

A Dorling Kindersley Book

Contents

DORLING KINDERSLEY

Senior Editor Nicki Lampon

Senior Art Editor Kevin Ryan

DTP Designer Sonia Charbonnier

Production Louise Daly

Picture Research Anna Grapes

Managing Editor Sharon Lucas

Senior Managing Art Editor Derek Coombes

Author's Project Manager Aylla Macphail

Canadian edition produced by
INTERNATIONAL BOOK PRODUCTIONS
25A Morrow Ave., Toronto, ON M6R 2H9, Canada

Project Editor Barbara Hopkinson

Researcher Terri Rothman

Editor Judy Phillips

DTP Designer Dietmar Kokemohr

Canadian Cataloguing in Publication Data
Ash, Russell
    The top 10 of everything
Annual.
Issues for 2002-   published: Toronto : Dorling Kindersley, 2001- .
Includes index.
ISSN 1209-3882
ISBN 1-55363-003-3 (2002 ed.)
    1. World records. 2. Curiosities and wonders. I. Title. II Title: Top
ten of everything.
AG243.A75   031.02'05   C97-301371-0

Reproduction by Colourscan, Singapore
Printed and bound by Printer Industria Grafica, S.A., Barcelona, Spain

01 02 03 3 2 1

See our website at

www.dk.com

Introduction

It's a Fact

If you have been buying *The Top 10 of Everything* every year since it was first published, you will now have 13 copies on your book shelf. Fortunately, I do not suffer from triskaidekaphobia (the fear of the number 13), but it is through researching and compiling Top 10 lists that I have discovered a wealth of unusual facts – such as the word triskaidekaphobia. In this year's volume, you too can discover facts, from the 10 places with the heaviest daily downpours to the Top 10 skateboarders, and from the first lie detector to the identity of the originals behind James Bond and Barbie.

A Changing World

During recent years, certain lists have become widely featured in the press, among them lists of school league tables and richest people, while the popularity of general knowledge is exemplified by the increasing number of TV quiz shows. Over the past 13 years, the information that this book presents has changed, and the nature of Top 10 lists has changed too. The Top 10 professions of cellular phone users was once of interest, but now that so many people in Western countries have cellular phones, such a list is synonymous with the Top 10 most common professions. Meanwhile, lists containing entries that have been valid for many centuries may alter: while work was in progress on this edition, the 5th tallest statue in the world, the 53-m (173-ft) Buddha at Bamian, Afghanistan, carved in the 3rd–4th centuries AD, was destroyed by the Taliban.

Information Superhighway

In the past, it often took years for data to be processed and disseminated. Today, the use of computers and the Internet means that information is more quickly and more readily available. One of the problems with information is that it piles up. Only a few hundred years ago, an educated person could be well informed about almost every aspect of the arts and sciences, but as each generation adds to the sum total of knowledge, so the task of sifting it for the items you require becomes an occupation in itself. I hope that *The Top 10 of Everything* offers some shortcuts through the information quagmire.

In and Out

To newcomers to *The Top 10 of Everything* it is worth mentioning that there are no "bests," other than bestsellers, and no "worsts" (with the exception of lists about disasters and murders, which are measurable by numbers of victims). The book focuses on superlatives in numerous categories, and also contains a variety of "firsts" or "latests,"

which recognize the pioneers and most recent achievers in various fields of endeavor. Top 10 lists of films are based on worldwide box office income, and those on such topics as recorded music, videos, DVDs, and books are based on sales, unless otherwise stated.

Thanks for Everything

My ever-expanding network of experts has enabled me to ensure that certain lists are constantly updated as new data become available. As ever, I want to thank the many people who have supplied information, especially private individuals, experts, and enthusiasts, who provide some of the most fascinating and otherwise quite unobtainable information. If you have any list ideas or comments, please write to me c/o the publishers or e-mail me direct at ash@pavilion.co.uk.

Other recent Dorling Kindersley books by Russell Ash:
  The Factastic Book of 1,001 Lists
  The Factastic Book of Comparisons
  Great Wonders of the World

Special Features

• More than 1,000 lists in many new categories make this the **most comprehensive** *Top 10 of Everything ever.*

• **Hundreds of new lists** are included, from the 10 countries with the most teenage brides to the Top 10 baked bean consumers.

• Interesting and unusual **2002 anniversaries** are celebrated throughout with "100 Years Ago" and "50 Years Ago" features.

• Numerous "Who Was...?" entries focus on the people behind **famous names**.

• "Did You Know?" entries offer **offbeat sidelights** on the subjects explored.

• **Quiz questions** with multichoice answers appear throughout the book.

THE UNIVERSE & THE EARTH

Star Gazing

STARS NEAREST TO THE EARTH*

	STAR	LIGHT-YEARS	MILES (MILLIONS)	KM (MILLIONS)
1	Proxima Centauri	4.22	24,792,500	39,923,310
2	Alpha Centauri	4.35	25,556,250	41,153,175
3	Barnard's Star	5.98	35,132,500	56,573,790
4	Wolf 359	7.75	45,531,250	73,318,875
5	Lalande 21185	8.22	48,292,500	77,765,310
6	Luyten 726-8	8.43	49,526,250	79,752,015
7	Sirius	8.65	50,818,750	81,833,325
8	Ross 154	9.45	55,518,750	89,401,725
9	Ross 248	10.40	61,100,000	98,389,200
10	Epsilon Eridani	10.80	63,450,000	102,173,400

* Excluding the Sun

A spaceship traveling at 40,237 km/h (25,000 mph) – which is faster than any human has yet reached in space – would take more than 113,200 years to reach the Earth's closest star, Proxima Centauri. While the nearest stars in this list lie just over four light-years away from the Earth, others within the Milky Way lie at a distance of 2,500 light-years. Our own galaxy may span as much as 100,000 light-years from end to end, with the Sun some 25,000 to 30,000 light-years from its center.

NEAR NEIGHBOR

Proxima Centauri, Earth's closest star beyond the Sun, was discovered in 1913 by Scottish astronomer Robert Thorburn Innes. It has 10 percent of the Sun's mass but only 0.006 percent of its luminosity.

BODIES IN THE SOLAR SYSTEM WITH THE GREATEST SURFACE GRAVITY*

	BODY	SURFACE GRAVITY	WEIGHT (KG)#
1	Sun	27.90	1813.50
2	Jupiter	2.64	171.6
3	Neptune	1.20	78.00
4	Uranus	1.17	76.05
5	Saturn	1.16	75.40
6	Earth	1.00	65.00
7	Venus	0.90	58.50
8 =	Mars	0.38	24.70
=	Mercury	0.38	24.70
10	Pluto	0.06	3.90

* Excluding satellites

 # Of a 65 kg (143 lb) adult on the body's surface

SMALL WONDER

Pluto is less than a fifth of the size of the Earth. Not only is it the smallest of the solar system's planets, it also has the lowest gravity. It was discovered in 1930 by American astronomer Clyde Tombaugh.

THIN ICE

Saturn is the furthest planet that can be seen with the naked eye. Its rings, which are composed of ice, are up to 270,000 km (167,770 miles) in diameter, but only a few meters thick.

TOP 10 ★
MOST MASSIVE BODIES IN THE SOLAR SYSTEM*

	BODY	MASS#
1	Sun	332,800.000
2	Jupiter	317.828
3	Saturn	95.161
4	Neptune	17.148
5	Uranus	14.536
6	Earth	1.000
7	Venus	0.815
8	Mars	0.10745
9	Mercury	0.05527
10	Pluto	0.0022

* *Excluding satellites*

Compared with the Earth = 1; the mass of Earth is approximately 72.6 trillion tonnes (80 trillion tons)

TOP 10 ★
GALAXIES NEAREST TO THE EARTH

	GALAXY	DISTANCE (LIGHT-YEARS)
1	Large Cloud of Magellan	169,000
2	Small Cloud of Magellan	190,000
3	Ursa Minor dwarf	250,000
4	Draco dwarf	260,000
5	Sculptor dwarf	280,000
6	Fornax dwarf	420,000
7	=Leo I dwarf	750,000
	=Leo II dwarf	750,000
9	Barnard's Galaxy	1,700,000
10	Andromeda Spiral	2,200,000

These, and other galaxies, are members of the so-called "Local Group," although with vast distances such as these, "local" is clearly a relative term.

TOP 10 ★
BODIES IN THE SOLAR SYSTEM WITH THE GREATEST ESCAPE VELOCITY*

	BODY	ESCAPE VELOCITY (KM/SEC)
1	Sun	617.50
2	Jupiter	60.22
3	Saturn	32.26
4	Neptune	23.90
5	Uranus	22.50
6	Earth	11.18
7	Venus	10.36
8	Mars	5.03
9	Mercury	4.25
10	Pluto	1.18

* *Excluding satellites*

Escape velocity is the speed a rocket has to attain upon launching to overcome the gravitational pull of the body it is leaving. The escape velocity of the Moon is 2.38 km/sec (1.48 miles/sec).

TOP 10 ★
LONGEST YEARS IN THE SOLAR SYSTEM

	BODY	LENGTH OF YEAR* YEARS	DAYS
1	Pluto	247	256
2	Neptune	164	298
3	Uranus	84	4
4	Saturn	29	168
5	Jupiter	11	314
6	Mars	1	322
7	Earth		365
8	Venus		225
9	Mercury		88
10	Sun		0

* *Period of orbit around the Sun, in Earth years/ days (based on a non-leap year of 365 days)*

TOP 10 ★
LARGEST BODIES IN THE SOLAR SYSTEM

	BODY	MAXIMUM DIAMETER MILES	KM
1	Sun	865,036	1,392,140
2	Jupiter	88,846	142,984
3	Saturn	74,898	120,536
4	Uranus	31,763	51,118
5	Neptune	30,778	49,532
6	Earth	7,926	12,756
7	Venus	7,520	12,103
8	Mars	4,222	6,794
9	Ganymede	3,274	5,269
10	Titan	3,200	5,150

Most of the planets are visible from the Earth with the naked eye and have been observed since ancient times. The exceptions are Uranus, discovered on March 13, 1781, by the British astronomer Sir William Herschel; Neptune, found by German astronomer Johann Galle on September 23, 1846 (Galle was led to his discovery by the independent calculations of the French astronomer Urbain Leverrier and the British mathematician John Adams); and, outside the Top 10, Pluto, located using photographic techniques by American astronomer Clyde Tombaugh on March 13, 1930.

Did You Know? The name of the planet Pluto was suggested two days after its discovery by Venetia Burney, an 11-year-old English schoolgirl. Pluto is the Roman god of the underworld, but the name also begins with the initials of Percival Lowell, the astronomer who had suggested its existence.

Asteroids, Meteorites & Comets

MOST FREQUENTLY SEEN COMETS

	COMET	YEARS BETWEEN APPEARANCES
1	Encke	3.302
2	Grigg-Skjellerup	4.908
3	Honda-Mrkós-Pajdusáková	5.210
4	Tempel 2	5.259
5	Neujmin 2	5.437
6	Brorsen	5.463
7	Tuttle-Giacobini-Kresák	5.489
8	Tempel-L. Swift	5.681
9	Tempel 1	5.982
10	Pons-Winnecke	6.125

These and several other comets return with regularity (although with some notable variations), while others have such long orbits that they may not be seen again for many thousands, or even millions, of years.

OBJECTS COMING CLOSEST TO THE EARTH

	NAME/DESIGNATION	DUE DATE*	DISTANCE# MILES	DISTANCE# KM
1	1999 RQ36	Sep 23, 2080	130,130	209,440
2	1998 HH49	Oct 17, 2023	232,393	374,000
3	1999 AN10	Aug 7, 2027	241,689	388,960
4	1999 RQ36	Sep 23, 2060	455,490	733,040
5	1999 MN	June 3, 2010	492,673	792,880
6	Hathor (2340)	Oct 21, 2086	520,560	837,760
7	1999 RM45	Mar 3, 2021	548,447	882,640
8	1997 XF11	Oct 26, 2028	567,038	912,560
9	2000 LF3	June 16, 2046	604,221	972,400
10	Hathor (2340)	Oct 21, 2069	613,517	987,360

* Of closest approach to the Earth

\# Closest distance from Earth

Source: *NASA*

It is believed that there are up to 2,000 "Near-Earth objects" (mostly asteroids and comets) over 1 km (0.6 miles) in diameter that approach the Earth's orbit.

COMETS THAT HAVE COME CLOSEST TO THE EARTH

	COMET	DATE*	DISTANCE# MILES	DISTANCE# KM
1	Comet of 1491	Feb 20, 1491	873,784	1,406,220
2	Lexell	July 1, 1770	1,403,633	2,258,928
3	Tempel-Tuttle	Oct 26, 1366	2,128,688	3,425,791
4	IRAS-Araki-Alcock	May 11, 1983	2,909,516	4,682,413
5	Halley	Apr 10, 837	3,104,724	4,996,569
6	Biela	Dec 9, 1805	3,402,182	5,475,282
7	Grischow	Feb 8, 1743	3,625,276	5,834,317
8	Pons-Winnecke	June 26, 1927	3,662,458	5,894,156
9	Comet of 1014	Feb 24, 1014	3,783,301	6,088,633
10	La Hire	Apr 20, 1702	4,062,168	6,537,427

* Of closest approach to the Earth

\# Closest distance from the Earth

HALLEY'S COMET

The predicted return of Halley's Comet, seen here during its most recent appearance in 1986, proved the theory that comets follow fixed orbits.

TOP 10 ⭐
LARGEST METEORITES EVER FOUND

LOCATION	ESTIMATED WEIGHT TONNES
1 Hoba West, Grootfontein, Namibia	more than 60.0
2 Ahnighito ("The Tent"), Cape York, West Greenland	57.3
3 Campo del Cielo, Argentina	41.4
4 Canyon Diablo*, Arizona	30.0
5 Sikhote-Alin, Russia	27.0
6 Chupaderos, Mexico	24.2
7 Bacuberito, Mexico	22.0
8 Armanty, Western Mongolia	20.0
9 Mundrabilla#, Western Australia	17.0
10 Mbosi, Tanzania	16.0

* Formed Meteor Crater; fragmented – total in public collections is around 11.5 tonnes
# In two parts

TOP 10 🍁
LARGEST METEORITES FOUND IN CANADA

LOCATION/YEAR FOUND	ESTIMATED WEIGHT KG
1 Madoc, Ontario, 1864	167.5
2 Iron Creek, Alberta, 1869	146.0
3 Abee, Alberta, 1952	107.0
4 Osseo, Ontario, 1931	46.3
5 Dresden, Ontario, 1939	39.9
6 Manitouwabing, Ontario, 1962	39.0
7 Springwater*, Saskatchewan, 1931	38.6
8 Bruderheim, Alberta, 1960	31.2
9 Vulcan, Alberta, 1962	19.0
10 Springwater#, Saskatchewan, 1931	18.6

* Largest mass of three masses
# Second largest mass of three masses
Source: Geological Survey of Canada

The number of meteorites falling has been calculated to amount to some 500 a year across the globe. The total number of meteorites found in Canada (falls or finds of complete masses) is 58.

TOP 10 ⭐
SOURCES OF ASTEROID NAMES

SOURCE	ASTEROIDS*
1 Astronomers, astrophysicists, and planetary scientists	1,040
2 Places and cultures	822
3 Scientists other than astronomers	551
4 Mythological characters	439
5 Astronomers' families and friends	406
6 Historical personalities	360
7 Writers and editors	275
8 Amateur astronomers	132
9 Musicians, composers, and film and TV directors	130
10 Literary characters	112

* Based on an analysis of 4,619 named asteroids within the first 6,000 discovered
Source: Jacob Schwartz, Asteroid Name Encyclopedia, 1995

Asteroid names have also been derived from individuals in such fields as singing and dancing, and art and architecture.

EARTH IMPACT

The Canyon Diablo, or Barringer meteorite crater, in Arizona, one of the largest on the Earth, was caused by the impact of a meteorite weighing 63,000 tonnes, of which some 30 tonnes have been recovered.

TOP 10 ⭐
LARGEST ASTEROIDS

NAME	YEAR DISCOVERED	DIAMETER MILES	KM
1 Ceres	1801	582	936
2 Pallas	1802	377	607
3 Vesta	1807	322	519
4 Hygeia	1849	279	450
5 Euphrosyne	1854	229	370
6 Interamnia	1910	217	349
7 Davida	1903	200	322
8 Cybele	1861	192	308
9 Europa	1858	179	288
10 Patientia	1899	171	275

Asteroids, sometimes known as "minor planets," are fragments of rock orbiting between Mars and Jupiter. There are perhaps 45,000 of them, but only about 10 percent have been named. The first and largest to be discovered was Ceres.

In 1946, an earthquake hit Vancouver Island. What was its magnitude on the Richter scale?
A 6.9
B 7.3
C 8.1
see p.29 for the answer

HUBBLE

American astronomer Edwin Powell Hubble (1889–1953) led a varied career, including heavyweight boxing and studying law at Oxford University, UK, before becoming a professional astronomer. After World War I, he worked at the Mount Wilson Observatory, home of the then most powerful telescope in the world. In 1923 he proved that the Universe extended beyond the Milky Way, and in 1929 that the universe is expanding. This became known as Hubble's Law. Named in his honor, the Hubble Telescope, launched in 1990 by Space Shuttle *Discovery*, has enabled exploration of distant galaxies without the atmospheric interference that is encountered on the Earth.

TOP 10 MOST RECENT PLANETARY MOONS TO BE DISCOVERED

(Moon/planet/year)

❶ **S/1999J1**, Jupiter, 2000
❷ = **Prospero**, Uranus, 1999; = **Setebos**, Uranus, 1999; = **Stephano**, Uranus, 1999
❺ = **Caliban**, Uranus, 1997;
= **Sycorax**, Uranus, 1997 ❼ **Pan**, Saturn, 1990
❽ = **Despina**, Neptune, 1989; = **Naiad**, Neptune, 1989; = **Thalassa**, Neptune, 1989

Space probe *Voyager 2* discovered six moons of Neptune on the same day (Aug 25, 1989). Those listed in the Top 10 were the first, followed by Galatea, Larissa, and Proteus.

TOP 10 ★ LARGEST REFLECTING TELESCOPES

	TELESCOPE/LOCATION	APERTURE FT	APERTURE M
1	**Keck I & II Telescopes***, Mauna Kea, Hawaii	32.8	10.0
2	**Hobby-Eberly Telescope**, Mount Fowlkes, Texas	30.9	9.2
3	**Subaru Telescope**, Mauna Kea, Hawaii	27.2	8.3
4	**Gemini North Telescope**, Mauna Kea, Hawaii	25.6	8.0
5	**MMT**#, Mount Hopkins, Arizona	21.3	6.5
6	**Bolshoi Teleskop Azimutalnyi**, Nizhny Arkhyz, Russia	19.6	6.0
7	**Hale Telescope**, Palomar Mountain, California	16.4	5.0
8	**William Herschel Telescope**, La Palma, Canary Islands, Spain	13.8	4.2
9	**Victor Blanco Telescope**, Gerro Tololo, Chile	13.1	4.0
10	**Anglo-Australian Telescope**, Coonabarabran, NSW, Australia	12.8	3.9

* *Identical telescopes that work in tandem to produce the largest reflecting surface*

Formerly the Multiple Mirror Telescope

Antu, Kueyen, and Melipal, three telescopes located in Cerro Paranal, Chile, are soon to be combined to form the appropriately named Very Large Telescope, which will take first place in this list with an aperture of 16.4 m (53.8 ft). The Keck telescopes will combine with several smaller scopes to form the 14.6 m (47.9 ft) Keck Interferometer.

GALILEAN DISCOVERY
Ganymede, largest of Jupiter's satellites, was among the four to be discovered by Galileo, on January 7, 1610, using the newly invented telescope.

THE 10 ★ FIRST PLANETARY MOONS TO BE DISCOVERED

	MOON/DISCOVERER	PLANET	YEAR
1	**Moon**	Earth	Ancient
2	=**Callisto**, Galileo Galilei	Jupiter	1610
	=**Europa**, Galileo Galilei	Jupiter	1610
	=**Ganymede**, Galileo Galilei	Jupiter	1610
	=**Io**, Galileo Galilei	Jupiter	1610
6	**Titan**, Christian Huygens	Saturn	1655
7	**Iapetus**, Giovanni Cassini	Saturn	1671
8	**Rhea**, Giovanni Cassini	Saturn	1672
9	=**Dione**, Giovanni Cassini	Saturn	1684
	=**Tethys**, Giovanni Cassini	Saturn	1684

While the Earth's moon has been observed since ancient times, it was not until the development of the telescope that Italian astronomer Galileo was able to discover (on January 7, 1610) the first moons of another planet. These, which are Jupiter's four largest, were named by German astronomer Simon Marius and are known as the Galileans.

HEAVENLY TWINS
Financed by US philanthropist W. M. Keck, twin telescopes Keck I (1993) and II (1996) on Mauna Kea, Hawaii, are the world's largest optical instruments.

Did You Know? Until 1986, Uranus was believed to have only five moons, but in that year interplanetary probe *Voyager 2* discovered 10 more, all but one of which were named after Shakespearean characters.

THE 10 ★
FIRST PLANETARY PROBES

PROBE/COUNTRY	PLANET	ARRIVAL*
1 *Venera 4*, USSR	Venus	Oct 18, 1967
2 *Venera 5*, USSR	Venus	May 16, 1969
3 *Venera 6*, USSR	Venus	May 17, 1969
4 *Venera 7*, USSR	Venus	Dec 15, 1970
5 *Mariner 9*, US	Mars	Nov 13, 1971
6 *Mars 2*, USSR	Mars	Nov 27, 1971
7 *Mars 3*, USSR	Mars	Dec 2, 1971
8 *Venera 8*, USSR	Venus	July 22, 1972
9 *Venera 9*, USSR	Venus	Oct 22, 1975
10 *Venera 10*, USSR	Venus	Oct 25, 1975

* *Successfully entered orbit or landed*

This list excludes "flybys" – probes that passed by but did not land on the surface of the planet. The US's *Pioneer 10*, for example, flew past Jupiter on December 3, 1973, but did not land.

VENUSIAN VOLCANOES

Mapped by the Magellan probe, the volcanoes of Sif Mons (left) and Gula Mons (right) stand out above the lava surface of the Eistla Regio area of Venus.

THE 10 ★
FIRST BODIES TO HAVE BEEN VISITED BY SPACECRAFT

BODY	SPACECRAFT/COUNTRY	DATE
1 Moon	*Luna 1*, USSR	Jan 2, 1959
2 Venus	*Venera 1*, USSR	May 19, 1961
3 Sun	*Pioneer 5*, US	Aug 10, 1961
4 Mars	*Mariner 4*, US	July 14, 1965
5 Jupiter	*Pioneer 10*, US	Dec 3, 1973
6 Mercury	*Mariner 10*, US	Mar 29, 1974
7 Saturn	*Pioneer 11*, US	Sep 1, 1979
8 Comet Giacobini- Zinner	*International Sun-Earth Explorer 3* (*International Cometary Explorer*) Europe/US	Sep 11, 1985
9 Uranus	*Voyager 2*, US	Jan 30, 1986
10 Halley's Comet	*Vega 1*, USSR	Mar 6, 1986

Only the first spacecraft successfully to approach or land on each body is included. Several of the bodies listed have since been visited on subsequent occasions, either by "flybys," orbiters, or landers. Other bodies also visited since the first 10 include Neptune (by *Voyager 2*, US, 1989).

THE 10 ★
FIRST UNMANNED MOON LANDINGS

NAME	COUNTRY	DATE (LAUNCH/IMPACT)
1 *Lunik 2*	USSR	Sep 12/14, 1959
2 *Ranger 4**	US	Apr 23/26, 1962
3 *Ranger 6*	US	Jan 30/Feb 2, 1964
4 *Ranger 7*	US	July 28/31, 1964
5 *Ranger 8*	US	Feb 17/20, 1965
6 *Ranger 9*	US	Mar 21/24, 1965
7 *Luna 5**	USSR	May 9/12, 1965
8 *Luna 7**	USSR	Oct 4/8, 1965
9 *Luna 8**	USSR	Dec 3/7, 1965
10 *Luna 9*	USSR	Jan 31/Feb 3, 1966

* *Crash landing*

In addition to these 10, debris left on the surface of the Moon includes the remains of several further *Luna* craft, including unmanned sample collectors and *Lunakhod 1* and *2* (1966–71; all Soviet), seven *Surveyors* (1966–68), and five *Lunar Orbiters* (1966–67; all US).

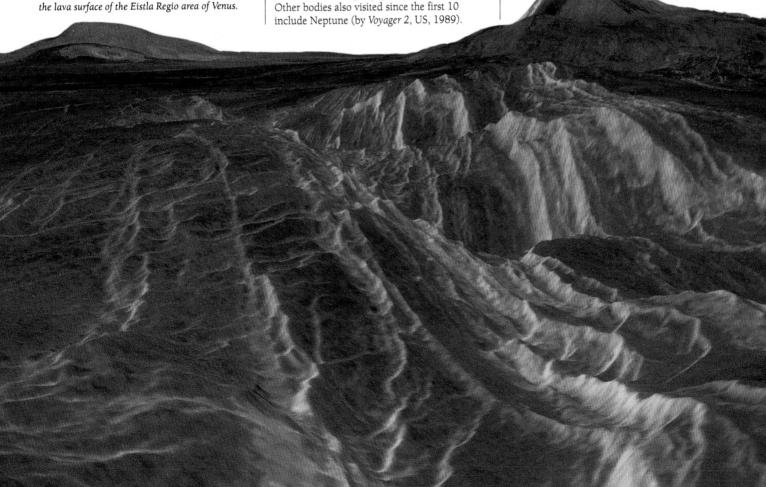

Space Explorers

FIRST MOONWALKERS

	ASTRONAUT	SPACECRAFT	TOTAL EVA* HR:MIN	MISSION DATES
1	Neil A. Armstrong	Apollo 11	2:32	July 16–24, 1969
2	Edwin E. ("Buzz") Aldrin	Apollo 11	2:15	July 16–24, 1969
3	Charles Conrad Jr.	Apollo 12	7:45	Nov 14–24, 1969
4	Alan L. Bean	Apollo 12	7:45	Nov 14–24, 1969
5	Alan B. Shepard	Apollo 14	9:23	Jan 31–Feb 9, 1971
6	Edgar D. Mitchell	Apollo 14	9:23	Jan 31–Feb 9, 1971
7	David R. Scott	Apollo 15	19:08	July 26–Aug 7, 1971
8	James B. Irwin	Apollo 15	18:35	July 26–Aug 7, 1971
9	John W. Young	Apollo 16	20:14	Apr 16–27, 1972
10	Charles M. Duke	Apollo 16	20:14	Apr 16–27, 1972

* Extra Vehicular Activity (i.e. time spent out of the lunar module on the Moon's surface)

Six US Apollo missions resulted in successful Moon landings (Apollo 13, April 11–17, 1970, was aborted after an oxygen tank exploded). During the last of these (Apollo 17, December 7–19, 1972), Eugene A. Cernan and Harrison H. Schmitt became the only other astronauts to date who have walked on the surface of the Moon.

FIRST CANADIAN ASTRONAUTS

	ASTRONAUT	PROFESSION	FLIGHT DATES
1	Marc Garneau	Electrical engineer	1) Oct 1984 2) May 1996 3) Nov 2000
2	Roberta Bondar	Neurologist	Jan 1992
3	Steven MacLean	Laser physicist	Oct 1992
	Robert Thirsk	Medical doctor, mech. engineer	Jun 1996
5	Bjarni Tryggvason	Eng. physicist, mathematician	Aug 1997
6	Ken Money	Physiologist	No space missions
7	Col. Chris Hadfield*	Mechanical engineer, test pilot	1) Nov 1995 2) Apr 2001
8	Capt. Mike McKay	Engineer	No space missions
9	Dave Williams	Emergency physician	Apr 1998
10	Julie Payette	Electrical/computer engineer	May 1999

* On April 22, 2001, Chris Hadfield became the first Canadian to walk in space.

Source: Canadian Space Agency

MAN ON THE MOON

On April 21, 1972, Apollo 16 commander John W. Young (shown here), along with Charles M. Duke (who took this photograph), became the 9th and 10th of the 12 people ever to set foot on the Moon.

TOP 10 ★
YOUNGEST ASTRONAUTS AND COSMONAUTS

	ASTRONAUT OR COSMONAUT*	FIRST FLIGHT	AGE#
1	Gherman S. Titov	June 17, 1970	25
2	Valentina V. Tereshkova	June 16, 1963	26
3	Boris B. Yegorov	Oct 15, 1964	26
4	Yuri A. Gagarin	Apr 12, 1961	27
5	Helen P. Sharman, UK	May 18, 1991	27
6	Dumitru D. Prunatiu, Romania	May 14, 1981	28
7	Valery F. Bykovsky	June 14, 1963	28
8	Salman Abdel Aziz Al-Saud, Saudi Arabia	June 17, 1985	28
9	Vladimir Remek, Czechoslovakia	Mar 2, 1978	29
10	Abdul Ahad Mohmand, Afghanistan	Aug 29, 1988	29

* All from Russia unless otherwise indicated

\# Those of apparently identical age have been ranked according to their precise age in days

TOP 10 ★
OLDEST ASTRONAUTS AND COSMONAUTS

	ASTRONAUT OR COSMONAUT*	LAST FLIGHT	AGE#
1	John H. Glenn	Nov 6, 1998	77
2	F. Story Musgrave	Dec 7, 1996	61
3	Vance D. Brand	Dec 11, 1990	59
4	Jean-Loup Chrétien, France	Oct 6, 1997	59
5	Valery V. Ryumin, Russia	June 12, 1998	58
6	Karl G. Henize	Aug 6, 1985	58
7	Roger K. Crouch	July 17, 1997	56
8	William E. Thornton	May 6, 1985	56
9	Claude Nicollier, Switzerland	Dec 28, 1999	55
10	Don L. Lind	May 6, 1985	54

* All from the US unless otherwise indicated

\# Those of apparently identical age have been ranked according to their precise age in days

THE 10 ★
FIRST COUNTRIES TO HAVE ASTRONAUTS OR COSMONAUTS IN ORBIT

	COUNTRY/ASTRONAUT OR COSMONAUT	DATE*
1	USSR, Yuri A. Gagarin	Apr 12, 1961
2	US, John H. Glenn	Feb 20, 1962
3	Czechoslovakia, Vladimir Remek	Mar 2, 1978
4	Poland, Miroslaw Hermaszewski	June 27, 1978
5	East Germany, Sigmund Jahn	Aug 26, 1978
6	Bulgaria, Georgi I. Ivanov	Apr 10, 1979
7	Hungary, Bertalan Farkas	May 26, 1980
8	Vietnam, Pham Tuan	July 23, 1980
9	Cuba, Arnaldo T. Mendez	Sep 18, 1980
10	Mongolia, Jugderdemidiyn Gurragcha	Mar 22, 1981

* Of first space entry of a national of that country

THE 10 ★
FIRST WOMEN IN SPACE

	ASTRONAUT OR COSMONAUT/ COUNTRY/SPACECRAFT	DATE
1	Valentina V. Tereshkova, USSR, *Vostok 6*	June 16–19, 1963
2	Svetlana Savitskaya, USSR, *Soyuz T7*	Aug 19, 1982
3	Sally K. Ride, US, *Challenger STS-7*	June 18–24, 1983
4	Judith A. Resnik, US, *Discovery STS-41-D*	Aug 30–Sep 5, 1984
5	Kathryn D. Sullivan, US, *Challenger STS-41-G*	Oct 5–13, 1984
6	Anna L. Fisher, US, *Discovery STS-51-A*	Nov 8–16, 1984
7	Margaret Rhea Seddon, US, *Discovery STS-51-D*	Apr 12–19, 1985
8	Shannon W. Lucid, US, *Discovery STS-51-G*	June 17–24, 1985
9	Bonnie J. Dunbar, US, *Challenger STS-61-A*	Oct 30–Nov 6, 1985
10	Mary L. Cleave, US, *Atlantis STS-61-B*	Nov 26–Dec 3, 1985

THE 10 ★
FIRST IN-FLIGHT SPACE FATALITIES

ASTRONAUT OR COSMONAUT(S)/INCIDENT

1 Vladimir M. Komarov
Launched on April 24, 1967, Soviet spaceship Soyuz 1 experienced various technical problems during its 18th orbit. After a successful re-entry, the capsule parachute was deployed at 7,010 m (23,000 ft), but its lines became tangled and it crash-landed near Orsk in the Urals, killing Komarov (the survivor of a previous one-day flight on October 12, 1964), who thus became the first-ever space fatality.

2 =Georgi T. Dobrovolsky
=Viktor I. Patsayev
=Vladislav N. Volkov
After a then-record 23 days in space, including a link-up with the Salyut space station, the Soviet Soyuz 9 mission ended in disaster on June 29, 1971, when the capsule depressurized during re-entry. Although it landed intact, all three cosmonauts – who were not wearing spacesuits – were found dead. The ashes of the three men were buried, along with those of fellow cosmonauts Yuri Gagarin and Vladimir Komarov, at the Kremlin, Moscow. Spacesuits have been worn during re-entry on all subsequent missions.

5 =Gregory B. Jarvis
=Sharon C. McAuliffe
=Ronald E. McNair
=Ellison S. Onizuka
=Judith A. Resnik
=Francis R. Scobee
=Michael J. Smith
The Challenger STS-51-L, the 25th Space Shuttle mission, exploded on take-off from Cape Canaveral, Florida, on January 28, 1986. The cause was determined to have been leakage of seals in the joint between rocket sections. The disaster, watched by thousands on the ground and millions on worldwide television, halted the US space program until a comprehensive review of the engineering problems and revision of the safety methods had been undertaken. It was not until September 29, 1988, that the next Space Shuttle, Discovery STS-26, was successfully launched.

The 11 cosmonauts and astronauts in this list are, to date, the only inflight space fatalities. They are not, however, the only victims of accidents during the space programs of the former USSR and the US. On October 24, 1960, for example, five months before the first manned flight, Field Marshal Mitrofan Nedelin, the commander of the USSR's Strategic Rocket Forces, and an unknown number of other personnel (165 according to some authorities), were killed in the catastrophic launchpad explosion of an unmanned space rocket at the Baikonur cosmodrome.

What is Manitoulin island's claim to fame?
see p.20 for the answer

A It has the largest island racoon population
B It is the largest island in a lake
C It has the highest island mountain

17

DEEPEST OCEANS AND SEAS

OCEAN OR SEA	GREATEST DEPTH		AVERAGE DEPTH	
	FT	M	FT	M
1 Pacific Ocean	35,837	10,924	13,215	4,028
2 Indian Ocean	24,460	7,455	13,002	3,963
3 Atlantic Ocean	30,246	9,219	12,880	3,926
4 Caribbean Sea	22,788	6,946	8,685	2,647
5 South China Sea	16,456	5,016	5,419	1,652
6 Bering Sea	15,659	4,773	5,075	1,547
7 Gulf of Mexico	12,425	3,787	4,874	1,486
8 Mediterranean Sea	15,197	4,632	4,688	1,429
9 Japan Sea	12,276	3,742	4,429	1,350
10 Arctic Ocean	18,456	5,625	3,953	1,205

The deepest point in the deepest ocean is the Marianas Trench in the Pacific Ocean, at a depth of 10,924 m (35,837 ft), according to a recent survey. The slightly lesser depth of 10,916 m (35,814 ft) was recorded on January 23, 1960, by Jacques Piccard and Donald Walsh in their 17.7-m (58-ft) long bathyscaphe *Trieste 2* during the deepest-ever ocean descent. Whichever is correct, it is close to 11 km (6.8 miles) down, or almost 29 times the height of the Empire State Building.

HIGHEST WATERFALLS

WATERFALL	RIVER	LOCATION	TOTAL DROP	
			FT	M
1 Angel	Carrao	Venezuela	3,212	979*
2 Tugela	Tugela	South Africa	3,107	947
3 Utigård	Jostedal Glacier	Norway	2,625	800
4 Mongefossen	Monge	Norway	2,540	774
5 Yosemite	Yosemite Creek	US	2,425	739
6 Østre Mardøla Foss	Mardals	Norway	2,152	656
7 Tyssestrengane	Tysso	Norway	2,120	646
8 Cuquenán	Arabopo	Venezuela	2,000	610
9 Sutherland	Arthur	New Zealand	1,904	580
10 Kjellfossen	Naero	Norway	1,841	561

* *Longest single drop 807 m (2,648 ft)*

FALL AND ANGEL

On November 16, 1933, American adventurer James Angel wrote in his diary, "I found myself a waterfall." He had discovered the world's highest falls, later named Angel Falls.

TOP 10 ★
DEEPEST DEEP-SEA TRENCHES*

	TRENCH	DEEPEST POINT FT	M
1	Marianas	35,837	10,924
2	Tonga#	35,430	10,800
3	Philippine	34,436	10,497
4	Kermadec#	32,960	10,047
5	Bonin	32,786	9,994
6	New Britain	32,609	9,940
7	Kuril	31,985	9,750
8	Izu	31,805	9,695
9	Puerto Rico	28,229	8,605
10	Yap	27,973	8,527

* With the exception of the Puerto Rico (Atlantic), all the trenches are in the Pacific.

\# Some authorities consider these to be parts of the same feature.

Each of the eight deepest ocean trenches would be deep enough to submerge Mount Everest, which is 8,850 m (29,035 ft) above sea level.

TOP 10 ★
LONGEST RIVERS

	RIVER/LOCATION	LENGTH MILES	KM
1	Nile, Tanzania/Uganda/ Sudan/Egypt	4,145	6,670
2	Amazon, Peru/Brazil	4,007	6,448
3	Yangtze–Kiang, China	3,915	6,300
4	Mississippi–Missouri– Red Rock, US	3,710	5,971
5	Yenisey–Angara– Selenga, Mongolia/Russia	3,442	5,540
6	Huang Ho (Yellow River), China	3,395	5,464
7	Ob'–Irtysh, Mongolia/ Kazakhstan/Russia	3,362	5,410
8	Congo, Angola/ Dem. Rep. of Congo	2,920	4,700
9	Lena–Kirenga, Russia	2,734	4,400
10	Mekong, Tibet/China/ Myanmar (Burma)/ Laos/Cambodia/Vietnam	2,703	4,350

AMAZON v NILE

Although the Amazon is ranked second in length, it is possible to sail from it up the Rio Pará, a total of 6,750 km (4,195 miles), which is a greater distance than the length of the Nile.

TOP 10 🍁
LONGEST RIVERS IN CANADA

	RIVER	LENGTH MILES	KM
1	Mackenzie	2,635	4,241
2	St. Lawrence	1,900	3,058
3	Nelson	1,600	2,575
4	Columbia	1,243	2,000
5	Saskatchewan	1,205	1,939
6	Peace	1,195	1,923
7	Churchill	1,000	1,609
8	South Saskatchewan	865	1,392
9	Fraser	851	1,370
10	Yukon*	714	1,149

* Canadian portion only, from the International Boundary to the head of the Nisutlin River. If the total length of the Yukon – 3,185 km (1,979 miles) – were considered, it would be second on this list.

Source: *Natural Resources Canada*

TOP 10 ★
COUNTRIES WITH THE GREATEST AREAS OF INLAND WATER

	COUNTRY	PERCENTAGE OF TOTAL AREA	WATER AREA SQ MILES	SQ KM
1	US*	4.88	292,125	756,600
2	Canada	7.60	291,573	755,170
3	India	9.56	121,391	314,400
4	China	2.82	104,460	270,550
5	Ethiopia	9.89	46,680	120,900
6	Colombia	8.80	38,691	100,210
7	Indonesia	4.88	35,908	93,000
8	Russia	0.47	30,657	79,400
9	Australia	0.90	26,610	68,920
10	Tanzania	6.25	22,799	59,050

* 50 states and District of Columbia

TOP 10 ★
LAKES WITH THE GREATEST VOLUME OF WATER

	LAKE/LOCATION	VOLUME CU MILES	CU KM
1	Caspian Sea, Azerbaijan/ Iran/Kazakhstan/Russia/ Turkmenistan	21,497	89,600
2	Baikal, Russia	5,517	22,995
3	Tanganyika, Burundi/ Tanzania/Dem. Rep. of Congo/Zambia	4,391	18,304
4	Superior, Canada/US	2,921	12,174
5	Michigan/Huron, US/Canada	2,642	8,449
6	Nyasa (Malawi), Malawi/Mozambique/ Tanzania	1,473	6,140
7	Victoria, Kenya/ Tanzania/Uganda	604	2,518
8	Great Bear, Canada	542	2,258
9	Great Slave, Canada	425	1,771
10	Issyk, Kyrgyzstan	420	1,752

Did You Know? Once the world's fourth largest lake, the Aral Sea has shrunk by over a third as a result of feeder rivers being diverted for irrigation and is in danger of disappearing completely.

Islands of the World

TOP 10 ★
LARGEST VOLCANIC ISLANDS

ISLAND/LOCATION/TYPE	AREA SQ MILES	SQ KM
1 **Sumatra**, Indonesia, Active volcanic	171,069	443,066
2 **Honshu**, Japan, Volcanic	87,182	225,800
3 **Java**, Indonesia, Volcanic	53,589	138,794
4 **North Island**, New Zealand, Volcanic	43,082	111,583
5 **Luzon**, Philippines, Active volcanic	42,458	109,965
6 **Iceland** Active volcanic	39,315	101,826
7 **Mindanao**, Philippines, Active volcanic	37,657	97,530
8 **Hokkaido**, Japan, Active volcanic	30,395	78,719
9 **New Britain**, Papua New Guinea, Volcanic	13,569	35,145
10 **Halmahera**, Indonesia, Active volcanic	6,965	18,040

Source: *United Nations*

TOP 10 ★
LARGEST ISLAND COUNTRIES

COUNTRY	AREA SQ MILES	SQ KM
1 **Indonesia**	735,358	1,904,569
2 **Madagascar**	226,917	587,713
3 **Papua New Guinea**	178,704	462,840
4 **Japan**	143,939	372,801
5 **Malaysia**	127,320	329,758
6 **Philippines**	115,831	300,000
7 **New Zealand***	103,883	269,057
8 **Great Britain**	88,787	229,957
9 **Cuba**	42,804	110,861
10 **Iceland**	39,769	103,000

* Total of all the islands

Greenland is not included in this Top 10 because it is part of Denmark.

TOP 10 ★
LARGEST LAKE ISLANDS

ISLAND/LAKE/LOCATION	AREA SQ MILES	SQ KM
1 **Manitoulin**, Huron, Ontario, Canada	1,068	2,766
2 **Vozrozhdeniya**, Aral Sea, Uzbekistan/Kazakhstan	888	2,300
3 **René-Lavasseur**, Manicouagan Reservoir, Quebec, Canada	780	2,020
4 **Olkhon**, Baykal, Russia	282	730
5 **Samosir**, Toba, Sumatra, Indonesia	243	630
6 **Isle Royale**, Superior, Michigan, US	209	541
7 **Ukerewe**, Victoria, Tanzania	205	530
8 **St. Joseph**, Huron, Ontario, Canada	141	365
9 **Drummond**, Huron, Michigan, US	134	347
10 **Idjwi**, Kivu, Dem. Rep. of Congo	110	285

Not all islands are surrounded by sea: many sizable islands are situated in lakes. The second largest in this list, Vozrozhdeniya, is growing as the Aral Sea contracts, and is set to link up with the surrounding land to become a peninsula.

TOP 10 ★
LARGEST ISLANDS IN THE US

ISLAND/LOCATION	AREA SQ MILES	SQ KM
1 **Hawaii**, Hawaii	4,037	10,456
2 **Kodiak**, Alaska	3,672	9,510
3 **Prince of Wales**, Alaska	2,587	6,700
4 **Chicagof**, Alaska	2,085	5,400
5 **Saint Lawrence**, Alaska	1,710	4,430
6 **Admiralty**, Alaska	1,649	4,270
7 **Baranof**, Alaska	1,636	4,237
8 **Nunivak**, Alaska	1,625	4,210
9 **Unimak**, Alaska	1,606	4,160
10 **Long Island**, New York	1,401	3,629

TOP 10 🍁
LARGEST ISLANDS IN CANADA

ISLAND	AREA SQ MILES	SQ KM
1 **Baffin**, NWT	195,942	507,451
2 **Victoria**, NWT	83,902	217,291
3 **Ellesmere**, NWT	75,772	196,236
4 **Newfoundland** (main island)	42,034	108,860
5 **Banks**, NWT	27,040	70,028
6 **Devon**, NWT	21,332	55,247
7 **Axel Heiberg**, NWT	16,672	43,178
8 **Melville**, NWT	16,275	42,149
9 **Southampton**, NWT	15,914	41,214
10 **Prince of Wales**, NWT	12,873	33,339

Source: *Natural Resources Canada*

Vancouver Island in British Columbia, covering 31,285 sq km (12,080 sq miles), would be No. 11 on the list. Canada has two island provinces: Prince Edward Island and Newfoundland (at No. 4). Prince Edward Island covers 5,620 sq km (2,170 sq miles) and is just over half the size of Cape Breton Island, Nova Scotia, which has a total area of 10,311 sq km (3,981 sq miles).

50TH STATE

Hawaii, the largest US island, is the largest of eight major and 124 smaller volcanic islands that make up the Hawaiian archipelago.

UNDER THE VOLCANO
Indonesia's highest active volcano, Gunung Kerinci, rises to 3,805 m (12,484 ft). It lies in the Barisan Mountains of Sumatra, the world's largest volcanic island.

TOP 10 ★
LARGEST ISLANDS

| ISLAND/LOCATION | APPROX. AREA* | |
	SQ MILES	SQ KM
1 Greenland (Kalaallit Nunaat)	840,004	2,175,600
2 New Guinea, Papua New Guinea/Indonesia	303,381	785,753
3 Borneo, Indonesia/Malaysia/Brunei	288,869	748,168
4 Madagascar	226,917	587,713
5 Baffin Island, Canada	194,574	503,944
6 Sumatra, Indonesia	171,069	443,066
7 Great Britain	88,787	229,957
8 Honshu, Japan	87,182	225,800
9 Victoria Island, Canada	85,154	220,548
10 Ellesmere Island, Canada	71,029	183,965

* *Mainlands, including areas of inland water, but excluding offshore islands*

Australia is regarded as a continental land mass rather than an island; otherwise it would rank first at 7,618,493 sq km (2,941,517 sq miles).

TOP 10 ★
LARGEST ISLANDS IN EUROPE

| ISLAND/LOCATION | AREA | |
	SQ MILES	SQ KM
1 Great Britain, North Atlantic	88,787	229,957
2 Iceland, North Atlantic	39,769	103,000
3 Ireland, North Atlantic	32,342	83,766
4 West Spitsbergen, Arctic Ocean	15,200	39,368
5 Sicily, Mediterranean Sea	9,807	25,400
6 Sardinia, Mediterranean Sea	9,189	23,800
7 North East Land, Barents Sea	5,792	15,000
8 Cyprus, Mediterranean Sea	3,572	9,251
9 Corsica, Mediterranean Sea	3,367	8,720
10 Crete, Mediterranean Sea	3,189	8,260

Great Britain became an island some 8,000 years ago, when the land bridge that had previously existed was inundated and the North Sea became connected with the English Channel.

TOP 10 ★
HIGHEST ISLANDS

| ISLAND/LOCATION | HIGHEST ELEVATION | |
	FT	M
1 New Guinea, Papua New Guinea/Indonesia	16,503	5,030
2 Akutan, Alaska, US	14,026	4,275
3 Hawaii, US	13,796	4,205
4 Borneo, Indonesia/Malaysia/Brunei	13,698	4,175
5 Formosa, China	13,114	3,997
6 Sumatra, Indonesia	12,484	3,805
7 Ross, Antarctica	12,448	3,794
8 Honshu, Japan	12,388	3,776
9 South Island, New Zealand	12,349	3,764
10 Lombok, Lesser Sunda Islands, Indonesia	12,224	3,726

Source: *United Nations*

The highest island peak is Puncak Jaya, Indonesia, which soars to 5,030 m (16,503 ft), making it also the highest mountain in the entire Pacific basin.

What is the most common element on Earth?
see p.27 for the answer

A Nitrogen
B Hydrogen
C Oxygen

The Face of the Earth

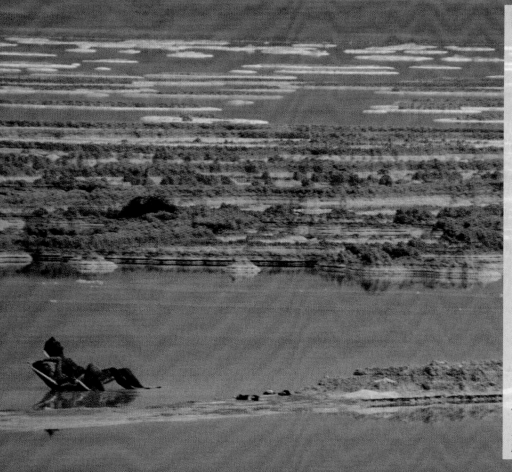

TOP 10 ★
HIGHEST ACTIVE VOLCANOES

VOLCANO/LOCATION	LATEST ACTIVITY	HEIGHT	
		FT	M
1 **Ojos del Salado**, Argentina/Chile	1981	22,588	6,895
2 **San Pedro**, Chile	1960	20,325	6,199
3 **Guallatiri**, Chile	1993	19,918	6,071
4 **Cotopaxi**, Ecuador	1975	19,347	5,897
5 **Tupungatito**, Chile	1986	18,504	5,640
6 **Láscar**, Chile	1995	18,346	5,591
7 **Popocatépetl**, Mexico	1998	17,802	5,426
8 **Nevado del Ruiz**, Colombia	1991	17,457	5,321
9 **Sangay**, Ecuador	1998	17,159	5,230
10 **Guagua Pichincha**, Ecuador	1993	15,696	4,784

This list includes only volcanoes that were active at some time during the 20th century. The tallest currently active volcano in Europe is Mt. Etna, Sicily (3,311 m/10,855 ft), which has been responsible for numerous deaths.

TOP 10 ★
LARGEST DESERTS

DESERT/LOCATION	APPROX. AREA	
	SQ MILES	SQ KM
1 **Sahara**, Northern Africa	3,500,000	9,100,000
2 **Australian**, Australia*	1,300,000	3,400,000
3 **Arabian Peninsula**, Southwest Asia#	1,000,000	2,600,000
4 **Turkestan**, Central Asia+	750,000	1,900,000
5 = **Gobi**, Central Asia	500,000	1,300,000
= **North American Desert**, US/Mexico★	500,000	1,300,000
7 **Patagonia**, Southern Argentina	260,000	670,000
8 **Thar**, Northwest India/Pakistan	230,000	600,000
9 **Kalahari**, Southwestern Africa	220,000	570,000
10 **Takla Makan**, Northwestern China	185,000	480,000

* Includes Gibson, Great Sandy, Great Victoria, and Simpson
# Includes an-Nafud and Rub alKhali   + Includes Kara-Kum and Kyzylkum
★ Includes Great Basin, Mojave, Sonora, and Chihuahuan

TOP 10 ★
HIGHEST MOUNTAINS

	MOUNTAIN/LOCATION	FIRST ASCENT /TEAM NATIONALITY	HEIGHT* FT	M
1	Everest, Nepal/China	May 29, 1953, British/New Zealand	29,035	8,850
2	K2 (Chogori), Pakistan/China	July 31, 1954, Italian	28,238	8,607
3	Kangchenjunga, Nepal/India	May 25, 1955, British	28,208	8,598
4	Lhotse, Nepal/China	May 18, 1956, Swiss	27,923	8,511
5	Makalu I, Nepal/China	May 15, 1955, French	27,824	8,481
6	Lhotse Shar (II), Nepal/China	May 12, 1970, Austrian	27,504	8,383
7	Dhaulagiri I, Nepal	May 13, 1960, Swiss/Austrian	26,810	8,172
8	Manaslu I (Kutang I), Nepal	May 9, 1956, Japanese	26,760	8,156
9	Cho Oyu, Nepal	Oct 19, 1954, Austrian	26,750	8,153
10	Nanga Parbat (Diamir), Pakistan	July 3, 1953, German/Austrian	26,660	8,126

* Height of principal peak; lower peaks of the same mountain are excluded

Dhaulagiri was once believed to be the world's tallest mountain, until Kangchenjunga was surveyed and declared to be even higher. When the results of the 19th-century Great Trigonometrical Survey of India were studied, however, it was realized that Everest was the tallest, its height being computed as 8,840 m (29,002 ft). Errors in measurement were corrected in 1955 to 8,848 m (29,029 ft), in April 1993 to 8,847 m (29,028 ft), and finally in November 1999 to its current record-breaking height.

TOP 10 ★
LONGEST CAVES

	CAVE/LOCATION	TOTAL KNOWN LENGTH MILES	KM
1	Mammoth cave system, Kentucky, US	352	567
2	Optimisticheskaya, Ukraine	130	208
3	Jewel Cave, South Dakota, US	122	195
4	Hölloch, Switzerland	103	166
5	Lechuguilla Cave, New Mexico, US	100	161
6	Fisher Ridge cave system, Kentucky, US	91	146
7	Siebenhengstehohle, Switzerland	87	140
8	Wind Cave, South Dakota, US	86	138
9	Ozernaya, Ukraine	69	111
10	Gua Air Jernih, Malaysia	68	109

Source: *Tony Waltham, BCRA*

TOP 10 ★
COUNTRIES WITH THE HIGHEST ELEVATIONS*

	COUNTRY/PEAK	HEIGHT FT	M
1 =	China, Everest	29,035	8,850
=	Nepal, Everest	29,035	8,850
3	Pakistan, K2	28,238	8,607
4	India, Kangchenjunga	28,208	8,598
5	Bhutan, Khula Kangri	24,784	7,554
6	Tajikistan, Mt. Garmo (formerly Kommunizma)	24,590	7,495
7	Afghanistan, Noshaq	24,581	7,490
8	Kyrgyzstan, Pik Pobedy	24,406	7,439
9	Kazakhstan, Khan Tengri	22,949	6,995
10	Argentina, Cerro Aconcagua	22,834	6,960

* Based on the tallest peak in each country

An elevation of more than 305 m (1,000 ft) is commonly regarded as a mountain, and using this criterion almost every country in the world can claim to have at least one mountain. There are some 54 countries in the world with elevations of greater than 3,048 m (10,000 ft).

TOP 10 ★
LARGEST METEORITE CRATERS

	CRATER/LOCATION	DIAMETER MILES	KM
1	Vredefort, South Africa	186	300
2	Sudbury, Ontario, Canada	140	225
3 =	Manicouagan, Quebec, Canada	62	100
=	Popigai, Russia	62	100
5	Puchezh-Katunki, Russia	50	80
6	Kara, Russia	40	65
7	Charlevoix, Quebec, Canada	34	54
8	Siljan, Sweden	32	52
9	Araguainha Dome, Brazil	25	40
10	Carswell, Saskatchewan, Canada	24	39

Source: *Geological Survey of Canada, Natural Resources Canada*

Many astroblemes (collision sites) on the Earth have been weathered over time and obscured. As a result, one of the ongoing debates in geology is whether or not certain craterlike structures discovered on our planet are of meteoric origin or are the remnants of long-extinct volcanoes.

TOP 10 ★
DEEPEST CAVES

	CAVE SYSTEM/LOCATION	DEPTH FT	M
1	Lamprechtsofen, Austria	5,354	1,632
2	Gouffre Mirolda, France	5,282	1,610
3	Réseau Jean Bernard, France	5,256	1,602
4	Torca del Cerro, Spain	5,213	1,589
5	Shakta Pantjukhina, Georgia	4,948	1,508
6	Ceki 2, Slovenia	4,511	1,480
7	Sistema Huautla, Mexico	4,839	1,475
8	Sistema de la Trave, Spain	4,738	1,444
9	Boj Bulok, Uzbekistan	4,642	1,415
10	Puerta di Illamina, Spain	4,619	1,408

Source: *Tony Waltham, BCRA*

How many of the ten tallest living trees in North America are found on Canadian soil?
see p.45 for the answer

A 2
B 3
C 6

World Weather

PLACES WITH THE MOST RAINY DAYS

LOCATION*	RAINY DAYS PER ANNUM#
1 Waialeale, Hawaii	335
2 Marion Island, South Africa	312
3 Pohnpei, Federated States of Micronesia	311
4 Andagoya, Colombia	306
5 Macquarie Island, Australia	299
6 Gough Island, Tristan da Cunha group, South Atlantic	291
7 Palau, Federated States of Micronesia	286
8 Heard Island, Australia	279
9 Camp Jacob, Guadeloupe	274
10 Atu Nau, Alaska	268

* Maximum of two places per country listed

Averaged over a period of many years

Source: Philip Eden

TOP 10 ★

WETTEST PLACES – AVERAGE

LOCATION*	AVERAGE ANNUAL RAINFALL# IN	MM
1 Cherrapunji, India	498.0	12,649
2 Mawsynram, India	467.4	11,872
3 Waialeale, Hawaii	451.0	11,455
4 Debundscha, Cameroon	404.6	10,277
5 Quibdó, Colombia	353.9	8,989
6 Bellenden Ker Range, Australia	340.0	8,636
7 Andagoya, Colombia	281.0	7,137
8 Henderson Lake, British Columbia, Canada	256.0	6,502
9 Kikori, Papua New Guinea	232.9	5,916
10 Tavoy, Myanmar (Burma)	214.6	5,451

* Maximum of two places per country listed

Annual rainfall total, averaged over a period of many years

Source: Philip Eden

TOP 10 PLACES WITH THE HEAVIEST DAILY DOWNPOURS*

(Location#/highest rainfall in 24 hours in in/mm)

1 Chilaos, Réunion, 73.6/1,870　2 Baguio, Philippines, 46.0/1,168
3 Alvin, Texas, 43.0/1,092　4 Cherrapunji, India, 41.0/1,041
5 Smithport, Pennsylvania, 39.9/1,013　6 Crohamhurst, Australia, 35.7/907
7 Finch-Hatton, Australia, 34.6/879　8 Suva, Fiji, 26.5/673
9 Cayenne, French Guiana, 23.5/597　10 Aitutaki, Cook Islands, 22.5/572

* Based on limited data　# Maximum of two places per country listed

Source: Philip Eden

TOP 10 ★

PLACES WITH THE FEWEST RAINY DAYS

LOCATION*	NUMBER OF RAINY DAYS#
1 Arica, Chile	1 day every 6 years
2 Asyût, Egypt	1 day every 5 years
3 Dakhla Oasis, Egypt	1 day every 4 years
4 Al'Kufrah, Libya	1 day every 2 years
5 = Bender Qaasim, Somalia	1 day per year
= Wadi Halfa, Sudan	1 day per year
7 Iquique, Chile	2 days per year
8 = Dongola, Sudan	3 days per year
= Faya-Largeau, Chad	3 days per year
= Masirāh Island, Oman	3 days per year

* Maximum of two places per country listed

Lowest number of days with rain per year, averaged over a period of many years

Source: Philip Eden

TOP 10 ★

HOTTEST PLACES – EXTREMES*

LOCATION#	HIGHEST TEMPERATURE °F	°C
1 Al'Azīzīyah, Libya	136.4	58.0
2 Greenland Ranch, Death Valley, California	134.0	56.7
3 = Ghudamis, Libya	131.0	55.0
= Kebili, Tunisia	131.0	55.0
5 Timbuktu, Mali	130.1	54.5
6 Araouane, Mali	130.0	54.4
7 Tirat Tavi, Israel	129.0	53.9
8 Ahwāz, Iran	128.3	53.5
9 Agha Jārī, Iran	128.0	53.3
10 Wadi Halfa, Sudan	127.0	52.8

* Highest individual temperatures

Maximum of two places per country listed

Source: Philip Eden

TOP 10 ★

DRIEST PLACES – AVERAGE

LOCATION*	AVERAGE ANNUAL RAINFALL# IN	MM	LOCATION*	AVERAGE ANNUAL RAINFALL# IN	MM
1 Arica, Chile	0.03	0.7	7 Iquique, Chile	0.20	5.0
2 = Al'Kufrah, Libya	0.03	0.8	8 Pelican Point, Namibia	0.32	8.0
= Aswân, Egypt	0.03	0.8	9 = Aoulef, Algeria	0.48	12.0
= Luxor, Egypt	0.03	0.8	= Callao, Peru	0.48	12.0
5 Ica, Peru	0.09	2.3			
6 Wadi Halfa, Sudan	0.10	2.6			

* Maximum of two places per country listed

Annual total averaged over a period of many years

Source: Philip Eden

TOP 10 ★
PLACES WITH THE MOST CONTRASTING SEASONS*

LOCATION #	WINTER °F	°C	SUMMER °F	°C	DIFFERENCE °F	°C
1 **Verkhoyansk**, Russia	-58.5	-50.3	56.5	13.6	115.0	63.9
2 **Yakutsk**, Russia	-49.0	-45.0	63.5	17.5	112.5	62.5
3 **Manzhouli**, China	-15.0	-26.1	69.0	20.6	84.0	46.7
4 **Fort Yukon**, Alaska	-20.2	-29.0	61.4	16.3	81.6	45.3
5 **Fort Good Hope**, Northwest Territories, Canada	-21.8	-29.9	59.5	15.3	81.3	45.2
6 **Brochet**, Manitoba, Canada	-20.5	-29.2	59.7	15.4	80.2	44.6
7 **Tunka**, Mongolia	-16.0	-26.7	61.0	16.1	77.0	42.8
8 **Fairbanks**, Alaska	-11.2	-24.0	60.1	15.6	71.3	39.6
9 **Semipalatinsk**, Kazakhstan	0.5	-17.7	69.0	20.6	68.5	38.3
10 **Jorgen Bronlund Fjørd**, Greenland	-23.6	-30.9	43.5	6.4	67.1	37.3

* *Biggest differences between mean monthly temperatures in summer and winter*

\# *Maximum of two places per country listed*

Source: *Philip Eden*

TOP 10 ★
COLDEST PLACES – EXTREMES*

LOCATION #	LOWEST TEMPERATURE °F	°C
1 **Vostok**+, Antarctica	-128.6	-89.2
2 **Plateau Station**+, Antarctica	-119.2	-84.0
3 **Oymyakon**, Russia	-96.0	-71.1
4 **Verkhoyansk**, Russia	-89.8	-67.7
5 **Northice**+, Greenland	-86.8	-66.0
6 **Eismitte**+, Greenland	-84.8	-64.9
7 **Snag**, Yukon, Canada	-81.4	-63.0
8 **Prospect Creek**, Alaska	-79.8	-62.1
9 **Fort Selkirk**, Yukon, Canada	-74.0	-58.9
10 **Rogers Pass**, Montana	-69.7	-56.5

* *Lowest individual temperatures*

\# *Maximum of two places per country listed*

\+ *Present or former scientific research base*

Source: *Philip Eden*

TOP 10 ★
CLOUDIEST PLACES*

LOCATION #	PERCENTAGE OF MAXIMUM POSSIBLE SUNSHINE	AVERAGE ANNUAL HOURS OF SUNSHINE
1 **Ben Nevis**, Scotland	16	736
2 **Hoyvik**, Faeroes, Denmark	19	902
3 **Maam**, Ireland	19	929
4 **Prince Rupert**, British Columbia, Canada	20	955
5 **Riksgransen**, Sweden	20	965
6 **Akureyri**, Iceland	20	973
7 **Raufarhöfn**, Iceland	21	995
8 **Nanortalik**, Greenland	22	1,000
9 **Dalwhinnie**, Scotland	22	1,032
10 **Karasjok**, Norway	23	1,090

* *Lowest annual sunshine total, averaged over a period of many years*

\# *Maximum of two places per country listed*

Source: *Philip Eden*

TOP 10 ★
SUNNIEST PLACES*

LOCATION #	PERCENTAGE OF MAXIMUM POSSIBLE SUNSHINE	AVERAGE ANNUAL HOURS OF SUNSHINE
1 **Yuma**, Arizona	91	4,127
2 **Phoenix**, Arizona	90	4,041
3 **Wadi Halfa**, Sudan	89	3,964
4 **Bordj Omar Driss**, Algeria	88	3,899
5 **Keetmanshoop**, Namibia	88	3,876
6 **Aoulef**, Algeria	86	3,784
7 **Upington**, South Africa	86	3,766
8 **Atbara**, Sudan	85	3,739
9 **Mariental**, Namibia	84	3,707
10 **Bilma**, Niger	84	3,699

* *Highest yearly sunshine total, averaged over a period of many years*

\# *Maximum of two places per country listed*

Source: *Philip Eden*

CELSIUS

Anders Celsius (1701–44) was a Swedish mathematician and, like his father before him, Professor of Astronomy at the University of Uppsala. While Celsius was on an expedition to Lapland, making measurements that proved that the Earth is flattened at the poles, he realized the need for an improved thermometer. In 1742 he devised a new temperature scale, taking two fixed points – 0° as the boiling point of water and 100° as the freezing point of water. It was not until 1750, after Celsius's death, that his pupil Martin Strömer proposed that the two be reversed. This scale became known as Centigrade, but was changed to Celsius in 1948 in honor of its inventor.

WHO WAS • WHO WAS • WHO WAS • WHO WAS •

Canada, Australia, and Namibia all produced the same amount of which commodity in 1999?
see p.204 for the answer
A Salt
B Diamonds
C Silver

Out of This World

HEAVIEST ELEMENTS

	ELEMENT	DISCOVERER/COUNTRY	YEAR DISCOVERED	DENSITY*
1	Osmium	Smithson Tennant, UK	1804	22.59
2	Iridium	Smithson Tennant, UK	1804	22.56
3	Platinum	J.C. Scaliger#, Italy/France; Charles Wood+, UK	1557 1741	21.45
4	Rhenium	W. Noddack *et al.*, Germany	1925	21.01
5	Neptunium	Edwin M. McMillan and Philip H. Abelson, US	1940	20.47
6	Plutonium	Glenn T. Seaborg *et al.*, US	1940	20.26
7	Gold	–	Prehistoric	19.29
8	Tungsten	Juan José and Fausto de Elhuijar, Spain	1783	19.26
9	Uranium	Martin J. Klaproth, Germany	1789	19.05
10	Tantalum	Anders G. Ekeberg, Sweden	1802	16.67

* Grams per cu cm at 20°C   # Made earliest reference to   + Discovered by

The two heaviest elements, the metals osmium and iridium, were discovered at the same time by the British chemist Smithson Tennant (1761–1815), who was also the first to prove that diamonds are made of carbon. Equivalent to 10 people each weighing 64 kg (141 lb), 0.028317 cu m (1 cu ft) of osmium weighs 640 kg (1,410 lb).

LIGHTEST ELEMENTS*

	ELEMENT	DISCOVERER/COUNTRY	YEAR DISCOVERED	DENSITY#
1	Lithium	J.A. Arfvedson, Sweden	1817	0.533
2	Potassium	Sir Humphry Davy, UK	1807	0.859
3	Sodium	Sir Humphry Davy, UK	1807	0.969
4	Calcium	Sir Humphry Davy, UK	1808	1.526
5	Rubidium	Robert W. Bunsen and Gustav Kirchoff, Germany	1861	1.534
6	Magnesium	Sir Humphry Davy	1808+	1.737
7	Phosphorus	Hennig Brandt, Germany	1669	1.825
8	Beryllium	Friedrich Wöhler, Germany; A.-A.B. Bussy, France	1828★	1.846
9	Cesium	Robert W. Bunsen and Gustav Kirchoff, Germany	1860	1.896
10	Sulfur	–	Prehistoric	2.070

* Solids only # Grams per cu cm at 20°C + Recognized by Joseph Black, 1755, but not isolated ★ Recognized by Nicholas Vauquelin, 1797, but not isolated

Osmium, the heaviest element, is over 42 times heavier than lithium, the lightest element. Lithium is not only extremely light, but it is also so soft that it can be easily cut with a knife. It is half as heavy as water, and even lighter than certain types of wood.

TOP 10 PRINCIPAL COMPONENTS OF AIR

(Component/volume percent)

1 Nitrogen, 78.110 **2** Oxygen, 20.953 **3** Argon, 0.934 **4** Carbon dioxide, 0.01–0.10 **5** Neon, 0.001818 **6** Helium, 0.000524 **7** Methane, 0.0002 **8** Krypton, 0.000114 **9** = Hydrogen, 0.00005; = Nitrous oxide, 0.00005

METALLIC ELEMENTS WITH THE GREATEST RESERVES

	ELEMENT	ESTIMATED GLOBAL RESERVES (TONNES)
1	Iron	110,000,000,000
2	Magnesium	20,000,000,000
3	Potassium	10,000,000,000
4	Aluminum	6,000,000,000
5	Manganese	3,355,000,000
6	Zirconium	over 1,000,000,000
7	Chromium	1,000,000,000
8	Barium	450,000,000
9	Titanium	440,000,000
10	Copper	310,000,000

COPPER BOTTOMED

Over 12.7 million tonnes (14 million tons) of copper have been removed from the Bingham Copper Mine, Utah, which is an all-time record for a single mine. This is the world's largest manmade excavation.

TOP 10 MOST COMMON ELEMENTS IN SEAWATER
(Element/tonnes per cu km)

❶ Oxygen*, 857,000,000 ❷ Hydrogen*, 107,800,000 ❸ Chlorine, 19,870,000
❹ Sodium, 11,050,000 ❺ Magnesium, 1,326,000 ❻ Sulfur, 928,000
❼ Calcium, 422,000 ❽ Potassium, 416,000 ❾ Bromine, 67,300 ❿ Carbon, 28,000
* Combined as water

TOP 10 ★ MOST COMMON ELEMENTS IN THE EARTH'S CRUST

ELEMENT	PARTS PER MILLION
1 Oxygen	474,000
2 Silicon	277,100
3 Aluminum	82,000
4 =Iron	41,000
=Calcium	41,000
6 =Magnesium	23,000
=Sodium	23,000
8 Potassium	21,000
9 Titanium	5,600
10 Hydrogen	1,520

This Top 10 is based on the average percentages of the elements in igneous rock. At an atomic level, out of every million atoms, some 205,000 are silicon, 62,600 are aluminum, and 29,000 are hydrogen. In the universe as a whole, however, hydrogen is by far the most common element, comprising some 927,000 out of every million atoms. It is followed in second place by helium at 72,000 per million.

LIGHT FANTASTIC
This computer-generated image shows a nucleus and orbiting electron, which make up a single atom of hydrogen, the lightest, simplest, most abundant, and most extracted of all elements.

TOP 10 ★ MOST COMMON ELEMENTS ON THE MOON

ELEMENT	PERCENTAGE
1 Oxygen	40.0
2 Silicon	19.2
3 Iron	14.3
4 Calcium	8.0
5 Titanium	5.9
6 Aluminum	5.6
7 Magnesium	4.5
8 Sodium	0.33
9 Potassium	0.14
10 Chromium	0.002

This list is based on the chemical analysis of the 20.77 kg (45.8 lb) of rock samples brought back to the Earth by the three-man crew of the 1969 *Apollo 11* lunar mission.

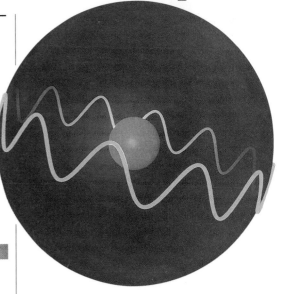

TOP 10 MOST COMMON ELEMENTS IN THE SUN
(Element/parts per million)

❶ Hydrogen, 745,000 ❷ Helium, 237,000
❸ Oxygen, 8,990 ❹ Carbon, 3,900
❺ Iron, 1,321 ❻ Neon, 1,200
❼ Nitrogen, 870 ❽ Silicon, 830
❾ Magnesium, 720 ❿ Sulfur, 380

TOP 10 ★ ELEMENTS WITH THE HIGHEST MELTING POINTS

ELEMENT	MELTING POINT °F	°C
1 Carbon	6,381	3,527
2 Tungsten	6,192	3,422
3 Rhenium	5,767	3,186
4 Osmium	5,491	3,033
5 Tantalum	5,463	3,017
6 Molybdenum	4,753	2,623
7 Niobium	4,491	2,477
8 Iridium	4,471	2,466
9 Ruthenium	4,233	2,334
10 Hafnium	4,051	2,233

Other elements that melt at high temperatures include chromium (1,907°C/3,465°F), iron (1,538°C/2,800°F), and gold (1,064°C/1,947°F).

THE DISCOVERY OF RADIUM

In 1898, Polish-born Marie Curie (1867–1934) and her French husband Pierre Curie detected radioactivity (a term Marie invented) in the mineral ore pitchblende, a waste product of mining. It took until 1902 before she had manually refined tonnes of ore to concentrate the radioactive content, producing about one tenth of a gram of radium chloride, an element that is a million times more radioactive than uranium. The following year, Marie and Pierre shared the Nobel Prize for Physics with Henry Becquerel. Marie eventually obtained pure radium in 1910. Marie was not only the first female Nobel winner, but also the first to achieve two Prizes, receiving the Chemistry Prize in 1911. Radium was subsequently used in the treatment of cancer, but, ironically, Marie died in 1934 from leukemia resulting from her prolonged contact with radium.

100 YEARS AGO · YEARS AGO · YEARS AGO · YEARS

Did You Know? Following the naming of the element Uranium after the planet Uranus, Neptunium and Plutonium were named after Neptune and Pluto, two more distant planets.

Natural Disasters

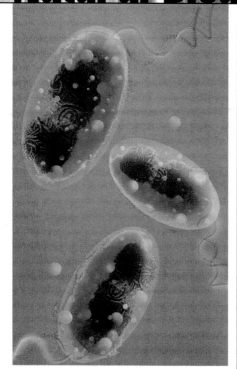

CHOLERA KILLER

One of the scourges of the 19th century, when it killed millions, the cholera bacteria continues to cause illness and death in human communities that lack modern sanitation.

THE 10 ★ WORST EPIDEMICS OF ALL TIME

	EPIDEMIC/LOCATION	DATE	ESTIMATED NO. KILLED
1	**Black Death,** Europe/Asia	1347–51	75,000,000
2	**Influenza,** worldwide	1918–20	21,640,000
3	**AIDS,** worldwide	1981–	16,300,000
4	**Bubonic plague,** India	1896–1948	12,000,000
5	**Typhus,** Eastern Europe	1914–15	3,000,000
6	**="Plague of Justinian,"** Europe/Asia	541–90	millions*
	=Cholera, worldwide	1846–60	millions*
	=Cholera, Europe	1826–37	millions*
	=Cholera, worldwide	1893–94	millions*
10	**Smallpox,** Mexico	1530–45	>1,000,000

* No precise figures available

THE 10 WORST YEARS FOR EPIDEMICS IN THE 1990s

(Year/deaths due to epidemics)

❶ 1991, 28,540 **❷ 1996**, 13,904 **❸ 1998**, 11,224 **❹ 1997**, 9,948 **❺ 1992**, 5,533 **❻ 1999**, 4,866 **❼ 1995**, 4,069 **❽ 1990**, 2,864 **❾ 1994**, 2,240 **❿ 1993**, 859

Source: *International Federation of Red Cross and Red Cross Societies*

Over two-thirds of those killed by epidemics in the 1990s were African. In 1991, 8,000 people died in Peru due to a diarrheal/enteric disease, and another 7,000 were killed by an epidemic of cholera in Nigeria.

THE 10 ★ WORST FLOODS OF ALL TIME

	LOCATION	DATE	ESTIMATED NO. KILLED
1	**Huang He River,** China	Aug 1931	3,700,000
2	**Huang He River,** China	Spring 1887	1,500,000
3	**Holland**	Nov 1, 1530	400,000
4	**Kaifong**, China	1642	300,000
5	**Henan**, China	Sep–Nov 1939	over 200,000
6	**Bengal**, India	1876	200,000
7	**Yangtze River,** China	Aug–Sep 1931	140,000
8	**Holland**	1646	110,000
9	**North Vietnam**	Aug 30, 1971	over 100,000
10	**=Friesland**, Holland	1228	100,000
	=Dort, Holland	Apr 16, 1421	100,000
	=Canton, China	June 12, 1915	100,000
	=Yangtze River, China	Sep 1911	100,000

China's Huang He, or Yellow River, has flooded at least 1,500 times since records began in 2297 BC.

THE 10 ★ COUNTRIES WITH MOST DEATHS DUE TO NATURAL DISASTERS

	COUNTRY	ESTIMATED DEATHS DUE TO NATURAL DISASTERS (1999)
1	**Venezuela**	30,021
2	**Turkey**	18,019
3	**India**	12,074
4	**China**	2,367
5	**Taiwan**	2,264
6	**Colombia**	1,284
7	**Nigeria**	1,190
8	**Mexico**	903
9	**Vietnam**	893
10	**US**	792
	World	212,544,647

Source: *International Federation of Red Cross and Red Cross Societies*

Deaths due to natural disasters in 1999 break down by continent to 6,294,514 in Africa, 13,494,780 in the Americas, 187,617,273 in Asia, 4,986,835 in Europe, and 151,245 in Oceania.

THE ERUPTION OF MONT PELÉE

After lying dormant for centuries, Mont Pelée, a 1,350-m (4,430-ft) volcano on the West Indian island of Martinique, began to erupt in April 1902. Assured that the volcano presented no danger to them, the residents of the main city, St. Pierre, stayed in their homes instead of being evacuated. As a result of this catastrophic misreading of the volcano's activity, they were still there when, at 7:30 am on May 8, the volcano burst apart and showered the port with molten lava, ash, and gas, destroying property, ships in the harbor, and virtually all life. A total of about 40,000 people were killed, which was more than twice as many as had been killed when Vesuvius engulfed Pompeii in AD 79. Raoul Sarteret, a prisoner in St. Pierre jail and the town's only survivor, provided a vivid eyewitness account of the event.

YEARS AGO · YEARS AGO · 100 · YEARS AGO · YEARS

AFTER THE STORM

Hurricane Andrew, the costliest for over 75 years, ravaged Miami, Florida, where it wrecked property and overturned vehicles to a cost of over US$35.4 million dollars.

THE 10 🍁

WORST CANADIAN EARTHQUAKES OF THE 20TH CENTURY

	LOCATION/YEAR	MAGNITUDE*
1	Queen Charlotte Islands, 1949	8.1
2	Off Queen Charlotte Islands, 1970	7.4
3	=Baffin Bay, 1933	7.3
	=Central Vancouver Island, 1946	7.3
5	Atlantic Ocean, south of Newfoundland, 1929	7.2
6	Vancouver Island, 1918	7.0
7	Nahanni region, Northwest Territories, 1985	6.9
8	Charlevoix-Kamouraska region, Quebec, 1925	6.2
9	Saguenay region, Quebec, 1988	5.9
10	Eastern Ontario-New York border, 1944	5.8

* On the Richter scale

Source: *Geological Survey of Canada*

THE 10 ★

MOST COSTLY TYPES OF DISASTER*

	TYPE OF DISASTER	ESTIMATED DAMAGE 1990–99 (US$)
1	Floods	243,561,900,000
2	Earthquakes	215,023,211,000
3	Wind storms	179,391,693,000
4	Forest/scrub fires	36,975,436,000
5	Non-natural disasters	28,066,406,000
6	Droughts	21,941,064,000
7	Extreme temperatures	14,362,550,000
8	Avalanches/landslides	929,028,000
9	Volcanoes	672,628,000
10	Other natural disasters (insect infestations, waves and surges, etc.)	109,467,000
	World total	741,033,383,000

* Includes natural and non-natural

Source: *International Federation of Red Cross and Red Cross Societies*

THE 10 ★

MOST DEADLY TYPES OF NATURAL DISASTER IN THE 1990s

	TYPE OF DISASTER	REPORTED DEATHS
1	Wind storms	201,790
2	Floods	103,870
3	Earthquakes	98,678
4	Epidemics*	84,047
5	Extreme temperatures	9,055
6	Avalanches/landslides	8,658
7	Droughts	2,790
8	Insect infestations, waves/surges	2,686
9	Volcanoes	1,080
10	Forest/scrub fires	575

* Excluding chronic public health disasters, such as the AIDS pandemic

Source: *International Federation of Red Cross and Red Cross Societies*

Did You Know? Since 1979, Atlantic hurricanes have been assigned men's and women's names, which alternate alphabetically and from year to year. Hurricane Bob, in July 1979, was the first.

LIFE ON EARTH

Land Animals

HEAVIEST TERRESTRIAL MAMMALS

	MAMMAL	LENGTH FT	LENGTH M	WEIGHT LB	WEIGHT KG
1	African elephant	24	7.3	14,432	7,000
2	White rhinoceros	14	4.2	7,937	3,600
3	Hippopotamus	13	4.0	5,512	2,500
4	Giraffe	19	5.8	3,527	1,600
5	American bison	13	3.9	2,205	1,000
6	Arabian camel (dromedary)	12	3.5	1,521	690
7	Polar bear	8	2.6	1,323	600
8	Moose	10	3.0	1,213	550
9	Siberian tiger	11	3.3	661	300
10	Gorilla	7	2.0	485	220

The list excludes domesticated cattle and horses. It also avoids comparing close kin such as the African and Indian elephants, highlighting instead the sumo stars within distinctive large mammal groups such as the bears, big cats, primates, and bovines (ox-like mammals).

MAMMALS WITH THE SHORTEST GESTATION PERIODS

	MAMMAL	AVERAGE GESTATION (DAYS)
1	Short-nosed bandicoot	12
2	Opossum	13
3	Shrew	14
4	Golden hamster	16
5	Lemming	20
6	Mouse	21
7	Rat	22
8	Gerbil	24
9	Rabbit	30
10	Mole	38

The short-nosed bandicoot and the opossum are both marsupial mammals whose newborn young transfer to a pouch to complete their natal development. The babies of marsupials are minute when born.

MOST ENDANGERED MAMMALS

	MAMMAL	ESTIMATED NO.
1 =	Ghana fat mouse	unknown
=	Halcon fruit bat	unknown
=	Tasmanian wolf	unknown
4	Javan rhinoceros	50
5	Iriomote cat	60
6	Black lion tamarin	130
7	Pygmy hog	150
8	Kouprey	100–200
9	Tamaraw	200
10	Indus dolphin	400

The first three mammals on the list have not been seen for many years and may well be extinct, but zoologists are hopeful of the possibility of their survival. The Tasmanian wolf, for example, has been technically extinct since the last specimen died in a zoo in 1936, but occasional unconfirmed sightings suggest that there may still be animals in the wild.

HEAVIEST PRIMATES

	PRIMATE	LENGTH* IN	LENGTH* CM	WEIGHT LB	WEIGHT KG
1	Gorilla	79	200	485	220
2	Man	70	177	170	77
3	Orangutan	54	137	165	75
4	Chimpanzee	36	92	110	50
5 =	Baboon	39	100	99	45
=	Mandrill	37	95	99	45
7	Gelada baboon	30	75	55	25
8	Proboscis monkey	30	76	53	24
9	Hanuman langur	42	107	44	20
10	Siamung gibbon	35	90	29	13

* Excluding tail

ORANGUTAN

Among the heaviest primates, and noted for its use of tools, the orangutan gets its name from the Malay words for "man of the woods."

TOP 10 ★
LONGEST LAND ANIMALS

ANIMAL*	LENGTH FT	M
1 Reticulated python	35	10.7
2 Tapeworm	33	10.0
3 African elephant	24	7.3
4 Estuarine crocodile	19	5.9
5 Giraffe	19	5.8
6 White rhinoceros	14	4.2
7 Hippopotamus	13	4.0
8 American bison	13	3.9
9 Arabian camel (dromedary)	12	3.5
10 Siberian tiger	11	3.3

* Longest representative of each species

NECK AND NECK

The giraffe is the tallest of all living animals. In 1937 a calf giraffe that measured 1.58 m (5 ft 2 in) at birth was found to be growing at an astonishing 1.3 cm (½ in) per hour.

TOP 10 ★
FASTEST MAMMALS

MAMMAL	MAXIMUM RECORDED SPEED MPH	KM/H
1 Cheetah	65	105
2 Pronghorn antelope	55	89
3 =Mongolian gazelle	50	80
=Springbok	50	80
5 =Grant's gazelle	47	76
=Thomson's gazelle	47	76
7 Brown hare	45	72
8 Horse	43	69
9 =Greyhound	42	68
=Red deer	42	68

QUICK OFF THE MARK

The speedy cheetah can accelerate to 96 km/h (60 mph) in just three seconds.

TOP 10 ★
LONGEST SNAKES

SNAKE	MAXIMUM LENGTH FT	M
1 Reticulated python	35	10.7
2 Anaconda	28	8.5
3 Indian python	25	7.6
4 Diamond python	21	6.4
5 King cobra	19	5.8
6 Boa constrictor	16	4.9
7 Bushmaster	12	3.7
8 Giant brown snake	11	3.4
9 Diamondback rattlesnake	9	2.7
10 Indigo or gopher snake	8	2.4

Did You Know? "Old Bet," the first elephant ever seen in the US, arrived from Bengal, India, on April 13, 1796, and was exhibited in New York. She was known for her ability to draw corks from bottles using only her trunk.

Marine Animals

HEAVIEST MARINE MAMMALS

MAMMAL	LENGTH FT	M	WEIGHT (TONNES)
1 Blue whale	110.0	33.5	137.0
2 Bowhead whale (Greenland right)	65.0	20.0	86.0
3 Northern Right whale (Black right)	60.0	18.6	77.7
4 Fin whale (Common rorqual)	82.0	25.0	63.4
5 Sperm whale	59.0	18.0	43.7
6 Gray whale	46.0	14.0	34.9
7 Humpback whale	49.2	15.0	34.6
8 Sei whale	60.0	18.5	29.4
9 Bryde's whale	47.9	14.6	20.0
10 Baird's whale	18.0	5.5	12.1

Source: *Lucy T. Verma*

Probably the largest animal that ever lived, the blue whale dwarfs even the other whales listed here, all but one of which far outweigh the biggest land animal, the elephant. The elephant seal, with a weight of 3.5 tonnes, is the heaviest marine mammal that is not a whale.

HEAVIEST TURTLES

TURTLE/TORTOISE	MAX. WEIGHT LB	KG
1 Pacific leatherback turtle*	1,552	704.4
2 Atlantic leatherback turtle*	1,018	463.0
3 Green sea turtle	783	355.3
4 Loggerhead turtle	568	257.8
5 Alligator snapping turtle#	220	100.0
6 Flatback (sea) turtle	171	78.2
7 Hawksbill (sea) turtle	138	62.7
8 Kemps ridley turtle	133	60.5
9 Olive ridley turtle	110	49.9
10 Common snapping turtle#	85	38.5

* One species, differing in size according to where they live

Freshwater species   Source: *Lucy T. Verma*

MARINE MONSTER

There are several species of right whale, with larger examples of Greenland rights topping 20 m (65 ft) and weighing 86 tonnes (95 tons). By contrast, the Pygmy right whale, found off New Zealand, rarely exceeds 6 m (20 ft).

TOP 10 LONGEST-LIVED MARINE MAMMALS

(Marine mammal/lifespan in years)

❶ Bowhead whale (*Balaena mysticetus*), 200
❷ Fin whale, 100 ❸ Orca (Killer whale), 90
❹ Baird's beaked whale, 82
❺ Sperm whale, 65 ❻ = Dugong, 60;
= Sei whale, 60 ❽ Bottlenose dolphin, 48
❾ Grey seal, 46 ❿ Blue whale, 45
Source: *Lucy T. Verma*

TOP 10

SPECIES OF FISH MOST CAUGHT

	SPECIES	TONNES CAUGHT (1998)
1	Anchoveta (Peruvian anchovy)	11,729,064
2	Alaska pollock	4,049,317
3	Japanese anchovy	2,093,888
4	Chilean jack mackerel	2,025,758
5	Chubb mackerel	1,910,254
6	Skipjack tuna	1,850,487
7	Largehead hairtail	1,214,470
8	Atlantic cod	1,191,184
9	Yellowfin tuna	1,152,586
10	Capelin	988,033
	World total all species	86,299,400

Source: *Food and Agriculture Organization of the United Nations*

The Food and Agriculture Organization of the United Nations estimates the volume of the world's fishing catch to be just over 86 million tonnes a year. Of this, about 75 million tonnes is estimated to be destined for human consumption – equivalent to approximately 13 kg (29 lb) a year for every inhabitant. The foremost species, anchoveta, are small anchovies used principally as bait to catch tuna.

TOP 10

HEAVIEST SPECIES OF FRESHWATER FISH CAUGHT

	SPECIES	ANGLER/LOCATION/DATE	WEIGHT LB	OZ	KG	G
1	White sturgeon	Joey Pallotta III, Benicia, California, July 9, 1983	468	0	212	28
2	Alligator gar	Bill Valverde, Rio Grande, Texas, Dec 2, 1951	279	0	126	55
3	Beluga sturgeon	Merete Lehne, Guryev, Kazakhstan, May 3, 1993	224	13	102	00
4	Nile perch	Adrian Brayshaw, Lake Nasser, Egypt, Dec 18, 1997	213	0	96	62
5	Flathead catfish	Ken Paulie, Withlacoochee River, Florida, May 14, 1998	123	9	55	79
6	Blue catfish	William P. McKinley, Wheeler Reservoir, Tennessee, July 5, 1996	111	0	50	35
7	Redtailed catfish	Gilberto Fernandes, Amazon River, Amazonia, Brazil, July 16, 1988	97	7	44	20
8	Chinook salmon	Les Anderson, Kenai River, Alaska, May 17, 1985	97	4	44	11
9	Giant tigerfish	Raymond Houtmans, Zaïre River, Kinshasa, Zaïre, July 9, 1988	97	0	44	00
10	Guilded catfish	Gilberto Fernandes, Amazon River, Amazonia Brazil, Nov 15, 1986	85	8	38	80

Source: *International Game Fish Association, World Record Game Fishes 2000*

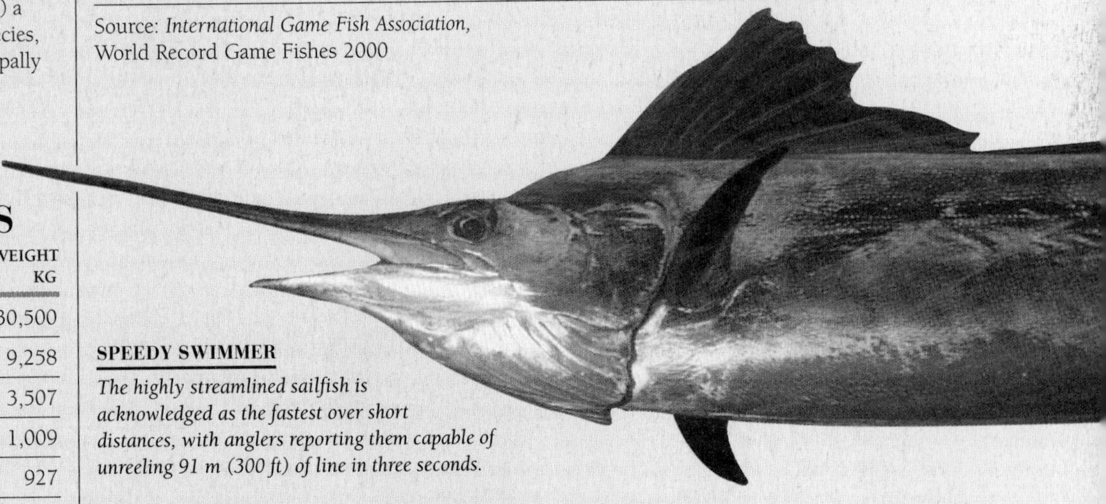

SPEEDY SWIMMER

The highly streamlined sailfish is acknowledged as the fastest over short distances, with anglers reporting them capable of unreeling 91 m (300 ft) of line in three seconds.

TOP 10

HEAVIEST SHARKS

	SHARK	MAXIMUM WEIGHT LB	KG
1	Whale shark	67,240	30,500
2	Basking shark	20,410	9,258
3	Great white shark	7,731	3,507
4	Greenland shark	2,224	1,009
5	Tiger shark	2,043	927
6	Great hammerhead shark	1,889	857
7	Six-gill shark	1,327	602
8	Gray nurse shark	1,243	564
9	Mako shark	1,221	554
10	Thresher shark	1,097	498

Source: *Lucy T. Verma*

TOP 10 FASTEST FISH

(Fish/maximum recorded speed in mph/km/h)

❶ **Sailfish**, 69/112 ❷ **Marlin**, 50/80 ❸ **Wahoo**, 48/77 ❹ **Bluefin tuna**, 47/76 ❺ **Yellowfin tuna**, 46/74 ❻ **Blue shark**, 43/69 ❼ = **Bonefish**, 40/64; = **Swordfish**, 40/64 ❾ **Tarpon**, 35/56 ❿ **Tiger shark**, 33/53

Source: *Lucy T. Verma*

Did You Know? In a survey of recorded shark attacks from 1580 to 2000, the Great White shark was alone responsible for 348 out of a total of 980, resulting in 67 fatalities.

Flying Animals

TOP 10 ★
FASTEST BIRDS

BIRD	SPEED MPH	KM/H
1 Common eider	47	76
2 Bewick's swan	44	72
3 =Barnacle goose	42	68
=Common crane	42	68
5 Mallard	40	65
6 =Red-throated diver	38	61
=Wood pigeon	38	61
8 Oyster catcher	36	58
9= Pheasant	33	54
=White-fronted goose	33	54

Source: *Chris Mead*

Recent research reveals that, contrary to popular belief, swifts are not fast fliers, but they are very efficient, with long thin wings like gliders and low wing-loading. Fast fliers generally have high wing-loading and fast wing beats.

TOP 10 🍁
MOST COMMON BREEDING BIRDS IN CANADA

BIRD	NUMBER REPORTED IN 2000*
1 American robin	17,819
2 Red-winged blackbird	16,194
3 American crow	14,879
4 European starling	13,399
5 Savannah sparrow	8,318
6 Song sparrow	7,761
7 Red-eyed vireo	7,485
8 House sparrow	6,437
9 White-throated sparrow	6,393
10 Mallard	5,617

* *A bird is counted if it is seen or heard by one of 360 volunteer skilled bird observers. Actual population figures are much higher. Since the survey takes place along roadways, regions with few roads may be underrepresented.*

Source: *Canadian Breeding Bird Survey 1966–2000, National Wildlife Research Centre, Canadian Wildlife Service*

TOP 10 ★
FARTHEST BIRD MIGRATIONS

SPECIES	APPROXIMATE DISTANCE MILES	KM
1 Pectoral sandpiper	11,806*	19,000
2 Wheatear	11,184	18,000
3 Slender-billed shearwater	10,874*	17,500
4 Ruff	10,314	16,600
5 Willow warbler	10,128	16,300
6 Arctic tern	10,066	16,200
7 Parasitic jaeger	9,693	15,600
8 Swainson's hawk	9,445	15,200
9 Knot	9,320	15,000
10 Barn swallow	9,258	14,900

* *Thought to be only half of the path taken during a whole year*

Source: *Chris Mead*

This list is of the likely extremes for a normal migrant, not one that has gotten lost and wandered into new territory. All migrant birds fly much farther than is indicated by the direct route.

TOP 10 ★
LARGEST FLIGHTLESS BIRDS

BIRD*	HEIGHT IN	CM	WEIGHT LB	OZ	KG
1 Ostrich (male)	100.4	255.0	343	9	156.0
2 Northern cassowary	59.1	150.0	127	9	58.0
3 Emu (female)	61.0	155.0	121	6	55.0
4 Emperor penguin (female)	45.3	115.0	101	4	46.0
5 Greater rhea	55.1	140.0	55	2	25.0
6 Flightless steamer# (duck)	33.1	84.0	13	7	6.2
7 Flightless cormorant	39.4	100.0	9	15	4.5
8 Kiwi (female)	25.6	65.0	8	4	3.8
9 Takahe (rail)	19.7	50.0	7	2	3.2
10 Kakapo (parrot)	25.2	64.0	7	1	3.2

* *By species*

\# *The flightless steamer is 84 cm (33 in) long but does not stand upright*

Source: *Chris Mead*

EMPEROR RULES

The emperor penguin is the largest of all penguins, with females as much as twice as heavy as males. There are estimated to be 220,000 breeding pairs in the Antarctic.

TOP 10 ★
SMALLEST BATS

BAT/HABITAT	LENGTH IN	LENGTH CM	WEIGHT OZ	WEIGHT G
1 Kitti's hognosed bat (*Craseonycteris thonglongyai*), Thailand	1.10	2.9	0.07	2.0
2 Proboscis bat (*Rhynchonycteris naso*), Central and South America	1.50	3.8	0.09	2.5
3 =Banana bat (*Pipistrellus nanus*), Africa	1.50	3.8	0.11	3.0
=Smoky bat (*Furipterus horrens*), Central and South America	1.50	3.8	0.11	3.0
5 =Little yellow bat (*Rhogeessa mira*), Central America	1.57	4.0	0.12	3.5
=Lesser bamboo bat (*Tylonycteris pachypus*), Southeast Asia	1.57	4.0	0.12	3.5
7 Disc-winged bat (*Thyroptera tricolor*), Central and South America	1.42	3.6	0.14	4.0
8 =Lesser horseshoe bat (*Rhinolophus hipposideros*), Europe and Western Asia	1.46	3.7	0.18	5.0
=California myotis (*Myotis californienses*), North America	1.69	4.3	0.18	5.0
10 Northern blossom bat (*Macroglossus minimus*), Southeast Asia to Australia	2.52	6.4	0.53	15.0

This list focuses on the smallest example of 10 different bat families. The weights shown are typical, rather than extreme – and as a bat can eat more than half its own weight, the weights of individual examples may vary considerably. Length is of head and body only, since tail lengths vary from zero (Kitti's hognosed bat and the northern blossom bat) to long (proboscis bat and lesser horseshoe bat).

JUST HANGING AROUND
The banana bat, the smallest found in Africa, roosts in small groups among the leaves of banana plants, using sucker pads to cling to the slippery leaf surfaces.

TOP 10 ★
LARGEST BIRDS OF PREY (BY LENGTH)

BIRD*	LENGTH IN	LENGTH CM
1 Himalayan griffon vulture	59	150
2 Californian condor	53	134
3 Andean condor	51	130
4 =Lammergeier	45	115
=Lappet-faced vulture	45	115
6 Eurasian griffon vulture	43	110
7 European black vulture	42	107
8 Harpy eagle	41	105
9 Wedge-tailed eagle	41	104
10 Ruppell's griffon	40	101

* Diurnal only – hence excluding owls

The entrants in this Top 10 all measure more than 1 m (39 in) from beak to tail. In all but the vultures, the female will be larger than the male. All these raptors, or aerial hunters, have remarkable eyesight and can spot their victims from great distances. If they kill animals heavier than themselves, they are generally unable to take wing with them, unless they take advantage of a powerful updraft of air to soar up.

TOP 10 ★
BIRDS WITH THE LARGEST WINGSPANS

BIRD*	MAXIMUM WINGSPAN IN	MAXIMUM WINGSPAN CM
1 Great white pelican	141	360
2 Wandering albatross#	138	351
3 Andean condor	126	320
4 Himalayan griffon (vulture)	122	310
5 Black vulture (Old World)	116	295
6 Marabou stork	113	287
7 Lammergeier	111	282
8 Sarus crane	110	280
9 Kori bustard	106	270
10 Stellers Sea eagle	104	265

* By species

 # The royal albatross, a close relative, is the same size

Source: Chris Mead

Very much bigger wingspans have been claimed for many species, but dead specimens of some species may easily be stretched by as much as 15 to 20 percent. The measurements given are, as far as can be ascertained, for wingtip to wingtip for live birds measured in a natural position.

TOP 10 ★
RAREST BIRDS

BIRD/COUNTRY	ESTIMATED NO.*
1 =Cebu flower pecker, Philippines	1
=Spix's macaw, Brazil	1
3 Hawaiian crow, Hawaii	5
4 Black stilt, New Zealand	12
5 Echo parakeet, Mauritius	13
6 Imperial Amazon parrot, Dominica	15
7 Magpie robin, Seychelles	20
8 Kakapo, New Zealand	24
9 Pink pigeon, Mauritius	70
10 Mauritius kestrel, Mauritius	100

* Of breeding pairs reported since 1986

Several rare bird species are known from old records or from only one specimen, but must be assumed to be extinct in the absence of recent sightings or records of breeding pairs.

Did You Know? On June 5, 1932, near Trondheim, Norway, a white-tailed sea eagle lifted 4-year-old Svanhild Hansen 244 m (800 ft) to its mountain eyrie. She was recovered unharmed.

Popular Pets

TOP 10 ★ CAT BREEDS IN CANADA

	BREED	NO. REGISTERED*
1	Himalayan	735
2	Persian	466
3	Ragdoll	186
4	Himalayan non-pointed	175
5	Exotic longhair	120
6	Birman	102
7	Maine coon	101
8	Abyssinian	82
9	Siamese	72
10	Bengal	64

* Year ending December 31, 2000

Source: Canadian Cat Association

TOP 10 ★ CAT POPULATIONS

	COUNTRY	ESTIMATED CAT POPULATION (1999)
1	US	72,600,000
2	China	46,800,000
3	Russia	12,500,000
4	Brazil	10,000,000
5	France	8,700,000
6	UK	7,700,000
7	Japan	7,540,000
8	Ukraine	7,150,000
9	Italy	7,000,000
10	Germany	6,500,000

Source: Euromonitor

Estimates of the number of domestic cats in the 20 leading countries reveal a total of 221 million, with the greatest increases experienced in China and other Asian countries.

TOP 10 ★ PETS IN THE US

	PET	ESTIMATED NUMBER
1	Cats	72,600,000
2	Dogs	58,500,000
3	Small animal pets*	13,080,000
4	Parakeets	11,000,000
5	Freshwater fish	10,800,000#
6	Reptiles	7,680,000
7	Finches	7,350,000
8	Cockatiels	6,320,000
9	Canaries	2,580,000
10	Parrots	1,550,000

* Includes small rodents – rabbits, ferrets, hamsters, guinea pigs, and gerbils

Number of households owning, rather than individual specimens

Source: Pet Industry Joint Advisory Council/ Euromonitor

The size of the pet population of the US is mirrored in the sales of dog food (US$6,169 million in 1999) and cat food (US$4,922 million), and total expenditure on pet food and care products (US$15,707,200,000).

TOP 10 CATS' NAMES IN THE US

❶ Tigger ❷ Tiger ❸ Smokey ❹ Shadow ❺ Sam ❻ Max ❼ Kitty ❽ Oreo ❾ Buddy ❿ Misty

Source: American Pet Classics

TOP 10 ★ DOG POPULATIONS

	COUNTRY	ESTIMATED DOG POPULATION (1999)
1	US	58,500,000
2	Brazil	23,000,000
3	China	19,380,000
4	Japan	9,567,000
5	Russia	9,375,000
6	France	8,100,000
7	South Africa	7,800,000
8	Poland	7,400,000
9	UK	6,700,000
10	Italy	6,300,000

Source: Euromonitor

WHAT'S NEW PUSSYCAT?

Although their role as household mouse exterminators is less significant today, cats maintain their place among the world's favorite animals.

TOP 10 DOGS' NAMES IN THE US

1 Max **2** Buddy **3** Maggie **4** Molly **5** Jake **6** Bailey **7** Lucy
8 Daisy **9** Lucky **10** Sadie

Source: *American Pet Classics*

TOP 10 🍁
DOG BREEDS IN CANADA

	BREED	NO. REGISTERED (2000)
1	Labrador retriever	9,336
2	Golden retriever	6,256
3	German shepherd	4,317
4	Poodle	2,995
5	Shetland sheepdog	2,830
6	Miniature schnauzer	2,116
7	Yorkshire terrier	2,074
8	Shih tzu	1,546
9	Bichon frise	1,520
10	Boxer	1,490

Source: *Canadian Kennel Club*

TOP 10 ⭐
FILMS STARRING DOGS

	FILM	YEAR
1	101 Dalmatians	1996
2	One Hundred and One Dalmatians*	1961
3	102 Dalmatians	2000
4	Lady and the Tramp*	1955
5	Oliver & Company	1988
6	Turner & Hooch	1989
7	The Fox and the Hound*	1981
8	Beethoven	1992
9	Homeward Bound II: Lost in San Francisco	1996
10	Beethoven's 2nd	1993

* Animated

Man's best friend has been stealing scenes since the earliest years of film-making, with the 1905 low-budget *Rescued by Rover* outstanding as one of the most successful productions of the pioneer period. The numerous silent era films starring Rin Tin Tin, an ex-German army dog who emigrated to the US, and his successor Lassie, whose long series of feature and TV films dates from the 1940s onward, are among the most enduring in cinematic history.

JACK RUSSELL

In 1819, according to legend, John "Jack" Russell (1795–1883) spotted a milkman accompanied by a distinctive-looking dog, which he persuaded its owner to sell to him and which he named Trump. He later became Curate of Swimbridge near Barnstaple, Devon, UK, where he devoted himself to breeding a type of fox terrier with short legs and a short white, black, and tan coat, ideally suited for hunting and able to follow animals into burrows. These dogs are today known in his honor as Jack Russell terriers.

WHO WAS · WHO WAS · WHO WAS · WHO WAS

THE 10 ⭐
LATEST BEST IN SHOW WINNERS AT THE WESTMINSTER KENNEL CLUB DOG SHOW

YEAR	BREED/CHAMPION
2001	Bichons frises, Special Times Just Right
2000	English springer spaniel, Salilyn 'N Erin's Shameless
1999	Papillon, Loteki Supernatural Being
1998	Norwich terrier, Fairewood Frolic
1997	Standard schnauzer, Parsifal Di Casa Netzer
1996	Clumber spaniel, Clussexx Country Sunrise
1995	Scottish terrier, Gaelforce Post Script
1994	Norwich terrier, Chidley Willum The Conqueror
1993	English springer spaniel, Salilyn's Condor
1992	Wire fox terrier, Registry's Lonesome Dove

Source: *Westminster Kennel Club*

TOP DOGS

Labrador retrievers are the most popular dogs in Canada, the US, and the UK, where they were first bred as gundogs in the 19th century.

Creepy Crawlies

FASTEST INSECT FLYERS

INSECT	MPH	KM/H
1 Hawkmoth (*Sphingidaei*)	33.3	53.6
2 =West Indian butterfly (*Nymphalidae prepona*)	30.0	48.0
=Deer bot fly (*Cephenemyia pratti*)	30.0	48.0
4 Deer bot fly (*Chrysops*)	25.0	40.0
5 West Indian butterfly (*Hesperiidae sp.*)	18.6	30.0
6 Dragonfly (*Anax parthenope*)	17.8	28.6
7 Hornet (*Vespa crabro*)	13.3	21.4
8 Bumble bee (*Bombus lapidarius*)	11.1	17.9
9 Horsefly (*Tabanus bovinus*)	8.9	14.3
10 Honey bee (*Apis millefera*)	7.2	11.6

Few accurate assessments of insect flying speeds have ever been attempted, and this Top 10 represents the results of only the handful of scientific studies that are widely recognized by entomologists. Some experts have also suggested that the male *Hybomitra linei wrighti* (*Diptera tabanidae*) is capable of traveling at 145 km/h (90 mph) when in pursuit of a female, while there are exceptional, one-time examples such as that of a dragonfly (*Austophlebia costalis*) allegedly recorded as flying at a speed of 98 km/h (61 mph).

LARGEST BUTTERFLIES

BUTTERFLY	AVERAGE WINGSPAN IN	MM
1 Queen Alexandra's birdwing	11.0	280
2 African giant swallowtail	9.1	230
3 Goliath birdwing	8.3	210
4 =Buru opalescent birdwing	7.9	200
=*Trogonoptera trojana*	7.9	200
=*Troides hypolitus*	7.9	200
7 =*Chimaera birdwing*	7.5	190
=*Ornithoptera lydius*	7.5	190
=*Troides magellanus*	7.5	190
=*Troides miranda*	7.5	190

CREATURES WITH THE MOST LEGS

CREATURE	AVERAGE LEGS
1 Millipede *Illacme plenipes*	750
2 Centipede *Himantarum gabrielis*	354
3 Centipede *Haplophilus subterraneus*	178
4 Millipedes*	30
5 Symphylans	24
6 Caterpillars*	16
7 Woodlice	14
8 Crabs, shrimps	10
9 Spiders	8
10 Insects	6

* Most species

Despite their names, centipedes, depending on their species, have anything from 28 to 354 legs and millipedes have up to 400 legs, with the record standing at around 750.

LARGEST MOLLUSCS

SPECIES/CLASS	AVERAGE LENGTH* IN	MM
1 Giant squid (*Architeuthis sp.*), Cephalopod	660	16,764#
2 Giant clam (*Tridacna gigas*), Marine bivalve	51	1,300
3 Australian trumpet, Marine snail	30	770
4 *Hexabranchus sanguineus*, Sea slug	20	520
5 *Carinaria cristata*, Heteropod	19	500
6 Steller's coat of mail shell (*Cryptochiton stelleri*), Chiton	18	470
7 Freshwater mussel (*Cristaria plicata*), Freshwater bivalve	11	300
8 Giant African snail (*Achatina achatina*), Land snail	7	200
9 Tusk shell (*Dentalium vernedi*), Scaphopod	5	138
10 Apple snail (*Pila werneri*), Freshwater snail	4	125

* Largest species within each class
# Estimated; actual length unknown

COUNTRIES WITH THE MOST THREATENED INVERTEBRATES

COUNTRY	THREATENED INVERTEBRATE SPECIES
1 US	594
2 Australia	281
3 South Africa	101
4 Portugal	67
5 France	61
6 Spain	57
7 Tanzania	46
8 =Dem. Rep. of Congo	45
=Japan	45
10 =Austria	41
=Italy	41

Source: *International Union for the Conservation of Nature*

LARGEST MOTHS

MOTH	AVERAGE WINGSPAN IN	MM
1 Atlas moth (*Attacus atlas*)	11.8	300
2 Owlet moth (*Thysania agrippina*)*	11.4	290
3 *Haematopis grataria*	10.2	260
4 Hercules emperor moth (*Coscinocera hercules*)	8.3	210
5 Malagasy silk moth (*Argema mitraei*)	7.1	180
6 *Eacles imperialis*	6.9	175
7 = Common emperor moth (*Bunaea alcinoe*)	6.3	160
=Giant peacock moth (*Saturnia pyri*)	6.3	160
9 Gray moth (*Brahmaea wallichii*)	6.1	155
10 =Black witch (*Ascalapha odorata*)	5.9	150
=Regal moth (*Citheronia regalis*)	5.9	150
=Polyphemus moth (*Antheraea polyphemus*)	5.9	150

* Exceptional specimen measured at 308 mm (12¼ in)

TOP 10 ★
DEADLIEST SPIDERS

SPIDER/LOCATION

1 Banana spider (*Phonenutria nigriventer*), Central and South America

2 Sydney funnel web (*Atrax robustus*), Australia

3 Wolf spider (*Lycosa raptoria/erythrognatha*), Central and South America

4 Black widow (*Latrodectus* species), Widespread

5 Violin spider/Recluse spider, Widespread

6 Sac spider, Southern Europe

7 Tarantula (*Eurypelma rubropilosum*), Neotropics

8 Tarantula (*Acanthoscurria atrox*), Neotropics

9 Tarantula (*Lasiodora klugi*), Neotropics

10 Tarantula (*Pamphobeteus* species), Neotropics

This list ranks spiders according to their "lethal potential" – their venom yield divided by their venom potency. The Banana spider, for example, yields 6 mg of venom, with 1 mg the estimated lethal dose in man.

THE 10 MOST ENDANGERED SPIDERS
(Spider/country)

1 Kauai cave wolf spider, US **2** Doloff cave spider, US **3** Empire cave pseudoscorpion, US **4** Glacier Bay wolf spider, US **5** Great raft spider, Europe **6** Kocevje subterranean spider (*Troglohyphantes gracilis*), Slovenia **7** Kocevje subterranean spider (*Troglohyphantes similis*), Slovenia **8** Kocevje subterranean spider (*Troglohyphantes spinipes*), Slovenia **9** Lake Placid funnel wolf spider, US **10** Melones cave harvestman, US

Source: *International Union for the Conservation of Nature*

THE FLY
The 120,000 known species of flies include houseflies, mosquitoes, midges, and gnats, all of which number among the insects humans consider the most irritating.

TOP 10 ★
MOST COMMON INSECTS*

SPECIES	APPROX. NO. OF KNOWN SPECIES
1 Beetles (*Coleoptera*)	400,000
2 Butterflies and moths (*Lepidoptera*)	165,000
3 Ants, bees, and wasps (*Hymenoptera*)	140,000
4 True flies (*Diptera*)	120,000
5 Bugs (*Hemiptera*)	90,000
6 Crickets, grasshoppers, and locusts (*Orthoptera*)	20,000
7 Caddisflies (*Trichoptera*)	10,000
8 Lice (*Phthiraptera/Psocoptera*)	7,000
9 Dragonflies and damselflies (*Odonata*)	5,500
10 Lacewings (*Neuroptera*)	4,700

* By number of known species

This list includes only species that have been discovered and named. It is surmised that many thousands of species still await discovery. It takes no account of the truly colossal numbers of each species: there are at least 1 million insects for each of the Earth's 6.1 billion humans.

The UK has over 44 million and Canada less than 700,000. What are they?
see p.42 for the answer

A Houses over 100 years old
B Sheep
C Lime trees

Livestock

CATTLE COUNTRIES

	COUNTRY	CATTLE (2000)
1	India	218,800,000
2	Brazil	167,471,000
3	China	104,169,000
4	US	98,048,000
5	Argentina	55,000,000
6	Sudan	35,300,000
7	Ethiopia	35,100,000
8	Mexico	30,293,000
9	Russian Federation	27,500,000
10	Colombia	26,000,000
	Canada	12,655,000
	World	1,343,794,190

Source: *Food and Agriculture Organization of the United Nations*

SHEEP COUNTRIES

	COUNTRY	SHEEP (2000)
1	China	131,095,415
2	Australia	116,900,000
3	India	57,900,000
4	Iran	55,000,000
5	New Zealand	45,497,000
6	UK	44,656,000
7	Sudan	42,800,000
8	Turkey	30,238,000
9	South Africa	28,700,000
10	Pakistan	24,084,000
	Canada	645,000
	World	1,064,377,000

Source: *Food and Agriculture Organization of the United Nations*

This is one of the few world lists in which the UK ranks considerably above the US (7,215,000).

CHICKEN COUNTRIES

	COUNTRY	CHICKENS (2000)
1	China	3,625,012,000
2	US	1,720,000,000
3	Indonesia	1,000,000,000
4	Brazil	950,000,000
5	Mexico	476,000,000
6	India	402,000,000
7	Russia	340,000,000
8	Japan	298,000,000
9	France	232,970,000
10	Iran	230,000,000
	Canada	145,000,000
	World	14,525,381,000

Source: *Food and Agriculture Organization of the United Nations*

The Top 10 countries have 65 percent of the world's chicken population, with almost half the world total being reared in Asian countries. In the UK, the estimated chicken population of 154,180,000 outnumbers the human population more than twice over.

TOP 10 MILK-PRODUCING COUNTRIES

(Country/production in tonnes*, 2000)

❶ US, 76,294,174 **❷ Russia**, 31,560,024 **❸ India**, 30,899,594 **❹ Germany**, 28,199,814
❺ France, 24,890,407 **❻ Brazil**, 22,495,441 **❼ UK**, 14,720,874
❽ Ukraine, 12,400,298 **❾ New Zealand**, 12,013,837 **❿ Poland**, 11,484,949
Canada 8,200,036 *World* 484,746,000

* *Fresh cows' milk* Source: *Food and Agriculture Organization of the United Nations*

GEESE COUNTRIES

	COUNTRY	GEESE (2000)
1	China	203,225,000
2	Egypt	9,100,000
3	Romania	4,000,000
4	Russia	3,300,000
5	Madagascar	3,100,000
6	Turkey	1,650,000
7	Hungary	1,226,000
8	Iran	1,200,000
9	Israel	1,100,000
10	France	1,000,000
	Canada	300,000
	World	235,087,000

Source: *Food and Agriculture Organization of the United Nations*

GOLDEN EGG

Some 86 percent of the world's geese reside in China, where they play an important part in culture and cuisine. China is also the top producer of goose down.

DONKEY COUNTRIES

	COUNTRY	DONKEYS (2000)
1	China	9,348,000
2	Ethiopia	5,200,000
3	Pakistan	4,500,000
4	Mexico	3,250,000
5	Egypt	3,050,000
6	Iran	1,600,000
7	Brazil	1,350,000
8	Afghanistan	1,160,000
9 =	India	1,000,000
=	Nigeria	1,000,000
	World	43,564,000

Source: *Food and Agriculture Organization of the United Nations*

BUFFALO

More than 95 percent of the world's buffalo population resides in the Top 10 countries. Only one European country has a significant herd: Italy, with 173,000.

TOP 10 ⭐

BUFFALO COUNTRIES

	COUNTRY	BUFFALOES (2000)
1	India	93,772,000
2	Pakistan	22,670,000
3	China	22,599,000
4	Nepal	3,470,600
5	Egypt	3,200,000
6	Indonesia	3,145,150
7	Philippines	3,018,000
8	Vietnam	3,000,000
9	Myanmar (Burma)	2,400,000
10	Thailand	2,100,000
	World	165,804,000

Source: *Food and Agriculture Organization of the United Nations*

TOP 10 ⭐

PIG COUNTRIES

	COUNTRY	PIGS (2000)
1	China	437,551,000
2	US	59,337,000
3	Brazil	27,320,000
4	Germany	27,049,000
5	Spain	23,682,000
6	Vietnam	19,586,000
7	Russia	18,300,000
8	Poland	18,200,000
9	India	16,005,000
10	France	14,635,000
	Canada	12,254,000
	World	909,486,000

Source: *Food and Agriculture Organization of the United Nations*

The distribution of the world's pig population reflects cultural, religious, and dietary factors. There are few pigs in African and Islamic countries and a disproportionate concentration of pigs in those countries that do not have such prohibitions.

TOP 10 ⭐

GOAT COUNTRIES

	COUNTRY	GOATS (2000)
1	China	148,400,500
2	India	123,000,000
3	Pakistan	47,425,000
4	Sudan	37,500,000
5	Bangladesh	33,800,000
6	Iran	26,000,000
7	Nigeria	24,300,000
8	Ethiopia	17,000,000
9	Indonesia	15,197,832
10	Brazil	12,600,000
	Canada	29,000
	World	715,297,550

Source: *Food and Agriculture Organization of the United Nations*

The goat is one of the most widely distributed of all domesticated animals. Its resilience to diseases, such as the tuberculosis that affects cattle, and its adaptability to harsh conditions make it ideally suited to the environments encountered in some of the less-developed parts of the world. Goat meat and milk figure in the national diets of many countries, and even some of the smaller African nations have one million or more goats.

DONKEY

The donkey is used extensively throughout the world as a beast of burden. It should not be confused with the mule (the offspring of a horse and a donkey).

Did You Know? The first pig to fly took to the air on November 4, 1909, the passenger of Claude Moore- (later Lord) Brabazon, in a wicker basket attached to his Voisin biplane.

43

TAPPING RUBBER

In the 20th century, world demand for natural rubber, especially for the automotive industry, increased from under 46,000 to over 5.4 million tonnes.

TOP 10 ★
RUBBER-PRODUCING COUNTRIES

	COUNTRY	1999 PRODUCTION (TONNES)
1	Thailand	2,197,786
2	Indonesia	1,563,880
3	Malaysia	885,424
4	India	549,844
5	China	439,875
6	Vietnam	214,766
7	Côte d'Ivoire	118,826
8	Sri Lanka	95,683
9	Nigeria	89,975
10	Philippines	63,982
	World total	*5,923,674*

Source: *Food and Agriculture Organization of the United Nations*

TOP 10 ★
MOST FORESTED COUNTRIES

	COUNTRY	PERCENTAGE FOREST COVER 2000
1	French Guiana	90.0
2	Solomon Islands	87.8
3	Suriname	86.4
4	Gabon	81.5
5	Guyana	78.5
6	Brunei	76.6
7	Palau	76.1
8	Finland	72.0
9	North Korea	68.1
10	Sweden	66.8
	Canada	*26.5*

Source: *Food and Agriculture Organization of the United Nations*

These are the 10 countries with the greatest area of forest and woodland as a percentage of their total land area. With increasing deforestation, the world average has fallen from about 32 percent in 1972 to its present 29 percent. The least forested large countries in the world are the desert lands of the Middle East and North Africa, such as Egypt with just 0.1 percent.

TOP 10 ★
COUNTRIES WITH THE LARGEST AREAS OF FOREST

	COUNTRY	AREA (2000) SQ MILES	AREA (2000) SQ KM
1	Russia	3,287,243	8,513,920
2	Brazil	2,055,921	5,324,810
3	Canada	944,294	2,445,710
4	US	872,564	2,259,930
5	China	631,200	1,634,800
6	Australia	610,350	1,580,800
7	Dem. Rep. of Congo	522,037	1,352,070
8	Indonesia	405,353	1,049,860
9	Angola	269,329	697,560
10	Peru	251,796	652,150
	World total	*14,888,715*	*38,561,590*

The world's forests occupy some 29 percent of the total land area of the planet.

TOP 10 ★
LARGEST NATIONAL FORESTS IN THE US

	FOREST/LOCATION	AREA SQ MILES	SQ KM
1	**Tongass National Forest,** Sitka, Alaska	25,920	67,133
2	**Chugach National Forest,** Anchorage, Alaska	8,439	21,856
3	**Toiyabe National Forest,** Sparks, Nevada	5,053	13,087
6	**Tonto National Forest,** Phoenix, Arizona	4,489	11,627
8	**Gila National Forest,** Silver City, New Mexico	4,231	10,961
7	**Boise National Forest,** Boise, Idaho	4,145	10,734
8	**Humboldt National Forest,** Elko, Nevada	3,878	10,044
9	**Challis National Forest,** Challis, Idaho	3,851	9,974
10	**Shoshone National Forest,** Cody, Wyoming	3,808	9,862

Source: *Land Areas of the National Forest System*

TREE TOPS
Canada is the 6th-largest producer of timber in the world, supplying the requirements of many industries such as construction and paper manufacture.

TOP 10 ★
TIMBER-PRODUCING COUNTRIES

	COUNTRY	CU FT	PRODUCTION 1998 CU M
1	US	17,478,536,826	494,937,000
2	China	11,054,092,059	313,017,000
3	India	10,822,357,195	306,455,000
4	Brazil	7,780,280,892	220,313,000
5	Indonesia	7,168,471,891	202,988,500
6	Canada	6,751,387,981	191,178,000
7	Nigeria	4,145,483,167	117,387,000
8	Russia	2,965,302,211	83,968,000
9	Sweden	2,126,790,686	60,224,000
10	Ethiopia	1,847,310,388	52,310,000
	World total	119,562,158,989	3,385,623,000

Source: *Food and Agriculture Organization of the United Nations*

TOP 10 🍁
MOST COMMON TREES IN CANADA

	TREE	RANGE AREA (SQ KM)
1	Bebb willow	5,984,482
2	White spruce	5,848,283
3	White birch	5,756,537
4	Black spruce	5,718,916
5	Trembling aspen	5,153,891
6	Balsam poplar	5,042,705
7	Tamarack	4,969,130
8	Speckled alder	4,865,415
9	Pin cherry	3,543,706
10	Water birch	3,499,059

Source: *Canadian Forest Service, Science Branch*

Canada's national emblem, the maple, does not make the Top 10. The most common type, the mountain maple (*Acer spicatum*), which covers 1,778,693 sq km, places at No. 20.

TOP 10 ★
TALLEST TREES IN NORTH AMERICA

	TREE/LOCATION	HEIGHT FT	M
1	**Coast redwood**, Jedidiah Smith State Park, California	321	97.8
2	**Sitka spruce**, Carmanah Creek, British Columbia	315	96.0
3	**Coast Douglas fir**, Coquitlam, British Columbia	309	94.3
4	**Coast Douglas fir**, Olympic National Forest, Washington	281	85.6
5	**General Sherman giant sequoia**, Sequoia National Park, California	275	83.8
6	=**Coast Douglas fir**, Puntledge River, British Columbia	272	82.9
	=**Noble fir**, Mount St. Helens National Monument, Washington	272	82.9
8	**Sitka spruce**, West Walbran Creek, British Columbia	265	80.8
9	**Western hemlock**, Tahsish River, British Columbia	248	75.6
10	**Grand fir**, Upper Chilliwack River, British Columbia	246	75.0

Source: *American Forests* and *British Columbia Register of Big Trees*

A Coast redwood known as the Dyerville Giant (from Dyerville, California), which stood 110.3 m (362 ft) high, fell in a storm on March 27, 1991, and a slightly taller (110.6-m/363-ft) Coast redwood, which formerly topped this list, fell during the winter of 1992.

Which is the largest island in Canada?
see p.20 for the answer
A Prince Edward Island
B Baffin Island
C Newfoundland

THE HUMAN WORLD

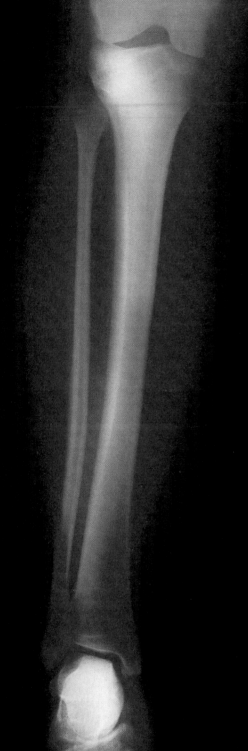

THE WINNING LEG

The second longest bone, the tibia is named after the Latin word for a flute, which it resembles in shape and length. The three longest bones are all in the leg.

TOP 10 ★
LONGEST BONES IN THE HUMAN BODY

BONE	AVERAGE LENGTH IN	CM
1 **Femur** (thighbone – upper leg)	19.88	50.50
2 **Tibia** (shinbone – inner lower leg)	16.94	43.03
3 **Fibula** (outer lower leg)	15.94	40.50
4 **Humerus** (upper arm)	14.35	36.46
5 **Ulna** (inner lower arm)	11.10	28.20
6 **Radius** (outer lower arm)	10.40	26.42
7 **7th rib**	9.45	24.00
8 **8th rib**	9.06	23.00
9 **Innominate bone** (hipbone – half pelvis)	7.28	18.50
10 **Sternum** (breastbone)	6.69	17.00

❀ TOP 10 REASONS CANADIANS VISIT THEIR DOCTORS

(reason for visit/visits to Canadian office-based doctors, 2000)

❶ **High blood pressure**, 16,622,000 ❷ **Depression**, 7,842,000 ❸ **Diabetes mellitus**, 7,158,000 ❹ **Routine check-up** 6,896,000 ❺ **Acute upper respiratory infection**, 6,087,000 ❻ **Anxiety**, 4,563,000 ❼ **Middle ear infection**, 4,256,000 ❽ **Normal pregnancy**, 4,253,000 ❾ **Acute bronchitis**, 3,382,000 ❿ **Asthma**, 3,090,000

Source: IMS Health, Canada

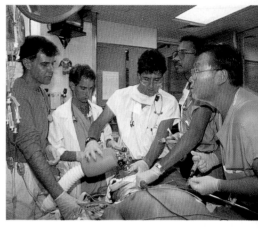

EMERGENCY ROOM

The world's hospital emergency rooms must treat all kinds of injuries and many are equipped to administer both gas-based and injection-based anesthetics.

THE 10 ★
COUNTRIES WITH THE MOST PATIENTS PER DOCTOR

	COUNTRY	PATIENTS PER DOCTOR
1	**Malawi**	49,118
2	**Eritrea**	46,200
3	**Mozambique**	36,320
4	**Niger**	35,141
5	**Ethiopia**	30,195
6	**Chad**	27,765
7	**Burkina Faso**	27,158
8	**Rwanda**	24,697
9	**Liberia**	24,600
10	**Ghana**	22,970
	Canada	465

Source: *World Bank*

THE FIRST INJECTABLE ANESTHETIC

The first anesthetics – ether, chloroform, and nitrous oxide ("laughing gas") – came into use in the mid-19th century. All were administered by the patient breathing in the vapors or gases, but all had their drawbacks, in particular the difficulty of safely controlling the precise quantity that was being administered. In 1902, German chemist Emil Fischer and pathologist Joseph Freiherr von Mering introduced the hypnotic drugs known as barbiturates, including Veronal, the first anesthetic that could be injected so that the anesthetist could control breathing. It is said that von Mering proposed that the new substance be called "Veronal," because the most peaceful place he knew was the Italian city of Verona.

100 YEARS AGO · YEARS AGO · YEARS AGO · YEARS AGO

Which is the fastest growing career in Canada?
see p.195 for the answer

A Nurse practitioner
B Physician/Surgeon
C In-home nurse

TOP 10 ★
COUNTRIES THAT SPEND THE MOST ON HEALTH CARE

COUNTRY	HEALTH SPENDING PER CAPITA (US$)
1 US	4,080
2 Switzerland	3,616
3 Germany	2,727
4 Norway	2,616
5 Denmark	2,576
6 Japan	2,379
7 France	2,287
8 Sweden	2,220
9 Austria	2,108
10 Netherlands	1,988
Canada	1,855

Source: *World Bank*, World Development Indicators 2000

THE 10 ★
GLOBAL DISEASES THAT CAUSE THE HIGHEST LEVEL OF DISABILITY

DISEASE	PERCENTAGE OF TOTAL BURDEN OF DISEASE * #
1 Neuropsychiatric disorders	11.0
2 Cardiovascular diseases	10.9
3 Respiratory infections	7.0
4 =HIV/AIDS	6.2
=Perinatal conditions	6.2
6 Malignant neoplasms (cancers)	5.9
7 Diarrheal diseases	5.0
8 Respiratory diseases (noncommunicable)	4.9
9 Childhood diseases	3.8
10 Malaria	3.1

* *Measured in Disability-Adjusted Life Years (DALYs): a measure of the difference between a population's actual level of health and a normative goal of living in full health*

\# *Total percentage includes injuries at 13.9 percent*

Source: *World Health Organization*, World Health Report 2000

TOP 10 ★
LARGEST HUMAN ORGANS

ORGAN		AVERAGE WEIGHT OZ	G
1 Skin		384.0	10,886
2 Liver		55.0	1,560
3 Brain	male	49.7	1,408
	female	44.6	1,263
4 Lungs	*right*	20.5	580
	left	18.0	510
	total	38.5	1,090
5 Heart	male	11.1	315
	female	9.3	265
6 Kidneys	*right*	4.9	140
	left	5.3	150
	total	10.2	290
7 Spleen		6.0	170
8 Pancreas		3.5	98
9 Thyroid		1.2	35
10 Prostate	male only	0.7	20

This list is based on average immediate post-mortem weights, as recorded by St. Bartholemew's Hospital, London, England, and other sources during a 10-year period.

BRAIN WAVE

The modern technique of Magnetic Resonance Imaging (MRI) enables us to view the human brain, the human body's third largest organ.

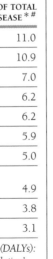
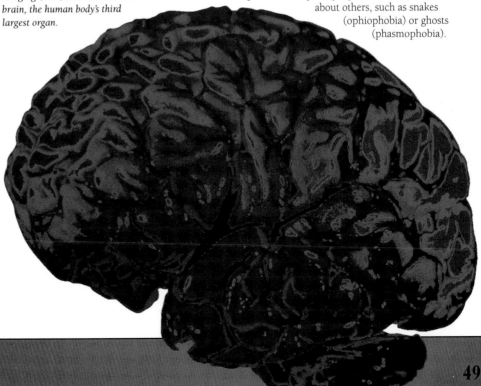

TOP 10 ★
MOST COMMON PHOBIAS

	OBJECT OF PHOBIA	MEDICAL TERM
1	Spiders	Arachnephobia or arachnophobia
2	People and social situations	Anthropophobia or sociophobia
3	Flying	Aerophobia or aviatophobia
4	Open spaces	Agoraphobia, cenophobia, or kenophobia
5	Confined spaces	Claustrophobia, cleisiophobia, cleithrophobia, or clithrophobia
6 =	Vomiting	Emetophobia or emitophobia
=	Heights	Acrophobia, altophobia, hypsophobia, or hypsiphobia
8	Cancer	Carcinomaphobia, carcinophobia, carcinomatophobia, cancerphobia, or cancerophobia
9	Thunderstorms	Brontophobia or keraunophobia
10 =	Death	Necrophobia or thanatophobia
=	Heart disease	Cardiophobia

A phobia is a morbid fear that is out of all proportion to the object of the fear. Many people would admit to being uncomfortable about the objects of these principal phobias, as well as about others, such as snakes (ophiophobia) or ghosts (phasmophobia).

Lifestyle

COUNTRIES WITH THE HEAVIEST SMOKERS

	COUNTRY	AVERAGE ANNUAL CIGARETTE CONSUMPTION PER SMOKER (1988–98)*
1	Iraq	5,751
2	Belgium	5,300
3	Australia	4,951
4	Hungary	4,949
5	US	4,938
6	Greece	4,877
7	Switzerland	4,618
8	Poland	4,544
9	Singapore	4,250
10	Japan	4,126

* Smokers aged over 15, in those countries for which data available

Source: *World Bank*, World Development Indicators 2000

CANADIAN PROVINCES WITH THE MOST PHYSICAL INACTIVITY

	PROVINCE	% OF POPULATION, INACTIVE
1	Quebec	72
2	Prince Edward Island	68
3	Newfoundland	67
4	=Nova Scotia	65
	=New Brunswick	65
	=Manitoba	65
7	Alberta	62
8	Ontario	61
9	Saskatchewan	60
10	British Columbia	57

Source: 1999 Physical Activity Monitor, *Canadian Fitness and Lifestyle Research Institute*

Physical inactivity is less pervasive in Canada's territories: the NWT/Nunavut places at No. 11 with 55 percent, and the Yukon trails at 47 percent.

FAT CONSUMERS

	COUNTRY	DAILY CONSUMPTION PER CAPITA OZ	G
1	France	5.80	164.7
2	Austria	5.64	159.9
3	Belgium and Luxembourg	5.58	158.6
4	Italy	5.37	152.3
5	Greece	5.35	151.7
6	Switzerland	5.19	147.3
7	Germany	5.18	147.0
8	Spain	5.17	146.8
9	US	5.16	146.4
10	UK	5.06	143.7
	Canada	4.57	129.6

Source: *Food and Agriculture Organization of the United Nations*

CALORIE CONSUMERS

	COUNTRY	AVERAGE DAILY CONSUMPTION PER CAPITA
1	US	3,756.8
2	Portugal	3,691.1
3	Greece	3,629.9
4	Ireland	3,622.0
5	Italy	3,608.3
6	Belgium and Luxembourg	3,606.3
7	Turkey	3,554.1
8	France	3,541.2
9	Austria	3,530.8
10	Cyprus	3,473.8
	Canada	3,167.4
	World	2,791.8

Source: *Food and Agriculture Organization of the United Nations*

The Calorie requirement of the average man is 2,700 and that of a woman 2,500. Inactive people need less, whereas those engaged in heavy labor might need even to double these figures.

FAT OF THE LAND

The ubiquitous burger and fries contribute to the US's place at the top of the table of high Calorie consumers.

TOP 10 MOST EFFECTIVE FITNESS ACTIVITIES

1 Swimming **2** Cycling **3** Rowing **4** Gymnastics **5** Judo **6** Dancing
7 Soccer **8** Jogging **9** Walking (briskly!) **10** Squash

These are the sports and activities recommended by fitness experts as the best means of acquiring all-around fitness, building stamina and strength, and increasing suppleness.

TOP 10 ★
MULTIVITAMIN CONSUMERS

	COUNTRY	PERCENTAGE OF HEALTH SUPPLEMENT MARKET
1	Mexico	34.8
2 =	Brazil	30.9
=	Spain	30.9
4	Switzerland	30.5
5	UK	30.4
6	Canada	27.1
7	Italy	24.8
8	US	24.0
9	Finland	22.0
10	Germany	20.5

Source: *Euromonitor*

TOP 10 ★
CAUSES OF STRESS-RELATED ILLNESS

	EVENT	VALUE
1	Death of spouse	100
2	Divorce	73
3	Marital separation	65
4 =	Death of close family member	63
=	Detention in prison or other institution	63
6	Major personal injury or illness	53
7	Marriage	50
8	Losing one's job	47
9 =	Marital reconciliation	45
=	Retirement	45

Psychiatrists Dr. Thomas Holmes and Dr. Richard Rahe devised what they called the "Social Readjustment Rating Scale" to place a value on the likelihood of illness occurring as a result of stress caused by various "life events." The cumulative effect of several incidents increases the risk factor.

TOP 10 ★
COUNTRIES SPENDING THE MOST ON WEIGHT MANAGEMENT PRODUCTS

	COUNTRY	VALUE OF SALES IN 1999 (US$)
1	US	3,546,300,000
2	Japan	896,000,000
3	France	142,700,000
4	UK	126,800,000
5	Italy	114,400,000
6	China	102,400,000
7	Canada	84,000,000
8	Australia	56,700,000
9	Brazil	56,600,000
10	Germany	44,200,000

Source: *Euromonitor*

TOP 10 ★
SPENDERS ON VITAMINS AND DIETARY SUPPLEMENTS

	COUNTRY	VALUE OF SALES IN 1999 (US$)
1	US	11,430,200,000
2	Japan	10,733,400,000
3	Germany	795,500,000
4	UK	630,500,000
5	China	523,300,000
6	France	511,700,000
7	Italy	510,400,000
8	Brazil	465,200,000
9	Canada	430,400,000
10	Russia	230,400,000

Source: *Euromonitor*

TWO WHEELS GOOD

Cycling's popularity has increased since the invention of the mountain bike. It is ranked second only to swimming as one of the most effective fitness activities.

TOP 10 ★
COSMETIC SURGERY PROCEDURES

1	Body reshaping by liposuction/liposculpture
2	Nose reshaping (rhinoplasty)
3	Upper or lower eye bag removal (blepharoplasty)
4	Face lift
5	Breast augmentation
6	Breast reduction
7	Ear reshaping (otoplasty)
8	Laser treatment for the removal of lines and wrinkles
9	Laser treatment for snoring problems
10	Varicose veins/thread vein removal

Source: *The Harley Medical Group*

Did You Know? Soon after the press identified 54-year-old Chao Boonchu as Thailand's champion chain-smoker (120 cigarettes a day for 30 years), he collapsed with severe breathing difficulties and heart problems and went into a coma.

Cradle to the Grave

COUNTRIES WITH THE HIGHEST BIRTH RATE

COUNTRY	LIVE BIRTH RATE PER 1,000 POPULATION (2002)
1 Niger	50.0
2 Mali	48.4
3 Chad	47.7
4 Uganda	47.1
5 Somalia	46.8
6 Angola	46.2
7 Liberia	46.0
8 Dem. Rep. of Congo	45.5
9 Marshall Islands	45.0
10 Sierra Leone	44.6
Canada	11.1

Source: *US Census Bureau International Data Base*

The countries with the highest birth rates are amongst the poorest countries in the world. In these countries, people often want to have large families so that the children can help earn income for the family when they are older.

CHILDREN FROM MALI

Mali is one of only a handful of countries with a birth rate of more than 45 per 1,000. The country also has the ninth highest fertility rate (the average number of children born to each woman) of 6.6.

TOP 10 COUNTRIES WITH THE LOWEST BIRTH RATE

(Country/live birth rate per 1,000 population, 2002)

❶ Bulgaria, 8.1 ❷ Latvia, 8.3 ❸ Italy, 8.9 ❹ = Estonia, 9.0; = Germany, 9.0 ❻ Czech Republic, 9.1 ❼ = Hungary, 9.3; = Slovenia, 9.3; = Spain, 9.3 ❿ = Austria, 9.6; = Monaco, 9.6; = Ukraine, 9.6

Source: *US Census Bureau International Data Base*

COUNTRIES WITH THE HIGHEST UNDER-5 MORTALITY RATE

COUNTRY	MORTALITY RATE PER 1,000 LIVE BIRTHS (1998)
1 Sierra Leone	316
2 Angola	292
3 Niger	280
4 Afghanistan	257
5 Mali	237
6 Liberia	235
7 Malawi	213
8 Somalia	211
9 Dem. Rep. of Congo	207
10 Mozambique	206

Source: *UNICEF, The State of the World's Children 2000*

COUNTRIES WITH THE HIGHEST DEATH RATE

COUNTRY	DEATH RATE PER 1,000 POPULATION
1 Angola	25.01
2 Mozambique	23.29
3 Niger	23.17
4 Malawi	22.44
5 Zimbabwe	22.43
6 = Botswana	22.08
= Zambia	22.08
8 Rwanda	20.95
9 Swaziland	20.40
10 Sierra Leone	19.58
Canada	7.00

Source: *Central Intelligence Agency*

The 15 countries with the highest death rates are all in Africa; the highest outside Africa is Afghanistan, with a rate of 18.01. Ukraine's 16.48 is the highest of any European country, and Haiti's 15.12 the highest of any in the Western hemisphere.

THE 10 MOST COMMON CAUSES OF DEATH

(Cause/approximate no. of deaths per annum)

❶ Ischemic heart disease, 7,089,000 ❷ Cancers*, 7,065,000 ❸ Cerebrovascular disease, 5,544,000 ❹ Acute lower respiratory infection, 3,963,000 ❺ HIV/AIDS, 2,673,000 ❻ Chronic obstructive pulmonary disease, 2,660,000 ❼ Diarrhea, including dysentery, 2,213,000 ❽ Tuberculosis, 1,669,000 ❾ Childhood diseases#, 1,554,000 ❿ Traffic accidents, 1,230,000

* Lung cancer deaths alone number 1,193,000
\# Childhood diseases include pertussis, polio, diphtheria, measles, and tetanus
Source: *WHO, World Health Report 2000*

GREEK GIFT

The country's traditional Mediterranean diet, high in olive oil, fruits and vegetables, and fish, may partly explain why Greek men enjoy one of the world's highest life expectancies.

TOP 10 ★
COUNTRIES WITH THE HIGHEST MALE LIFE EXPECTANCY

COUNTRY	LIFE EXPECTANCY AT BIRTH, 2002 (YEARS)
1 =Andorra	80.6
=San Marino	77.8
3 Japan	77.7
4 Iceland	77.4
5 Singapore	77.3
6 =Australia	77.2
=Sweden	77.2
8 Switzerland	77.0
9 Israel	76.8
10 Canada	76.3

Source: *US Census Bureau International Data Base*

TOP 10 ★
COUNTRIES WITH THE HIGHEST FEMALE LIFE EXPECTANCY

COUNTRY	LIFE EXPECTANCY AT BIRTH, 2002 (YEARS)
1 Andorra	86.6
2 San Marino	85.2
3 Japan	84.2
4 Singapore	83.5
5 =Canada	83.2
=Monaco	83.2
7 France	83.1
8 Australia	83.0
9 Switzerland	82.9
10 Spain	82.8

Source: *US Census Bureau International Data Base*

THE 10 ★
COUNTRIES WITH THE MOST CASES OF AIDS

COUNTRY	DEATHS	NO. OF CASES
1 South Africa	250,000	4,200,000
2 India	310,000	3,700,000
3 Ethiopia	280,000	3,000,000
4 Nigeria	250,000	2,700,000
5 Kenya	180,000	2,100,000
6 Zimbabwe	160,000	1,500,000
7 Tanzania	140,000	1,300,000
8 Mozambique	98,000	1,200,000
9 Dem. Rep. of Congo	95,000	1,100,000
10 Zambia	99,000	870,000
Canada	400	49,000
World	2,800,000	34,300,000

Source: *UNAIDS*, Report on the Global HIV/AIDS Epidemic, June 2000

THE 10 ★
MOST COMMON TYPES OF CANCER

TYPE	ANNUAL DEATHS
1 Trachea, bronchus, and lung	1,193,000
2 Stomach	801,000
3 Liver	589,000
4 Colon and rectum	509,000
5 Breast	467,000
6 Esophagus	381,000
7 Lymphomas	295,000
8 Mouth and pharynx	282,000
9 Leukemias	268,000
10 Prostate	255,000

Source: *WHO*, World Health Report 2000

Globally, a clear trend is emerging: the gradual elimination of other fatal diseases, combined with rising life expectancy, means that the risks of developing cancer are steadily growing. One of the most noticeable changes in the ranking compared with 10 years ago is the increase in lung cancer.

THE 10 MOST SUICIDAL COUNTRIES
(Country/suicides per 100,000 population)

1 Lithuania, 45.8 **2** Russia, 41.8 **3** Estonia, 41.0 **4** Latvia, 40.7 **5** Hungary, 32.9
6 Slovenia, 28.4 **7** Belarus, 27.9 **8** Finland, 27.3 **9** Kazakstan, 23.8
10 Croatia, 22.8 *Canada*, 12.8

It is perhaps surprising that the highest suicide rates are not generally recorded in the poorest countries in the world. In fact, the lowest suicide rate recorded is in Egypt – fewer than one suicide per 1 million people.   Source: UN Demographic Yearbook

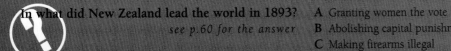

In what did New Zealand lead the world in 1893?
see p.60 for the answer

A Granting women the vote
B Abolishing capital punishment
C Making firearms illegal

Marriage & Divorce

COUNTRIES WITH THE MOST MARRIAGES

	COUNTRY	MARRIAGES PER ANNUM
1	China	9,121,622
2	US	2,362,000
3	Bangladesh	1,200,000
4	Russia	1,080,600
5	Japan	782,738
6	Brazil	763,129
7	Mexico	671,640
8	Egypt	530,746
9	Thailand	484,569
10	Iran	460,888
	Canada	158,200

Source: *United Nations*

This list, based on United Nations statistics, regrettably excludes certain large countries such as Indonesia, India, and Pakistan, which fail to provide accurate data.

COUNTRIES WITH THE HIGHEST PROPORTION OF TEENAGE BRIDES

	COUNTRY	PERCENTAGE OF 15–19-YEAR-OLD GIRLS WHO HAVE EVER BEEN MARRIED*
1	Dem. Rep. of Congo	74.2
2	Congo	55.0
3	Afghanistan	53.7
4	Bangladesh	51.3
5	Uganda	49.8
6	Mali	49.7
7	Guinea	49.0
8	Chad	48.6
9	Mozambique	47.1
10	Senegal	43.8
	Canada	1.3

* In latest year for which data available

Source: *United Nations*

COUNTRIES WITH THE HIGHEST PROPORTION OF TEENAGE GROOMS

	COUNTRY	PERCENTAGE OF 15–19-YEAR-OLD BOYS WHO HAVE EVER BEEN MARRIED*
1	Iraq	14.9
2	Nepal	13.5
3	Congo	11.8
4	Uganda	11.4
5	India	9.5
6	Afghanistan	9.2
7	Guinea	8.2
8	Central African Republic	8.1
9	Guatemala	7.8
10	Columbia	7.7
	Canada	0.3

* In latest year for which data available

Source: *United Nations*

COUNTRIES WITH THE LOWEST MARRIAGE RATE

	COUNTRY	ANNUAL MARRIAGES PER 1,000
1	Andorra	2.0
2	Malaysia	3.2
3	South Africa	3.3
4	St. Lucia	3.4
5 =	Dominican Republic	3.6
=	Paraguay	3.6
7	Cape Verde	3.8
8 =	Bulgaria	4.0
=	United Arab Emirates	4.0
10	El Salvador	4.2

Source: *United Nations*

Marriage rates around the world vary according to a variety of religious and cultural factors. At the other end of the scale is Antigua and Barbuda, with an annual rate of 21 marriages per 1,000.

COUNTRIES WHERE MOST WOMEN MARRY

	COUNTRY	PERCENTAGE OF WOMEN MARRIED BY AGE 50*
1 =	Comoros	100.0
=	The Gambia	100.0
=	Ghana	100.0
=	Nauru	100.0
5	Chad	99.9
6 =	China	99.8
=	Guinea	99.8
=	Mali	99.8
=	Papua New Guinea	99.8
10	Benin	99.7
	Canada	93.0

* In latest year for which data available

Source: *United Nations*

Marriage in these countries can be considered the norm, contrasting with others where almost half the female population never marry.

COUNTRIES WHERE MOST MEN MARRY

	COUNTRY	PERCENTAGE OF MEN MARRIED BY AGE 50*
1 =	Chad	100.0
=	The Gambia	100.0
3	Guinea	99.7
4 =	Mali	99.6
=	Niger	99.6
6 =	Bangladesh	99.3
=	Mozambique	99.3
8	Cameroon	99.2
9	Nepal	99.1
10 =	Central African Republic	99.0
=	Eritrea	99.0
=	Tajikistan	99.0
	Canada	91.5

* In latest year for which data available

Source: *United Nations*

What was the first Canadian invention, in 1796?
see p.208 for the answer

A A steamship
B An apple
C Kerosene

TOP 10 ★
COUNTRIES WHERE WOMEN MARRY THE LATEST

COUNTRY	AVERAGE AGE AT FIRST MARRIAGE
1 Jamaica	33.1
2 =Barbados	31.8
=Sweden	31.8
4 Iceland	31.7
5 =Antigua and Barbuda	31.5
=Dominica	31.5
=Greenland	31.5
8 St. Kitts and Nevis	31.3
9 Martinique	31.0
10 =Grenada	30.9
=St. Vincent and the Grenadines	30.9
Canada	26.2

Source: *United Nations*

This list is based on the "singulate mean age at marriage" (SMAM), or average age for first marriage among those who marry by the age of 50, after which first marriages are so rare as to be statistically insignificant.

TOP 10 ★
COUNTRIES WITH THE HIGHEST DIVORCE RATES

COUNTRY	DIVORCE RATE PER 1,000
1 Maldives	10.75
2 =Belarus	4.63
=China	4.63
4 Russia	4.51
5 US	4.33
6 Surinam	4.26
7 Estonia	3.85
8 Cuba	3.72
9 Ukraine	3.71
10 Puerto Rico	3.49

Source: *United Nations*

The UK has the highest divorce rate in Europe (excluding republics of the former Soviet Union) at 2.89 per 1,000. According to UN statistics, Britain's Isle of Man, if it were an independent country, would appear in seventh place in this list, with a divorce rate of 4.04 per 1,000 population.

TOP 10 ★
COUNTRIES WITH THE LOWEST DIVORCE RATES

COUNTRY	DIVORCE RATE PER 1,000
1 Guatemala	0.15
2 Macedonia	0.27
3 Mexico	0.35
4 =Chile	0.46
=Turkey	0.46
6 Italy	0.48
7 =Iran	0.50
=Libya	0.50
9 El Salvador	0.51
10 Jamaica	0.54

Source: *United Nations*

The UN data on divorce rates omit a number of large countries and ones that we might expect to have a very low divorce rate, such as Ireland. The data are very difficult to collect, given the different laws relating to divorce in each country. In some, such as certain Muslim countries, no legal document has to be signed for a divorce. In others, divorce rates are rarely accurately recorded.

TOP 10 ★
COUNTRIES WHERE MEN MARRY THE LATEST

COUNTRY	AVERAGE AGE AT FIRST MARRIAGE
1 Dominica	35.4
2 Jamaica	34.6
3 St. Vincent and the Grenadines	34.5
4 Grenada	34.4
5 Barbados	34.3
6 Sweden	34.0
7 Greenland	33.7
8 Iceland	33.3
9 Antigua and Barbuda	33.2
10 Martinique	33.0
Canada	28.9

Source: *United Nations*

TOP 10 ★
COUNTRIES WHERE THE FEWEST WOMEN MARRY

COUNTRY	PERCENTAGE OF WOMEN MARRIED BY AGE 50[*]
1 =French Guiana	54.2
=Jamaica	54.2
3 Grenada	57.4
4 St. Vincent and the Grenadines	58.3
5 Dominica	59.7
6 Barbados	59.8
7 St. Kitts and Nevis	62.1
8 Antigua and Barbuda	62.6
9 Martinique	67.1
10 Netherlands Antilles	72.4

[*] *In latest year for which data available*

Source: *United Nations*

TOP 10 ★
COUNTRIES WHERE THE FEWEST MEN MARRY

COUNTRY	PERCENTAGE OF MEN MARRIED BY AGE 50[*]
1 St. Kitts and Nevis	51.1
2 Jamaica	51.8
3 French Guiana	53.9
4 Grenada	59.8
5 =Montserrat	60.7
=St. Vincent and the Grenadines	60.7
7 Barbados	62.8
8 =Dominica	63.4
=Greenland	63.4
10 Antigua and Barbuda	68.1

[*] *In latest year for which data available*

Source: *United Nations*

People on the Move

PLACES RECEIVING THE MOST REFUGEES AND ASYLUM SEEKERS

COUNTRY OR TERRITORY	REFUGEES/ASYLUM SEEKERS, 1999
1 Iran	1,980,000
2 Jordan	1,518,000
3 Pakistan	1,125,000
4 Gaza Strip	798,000
5 West Bank	570,000
6 US	505,000
7 Yugoslavia	480,000
8 Guinea	450,000
9 Tanzania	400,000
10 Syria	379,200

Source: *US Committee for Refugees*

SEEKING REFUGE

Refugees displaced during the 1990 Iraq–Kuwait War are among the millions who fled from the many conflicts that beset the 1990s.

COUNTRIES WITH THE MOST INTERNALLY DISPLACED PEOPLE

COUNTRY	INTERNALLY DISPLACED PEOPLE, 1999
1 Sudan	4,000,000
2 Colombia	1,800,000
3 Angola	1,500,000
4 Russia	1,000,000
5 Iraq	900,000
6 Bosnia and Herzegovina	830,000
7 Dem. Rep. of Congo	800,000
8 Afghanistan	750,000
9 Yugoslavia	640,000
10 =Burundi	600,000
=Myanmar (Burma)	600,000
=Rwanda	600,000
=Turkey	600,000

Source: *US Committee for Refugees*

ETHNIC ORIGINS OF CANADIANS

	ETHNIC ORIGIN	TOTAL RESPONSES*
1	Canadian#	8,806,275
2	English	6,832,095
3	French	5,597,845
4	Scottish	4,260,840
5	Irish	3,767,610
6	German	2,757,140
7	Italian	1,207,475
8	Aboriginal origins+	1,101,955
9	Ukranian	1,026,475
10	Chinese	921,585

* *Total of reportings of one ethnic origin and reportings of more than one ethnic origin*

\# *Response of "Canadian" has impacted English, Irish, Scottish, and French totals in particular*

+ *Includes North American Indian, Métis, and Inuit*

Source: *1996 Census, Statistics Canada*

TOP 10 ★
ANCESTRIES OF THE US POPULATION

	ANCESTRY GROUP	NUMBER
1	German	57,947,873
2	Irish	38,735,539
3	English	32,651,788
4	Afro-American	23,777,098
5	Italian	14,664,550
6	American	12,395,999
7	Mexican	11,586,983
8	French	10,320,935
9	Polish	9,366,106
10	Native Americans	8,708,220

The 1990 US Census asked people to identify the ancestry group to which they believed themselves to belong. Five percent were unable to define their family origin more precisely than "American," while many claimed multiple ancestry.

TOP 10 🍁
CANADIAN CITIES WITH THE MOST IMMIGRANTS

	CITY*	IMMIGRANTS, 1999#
1	Toronto	83,267
2	Vancouver	27,785
3	Montreal	23,522
4	Calgary	6,749
5	Ottawa-Carleton	6,401
6	Edmonton	3,755
7	Winnipeg	2,928
8	Hamilton	2,695
9	London	1,535
10	Quebec	1,333
	Total 1999 arrivals in Canada	189,816

* Figures reflect the immigrant population in census metropolitan areas (CMAs)

Principal applicants for Canadian citizenship and their dependents

Source: Facts and Figures 1999, Citizenship and Immigration Canada. Adapted with the permission of the Minister of Public Works and Government Services Canada, 2001.

HEADING DOWN UNDER

A young British emigrant waits to embark for Australia in 1950. The two countries' longstanding links have been maintained over the decades.

TOP 10 ★
COUNTRIES OF ORIGIN OF UK IMMIGRANTS

	COUNTRY	IMMIGRANTS, 1999
1	Pakistan	11,860
2	Former Yugoslavia	6,650
3	India	6,290
4	Sri Lanka	5,370
5	Turkey	5,220
6	US	3,760
7	Ghana	3,480
8	Bangladesh	3,280
9 =Nigeria		3,180
=Somalia		3,180

Source: Home Office

TOP 10 ★
COUNTRIES OF ORIGIN OF IMMIGRANTS TO AUSTRALIA

	COUNTRY OF BIRTH	IMMIGRANTS, 1999
1	UK	8,876
2	China*	5,982
3	South Africa	5,558
4	Philippines	3,409
5	Indonesia	3,313
6	India	3,156
7	Iraq	2,307
8	Former Yugoslavia	1,998
9	Vietnam	1,889
10	Fiji	1,554

* Excluding Taiwan and Special Administrative Regions

Source: Australian Department of Immigration and Multicultural Affairs

Since the era of the first settlement of Australia the UK has always been the principal country of origin of immigrants, and it still provides 13.5 percent of the total. In 1999, a further 27,911 immigrants were recorded as having arrived from other countries not listed in the Top 10, together with 1,272 whose birthplace was unknown, making an overall total of 67,215.

TOP 10 🍁
COUNTRIES OF ORIGIN OF IMMIGRANTS TO CANADA

	COUNTRY	IMMIGRANTS, 1999
1	China	29,095
2	India	17,415
3	Pakistan	9,285
4	Philippines	9,160
5	Korea, Republic of	7,212
6	Iran	5,903
7	US	5,514
8	Taiwan	5,461
9	Sri Lanka	4,719
10	UK	4,476

Source: Citizenship and Immigration Canada

Did You Know? The top single year for immigration to the US was 1907, with 1,285,349 arrivals; Italy was the leading country of origin, with 285,731 emigrants.

What's in a Name?

BOYS' NAMES IN THE US, 1990–2000

1990		2000
Michael	1	Michael
Christopher	2	Jacob
Joshua	3	Matthew
Matthew	4	Joseph
David	5	Nicholas
Daniel	6	Christopher
Andrew	7	Andrew
Joseph	8	William
Justin	9	Joshua
James	10	Daniel

TOP 10 MOST COMMON FEMALE FIRST NAMES IN THE US

(Name/% of all first names)

❶ Mary, 2.629 ❷ Patricia, 1.073
❸ Linda, 1.035 ❹ Barbara, 0.980
❺ Elizabeth, 0.937 ❻ Jennifer, 0.932
❼ Maria, 0.828 ❽ Susan, 0.794
❾ Margaret, 0.768 ❿ Dorothy, 0.727

Source: *US Census Bureau*
According to an analysis of the 1990 US Census, the Top 10 female names account for 10.703 percent of all names, while the male names (listed below) account for 23.185 percent. It should be noted that these lists represent names of people of all age groups enumerated, and not the current popularity of first names.

TOP 10 MOST COMMON MALE FIRST NAMES IN THE US

(Name/% of all first names)

❶ James, 3.318 ❷ John, 3.271
❸ Robert, 3.143 ❹ Michael, 2.629
❺ William, 2.451 ❻ David, 2.363
❼ Richard, 1.703 ❽ Charles, 1.523
❾ Joseph, 1.404 ❿ Thomas, 1.380

Source: *US Census Bureau*

GIRLS' NAMES IN THE US, 1990–2000

1990		2000
Jessica	1	Hannah
Ashley	2	Emily
Brittany	3	Madison
Amanda	4	Elizabeth
Stephanie	5	Alexis
Jennifer	6	Sarah
Samantha	7	Taylor
Sarah	8	Lauren
Megan	9	Jessica
Lauren	10	Ashley

MOST COMMON SURNAMES IN NOVA SCOTIA, 1864–77*

	SURNAME	ESTIMATED NUMBER
1	McDonald	4,134
2	Smith	1,570
3	McNeil	1,184
4	McLean	1,171
5	McLeod	1,074
6	Fraser	999
7	McKenzie	918
8	McKay	844
9	Campbell	821
10	Le Blanc	777

* *Most common surname groups (encompassing variant spellings) in 12 or more counties in Nova Scotia, out of a total of 18 counties; based on reported births 1864–77*

Source: In Which County? Nova Scotia Surnames from Birth Registers: 1864 to 1877, *Genealogical Assn. of the Royal Nova Scotia Historical Society, 1985*

In 1877, cuts to government spending, along with a lack of public response, prompted the Province of Nova Scotia to quit maintaining the registry of births and deaths it had created 13 years earlier.

❶ Tremblay ❷ Gagnon ❸ Roy
❹ Côté ❺ Bouchard ❻ Morin
❼ Gauthier ❽ Pelletier
❾ Fortin ❿ Lavoie

Source: *Louis Duchesne, Le choix du nom de famille en 1996, Données sociodémographiques en bref, vol. 3, no. 2, 1999*

FIRST NAMES IN SCOTLAND, 2000

GIRLS/RISE OR FALL		BOYS/RISE OR FALL
Chloe	1	Jack
Amy (+3)	2	Lewis
Lauren (+2)	3	Ryan
Emma (−1)	4	Cameron
Rebecca (−3)	5	James (+2)
Megan	6	Andrew
Caitlin	7	Matthew (+6)
Rachel	8	Liam
Erin	9	Callum (+3)
Hannah (+2)	10	Jamie (+6)

+ *Indicates rise in popularity since previous year*

− *Represents decline in popularity since previous year*

FIRST NAMES IN AUSTRALIA*

GIRLS		BOYS
Jessica	1	Joshua
Emily	2	Jack
Sarah	3	Thomas
Georgia	4	Lachlan
Olivia	5	Matthew
Chloe	6	James
Emma	7	Daniel
Sophie	8	Benjamin
Hannah	9	Nicholas
Isabella	10	William

* *Based on births registered in New South Wales*

TOP 10 ★
FIRST NAMES IN IRELAND

GIRLS		BOYS
Chloe	1	Conor
Aoife	2	Sean
Sarah	3	Jack
Ciara	4	James
Niamh	5	Adam
Emma	6	Michael
Rachel	7	David
Rebecca	8	Aaron
Lauren	9	Daniel
Megan	10	Dylan

While these were the Top 10 girls' and boys' names among the total of 53,354 births registered in Ireland in 1999, there are certain regional variations: Rachel was the most popular girls' name in the West, and Sean was the most popular boy's name in the West and Dublin. As with other first name lists, boys' names remain more static than girls': the top five are identical to the previous year.

TOP 10 🍁
FIRST NAMES IN BRITISH COLUMBIA, 1999

GIRLS		BOYS
Emily	1	Matthew
Sarah	2	Joshua
Emma	3	Jacob
Hannah	4	Nicholas
Taylor	5	Ryan
Jessica	6	Brandon
Megan	7	Michael
Samantha	8	Jordan
Ashley	9	Alexander
Madison	10	Liam

TOP 10 ★
FIRST NAMES IN WALES, 2000

GIRLS/RISE OR FALL		BOYS/RISE OR FALL
Chloe	1	Thomas
Megan	2	Jack
Emily	3	Joshua
Sophie	4	Callum ($^+$1)
Lauren	5	Rhys ($^+$8)
Hannah ($^+$3)	6	Daniel (–2)
Jessica (–1)	7	Jordan ($^+$5)
Georgina (–1)	8	Ryan ($^+$1)
Ffion (–1)	9	Liam (–2)
Olivia ($^+$1)	10	James (–4)

$^+$ *Indicates rise in popularity since previous year*

– *Represents decline in popularity since previous year*

Among girls' names, all those in the Top 10 also appear, though in different order of popularity, in the combined England and Wales Top 10, with the exception of Georgina (No. 11 in England and Wales) and Ffion, which does not even appear in the Top 50.

TOP 10 ★
NAMES IN THE US 100 YEARS AGO

GIRLS		BOYS
Mary	1	John
Helen	2	William
Anna	3	James
Margaret	4	George
Ruth	5	Joseph
Elizabeth	6	Charles
Marie	7	Robert
Lillian	8	Frank
Florence	9	Edward
Alice	10	Walter
Rose	=	

TOP 10 SURNAMES IN CHINA
❶ Zhang ❷ Whang ❸ Li ❹ Zhao ❺ Chen ❻ Yang ❼ Wu ❽ Liu
❾ Huang ❿ Zhou

It has been estimated that there are more than 100 million people with the surname Zhang in China.

THE JONESES
San Diego-born artist Arthur R. "Pop" Momand (1886–1987) settled in Cedarhurst, New York, where he rubbed shoulders with a group of wealthy people, each of whom he noticed was competing with those with even more money. After moving to Manhattan, he devised a comic strip featuring the exploits of such people, which he called "Keeping up with the Joneses" – perhaps named after American novelist Edith Wharton's rich aunt Elizabeth Schermerhorn Jones, owner of a large New York estate. The strip ran for many years, and the phrase became an idiom in the English language.

WHO WAS • WHO WAS • WHO WAS • WHO WAS

TOP 10 ★
MOST COMMON SURNAMES IN THE UK

	SURNAME	NUMBER
1	Smith	538,369
2	Jones	402,489
3	Williams	279,150
4	Brown	260,652
5	Taylor	251,058
6	Davies/Davis	209,584
7	Wilson	191,006
8	Evans	170,391
9	Thomas	152,945
10	Johnson	146,535

This survey of British surnames is based on an analysis of almost 50 million appearing in the British electoral rolls – hence enumerating only those aged over 18 and eligible to vote. Some 10.77 people out of every 1,000 in the UK are called Smith, compared with 14.55 per 1,000 of names appearing in a sample from the 1851 Census. This decline may be accounted for by considering the diluting effect of immigrant names, the same survey indicating, for example, that 66,663 people, or 1.33 per 1,000, now bear the name Patel, whereas none with that name was listed in 1851.

Did You Know? Although it is often claimed that J.M. Barrie invented the name Wendy in his 1904 play *Peter Pan*, researchers have uncovered a record of a 21-year-old woman and two girls with this name in the 1851 British census.

World Leaders & Politics

FIRST COUNTRIES TO GIVE WOMEN THE VOTE

	COUNTRY	YEAR
1	New Zealand	1893
2	Australia (South Australia 1894; Western Australia 1898)	1902
3	Finland (then a Grand Duchy under the Russian Crown)	1906
4	Norway (restricted franchise; all women over 25 in 1913)	1907
5	Denmark and Iceland (a Danish dependency until 1918)	1915
6 =	Netherlands	1917
=	USSR	1917
8 =	Austria	1918
=	Canada	1918
=	Germany	1918
=	Great Britain and Ireland (Ireland part of the United Kingdom until 1921; women over 30 only – lowered to 21 in 1928)	1918
=	Poland	1918

Until 1920, the only other European countries to enfranchise women were Sweden in 1919 and Czechoslovakia in 1920.

VOTES FOR WOMEN
The women of New Zealand, granted suffrage on September 19, 1893, were able to cast their votes at the country's General Election on November 28.

★ TOP 10 LONGEST-SERVING PRIME MINISTERS IN CANADA

(Prime Minister/months in office)

1. William Lyon Mackenzie King, 258
2. Sir John Alexander Macdonald, 229
3. Pierre Elliott Trudeau, 185
4. Sir Wilfrid Laurier, 183
5. =Sir Robert Laird Borden; 105
   =Martin Brian Mulroney, 105
7. Louis Stephen Saint Laurent, 103
8. Joseph Jacques Jean Chrétien, 91*
9. John George Diefenbaker, 70
10. Lester Bowles Pearson, 60

* As at May 2001, still in office

Source: *National Archives of Canada*

PARLIAMENTS WITH THE HIGHEST PERCENTAGE OF WOMEN MEMBERS*

	PARLIAMENT/ ELECTION DATE	WOMEN MEMBERS	TOTAL MEMBERS	% WOMEN		PARLIAMENT/ ELECTION DATE	WOMEN MEMBERS	TOTAL MEMBERS	% WOMEN
1	Sweden, 1998	149	349	42.7	7	Germany, 1998	207	669	30.9
2	Denmark, 1998	67	179	37.4	8	New Zealand, 1999	37	120	30.8
3	Finland, 1999	73	200	36.5	9	Mozambique, 1999	75	250	30.0
4	Norway, 1997	60	165	36.4	10	South Africa, 1999	119	399	29.8
5	Netherlands, 1998	54	150	36.0					
6	Iceland, 1999	22	63	34.9					

* As at April 25, 2001

Source: *Inter-Parliamentary Union*

AUSTRALIAN WOMEN GET THE VOTE

Following pressure exerted by the Womanhood Suffrage League, Australia followed the lead of New Zealand (the first country to grant women suffrage) when, on June 12, 1902, Melbourne Governor-General Lord Hopetoun signed the Uniform Franchise Act. Although a major advance, it still imposed a number of limitations: it was restricted to federal elections and was granted only to British subjects aged over 21 and with a minimum of six months' residence; "Aboriginal natives of Australia, Asia, Africa, or the Islands of the Pacific" were excluded. Over the next few years, all women aged over 21 were progressively granted the vote; though it was not until 1962 that aboriginal women (and men) were given the vote.

100 YEARS AGO · YEARS AGO · YEARS · YEARS AGO ·

TOP 10 ★
LONGEST-SERVING PRESIDENTS TODAY

	PRESIDENT/COUNTRY	TOOK OFFICE
1	General Gnassingbé Eyadéma, Togo	Apr 14, 1967
2	El Hadj Omar Bongo, Gabon	Dec 2, 1967
3	Colonel Mu'ammar Gadhafi, Libya*	Sep 1, 1969
4	Zayid ibn Sultan al-Nuhayyan, United Arab Emirates	Dec 2, 1971
5	Fidel Castro, Cuba	Nov 2, 1976
6	France-Albert René, Seychelles	June 5, 1977
7	Al Abdullah Saleh, Yemen	July 17, 1978
8	Daniel Teroitich arap Moi, Kenya	Oct 14, 1978
9	Maumoon Abdul Gayoom, Maldives	Nov 11, 1978
10	Saddam Hussein, Iraq	July 16, 1979

* Since a reorganization in 1979, Colonel Gadhafi has held no formal position, but continues to rule under the ceremonial title of "Leader of the Revolution."

All the presidents in this list have been in power for more than 20 years, some for over 30. Fidel Castro was prime minister of Cuba from February 1959 onwards. As he was also chief of the army, and there was no opposition party, he effectively ruled as dictator from then on, but he was not technically president until the Cuban constitution was revised in 1976. Among those presidents no longer in office, Abu Sulayman Hafiz al-Assad, president of Syria, died on June 10, 2000, after serving as leader of his country since February 22, 1971, a total of 29 years.

TOP 10 ★
LONGEST-REIGNING LIVING MONARCHS*

	MONARCH#/COUNTRY	DATE OF BIRTH	ACCESSION
1	Bhumibol Adulyadej, Thailand	Dec 5, 1927	June 9, 1946
2	Prince Rainier III, Monaco	May 31, 1923	May 9, 1949
3	Elizabeth II, UK	Apr 21, 1926	Feb 6, 1952
4	Malietoa Tanumafili II, Western Samoa	Jan 4, 1913	Jan 1, 1962#
5	Taufa'ahau Tupou IV, Tonga	July 4, 1918	Dec 16, 1965+
6	Haji Hassanal Bolkiah, Brunei	July 15, 1946	Oct 5, 1967
7	Sayyid Qaboos ibn Said al-Said, Oman	Nov 18, 1942	July 23, 1970
8	Margrethe II, Denmark	Apr 16, 1940	Jan 14, 1972
9	Birendra Bir Bikram Shah Dev, Nepal	Dec 28, 1945	Jan 31, 1972
10	Jigme Singye Wangchuk, Bhutan	Nov 11, 1955	July 24, 1972

* Including hereditary rulers of principalities, dukedoms, etc.

 # Sole ruler since April 15, 1963

+ Full sovereignty from June 5, 1970, when British protectorate ended

Twenty-eight countries have emperors, kings, queens, princes, dukes, sultans, or other hereditary rulers as their heads of state. This list formerly included Grand Duke Jean of Luxembourg, who abdicated September 28, 2000.

THE 10 ★
FIRST COUNTRIES TO RATIFY THE UN CHARTER

	COUNTRY	DATE
1	Nicaragua	July 6, 1945
2	US	Aug 8, 1945
3	France	Aug 31, 1945
4	Dominican Republic	Sep 4, 1945
5	New Zealand	Sep 19, 1945
6	Brazil	Sep 21, 1945
7	Argentina	Sep 24, 1945
8	China	Sep 28, 1945
9	Denmark	Oct 9, 1945
10	Chile	Oct 11, 1945

In New York on June 26, 1945, 50 nations signed the World Security Charter, thus establishing the UN as an international peacekeeping organization.

WORLD PEACE
While World War II still raged in the Far East, delegates signed the charter that inaugurated the United Nations as the world's peacekeepers.

What was unusual about the transatlantic balloon crossing reported in 1844?
see p.63 for the answer

A It was kept secret for over 100 years
B It was the first
C It was a hoax

Human Achievements

THE 10 ★
FIRST MOUNTAINEERS TO CLIMB EVEREST

	MOUNTAINEER/NATIONALITY	DATE
1	Edmund Hillary, New Zealander	May 29, 1953
2	Tenzing Norgay, Nepalese	May 29, 1953
3	Jürg Marmet, Swiss	May 23, 1956
4	Ernst Schmied, Swiss	May 23, 1956
5	Hans-Rudolf von Gunten, Swiss	May 24, 1956
6	Adolf Reist, Swiss	May 24, 1956
7	Wang Fu-chou, Chinese	May 25, 1960
8	Chu Ying-hua, Chinese	May 25, 1960
9	Konbu, Tibetan	May 25, 1960
10=	Nawang Gombu, Indian	May 1, 1963
=	James Whittaker, American	May 1, 1963

Nawang Gombu and James Whittaker are 10th equal because, neither wishing to deny the other the privilege of being first, they ascended the last feet to the summit side by side.

THE 10 ★
FIRST PEOPLE TO REACH THE SOUTH POLE

	NAME/NATIONALITY	DATE
1=	Roald Amundsen*, Norwegian	Dec 14, 1911
=	Olav Olavsen Bjaaland, Norwegian	Dec 14, 1911
=	Helmer Julius Hanssen, Norwegian	Dec 14, 1911
=	Helge Sverre Hassel, Norwegian	Dec 14, 1911
=	Oscar Wisting, Norwegian	Dec 14, 1911
6=	Robert Falcon Scott*, British	Jan 17, 1912
=	Henry Robertson Bowers, British	Jan 17, 1912
=	Edgar Evans, British	Jan 17, 1912
=	Lawrence Edward Grace Oates, British	Jan 17, 1912
=	Edward Adrian Wilson, British	Jan 17, 1912

* Expedition leader

THE 10 ★
FIRST EXPEDITIONS TO REACH THE NORTH POLE*

	NAME[#]/NATIONALITY	DATE
1	Ralph S. Plaisted, American	Apr 19, 1968
2	Wally W. Herbert, British	Apr 5, 1969
3	Naomi Uemura, Japanese	May 1, 1978
4	Dmitri Shparo, Soviet	May 31, 1979
5	Sir Ranulph Fiennes/ Charles Burton, British	Apr 11, 1982
6	Will Steger/Paul Schurke, American	May 1, 1986
7	Jean-Louis Etienne, French	May 11, 1986
8	Fukashi Kazami, Japanese	Apr 20, 1987
9	Helen Thayer[+], American	Apr 20, 1988
10	Robert Swan, British	May 14, 1989

* Overland expeditions
# Expedition leader or co-leader
+ New Zealand-born

THE 10 ★
LATEST WINNERS OF *TIME MAGAZINE*'S "PERSON OF THE YEAR" AWARD

	RECIPIENT	YEAR
1	George W. Bush (1946–), US President elect	2000
2	Jeffrey T. Bezos (1964–), entrepreneur, founder of Amazon.com	1999
3	Bill Clinton (1946–), US President, Kenneth Starr (1946–), Independent Counsel	1998
4	Andrew S. Grove (1936–), CEO of Intel microchip company	1997
5	David Ho (1952–), AIDS researcher	1996
6	Newt Gingrich (1943–), US politician	1995
7	Pope John Paul II (1920–)	1994
8	Yasser Arafat (1929–), F. W. de Klerk (1936–), Nelson Mandela (1918–), Yitzhak Rabin (1922–95), "Peacemakers"	1993
9	Bill Clinton (1946–), US President	1992
10	George Bush (1924–), US President	1991

THE 10 🍁
FIRST SWIMMERS TO CROSS LAKE ONTARIO

	SWIMMER/NATIONALITY	YEAR	TIME HR:MIN			SWIMMER/NATIONALITY	YEAR	TIME HR:MIN
1	Marilyn Bell, Canadian	1954	20:55		6	Jim Woods, American	1961	17:07
2	John Jaremey, Canadian	1956	21:13		7	Cindy Nicholas, Canadian	1974	15:10
3	Brenda Fisher, British	1956	18:51		8	Diana Nyad, American	1974	18:15
4	Bill Sadlo, American	1957	25:01		9	Debbie Roach, Canadian	1975	18:30
5	Jim Woods, American	1957	18:35		10	Angela Kondrak, Canadian	1976	23:48

Source: *Solo Swims of Ontario*

FIRST US LANDING AT THE NORTH POLE

The first US landing at the Pole was that of Lt.-Col. William Pershing Benedict, with a team of 10 US Air Force scientists. They flew in a C-47 fitted with skis, landing on May 3, 1952. Co-pilot Lt.-Col. Joseph Otis Fletcher became the first American undisputedly to set foot on the North Pole. (This achievement had previously been claimed by American Robert Peary and his companions, who were reported to have reached the Pole in 1909. This claim has since been widely discredited.) Dr. Albert Paddock Crary, one of the scientists on the American expedition, later trekked to the South Pole, arriving there on February 12, 1961, thus becoming the first man to set foot on both North and South Poles.

50 YEARS AGO · YEARS AGO · YEARS AGO ·

TOP 10 ★
CIRCUMNAVIGATION FIRSTS

CIRCUMNAVIGATION	CRAFT	CAPTAIN(S)	RETURN DATE
1 First voyage	Vittoria	Juan Sebastian de Elcano	Sep 6, 1522
2 First in less than 80 days	Various	"Nellie Bly" (Elizabeth Cochrane)	Jan 25, 1890
3 First solo voyage	Spray	Capt. Joshua Slocum	July 3, 1898
4 First by air	Chicago and New Orleans	Lt. Lowell Smith and Lt. Leslie P. Arnold	Sep 28, 1924
5 First nonstop by air	Lucky Lady I	Capt. James Gallagher	Mar 2, 1949
6 First underwater voyage	Triton	Capt. Edward Latimer Beach	Apr 25, 1960
7 First nonstop solo voyage	Suhaili	Robin Knox-Johnston	Apr 22, 1969
8 First helicopter	Spirit of Texas	H. Ross Perot Jr. and Jay Coburn	Sep 30, 1982
9 First air without refueling	Voyager	Richard Rutan and Jeana Yeager	Dec 23, 1986
10 First by balloon	Breitling Orbiter 3	Brian Jones and Bertrand Piccard	Mar 21, 1999

The first ever circumnavigation, by Juan Sebastian de Elcano and his crew of 17, sailed from Spain, returning to Italy. US journalist "Nellie Bly" (Elizabeth Cochrane) set out to beat the fictitious "record" established in Jules Verne's novel *Around the World in 80 Days*, traveling from New York and returning on January 25, 1890 – a record circumnavigation of 72 days, 6 hours, 11 minutes, and 14 seconds.

AROUND THE WORLD IN 19 DAYS
In 1999, traveling from Switzerland to Egypt, the 55-m (180-ft) tall Breitling Orbiter 3 achieved the first balloon circumnavigation of the Earth.

THE 10 ★
FIRST SUCCESSFUL HUMAN DESCENTS OVER NIAGARA FALLS

NAME/METHOD	DATE
1 Annie Edson Taylor, Wooden barrel	Oct 24, 1901
2 Bobby Leach, Steel barrel	July 25, 1911
3 Jean Lussier, Steel and rubber ball fitted with oxygen cylinders	July 4, 1928
4 William Fitzgerald (aka Nathan Boya), Steel and rubber ball fitted with oxygen cylinders	July 15, 1961
5 Karel Soucek, Barrel	July 3, 1984
6 Steven Trotter, Barrel	Aug 18, 1985
7 Dave Mundy, Barrel	Oct 5, 1985
8 =Peter deBernardi, Metal container	Sep 28, 1989
=Jeffrey Petkovich, Metal container	Sep 28, 1989
10 Dave Mundy, Diving bell	Sep 26, 1993

Source: *Niagara Falls Museum*

WITH KIND AUTHORIZATION OF BREITLING SA

Did You Know? The first transatlantic crossing by balloon, reported in the *New York Sun* of April 13, 1844, was a hoax perpetrated by novelist Edgar Allan Poe. It was another 134 years before balloonists truly achieved the feat.

THE 10 ★
LATEST WINNERS OF THE NOBEL PRIZE FOR ECONOMIC SCIENCES

WINNER	COUNTRY	YEAR
1 =James J. Heckman	US	2000
=Daniel L. McFadden	US	2000
3 Robert A. Mundell	Canada	1999
4 Amartya Sen	India	1998
5 =Robert C. Merton	US	1997
=Myron S. Scholes	US	1997
7 =James A. Mirrlees	UK	1996
=William Vickrey	Canada	1996
9 Robert E. Lucas	US	1995
10 =John C. Harsanyi	Hungary/US	1994
=Reinhard Selten	Germany	1994
=John F. Nash	US	1994

Correctly called the Bank of Sweden Prize in Economic Sciences in Memory of Alfred Nobel, this is a recent addition to the Nobel Prizes. It is presented annually by the Royal Swedish Academy of Sciences and consists of a gold medal, a diploma, and a sum of money. The presentation of this and the other Prizes is made on December 10, the anniversary of Alfred Nobel's death.

NOBEL

Swedish scientist Alfred Bernhard Nobel (1833–96) studied widely in Europe and the US. He perfected a way of stabilizing nitroglycerine, a dangerous explosive. The result was dynamite, which Nobel patented in 1866. It was used extensively in quarrying and railway construction. At his death in 1896, the unmarried Nobel left a will establishing a trust fund, which is now estimated to be worth over US$420 million. Interest earned from this fund has enabled annual prizes to be awarded to those deemed to have achieved the greatest common good in the six fields of Physics, Chemistry, Physiology or Medicine, Literature, Peace, and, since 1969, Economic Sciences.

TOP 10 ★
NOBEL LITERATURE PRIZE-WINNING COUNTRIES

COUNTRY	LITERATURE PRIZES
1 France	12
2 US	10
3 UK	8
4 =Germany	7
=Sweden	7
6 Italy	6
7 Spain	5
8 =Denmark	3
=Ireland	3
=Norway	3
=Poland	3
=USSR	3

TOP 10 ★
NOBEL PHYSIOLOGY OR MEDICINE PRIZE-WINNING COUNTRIES

COUNTRY	PHYSIOLOGY OR MEDICINE PRIZES
1 US	80
2 UK	24
3 Germany	16
4 Sweden	8
5 France	7
6 Switzerland	6
7 Denmark	5
8 =Austria	4
=Belgium	4
10 =Italy	3
=Australia	3

THE 10 ★
LATEST WINNERS OF THE NOBEL PRIZE FOR LITERATURE

WINNER	COUNTRY	YEAR
1 Gao Xingjian	China	2000
2 Günter Grass	Germany	1999
3 José Saramago	Portugal	1998
4 Dario Fo	Italy	1997
5 Wislawa Szymborska	Poland	1996
6 Seamus Heaney	Ireland	1995
7 Kenzaburo Oe	Japan	1994
8 Toni Morrison	US	1993
9 Derek Walcott	Saint Lucia	1992
10 Nadine Gordimer	South Africa	1991

THE 10 ★
LATEST WINNERS OF THE NOBEL PRIZE FOR PHYSICS

WINNER	COUNTRY	YEAR
1 =Zhores I. Alferov	Russia	2000
=Herbert Kroemer	US	2000
=Jack S. Kilby	US	2000
4 =Gerardus 't Hooft	Netherlands	1999
=Martinus J.G. Veltman	Netherlands	1999
6 =Robert B. Laughlin	US	1998
=Horst L. Störmer	Germany	1998
=Daniel C. Tsui	US	1998
9 = Steven Chu	US	1997
=William D. Phillips	US	1997
=Claude Cohen-Tannoudji	France	1997

TOP 10 NOBEL PHYSICS PRIZE-WINNING COUNTRIES
(Country/physics prizes)

❶ US, 69 ❷ UK, 21 ❸ Germany, 20 ❹ France, 12 ❺ Netherlands, 8 ❻ USSR, 7 ❼ Sweden, 4 ❽ = Austria, 3; = Denmark, 3; = Italy, 3; = Japan, 3

Which country has the highest proportion of adults in higher education?
see p.105 for the answer

A South Korea
B Canada
C Norway

TOP 10 ★
NOBEL PRIZE-WINNING COUNTRIES

	COUNTRY	PHY	CHE	PH/MED	LIT	PCE	ECO	TOTAL
1	US	69	45	80	10	18	27	249
2	UK	21	25	24	8	13	7	98
3	Germany*	20	27	16	7	4	1	75
4	France	12	7	7	12	9	–	48
5	Sweden	4	4	8	7	5	2	30
6	Switzerland	2	5	6	2	3	–	18
7 =	USSR	7	1	2	3	2	1	16
=	Institutions	–	–	–	–	16	–	16
9	Netherlands	8	3	2	–	1	1	15
10	Italy	3	1	3	6	1	–	14

Phy – Physics; Che – Chemistry; Ph/Med – Physiology or Medicine; Lit – Literature; Pce – Peace; Eco – Economic Sciences

* Includes the united country before 1948, West Germany to 1990, and the united country since 1990

PEACE OF MIND

Selected from a record 150 nominees, South Korean president Kim Dae Jung was awarded the first Nobel Peace Prize of the 21st century for his work in forging ties with North Korea.

TOP 10 NOBEL PEACE PRIZE-WINNING COUNTRIES

(Country/peace prizes)

1 US, 18 **2** International institutions, 16 **3** UK, 13 **4** France, 9 **5** Sweden, 5
6 = Belgium, 4; = Germany, 4; = South Africa, 4 **9** = Israel, 3; = Switzerland, 3

THE 10 ★
LATEST WINNERS OF THE NOBEL PRIZE FOR CHEMISTRY

	WINNER	COUNTRY	YEAR
1 =	Alan J. Heeger	US	2000
=	Alan G. MacDiarmid	US	2000
=	Hideki Shirakawa	Japan	2000
4	Ahmed Zewail	Egypt	1999
5 =	Walter Kohn	US	1998
=	John A. Pople	UK	1998
7 =	Paul D. Boyer	US	1997
=	John E. Walker	UK	1997
=	Jens C. Skou	Denmark	1997
10 =	Sir Harold W. Kroto	UK	1996
=	Richard E. Smalley	US	1996

THE 10 ★
LATEST WINNERS OF THE NOBEL PRIZE FOR PHYSIOLOGY OR MEDICINE

	WINNER	COUNTRY	YEAR
1 =	Arvid Carlsson	Sweden	2000
=	Paul Greengard	US	2000
=	Eric Kandel	US	2000
4	Günter Blobel	Germany	1999
5 =	Robert F. Furchgott	US	1998
=	Louis J. Ignarro	US	1998
=	Ferid Murad	US	1998
8	Stanley B. Prusiner	US	1997
9 =	Peter C. Doherty	Australia	1996
=	Rolf M. Zinkernagel	Switzerland	1996

THE 10 ★
LATEST WINNERS OF THE NOBEL PEACE PRIZE

	WINNER	COUNTRY	YEAR
1	Kim Dae Jung	South Korea	2000
2	Médecins Sans Frontières	Belgium	1999
3 =	John Hume	UK	1998
=	David Trimble	UK	1998
5 =	International Campaign to Ban Landmines	–	1997
=	Jody Williams	US	1997
7 =	Carlos Filipe Ximenes Belo	East Timor	1996
=	José Ramos-Horta	East Timor	1996
9	Joseph Rotblat	UK	1995
10 =	Yasir Arafat	Palestine	1994
=	Shimon Peres	Israel	1994
=	Itzhak Rabin	Israel	1994

Criminal Records

COUNTRIES WITH THE HIGHEST PRISON POPULATION RATES

	COUNTRY	TOTAL PRISON POPULATION*	PRISONERS PER 100,000#
1	Russia	1,060,085	730
2	US	1,860,520	680
3	Belarus	58,879	575
4	Kazakhstan	82,945	495
5	Bahamas	1,401	485
6	Belize	1,097	460
7	Kyrgyzstan	19,857	440
8	Suriname	1,933	435
9	Ukraine	217,400	430
10	Dominica	298	420
	Canada	32,970	110

* Including pretrial detainees
# In latest year for which figures are available
Source: British Home Office

COUNTRIES WITH THE MOST PRISONERS

	COUNTRY	PRISONERS*
1	US	1,860,520
2	China	1,408,860
3	Russia	1,060,085
4	India	381,147
5	Ukraine	217,400
6	Thailand	197,214
7	Brazil	194,074
8	South Africa	161,163
9	Rwanda	143,021#
10	Mexico	139,707
	Canada	32,970

* In latest year for which figures are available
# Includes 135,000 held on suspicion of participation in genocide
Source: British Home Office

MOST COMMON FEDERAL STATUTE INCIDENTS IN CANADA*

	TYPE OF OFFENSE	NUMBER OF INCIDENTS (1999)
1	Theft ($5,000 and under)	679,095
2	Breaking and entering	318,448
3	Mischief	312,563
4	Assault	221,281
5	Motor vehicle theft	161,405
6	Fraud	90,568
7	Impaired driving#	85,984
8	Drugs	79,871
9	Bail violation	72,223
10	Disturbing the peace	69,982

* Reported to police in 1999
# Includes impaired operation of a vehicle causing death or bodily harm, alcohol rate over 80 mg, failure/refusal to provide a breath/blood sample
Source: Statistics Canada

THE 10 COUNTRIES WITH THE HIGHEST CRIME RATES

(Country/crime rate)*

❶ Gibraltar, 18,316 ❷ Suriname, 17,819 ❸ St. Kitts and Nevis, 15,468
❹ Finland, 14,799 ❺ Rwanda, 14,550 ❻ New Zealand, 13,854 ❼ Sweden, 12,982
❽ Denmark, 10,525 ❾ Canada, 10,451 ❿ US Virgin Islands, 10,441

* Reported crime per 100,000 population

CANADIAN CITIES WITH THE MOST POLICE OFFICERS*

	CITY (CMA)	NO. OF OFFICERS	OFFICERS PER 100,000
1	Thunder Bay, ON	240	186.2
2	Winnipeg, MB	1,230	181.6
3	Saint John, NB	225	174.5
4	Regina, SK	345	173.5
5	Montreal, QC	5,841	172.6
6	Windsor, ON	508	170.4
7	Toronto, ON	7,375	163.5
8	Saskatoon, SK	345	154.8
9	Halifax, NS	526	150.6
10	Victoria, BC	475	148.3

* In 1998; only those involved in municipal and provincial policing included
Source: Canadian Centre for Justice Statistics

THE FIRST MECHANICAL LIE DETECTOR

Italian criminologist Cesare Lombroso first described using blood pressure changes to measure the reactions of suspects during questioning in 1895, but it was not until 1902 that this proposal was put into practice. Working in Burnley, UK, Scottish doctor James MacKenzie (1853–1925) published a book, *The Study of the Pulse*, and, with the aid of a local watchmaker, invented the polygraph, a machine to record the rhythms of the heart. Although MacKenzie's instrument, which was later produced commercially, was primarily designed for medical purposes, its principles were used by subsequent researchers to develop increasingly sophisticated devices to relate such phenomena as blood pressure, respiratory changes, and even voice frequencies to lying, and thus to create lie detectors. However, since the results of tests using such devices can be literally a matter of life or death, to this day few jurisdictions accept their results.

100 YEARS AGO • YEARS AGO • YEARS AGO

THE 10 🍁
CANADIAN CITIES WITH THE HIGHEST CRIME RATES*

CITY (CMA)/PROVINCE#	CRIME RATE (1999)
1 **Regina**, Saskatchewan	15,191
2 **Victoria**, British Columbia	11,865
3 **Saskatoon**, Saskatchewan	11,640
4 **Vancouver**, British Columbia	11,562
5 **Winnipeg**, Manitoba	9,763
6 **Halifax**, Nova Scotia	9,551
7 **Thunder Bay**, Ontario	9,109
8 **London**, Ontario	8,581
9 **Edmonton**, Alberta	8,533
10 **Calgary**, Alberta	7,554

* Includes violent, property, and other crimes, 1999

Census metropolitan area with population over 100,000   Source: *Statistics Canada*

Quebec City has the lowest crime rate in Canada: 4,790 incidences per 100,000 people.

THE 10 🍁
TYPES OF SPOUSAL VIOLENCE IN CANADA*

TYPE OF VIOLENCE	FEMALE VICTIMS, %	MALE VICTIMS, %
1 Pushed, grabbed, or shoved	81	43
2 Threatened to hit	65	61
3 Threw something	44	56
4 Slapped	40	57
5 Kicked, bit, or hit	33	51
6 Beat	25	10
7 Hit with something	23	26
8 Choked	20	4
9 Sexual assault	20	3
10 Used or threatened to use a gun or knife	13	7

* Victims 15 years and older who reported violence by a current or previous spouse between 1994 and 1999; includes common-law partners. Ranked by female victims

Source: *General Social Survey, Statistics Canada*

🍁 TOP 10 PROVINCES AND TERRITORIES WITH THE HIGHEST RATE OF CAR THEFTS
(Province or territory/rate per 100,000 population, 1997)

❶ **Manitoba**, 989   ❷ **British Columbia**, 833   ❸ **Saskatchewan**, 685
❹ **Yukon Territory**, 677   ❺ **Quebec**, 665   ❻ **Northwest Territories**, 579   ❼ **Alberta**, 546
❽ **Ontario**, 490   ❾ **Nova Scotia**, 270   ❿ **New Brunswick**, 200

Canada, 585   Source: *Statistics Canada*

THE 10 ⭐
US STATES WITH THE HIGHEST CRIME RATES

STATE	CRIMES PER 100,000 (1999)
1 **Florida**	6,205.5
2 **New Mexico**	5,962.1
3 **Arizona**	5,896.5
4 **Louisiana**	5,746.8
5 **South Carolina**	5,324.4
6 **Washington**	5,255.5
7 **North Carolina**	5,175.4
8 **Georgia**	5,148.5
9 **Texas**	5,031.8
10 **Oregon**	5,002.0

Source: *FBI Uniform Crime Reports*

TOP 10 🍁
CARS MOST STOLEN IN CANADA

MODEL	THEFT FREQUENCY (1998–99)*
1 **Hyundai Tiburon FX**	850
2 **Volkswagen Golf** (two door)	484
3 **Acura Integra** (two door)	479
4 **Jeep TJ** (four-wheel drive)	324
5 **Hyundai Accent** (two door)	313
6 **Chevrolet Cavalier Z24**	294
7 **Dodge Durango** (four-wheel drive)	251
8 **Dodge Dakota** (four-wheel drive)	250
9 **Toyota 4Runner** (four-wheel drive)	244
10 **Dodge Ram 1500** (four-wheel drive)	234

* Relative theft claim frequency: 100 represents the average (eg, 850 is 750% above the average)

Source: *Vehicle Information Centre of Canada*

THE 10 🍁
PROVINCES AND TERRITORIES WITH THE HIGHEST PENITENTIARY OCCUPANCY*

PROVINCE OR TERRITORY	NO. OF FACILITIES	TOTAL CAPACITY	NO. OF INMATES
1 **Ontario**	47	7,914	8,416
2 **Quebec**	19	3,483	3,424
3 **British Columbia**	19	2,259	2,324
4 **Alberta**	10	2,412	2,176
5 **Saskatchewan**	15	1,228	1,117
6 **Manitoba**	8	976	942
7 **Nova Scotia**	9	512	432
8 **New Brunswick**	10	388	396
9 **Newfoundland**	6	351	299
10 **Northwest Territories**	4	244	273

* As at October 5, 1996; ranked by number of inmates

Source: *Canadian Centre for Justice Statistics*

Did You Know? Although regarded as "priceless," Leonardo da Vinci's *Mona Lisa* is believed to be the most valuable single object ever stolen. It was taken from the Louvre Museum on August 21, 1911, and returned on January 4, 1914.

Capital Punishment

LAST PUBLIC HANGINGS IN THE UK

HANGED/CRIME	DATE
1 Michael Barrett *Murder of Sarah Ann Hodgkinson, one of 12 victims of bombing in Clerkenwell, London*	May 26, 1868
2 Robert Smith *Murder of a girl (the last public hanging in Scotland)*	May 12, 1868
3 Richard Bishop *Stabbing of Alfred Cartwright*	Apr 30, 1868
4 John Mapp *Murder of a girl*	Apr 9, 1868
5 Frederick Parker *Murder of Daniel Driscoll*	Apr 4, 1868
6 Timothy Faherty *Murder of Mary Hanmer*	Apr 4, 1868
7 Miles Wetherill or **Weatherill** *Murder of Rev. Plow and his maid*	Apr 4, 1868
8 Frances Kidder *Murder of 12-year-old Louise Kidder-Staple (the last public hanging of a woman)*	Apr 2, 1868
9 William Worsley *Murder of William Bradbury*	Mar 31, 1868
10 Frederick Baker *Murder and mutilation of 8-year-old Fanny Adams*	Dec 24, 1867

FIRST COUNTRIES TO ABOLISH CAPITAL PUNISHMENT

COUNTRY	ABOLISHED
1 Russia	1826
2 Venezuela	1863
3 Portugal	1867
4 =Brazil	1882
=Costa Rica	1882
6 Ecuador	1897
7 Panama	1903
8 Norway	1905
9 Uruguay	1907
10 Colombia	1910

PRISONS WITH THE MOST HANGINGS IN ENGLAND AND WALES, 1868–1964

PRISON	HANGINGS 1868–99	1900–64	TOTAL
1 Wandsworth, London	18	98	116
2 Pentonville, London	–	105	105
3 Manchester (Strangeways)	28	71	99
4 Liverpool (Walton)	39	52	91
5 Leeds (Armley)	23	66	89
6 Durham	21	54	75
7 Newgate, London	50	9	59
8 Birmingham (Winson Green)	6	34	40
9 Lincoln	12	18	30
10=Maidstone	17	11	28
=Winchester	14	14	28

WORST YEARS FOR LYNCHINGS IN THE US*

YEAR	LYNCHING VICTIMS WHITE	BLACK	TOTAL
1 1892	69	161	230
2 1884	160	51	211
3 1894	58	134	192
4 =1885	110	74	184
=1891	71	113	184
6 1895	66	113	179
7 1889	76	94	170
8 1897	35	123	158
9 1893	34	118	152
10 1886	64	74	138

* *Since 1882*

Lynching is the "rough justice" of a mob seizing a crime suspect and hanging him or her (92 women were lynched between 1882 and 1927) without trial. Although lynching progressively became a racial crime, in its early years white victims actually outnumbered black.

FIRST EXECUTIONS BY LETHAL INJECTION IN THE US

NAME	EXECUTION
1 Charles Brooks	Dec 7, 1982
2 James Autry	Mar 14, 1984
3 Ronald O'Bryan	Mar 31, 1984
4 Thomas Barefoot	Oct 30, 1984
5 Dovle Skillem	Jan 16, 1985
6 Stephen Morin	Mar 13, 1985
7 Jesse de la Rosa	May 15, 1985
8 Charles Milton	June 25, 1985
9 Henry M. Porter	July 9, 1985
10 Charles Rumbaugh	Sep 11, 1985

Source: *Death Penalty Information Center*

Although Oklahoma was the first state to legalize execution by lethal injection, the option was not taken there until 1990. All of the above were executed in Texas (where, curiously, death row inmates with the first name of Charles figure prominently). Lethal injection is now the most commonly used method of execution in the US.

COUNTRIES WITH THE MOST EXECUTIONS

COUNTRY	EXECUTIONS (1998)
1 China	1,067
2 Dem. Rep. of Congo	100
3 US	68
4 Iran	66
5 Egypt	48
6 Belarus	33
7 Taiwan	32
8 Saudi Arabia	29
9 Singapore	28
10=Rwanda	24
=Sierra Leone	24

Source: *Amnesty International*

Although unconfirmed, Amnesty International also received reports of many hundreds of executions in Iraq.

THE 10 ★
STATES WITH THE MOST PRISONERS ON DEATH ROW

STATE	PRISONERS UNDER DEATH SENTENCE*
1 California	582
2 Texas	448
3 Florida	385
4 Pennsylvania	238
5 North Carolina	237
6 Ohio	202
7 Alabama	185
8 Illinois	172
9 Oklahoma	137
10 Georgia	136

* As at October 1, 2000

Source: *Death Penalty Information Center*

A total of 3,703 prisoners were on death row at the end of 2000. Some were sentenced in more than one state, causing a higher total to be achieved by adding individual state figures together.

THE 10 ★
STATES WITH THE MOST EXECUTIONS, 1977–2000*

STATE	EXECUTIONS
1 Texas	239
2 Virginia	81
3 Florida	50
4 Missouri	46
5 Oklahoma	30
6 Louisiana	26
7 South Carolina	25
8 =Alabama	23
=Arkansas	23
=Georgia	23

* To December 19, 2000

Source: *Death Penalty Information Center*

A total of 557 people have been executed since 1977, when the death penalty was reintroduced after a 10-year moratorium. During this period, 20 states have not carried out any executions.

THE 10 🍁
HANGINGS ON PRINCE EDWARD ISLAND*

PERSON HANGED	CRIME	DATE
1 Joseph Farrow	Rape	1792
2 =John Nicholson	Murder	1813
=Samuel Nicholson	Murder	1813
4 =Sancho Byers	Theft	1815
=Peter Byers	Theft	1815
6 =James Cash	Rape	1821
=James Christie	Theft	1821
8 George Dowey	Murder	1869

PERSON HANGED	CRIME	DATE
9 William Millman	Murder	1888
10 =Frederick Phillips	Murder	1941
=Earl Lund	Murder	1941

* There have been a total of 11 hangings in PEI, carried out between 1792, when the island was known as the Island of St. John (it was renamed Prince Edward Island in 1799), and 1976, when capital punishment was abolished from Canada's Criminal Code.

Source: In the Shadow of the Gallows by Jim Hornby

THE 10 ★
STATES WITH THE MOST WOMEN SENTENCED TO DEATH, 1973–2000

STATE	WOMEN SENTENCED TO DEATH*
1 North Carolina	16
2 Florida	15
3 =California	14
=Texas	13
5 Ohio	9
6 Alabama	8
7 =Illinois	7
=Mississippi	7
=Oklahoma	7
10 Georgia	6

* As at June 30, 2000

Source: *Death Penalty Information Center*

In the US, the sentencing of women to death is comparatively rare, and occasions when the sentence is actually carried out are even rarer. There are only 561 known instances since 1632 out of a total of some 19,200 executions. Forty-five executions of women have been carried out since 1900. Of these, only 7 have occurred since May 2, 1962, when Elizabeth Ann Duncan was executed. The most recent execution was of Wanda Jean Allen in Oklahoma on January 11, 2001.

THE 10 🍁
LAST HANGINGS IN EACH PROVINCE

PERSON HANGED/PROVINCE	DATE
1 Arthur Lucas and Ronald Turpin, Ontario	Dec 11, 1962
2 Robert Rae Cook, Alberta	Nov 14, 1960
3 Leo Anthony Mantha, British Columbia	Apr 27, 1959
4 Henri Hector Legault, Quebec	Feb 27, 1959
5 Joseph Pierre Richard, New Brunswick	Dec 11, 1957
6 Henry Malanik, Manitoba	Jan 17, 1951
7 Jack Loran, Saskatchewan	Feb 20, 1946
8 Robert Spratt, Newfoundland*	May 22, 1942
9 Frederick Phillips and Earl Lund, Prince Edward Island	Aug 20, 1941
Everett Farmer, Nova Scotia	Mar 28, 1935

* There have been no hangings in Newfoundland since it became part of Canada in 1949.

Source: They Were Hanged by Alan Hustak

Marguerite Pitre, hung in Quebec on January 8, 1953, was the last woman to be executed in Canada.

 What is Charles W. Furnas's claim to aviation fame?
see p.236 for the answer

A The first airplane passenger in the US
B The first to use a parachute over the Himalayas
C The first to land an aircraft on the Fraser River

69

Murder File

WORST GUN MASSACRES*

PERPETRATOR/LOCATION/DATE/CIRCUMSTANCES   VICTIMS

1 Woo Bum Kong, Sang-Namdo, South Korea, Apr 28, 1982   57
Off-duty policeman Woo Bum Kong (or Wou Bom-Kon), 27, went on a drunken rampage with rifles and hand grenades, killing 57 and injuring 38 before blowing himself up with a grenade.

2 Martin Bryant, Port Arthur, Tasmania, Australia, Apr 28, 1996   35
Bryant, a 28-year-old Hobart resident, used a rifle in a horrific spree that began in a restaurant and ended with a siege in a guesthouse in which he held hostages. He set the building on fire before being captured by police.

3 Baruch Goldstein, Hebron, occupied West Bank,
    Israel, Feb 25, 1994   29
Goldstein, a 42-year-old US immigrant doctor, carried out a gun massacre of Palestinians at prayer at the Tomb of the Patriarchs before being beaten to death by the crowd.

4 Campo Elias Delgado, Bogota, Colombia, Dec 4, 1986   28
Delgado, a Vietnamese war veteran and electronics engineer, stabbed two and shot a further 26 people before being killed by police.

5 =James Oliver Huberty, San Ysidro, California, July 18, 1984   22
Huberty, aged 41, opened fire in a McDonald's restaurant, killing 21 before being shot dead by a SWAT marksman. A further 19 were wounded, including a victim who died the following day.

=George Jo Hennard, Killeen, Texas, Oct 16, 1991   22
Hennard drove his pick-up truck through the window of Luby's Cafeteria and, in 11 minutes, killed 22 with semiautomatic pistols before shooting himself.

7 Thomas Hamilton, Dunblane, Stirling, UK, Mar 13, 1996   17
Hamilton, 43, shot 16 children and a teacher in Dunblane Primary School before killing himself in the UK's worst-ever shooting incident.

8 =Charles Joseph Whitman,
    Austin, Texas, July 31–Aug 1, 1966   16
25-year-old ex-Marine marksman Whitman killed his mother and wife; the following day he shot 14 and wounded 34 from the observation deck at the University of Texas at Austin, before being shot dead by police.

=Michael Ryan, Hungerford, Berkshire, UK, Aug 19, 1987   16
Ryan, 26, shot 14 dead and wounded 16 others (two of whom died later) before shooting himself.

=Ronald Gene Simmons, Russellville, Arkansas, Dec 28, 1987   16
47-year-old Simmons killed 16, including 14 members of his own family, by shooting or strangling. He was caught and then sentenced to death on Feb 10, 1989.

* *By individuals, excluding terrorist and military actions; totals exclude perpetrator*

Gun massacres at workplaces in the US have attracted considerable attention in recent years, with post offices being especially notable: on August 20, 1986, in Edmond, Oklahoma, 44-year-old postal worker Patrick Henry Sherrill shot 14 dead and wounded six others at the post office where he worked, before killing himself. Since then, there have been some 15 such incidents perpetrated by postal workers, in which 40 victims have been killed. Equally distressing have been a number of shootings at schools and other educational establishments, among the worst of which – and Canada's worst gun massacre – was that committed by Marc Lépine, a student at the Université de Montreal, Quebec, Canada. On December 6, 1989, he went on an armed rampage, shooting 14 women before killing himself.

MOST PROLIFIC SERIAL KILLERS OF THE 20TH CENTURY

KILLER/COUNTRY/CRIME   VICTIMS*

1 Pedro Alonso López, Colombia   300
Captured in 1980, López, nicknamed the "Monster of the Andes," led police to 53 graves, but probably murdered at least 300 in Colombia, Ecuador, and Peru. He was sentenced to life imprisonment.

2 Dr. Harold Shipman, UK   236
In January 2000, Manchester doctor Shipman was found guilty of the murder of 15 women patients, but an official report published in January 2001 suggested that the potential figure could be at least 236 and perhaps as high as 345 .

3 Henry Lee Lucas, US   200
Lucas confessed in 1983 to 360 murders, although the number of murder sites to which he led police was "only" 200. He committed many crimes with his partner-in-crime Ottis Toole, who died in jail in 1996. He remains on death row in Huntsville Prison, Texas.

4 Hu Wanlin, China   196
Posing as a doctor specializing in ancient Chinese medicine, Hu Wanlin was sentenced on October 1, 2000, to 15 years imprisonment for three deaths, but authorities believe he was responsible for considerably more, an estimated 20 in Taiyuan, 146 in Shanxi, and 30 in Shangqiu.

5 Luis Alfredo Gavarito, Colombia   140
Gavarito confessed in 1999 to a spate of murders that are still the subject of investigation.

6 Dr. Jack Kevorkian, US   130
In 1999 Kevorkian, who admitted to assisting in 130 suicides since 1990, was convicted of second-degree murder. His 10- to 25-year prison sentence is subject to appeal.

7 =Donald Henry "Pee Wee" Gaskins, US   100
Gaskins was executed in 1991 for a series of murders that may have reached 200.

=Javed Iqbal, Pakistan   100
Iqbal and two accomplices were found guilty in March 2000 of murdering boys in Lahore. Iqbal was sentenced to be publicly strangled, dismembered, and his body dissolved in acid.

9 Delfina and Maria de Jesús Gonzales, Mexico   91
In 1964 the Gonzales sisters were sentenced to 40 years' imprisonment after the remains of 80 women and 11 men were discovered on their property.

10 Bruno Lüdke, Germany   86
Lüdke confessed to murdering 86 women between 1928 and 1943. He died in the hospital in 1944 after a lethal injection.

* *Estimated minimum; includes only individual and partnership murderers; excludes "mercy killings" by doctors, murders by bandits, those carried out by groups, such as political and military atrocities, and gangland slayings.*

Serial killers are mass murderers who kill repeatedly, often over long periods, in contrast to the so-called "spree killers" who have been responsible for single occasion massacres, usually with guns, and other perpetrators of single outrages, often by means of bombs, resulting in multiple deaths. Because of the secrecy surrounding their horrific crimes, and the time-spans involved, it is almost impossible to calculate the precise numbers of their victims.

TOP 10

RELATIONSHIPS OF ACCUSED TO VICTIM IN SOLVED HOMICIDES IN CANADA

	RELATIONSHIP	PERCENT OF SOLVED HOMICIDES (1999)
1	Casual acquaintance	22.5
2	Stranger	14.9
3	Husband (legal and common-law)	9.4
4	Close acquaintance	7.2
5	Criminal relationships*	6.9
6	Father	5.4
7 =	(ex) Boyfriend/girlfriend	5.0
=	Husband (separated/divorced)	5.0
9	Child	4.5
10	Other family relation#	4.0

* Includes prostitutes, drug dealers, and their clients
\# Excludes father, mother, child, and siblings
Source: Homicide Survey, *Canadian Centre for Justice Statistics, October 2000*

FIREPOWER
While handguns are the most common murder weapons in the US and certain other countries, restrictions on their use elsewhere relegates them to a less significant position.

THE 10

MOST COMMON MURDER METHODS IN CANADA

	METHOD	VICTIMS (1999)
1	Shooting	165
2	Stabbing	143
3	Beating	123
4	Strangulation	55
5	Vehicles	13
6	Fire (burns, suffocation)	11
7	Unknown	8
8	Shaken Baby Syndrome	7
9	Other*	6
10	Poisoning	5

* Includes heart attacks and exposure
Source: Homicide Survey, *Canadian Centre for Justice Statistics, October 2000*

Firearms have accounted for approximately 30 percent of all homicides in Canada since 1976.

THE 10

CANADIAN CITIES WITH THE HIGHEST HOMICIDE RATES*

	CITY (CMA)	HOMICIDES (1999)
1	Thunder Bay, ON	3.16
2	Victoria, BC	2.85
3	Vancouver, BC	2.83
4	Sudbury, ON	2.49
5	Hamilton, ON	2.41
6	Windsor, ON	2.33
7	Winnipeg, MB	2.21
8	Edmonton, AB	2.15
9	Montreal, QC#	2.04
10	Halifax, NS	1.99

* Calculated per 100,000 population
\# Montreal had the most homicides in 1999: 70.
Source: *Canadian Centre for Justice Statistics*

THE 10

WORST CITIES FOR MURDER IN THE US

	CITY/STATE	MURDERS, 1999*
1	New York, New York	671
2	Chicago, Illinois	642
3	Los Angeles, California	425
4	Detroit, Michigan	415
5	Philadelphia, Pennsylvania	292
6 =	Houston, Texas	241
=	Washington, DC	241
8	Dallas, Texas	191
9	New Orleans, Louisiana	158
10	Atlanta, Georgia	143

* Murders and non-negligent manslaughter
Source: *FBI Uniform Crime Reports*

New York's status as the murder capital of the US improved in the 1990s.

Did You Know? The peak year for murder in the US was 1994, when 22,084 cases were recorded, 14,463 of them, or 65 percent, involving firearms.

Military Matters

CHINESE ARMED FORCES

Members of the Chinese army, the largest military force in the world, parade in the now infamous Tiananmen Square, Beijing.

THE 10 YEARS WITH THE MOST NUCLEAR EXPLOSIONS

(Year/explosions)

❶ 1962, 178 ❷ 1958, 116 ❸ 1968, 79 ❹ 1966, 76 ❺ 1961, 71
❻ 1969, 67 ❼ 1978, 66 ❽ = 1967, 64; = 1970, 64 ❿ 1964, 60

TOP 10 ★
COUNTRIES WITH THE LARGEST DEFENCE BUDGETS

	COUNTRY	BUDGET (US$)
1	US	291,200,000,000
2	Japan	45,600,000,000
3	UK	34,500,000,000
4	Russia	29,000,000,000
5	France	27,000,000,000
6	Germany	23,300,000,000
7	Saudi Arabia	18,700,000,000
8	Italy	16,000,000,000
9	India	15,900,000,000
10	China	14,500,000,000

The savings made as a consequence of the end of the Cold War between the West and the former Soviet Union mean that both the numbers of personnel and the defence budgets of many countries have been cut.

TOP 10 ★
LARGEST ARMED FORCES

	COUNTRY	ESTIMATED ACTIVE FORCES			
		ARMY	NAVY	AIR	TOTAL
1	China	1,700,000	220,000	420,000	2,340,000
2	US	471,700	370,700	353,600	1,365,800*
3	India	1,100,000	53,000	150,000	1,303,000
6	North Korea	950,000	46,000	86,000	1,082,000
5	Russia	348,000	171,500	184,600	1,004,100#
6	South Korea	560,000	60,000	63,000	683,000
7	Pakistan	550,000	22,000	40,000	612,000
8	Turkey	495,000	54,600	60,100	609,700
9	Iran	325,000	18,000	45,000	513,000+
10	Vietnam	412,000	42,000	30,000	484,000
	Canada	20,900	9,000	13,500	59,100*

* *Includes 169,800 Marine Corps*
\# *Includes Strategic Deterrent Forces, Paramilitary, National Guard, etc.*
\+ *Includes 125,000 Revolutionary Guards*
⋆ *15,700 not identified by service*

TOP 10 COUNTRIES WITH THE HIGHEST MILITARY/CIVILIAN RATIO

(Country/ratio* in 2000)

1 North Korea, 503 **2** Israel, 278 **3** United Arab Emirates, 240 **4** Jordan, 201
5 Iraq, 192 **6** Oman, 189 **7** Syria, 187 **8** Qatar, 178
9 Bahrain, 172 **10** Taiwan, 168

* Military personnel per 10,000 population

TOP 10 ★
COUNTRIES WITH THE HIGHEST PER CAPITA DEFENCE EXPENDITURE

	COUNTRY	EXPENDITURE PER CAPITA, 1999 (US$)
1	Qatar	2,026
2	Israel	1,435
3	Kuwait	1,407
4	Brunei	1,211
5	United Arab Emirates	1,185
6	Singapore	1,138
7	Saudi Arabia	1,006
8	US	1,000
9	Norway	743
10	Oman	696

THOMPSON OF THE TOMMY GUN

The "Tommy gun," or Thompson sub-machine gun, was originally produced as a military weapon. It takes its name from US Army ordnance officer John Taliaferro Thompson (1860–1940), but the operating mechanism of the .45-caliber weapon was the brainchild of naval officer John N. Blish, from whom John Thompson acquired the patent. The gun was manufactured by Thompson's Auto-Ordnance Company from 1919 but was not widely used until World War II, when over 2 million were made. Unusually, the nickname "Tommy Gun" was registered as a trademark.

TOP 10 ★
COUNTRIES WITH THE LARGEST NAVIES

	COUNTRY	MANPOWER, 2000*
1	US	370,700
2	China	220,000
3	Russia	171,500
4	Taiwan	62,000
5	South Korea	60,000
6	Turkey	54,600
7	India	53,000
8	France	49,490
9	North Korea	46,000
10	UK	43,770
	Canada	*9,000*

* Including naval air forces and marines

TOP 10 ★
ARMS IMPORTERS

	COUNTRY	ANNUAL IMPORTS (US$)
1	Saudi Arabia	6,103,000,000
2	Taiwan	2,604,000,000
3	Japan	1,866,000,000
4	South Korea	1,847,000,000
5	Israel	1,504,000,000
6	Egypt	800,000,000
7	Indonesia	767,000,000
8	Canada	583,000,000
9	=China	500,000,000
	=US*	500,000,000

* Imports from Europe only

CRUISE SHIP
The US Navy is the world's largest. Here, the destroyer USS Merrill *launches a Tomahawk cruise missile.*

TOP 10 ★
COUNTRIES WITH THE MOST COMBAT AIRCRAFT*

	COUNTRY	COMBAT AIRCRAFT
1	China	3,000
2	Russia	2,733
3	US	2,529
4	Ukraine	911
5	India	774
6	North Korea	621
7	Egypt	580
8	Taiwan	570
9	South Korea	555
10	France	517
	Canada	*140*

* Air force only, excluding long-range strike/attack aircraft

TOP 10 ★
LARGEST ARMED FORCES OF WORLD WAR I

COUNTRY	PERSONNEL*
1 Russia	12,000,000
2 Germany	11,000,000
3 British Empire	8,904,000
4 France	8,410,000
5 Austria–Hungary	7,800,000
6 Italy	5,615,000
7 US	4,355,000
8 Turkey	2,850,000
9 Bulgaria	1,200,000
10 Japan	800,000

*Total at peak strength

Russia's armed forces were relatively small in relation to the country's population – some 6 percent, compared with 17 percent in Germany. Several other European nations had forces that were similarly substantial in relation to their populations: Serbia's army was equivalent to 4 percent of its population. In total, more than 65 million combatants were involved in fighting some of the costliest battles, in terms of numbers killed, that the world has ever known.

TOP 10 ★
SMALLEST ARMED FORCES OF WORLD WAR I

COUNTRY	PERSONNEL*
1 Montenegro	50,000
2 Portugal	100,000
3 Greece	230,000
4 Belgium	267,000
5 Serbia	707,000
6 Romania	750,000
7 Japan	800,000
8 Bulgaria	1,200,000
9 Turkey	2,850,000
10 US	4,355,000

*Total at peak strength

THE 10 COUNTRIES WITH THE MOST PRISONERS OF WAR, 1914–18
(Country/captured)

❶ Russia, 2,500,000 ❷ Austria–Hungary, 2,200,000 ❸ Germany, 1,152,800 ❹ Italy, 600,000 ❺ France, 537,000 ❻ Turkey, 250,000 ❼ British Empire, 191,652 ❽ Serbia, 152,958 ❾ Romania, 80,000 ❿ Belgium, 34,659

THE 10 ★
COUNTRIES SUFFERING THE GREATEST MILITARY LOSSES IN WORLD WAR I

COUNTRY	KILLED
1 Germany	1,773,700
2 Russia	1,700,000
3 France	1,357,800
4 Austria–Hungary	1,200,000
5 British Empire*	908,371
6 Italy	650,000
7 Romania	335,706
8 Turkey	325,000
9 US	116,516
10 Bulgaria	87,500

* Including Australia, Canada, India, New Zealand, South Africa, etc.

The number of battle fatalities and deaths from other causes among military personnel varied enormously from country to country. Romania's death rate was highest at 45 percent of its total mobilized forces; Germany's was 16 percent, Austria–Hungary's and Russia's 15 percent, and the British Empire's 10 percent, with the US's 2 percent and Japan's 0.04 percent among the lowest. Japan's forces totalled only 800,000, of which an estimated 300 were killed, 907 wounded, and just three taken prisoner or reported missing.

WAR GRAVES
The first Battle of the Somme (July 1 to November 18, 1916) resulted in some 1,265,000 casualties, with no significant territorial gain.

THE 10 ★
COUNTRIES SUFFERING THE GREATEST MILITARY LOSSES IN WORLD WAR II

	COUNTRY	KILLED
1	USSR	13,600,000*
2	Germany	3,300,000
3	China	1,324,516
4	Japan	1,140,429
5	British Empire#	357,116
6	Romania	350,000
7	Poland	320,000
8	Yugoslavia	305,000
9	US	292,131
10	Italy	279,800
	Total	21,268,992

* Total, of which 7,800,000 battlefield deaths

Including Australia, Canada, India, New Zealand, etc.; UK figure 264,000

The actual numbers killed in World War II have been the subject of intense argument for over 50 years. Most authorities now agree that of the 30 million Soviets who bore arms, there were 13.6 million military deaths.

TOP 10 ★
LARGEST ARMED FORCES OF WORLD WAR II

	COUNTRY	PERSONNEL*
1	USSR	12,500,000
2	US	12,364,000
3	Germany	10,000,000
4	Japan	6,095,000
5	France	5,700,000
6	UK	4,683,000
7	Italy	4,500,000
8	China	3,800,000
9	India	2,150,000
10	Poland	1,000,000

* Total at peak strength

THE 10 ★
COUNTRIES SUFFERING THE GREATEST CIVILIAN LOSSES IN WORLD WAR II

	COUNTRY	KILLED
1	China	8,000,000
2	USSR	6,500,000
3	Poland	5,300,000
4	Germany	2,350,000
5	Yugoslavia	1,500,000
6	France	470,000
7	Greece	415,000
8	Japan	393,400
9	Romania	340,000
10	Hungary	300,000

Deaths among civilians during this war – many resulting from famine and internal purges, such as those in China and the USSR – were colossal, but they were less well documented than those among fighting forces. Although the figures are the best available from authoritative sources, and present a broad picture of the scale of civilian losses, the precise numbers will never be known.

TOP 10 ★
LARGEST SUBMARINE FLEETS OF WORLD WAR II

	COUNTRY	SUBMARINES
1	Japan*	163
2	US*	112
3	France	77
4	USSR	75
5	Germany	57
6	UK	38
7	Netherlands	21
8	Italy	15
9	Denmark	12
10	Greece	6

* Strength at December 1941

These show submarine strengths at the outbreak of the war. During hostilities, production rose sharply.

THE 10 ★
COUNTRIES SUFFERING THE GREATEST NUMBER OF WARSHIP LOSSES IN WORLD WAR II

	COUNTRY	WARSHIPS SUNK
1	UK	213
2	Japan	198
3	US	105
4	Italy	97
5	Germany	60
6	USSR	37
7	Canada	17
8	France	11
9	Australia	9
10	Norway	2

TOP 10 ★
TANKS OF WORLD WAR II

	TANK	COUNTRY	WEIGHT (TONNES)	NO. PRODUCED
1	M4A3 Sherman	US	31.5	41,530
2	T34 Model 42	USSR	28.9	35,120
3	T34/85	USSR	32.5	29,430
4	M3 General Stuart	US	12.4	14,000
5	Valentine II	UK	17.8	8,280
6	M3A1 Lee/Grant	US	27.2	7,400
7	Churchill VII	UK	40.6	5,640
8 =	Panzer IVD	Germany	20.3	5,500
=	Panzer VG	Germany	45.5	5,500
10	Crusader I	UK	19.3	4,750

The tank named after US Civil War General William Tecumseh Sherman was used in large numbers by both US and British troops during World War II. It carried a crew of five and could cruise over a distance of 230 km (143 miles) at up to 40 km/h (25 mph). Its weaponry comprised two machine guns and, originally, a 75-mm (3-in) cannon, but after 1944 about half the Shermans in operation had their cannons replaced by one capable of firing a powerful 7.7-kg (17-lb) shell or a 5.5-kg (12-lb) armor-piercing shell.

Did You Know? Argentina, the 53rd country to enter World War II, did not declare war on Germany and Japan until March 27, 1945 – just six weeks before Germany was defeated.

TOP 10
RELIGIOUS GROUPS IN CANADA

	RELIGIOUS GROUP	POPULATION 1991
1	Roman Catholic	12,203,600
2	Protestant*	4,499,500
3	United Church	3,093,100
4	Anglican	2,188,100
5	Eastern Orthodox	387,400
6	Jewish	318,100
7	Islam	253,300
8	Buddhist	163,400
9	Hindu	157,000
10	Sikh	147,000

* Includes Baptist, Presbyterian, Lutheran, Pentecostal, and other, smaller denominations

Source: 1991 Census, Statistics Canada

According to the latest census that asked about religious affiliation, 3,386,400 Canadians, or 12.5 percent of the population, have no religious persuasion. The only single denomination able to claim higher numbers is Roman Catholicism. Although membership in many non-Christian groups has risen dramatically over the last 30 years, Christianity remains Canada's dominant religion, a faith held by some 80 percent of the population.

TOP 10
COUNTRIES WITH THE HIGHEST PROPORTION OF HINDUS

	COUNTRY	HINDU PERCENTAGE OF POPULATION
1	Nepal	89
2	India	79
3	Mauritius	52
4	Guyana	40
5	Fiji	38
6	Suriname	30
7	Bhutan	25
8	Trinidad and Tobago	24
9	Sri Lanka	15
10	Bangladesh	11

Source: Adherents.com

THE 10 LATEST DALAI LAMAS
(Dalai Lama/lifespan)

1 Tenzin Gyatso, 1935– 2 Thupten Gyatso, 1876–1933
3 Trinley Gyatso, 1856–1875 4 Khendrup Gyatso, 1838–1856
5 Tsultrim Gyatso, 1816–1837 6 Luntok Gyatso, 1806–1815 7 Jampel Gyatso, 1758–1804 8 Kesang Gyatso, 1708–1757 9 Tsangyang Gyatso, 1683–1706
10 Ngawang Lobsang Gyatso, 1617–1682

The current Dalai Lama is the fourteenth in line since the first head of the "Yellow Hat Order" of Tibetan Buddhists (1391–1475).

TOP 10
LARGEST CHRISTIAN POPULATIONS

	COUNTRY	TOTAL CHRISTIAN POPULATION
1	US	189,983,000
2	Brazil	170,405,000
3	Mexico	96,614,000
4	China	86,801,000
5	Philippines	72,255,000
6	Germany	60,712,000
7	Nigeria	54,012,000
8	Italy	47,704,000
9	France	45,505,000
10	Dem. Rep. of Congo	42,283,000
	World total	2,094,371,000

Source: Christian Research

TOP 10
CHRISTIAN DENOMINATIONS

	DENOMINATION	MEMBERS
1	Roman Catholic	936,192,000
2	Orthodox	139,469,000
3	Pentecostal	122,096,000
4	Lutheran	82,943,000
5	Anglican	78,395,000
6	Baptist	71,590,000
7	Presbyterian	49,286,000
8	Methodist	26,374,000
9	Seventh Day Adventist	11,589,000
10	Churches of Christ	6,759,000

Source: Christian Research

TOP 10
RELIGIOUS BELIEFS

	RELIGION	FOLLOWERS*
1	Christianity	2,094,371,000
2	Islam	1,155,109,000
3	Hinduism	850,000,000
4	Non-religions	768,159,000
5	Buddhism	356,270,000
6	Tribal religions	228,367,000
7	Atheism	150,090,000
8	New religions	102,356,000
9	Sikhism	23,258,000
10	Judaism	13,000,000

* Estimates for mid-2000

TOP 10
LARGEST JEWISH POPULATIONS

	COUNTRY	TOTAL JEWISH POPULATION
1	US	5,800,000
2	Israel	4,600,000
3	France	600,000
4	Russia	550,000
5	Ukraine	400,000
6	Canada	360,000
7	UK	300,000
8	Argentina	250,000
9	Brazil	130,000
10	South Africa	106,000
	World total	13,000,000

As a result of the Diaspora, or scattering of Jewish people, Jewish communities are found in virtually every country in the world.

Did You Know? Completed in 1989, the world's largest church, Our Lady of Peace Basilica in Yamoussoukro, Côte d'Ivoire, is taller than and has double the floor area of St. Peter's, Rome, the previous record holder.

LARGEST MUSLIM POPULATIONS

	COUNTRY	TOTAL MUSLIM POPULATION
1	Indonesia	179,780,000
2	Pakistan	144,620,000
3	India	120,000,000
4	Bangladesh	112,250,000
5	Turkey	64,280,000
6	Iran	61,600,000
7	Egypt	57,460,000
8	Nigeria	48,900,000
9	Algeria	29,880,000
10	Morocco	28,260,000
	World total	1,155,109,000

There are at least 15 countries where the population is 95 percent Muslim, including Bahrain, Kuwait, Somalia, and Yemen. Historically, Islam spread both as a result of missionary activity and through contacts with Muslim traders.

BOWING TO MECCA

Islam places many strictures on its female members but is nonetheless the world's fastest-growing religion. Here, hundreds of Muslim women unite in prayers.

COUNTRIES WITH THE HIGHEST PROPORTION OF BUDDHISTS

	COUNTRY	BUDDHIST PERCENTAGE OF POPULATION
1	Thailand	95
2	Cambodia	90
3	Myanmar (Burma)	88
4	Bhutan	75
5	Sri Lanka	70
6	Tibet*	65
7	Laos	60
8	Vietnam	55
9	Japan*	50
10	Macau	45

* No accurate figures available
Source: *Adherents.com*

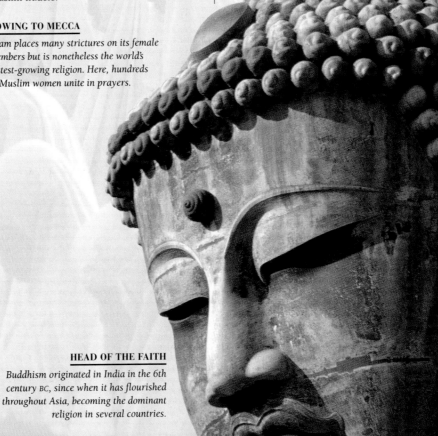

HEAD OF THE FAITH

Buddhism originated in India in the 6th century BC, since when it has flourished throughout Asia, becoming the dominant religion in several countries.

TOWN & COUNTRY

Country Matters

LARGEST COUNTRIES IN EUROPE

	COUNTRY	AREA SQ MILES	SQ KM
1	Russia (in Europe)	1,818,629	4,710,227
2	Ukraine	233,090	603,700
3	France	212,935	551,500
4	Spain*	194,897	504,781
5	Sweden	173,732	449,964
6	Germany	137,735	356,733
7	Finland	130,559	338,145
8	Norway	125,050	323,877
9	Poland	124,808	323,250
10	Italy	116,320	301,268

* Including offshore islands

The UK falls just outside the Top 10 at 244,101 sq km (94,247 sq miles). Excluding the Isle of Man and Channel Islands, its area comprises: England (130,410 sq km/50,351 sq miles), Scotland (78,789 sq km/30,420 sq miles), Wales (20,758 sq km/8,015 sq miles), and Northern Ireland (14,144 sq km/5,461 sq miles).

SPANISH MAIN STREET

Spain covers most of the Iberian Peninsula in southwestern Europe. At its center lies Madrid, which has been Spain's capital city since 1561.

LARGEST COUNTRIES

	COUNTRY	AREA SQ MILES	SQ KM	PERCENTAGE OF WORLD TOTAL
1	Russia	6,590,876	17,070,289	11.46
2	Canada	3,849,670	9,970,599	6.69
3	US	3,717,813	9,629,091	6.46
4	China	3,705,408	9,596,961	6.44
5	Brazil	3,286,488	8,511,965	5.71
6	Australia	2,967,909	7,686,848	5.16
7	India	1,269,346	3,287,590	2.20
8	Argentina	1,068,302	2,766,890	1.85
9	Kazakhstan	1,049,156	2,717,300	1.82
10	Sudan	967,500	2,505,813	1.68
	World total	57,506,061	148,940,000	100.00

The world's largest countries, the Top 10 of which comprise more than 50 percent of the Earth's land, have undergone substantial revision lately. The breakup of the former Soviet Union has effectively introduced two new countries into the list, with Russia taking preeminent position (since it occupies a vast 76 percent of the area of the old USSR, which it replaces, and, for comparison, is 70 times the size of the UK), while Kazakhstan, which enters in 9th position, ousts Algeria from the bottom of the previous list.

WESTWARD EXPANSION

The land area of the United States 200 years ago, at 2,239,682 sq km (864,746 sq miles), was less than a quarter of its present extent.

COUNTRIES WITH THE LONGEST COASTLINES

	COUNTRY	TOTAL COASTLINE LENGTH MILES	KM
1	Canada	151,485	243,791
2	Indonesia	33,999	54,716
3	Russia	23,396	37,653
4	Philippines	22,559	36,289
5	Japan	18,486	29,751
6	Australia	16,007	25,760
7	Norway	13,624	21,925
8	US	12,380	19,924
9	New Zealand	9,404	15,134
10	China	9,010	14,500

Including all of its islands, the coastline of Canada is more than six times as long as the distance around the Earth at the equator (40,076 km/24,902 miles). The coastline of the UK (12,429 km/7,723 miles – greater than the distance from London to Honolulu) puts it in 13th place after Greece (13,676 km/8,498 miles). Were it included as a country, Greenland (44,087 km/27,394 miles) would be in 3rd place.

TOP 10 ★
COUNTRIES WITH THE MOST NEIGHBORS

COUNTRY/NEIGHBORS	NO.
1 China	15

Afghanistan, Bhutan, India, Kazakhstan, Kyrgyzstan, Laos, Mongolia, Myanmar (Burma), Nepal, North Korea, Pakistan, Russia, Tajikstan, Thailand, Vietnam

2 Russia	14

Azerbaijan, Belarus, China, Estonia, Finland, Georgia, Kazakhstan, Latvia, Lithuania, Mongolia, North Korea, Norway, Poland, Ukraine

3 Brazil	10

Argentina, Bolivia, Colombia, French Guiana, Guyana, Paraguay, Peru, Suriname, Uruguay, Venezuela

4 = Dem. Rep. of Congo	9

Angola, Burundi, Central African Republic, Congo, Rwanda, Sudan, Tanzania, Uganda, Zambia

= Germany	9

Austria, Belgium, Czech Republic, Denmark, France, Luxembourg, Netherlands, Poland, Switzerland

= Sudan	9

Central African Republic, Chad, Dem. Rep. of Congo, Egypt, Eritrea, Ethiopia, Kenya, Libya, Uganda

7 = Austria	8

Czech Republic, Germany, Hungary, Italy, Liechtenstein, Slovac Republic, Slovenia, Switzerland

= France	8

Andorra, Belgium, Germany, Italy, Luxembourg, Monaco, Spain, Switzerland

= Saudi Arabia	8

Iraq, Jordan, Kuwait, Oman, People's Democratic Republic of Yemen, Qatar, United Arab Emirates, Yemen Arab Republic

= Tanzania	8

Burundi, Dem. Rep. of Congo, Kenya, Malawi, Mozambique, Rwanda, Uganda, Zambia

= Turkey	8

Armenia, Azerbaijan, Bulgaria, Georgia, Greece, Iran, Iraq, Syria

Some countries have more than one discontinuous border with the same country; this has been counted only once. Outside the Top 10, five countries – Mali, Niger, Ukraine, Zambia, and Yugoslavia – each have seven neighbors. Political changes make this a volatile list: the former Soviet Union had 12 neighbors, but since its breakup Russia has 14, while Eritrea's separation from Ethiopia in 1993 increased Sudan's total.

TOP 10 ★
LARGEST LANDLOCKED COUNTRIES

	COUNTRY	AREA SQ MILES	AREA SQ KM
1	Kazakhstan	1,049,156	2,717,300
2	Mongolia	604,829	1,566,500
3	Chad	495,755	1,284,000
4	Niger	489,191	1,267,000
5	Mali	478,841	1,240,192
6	Ethiopia	426,373	1,104,300
7	Bolivia	424,165	1,098,581
8	Zambia	290,587	752,618
9	Afghanistan	251,773	652,090
10	Central African Republic	240,535	622,984

There are more than 40 landlocked countries, although the largest, Kazakhstan, and the 12th largest, Turkmenistan, both have coasts on the Caspian Sea – which is itself landlocked. The largest landlocked state in Europe is Hungary (93,030 sq km/35,919 sq miles). Europe contains the world's smallest landlocked states: Andorra, Liechtenstein, San Marino, and Vatican City.

MONACO GRAND PRIX

An enclave within France, Monaco's wealth, from tourism, gambling, and other sources, is out of proportion to its status as one of the world's smallest sovereign states.

TOP 10 SMALLEST COUNTRIES
(Country/area in sq miles/sq km)

1 Vatican City, 0.17/0.44   **2** Monaco, 0.38/1.00   **3** Gibraltar, 2.49/6.47
4 Nauru, 8.19/21.23   **5** Tuvalu, 10.00/25.90   **6** Bermuda, 20.59/53.35
7 San Marino, 23.00/59.57   **8** Liechtenstein, 61.00/157.99
9 Marshall Islands, 70.00/181.00   **10** Antigua, 108.00/279.72

The "country" status of several of these microstates is questionable, since their government, defense, currency, and other features are often intricately linked with those of larger countries – the Vatican City with Italy, and Monaco with France, for example, while Gibraltar and Bermuda are dependent territories of the UK.

THE FOUNDATION OF SAUDI ARABIA

One of the largest and, through its oil wealth, richest countries in the world, Saudi Arabia has a history that dates back just 100 years. The territory had long been subject to rule by Egypt, the Ottoman Empire, and competing Arab families, with the head of one, Abdul Aziz Bin Abdul Rahman Al-Saud (known in the West as Ibn Saud), living in exile in Kuwait. At the age of just 21, he became the leader of a small group that in 1902 captured the city of Riyadh from the rival Al-Rashid family. This conquest marks the beginning of the formation of the modern state, but it took 30 years to incorporate all the regions into one kingdom, which, in honor of its founder, was named Saudi Arabia. Oil was discovered in 1938, and Ibn Saud ruled until 1953, fathering 45 sons and over 200 daughters.

100 YEARS AGO · YEARS AGO · YEARS AGO · YEARS AGO

Did You Know? Greenland is part of Danish territory, but if regarded as a country, its 2,175,600 sq km (840,004 sq miles) would make it the 12th largest in the world.

81

World & Country Populations

FASTEST GROWING COUNTRIES

COUNTRY	ANNUAL GROWTH RATE, 1998–2015 (%)
1 Yemen	3.4
2 Oman	3.2
3 Niger	3.0
4 =Angola	2.9
=Dem. Rep. of Congo	2.9
=Saudi Arabia	2.9
7 =Burkino Faso	2.8
=Rwanda	2.8
=Solomon Islands	2.8
10 =Congo	2.7
=Iraq	2.7
=Jordan	2.7
Canada	0.9

Source: *UN, Human Development Report 2000*

FASTEST SHRINKING COUNTRIES

COUNTRY	ANNUAL GROWTH RATE, 1998–2015 (%)
1 =Estonia	-0.9
=Latvia	-0.9
3 Bulgaria	-0.6
4 St. Kitts and Nevis	-0.5
5 =Hungary	-0.4
=Romania	-0.4
=Ukraine	-0.4
8 =Belarus	-0.3
=Italy	-0.3
=Lithuania	-0.3

Source: *UN, Human Development Report 2000*

Many of the countries in this Top 10 are in the former Soviet Union or Eastern Europe. They have a negative population growth rate, which means that their populations are actually shrinking, in the case of Estonia and Latvia at almost 1 percent a year. This is probably related to the rapid social and economic changes that these countries experienced in the final years of the 20th century.

COUNTRIES WITH THE YOUNGEST POPULATIONS

COUNTRY	PERCENTAGE UNDER 15 (2002)
1 Uganda	50.9
2 Marshall Islands	49.1
3 Dem. Rep. of Congo	48.2
4 Niger	47.9
5 Chad	47.8
6 São Tomé and Príncipe	47.7
7 Burkino Faso	47.4
8 Ethiopia	47.3
9 Benin	47.2
10 =Mali	47.1
=Zambia	47.1
Canada	18.7

Source: *US Census Bureau International Data Base*

Countries with high proportions of their population under the age of 15 are usually characterized by high birth rates and high death rates.

COUNTRIES WITH THE OLDEST POPULATIONS

COUNTRY	PERCENTAGE OVER 65 (2002)
1 Monaco	22.4
2 Italy	18.6
3 =Greece	18.0
=Japan	18.0
5 Spain	17.4
6 Sweden	17.3
7 Belgium	17.1
8 Germany	17.0
9 Bulgaria	16.9
10 San Marino	16.4
Canada	12.9

Source: *US Census Bureau International Data Base*

Nine of the 10 countries with the oldest populations are in Europe, implying that this region has lower death rates and a higher life expectancy than the rest of the world. On average, one in every 6.6 people (15.2 percent) in Europe is over 65.

COUNTRIES IN WHICH MEN MOST OUTNUMBER WOMEN

COUNTRY	MEN PER 100 WOMEN (2000)
1 Qatar	187
2 United Arab Emirates	172
3 Bahrain	132
4 Saudi Arabia	123
5 Oman	113
6 =Cook Islands	111
=Guam	111
=Kuwait	111
9 =Brunei	110
=Northern Mariana Islands	110

Source: *United Nations*

The world male/female ratio is balanced virtually 50:50, although in many Western countries male births slightly outnumber female by a very small percentage. There are certain countries, however, where one sex dominates more obviously. No one knows why these imbalances occur, or even if such apparent differentials represent a true picture.

COUNTRIES IN WHICH WOMEN MOST OUTNUMBER MEN

COUNTRY	WOMEN PER 100 MEN (2000)
1 Latvia	120
2 Ukraine	115
3 =Cape Verde	114
=Russia	114
5 =Belarus	112
=Estonia	112
=Lithuania	112
8 =Georgia	109
=Hungary	109
=Moldova	109
Canada	102

Source: *United Nations*

TOP 10 ★
MOST DENSELY POPULATED COUNTRIES

	COUNTRY	AREA (SQ KM)	ESTIMATED POPULATION (2002)	POPULATION PER SQ KM
1	Monaco	1.95	31,987	15,993.5
2	Singapore	624	4,452,732	7,135.8
3	Malta	321	397,499	1,238.3
4	Maldives	300	320,165	1,067.2
5	Bahrain	619	656,397	1,060.4
6	Bangladesh	133,911	133,376,684	996.0
7	Taiwan	32,261	22,548,009	698.9
8	Mauritius	1,849	1,196,172	649.1
9	Barbados	430	276,607	643.3
10	Nauru	21	12,329	587.1
	Canada	9,220,302	31,330,255	3.5
	World	131,003,055	6,234,250,387	47.6

Source: *US Census Bureau, International Data Base*

TOP 10 ★
MOST HIGHLY POPULATED COUNTRIES

	COUNTRY	1980	POPULATION 1990	2000*
1	China	984,736,000	1,138,895,000	1,256,168,000
2	India	690,462,000	850,558,000	1,017,645,000
3	US	227,726,000	249,949,000	274,943,000
4	Indonesia	154,936,000	187,728,000	219,267,000
5	Brazil	122,936,000	151,040,000	173,791,000
6	Russia	139,045,000	148,088,000	145,905,000
7	Pakistan	85,219,000	113,914,000	141,145,000
8	Bangladesh	88,077,000	110,118,000	129,147,000
9	Japan	116,807,000	123,537,000	126,434,000
10	Nigeria	65,699,000	86,530,000	117,171,000
	Canada	24,593,000	27,791,000	31,330,000
	World	4,453,778,000	5,276,992,000	6,073,099,000

* Estimated

Source: *US Census Bureau*

According to estimates by the US Census Bureau, the world entered the 21st century with a total population topping 6 billion. In 1999, India joined China as the second country to achieve a population in excess of 1 billion, while Mexico ascended to the 100-million-plus club in 11th place, with a population of 102,027,000. In contrast, the populations of some countries, such as Russia and (in 22nd place) Italy, declined during the 1990s as their birth rates fell.

TOP 10 ★
MOST POPULOUS ISLAND COUNTRIES

	ISLAND COUNTRY	POPULATION PER SQ MILE	SQ KM	POPULATION
1	Indonesia	305.6	118.0	224,784,210
2	Japan	879.1	339.4	126,549,976
3	Philippines	700.6	270.5	81,159,644
4	UK	631.4	243.7	59,508,382
5	Taiwan	1,608.0	620.8	22,191,087
6	Sri Lanka	759.4	293.2	19,238,575
7	Madagascar	68.4	26.4	15,506,472
8	Cuba	260.3	100.5	11,141,997
9	Dominican Republic	448.6	173.2	8,442,533
10	Haiti	641.0	247.4	6,867,995

TOP 10 ★
LEAST DENSELY POPULATED COUNTRIES

	COUNTRY	AREA (SQ KM)	ESTIMATED POPULATION (2002)	POPULATION PER SQ KM
1	Mongolia	1,565,000	2,694,432	1.7
2	Namibia	823,291	1,820,916	2.2
3	Australia	7,617,931	19,546,792	2.6
4 =	Botswana	585,371	1,591,232	2.7
=	Mauritania	1,030,400	2,828,858	2.7
6	Suriname	161,471	436,494	2.7
7	Iceland	100,251	279,384	2.8
8	Libya	1,759,540	5,368,585	3.2
9 =	Canada	9,220,970	31,902,268	3.5
=	Guyana	196,850	698,209	3.5

Source: *US Census Bureau, International Data Base*

TOP 10 MOST HIGHLY POPULATED COUNTRIES 100 YEARS AGO
(Country/population)

1 China, 372,563,000 **2** India, 287,223,431 **3** Russia, 147,277,000 **4** US, 76,356,000 **5** Germany, 56,345,014 **6** Austro-Hungarian Empire, 47,013,835 **7** Japan, 43,759,577 **8** UK, 41,605,220 **9** France, 38,641,333 **10** Italy, 32,100,000

The extensive Austro-Hungarian Empire included all its territories in its census, the largest being Austria, with a population of 26,150,708.

Did You Know? China has led the world as the most highly populated country since ancient times: as early as 1393 a figure of 60 million was recorded.

Future Shock

TOP 10 ★
MOST POPULATED COUNTRIES IN EUROPE IN 2050

	COUNTRY	EST. POPULATION IN 2050
1	Russia (including in Asia)	118,233,243
2	Germany	79,702,511
3	France	58,967,418
4	UK	58,210,627
5	Italy	45,016,465
6	Ukraine	37,726,401
7	Poland	33,779,568
8	Spain	32,562,163
9	Romania	18,340,400
10	Netherlands	16,721,036

Source: *US Census Bureau, International Data Base*

THE 10 ★
DECADES OF WORLD POPULATION, 1960–2050

YEAR	WORLD POPULATION
1960	3,039,332,401
1970	3,707,610,112
1980	4,456,705,217
1990	5,283,755,345
2000	6,080,141,683
2010	6,823,634,553
2020	7,518,010,600
2030	8,140,344,240
2040	8,668,391,454
2050	9,104,205,830

Source: *US Census Bureau, International Data Base*

TOP 10 🍁
MOST POPULATED METROPOLITAN AREAS IN CANADA IN 2010

	CITY*/PROVINCE	EST. POPULATION IN 2010
1	Toronto, Ontario	5,704,059
2	Montreal, Quebec	3,597,202
3	Vancouver, British Columbia	2,470,830
4	Ottawa-Hull, Ontario-Quebec	1,178,690
5	Calgary, Alberta	1,103,024
6	Edmonton, Alberta	1,028,509
7	Hamilton, Ontario	735,959
8	Quebec, Quebec	687,481
9	Winnipeg, Manitoba	671,132
10	Kitchener, Ontario	475,111

Census metropolitan areas

Source: *Statistics Canada*

The most marked change in Canada's demographics over the next two decades will be the increase in the number of seniors. Improved health care will contribute to greater longevity, benefiting especially the baby boom generation. This, combined with low fertility rates, means that by 2025, seniors will greatly outnumber the country's youth – a first for Canada's recordkeepers. Immigration levels, expected to be high in the 21st century, are also an important factor in growth projections.

🍁 TOP 10 MOST POPULATED PROVINCES IN 2025

(Province/estimated population in 2025)

❶ Ontario, 14,823,363 ❷ Quebec, 7,487,350 ❸ British Columbia, 5,475,901
❹ Alberta, 3,576,602 ❺ Manitoba, 1,191,839 ❻ Saskatchewan, 1,012,278
❼ Nova Scotia, 975,052 ❽ New Brunswick, 734,997 ❾ Newfoundland, 496,050
❿ Prince Edward Island, 150,142

Source: *Statistics Canada*

TOP 10 ★
MOST POPULATED WORLD CITIES IN 2015

	CITY	COUNTRY	% GROWTH 2000–2015	ESTIMATED POPULATION IN 2015
1	Tokyo	Japan	0.0	26,400,000
2	Bombay	India	2.4	26,100,000
3	Lagos	Nigeria	3.7	23,200,000
4	Dhaka	Bangladesh	3.6	21,100,000
5	São Paulo	Brazil	0.9	20,400,000
6 =	Karachi	Pakistan	3.2	19,200,000
=	Mexico City	Mexico	0.4	19,200,000
8	New York	US	0.3	17,400,000
9 =	Calcutta	India	1.9	17,300,000
=	Jakarta	Indonesia	3.0	17,300,000

Source: *United Nations, World Urbanization Prospects: The 1999 Revision*

TOP 10 ★
FASTEST-GROWING CITIES*

	CITY	COUNTRY	INCREASE (%) 1975–95	ESTIMATED INCREASE (%) 1995–2010
1	Hangzhou	China	283.5	171.1
2	Addis Ababa	Ethiopia	161.6	170.7
3	Kabul	Afghanistan	200.9	156.3
4	Handan	China	245.9	141.6
5	Isfahan	Iran	150.9	141.3
6	Maputo	Mozambique	318.6	139.9
7	Lagos	Nigeria	211.7	139.5
8	Luanda	Angola	210.9	138.8
9	Nairobi	Kenya	167.4	133.6
10	Qingdao	China	183.8	132.4

* *Urban agglomerations of over 1 million population only*

Source: *United Nations*

TEEMING MILLIONS
China began the 20th century with a population of some 400 million and ended it with 1.2 billion – about one fifth of the world's population.

TOP 10 ★

MOST POPULATED COUNTRIES IN 2005

	COUNTRY	ESTIMATED POPULATION IN 2005
1	China	1,315,507,068
2	India	1,092,502,123
3	US	287,972,263
4	Indonesia	242,799,696
5	Brazil	180,395,927
6	Pakistan	156,689,148
7	Russia	143,736,793
8	Bangladesh	139,794,159
9	Nigeria	139,779,647
10	Japan	127,404,212
	Canada	*32,805,041*

Source: *US Census Bureau, International Data Base*
China and India entered the 21st century as the first countries ever with billion-plus populations.

TOP 10 ★

MOST POPULATED COUNTRIES IN 2025

	COUNTRY	ESTIMATED POPULATION IN 2025
1	China	1,464,028,860
2	India	1,377,264,176
3	US	338,070,951
4	Indonesia	301,461,556
5	Pakistan	213,338,252
6	Nigeria	204,453,333
7	Brazil	200,606,553
8	Bangladesh	177,499,122
9	Russia	135,951,626
10	Mexico	133,834,712
	Canada	*38,164,606*

Source: *US Census Bureau, International Data Base*
In a single generation (2000–2025), Nigeria's population is set to increase by almost 75 percent.

TOP 10 ★

MOST POPULATED COUNTRIES IN 2050

	COUNTRY	ESTIMATED POPULATION IN 2050
1	India	1,619,582,271
2	China	1,470,468,924
3	US	403,943,147
4	Indonesia	337,807,011
5	Nigeria	303,586,770
6	Pakistan	267,813,495
7	Brazil	206,751,477
8	Bangladesh	205,093,861
9	Ethiopia	187,892,174
10	Dem. Rep. of Congo	181,922,656
	Canada	*41,429,579*

Source: *US Census Bureau, International Data Base*
Estimates of populations in 2050 present a striking change: China should be eclipsed by India in 2036.

Where does Canada rank as a paper-recycling country? *see p.206 for the answer* A At no. 4 B At no. 9 C At no. 2

🍁 THE 10 FIRST UNESCO HERITAGE SITES IN CANADA

(Site/location/year designated)

1 = Nahanni National Park, NWT, 1978; = L'Anse aux Meadows Archaeological Site, NF, 1978 **3** = Kluane/Wrangell–St. Elias/Glacier Bay/Tatshenshini-Alsek Park, Can/US, 1979; = Dinosaur Provincial Park, AB, 1979; **5** Head-Smashed-In Buffalo Jump Provincial Historic Site, AB, 1982 **6** SGaang Gwaii, BC, 1981 **7** Wood Buffalo National Park, AB/NWT, 1983; **8** Canadian Rocky Mountain Parks*, AB/BC, 1984 **9** Historic District of Quebec#, QC, 1985 **10** Gros Morne National Park, NF, 1987

* Includes Banff National Park, Jasper National Park, Kootenay National Park, Yoho National Park, Mount Robson Provincial Park, Mount Assiniboine Provincial Park, and Hamber Provincial Park
 # Includes Fortifications of Quebec National Historic Site and Artillery Park National Historic Site
Source: *Natural Resources Canada*

THE 10 🍁 OLDEST NATIONAL HISTORIC SITES*

SITE/SIGNIFICANCE/LOCATION	DATE
1 Fort Anne#, fortifications; Annapolis Royal, Nova Scotia	1695–1708
2 Fort Chambly, stone fort built as defense against English attack; Chambly, Quebec	1709
3 Prince of Wales Fort, Hudson's Bay Company fort to protect against French; Churchill, Manitoba	1732
4 Fortress of Louisbourg (reconstruction), important French military center and harbor; Louisbourg, Nova Scotia	1744
5 Fort Edward, oldest blockhouse in Canada; Windsor, Nova Scotia	1750
6 Fort Beauséjour, remnants of French fort; Aulac, New Brunswick	1751
7 Fort Wellington, military fortifications during War of 1812 and later uprisings; Prescott, Ontario	1812–38

SITE/SIGNIFICANCE	DATE
8 Battle of the Châteauguay, Site of 1813 battle in defense of Lower Canada, War of 1812; Allans Corners, Quebec	1813
9 Fort Lennox, early 19th-century English fortification against Americans; Île-aux-Noix, Quebec	1819–29
10 Battle of the Windmill, American invasion foiled; Prescott, Ontario	1838

* Administered by Parks Canada; designated 1919–20. Parks Canada administers 145 national historic sites out of a total of 863. Owners of sites not administered by Parks Canada and not on this Top 10 list include the provinces, municipalities, and the private sector.

 # First national historic site to be administered in Canada

Source: *Historic Sites and Monuments Board of Canada*

CRATER LAKE BECOMES A US NATIONAL PARK

According to Native American legend, the collapse of Mount Mazama and the creation of Crater Lake, Oregon, resulted from a battle between rival chiefs: Llao of the Below World and Skell of the Above World. Revered as a sacred place, it lay undiscovered by outsiders until 1853, when three gold prospectors, John Wesley Hillman, Henry Klippel, and Isaac Skeeters, stumbled upon it, naming it Deep Blue Lake. In 1886, it was explored by Captain Clarence Dutton, who carried the survey ship *Cleetwood* overland and took soundings that established the lake to be the world's sixth deepest. Crater Lake became a popular tourist attraction and, following the efforts of William Gladstone Steel, who named many of its features, achieved US national park status on May 22, 1902.

100 YEARS AGO

TOP 10 🍁 MOST VISITED NATIONAL PARKS IN CANADA*

NATIONAL PARK/ LOCATION	VISITORS (1999–2000)
1 Banff, AB	4,677,466
2 Kootenay, BC	1,590,596
3 Jasper, AB	1,585,412
4 Yoho, BC	1,371,105
5 Prince Edward Island, PEI	954,873
6 Pacific Rim National Park Reserve, BC	560,309
7 Mount Revelstoke and Glacier#, BC	530,638
8 Fathom Five National Marine Park, ON	456,809
9 Cape Breton Highlands, NS	440,663
10 Saguenay–St. Lawrence Marine Park, QC	431,498

* National Parks include National Park Reserves and National Marine Conservation Areas.

 # Although Mount Revelstoke and Glacier are two distinct parks, their proximity to each other does not allow for separate reporting.

Source: *Parks Canada*

THE 10 🍁 FIRST NATIONAL PARKS IN CANADA

NATIONAL PARK/LOCATION	ESTABLISHED
1 Banff, Alberta	1885
2 =Glacier, British Columbia	1886
=Yoho, British Columbia	1886
4 Waterton Lakes, Alberta	1895
5 Jasper, Alberta	1907
6 Elk Island, Alberta	1913
7 =Mount Revelstoke, British Columbia	1914
=St. Lawrence Islands, Ontario	1914
9 Point Pelee, Ontario	1918
10 Kootenay, British Columbia	1920

Source: *Parks Canada*

TOP 10 🍁
LARGEST NATIONAL PARKS IN CANADA

	NATIONAL PARK/LOCATION	ESTABLISHED	AREA (SQ KM)
1	**Wood Buffalo**, Alberta/Northwest Territories	1922	44,802.0
2	**Quttinirpaaq (Ellesmere Island)**, Nunavut	1986	37,775.0
3	**Sirmilik**, Nunavut	1992	22,252.0
4	**Kluane**, Yukon Territories	1972	22,013.3
5	**Auyuittuq**, Nunavut	1972	19,707.4
6	**Tuktut Nogait**, Northwest Territories	1996	16,340.0
7	**Aulavik**, Northwest Territories	1992	12,200.0
8	**Wapusk**, Manitoba	1996	11,475.0
9	**Jasper**, Alberta	1907	10,878.0
10	**Ivvavik**, Yukon Territories	1984	9,750.0

Source: *Natural Resources Canada* and *Parks Canada*

Wood Buffalo National Park, the country's largest national park and one of the world's largest, was established to protect a small herd of wood buffalo – the last of its kind in Canada's North. The park is now also home to one of the largest free-roaming bison (buffalo) herds in the world. At Quttinirpaaq (Inukituk for "top of the world"), No. 2 on the Top 10, and at Sirmilik, No. 3, there is evidence of both prehistoric and historic occupation. You may, for instance, happen upon a tent ring – a circle of boulders used some 4,000 years ago, possibly by forebears of the Inuit, to anchor a tent. Today, Sirmilik National Park is home to Inuit, many of whom continue to practice traditional

TOP 10 ⭐
COUNTRIES WITH THE LARGEST PROTECTED AREAS

	COUNTRY	PERCENTAGE OF TOTAL AREA	DESIGNATED AREA SQ MILES	SQ KM
1	**US**	24.9	902,091	2,336,406
2	**Australia**	13.4	395,911	1,025,405
3	**Greenland**	45.2	379,345	982,500
4	**Canada**	9.3	357,231	925,226
5	**Saudi Arabia**	34.4	318,811	825,717
6	**China**	7.1	263,480	682,410
7	**Venezuela**	61.7	217,397	563,056
8	**Brazil**	6.6	215,312	557,656
9	**Russia**	3.1	204,273	529,067
10	**Indonesia**	18.6	138,002	357,425

Protected Areas encompass national parks, nature reserves, national monuments, and other sites. There are at least 44,300 protected areas around the world, covering more than 10 percent of the total land area. In the case of some islands, such as Easter Island, almost 100 percent of the land is designated a protected area.

JOSHUA TREE NATIONAL PARK
Over 20 percent of the US land area is protected. National parks, such as that of the Biosphere Reserve of Joshua Tree National Monument in the Californian desert, comprise some 80 percent of the total.

Toronto's CN Tower is the world's tallest communications tower. Which is the world's tallest habitable building?
see p.95 for the answer

A World Trade Center, New York, US
B T & C Tower, Kao-hsiung, Taiwan
C Petronas Towers, Kuala Lumpur, Malaysia

World Cities

RUSH HOUR, NIGERIAN STYLE

Former capital Lagos, one of the world's largest, most densely populated, and fastest growing cities, suffers from massive traffic congestion, overcrowding, and slum dwellings.

TOP 10 ★
LARGEST NONCAPITAL CITIES

CITY/COUNTRY/CAPITAL CITY	POPULATIONS*
1 **Bombay**, India *New Delhi*	15,138,000 *8,419,000*
2 **Shanghai**, China *Beijing*	13,584,000 *11,299,000*
3 **Calcutta#**, India *New Delhi*	11,923,000 *8,419,000*
4 **Lagos#**, Nigeria *Abuja*	10,287,000 *378,671*
5 **São Paulo**, Brazil *Brasília*	10,017,821 *1,864,000*
6 **Karachi#**, Pakistan *Islamabad*	9,733,000 *350,000*
7 **Tianjin**, China *Beijing*	9,415,000 *11,299,000*
8 **Istanbul#**, Turkey *Ankara*	8,274,921 *2,937,524*
9 **New York**, US *Washington, DC*	7,420,166 *523,124*
10 **Madras**, India *New Delhi*	6,002,000 *8,419,000*

* *Based on comparison of population within administrative boundaries*

\# *Former capital*

TOP 10 ★
MOST CROWDED CITIES

CITY/COUNTRY	AVERAGE FLOOR SPACE PER PERSON*	
	SQ FT	SQ M
1 =**Lahore**, Pakistan	12.9	1.2
=**Tangail**, Bangladesh	12.9	1.2
3 **Bhiwandi**, India	25.8	2.4
4 **Dhaka**, Bangladesh	29.1	2.7
5 **Kano**, Nigeria	30.1	2.8
6 **Bamako**, Mali	34.4	3.2
7 **Bombay**, India	37.7	3.5
8 =**Mwanza**, Tanzania	43.1	4.0
=**Kampala**, Uganda	43.1	4.0
=**Sana'a**, Yemen	43.1	4.0

* *In those countries for which data available*

Source: *World Bank*, World Development Indicators 2000

TOP 10 ★
MOST DECLINED CITIES

CITY/COUNTRY	PEAK	LATEST	% DECLINE FROM PEAK
1 **St. Louis**, US	875,000	334,000	-61.0
2 **Pittsburgh**, US	677,000	341,000	-49.6
3 **Buffalo**, US	580,000	301,000	-48.1
4 **Detroit**, US	1,850,000	970,000	-47.6
5 **Manchester**, UK	766,000	403,000	-47.4
6 **Cleveland**, US	915,000	496,000	-45.8
7 **Liverpool**, UK	857,000	479,000	-44.1
8 **Copenhagen**, Denmark	768,000	456,000	-39.5
9 **Newark**, US	442,000	268,000	-39.4
10 **Glasgow**, UK	1,088,000	681,000	-37.4

THE 10 FIRST CITIES WITH POPULATIONS OF MORE THAN ONE MILLION

(City/country)

❶ **Rome**, Italy ❷ **Alexandria**, Egypt
❸ **Angkor**, Cambodia ❹ **Hangchow**, China
❺ **London**, UK ❻ **Paris**, France
❼ **Peking**, China ❽ **Canton**, China
❾ **Berlin**, Prussia ❿ **New York**, US

Rome's population is believed to have exceeded 1 million some time in the 2nd century BC. Alexandria was soon after.

Which is Canada's busiest port?
see p.234 for the answer
A Halifax
B Vancouver
C Montreal/Contrecoeur

TOP 10 ★
HIGHEST CITIES

CITY/COUNTRY	HEIGHT FT	M
1 **Wenchuan**, China	16,730	5,099
2 **Potosí**, Bolivia	13,045	3,976
3 **Oruro**, Bolivia	12,146	3,702
4 **Lhasa**, Tibet	12,087	3,684
5 **La Paz**, Bolivia	11,916	3,632
6 **Cuzco**, Peru	11,152	3,399
7 **Huancayo**, Peru	10,660	3,249
8 **Sucre**, Bolivia	9,301	2,835
9 **Tunja**, Colombia	9,252	2,820
10 **Quito**, Ecuador	9,249	2,819

Lhasa was formerly the highest capital city in the world, a role now occupied by La Paz, the capital of Bolivia. Wenchuan is situated at more than half the elevation of Everest, and even the cities at the bottom of this list are more than one-third as high as Everest.

TOP 10 🍁
LARGEST CITIES IN CANADA*

CITY/PROVINCE	POPULATION#
1 **Toronto**, Ontario	4,751,400
2 **Montreal**, Quebec	3,480,300
3 **Vancouver**, British Columbia	2,048,800
4 **Ottawa-Hull**, (Ontario-Quebec)	1,081,000
5 **Calgary**, Alberta	953,000
6 **Edmonton**, Alberta	944,200
7 **Quebec**, Quebec	689,700
8 **Winnipeg**, Manitoba	681,100
9 **Hamilton**, Ontario	671,700
10 **London**, Ontario	421,300

* Based on census metropolitan area (CMA), which is defined as a large urban area, or urban core, along with the adjacent urban and rural areas that are highly integrated both socially and economically with that urban core

Estimated figures on July 1, 2000

Source: Statistics Canada

TOP 10 ★
MOST URBANIZED COUNTRIES

COUNTRY	PERCENTAGE OF POPULATION LIVING IN URBAN AREAS, 1998
1 **Singapore**	100.0
2 **Kuwait**	97.4
3 **Belgium**	97.2
4 **Qatar**	92.1
5 **Iceland**	92.0
6 **Uruguay**	90.9
7 **Luxembourg**	90.4
8 **Malta**	90.1
9 = **Argentina**	88.9
= **Lebanon**	88.9

Source: UN, Human Development Report 2000

The last few decades have brought about a world that is far more urbanized, with a much higher proportion of the world's population living in large cities and metropolitan areas. There are also tens of millions of "rural-urban dwellers," who live in rural settlements but work in urban areas.

TOP 10 ★
LEAST URBANIZED COUNTRIES

COUNTRY	PERCENTAGE OF POPULATION LIVING IN URBAN AREAS, 1998
1 **Rwanda**	5.9
2 **Bhutan**	6.7
3 **Burundi**	8.4
4 **Nepal**	11.2
5 **Uganda**	13.5
6 **Malawi**	14.6
7 **Ethiopia**	16.7
8 **Papua New Guinea**	16.8
9 **Burkino Faso**	17.4
10 **Eritrea**	18.0

Source: United Nations

TOP 10 ★
LARGEST CITIES IN EUROPE, 2000

CITY/COUNTRY	EST. POPULATION, 2000*
1 **Moscow**, Russia	13,200,000
2 **London**, UK	11,800,000
3 **Paris**, France	10,150,000
4 **Essen**, Germany	6,050,000
5 **St. Petersburg**, Russia	5,550,000
6 **Madrid**, Spain	5,050,000
7 **Barcelona**, Spain	4,200,000
8 **Berlin**, Germany	4,150,000
9 **Milan**, Italy	3,800,000
10 **Athens**, Greece	3,500,000

* Of urban agglomeration

Source: Th. Brinkhoff: Principal Agglomerations and Cities of the World, www.citypopulation.de, 4.6.00

CAPITAL CITY

Paris grew from 2.7 million at the turn of the 20th century to just over 10 million in 2000, making it Europe's third largest city.

TOP 10 ❦
LARGEST PROVINCES AND TERRITORIES*

	PROVINCE OR TERRITORY	LAND (SQ KM)	WATER (SQ KM)	TOTAL (SQ KM)	% OF TOTAL
1	Nunavut	1,936,113	157,077	2,093,190	20.96
2	Quebec	1,365,128	176,928	1,542,056	15.44
3	Northwest Territories	1,183,085	163,021	1,346,106	13.48
4	Ontario	917,741	158,654	1,076,395	10.78
5	British Columbia	925,186	19,549	944,735	9.46
6	Alberta	642,317	19,531	661,848	6.63
7	Saskatchewan	591,670	59,366	651,036	6.52
8	Manitoba	553,556	94,241	647,797	6.49
9	Yukon Territory	474,391	8,052	482,443	4.83
10	Newfoundland and Labrador	373,872	31,340	405,212	4.06
	Canada	9,093,507	891,163	9,984,670	100.00

* Figures estimated from the National Atlas of Canada 1:1,000,000 scale hydrology base. They lie within +/-1% of the true value.   Source: Natural Resources Canada

❦ THE 10 FIRST PROVINCES AND TERRITORIES TO ENTER CONFEDERATION

(Province or territory/date)

❶ = **New Brunswick**, July 1, 1867; = **Nova Scotia**, July 1, 1867; = **Ontario**, July 1, 1867; = **Quebec**, July 1, 1867 ❺ = **Manitoba**, July 15, 1870; = **Northwest Territories**, July 15, 1870 ❼ **British Columbia**, July 20, 1871 ❽ **Prince Edward Island**, July 1, 1873 ❾ **Yukon Territory**, June 13, 1898 ❿ = **Alberta**, Sep 1, 1905; = **Saskatchewan**, Sep 1, 1905

Newfoundland entered Confederation on March 31, 1949; the territory of Nunavut was created on April 1, 1999.

THE 10 ❦
FIRST OFFICIAL FLORAL EMBLEMS

	PROVINCE OR TERRITORY	FLOWER	YEAR ADOPTED
1	Nova Scotia	Mayflower	1901
2	Manitoba	Prairie crocus	1906
3	=Alberta	Wild rose	1930
4	New Brunswick	Purple violet	1936
5	Ontario	White trillium	1937
6	Saskatchewan	Western red or prairie lily	1941
7	Prince Edward Island	Showy lady's slipper*	1947
8	Newfoundland	Pitcher plant	1954
9	British Columbia	Pacific dogwood	1956
10	=Northwest Territories	Mountain avens	1957
	=Yukon Territory	Fireweed	1957

* Replaced by pink lady's slipper in 1965

Quebec adopted the white garden (Madonna) lily as its flower in 1963. The sugar maple, the floral emblem of Canada, was adopted in 1867.

THE 10 ❦
PROVINCES WITH THE LARGEST POPULATIONS

	PROVINCE	POPULATION*
1	Ontario	11,669,344
2	Quebec	7,372,448
3	British Columbia	4,063,760
4	Alberta	2,997,236
5	Manitoba	1,147,880
6	Saskatchewan	1,023,636
7	Nova Scotia	940,996
8	New Brunswick	756,598
9	Newfoundland	538,823
10	Prince Edward Island	138,928
	Canada	30,750,087

* On July 1, 2000   Source: Statistics Canada

TOP 10 ❦
PROVINCES AND TERRITORIES WITH THE HIGHEST BIRTH RATES

	PROVINCE OR TERRITORY	1999–2000 BIRTH RATE*
1	Nunavut	28.5
2	Northwest Territories	18.2
3	Alberta	12.7
4	Manitoba	12.4
5	Saskatchewan	12.3
6	Yukon Territory	11.9
7	Ontario	11.1
8	Prince Edward Island	10.7
9	British Columbia	10.3
10	New Brunswick	10.1

* Per 1,000 population

Source: Statistics Canada

2001 CENSUS

On May 15, 2001, all Canadians participated in the latest compilation of social and economic statistics. The census is conducted every five years. Most households received the short form of the census, with just seven questions, while one fifth of the population was requested to answer an additional 52 questions in order to gather more detailed information.

TOP 10 🍁
RESIDENTIAL AVERAGE HOUSE PRICES, 2000*

	RESIDENTIAL AREA	AVERAGE PRICE $
1	Greater Vancouver	295,978
2	Toronto	243,249
3	Victoria	225,731
4	Durham Region	179,241
5	Calgary	176,305
6	Hamilton-Burlington	164,168
7	Ottawa-Carleton	159,511
8	Kitchener-Waterloo	157,317
9	Windsor-Essex	137,453
10	St. Catharines and district	136,932

Based on data collected from 106 real estate boards across Canada for properties sold through the Multiple Listing Service (MLS)

Source: *Canadian Real Estate Association*

THE 10 🍁
PROVINCES WITH THE HIGHEST AVERAGE FAMILY INCOME

	PROVINCE	INCOME $ (1998)
1	Ontario	55,619
2	Alberta	52,388
3	British Columbia	51,424
4	Manitoba	45,373
5	Saskatchewan	43,407
6	Quebec	42,787
7	Prince Edward Island	42,270
8	Nova Scotia	41,499
9	New Brunswick	41,131
10	Newfoundland	37,731
	Canada	49,626

Source: *Statistics Canada*

THE 10 🍁
PROVINCES WITH THE GREATEST CHANGE IN CONSUMER PRICE INDEX, 1999–2000

	PROVINCE	DEC 1999	DEC 2000	% CHANGE
1	Saskatchewan	114.5	119.1	4.0
2	Alberta	115.1	119.6	3.9
3	Prince Edward Island	109.4	113.4	3.7
4	Nova Scotia	112.0	116.0	3.6
5	Ontario	112.1	116.0	3.5
6	Manitoba	116.5	119.9	2.9
7	Quebec	108.7	111.8	2.9
8	New Brunswick	110.7	113.8	2.8
9	Newfoundland	111.1	114.0	2.6
10	British Columbia	111.6	114.3	2.4

Source: *Statistics Canada*

The Canadian Price Index (CPI) tracks the price of standard goods and services consumers purchase each month.

TOP 10 🍁
UNIVERSITIES RECEIVING FEDERAL RESEARCH GRANTS, 1998–99*

	UNIVERSITY	SSHRC $[#]	CIHR $[+]	NSERC $[*]	TOTAL $
1	Toronto	9,900,000	51,100,000	45,900,000	106,900,000
2	British Columbia	6,500,000	18,800,000	39,300,000	64,600,000
3	McGill	4,000,000	35,100,000	24,600,000	63,700,000
4	Montreal	5,600,000	22,700,000	26,800,000	55,100,000
5	Alberta	3,800,000	15,700,000	26,600,000	46,100,000
6	Laval	4,800,000	11,400,000	22,000,000	38,200,000
7	McMaster	2,800,000	10,400,000	16,200,000	29,400,000
8	Western Ontario	2,900,000	12,500,000	13,800,000	29,200,000
9	Calgary	1,600,000	11,700,000	14,600,000	27,900,000
10	Queen's	2,900,000	6,200,000	17,500,000	26,600,000

Rankings are based on combined funding from the three councils (listed below). At April 2000, only 1998–99 figures were available for all councils. Figures exclude the Federal Networks of Centres of Excellence. Payments to affiliates are included with those of each parent university.

[#] *Social Sciences and Humanities Research Council of Canada* [+] *Canadian Institutes of Health Research (formerly the Medical Research Council of Canada)* [*] *Natural Sciences and Engineering Research Council of Canada*

Source: *Federal granting councils' annual reports; data compiled by the University of Toronto*

Nearly 25 percent of national research and development is carried out at Canada's universities – more than that of any other G-7 country, and twice that of the US. According to the Association of Universities and Colleges of Canada, in 1997, 12 percent – approximately $76 billion – of the country's gross national product was attributable to the goods and services produced because of university research.

THE 10 🍁
FIRST CITIES TO ESTABLISH FREE POSTAL DELIVERY

	CITY	YEAR
1	Montreal, QC	1874
2 =	Halifax, NS	1875
=	Hamilton, ON	1875
=	Ottawa, ON	1875
=	Quebec, QC	1875
=	Saint John, NB	1875
=	Toronto, ON	1875
8	London, ON	1876
9 =	Kingston, ON	1882
=	Winnipeg, MB	1882

Source: *Special Delivery: Canada's Postal Heritage, by Elaine Amyot, Chantal Dufour, and John Willis, Goose Lane Editions, Canadian Museum of Civilization and Canadian Postal Museum, 2000*

Where is the world's longest cantilever bridge?
see p.96 for the answer
A Quebec, Canada
B San Francisco, US
C Firth of Forth, Scotland

♦ TOP 10 MOST COMMON PLACE NAMES IN CANADA

(Name/occurrences, August 1999)

① Mount Pleasant, 16 **②** = Centreville, 15 = Lakeview, 15
④ Pleasant Valley, 14 **⑤** Fairview, 13 **⑥** = Rosedale, 10;
= Salem, 10; = Westmount, 10; = Bellevue, 10; = Notre-Dame, 10;
= Victoria, 10; = Springfield, 10; = Glenwood, 10;
= Richmond, 10; = Riverside, 10

Source: *National Resources Canada, Geomatics Canada*

TOP 10 ★
COUNTRIES WITH THE LONGEST OFFICIAL NAMES

	OFFICIAL NAME*	COMMON ENGLISH NAME	LETTERS
1	al-Jamāhīrīyah al-'Arabīyah al-Lībīyah ash-Sha'bīyah al-Ishtirākīyah	Libya	59
2	al-Jumhūrīyah al-Jazā'irīyah ad-Dīmuqrātīyah ash-Sha'bīyah	Algeria	51
3	United Kingdom of Great Britain and Northern Ireland	United Kingdom	45
4	=Śrī Lankā Prajātāntrika Samājavādī Janarajaya	Sri Lanka	41
	=Jumhurīyat al-Qumur al-Ittihādīyah al-Islāmīyah	The Comoros	41
6	República Democrática de São Tomé e Príncipe	São Tomé and Príncipe	38
7	al-Jūmhurīyah al-Islāmīyah al-Mūrītānīyah	Mauritania	36
8	=al-Mamlakah al-Urdunnīyah al-Hāshimīyah	Jordan	34
	=Sathalanalat Paxathipatai Paxaxôn Lao	Laos	34
10	Federation of St. Christopher and Nevis	St. Kitts and Nevis	33

* *Some official names have been transliterated from languages that do not use the Roman alphabet; their length may vary according to the method used.*

Since this list was first published in 1991, three nation-states that at one time placed on it have ceased to exist: Socijalisticka Federativna Republika Jugoslavija (Yugoslavia, 45 letters), Soyuz Sovetskikh Sotsialisticheskikh Respublik (USSR, 43), and Ceskoslovenská Socialistická Republika (Czechoslovakia, 36).

♦ TOP 10 MOST COMMON FEATURE NAMES IN CANADA

(Name/occurrences, February 1998)

① Long Lake, 204 **②** Mud Lake, 182 **③** Lac Long, 152
④ Long Pond, 144 **⑤** Lac Rond, 132 **⑥** Green Island, 125
⑦ Long Point, 120 **⑧** Big Island, 119 **⑨** The Narrows, 113
⑩ Lac à la Truite, 109

TOP 10 ★
LARGEST COUNTRIES THAT CHANGED THEIR NAMES IN THE 20TH CENTURY

	FORMER NAME	CURRENT NAME	YEAR CHANGED	AREA SQ MILES	AREA SQ KM
1	Zaïre	Dem. Rep. of Congo	1997	905,567	2,345,409
2	Persia	Iran	1935	630,577	1,633,188
3	Tanganyika/Zanzibar	Tanzania	1964	364,900	945,087
4	South West Africa	Namibia	1990	318,261	824,292
5	Northern Rhodesia	Zambia	1964	290,586	752,614
6	Burma	Myanmar	1989	261,218	676,552
7	Ubanghi Shari	Central African Republic	1960	240,535	622,984
8	Bechuanaland	Botswana	1966	224,607	581,730
9	Siam	Thailand	1939	198,115	513,115
10	Mesopotamia	Iraq	1921	169,235	438,317

Although not a country, Greenland (2,175,600 sq km/840,004 sq miles) has been officially known as Kalaallit Nunaat since 1979. Some old names die hard: it is still common for Myanmar to be written as "Myanmar (Burma)."

TOP 10 ★
LARGEST COUNTRIES NAMED AFTER REAL PEOPLE

	COUNTRY	NAMED AFTER	AREA SQ MILES	AREA SQ KM
1	United States of America	Amerigo Vespucci (Italy; 1451–1512)	3,717,813	9,629,091
2	Saudi Arabia	Abdul Aziz Ibn Saud (Nejd; 1882–1953)	830,000	2,149,690
3	Colombia	Christopher Columbus (Italy; 1451–1506)	439,737	1,138,914
4	Bolivia	Simon Bolivar (Venezuela; 1783–1830)	424,165	1,098,581
5	Philippines	Philip II (Spain; 1527–98)	115,831	300,000
6	Falkland Islands	Lucius Cary, 2nd Viscount Falkland (UK; c.1610–43)	4,700	12,173
7	Northern Mariana	Maria Theresa (Austria; 1717–80)	179	464
8	Cook Islands	Capt. James Cook (UK; 1728–79)	91	236
9	Wallis & Futuna	Samuel Wallis (UK; 1728–95)	77	200
10	Marshall Islands	Capt. John Marshall (UK; 1748–after 1818)	70	181

TOP 10 ★
LONGEST PLACE NAMES*

NAME	LETTERS

1 Krung thep mahanakhon bovorn ratanakosin mahintharayutthaya mahadilok pop noparatratchathani burirom udomratchanivetmahasathan amornpiman avatarnsathit sakkathattiyavisnukarmprasit — 167

When the poetic name of Bangkok, capital of Thailand, is used, it is usually abbreviated to "Krung Thep" (city of angels).

2 Taumatawhakatangihangakoauauotamateaturipukakapiki-maungahoronukupokaiwhenuakitanatahu — 85

This is the longer version (the other has a mere 83 letters) of the Maori name of a hill in New Zealand. It translates as "The place where Tamatea, the man with the big knees, who slid, climbed, and swallowed mountains, known as land-eater, played on the flute to his loved one."

3 Gorsafawddachaidraigddanheddogleddollônpenrhynareurdraethceredigion — 67

A name contrived by the Fairbourne Steam Railway, Gwynedd, North Wales, for publicity purposes and in order to outdo its rival, No. 5. It means "The Mawddach station and its dragon teeth at the Northern Penrhyn Road on the golden beach of Cardigan Bay."

4 Cape St. George-Petit Jardin-Grand Jardin-De Grau-Marches Point-Loretto — 59

Canada's longest place name belongs to a community in Newfoundland.

5 Llanfairpwllgwyngyllgogerychwyrndrobwllllantysiliogogogoch — 58

This is the place in Gwynedd famed especially for the length of its railroad tickets. It means "St. Mary's Church in the hollow of the white hazel near to the rapid whirlpool of the church of St. Tysilo near the Red Cave." Questions have been raised about its authenticity, since its official name comprises only the first 20 letters and the full name appears to have been invented as a hoax in the 19th century by a local tailor.

6 El Pueblo de Nuestra Señora la Reina de los Ángeles de la Porciúncula — 57

The site of a Franciscan mission and the full Spanish name of Los Angeles; it means "The town of Our Lady the Queen of the Angels of the Little Portion." Nowadays it is customarily known by its initial letters, "LA," making it also one of the shortest-named cities in the world.

7 Cours d'eau du Cordon des Terres des Sixième et Septième Rangs — 51

When translated from French, this Quebec waterway indicates its location on "the lands of the sixth and seventh rows" – a name that harks back to the seigneurial days of New France, when farmland was settled in very narrow strips facing a river or stream.

8 Ruisseau Katakuschuwepaishit Kachikuschikepaisham — 47

This stream or "ruisseau" is located in Quebec. The name stems from a Native Indian language; the words katakuschuwepaishit kachikuschikepaisham mean, quite simply, "short creek."

9 Décharge des Neuvième, Dixième et Onzième Concessions — 46

Located in Quebec, this stream travels through three different parcels of land, or "concessions."

10 Cours d'eau de la Concession Sud-Est du Rang Saint-David — 45

This is a stream located near the town of Saint-David in Quebec. The town was named after Jacques David de Saint du Lac, a beaver trapper who hunted in the area in the 1690s.

* Including single-word, hyphenated, and multiple-word names

THE LONG AND THE SHORT OF IT

The original 57-letter Spanish name of Los Angeles contrasts with its more common designation as "LA."

Which country has the world's longest coastline?
see p.80 for the answer
A Australia
B Canada
C Russia

The Tallest Buildings

TOP 10 ★
TALLEST APARTMENT BUILDINGS

BUILDING/LOCATION/YEAR COMPLETED	STORIES	HEIGHT FT	M
1 Trump World Tower, New York City, US, 2000	72	863	263
2 Tregunter Tower III, Hong Kong, China, 1994	70	656	200
3 Lake Point Tower, Chicago, US, 1968	70	645	197
4 Central Park Place, New York City, US, 1988	56	628	191
5 Huron Plaza Apartments, Chicago, US, 1983	61	599	183
6 3 Lincoln Center, New York City, US, 1993	60	593	181
7 =May Road Apartments, Hong Kong, China, 1993	58	590	180
=1000 Lake Shore Plaza, Chicago, US, 1964	55	590	180
9 Marina City Apartments, Chicago, US, 1968	61	588	179
10 North Pier Apartments, Chicago, US, 1990	61	581	177

These towers are all purely residential, rather than office buildings with a proportion given over to residential use. Above its 50 levels of office suites, the 343-m (1,127-ft) John Hancock Center, Chicago, built in 1968, has 48 levels of apartments (floors 44 through to 92, at 155 m/509 ft to 315 m/1,033 ft above street level), which are thus the "highest" apartments in the world.

TOP 10 ★
TALLEST BUILDINGS ERECTED MORE THAN 100 YEARS AGO

BUILDING/LOCATION/YEAR COMPLETED	HEIGHT FT	M
1 Eiffel Tower, Paris, France, 1889	984	300
2 Washington Monument, Washington, DC, US, 1885	555	169
3 Ulm Cathedral, Ulm, Germany, 1890	528	161
4 Lincoln Cathedral, Lincoln, England, c.1307 (destroyed 1548)	525	160
5 Cologne Cathedral, Cologne, Germany, 1880	513	156
6 Rouen Cathedral I, Rouen, France, 1530 (destroyed 1822)	512	156
7 St. Pierre Church, Beauvais, France, 1568 (collapsed 1573)	502	153
8 St. Paul's Cathedral, London, England, 1315 (destroyed 1561)	489	149
9 Rouen Cathedral II, Rouen, France, 1876	485	148
10 Great Pyramid, Giza, Egypt, c.2580 BC	480	146

The height of the Washington Monument is less than it was when it was erected because it has steadily sunk into the ground.

TOP 10 ★
TALLEST TELECOMMUNICATIONS TOWERS

TOWER/YEAR/LOCATION	HEIGHT FT	M
1 CN Tower, 1975, Toronto, Canada	1,821	555
2 Ostankino Tower, 1967, Moscow, Russia	1,762	537
3 Oriental Pearl Broadcasting Tower, 1995, Shanghai, China	1,535	468
4 Menara Telecom Tower, 1996, Kuala Lumpur, Malaysia	1,381	421
5 Tianjin TV and Radio Tower, 1991, Tianjin, China	1,362	415
6 Central Radio and TV Tower, 1994, Beijing, China	1,328	405
7 TV Tower, 1983, Tashkent, Uzbekistan	1,230	375
8 Liberation Tower, 1998, Kuwait City, Kuwait	1,220	372
9 Alma-Ata Tower, 1983, Almaty, Kazakhstan	1,214	370
10 TV Tower, 1969, Berlin, Germany	1,198	365

TOP 10 ★
WORLD CITIES WITH MOST SKYSCRAPERS

CITY/LOCATION	SKYSCRAPERS*
1 New York City, US	162
2 Chicago, US	75
3 Hong Kong, China	42
4 Shanghai, China	38
5 =Houston, US	30
=Tokyo, Japan	30
7 Singapore City, Singapore	26
8 Los Angeles, US	22
9 Dallas, US	20
10 =Melbourne, Australia	18
=Sydney, Australia	18

* Habitable buildings of more than 152 m (500 ft)

SKY HIGH
Despite the ever-attendant earthquake threat to tall buildings, Tokyo boasts one of the world's highest city skylines.

EIFFEL

French engineer Alexandre Gustave Eiffel (1832–1923) is one of the few people after whom a world famous structure has been named. Drawing on his experience as a bridge designer, Eiffel built the Eiffel Tower as a temporary structure for the 1889 Universal Exhibition. It proved so popular that it was decided to retain it. It remained the world's tallest structure until 1930, when it was overtaken by New York's Chrysler Building. Eiffel also designed the iron framework that supports the Statue of Liberty. In 1893, when a project to build a Panama Canal collapsed, Eiffel was implicated in a scandal and was sent to prison for two years.

WHO WAS · WHO WAS · WHO WAS · WHO WAS ?

TOP 10 ★
TALLEST HOTELS

BUILDING/LOCATION/ YEAR COMPLETED	STORIES	HEIGHT FT	M
1 Baiyoke II Tower, Bangkok, Thailand, 1997	89	1,046	319
2 Yu Kyong, Pyong Yang, North Korea, 1993	105	985	300
3 Emirates Tower 2, Dubai, United Arab Emirates, 1999 *with spire*	50	858 1,010	262 308
4 Shangri-la, Hong Kong, China, 1990	60	748	228
5 Raffles Western Hotel, Singapore, 1986	73	742	226
6 Westin Peachtree Hotel, Atlanta, US, 1973	71	723	220
7 Westin Hotel, Detroit, US, 1973	71	720	219
8 Four Seasons Hotel, New York City, US, 1993	52	682	208
9 Trump International Hotel, New York City, US, 1995	45	679	207
10 Trump Tower, New York City, US, 1983	68	664	202

TOP 10 ★
TALLEST HABITABLE BUILDINGS

BUILDING/LOCATION/ YEAR COMPLETED	STORIES	HEIGHT FT	M
1 Petronas Towers, Kuala Lumpur, Malaysia, 1996	96	1,482	452
2 Taipei Financial Centre, Taipei, China, 2003* *with spire*	101	1,460 1,666	445 508
3 Sears Tower, Chicago, US, 1974 *with spires*	110	1,454 1,730	443 527
4 World Trade Center[#], New York, US, 1972	110	1,368	417
5 Jin Mao Building, Shanghai, China, 1997 *with spire*	93	1,255 1,378	382 420
6 Empire State Building, New York, US, 1931 *with spire*	102	1,250 1,472	381 449
7 T & C Tower, Kao-hsiung, Taiwan, 1997	85	1,142	348
8 Amoco Building, Chicago, US, 1973	80	1,136	346
9 John Hancock Center, Chicago, US, 1969 *with spires*	100	1,127 1,470	343 449
10 Shun Hing Square, Shenzen, China, 1996 *with spires*	80	1,082 1,260	330 384

* *Under construction; scheduled completion date*

[#] *Twin towers; the second tower, completed in 1973, has the same number of stories but is slightly smaller at 415 m (1,362 ft) – although its spire takes it up to 521 m (1,710 ft)*

Heights do not include television and radio antennas and uninhabited extensions. Although the twin Petronas Towers are now officially accepted as the world's tallest, their completion generated a controversy when it became clear that their overall measurement includes their spires, and that their roof height (at the point where the two towers are connected) is "only" 379 m (1,244 ft).

EMPIRE BUILDING

Over 70 years old and still going strong, the majestic 102-story Empire State Building has become a symbol of New York, dominating its skyline.

Did You Know? Lightning does strike (at least) twice: the lightning conductor on the Empire State Building was struck 68 times in the structure's first 10 years.

Bridges & Other Structures

LONGEST SUSPENSION BRIDGES

	BRIDGE/LOCATION	YEAR COMPLETED	LENGTH OF MAIN SPAN FT	M
1	**Akashi-Kaiko**, Kobe–Naruto, Japan	1998	6,532	1,991
2	**Great Belt**, Denmark	1997	5,328	1,624
3	**Humber Estuary**, UK	1980	4,626	1,410
4	**Jiangyin**, China	1998	4,544	1,385
5	**Tsing Ma**, Hong Kong, China	1997	4,518	1,377
6	**Verrazano Narrows**, New York, NY	1964	4,260	1,298
7	**Golden Gate**, San Francisco, CA	1937	4,200	1,280
8	**Höga Kusten (High Coast)**, Veda, Sweden	1997	3,970	1,210
9	**Mackinac Straits**, Michigan	1957	3,800	1,158
10	**Minami Bisan-seto**, Kojima–Sakaide, Japan	1988	3,609	1,100

The Messina Strait Bridge between Sicily and Calabria, Italy, remains a speculative project but, if constructed according to plan, it will have by far the longest center span of any bridge at 3,300 m (10,827 ft).

LONGEST CANTILEVER BRIDGES

	BRIDGE/LOCATION	YEAR COMPLETED	LONGEST SPAN FT	M
1	**Pont de Quebec**, Quebec, Canada	1917	1,800	549
2	**Firth of Forth**, Scotland	1890	1,710	521
3	**Minato**, Osaka, Japan	1974	1,673	510
4	**Commodore John Barry**, New Jersey/Pennsylvania	1974	1,622	494
5 =	**Greater New Orleans 1**, Louisiana	1958	1,575	480
=	**Greater New Orleans 2**, Louisiana	1988	1,575	480
7	**Howrah**, Calcutta, India	1943	1,500	457
8	**Gramercy**, Louisiana	1995	1,460	445
9	**Transbay**, San Francisco, CA	1936	1,400	427
10	**Baton Rouge**, Louisiana	1969	1,235	376

SHANGHAI SURPRISE

One of the world's longest cable-stayed bridges, Shanghai's Yang Pu was built to ease traffic congestion on the city's busy inner ring road.

LONGEST CABLE-STAYED BRIDGES

	BRIDGE/LOCATION	YEAR COMPLETED	LENGTH OF MAIN SPAN FT	M
1	**Tatara**, Onomichi–Imabari, Japan	1999	2,920	890
2	**Pont de Normandie**, Le Havre, France	1994	2,808	856
3	**Qinghzhou Minjiang**, Fozhou, China	1996	1,985	605
4	**Yang Pu**, Shanghai, China	1993	1,975	602
5 =	**Meiko-chuo**, Nagoya, Japan	1997	1,936	590
=	**Xu Pu**, Shanghai, China	1997	1,936	590
7	**Skarnsundet**, Trondheim Fjord, Norway	1991	1,739	530
8	**Tsurumi Tsubasa**, Yokohama, Japan	1994	1,673	510
9 =	**Ikuchi**, Onomichi–Imabari, Japan	1994	1,608	490
=	**Öresund**, Copenhagen–Malmö, Denmark/Sweden	2000	1,608	490

LARGEST DAMS

	DAM/LOCATION	YEAR COMPLETED*	VOLUME (THOUSANDS) CUBIC YD	CUBIC M
1	**Syncrude Tailings**, Canada	2001	706,293	540,000
2	**Chapetón**, Argentina	U/C	387,415	296,200
3	**Pati**, Argentina	U/C	311,528	238,180
4	**New Cornelia Tailings**, US	1973	274,016	209,500
5	**Tarbela**, Pakistan	1976	159,204	121,720
6	**Kambaratinsk**, Kyrgyzstan	U/C	146,752	112,200
7	**Fort Peck**, US	1940	125,628	96,049
8	**Lower Usuma**, Nigeria	1990	121,639	93,000
9	**Cipasang**, Indonesia	U/C	117,715	90,000
10	**Atatürk**, Turkey	1990	110,521	84,500

* *U/C = under construction*

Source: International Water Power and Dam Construction

These figures represent the volume of water that is impounded by the dam. Dams are commonly built to irrigate land, aid flood control, and to hold back water, thereby forming a reservoir or lake.

TOP 10 ★
LONGEST CANAL TUNNELS

TUNNEL/CANAL/LOCATION	LENGTH FT	M
1 Rôve, Canal de Marseille au Rhône, France	23,360	7,120
2 Bony ("Le Grand Souterrain"), Canal de St. Quentin, France	18,625	5,677
3 Standedge, Huddersfield Narrow, UK	17,093	5,210
4 Mauvages, Canal de la Marne et Rhin, France	16,306	4,970
5 Balesmes, Canal Marne à la Saône, France	15,748	4,800
6 Ruyaulcourt, Canal du Nord, France	14,764	4,500
7 Strood*, Thames and Medway, UK	11,837	3,608
8 Lapal, Birmingham, UK	11,713	3,570
9 Sapperton, Thames and Severn, UK	11,444	3,488
10 Pouilly-en-Auxois, Canal de Bourgogne, France	10,935	3,333

* *Later converted to a rail tunnel*

TOP 10 ★
LONGEST RAIL TUNNELS

TUNNEL/LOCATION/ YEAR COMPLETED*	LENGTH MILES	KM
1 Seikan, Japan, 1988	33.49	53.90
2 Channel Tunnel, France–England, 1994	31.03	49.94
3 Moscow Metro (Medvedkovo/ Belyaevo section), Russia, 1979	19.07	30.70
4 London Underground (East Finchley–Morden, Northern Line), UK, 1939	17.30	27.84
5 Hakkoda, Japan, U/C	16.44	26.46
6 Iwate, Japan, U/C	16.04	25.81
7 Iiyama, Japan, U/C	13.98	22.50
8 Dai-Shimizu, Japan, 1982	13.78	22.17
9 Simplon II, Italy– Switzerland, 1922	12.31	19.82
10 Simplon I, Italy– Switzerland, 1906	12.30	19.80

* *U/C = under construction*

The longest railroad tunnel in the US is the 12.6-km (7.8-mile) Cascade, east of Seattle, Washington, completed on January 12, 1929.

TOP 10 ★
LARGEST SPORTS STADIUMS

STADIUM/LOCATION	CAPACITY
1 Strahov Stadium, Prague, Czech Republic	240,000
2 Maracaña Municipal Stadium, Rio de Janeiro, Brazil	220,000
3 Rungnado Stadium, Pyongyang, South Korea	150,000
4 Mineiro Stadium, Belo Horizonte, Brazil	130,000
5 National Stadium of Iran, Azadi, Iran	128,000
6 Estádio Maghalaes Pinto, Belo Horizonte, Brazil	125,000
7= Estádio da Luz, Lisbon, Portugal	120,000
= Estádio Morumbi, São Paulo, Brazil	120,000
= Saltlake Stadium, Calcutta, India	120,000
= Senayan Main Stadium, Jakarta, Indonesia	120,000
= Yuba Bharati Krirangan, Nr. Calcutta, India	120,000

TOP 10 ★
HIGHEST DAMS

DAM/RIVER/LOCATION	YEAR COMPLETED*	HEIGHT FT	M
1 Rogun, Vakhsh, Tajikistan	U/C	1,099	335
2 Nurek, Vakhsh, Tajikistan	1980	984	300
3 Grande Dixence, Dixence, Switzerland	1961	935	285
4 Inguri, Inguri, Georgia	1980	892	272
5 Vajont, Vajont, Italy	1960	860	262
6 = Manuel M. Torres, Chicoasén, Grijalva, Mexico	1980	856	261
= Tehri, Bhagirathi, India	U/C	856	261
8 Alvaro Obregon, El Gallinero, Tenasco, Mexico	1946	853	260
9 Mauvoisin, Drance de Bagnes, Switzerland	1957	820	250
10 Alberto Lleras C., Guavio, Colombia	1989	797	243

* *U/C = under construction*

Source: *International Commission on Large Dams (ICOLD)*

DAM RECORD BUSTER

An incongruous mural depicting Lenin celebrates this Soviet engineering accomplishment, the building of the world's second highest dam, the Nurek in Tajikistan.

Did You Know? So vast is the 3,360,000 cu m (4,400,000 cu yd) volume of concrete in the Hoover Dam (1936), Colorado River, on the Arizona/Nevada border, that it will take until the year 2030 for it to set completely.

Angeles T

MONDAY, JULY 29, 1996
COPYRIGHT 1996 / THE TIMES MIRROR COMPANY / CC† /86 PAGES

n Lasorda's

8, '94, '95)

VINCE COMPAGNONE / Los Angeles Times

ames,
3).

TECHNOLOGY

DGETS
T FOR SPIES

ce products are
popularity
▶ *See Page C4*

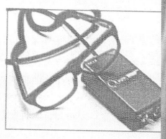

San Fran

NORTHERN CAL

g a
nt

Olympic He

Atlanta 1996.

s basketball
gold, respect

ael Wilbon
gton Post

esn't feel the dominance,
U.S. women's basketball
mpic games by an average
art of the Summer Games
nlike the so-called Dream
't a certainty to win a gold
e in fact of winning any

CULTURE & LEARNING

Word Power

TOP 10 ★
MOST WIDELY SPOKEN LANGUAGES

LANGUAGE	APPROXIMATE NO. OF SPEAKERS
1 Chinese (Mandarin)	1,075,000,000
2 Hindustani*	602,000,000
3 English	514,000,000
4 Spanish	425,000,000
5 Russian	275,000,000
6 Arabic	256,000,000
7 Bengali	215,000,000
8 Portuguese	194,000,000
9 Malay-Indonesian	176,000,000
10 French	129,000,000

* Hindi and Urdu are essentially the same language, Hindustani. As the official language of Pakistan, it is written in modified Arabic script and called Urdu. As the official language of India, it is written in the Devanagari script and called Hindi.

According to mid-1999 estimates by Emeritus Professor Sidney S. Culbert of the University of Washington, Seattle, in addition to those languages appearing in the Top 10, there are two further languages that are spoken by more than 100 million individuals: German and Japanese.

THE 10 🍁
LARGEST LANGUAGE GROUPS IN CANADA BY MOTHER TONGUE*

LANGUAGE	APPROXIMATE NO. OF SPEAKERS
1 English	16,890,615
2 French	6,636,660
3 Chinese	715,640
4 Italian	484,500
5 German	450,140
6 Polish	213,410
7 Spanish	212,890
8 Portuguese	211,290
9 Punjabi	201,785
10 Ukrainian	162,695

* First language learned and still understood
Source: 1996 Census, Statistics Canada

TOP 10 ★
LANGUAGES OFFICIALLY SPOKEN IN THE MOST COUNTRIES

LANGUAGE	COUNTRIES
1 English	57
2 French	33
3 Arabic	23
4 Spanish	21
5 Portuguese	7
6 Dutch	5
=German	5
8 =Chinese (Mandarin)	3
=Danish	3
=Italian	3
=Malay	3

TOP 10 ★
COUNTRIES WITH THE MOST ENGLISH-LANGUAGE SPEAKERS*

COUNTRY	APPROXIMATE NO. OF SPEAKERS
1 US	237,320,000
2 UK	58,090,000
3 Canada	18,218,000
4 Australia	15,561,000
5 Ireland	3,720,000
6 South Africa	3,700,000
7 New Zealand	3,338,000
8 Jamaica#	2,460,000
9 Trinidad and Tobago#+	1,245,000
10 Guyana+	764,000

* Inhabitants for whom English is their mother tongue

Includes English Creole

+ Trinidad English

This Top 10 represents the countries with the greatest numbers of inhabitants who speak English as their mother tongue. The world total is probably in excess of 500 million. However, there are perhaps as many as 1 billion people who speak English as a second language.

TOP 10 ★
MOST COMMON WORDS IN ENGLISH

SPOKEN ENGLISH		WRITTEN ENGLISH
the	1	the
and	2	of
I	3	to
to	4	in
of	5	and
a	6	a
you	7	for
that	8	was
in	9	is
it	10	that

Various surveys have been conducted to establish the most common words in spoken English, from telephone conversations to broadcast commentaries.

THE 10 ★
EARLIEST DATED WORDS IN THE OXFORD ENGLISH DICTIONARY

WORD	SOURCE	DATE
1 =priest	Laws of Ethelbert	601–4
=town	Laws of Ethelbert	601–4
3 earl	Laws of Ethelbert	616
4 this	Bewcastle Column	c.670
5 streale	Ruthwell Cross	c.680
6 ward	Caedmon, Hymn	680
7 thing	Laws of Hlothaer and Eadric	685–6
8 theft	Laws of Ine	688–95
9 worth	Laws of Ine	695
10 then	Laws of King Wihtraed	695–6

The 10 earliest citations in the Oxford English Dictionary (OED) come from 7th-century Anglo-Saxon documents and stone inscriptions. All have survived as commonly used English words, with the exception of "streale," which is another name for an arrow. A few other English words can be definitely dated to before 700, among them "church," which, like "then," appears in a law of King Wihtraed.

TOP 10 🍁

MOST COMMON ABORIGINAL LANGUAGES IN CANADA*

LANGUAGE	APPROXIMATE NO. OF SPEAKERS
1 Cree	76,475
2 Inuktitut	26,840
3 Ojibway	22,625
4 Montagnais-Naskapi	8,745
5 Micmac	6,720
6 Dakota/Sioux	4,020
7 Blackfoot	3,450
8 Salish languages	2,520
9 South Slave	2,425
10 Dogrib	2,030

* Includes North American Indians, Métis, and Inuit

Source: 1996 Census, Statistics Canada

TOP 10 ★

MOST USED LETTERS IN WRITTEN ENGLISH

SURVEY*		MORSE #
e	1	e
t	2	t
a	3	a
o	4	i
i	5	n
n	6	o
s	7	s
r	8	h
h	9	r
l	10	d

* *The order as indicated by a survey across approximately 1 million words appearing in a wide variety of printed texts, ranging from newspapers to novels*

\# *The order estimated by Samuel Morse, the inventor in the 1830s of Morse Code, based on his calculations of the respective quantities of type used by a printer. The number of letters in the printer's type trays ranged from 12,000 for "e" to 4,400 for "d," with only 200 for "z."*

TOP 10 ★

LONGEST WORDS IN THE ENGLISH LANGUAGE*

WORD/MEANING — LETTERS

1 Ornicopytheobibliopsychocrystarroscioaerogenethliometeoroaustrohiero-anthropoichthyopyrosiderochpnomyoalectryoophiobotanopegohydrorhab-docrithoaleuroalphitohalomolybdoclerobeloaxinocoscinodactyliogeolitho-pessopsephocatoptrotephraoneirochiroonychodactyloarithstichooxogelo-scogastrogyroceroabletonooenoscapulinaniac — 310

Medieval scribes used this word to refer to "A deluded human who practises divination or forecasting by means of phenomena, interpretation of acts, or other manifestations related to the following animate or inanimate objects and appearances: birds, oracles, Bible, ghosts, crystal gazing, shadows, air appearances, birth stars, meteors, winds, sacrificial appearances, entrails of humans and fishes, fire, red-hot irons, altar smoke, mice, grain picking by rooster, snakes, herbs, fountains, water, wands, dough, meal, barley, salt, lead, dice, arrows, hatchet balance, sieve, ring suspension, random dots, precious stones, pebbles, pebble heaps, mirrors, ash writing, dreams, palmistry, nail rays, finger rings, numbers, book passages, name letterings, laughing manners, ventriloquism, circle walking, wax, susceptibility to hidden springs, wine, and shoulder blades."

2 Lopadotemachoselachogaleokranioleipsanodrimhypotrimmatosilphioparao-melitokatakechymenokichlepikossyphophattoperisteralektryonoptekephall-iokigklopeleiolagoiosiraiobaphetraganopterygon — 182

The English transliteration of a 170-letter Greek word that appears in The Ecclesiazusae (a comedy by the Greek playwright Aristophanes, c.448–380 BC). It is used as a description of a 17-ingredient dish.

3 Aequeosalinocalcalinosetaceoaluminosocupreovitriolic — 52

Invented by a medical writer, Dr. Edward Strother (1675–1737), to describe the spa waters at Bath.

4 Osseocarnisanguineovisceiricartilaginonervomedullary — 51

Coined by writer and East India Company official Thomas Love Peacock (1785–1866), and used in his satire Headlong Hall (1816) as a description of the structure of the human body.

5 Pneumonoultramicroscopicsilicovolcanoconiosis — 45

It first appeared in print (though ending in "-koniosis") in F. Scully's Bedside Manna [sic] (1936), then found its way into Webster's Dictionary and is now in the Oxford English Dictionary. It is said to mean a lung disease caused by breathing fine dust.

6 Hepaticocholecystostcholecystenterostomies — 42

Surgical operations to create channels of communication between gall bladders and hepatic ducts or intestines.

7 Praetertranssubstantiationalistically — 37

The adverb describing the act of surpassing the act of transubstantiation; the word is found in Mark McShane's novel Untimely Ripped (1963).

8 = Pseudoantidisestablishmentarianism — 34

A word meaning "false opposition to the withdrawal of state support from a Church," derived from that perennial favorite long word, antidisestablishmentarianism (a mere 28 letters).

= Supercalifragilisticexpialidocious — 34

An invented word, but perhaps now eligible since it has appeared in the Oxford English Dictionary. It was popularized by the song of this title in the film Mary Poppins (1964), where it is used to mean "wonderful," but it was originally written in 1949 in an unpublished song by Parker and Young who spelled it "supercalafajalisticespialadojus" (32 letters).

10 = Encephalomyeloradiculoneuritis — 30

Inflammation of the whole nervous system.

= Hippopotomonstrosesquipedalian — 30

Appropriately, the word that means "pertaining to an extremely long word."

= Pseudopseudohypoparathyroidism — 30

First used (hyphenated) in the US in 1952 and (unhyphenated) in Great Britain in The Lancet in 1962 to describe a medical case in which a patient appeared to have symptoms of pseudohypoparathyroidism, but with "no manifestations suggesting hypoparathyroidism."

* *Excluding names of chemical compounds*

 When was Canada's first railway built?
see p.232 for the answer

A 1827
B 1836
C 1852

EASTERN PROMISE

China has the most children in school and the world's longest school year, but spends just 2 percent of its GNP on education – less than half that of Western countries.

TOP 10 ★
COUNTRIES WITH THE HIGHEST NUMBER OF PRIMARY SCHOOL PUPILS PER TEACHER

COUNTRY	PUPIL/TEACHER RATIO IN PRIMARY SCHOOLS*
1 Central African Republic	77
2 Congo	70
3 Chad	67
4 Bangladesh	63
5 Malawi	59
6 =Afghanistan	58
=Mozambique	58
=Rwanda	58
9 =Benin	56
=Senegal	56
Canada	16

* *In latest year for which figures available*

TOP 10 🍁
OLDEST SCHOOLS IN QUEBEC*

SCHOOL/CITY	YEAR FOUNDED
1 Collège des Jésuites, Quebec	1635
=Petite école des Jésuites, Quebec	1635
3 École tenue par Ameau, Trois-Rivières	1652
4 Marguerite Bourgeoys, Montreal	1657
5 Sulpiciens, Montreal	1666
6 Le Petit Séminaire de Québec, Quebec	1668
7 Sainte-Foy, Quebec	1673
8 Château-Richer, Quebec	1674
9 Saint-Joachim, Quebec	before 1676
10 Île d'Orléans, Quebec	1676

* *Includes primary and secondary schools for boys, when under French rule, 1635–1760*

Source: L'Instruction au Canada, *TYP Laflamme & Proulx, 1911*

TOP 10 ★
COUNTRIES SPENDING THE MOST ON EDUCATION

COUNTRY	EXPENDITURE AS PERCENTAGE OF GNP*
1 Kiribati	11.4
2 Moldova	10.3
3 Namibia	8.5
4 Denmark	7.7
5 Sweden	7.6
6 =South Africa	7.5
=Zimbabwe	7.5
8 Uzbekistan	7.4
9 Barbados	7.3
10 Saudi Arabia	7.2
Canada	6.4

* *GNP in latest year for which data available*
Source: *UNESCO*

TOP 10 ★
COUNTRIES WITH THE MOST PRIMARY SCHOOLS

COUNTRY	PRIMARY SCHOOLS
1 China	628,840
2 India	598,354
3 Brazil	196,479
4 Indonesia	173,893
5 Mexico	95,855
6 Pakistan	77,207
7 US	72,000
8 Russia	66,235
9 Iran	63,101
10 Colombia	48,933
Canada	12,685

Source: *UNESCO*

TOP 10 COUNTRIES WITH THE LONGEST SCHOOL YEARS

(Country/school year in days)

❶ China, 251 ❷ Japan, 243 ❸ South Korea, 220 ❹ Israel, 215 ❺ = Germany, 210;
= Russia, 210 ❼ Switzerland, 207 ❽ = Netherlands, 200;
= Scotland, 200; = Thailand, 200
Canada, 186

EDUCATING THE MASSES

Indian culture places a high value on education, and consequently some 7 percent of the country's entire population attends secondary school.

TOP 10 ★
COUNTRIES WITH THE MOST SECONDARY SCHOOL PUPILS

	COUNTRY	PERCENTAGE FEMALE	SECONDARY SCHOOL PUPILS
1	China	45	71,883,000
2	India	38	68,872,393
3	US	49	21,473,692
4	Indonesia	46	14,209,974
5	Russia	50	13,732,000
6	Japan	49	9,878,568
7	Iran	46	8,776,792
8	Germany	48	8,382,335
9	Mexico	49	7,914,165
10	UK	52	6,548,786

Source: *UNESCO*

The number of pupils enrolled at secondary schools as a percentage of the total population in those countries in this Top 10 list varies from 6 percent in China to 14 percent in both Iran and Germany.

TOP 10 🍁
EXPENDITURES PER STUDENT IN CANADA*

	PROVINCE OR TERRITORY	SPENDING PER STUDENT, 1996 ($)
1	Northwest Territories	12,390
2	Yukon	11,879
3	Quebec	7,372
4	Ontario	7,133
5	British Columbia	7,110
6	Manitoba	6,786
7	Alberta	5,987
8	New Brunswick	5,787
9	Saskatchewan	5,740
10	Newfoundland	5,477

* School board expenditure per student on public and private institutions for pre-elementary and elementary–secondary level

Source: *Centre for Education Statistics, Canada*

TOP 10 🍁
PROVINCES WITH THE HIGHEST HIGH SCHOOL GRADUATION RATE

	PROVINCE	1997 PERCENTAGE RATE
1	Prince Edward Island	86.5
2	New Brunswick	83.1
3	Nova Scotia	81.7
4	Newfoundland	81.5
5	Quebec	78.0
6	Manitoba	75.9
7	Saskatchewan	73.0
8	British Columbia	71.4
9	Ontario	68.8
10	Alberta	62.8

Source: *Statistics Canada*

Graduation rates in Yukon and the Northwest Territories are lower than that of the provinces: 57.9 and 34.1 respectively.

TOP 10 ★
COUNTRIES WITH THE HIGHEST ILLITERACY RATES

	COUNTRY	PERCENTAGE ADULT ILLITERACY RATE*
1	Niger	84.3
2	Burkina Faso	77.0
3 =	Afghanistan	63.7
=	Sierra Leone	63.7
5	Gambia	63.5
6	Guinea-Bissau	63.2
7	Senegal	62.7
8	Benin	62.5
9	Ethiopia	61.3
10	Mauritania	60.1

* Age over 15; estimates for 2000

Source: *UNESCO*

Did You Know? The first blackboards used in schools were invented in Skippack, Pennsylvania, in 1714 by Christopher Dock (1698–1771), a German immigrant schoolmaster who also wrote the first teaching manual published in America.

TOP 10 ★
LARGEST UNIVERSITIES

	UNIVERSITY	STUDENTS
1	**University of Paris**, France	311,163
2	**University of Calcutta**, India	300,000
3	**University of Mexico**, Mexico	269,000
4	**University of Bombay**, India	262,350
5	**University of Guadalajara**, Mexico	214,986
6	**University of Rome**, Italy	189,000
7	**University of Buenos Aires**, Argentina	183,397
8	**University of Rajasthan**, India	175,000
9	**University of California**, US	157,331
10	**University of Wisconsin**, US	155,298

Several universities in India, Egypt, Italy, and the US that didn't place on the Top 10 have a student population of more than 100,000. It should be noted that certain universities on this list consist of numerous separate centers. The University of Wisconsin, for example, comprises 14 campuses, with more than 40,000 students enrolled at the Madison campus, the university's largest.

TOP 10 ★
COUNTRIES WITH THE HIGHEST PERCENTAGE OF FEMALE UNIVERSITY STUDENTS

	COUNTRY	% OF FEMALE STUDENTS*
1	Cyprus	75
2	US Virgin Islands	74
3	Qatar	73
4 =	St. Lucia	72
=	United Arab Emirates	72
6	Kuwait	67
7	Myanmar (Burma)	64
8	Barbados	62
9	Namibia	61
10 =	Bulgaria	60
=	Cuba	60
=	Latvia	60
=	Lesotho	60
=	Mongolia	60
=	Panama	60
	Canada	53

* In latest year for which data available
Source: *UNESCO*

TOP 10 ★
COUNTRIES WITH THE LOWEST PERCENTAGE OF FEMALE UNIVERSITY STUDENTS

	COUNTRY	% OF FEMALE STUDENTS*
1	Samoa	3
2	Equatorial Guinea	4
3	Central African Republic	9
4	Somalia	10
5	Guinea	11
6	Chad	12
7	Yemen	13
8	Eritrea	14
9	Rwanda	15
10	Cambodia	16

* In latest year for which data available
Source: *UNESCO*

HARVARD

Harvard, the first college founded in the US, takes its name from John Harvard (1607–38). Born in Southwark, London, he graduated from Emmanuel College, Cambridge, in 1631, and in 1637 married Ann Sadler, a clergyman's daughter, in Lewes, England. He later emigrated to Charlestown, Massachusetts, where he worked as a preacher. Barely a year after his arrival, he died of consumption. In his will he bequeathed his library of 300 books and a sum of £779 to Cambridge College, which had been founded in 1636. Two years later, it was renamed as Harvard College in honor of its benefactor.

WHO WAS • WHO WAS • WHO WAS • WHO WAS

TOP 10 ★
COUNTRIES WITH THE HIGHEST PROPORTION OF ADULTS IN HIGHER EDUCATION

	COUNTRY	TOTAL	STUDENTS PER 100,000*
1	Canada	1,763,105	5,997
2	South Korea	2,541,659	5,609
3	Australia	1,002,476	5,552
4	US	14,261,778	5,339
5	New Zealand	162,350	4,508
6	Finland	213,995	4,190
7	Norway	180,383	4,164
8	Spain	1,591,863	4,017
9	Ireland	47,955	3,618
10	France	2,091,688	3,600

* In latest year for which data available
Source: *UNESCO*

TOP 10 ★
COUNTRIES WITH THE MOST UNIVERSITY STUDENTS

	COUNTRY	PERCENTAGE FEMALE	UNIVERSITY STUDENTS*
1	US	56	14,261,778
2	India	36	6,060,418
3	Japan	44	3,917,709
4	China	36	3,350,715
5	Russia	53	2,587,510
6	France	55	2,091,688
7	Philippines	57	2,017,972
8	Italy	54	1,892,542
9	Indonesia	31	1,889,408
10	Brazil	52	1,868,529
	Canada	*53*	*1,763,105*

* In latest year for which data available
Source: *UNESCO*

TOP 10 ★
COUNTRIES WITH THE MOST UNIVERSITIES

	COUNTRY	UNIVERSITIES
1	India	8,407
2	US	5,758
3	Argentina	1,705
4	Spain	1,415
5	Mexico	1,341
6	Bangladesh	1,268
7	Indonesia	1,236
8	Japan	1,223
9	France	1,062
10	China	1,054
	Canada	*265*

Although the number of universities in Canada seems low when compared with that of other countries, the number of people attending universities in Canada in proportion to its population is the highest in the world.

GRADUATION DAY

Decked in their traditional tasseled mortar boards and gowns, more students graduate from US universities than from those of any other country.

Libraries of the World

THE 10 ★
FIRST PUBLIC LIBRARIES IN THE US

LIBRARY/LOCATION	FOUNDED
1 Peterboro Public Library, Peterboro, NH	1833
2 New Orleans Public Library, New Orleans, LA	1843
3 Boston Public Library, Boston, MA	1852
4 Public Library of Cincinnati and Hamilton County, Cincinnati, OH	1853
5 Springfield City Library, Springfield, MA	1857
6 Worcester Public Library, Worcester, MA	1859
7 Multnomah County Library, Portland, OR	1864
8 =Detroit Public Library, Detroit, MI	1865
=St. Louis Public Library, St. Louis, MO	1865
10 Atlanta-Fulton Public Library, Atlanta, GA	1867

Source: *Public Library Association*

Although Medford Public Library in Medford, MA, claims to have been founded as early as 1825, evidence exists that Peterboro Public Library, founded on April 9, 1833, with 700 volumes, was the first public library (in that it was the first supported by local taxes) in the US.

DEWEY

Any visitor to a library will have noticed the system by which books are organized into 10 subject groups and a series of sub-groups, each bearing a decimal number. This was the brainchild of American-born Melville Louis Kossuth Dewey (1851–1931). At the age of 21, Dewey devised the system that bears his name. Published in 1876, it became adopted throughout the world and still remains the most widely used book classification system. Dewey also helped establish the ALA (American Library Association).

WHO WAS • WHO WAS • WHO WAS • WHO WAS

TOP 10 ★
OLDEST NATIONAL LIBRARIES

	LIBRARY	LOCATION	FOUNDED
1	National Library of the Czech Republic	Prague, Czech Republic	1366
2	National Library of Austria	Vienna, Austria	1368
3	Biblioteca Nazionale Marciana	Venice, Italy	1468
4	Bibliothèque Nationale de France	Paris, France	1480
5	National Library of Malta	Valetta, Malta	1555
6	Bayericsche Staatsbibliothek	Munich, Germany	1558
7	National Library of Belgium	Brussels, Belgium	1559
8	Zagreb National and University Library	Zagreb, Croatia	1606
9	National Library of Finland	Helsinki, Finland	1640
10	National Library of Denmark	Copenhagen, Denmark	1653

What may claim to be the world's first national library was that in Alexandria, Egypt, founded in about 307 BC by King Ptolemy I Soter. The library assembled the world's largest collection of scrolls, which were partly destroyed during Julius Caesar's invasion of 47 BC, and totally by Arab invaders in AD 642, an event that is considered one of the greatest ever losses to scholarship. Among national libraries in the English-speaking world, Scotland's dates from 1682 (thus pre-dating the British Library, part of the British Museum, established in 1753). The US Library of Congress was founded in 1800.

TOP 10 🍁
LARGEST PUBLIC LIBRARIES IN CANADA

	LIBRARY/PROVINCE	NO. OF BRANCHES	HOLDINGS (1999)*
1	Toronto Public Library, Ontario	98	12,037,529
2	Bibliothèque de Montreal, Quebec	25	2,742,408
3	Vancouver Public Library, British Columbia	20	2,361,044
4	Calgary Public Library, Alberta	16	2,173,905
5	Winnipeg Public Library, Manitoba	20	1,624,462
6	Edmonton Public Library, Alberta	16	1,617,717
7	Mississauga Library System, Ontario	15	1,456,850
8	London Public Library, Ontario	17	1,245,234
9	Halifax Regional Library, Nova Scotia	13	1,200,152
10	Hamilton Public Library, Ontario	26	1,112,470

* Holdings include books, magazines, newspapers, manuscripts, CDs, cassettes, videos, games, toys, and maps. Books represent the largest proportion of the holdings.

Source: *Council of Administrators of Large Urban Public Libraries*

TOP 10 COUNTRIES WITH THE MOST PUBLIC LIBRARIES
(Country/public libraries)

❶ Russia, 33,200   ❷ UK, 23,678   ❸ Germany, 20,448   ❹ US, 9,097
❺ Czech Republic, 8,398   ❻ Romania, 7,181   ❼ Bulgaria, 5,591   ❽ Hungary, 4,765
❾ Brazil, 3,600   ❿ China, 2,406

TOP 10 ★
LARGEST LIBRARIES

LIBRARY	LOCATION	FOUNDED	BOOKS
1 Library of Congress	Washington, DC, US	1800	24,616,867
2 National Library of China	Beijing, China	1909	20,000,000
3 National Library of Canada	Ottawa, Canada	1953	16,000,000
4 Deutsche Bibliothek*	Frankfurt, Germany	1990	15,997,000
5 British Library#	London, UK	1753	15,000,000
6 Harvard University Library	Cambridge, Massachusetts, US	1638	14,190,704
7 Vernadsky Central Scientific Library of the National Academy of Sciences	Kiev, Ukraine	1919	13,000,000
8 Russian State Library+	Moscow, Russia	1862	11,750,000
9 Bibliothèque Nationale de Paris	Paris, France	1400	11,000,000
10 New York Public Library★	New York, US	1895	10,421,691

* *Formed in 1990 through the unification of the Deutsche Bibliothek, Frankfurt (founded 1947) and the Deutsche Bucherei, Leipzig*

\# *Founded as part of the British Museum, 1753; became an independent body in 1973*

\+ *Founded 1862 as Rumyantsev Library, formerly State V.I. Lenin Library*

★ *Astor Library founded 1848, consolidated with Lenox Library and Tilden Trust to form New York Public Library in 1895*

The figures for books in such vast collections as held by these libraries represent only a fraction of the total collections, which include manuscripts, microfilms, maps, prints, and records. The Library of Congress has perhaps more than 100 million catalogued items.

DEUTSCHE BIBLIOTHEK

Formed in October 1990 through the merging of West and East German libraries, the Deutsche Bibliothek contains unified Germany's largest collection of books and other printed and recorded material.

TOP 10 🍁
LARGEST RESEARCH LIBRARIES IN CANADA

UNIVERSITY LIBRARY/INSTITUTION	VOLUMES
1 Toronto	9,195,841
2 National Library of Canada	7,267,860
3 Alberta	5,527,712
4 British Columbia	4,106,011
5 McGill	3,199,896
6 Montreal	2,571,577
7 CISTI*	2,562,988
8 Western Ontario	2,465,089
9 Laval	2,410,202
10 York	2,359,201

* *Canada Institute for Scientific and Technical Information*

Source: *Canadian Association of Research Libraries*

Whose valuable notebooks are known as the Codex Hammer?
see p.109 for the answer

A Leonardo da Vinci
B William Shakespeare
C Martin Luther

Book Firsts & Records

TOP 10 ★
MOST-PUBLISHED AUTHORS OF ALL TIME

AUTHOR/NATIONALITY

1 **William Shakespeare** (British; 1564–1616)
2 **Charles Dickens** (British; 1812–70)
3 **Sir Walter Scott** (British; 1771–1832)
4 **Johann Goethe** (German; 1749–1832)
5 **Aristotle** (Greek; 384–322 BC)
6 **Alexandre Dumas** (père) (French; 1802–70)
7 **Robert Louis Stevenson** (British; 1850–94)
8 **Mark Twain** (American; 1835–1910)
9 **Marcus Tullius Cicero** (Roman; 106–43 BC)
10 **Honoré de Balzac** (French; 1799–1850)

TOP 10 ★
BOOK PRODUCING COUNTRIES

	COUNTRY	TITLES PUBLISHED*
1	UK	110,155
2	China	73,923
3	Germany	62,277
4	US	49,276
5	France	45,379
6	Japan	42,245
7	Spain	37,325
8	Italy	26,620
9	South Korea	25,017
10	Russia	22,028

* Total of new titles, new editions, and reprints in latest year for which figures are available

TOP 10 ★
BOOK MARKETS

	COUNTRY	ANNUAL BOOK SALES (US$)
1	US	25,490,000,000
2	Japan	10,467,000,000
3	Germany	9,962,000,000
4	UK	3,651,000,000
5	France	3,380,000,000
6	Spain	2,992,000,000
7	South Korea	2,805,000,000
8	Brazil	2,526,000,000
9	Italy	2,246,000,000
10	China	1,760,000,000

TOP 10 ★
BOOK-BUYING COUNTRIES*

	COUNTRY	BOOK SALES PER PERSON, 2001 (US$)
1	Norway	134.40
2	Germany	119.20
3	US	102.60
4	Finland	101.30
5	Switzerland	100.70
6	Belgium	98.40
7	Japan	85.60
8	UK	81.80
9	Singapore	76.50
10	Denmark	73.00
	Canada	50.70

* Estimate based on 1999 prices

Source: Euromonitor

TOP 10 ★
BEST-SELLING PAPERBACKS PUBLISHED OVER 50 YEARS AGO

	BOOK/AUTHOR/YEAR	US SALES (US$)*
1	*The Common Sense Book of Baby and Child Care*, Benjamin Spock, 1946	23,285,000
2	*The Merriam-Webster Pocket Dictionary*, 1947	15,500,000
3	*English–Spanish, Spanish–English Dictionary*, Carlos Castillo and Otto F. Bond, 1948	10,187,000
4	*Gone With the Wind*, Margaret Mitchell, 1936	8,630,000
5	*God's Little Acre*, Erskine Caldwell, 1946	8,258,400
6	*1984*, George Orwell, 1949	8,147,629
7	*Animal Farm*, George Orwell, 1946	7,070,892
8	*Roget's Pocket Thesaurus*, 1946	7,020,000
9	*How to Win Friends and Influence People*, Dale Carnegie, 1940	6,578,314
10	*Lady Chatterley's Lover*, D. H. Lawrence, 1932	6,326,470

* Includes hardback sales where relevant, estimated to 1975

UNDER THE HAMMER

The Codex Hammer, *a collection of Leonardo da Vinci's scientific writings, was compiled c.1508–10. It contains over 350 drawings illustrating the artist's scientific theories. In 1994 it achieved a record price at auction when bought by Bill Gates.*

DR. SPOCK

Dr. Benjamin McLane Spock (1903–98) was the eldest of six children. Born in New Haven, Connecticut, he became a pediatric specialist and studied psychoanalysis, but his chief celebrity came from his *The Common Sense Book of Baby and Child Care*, which was published in 1946. Originally sold for 25 cents, this manual became the bestselling paperback of all time in the US. Translated into some 40 languages, it sold over 50 million copies worldwide, making Dr. Spock the most famous of all childcare experts.

WHO WAS • WHO WAS • WHO WAS • WHO WAS

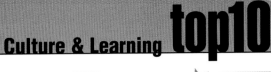

BEST RED BOOK

During the Cultural Revolution, Chinese Communist leader Mao Tse-tung (Zedong) became the subject of a personality cult, with his bestselling Quotations ... (Little Red Book) its most potent symbol.

THE 10
FIRST BOOKS PUBLISHED IN CANADA

BOOK	YEAR
1=Catholic Church Catechism (French)	1765
=Quebec Primer (French alphabet)	1765
3 Quebec Primer (Latin alphabet)	1766
4 A devotional book in the Mohawk language, Jean Baptiste de la Brosse	1767
5 *Nova Scotia Almanac**	1769
6 *The Universal Prayer*, William Doyle	1770
7 Catholic Church Liturgy and Ritual (French)	1772
8=*The Gospel of Christ Preached to the Poor*, Peter Delaroche	1773
=Catholic Church Psalter (French)	1773
10 A three-volume treatise on the French laws of Quebec, François Joseph Cugnet	1775

* Reprinted 1772, 1773, and 1775 (the latter thought to be the first illustrated Canadian printed book)

Source: Bibliography of Canadian Imprints 1751–1800

TOP 10
BEST-SELLING BOOKS OF ALL TIME

BOOK/AUTHOR	FIRST PUBLISHED	APPROX. SALES
1 *The Bible*	c.1451–55	more than 6,000,000,000
2 *Quotations from the Works of Mao Tse-tung* (dubbed *Little Red Book* by the Western press)	1966	900,000,000
3 *American Spelling Book*, Noah Webster	1783	up to 100,000,000
4 *The Guinness Book of Records* (now *Guinness World Records*)	1955	more than 90,000,000*
5 *World Almanac*	1868	73,500,000*
6 *The McGuffey Readers*, William Holmes McGuffey	1836	60,000,000
7 *The Common Sense Book of Baby and Child Care*, Benjamin Spock	1946	more than 50,000,000
8 *A Message to Garcia*, Elbert Hubbard	1899	up to 40,000,000
9=*In His Steps: "What Would Jesus Do?"*, Rev. Charles Monroe Sheldon	1896	more than 30,000,000
=*Valley of the Dolls*, Jacqueline Susann	1966	more than 30,000,000

* Aggregate sales of annual publication

TOP 10
MOST EXPENSIVE BOOKS AND MANUSCRIPTS EVER SOLD AT AUCTION

BOOK OR MANUSCRIPT/SALE	PRICE (US$)*
1 *The Codex Hammer*, c.1508–10, Christie's, New York, Nov 11, 1994	28,800,000

This Leonardo da Vinci notebook was purchased by Bill Gates, the billionaire founder of Microsoft.

2 *The Rothschild Prayerbook*, c.1505, Christie's, London, July 8, 1999	12,557,220

This prayerbook holds the world record price for an illuminated manuscript.

3 *The Gospels of Henry the Lion*, c.1173–75, Sotheby's, London, Dec 6, 1983	10,841,000

At the time of sale, this was the most expensive manuscript or book ever sold.

4 *The Birds of America* (John James Audubon), 1827–38, Christie's, New York, Mar 10, 2000	8,000,000

This holds the record for any natural history book.

5 *The Canterbury Tales* (Geoffrey Chaucer), c.1476–77, Christie's, London, July 8, 1998	7,696,720

Printed by William Caxton and bought by Paul Getty.

6 *The Gutenberg Bible*, 1455, Christie's, New York, Oct 22, 1987	5,390,000

One of the first books ever printed, by Johann Gutenberg and Johann Fust in 1455.

7 *The Northumberland Bestiary*, c.1250–60, Sotheby's, London, Nov 29, 1990	5,049,000

This achieved the highest price ever paid for an English manuscript.

8 *The Burdett Psalter and Hours*, 1282–86, Sotheby's, London, June 23, 1998	4,517,640

This is the third most expensive illuminated manuscript.

9 *The Cornaro Missal*, c.1503, Christie's, London, July 8, 1999	4,185,740

This achieved the record price for an Italian manuscript.

10 *Autographed manuscript of nine symphonies by Wolfgang Amadeus Mozart*, c.1773–74, Sotheby's, London, May 22, 1987	3,854,000

This garnered the highest price ever paid for a music manuscript.

* Excluding premiums

Did You Know? John James Audubon's *The Birds of America* is not only one of the most expensive books ever published, but it is also one of the largest: its pages measure 63.5 x 96.5 cm (25 x 38 in).

Best-sellers & Literary Awards

PULITZER

Joseph Pulitzer (1847–1911) was born in Makó, Hungary. He settled in St. Louis, US, where he became a journalist and within a few years publisher of the *St. Louis Post-Dispatch*. He then purchased the *New York World*, which became America's largest circulation newspaper. In his publications, he had waged war against corruption in business and government and promoted freedom of the press and journalistic professionalism. He left a US$2 million endowment to establish the Columbia School of Journalism, which since 1917 has administered the Pulitzer Prizes in a range of categories for journalism, literature, music, and drama.

WHO WAS • WHO WAS • WHO WAS • WHO WAS •

TOP 10 ★
CHILDREN'S BOOKS IN THE US, 2000

AUTHOR/TITLE	SALES
1 **J.K. Rowling**, *Harry Potter and the Goblet of Fire*	7,900,000
2 **Jack Canfield**, *et al.*, *Chicken Soup for the Teenage Soul*	5,250,566
3 **J.K. Rowling**, *Harry Potter and the Chamber of Secrets* (pb)	4,500,000
4 **J.K. Rowling**, *Harry Potter and the Sorcerer's Stone* (pb)	3,400,000
5 **Jack Canfield**, *et al.*, *Chicken Soup for the Teenage Soul II*	3,036,879
6 **J.K. Rowling**, *Harry Potter and the Chamber of Secrets* (hb)	2,900,000
7 **J.K. Rowling**, *Harry Potter and the Prisoner of Azkaban*	2,700,000
8 **Jack Canfield**, *et al.*, *Chicken Soup for the Kid's Soul*	2,053,897
9 **J.K. Rowling**, *Harry Potter and the Sorcerer's Stone* (hb)	1,800,000
10 **Jack Canfield**, *et al.*, *Chicken Soup for the Teenage Soul III*	1,326,652

Source: Publishers Weekly

TOP 10 🍁
NON-FICTION BEST-SELLERS IN CANADA, 2000

TITLE	AUTHOR
1 *Tuesdays with Morrie*	Mitch Albom
2 *'Tis*	Frank McCourt
3 *The Rock Says*	The Rock
4 *Have a Nice Day*	Mick (Mankind) Foley
5 *In a Sunburned Country*	Bill Bryson
6 *Canada: A People's History**	Don Gillmor and Pierre Turgeon
7 *The Beatles Anthology*	The Beatles
8 *Ten Things I Wish I'd Known – Before I Went Out Into the Real World*	Maria Shriver
9 *On Writing*	Stephen King
10 *Trudeau Albums**	Peter Gzowski et al.

* *Canadian books*

Source: The Globe and Mail

TOP 10 🍁
FICTION BEST-SELLERS IN CANADA, 2000

TITLE	AUTHOR
1 *Scarlet Feather*	Maeve Binchy
2 *Anil's Ghost**	Michael Ondaatje
3 *The Blind Assassin**	Margaret Atwood
4 *The Brethren*	John Grisham
5 *The Bear and the Dragon*	Tom Clancy
6 *Winter's Heart*	Robert Jordan
7 *Vinyl Café: Unplugged**	Stuart McLean
8 *No Great Mischief**	Alistair MacLeod
9 *A Good House**	Bonnie Burnard
10 *Mercy Among the Children**	David Adams

* *By Canadian authors*

Source: The Globe and Mail

According to a 1998 survey, over 61 percent of Canadians read at least one book a week, while just over 31 percent reported that they read at least one book a month.

THE 10 🍁
LATEST WINNERS OF THE GOVERNOR GENERAL'S AWARD FOR ENGLISH FICTION

YEAR	AUTHOR/TITLE
2000	Michael Ondaatje, *Anil's Ghost*
1999	Matt Cohen, *Elizabeth and After*
1998	Diane Schoemperlen, *Forms of Devotion*
1997	Jane Urquart, *The Underpainter*
1996	Guy Vanderhaeghe, *The Englishman's Boy*
1995	Greg Hollingshead, *The Roaring Girl*
1994	Rudy Wiebe, *A Discovery of Strangers*
1993	Carol Shields, *The Stone Diaries*
1992	Michael Ondaatje, *The English Patient*
1991	Rohinton Mistry, *Such a Long Journey*

The Governor General Literary Awards have been honoring Canadian authors since 1937. Today, there are seven categories, including drama, poetry, and translation, each with a cash prize of $15,000.

THE 10 🍁
LATEST WINNERS OF THE GOVERNOR GENERAL'S AWARD FOR FRENCH FICTION

YEAR	AUTHOR/TITLE
2000	Jean Marc Dalpé, *Un vent se lève qui éparpille*
1999	Lise Tremblay, *La danse juive*
1998	Christiane Frenette, *La terre ferme*
1997	Aude, *Cet imperceptible mouvement*
1996	Marie-Claire Blais, *Soifs*
1995	Nicole Houde, *Les oiseaux de Saint-John Perse*
1994	Robert Lalonde, *Le petit aigle à tête blanche*
1993	Nancy Huston, *Cantique des plaines*
1992	Anne Hébert, *L'enfant chargé de songes Andromède attendra*
1991	André Brochu, *La croix du nord*

Which Canadian daily newspaper has the highest circulation?   **A** National Post
see p.113 for the answer   **B** Globe and Mail
   C Toronto Star

THE 10 ★

LATEST WINNERS OF THE PULITZER PRIZE FOR FICTION

YEAR	AUTHOR/TITLE
2001	Michael Chabon, *The Amazing Adventures of Kavalier & Clay*
2000	Jhumpa Lhiri, *Interpreter of Maladies*
1999	Michael Cunningham, *The Hours*
1998	Philip Roth, *American Pastoral*
1997	Steven Millhauser, *Martin Dressler: The Tale of an American Dreamer*
1996	Richard Ford, *Independence Day*
1995	Carol Shields, *The Stone Diaries*
1994	E. Annie Proulx, *The Shipping News*
1993	Robert Olen Butler, *A Good Scent From a Strange Mountain: Stories*
1992	Jane Smiley, *A Thousand Acres*

THE 10 ★

LATEST BOOKER PRIZE WINNERS

YEAR	AUTHOR/TITLE
2000	Margaret Atwood, *The Blind Assassin*
1999	J.M. Coetzee, *Disgrace*
1998	Ian McEwan, *Amsterdam*
1997	Arundhati Roy, *The God of Small Things*
1996	Graham Swift, *Last Orders*
1995	Pat Barker, *The Ghost Road*
1994	James Kelman, *How Late It Was, How Late*
1993	Roddy Doyle, *Paddy Clarke Ha Ha Ha*
1992	= Michael Ondaatje, *The English Patient* = Barry Unsworth, *Sacred Hunger*

The South African writer J.M. Coetzee is the only person to have won the Booker prize twice, in 1999 with *Disgrace* and in 1983 with *Life and Times of Michael K.*

MARGARET ATWOOD

Canadian poet and novelist Margaret Atwood joins the list of Booker Prize winners for her tenth novel, The Blind Assassin. Two of her previous books, The Handmaid's Tale and Cat's Eye, were shortlisted.

THE 10 ★

LATEST WINNERS OF HUGO AWARDS FOR THE BEST SCIENCE FICTION NOVEL

YEAR	AUTHOR/TITLE
2000	Vernor Vinge, *A Deepness in the Sky*
1999	Connie Willis, *To Say Nothing of the Dog*
1998	Joe Haldeman, *Forever Peace*
1997	Kim Stanley Robinson, *Blue Mars*
1996	Neal Stephenson, *The Diamond Age*
1995	Lois McMaster Bujold, *Mirror Dance*
1994	Kim Stanley Robinson, *Green Mars*
1993	= Vernor Vinge, *A Fire Upon the Deep* = Connie Willis, *Doomsday Book*
1992	Lois McMaster Bujold, *Barrayar*

THE 10 🍁

LATEST WINNERS OF STEPHEN LEACOCK MEDAL FOR HUMOUR

YEAR	AUTHOR/TITLE
2001	Stuart McLean, *Vinyl Café: Unplugged*
2000	Arthur Black, *Black Tie and Tales*
1999	Stuart McLean, *Home from the Vinyl Café*
1998	Mordecai Richler, *Barney's Version*
1997	Arthur Black, *Black in the Saddle Again*
1996	Marsha Boulton, *Letters from the Country*
1995	Josh Freed, *Fear of Frying and Other Fax of Life*
1994	Bill Richardson, *Bachelor Brothers' Bed & Breakfast*
1993	John Levesque, *Waiting for Aquarius*
1992	Roch Carrier, *Prayers of a Very Wise Child*

TOP 10 ★
NON-ENGLISH-LANGUAGE DAILY NEWSPAPERS

	NEWSPAPER	COUNTRY	AVERAGE DAILY CIRCULATION
1	Yomiuri Shimbun	Japan	14,476,000
2	Asahi Shimbun	Japan	12,475,000
3	Mainichi Shimbun	Japan	5,785,000
4	Nihon Keizai Shimbun	Japan	4,674,000
5	Chunichi Shimbun	Japan	4,667,000
6	Bild-Zeitung	Germany	4,256,000
7	Sankei Shimbun	Japan	2,890,000
8	Reference News	China	2,800,000
9	Chosen Ilbo	South Korea	2,348,000
10	People's Daily	China	2,300,000

Source: *World Association of Newspapers*

TOP 10 ★
ENGLISH-LANGUAGE DAILY NEWSPAPERS

	NEWSPAPER	COUNTRY	AVERAGE DAILY CIRCULATION
1	The Sun	UK	3,554,000
2	Daily Mail	UK	2,367,000
3	The Mirror	UK	2,262,000
4	Wall Street Journal	US	1,753,000
5	USA Today	US	1,672,000
6	Times of India	India	1,479,000
7	The New York Times	US	1,086,000
8	Los Angeles Times	US	1,078,000
9	Daily Express	UK	1,044,000
10	Daily Telegraph	UK	1,033,000

Source: *World Association of Newspapers*

TOP 10 ★
MAGAZINES IN THE US

	MAGAZINE/ISSUES PER YEAR	CIRCULATION*
1	NRTA/AARP Bulletin, 10	20,826,083
2	Modern Maturity, 36	20,824,815
3	Reader's Digest, 12	12,613,790
4	TV Guide, 52	10,844,269
5	National Geographic Magazine, 12	7,957,062
6	Better Homes and Gardens, 12	7,627,977
7	Family Circle, 17	5,002,383
8	Good Housekeeping, 12	4,507,306
9	McCall's, 12	4,204,022
10	Ladies Home Journal, 12	4,173,295

* Average for the first six months of 2000

Source: *Magazine Publishers of America*

TOP 10 ★
NEWSPAPER-READING COUNTRIES

	COUNTRY	DAILY COPIES PER 1,000 PEOPLE		COUNTRY	DAILY COPIES PER 1,000 PEOPLE
1	Norway	583	6	Austria	356
2	Japan	574	7	Iceland	341
3	Finland	452	8	Singapore	334
4	Sweden	420	9	UK	321
5	Switzerland	376	10	Germany	300

Source: *World Association of Newspapers*

TOP 10 COUNTRIES WITH THE HIGHEST NEWSPAPER CIRCULATIONS
(Country/average daily circulation)

❶ Japan, 72,218,000 ❷ US, 55,979,000 ❸ China, 50,000,000
❹ India, 25,587,000 ❺ Germany, 24,565,000 ❻ Russia, 23,800,000
❼ UK, 18,939,000 ❽ France, 8,799,000 ❾ Brazil, 7,245,000
❿ Italy, 5,937,000

Source: *World Association of Newspapers*

HOLD THE FRONT PAGE

Unlike Canada, with its two major national papers, the US has few newspapers that can claim national readership. The circulations of the major publications shown here tend to be as regional as their titles imply.

TOP 10 ⚜
DAILY NEWSPAPERS IN CANADA

NEWSPAPER	WEEKLY CIRCULATION*
1 Toronto Star	3,469,255
2 Globe and Mail	2,003,935
3 Journal de Montreal	1,949,429
4 Toronto Sun	1,785,626
5 National Post	1,763,934
6 La Press, Montreal	1,419,204
7 Vancouver Sun	1,199,776
8 Ottawa Citizen	1,026,662
9 Gazette, Montreal	1,026,278
10 Province, Vancouver	999,716

* As at March 31, 2000

Source: *Canadian Newspaper Association*

The newspaper wars continue in major cities across Canada. In 2000, three free subway papers joined the competition in Toronto: *Today* (produced by TorStar Corp.); *F.Y.I.* (produced by Quebecor, publisher of *Toronto Sun*); and *Metro* (produced by Metro International SA of Sweden).

TOP 10 ★
SUNDAY NEWSPAPERS IN THE US

NEWSPAPER	AVERAGE SUNDAY CIRCULATION*
1 The New York Times	1,682,208
2 Los Angeles Times	1,379,564
3 Washington Post	1,065,011
4 Chicago Tribune	1,007,236
5 Philadelphia Inquirer	798,252
6 New York Sunday News	790,935
7 Dallas News	785,758
8 Detroit News & Free Press	748,383
9 Houston Chronicle	743,009
10 Boston Globe	721,859

* Through September 30, 2000

Source: *Audit Bureau of Circulations*

America's first ever Sunday newspaper was the Baltimore, MD, *Sunday Monitor*. Its first issue appeared on December 18, 1796, and comprised just four pages. Of those in the Top 10, the oldest-established is the *Philadelphia Inquirer*, founded in 1830 by printer Jasper Harding as the *Pennsylvania Inquirer*.

THE 10 ⚜
OLDEST NEWSPAPERS IN CANADA*

NEWSPAPER	YEAR ESTABLISHED
1 Chronicle-Telegraph, Quebec, QC	1764
2 Gazette, Montreal, QC	1778
3 Recorder & Times, Brockville, ON	1821
4 Vanguard#, Yarmouth, NS	1833
5 Whig-Standard, Kingston, ON	1834
6 =Globe and Mail+, Toronto, ON	1844
=Herald*, Halifax, NS	1844
=Ottawa Citizen, Ottawa, ON	1844
=Standard-Freeholder, Cornwall, ON	1844
10 =Cambridge Reporter†, Galt, ON	1846
=Spectator, Hamilton, ON	1846

* Still publishing # Originally Yarmouth Herald
+ In 1936, the Globe purchased the Mail and Empire, established in 1872, creating the current national newspaper, the Globe and Mail.
* Originally Chronicle-Herald † Originally Galt Evening Reporter

Source: *Early Canadian Companies, Toronto Public Library*, 1967

TOP 10 ★
COUNTRIES WITH THE MOST NEWSPAPER TITLES PER CAPITA

COUNTRY	DAILY TITLES PER 1,000,000 PEOPLE
1 Uruguay	24.79
2 Norway	18.67
3 Russia	18.00
4 Switzerland	14.74
5 Cyprus	12.27
6 Estonia	11.76
7 Luxembourg	11.48
8 =Iceland	10.87
=Sweden	10.87
10 Finland	10.85

Source: *World Association of Newspapers*

TOP 10 ⚜
MAGAZINES IN CANADA

MAGAZINE	CIRCULATION*
1 Reader's Digest, (Canadian English edition)	1,083,413
2 Chatelaine, (English-language edition)	763,778
3 TV Guide	630,739
4 Canadian Living	551,884
5 Maclean's	503,369
6 Time (Canadian edition)	319,041
7 Séléction du Reader's Digest, (Canadian French edition)	226,533
8 Canadian Geographic	205,488
9 TV Hebdo (French-language edition of TV Guide)	200,672
10 Châtelaine, (French-language edition)	187,913

* Average total paid circulation for most recently reported six month period as of August 2000

Source: *CARD, Media Information Network*

THE 10 ⚜
OLDEST CANADIAN MAGAZINES*

MAGAZINE	FIRST PUBLISHED
1 United Church Observer#	1829
2 =Canadian Entomologist	1868
=Canadian Pharmaceutical Journal	1868
4 =Canadian Mining Journal	1879
=Watchtower	1879
6 Canadian Forest Industries	1880
7 Canadian Textile Journal	1883
8 Canadian Grocer	1886
9 Saturday Night+	1887
10 Hardware Merchandising	1888

* Still publishing; excluding magazines without initial publishing dates # Originally New Outlook; then Christian Guardian + Originally Toronto Saturday Night, 1887–1889

Source: *Canadian Serials Index*

Did You Know? British writer Rudyard Kipling was fired as a reporter on the *San Francisco Examiner*, which told him "You just don't know how to use the English language." In 1907, he won the Nobel Prize for Literature.

Toys & Games

TOY-BUYING COUNTRIES

	COUNTRY*	SPENDING ON TOYS, 2000 (US$)
1	US	34,554,900,000
2	Japan	9,190,600,000
3	UK	5,348,100,000
4	France	3,397,200,000
5	Germany	3,117,900,000
6	Canada	2,689,500,000
7	Italy	1,941,000,000
8	Australia	937,100,000
9	Spain	933,600,000
10	Belgium	754,700,000

* Of those covered by survey

Source: Euromonitor

CHILDREN'S CHOICE TOYS FOR 2001*

	TOY/AGE CATEGORY	MANUFACTURER
1	Bebe Do, 3+	Corolle
2	Jumpstart Phonics Learning System, 3+	Knowledge Adventure
3	Large Carry Bed, 3+	Corolle
4	Little Smart DJ Jazz 'n Jam, 3–6	VTech Electronics Canada
5	Making Faces, 4+	Roylco
6	Non-Stop Girl, 6+	VTech Electronics Canada
7	Lego Championship Challenge, 7+	Lego Canada
8	A Book of Artrageous Projects, 8+	Klutz Inc.
9	Air Hogs Hydro Rockets, 8+	Spin Master
10	=Make Your Own Lip Balm, 8+	Klutz Inc.
	=Roller Coaster Tycoon, 9+	Hasbro Interactive

* Ranked by age category, ages three and older. This award is given to new toys introduced during the year that are "fun, innovative and the absolute best in their area of play."

Source: Canadian Toy Testing Council

TOYS IN THE US BY DOLLAR SALES, 2000

	TOY	MANUFACTURER
1	Hot Wheels basic cars	Mattel
2	Poo-chi robotic dog	Tiger Electronics
3	Leap pad	Leapfrog
4	Barbie cruisin' jeep	Fisher-Price
5	Tekno robot dog	Manley Toy Quest
6	Celebration Barbie	Mattel
7	Pokémon series number 2	Wizards of the Coast
8	Who Wants to be a Millionaire?	Pressman
9	Pokémon rocket booster	Wizards of the Coast
10	Barbie cash register	Kid Designs

Source: NPD TRSTS Toys Tracking Service

MOST LANDED-ON SQUARES IN MONOPOLY®*

US GAME		UK GAME
Illinois Avenue	1	Trafalgar Square
Go	2	Go
B. & O. Railroad	3	Fenchurch Street Station
Free Parking	4	Free Parking
Tennessee Avenue	5	Marlborough Street
New York Avenue	6	Vine Street
Reading Railroad	7	King's Cross Station
St. James Place	8	Bow Street
Water Works	9	Water Works
Pennsylvania Railroad	10	Marylebone Station

* Based on a computer analysis of the probability of landing on each square

Monopoly® is a registered trademark of Parker Brothers division of Tonka Corporation, USA.

MOST EXPENSIVE TEDDY BEARS SOLD AT AUCTION IN THE UK

	BEAR/SALE	PRICE (US$)*
1	"Teddy Girl", Steiff cinnamon teddy bear, 1904, Christie's, London, Dec 5, 1994	169,928 (£110,000)

Formerly owned by Lt-Col Bob Henderson, this sale precisely doubled the previous world record for a teddy bear when it was acquired by Yoshiro Sekiguchi for display at his teddy bear museum near Tokyo.

2	Black mohair Steiff teddy bear, c.1912, Christie's, London, Dec 4, 2000	132,157 (£91,750)

One of a number of black Steiff teddy bears brought out in the UK after the sinking of the Titanic; these have since become known as "mourning" teddies.

3	"Happy", dual-plush Steiff teddy bear, 1926, Sotheby's, London, Sep 19, 1989	85,470 (£55,000)

Although estimated at £700–900, competitive bidding pushed the price up to the then world record, when it was acquired by collector Paul Volpp.

4	"Elliot", blue Steiff bear, 1908, Christie's, London, Dec 6, 1993	74,275 (£49,500)

Produced as a sample for Harrods, but never manufactured commercially.

5	"Teddy Edward", golden mohair teddy bear, Christie's, London, Dec 9, 1996	60,176 (£38,500)
6	Black mohair Steiff teddy bear, c.1912, Sotheby's, London, May 18, 1990 See entry no. 2	45,327 (£24,200)
7	Blank button, brown Steiff teddy bear, c.1905, Christie's, London, Dec 8, 1997	35,948 (£23,000)
8	Black mohair Steiff teddy bear, c.1912, Christie's, London, Dec 5, 1994 See entry no. 2	34,331 (£22,000)
9	"Albert", Steiff teddy bear c.1910, Christie's, London, Dec 9, 1996	28,759 (£18,400)
10	Steiff teddy bear, Christie's, London, Dec 9, 1996	26,962 (£17,250)

* Prices include buyer's premium where appropriate

It is said that, while on a hunting trip, US President Theodore ("Teddy") Roosevelt refused to shoot a young bear. A New York shopkeeper made some stuffed bears and sold them as "Teddy's Bears."

TOP 10 ★
MOST EXPENSIVE TOYS EVER SOLD BY CHRISTIE'S EAST, NY

	TOY/SALE	PRICE (US$)*
1	**The Charles**, a fire hose-reel made by American manufacturer George Brown & Co, c.1875, Dec 1991	231,000
2	**Märklin fire station**, Dec 1991	79,200
3	**Horse-drawn double-decker tram**, Dec 1991	71,500
4	**Mikado mechanical bank**, Dec 1993	63,000
5	**Märklin Ferris wheel**, June 1994	55,200
6	**Girl skipping rope mechanical bank**, June 1994	48,300
7	**Märklin battleship**, June 1994	33,350
8	**Märklin battleship**, June 1994	32,200
9=	**Bing keywind open phaeton tinplate automobile**, Dec 1991	24,200
=	**Märklin fire pumper**, Dec 1991	24,200

* Including 10 percent buyer's premium

The fire hose-reel at No. 1 in this list is the record price paid at auction for a toy other than a doll. Models by the German tinplate maker Märklin, regarded by collectors as the Rolls-Royce of toys, similarly feature among the record prices of auction houses in the UK and other countries, where high prices have also been attained. On both sides of the Atlantic, pristine examples of high quality mechanical toys (ideally in their original boxes, and unplayed with by the children for whom they were designed) command top dollar.

TOP 10 MOST POPULAR TYPES OF TOY
(Type of toy/market share percentage, 1998)

❶ Video games, 21.5 ❷ Activity toys, 13.0 ❸ Infant/pre-school toys, 11.0 ❹ = Dolls, 10.5; = Games/puzzles, 10.5; = Other toys, 10.5 ❼ Toy vehicles, 9.0 ❽ = Action figures, 5.0; = Plush toys, 5.0 ❿ Ride-on toys, 4.0

Source: *Eurotoys/The NPD Group Worldwide*

This list is based on a survey of toy consumption in the European Union and can be taken as a reliable guide to the most popular types of toy in the developed world.

TOP 10 TRADITIONAL TOY RETAILERS IN THE US
(Retailer/type/market share percentage, 1999)

❶ **Wal-Mart**, discount, 17.4 ❷ **Toys R Us**, toy, 15.6 ❸ **Kmart**, discount, 7.2 ❹ **Target**, discount, 6.8 ❺ **KB Toys/Toy Works**, toy, 5.1 ❻ **Ames**, discount, 1.6 ❼ **J.C. Penney**, department, 1.2 ❽ **Hallmark**, card, 1.1 ❾ **Meijer**, discount, 1.0 ❿ **Shopko**, discount, 0.8

Source: *NPD Toy Market Index Service*

TOP 10 ★
INTERACTIVE ENTERTAINMENT SOFTWARE TITLES IN THE US, 2000*

	GAME/FORMAT	PUBLISHER
1	**Pokémon Silver**, Gameboy Color	Nintendo of America
2	**Pokémon Gold**, Gameboy Color	Nintendo of America
3	**Pokémon Yellow**, Gameboy	Nintendo of America
4	**Pokémon Stadium**, Nintendo 64	Nintendo of America
5	**Tony Hawks Pro Skater 2**, Playstation	Activision
6	**Legend Zelda: Majora's Mask**, Nintendo 64	Nintendo of America
7	**Tony Hawks Pro Skater**, Playstation	Activision
8	**Gran Turismo 2**, Playstation	Sony Computer Entertainment
9	**Pokémon Blue**, Gameboy	Nintendo of America
10	**Pokémon Red**, Gameboy	Nintendo of America

* Ranked by units sold

Source: *NPD TRSTS Toys Tracking Service*

TOP 10 🍁
BOARD GAMES IN CANADA, 2000

	GAME*	MANUFACTURER
1	**Monopoly**	Parker Brothers
2	**Yahtzee**	Milton Bradley
3	**Operation**	Milton Bradley
4	**Trouble**	Milton Bradley
5	**Candyland**	Milton Bradley
6	**Twister**	Milton Bradley
7	**Chutes & Ladders**	Milton Bradley
8	**Connect Four**	Milton Bradley
9	**Scrabble**	Milton Bradley
10	**Life**	Milton Bradley

* Includes children's, family, and adult board games

Source: *Hasbro Canada*

Over 200 million Monopoly games have been bought worldwide since 1935. The longest game on record lasted 70 days.

BARBIE

Ruth and Elliot Handler, co-founders of American toy manufacturers Mattel, introduced the first Barbie doll in February 1959. Previously, most dolls were babies, but Ruth Handler had seen her daughter Barbara – who provided the doll's name – playing with paper dolls with adult attributes and realized that there would be a market for a grown-up doll, complete with an extensive wardrobe of clothes and accessories. The first Barbie was dressed in a striped swimsuit, with high heels, sunglasses, and gold hoop earrings. Sold at $3.00 each, 351,000 Barbies were sold in the first year.

Which flower is Newfoundland's official floral emblem?
see p.90 for the answer
A Pitcher plant
B Wild rose
C Purple violet

Art on Show

TOP 10 ★
BEST-ATTENDED ART EXHIBITIONS IN 2000

EXHIBITION/VENUE/CITY	TOTAL VISITORS
1 The Glory of the Golden Age, Rijksmuseum, Amsterdam, Netherlands	594,122
2 Earthly Art–Heavenly Beauty, State Hermitage, St. Petersburg, Russia	570,000*
3 Triumph of the Baroque, National Gallery of Art, Washington, DC, US	526,050
4 Sinai: Byzantium, Russia, State Hermitage, St. Petersburg, Russia	500,000*
5 Picasso's World of Children, National Museum of Western Art, Tokyo, Japan	386,086
6 Seeing Salvation: The Image of Christ, National Gallery, London, UK	355,175
7 Van Gogh: Face to Face, Museum of Fine Arts, Boston, US	316,049
8 Van Gogh: Face to Face, Detroit Institute of Arts, Detroit, US	315,000*
9 Amazons of the Avant-Garde, Guggenheim Museum, Bilbao, Spain	283,181
10 Dutch Art: Rembrandt and Vermeer, Metropolitan Museum of Art, New York, US	280,259

* Approximate total provided by museum

Source: The Art Newspaper

TOP 10 🍁
BEST-ATTENDED EXHIBITIONS AT THE MONTREAL MUSEUM OF FINE ARTS

EXHIBITION/YEAR	ATTENDANCE
1 Pablo Picasso: Meeting in Montreal, 1985	517,000
2 Leonardo da Vinci: Engineer and Architect, 1987	436,419
3 From Renoir to Picasso, 2000	327,644
4 Monet at Giverny, 1999	256,738
5 Marc Chagall, 1988–89	245,883
6 The 1920s: Age of the Metropolis, 1991	245,286
7 The Passionate Eye: Impressionist and Other Master Paintings from the Emil G. Bührle Collection, 1990	201,205
8 Salvador Dali, 1990	192,963
9 Moving Beauty, 1995	184,473
10 Magritte, 1996	163,577

Source: Montreal Museum of Fine Arts

TOP 10 ★
BEST-ATTENDED ART EXHIBITIONS IN NEW YORK, 2000

EXHIBITION	ATTENDANCE
1 Egyptian Art in the Age of the Pyramids, Metropolitan Museum of Art	462,757
2 American Century Part II, Whitney Museum	274,714
3 Rock Style, Metropolitan Museum of Art	248,145
4 Portraits by Ingres: Image of an Epoch, Metropolitan Museum of Art	232,191
5 Walker Evans, Metropolitan Museum of Art	212,487
6 Ancient Faces: Mummy Portraits from Roman Egypt, Metropolitan Museum of Art	186,272
7 Barbara Kruger, Whitney Museum	184,395
8 Chardin, Metropolitan Museum of Art	182,040
9 World of Nam June Paik, Solomon R. Guggenheim	22,078
10 1900: Art at the Crossroads, Solomon R. Guggenheim	20,290

Source: The Art Newspaper

The impressive attendance figures achieved by New York's Guggenheim museum were actually lower than those of the relatively new (1997) Guggenheim in Bilbao, Spain. This list of Manhattan's most popular shows excludes two staged by the Museum of Modern Art, *Modern Starts* and *Making Choices*, which attracted over 4,000 visitors a day, since both were based on the museum's own collections and thus do not constitute temporary exhibitions.

TOP 10 ★
BEST-ATTENDED EXHIBITIONS AT THE NATIONAL GALLERY OF ART, WASHINGTON, DC

EXHIBITION/YEAR	ATTENDANCE
1 Rodin Rediscovered, 1981–82	1,053,223
2 Treasure Houses of Britain, 1985–86	990,474
3 The Treasures of Tutankhamun, 1976–77	835,924
4 Archaeological Finds of the People's Republic of China, 1974–75	684,238
5 Ansel Adams: Classic Images, 1985–86	651,652
6 The Splendor of Dresden, 1978	620,089
7 The Art of Paul Gauguin, 1988	596,058
8 Circa 1492: Art in the Age of Exploration, 1991–92	568,192
9 Andrew Wyeth: The Helga Pictures, 1987	558,433
10 Post Impressionism: Cross Currents in European & American Painting, 1980	557,533

Source: National Gallery of Art

The inhabitants of which province are the least physically active? **A** Quebec
see p.50 for the answer **B** Ontario **C** Alberta

see p.50 for the answer

TOP 10 ★

TALLEST FREESTANDING STATUES

STATUE/LOCATION	HEIGHT FT	M
1 Chief Crazy Horse, Thunderhead Mountain, South Dakota, US	563	172

Started in 1948 by Polish-American sculptor Korczak Ziolkowski and continued after his death in 1982 by his widow and eight of his children, this gigantic equestrian statue is even longer (195 m/641 ft) than it is high. It is being carved out of the granite mountain by dynamiting and drilling, and is not expected to be completed for several more years.

2 Buddha, Tokyo, Japan	394	120

This Japanese-Taiwanese project, unveiled in 1993, took seven years to complete and weighs 1,000 tonnes.

3 The Indian Rope Trick, Riddersberg Säteri, Jönköping, Sweden	337	103

Sculptor Calle Örnemark's 144-tonne wooden sculpture depicts a long strand of "rope" held by a fakir, while another figure ascends.

4 Motherland, Volgograd, Russia	270	82

This concrete statue of a woman with a raised sword, designed by Yevgeniy Vuchetich, commemorates the Soviet victory at the Battle of Stalingrad (1942–43).

5 Kannon, Otsubo-yama, near Tokyo, Japan	170	52

The immense statue of the goddess of mercy was unveiled in 1961 in honor of the dead of World War II.

6 Statue of Liberty, New York, US	151	46

Designed by Auguste Bartholdi and presented to the US by the people of France, the statue was shipped in sections to Liberty (formerly Bedloes) Island, where it was assembled before being unveiled on October 28, 1886.

7 Christ, Rio de Janeiro, Brazil	125	38

The work of sculptor Paul Landowski and engineer Heitor da Silva Costa, the figure of Christ was unveiled in 1931.

8 Tian Tan (Temple of Heaven) Buddha, Po Lin Monastery, Lantau Island, Hong Kong, China	112	34

This statue was completed after 20 years of work and unveiled on December 29, 1993.

9 Quantum Cloud, Greenwich, London, UK	95	29

A gigantic steel human figure surrounded by a matrix of steel struts, it was created in 1999 by Antony Gormley, the sculptor of the similarly gigantic 20-m (66-ft) Angel of the North, Gateshead, UK.

10 Colossi of Memnon, Karnak, Egypt	70	21

This statue portrays two seated sandstone figures of Pharaoh Amenhotep III.

Various projects are in the planning stages, including a 169-m (555-ft) statue of a woman, the Spirit of Houston, and even taller statues of Buddha. If realized, these will enter this Top 10 in the future.

STATUE OF LIBERTY

Originally called "Liberty Enlightening the World," the Statue of Liberty was a gift to the people of the United States of America from France.

TOP 10 ★
MOST EXPENSIVE PAINTINGS EVER SOLD AT AUCTION

PAINTING/ARTIST/SALE	PRICE (US$)
1 *Portrait of Dr. Gachet*, **Vincent van Gogh** (Dutch; 1853–90), Christie's, New York, May 15, 1990	75,000,000
2 *Au Moulin de la Galette*, **Pierre-Auguste Renoir** (French; 1841–1919), Sotheby's, New York, May 17, 1990	71,000,000
3 *Portrait de l'Artiste sans Barbe*, **Vincent van Gogh**, Christie's, New York, Nov 19, 1998	65,000,000
4 *Rideau, Cruchon et Compotier*, **Paul Cézanne** (French; 1839–1906), Sotheby's, New York, May 10, 1999	55,000,000
5 *Les Noces de Pierrette, 1905*, **Pablo Picasso** (Spanish; 1881–1973), Binoche et Godeau, Paris, Nov 30, 1989	51,671,920 (F.Fr315,000,000)
6 *Femme aux Bras Croisés*, **Pablo Picasso**, Christie's Rockefeller, New York, Nov 8, 2000	50,000,000
7 *Irises*, **Vincent van Gogh**, Sotheby's, New York, Nov 11, 1987	49,000,000
8 *Femme Assise dans un Jardin*, **Pablo Picasso**, Sotheby's, New York, Nov 10, 1999	45,000,000
9 *Le Rêve*, **Pablo Picasso**, Christie's, New York, Nov 10, 1997	44,000,000
10 *Self Portrait: Yo Picasso*, **Pablo Picasso**, Sotheby's, New York, May 9, 1989	43,500,000

RAGS TO RICHES

The impoverished van Gogh painted this self-portrait, Portrait de l'Artiste sans Barbe, *at Arles in September 1888. Just over a century later, it realized US$65 million, making it the third most expensive painting ever sold at auction.*

TOP 10 ★
MOST EXPENSIVE PIECES OF SCULPTURE EVER SOLD AT AUCTION

SCULPTURE/ARTIST/SALE	PRICE (US$)
1 *Grande Femme Debout I*, **Alberto Giacometti** (Swiss; 1901–66), Christie's Rockefeller, New York, Nov 8, 2000	13,000,000
2 *La Serpentine Femme à la Stèle – l'Araignée*, **Henri Matisse** (French; 1869–1954), Sotheby's, New York, May 10, 2000	12,750,000
3 *Petite Danseuse de Quatorze Ans*, **Edgar Degas** (French; 1834–1917), Sotheby's, New York, Nov 11, 1999	11,250,000
4 *Petite Danseuse de Quatorze Ans*, **Edgar Degas**, Sotheby's, New York, Nov 12, 1996	10,800,000
5 *Petite Danseuse de Quatorze Ans*, **Edgar Degas**, Sotheby's, London, June 27, 2000	10,222,100 (£7,000,000)
6 *The Dancing Faun*, **Adriaen de Vries** (Dutch; c.1550–1626), Sotheby's, London, Dec 7, 1989	9,634,800 (£6,200,000)
7 *Petite Danseuse de Quatorze Ans*, **Edgar Degas**, Christie's, New York, Nov 14, 1988	9,250,000
8 *Petite Danseuse de Quatorze Ans*, **Edgar Degas**, Sotheby's, New York, May 10, 1988	9,200,000
9 *Nu Couché, Aurore*, **Henri Matisse**, Christie's Rockefeller, New York, Nov 9, 1999	8,400,000
10 *La Muse Endormie III*, **Constantin Brancusi** (Romanian; 1876–1957), Christie's, New York, Nov 14, 1989	7,500,000

TOP 10 🍁
MOST EXPENSIVE CANADIAN PAINTINGS EVER SOLD AT AUCTION

PAINTING/ARTIST/SALE	PRICE ($)
1 *Untitled (1955)*, **Jean-Paul Riopelle**, May 5, 1989	1,610,000
2 *Lake Superior III*, **Lawren Harris**, June 1, 1999	960,000
3 *War Canoes, Alert Bay*, **Emily Carr**, May 10, 2000	925,000
4 *Untitled (1950)*, **Jean-Paul Riopelle**, Nov 30, 1989	798,000
5 *Untitled*, **Jean-Paul Riopelle**, May 22, 1991	700,000
6 *L'Autriche*, **Jean-Paul Riopelle**, June 29, 1989	532,000
7 *Lake, North Labrador*, **Lawren Harris**, May 24, 2000	525,000
8 *Bull Ring, Marseilles*, **James Morrice**, May 26, 1995	520,000
9 *Portrait of Maungwudaus*, **Paul Kane**, June 2, 1999	475,000
10 *Filets Frontiere*, **Jean-Paul Riopelle**, June 30, 1988	462,000

Source: Canadian Art Sales Index, *Westbridge Publications, BC*

Which exhibition was the best attended at the Montreal Museum of Fine Arts?
see p.116 for the answer
A Monet at Giverny
B Salvador Dali
C Pablo Picasso: Meeting in Montreal

MOST EXPENSIVE OLD MASTER PAINTINGS EVER SOLD AT AUCTION

PAINTING/ARTIST/SALE	PRICE (US$)

1 *Portrait of Duke Cosimo I de Medici*, **Jacopo da Carucci (Pontormo)**
(Italian; 1493–1558), Christie's,
New York, May 31, 1989 — 32,000,000

2 *The Old Horse Guards, London, from St. James's Park*, **Canaletto**
(Italian; 1697–1768), Christie's, — 16,008,000
London, Apr 15, 1992 — (£9,200,000)

3 *Vue de la Giudecca et du Zattere à Venise*, **Francesco Guardi**
(Italian; 1712–93), Sotheby's, — 13,943,218
Monaco, Dec 1, 1989 — (F.Fr85,000,000)

4 *Venus and Adonis*, **Titian**
(Italian; c.1488–1576), Christie's, — 12,376,000
London, Dec 13, 1991 — (£6,800,000)

5 *Tieleman Roosterman in Black Doublet, White Ruff*, **Frans Hals the Elder**
(Dutch; c.1580–1666), Christie's, — 11,625,001
London, July 8, 1999 — (£7,500,000)

6 *Le Retour du Bucentaure le Jour de l'Ascension*, **Canaletto**, Ader Tajan, — 11,316,457
Paris, Dec 15, 1993 — (F.Fr66,000,000)

7 *The Risen Christ*, **Michelangelo**
(Italian; 1475–1564), Christie's, — 11,174,001
London, July 4, 2000 — (£7,400,000)

8 *View of Molo from Bacino di San Marco, Venice* and *View of the Grand Canal Facing East from Campo di Santi, Venice* (pair), **Canaletto**, Sotheby's,
New York, June 1, 1990 — 10,000,000

9 *Adoration of the Magi*, **Andrea Mantegna**
(Italian; 1431–1506), Christie's, — 9,525,000
London, Apr 18, 1985 — (£7,500,000)

10 *Portrait of a Girl Wearing a Gold-trimmed Cloak*, **Rembrandt**
(Dutch; 1606–69), Sotheby's, — 9,372,000
London, Dec 10, 1986 — (£6,600,000)

PRICEY PRE-RAPHAELITE

Although popular in their day, the Pre-Raphaelites fell out of favor until the late 20th century, when works such as Sleeping *by Sir John Everett Millais began to command record prices.*

MOST EXPENSIVE PRE-RAPHAELITE PAINTINGS EVER SOLD AT AUCTION

PAINTING/ARTIST*/SALE	PRICE (US$)

1 *St. Cecilia*, **John William Waterhouse** (1849–1917), — 9,060,001
Christie's, London, June 14, 2000 (£6,000,000)

2 *Pandora*, **Dante Gabriel Rossetti** (1828–82), Christie's, — 3,624,000
London, June 14, 2000 — (£2,400,000)

3 *Sleeping*, **Sir John Everett Millais** (1829–96), Christie's, — 3,040,000
London, June 10, 1999 — (£1,900,000)

4 *The Shadow of Death*, **William Holman Hunt**,
(1827–1910), Sotheby's, — 2,720,000
London, Nov 2, 1994 — (£1,700,000)

5 *Proserpine*, **Dante Gabriel Rossetti**, Christie's, — 2,366,000
London, Nov 27, 1987 — (£1,300,000)

PAINTING/ARTIST*/SALE	PRICE (US$)

6 *Ophelia*, **John William Waterhouse**, Phillips, — 2,265,000
London, June 14, 2000 — (£1,500,000)

7 *The Awakening of Adonis*, **John William Waterhouse**, Sotheby's, New York,
Nov 10, 1998 — 2,125,000

8= *Val d'Aosta*, **John Brett**
(1830–1902), Sotheby's, — 1,932,000
London, June 20, 1989 — (£1,200,000)

= *Joan of Arc*, **Sir John Everett Millais**, Sotheby's, London, — 1,848,000
Nov 10, 1999 — (£1,200,000)

10 *Master Hilary – The Tracer*, **William Holman Hunt**, — 1,320,000
Christie's, London, June 3, 1994 (£880,000)

* All British

20th-Century Artists

TOP 10 ★
MOST EXPENSIVE WORKS BY ALEXANDER CALDER

MOBILE OR SCULPTURE/SALE	PRICE (US$)
1 Brazilian Fish, Sotheby's, New York, Nov 17, 1999	3,550,000
2 The Tree, Selkirks, St. Louis, May 22, 1989	1,900,000
3 Constellation, Sotheby's, New York, May 18, 1999	1,800,000
4 Constellation, Sotheby's, New York, Nov 10, 1993	1,650,000
5 Trépied, Sotheby's, New York, May 18, 1999	1,400,000
6 Eighteen Numbered Black, Sotheby's, New York, Nov 17, 1998	1,150,000
7 Mobile au Plomb, Christie's, London, June 28, 2000	1,087,000 (£720,000)
8 Haverford Monster, Sotheby's, New York, May 4, 1994	980,000
9 =Laocoon, Christie's, New York, Nov 14, 1995	900,000
=Hanging Apricot, Christie's Rockefeller, New York, May 13, 1999	900,000

TOP 10 🍁
MOST EXPENSIVE PAINTINGS BY JEAN-PAUL RIOPELLE

PAINTING/SALE	PRICE ($)
1 Untitled (1955), May 5, 1989	1,610,000
2 Untitled (1950), Nov 30, 1989	798,000
3 Untitled, May 22, 1991	700,000
4 L'Autriche, June 29, 1989	532,000
5 Filets Frontiere, June 30, 1988	462,000
6 ...et plus..., Nov 30, 1989	456,000
7 Tryptique, May 11, 1994	420,000
8 Composition, May 15, 1990	380,000
9 Composition 1953, Oct 16, 1990	375,000
10 Le Reveil, Nov 30, 1989	361,000

Source: Canadian Art Sales Index, *Westbridge Publications, BC*

Born in 1923 in Montreal, Jean-Paul Riopelle is considered by many to be the leading Canadian abstract painter of his generation. In the late 1940s, he studied painting in Paris, where he was influenced by Joan Miró and André Breton. Riopelle uses his unusual technique of literally throwing paint onto canvas, then cutting through it with a spatula, to create Surrealist masterpieces.

TOP 10 ★
MOST EXPENSIVE PAINTINGS BY PABLO PICASSO

PAINTING/SALE	PRICE (US$)
1 Les Noces de Pierrette, 1905, Binoche et Godeau, Paris, Nov 30, 1989	51,671,920 (F.Fr315,000,000)
2 Femme aux Bras Croisés, Christie's Rockefeller, New York, Nov 8, 2000	50,000,000
3 Femme Assise dans un Jardin, Sotheby's, New York, Nov 10, 1999	45,000,000
4 Le Rêve, Christie's, New York, Nov 10, 1997	44,000,000
5 Self Portrait: Yo Picasso, Sotheby's, New York, May 9, 1989	43,500,000
6 Nu au Fauteuil Noir, Christie's Rockefeller, New York, Nov 9, 1999	41,000,000
7 Au Lapin Agile, Sotheby's, New York, Nov 15, 1989	37,000,000
8 Acrobate et Jeune Arlequin, Christie's, London, Nov 28, 1988	35,530,000 (£19,000,000)
9 Les Femmes d'Alger, Version O, Christie's, New York, Nov 10, 1997	29,000,000
10 Angel Fernandez de Soto, Sotheby's, New York, May 8, 1995	26,500,000

TOP 10 ★
MOST EXPENSIVE PAINTINGS BY MARC CHAGALL

PAINTING/SALE	PRICE (US$)
1 Anniversaire, Sotheby's, New York, May 17, 1990	13,500,000
2 Au Dessus de la Ville, Christie's, New York, May 15, 1990	9,000,000
3 Le Village Russe de la Lune, Sotheby's, New York, Nov 11, 1999	7,500,000
4 La Mariée sous le Baldaquin, Sotheby's, London, Apr 3, 1990	5,542,000 (£3,400,000)
5 =Le Buveur – Le Saoul, Christie's, New York, Nov 14, 1990	5,000,000
=La Chambre Jaune, Christie's Rockefeller, New York, Nov 9, 1999	5,000,000
7 Le Bouquet des Fermiers, Sotheby's, London, Apr 3, 1990	4,564,000 (£2,800,000)
8 Two Bouquets, Sotheby's, New York, May 17, 1990	4,400,000
9 Le Violoniste au Monde Renversé, Habsburg, New York, May 8, 1989	4,200,000
10 Les Amoureux, Sotheby's, London, June 24, 1996	3,850,000 (£2,500,000)

Did You Know? Alexander Calder's *White Cascade* mobile, installed in Philadelphia, PA, in 1976, is one of the biggest works of art ever constructed: it is 30.5 m (100 ft) tall and weighs 8.9 tonnes.

TOP 10 ⭐

MOST EXPENSIVE PAINTINGS BY FRANCIS BACON

	PAINTING/SALE	PRICE (US$)
1	*Triptych May–June*, Sotheby's, New York, May 2, 1989	5,700,000
2	*Study for Portrait of van Gogh II*, Sotheby's, New York, May 2, 1989	5,300,000
3	*Study for Pope*, Christie's, New York, Nov 7, 1989	5,200,000
4	*Study for Portrait*, Sotheby's, New York, May 8, 1990	5,000,000
5	*Study for a Portrait – Man Screaming*, Christie's, London, June 28, 2000	4,077,000 (£2,700,000)
6	*Portrait of George Dyer Staring into Mirror*, Christie's, New York, Nov 7, 1990	3,500,000
7	*Portrait of Lucian Freud*, Sotheby's, New York, Nov 8, 1989	3,300,000
8	*Study for Portrait VIII, 1953*, Sotheby's, London, Dec 5, 1991	3,258,000 (£1,800,000)
9	*Turning Figure*, Sotheby's, New York, Nov 8, 1989	3,000,000
10	*Studies for Self-Portrait*, Christie's, London, June 30, 1999	2,686,000 (£1,700,000)

TOP 10 ⭐

MOST EXPENSIVE WORKS BY JASPER JOHNS

	WORK/SALE	PRICE (US$)
1	*False Start*, Sotheby's, New York, Nov 10, 1988	15,500,000
2	*Two Flags*, Christie's Rockefeller, New York, May 13, 1999	6,500,000
3	*Jubilee*, Sotheby's, New York, Nov 13, 1991	4,500,000
4	*Device Circle*, Christie's, New York, Nov 12, 1991	4,000,000
5	*Alphabets*, Sotheby's, New York, May 2, 1989	2,600,000
6	*0 Through 9*, Christie's, New York, Nov 18, 1992	2,100,000
7	*Double Flag*, Sotheby's, New York, Dec 11, 1986	1,600,000
8	*Screen Piece II*, Sotheby's, New York, Nov 10, 1988	1,250,000
9	*Screen Piece No. 3, The Sonnets*, Sotheby's, New York, Nov 1, 1994	600,000
10	*Untitled*, Christie's, New York, May 4, 1993	550,000

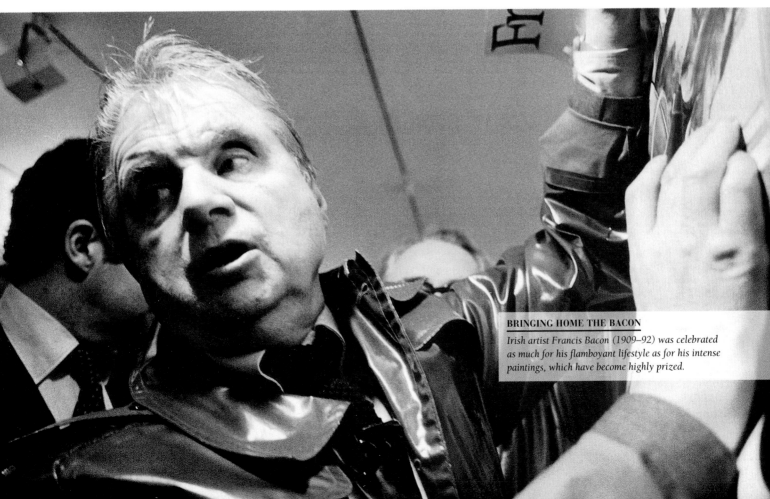

BRINGING HOME THE BACON
Irish artist Francis Bacon (1909–92) was celebrated as much for his flamboyant lifestyle as for his intense paintings, which have become highly prized.

GEORGIA ON MY MIND

Georgia O'Keeffe (1887–1986), who specialized in richly colored paintings of plants and natural forms, is ranked high in the pantheon of 20th-century American painters.

TOP 10 ★
MOST EXPENSIVE PAINTINGS BY FRIDA KAHLO

PAINTING/SALE	PRICE (US$)
1 **Autoretrato con Chango y Loro**, Sotheby's, New York, May 17, 1995	2,900,000
2 **Autorretrato con Pelo Suelto**, Christie's, New York, May 15, 1991	1,500,000
3 **Diego and I**, Sotheby's, New York, May 2, 1990	1,300,000
4 **Recuerdo**, Christie's, New York, May 18, 1992	850,000
5 **Los Cuatro Habitantes de Mexico**, Sotheby's, New York, May 14, 1996	800,000
6 **Parade in a Street in Detroit**, Gary Nader, Miami, Jan 23, 2000	750,000
7 **La Tierra Misma o Dos Desnudos en la Jungla**, Christie's, New York, Nov 21, 1989	460,000
8 **What the Water Gave Me**, Sotheby's, New York, Nov 29, 1983	235,000
9 **Ella Juega Sola o Nina con Mascara de la Muerte**, Christie's, New York, Nov 21, 1989	220,000
10 **Moses**, Sotheby's, New York, Nov 26, 1985	210,000

TOP 10 ★
MOST EXPENSIVE PAINTINGS BY GEORGIA O'KEEFFE

PAINTING/SALE	PRICE (US$)
1 **From the Plains**, Sotheby's, New York, Dec 3, 1997	3,300,000
2 **Calla Lily with Red Roses**, Sotheby's, New York, May 20, 1998	2,400,000
3 **Black Hollyhocks with Blue Larkspur**, Sotheby's, New York, Dec 3, 1987	1,800,000
4 **Dark Iris, No. 2**, Sotheby's, New York, May 24, 1989	1,500,000
5 **At the Rodeo, New Mexico**, Sotheby's, New York, Dec 3, 1987	1,430,000
6 **Yellow Cactus Flowers**, Sotheby's, New York, May 24, 1989	1,200,000
7 **White Rose, New Mexico**, Sotheby's, New York, Dec 5, 1985	1,150,000
8 =**Ritz Tower, Night**, Christie's, New York, Dec 4, 1992	1,100,000
=**Two Jimson Weeds**, Sotheby's, New York, Dec 3, 1987	1,100,000
10 =**Black Iris II – Black Iris VI**, Christie's, New York, May 21, 1998	1,000,000
=**Cow's Skull on Red**, Christie's, New York, Nov 30, 1994	1,000,000
=**Red Poppy, No. VI**, Christie's, New York, May 23, 1990	1,000,000
=**Slightly Open Clam Shell**, Christie's, New York, Dec 4, 1997	1,000,000

TOP 10 🍁
MOST EXPENSIVE PAINTINGS BY EMILY CARR

PAINTING/SALE	PRICE ($)
1 **War Canoes, Alert Bay**, May 10, 2000	925,000
2 **In a Circle**, Nov 25, 1987	270,000
3 **The Path**, Nov 17, 1999	265,000
4 **Thunderbird**, Nov 25, 1987	160,000
5 **British Columbia, Forest Interior**, May 24, 2000	145,000
6 **Alert Bay**, May 31, 1990	120,000
7 **Summer, Mount Douglas, No. 12**, Nov 20, 1990	105,000
8 **Kispiox**, Nov 24, 1992	90,000
9 **Swirl**, Nov 8, 1988	82,500
10 **Sea and Sky**, Nov 8, 1988	75,000

Source: Canadian Art Sales Index, *Westbridge Publications, BC*

Emily Carr (1871–1945) was born in Victoria, BC. Early paintings of Indian villages and totem poles, rendered in a Post-Impressionist style, served as a record of disappearing Native cultures. At age 57, Carr met Lawren Harris and other members of the Group of Seven, who greatly influenced her later works. Indian themes were replaced by scenes of nature in her home province – particularly those of forests and beaches. After a heart attack in 1932, Carr devoted her time to writing.

Mexican painter Frida Kahlo (1907–54) overcame disabilities resulting from childhood polio and a car accident to become a talented artist whose work was much revered by the Surrealists. She was married to the artist Diego Rivera, and their turbulent life together (they divorced in 1939 and married again the following year) and Kahlo's personal joys and suffering are revealed in her vivid, often autobiographical paintings.

Did You Know? In 1947, Madame Claude Latour was convicted of producing forgeries of paintings by Pablo Picasso and Maurice Utrillo that were so skillful that Utrillo himself could not tell which were his and which she had painted.

TOP 10 ★

MOST EXPENSIVE PAINTINGS BY BERTHE MORISOT

PAINTING/SALE	PRICE (US$)
1 *Cache-cache*, Sotheby's, New York, Nov 9, 2000	4,000,000
2 *Cache-cache*, Sotheby's, New York, May 10, 1999	3,500,000
3 *Après le Déjeuner*, Christie's, New York, May 14, 1997	3,250,000
4 *La Femme au Gant, ou La Parisienne*, Sotheby's, New York, Nov 16, 1998	1,500,000
5 *Derrière la Jalousie*, Sotheby's, New York, May 10, 2000	1,200,000
6 *Le Thé*, Sotheby's, New York, May 9, 1995	1,150,000
7 =*Derrière la Jalousie*, Christie's, New York, May 5, 1998	1,100,000
=*Fillettes à la Fenêtre, Jeanne et Edma Bodeau*, Christie's, New York, Nov 11, 1997	1,100,000
9 *Julie Manet à la Perruche*, Sotheby's, New York, May 17, 1990	950,000
10 *La Leçon au Jardin*, Christie's, New York, May 10, 1989	900,000

Berthe Morisot (1841–95) was a French Impressionist painter who was closely associated with the leading figures in the movement (and married to Manet's brother). Landscapes and women and children chiefly feature in her work, which has commanded escalating prices in the world's salesrooms.

THERE'S SOMETHING ABOUT MARY

Five paintings by Mary Cassatt, including her Mother, Sara and the Baby, *are numbered among the 10 highest-priced paintings by a woman.*

TOP 10 ★

MOST EXPENSIVE PAINTINGS BY WOMEN ARTISTS EVER SOLD AT AUCTION

PAINTING/ARTIST/SALE	PRICE (US$)	PAINTING/ARTIST/SALE	PRICE (US$)
1 *The Conversation*, Mary Cassatt (American; 1844–1926), Christie's, New York, May 11, 1988	4,100,000	**6** *From the Plains*, Georgia O'Keeffe (American; 1887–1986), Sotheby's, New York, Dec 3, 1997	3,300,000
2 *Cache-cache*, Berthe Morisot (French; 1841–95), Sotheby's, New York, Nov 9, 2000	4,000,000	**7** *Après le Déjeuner*, Berthe Morisot, Christie's, New York, May 14, 1997	3,250,000
3 *In the Box*, Mary Cassatt, Christie's, New York, May 23, 1996	3,700,000	**8** *Autoretrato con Chango y Loro*, Frida Kahlo (Mexican; 1907–54), Sotheby's, New York, May 17, 1995	2,900,000
4 =*Cache-cache*, Berthe Morisot, Sotheby's, New York, May 10, 1999	3,500,000	**9** *Augusta Reading to Her Daughter*, Mary Cassatt, Sotheby's, New York, May 9, 1989	2,800,000
=*Mother, Sara and the Baby*, Mary Cassatt, Christie's, New York, May 10, 1989	3,500,000	**10** *Children Playing with Cat*, Mary Cassatt, Sotheby's, New York, Dec 3, 1998	2,700,000

Objects of Desire

TOP 10 ★
MOST EXPENSIVE ITEMS OF AMERICAN FURNITURE

ITEM/SALE	PRICE (US$)
1 The Nicholas Brown Chippendale mahogany block and shell desk and bookcase, c.1760–70, attributed to John Goddard, Christie's, New York, June 3, 1989	12,100,000
2 Richard Edwards Chippendale carved mahogany pier table, by Thomas Tufft, c.1775–76, Christie's, New York, Jan 20, 1990	4,620,000
3 The Samuel Whitehorne Queen Anne block-and-shell carved mahogany kneehole desk, attributed to Edmund Townsend, c.1780, Sotheby's, New York, Jan 20, 1996	3,632,500
4 Chippendale carved mahogany tea table, c.1760–80, Christie's, New York, May 28, 1987	2,422,500
5 The Edwards-Harrison family Chippendale carved mahogany high chest-of-drawers, dressing table and pair of side chairs, by Thomas Tufft, c.1775–76, Christie's, New York, May 28, 1987	1,760,000
6 The Edward Jackson parcel gilt inlaid and figured mahogany mirrored bonnet-top secretary bookcase, c.1738–48, Sotheby's, New York, Jan 20, 1996	1,432,500
7 Cornelius Stevenson Chippendale carved mahogany tea table, attributed to Thomas Affleck, carving attributed to Nicholas Bernard & Martin Jugiez, c.1760–80, Christie's, New York, Jan 20, 1990	1,210,000
8 Chippendale carved mahogany tea table, c.1760–80, Christie's, New York, Jan 25, 1986	1,045,000
9 Chipppendale carved mahogany tea table, c.1770, Christie's, New York, Jan 26, 1995	695,500
10 Chippendale mahogany block front and shell-carved kneehole desk, c.1760–85, Christie's, New York, June 2, 1983	627,000

TOP 10 ★
MOST EXPENSIVE PRINTS

PRINT/ARTIST/SALE	PRICE (US$)
1 Diehard, Robert Rauschenberg (American; 1925–), Sotheby's, New York, May 2, 1989	1,600,000
2 Mao, Andy Warhol (American; 1928–87), Sotheby's, London, June 26, 1996	939,400 (£610,000)
3 Famille Tahitienne, Paul Gauguin (French; 1848–1903), Francis Briest, Paris, Dec 4, 1998	806,922 (F.Fr4,545,010)
4 Elles*, Henri de Toulouse-Lautrec (French; 1864–1901), Sotheby's, New York, May 10, 1999	800,000
5 Glider, Robert Rauschenberg, Christie's, New York, Nov 14, 1995	750,000
6 The Kiss – Bela Lugosi, Andy Warhol, Christie's Rockefeller, New York, May 9, 2000	720,000
7 Elles*, Henri de Toulouse-Lautrec, Sotheby's, New York, Nov 7, 1997	695,000
8 =La Suite Vollard, Pablo Picasso (Spanish; 1881–1973), Christie's, New York, Nov 2, 1999	650,000
=Suicide, Andy Warhol, Sotheby's, New York, May 18, 1999	650,000
10 Head of Marilyn Monroe, Andy Warhol, Beijers, Stockholm, May 21, 1990	640,525 (SKR 3,900,000)

* A collection of 10 lithographs

Included within the classification of prints are silkscreens, lithographs, monotypes, aquatints, woodcuts, engravings, and etchings.

TOP 10 ★
MOST EXPENSIVE PHOTOGRAPHS

PHOTOGRAPH/PHOTOGRAPHER/SALE	PRICE (US$)
1 Egypte et Nubie: Sites et monuments les plus intéressants pour l'étude de l'art et de l'histoire* (1858), **Félix Teynard** (French; 1817–92), Laurin Guilloux Buffetaud Tailleur, Paris, Dec 21, 1990	707,000 (F.Fr3,700,000)
2 The North American Indian* (1907–30), **Edward S. Curtis** (American; 1868–1952), Sotheby's, New York, Oct 7, 1993	662,500
3 Noire et Blanche (1926), **Man Ray** (American; 1890–1976), Christie's, New York, Oct 4, 1998	607,500
4 Light Trap for Henry Moore No. 1, Bruce Nauman (American; 1941–), Sotheby's, New York, May 17, 2000	480,000
5 The North American Indian* (1907–30), **Edward S. Curtis**, Christie's, New York, Apr 6, 1995	464,500
6 Georgia O'Keeffe: A Portrait – Hands with Thimble (1930), **Alfred Stieglitz** (American; 1864–1946), Christie's, New York, Oct 8, 1993	398,500
7 =Equivalents (21)* (1920s), **Alfred Stieglitz**, Christie's, New York, Oct 30, 1989	396,000
=The North American Indian* (1907–30), **Edward S. Curtis**, Christie's, New York, Oct 13, 1992	396,000
9 Arrival of the Body of Admiral Bruat and Flagship Montebello at Toulon (1855), **Gustave le Gray** (French; 1820–82), Bearnes, Exeter, May 6, 2000	380,000 (£250,000)
10 Mondrian's Pipe and Glasses (1926), **André Kertész** (Hungarian-American; 1894–1985), Christie's, New York, Apr 17, 1997	376,500

* Collections; all others are single prints

LENNON'S LIMO
Repainted in 1967, John Lennon's Rolls-Royce was eventually donated to Queen Elizabeth and is preserved by the Royal British Columbia Museum in Victoria, British Columbia.

TOP 10 ★
MOST EXPENSIVE MUSICAL INSTRUMENTS

INSTRUMENT*/SALE	PRICE (US$)
1 John Lennon's Steinway Model Z upright piano (on which he composed *Imagine*), teak veneered, complete with cigarette burns, Fleetwood-Owen online auction, Hard Rock Café, London and New York, Oct 17, 2000	2,150,000
2 "Kreutzer" violin by Antonio Stradivari, Christie's, London, Apr 1, 1998	1,582,847 (£946,000)
3 "Cholmondeley" violincello by Antonio Stradivari, Sotheby's, London, June 22, 1998	1,141,122 (£682,000)
4 "Brownie," one of Eric Clapton's favorite guitars, Christie's, New York, June 24, 1999	497,500

Clapton used the 1956 sunburst Fender to record his definitive guitar track, Layla. It was sold to an anonymous telephone bidder for double the expected price, making it the most expensive guitar ever bought at auction.

5 Jimi Hendrix's Fender *Stratocaster* electric guitar, Sotheby's, London, Apr 25, 1990	370,854 (£198,000)
6 Double bass by Domenico Montagnana, Sotheby's, London, Mar 16, 1999	250,339 (£155,500)
7 Verne Powell's platinum flute, Christie's, New York, Oct 18, 1986	187,000
8 English double-manual harpsichord by Burkat Shudi and John Broadwood, Sotheby's, London, Oct 27, 1999	170,649 (£106,000)
9 Viola by Giovanni Paolo Maggini, Christie's, London, Nov 20, 1984	161,121 (£129,000)
10 Bundfrei clavichord by Marcus Gabriel Sondermann, late 18th/early 19th century, Sotheby's, London, Nov 16, 2000	29,370 (£20,625)

* *Most expensive example only for each category of instrument*

TOP 10 ★
MOST EXPENSIVE ITEMS OF POP MEMORABILIA

ITEM/SALE	PRICE (US$)*
1 John Lennon's 1965 Rolls-Royce Phantom V touring limousine, finished in psychedelic paintwork, Sotheby's, New York, June 29, 1985	2,299,000
2 John Lennon's Steinway Model Z upright piano (on which he composed *Imagine*), teak veneered, complete with cigarette burns, Fleetwood-Owen online auction, Hard Rock Café, London and New York, Oct 17, 2000	2,150,000
3 "Brownie," one of Eric Clapton's favorite guitars (on which he recorded *Layla*), Christie's, New York, June 24, 1999	497,500
4 Bernie Taupin's handwritten lyrics for the rewritten *Candle in the Wind*, Christie's, Los Angeles, Feb 11, 1998	400,000
5 Jimi Hendrix's Fender *Stratocaster* electric guitar, which he played at Woodstock in 1969, Sotheby's, London, Apr 25, 1990	370,260 (£198,000)
6 Paul McCartney's handwritten lyrics for *Getting Better*, 1967, Sotheby's, London, Sep 14, 1995	251,643 (£161,000)
7 Buddy Holly's Gibson acoustic guitar, *c.*1945, in a tooled leather case made by Holly, Sotheby's, New York, June 23, 1990	242,000
8 John Lennon's 1970 Mercedes-Benz 600 Pullman four-door limousine, Christie's, London, Apr 27, 1989	213,125 (£137,500)
9 John Lennon's 1965 Ferrari 330 GT 2+2 two-door coupe, right-hand drive, Fleetwood-Owen online auction, Hard Rock Café, London and New York, Oct 17, 2000	190,750
10 Mal Evan's notebook, compiled 1967–68, which includes a draft by Paul McCartney of the lyrics for *Hey Jude*, Sotheby's, London, Sep 15, 1998	185,202 (£111,500)

* *Including 10 percent buyer's premium, where appropriate*

What was the nationality of the painter Frida Kahlo?   A German
see p.122 for the answer   B Mexican
C Canadian

MUSIC & MUSICIANS

Popular Songs

CANADIAN HITS COMPOSED BY SARAH MCLACHLAN*

	TITLE	YEAR
1	Building a Mystery	1997
2	Adia	1998
3	Sweet Surrender	1998
4	Angel	1999
5	I Will Remember You (Live)	1999
6	Good Enough	1994
7	I Will Remember You	1995
8	Silence	1999
9	Possession	1993
10	Into the Fire	1991

* All songs recorded by Sarah McLachlan, except No. 8, which was recorded by Delirium

Source: *Music Data Research*

Even though Sarah McLachlan has been recording since 1988, she became a pop music superstar only in the late 1990s. The top three hits are from her 1997 No. 1 album *Surfacing*.

CANADIAN HITS COMPOSED BY BRYAN ADAMS*

	TITLE	YEAR
1	(Everything I Do) I Do It For You	1991
2	Christmas Time	1985
3	Can't Stop This Thing We Started	1991
4	Heat of the Night	1987
5	Heaven	1985
6	Run to You	1985
7	Have You Ever Really Loved a Woman?	1995
8	Please Forgive Me	1993
9	The Only Thing That Looks Good On Me Is You	1996
10	Thought I'd Died and Gone to Heaven	1992

* All songs recorded by Bryan Adams

Source: *Music Data Research*

CANADIAN HITS COMPOSED BY BRUCE SPRINGSTEEN*

	TITLE	YEAR
1	Dancing in the Dark	1984
2	Pink Cadillac#	1988
3	My Hometown	1986
4	Streets of Philadelphia	1994
5	Hungry Heart	1980
6	Human Touch	1992
7	Fire+	1979
8	Brilliant Disguise	1987
9	I'm Goin' Down	1985
10	Born in the USA	1985

* Recorded by Bruce Springsteen unless otherwise noted

Recorded by Natalie Cole

+ Recorded by the Pointer Sisters

Source: *Music Data Research*

Bruce Springsteen, born in New Jersey in 1949, began his music career playing in local clubs during the 1960s. In 1972 he formed the E-Street Band, with which he performed until 1989.

CANADIAN HITS COMPOSED BY GEORGE MICHAEL*

	TITLE	YEAR
1	Wake Me Up Before You Go-Go#	1984
2	Careless Whisper+	1985
3	Faith	1987
4	I Want Your Sex	1987
5	Everything She Wants#	1985
6	I'm Your Man#	1986
7	Praying for Time	1990
8	Freedom	1991
9	One More Try	1998
10	A Different Corner	1986

* Recorded by George Michael unless otherwise noted

Recorded by Wham!

+ Recorded by Wham! featuring George Michael

CANADIAN HITS COMPOSED BY PRINCE*

	TITLE	YEAR
1	When Doves Cry	1984
2	Batdance	1989
3	Cream#	1991
4	I Feel for You+	1984
5	7#	1993
6	Purple Rain★	1984
7	Kiss★	1986
8	Let's Go Crazy★	1984
9	My Name is Prince	1992
10	Little Red Corvette	1983

* Recorded by Prince unless otherwise noted

Recorded by Prince & the New Power Generation

+ Recorded by Chaka Khan

★ Recorded by Prince and the Revolution

Topping the list of Prince compositions is *When Doves Cry*, a recording whose rhythm track was used on the 1990 hit *Pray* by Hammer. *Pray* was never released as a single and subsequently did not appear on the sales chart. However, it did hit No. 7 on the radio airplay chart. In 1993, Prince, born Prince Rogers Nelson, changed his name to an unpronounceable symbol combining both male and female symbols.

♦ TOP 10 SINGER-SONGWRITERS IN CANADA

1 Elton John **2** Bryan Adams **3** Prince **4** John Cougar Mellencamp **5** Phil Collins **6** Billy Joel **7** Paul McCartney **8** George Michael **9** Michael Bolton **10** Lionel Richie

Based on an analysis of consistent Canadian singles chart success, these are the artists whose songs were largely or entirely self-penned. However, Elton John's recordings include those that he wrote with long-time collaborator, lyricist Bernie Taupin. Bryan Adams' 1984 album *Reckless*, cowritten with Jim Vallance, Adams' songwriting partner from 1978 to 1989, was the first Canadian album to receive a Diamond award from the Canadian Recording Industry Association for sales of one million copies.

TOP 10 🍁
CANADIAN HITS COMPOSED BY DIANE WARREN

	TITLE/YEAR	RECORDING ARTIST
1	Nothing's Gonna Stop Us Now (1987)	Starship
2	Blame It On the Rain (1990)	Milli Vanilli
3	Because You Loved Me (1996)	Celine Dion
4	Unbreak My Heart (1997)	Toni Braxton
5	How Do I Live (1997)	Leann Rimes
6	Love Will Lead You Back (1990)	Taylor Dayne
7	Rhythm of the Night (1985)	DeBarge
8	I'll Be Your Shelter (1990)	Taylor Dayne
9	If You Asked Me To (1992)	Celine Dion
10	How Can We Be Lovers (1990)	Michael Bolton

Source: *Music Data Research*

Although American Diane Warren may not be a household name, she just might be one of the most prolific songwriters of our time. Her ballads have been performed by a diverse array of artists, from Celine Dion to Aerosmith.

THE 10 ★
LATEST GRAMMY SONGS OF THE YEAR

YEAR	SONG/SONGWRITER
2000	Beautiful Day, U2
1999	Smooth, Itaal Shur and Rob Thomas
1998	My Heart Will Go On, James Horner and Will Jennings
1997	Sunny Came Home, Shawn Colvin
1996	Change the World, Gordon Kennedy, Wayne Kirkpatrick, and Tommy Sims
1995	Kiss From a Rose, Seal
1994	Streets of Philadelphia, Bruce Springsteen
1993	A Whole New World, Alan Menken and Tim Rice
1992	Tears in Heaven, Eric Clapton
1991	Unforgettable, Irving Gordon

THE 10 🍁
LAST JUNO AWARD-WINNING SONGWRITERS OF THE YEAR

YEAR	ARTIST
2001	Nelly Furtado
2000	Shania Twain/Robert John "Mutt" Lange
1999	Bryan Adams/ Phil Thornally and Eliot Kennedy
1998	Sarah McLachlan/Pierre Marchand
1997	Alanis Morissette
1996	Alanis Morissette
1995	Jann Arden
1994	Leonard Cohen
1993	k.d. lang/Ben Mink
1992	Tom Cochrane

Source: *Canadian Academy of Recording Arts and Sciences*

Nelly Furtado shot to fame in late 2000 with her No. 3 hit, *I'm Like a Bird*, which snared Single of the Year at the 2001 ceremonies. Nominated in five categories, Furtado netted a total of four Junos.

THE 10 ★
LATEST WINNERS OF THE ASCAP SONGWRITER OF THE YEAR (POP CATEGORY)

YEAR	ARTIST
2000	Max Martin
1999	Diane Warren and Max Martin
1998	Diane Warren
1997	Glen Ballard
1996	Melissa Etheridge/Hootie and the Blowfish
1995	Robert John "Mutt" Lange
1994	Elton John and Bernie Taupin
1993	Diane Warren
1992	Jimmy Jam and Terry Lewis
1991	Diane Warren

Source: *American Society of Composers, Authors, and Publishers*

TOP 10 ★
ROCK SONGS OF ALL TIME*

	SONG	ARTIST OR GROUP
1	(I Can't Get No) Satisfaction	The Rolling Stones
2	Respect	Aretha Franklin
3	Stairway to Heaven	Led Zeppelin
4	Like a Rolling Stone	Bob Dylan
5	Born to Run	Bruce Springsteen
6	Hotel California	The Eagles
7	Light My Fire	The Doors
8	Good Vibrations	The Beach Boys
9	Hey Jude	The Beatles
10	Imagine	John Lennon

* Determined by a panel of 700 voters assembled by the music network VH1

The all-time Top 100 list, from which this Top 10 is taken, is dominated by songs dating from the 1960s. Within it, there are no fewer than nine Beatles songs, as well as five by the Rolling Stones and three by Bob Dylan.

TOP 10 ★
MOST COVERED BEATLES SONGS

	SONG	WRITTEN
1	Yesterday	1965
2	Eleanor Rigby	1966
3	Something	1969
4	Hey Jude	1968
5	Let It Be	1969
6	Michelle	1965
7	With a Little Help from My Friends	1967
8	Day Tripper	1965
9	Come Together	1969
10	The Long and Winding Road	1969

Yesterday is one of the most-covered songs of all time, with the number of recorded versions now in four figures. Although most of these songs are Lennon and McCartney compositions, the No. 3 song, *Something*, was written by George Harrison. *Hey Jude* and *Day Tripper* were both No. 1 hits.

Who recorded the two "greatest hits" albums that are among the bestselling of all time?
see p.130 for the answer

A The Beatles and the Rolling Stones
B Michael Jackson and Elvis Presley
C The Eagles and Elton John

Chart Hits

TOP 10 ALBUMS IN CANADA

	ALBUM/ARTIST	YEAR
1	*Thriller*, Michael Jackson	1983
2	*Jagged Little Pill*, Alanis Morissette	1996
3	*Rumours*, Fleetwood Mac	1977
4	*The Woman in Me*, Shania Twain	1995
5	*Come on Over*, Shania Twain	1997
6	*The Wall*, Pink Floyd	1980
7	*Their Greatest Hits 1971–1975*, The Eagles	1976
8	*Led Zeppelin IV*, Led Zeppelin	1971
9	*Bat Out of Hell*, Meat Loaf	1978
10	*Brothers in Arms*, Dire Straits	1985

Source: *Music Data Research*

TOP 10 ALBUMS OF ALL TIME

	ALBUM/ARTIST	YEAR
1	*Thriller*, Michael Jackson	1982
2	*Dark Side of the Moon*, Pink Floyd	1973
3	*Their Greatest Hits 1971–1975*, The Eagles	1976
4	*The Bodyguard*, Soundtrack	1992
5	*Rumours*, Fleetwood Mac	1977
6	*Sgt. Pepper's Lonely Hearts Club Band*, The Beatles	1967
7	*Led Zeppelin IV*, Led Zeppelin	1971
8	*Greatest Hits*, Elton John	1974
9	*Jagged Little Pill*, Alanis Morissette	1995
10	*Bat Out of Hell*, Meat Loaf	1977

BEAT ALL

Although disbanded over 30 years ago, the Beatles remain prominent in many all-time Top 10 lists and continue to achieve chart success in the 21st century.

TOP 10 SINGLES OF ALL TIME IN CANADA

	SINGLE/ARTIST	YEAR
1	*Candle in the Wind (1997)/Something about the Way You Look Tonight*, Elton John	1997
2	*I Just Called to Say I Love You*, Stevie Wonder	1984
3	*Tears Are Not Enough*, Northern Lights	1985
4	*We Are the World*, USA for Africa	1985
5	*YMCA*, Village People	1979
6	*Le Freak*, Chic	1979
7	*(Everything I Do) I Do It for You*, Bryan Adams	1991
8	*Heart of Glass*, Blondie	1979
9	*Flashdance*, Irene Cara	1983
10	*Live is Life*, Opus	1986

Source: *Music Data Canada*

TOP 10 SINGLES THAT PEAKED AT NO. 2 IN CANADA*

	SINGLE/ARTIST	WEEKS AT NO. 2
1	*Mo Money, Mo Problems*, Notorious B.I.G.	11
2	=*Wake Me Up Before You Go Go*, Wham!	9
	=*All Night Long (All Night)*, Lionel Richie	9
4	*Total Eclipse of the Heart*, Bonnie Tyler	8
5	=*You Are Not Alone*, Michael Jackson	7
	=*Careless Whisper*, Wham! featuring George Michael	7
	=*Believe*, Cher	7
	=*Can't Stop This Thing We Started*, Bryan Adams	7
	=*You Could Be Mine*, Guns 'N' Roses	7
10	*Been Around the World*, Puff Daddy	6

* Number of weeks at No. 2 and on the chart

Source: *Music Data Canada*

TOP 10 ARTISTS WITH MOST WEEKS AT NO. 1 ON THE CANADIAN SINGLES CHART

(Artist/weeks)

1 Elton John, 76 **2** Madonna, 73 **3** Stevie Wonder, 28 **4** Bryan Adams, 27 **5** = Puff Daddy, 21; = Rod Stewart, 21; = Mariah Carey, 21 **8** = Paula Abdul, 20; = Phil Collins, 20 **10** = Blondie, 19; = Michael Jackson, 19

Source: *Music Data Canada*

CANDLE POWER

Elton John's Candle in the Wind (1997) tribute to Princess Diana overtook White Christmas, the world's bestselling single for over 50 years.

TOP 10 🍁

SINGLES WITH THE MOST WEEKS ON THE CANADIAN CHARTS*

SINGLE/ARTIST/YEAR	WEEKS
1 *Candle in the Wind (1997)/Something about the Way You Look Tonight*, Elton John, 1997	157
2 *Glorytimes*, Portishead, 1997#	116
3 *Paradoxx*, 666, 1998	96
4 *Quit Playing Games (with My Heart)*, Backstreet Boys, 1997	85
5 *The Power of Love*, Celine Dion, 1994	70
6 =*Anytime, Anyplace*, Janet Jackson, 1994	59
=*God Bless the Child*, Shania Twain, 1996	59
8 =*Wild Night*, John Cougar Mellencamp, 1994	53
=*Get Down (You're the One for Me)*, Backstreet Boys, 1996	53
10 *Streets of Philadelphia*, Bruce Springsteen, 1994	52

* Up to March 2001

Still charting as of March 3, 2001

FENDER OF THE FENDER STRATOCASTER GUITAR

Californian-born Leo Fender (1909–91) set up the Fender Electrical Instrument Company in 1946, launching the Broadcaster (later Telecaster) electric guitar in 1948. He then developed the solid-bodied, contoured, double cutaway Stratocaster (the "Strat"), with his patented tremolo, which first went on sale in 1954. It was immediately and enduringly popular with rock musicians from Buddy Holly to Eric Clapton and Jimi Hendrix. The Fender Company was sold for $13 million to CBS in 1965, but Fender continued designing guitars until his death.

TOP 10 🍁

OLDEST ARTISTS TO HAVE A N0. 1 HIT SINGLE IN CANADA

	ARTIST/SINGLE	AGE YRS	MTHS
1	Eric Clapton, *Change the World*	51	4
2	Willie Nelson*, *To All the Girls I've Loved Before*	51	1
3	Elton John, *Candle in the Wind (1997)/Something about the Way You Look Tonight*	50	5
4	Tina Turner, *We Don't Need Another Hero*	45	9
5	Kenny Rogers, *Islands in the Stream*	45	2
6	John Cougar Mellencamp#, *Key West Intermezzo*	44	11
7	Bruce Springsteen, *Streets of Philadelphia*	44	7
8	Madonna, *Music*	42	1
9	Paul McCartney+, *Say, Say, Say*	41	6
10	Michael Bolton, *Said I Loved You ... But I Lied*	40	9

* Duet with Julio Iglesias # Duet with Dolly Parton

+ Duet with Michael Jackson

Source: *Music Data Canada*

TOP 10 ⭐

SINGLES OF ALL TIME

SINGLE/ARTIST/YEAR	SALES EXCEED
1 *Candle in the Wind (1997)/Something about the Way You Look Tonight*, Elton John, 1997	37,000,000
2 *White Christmas*, Bing Crosby, 1945	30,000,000
3 *Rock Around the Clock*, Bill Haley and His Comets, 1954	17,000,000
4 *I Want to Hold Your Hand*, The Beatles, 1963	12,000,000
5 =*Hey Jude*, The Beatles, 1968	10,000,000
=*It's Now or Never*, Elvis Presley, 1960	10,000,000
=*I Will Always Love You*, Whitney Houston, 1993	10,000,000
8 =*Hound Dog/Don't Be Cruel*, Elvis Presley, 1956	9,000,000
=*Diana*, Paul Anka, 1957	9,000,000
10 =*I'm a Believer*, The Monkees, 1966	8,000,000
=*(Everything I Do) I Do It for You*, Bryan Adams, 1991	8,000,000

Which Canadian artist has won the largest number of Juno awards?

see p.143 for the answer

A Anne Murray
B Bryan Adams
C Celine Dion

THE KING

Many of Elvis Presley's early hits predate Canadian charts. His first single was released in 1954, and he continued to record until 1976, a year before his death.

THE 10
FIRST MILLION-SELLING ALBUMS IN CANADA

	ALBUM/ARTIST OR GROUP	DATE
1	*Rumours*, Fleetwood Mac	May 1978
2	*Saturday Night Fever* (Soundtrack), Various	June 1978
3	*Grease* (Soundtrack), Various	Nov 1978
4	*Bat Out of Hell*, Meat Loaf	Mar 1979
5	*Breakfast in America*, Supertramp	Oct 1979
6	*Crime of the Century*, Supertramp	Nov 1979
7	*Dark Side of the Moon*, Pink Floyd	Aug 1980
8	*Kenny Rogers' Greatest Hits*, Kenny Rogers	May 1981
9	*Led Zeppelin IV*, Led Zeppelin	Dec 1982
10	*Thriller*, Michael Jackson	Nov 1983

Source: *Canadian Recording Industry Association*

THE 10
FIRST CANADIAN CHART SINGLES

	SINGLE	ARTIST OR GROUP
1	*Pinball Wizard*	Elton John
2	*Sister Golden Hair*	America
3	*How Long*	Ace
4	*Old Days*	Chicago
5	*Thank God I'm a Country Boy*	John Denver
6	*Bad Time*	Grand Funk Railroad
7	*Jackie Blue*	Ozark Mountain Devils
8	*Only Yesterday*	The Carpenters
9	*Philadelphia Freedom*	Elton John
10	*Shining Star*	Earth Wind & Fire

Earlier charts exist, but this, from *The Steede Report*, reflecting radio airplay for the week ending May 31, 1975, is the first used by Music Data Research.

THE 10
FIRST CANADIAN CHART ALBUMS

	ALBUM	ARTIST OR GROUP
1	*Rumours*	Fleetwood Mac
2	*Hotel California*	The Eagles
3	*Even in the Quietest Moments*	Supertramp
4	*Endless Flight*	Leo Sayer
5	*Live*	Barry Manilow
6	*Greatest Hits*	ABBA
7	*Little Queen*	Heart
8	*Arrival*	ABBA
9	*Their Greatest Hits 1971–75*	The Eagles
10	*I'm in You*	Peter Frampton

Even though earlier national charts exist, this is the first Top 10 list used for research purposes by Music Data Research. It is excerpted from Canadian Recording Industry Association national best-selling chart of August 10, 1977.

THE 10
FIRST FEMALE SINGERS WITH A CANADIAN NO. 1

	ARTIST/SINGLE	DATE AT NO. 1
1	**Maxine Nightingale**, *Right Back Where We Started from*	Apr 24, 1976
2	**Diana Ross**, *Love Hangover*	July 3, 1976
3	**Barbra Streisand**, *Evergreen*	Mar 19, 1977
4	**Debby Boone**, *You Light Up My Life*	Nov 16, 1977
5	**Bonnie Tyler**, *It's a Heartache*	June 14, 1978
6	**Donna Summer**, *MacArthur Park*	Nov 29, 1978
7	**Donna Summer**, *Hot Stuff*	June 27, 1979
8	**Anita Ward**, *Ring My Bell*	July 25, 1979
9	**Barbra Streisand**, *Woman in Love*	Nov 15, 1980
10	**Sheena Easton**, *Morning Train*	Apr 25, 1981

Source: *Music Data Research*

What is unusual about John Lennon's single *Imagine*?
see p.143 for the answer

A It was a posthumous hit
B It has the shortest title of a No. 1 single
C It was the first ever CD single

THE 10 🍁
FIRST CANADIAN SINGLES TO HIT NO. 1 IN THE US IN THE ROCK ERA

	SINGLE/ARTIST OR GROUP	DATE
1	*Diana*, Paul Anka	Sep 9, 1957
2	*Lonely Boy*, Paul Anka	July 13, 1959
3	*Theme from "A Summer Place,"* Percy Faith	Feb 22, 1960
4	*Ringo*, Lorne Greene	Dec 5, 1964
5	*American Woman*, Guess Who	May 9, 1969
6	*Heart of Gold*, Neil Young	Mar 18, 1972
7	*Seasons in the Sun*, Terry Jacks	Mar 2, 1974
8	*Sundown*, Gordon Lightfoot	June 29, 1974
9	*(You're) Having My Baby*, Paul Anka	Aug 24, 1974
10	*Rock Me Gently*, Andy Kim	Sep 28, 1974

Source: *Billboard*

The rock era began in July 1955 when Bill Haley's *Rock Around the Clock* went to No. 1 in the US.

THE 10 ★
FIRST AMERICAN GROUPS TO HAVE A NO. 1 SINGLE IN THE UK

	GROUP/SINGLE	DATE AT NO. 1
1	Bill Haley & His Comets, *Rock Around the Clock*	Nov 25, 1955
2	Dream Weavers, *It's Almost Tomorrow*	Mar 16, 1956
3	Teenagers featuring Frankie Lymon, *Why Do Fools Fall in Love?*	July 20, 1956
4	Crickets, *That'll Be the Day*	Nov 1, 1957
5	Platters, *Smoke Gets in Your Eyes*	Mar 20, 1959
6	Marcels, *Blue Moon*	May 4, 1961
7	Highwaymen, *Michael*	Oct 12, 1961
8	B. Bumble & the Stingers, *Nut Rocker*	May 17, 1962
9	Supremes, *Baby Love*	Nov 19, 1964
10	Byrds, *Mr. Tambourine Man*	July 22, 1965

Source: *The Popular Music Database*

THE 10 🍁
FIRST PLATINUM SINGLES IN CANADA

	SINGLE/ARTIST OR GROUP	YEAR
1	*That's the Way I Like It*, K.C. and the Sunshine Band	1976
2	*Feelings*, Morris Albert	1976
3	*I Love to Love*, Tina Charles	1976
4	*Love Hurts*, Nazareth	1976
5	*A Fifth of Beethoven*, Walter Murphy and the Big Apple Band	1976
6	*Don't Go Breaking My Heart*, Elton John and Kiki Dee	1976
7	*Disco Duck*, Rick Dees and His Cast of Idiots	1976
8	*I Feel Love*, Donna Summer	1977
9	*You Light Up My Life*, Debby Boone	1977
10	*The Unicorn*, The Irish Rovers	1978

Source: *Canadian Recording Industry Association*

THE 10 🍁
FIRST BRITISH SINGLES TO HIT NO. 1 IN CANADA

	SINGLE	ARTIST	DATE AT NO. 1
1	*Pinball Wizard*	Elton John	May 31, 1975
2	*Listen to What the Man Said*	Paul McCartney & Wings	July 26, 1975
3	*Jive Talkin'*	Bee Gees	Aug 16, 1975
4	*Ballroom Blitz*	Sweet	Oct 4, 1975
5	*Fame*	David Bowie	Oct 18, 1975
6	*Island Girl*	Elton John	Nov 29, 1975
7	*Saturday Night*	Bay City Rollers	Jan 17, 1976
8	*You Sexy Thing*	Hot Chocolate	Feb 14, 1976
9	*Right Back Where You Started*	Maxine Nightingale	Apr 24, 1976
10	*Silly Love Songs*	Paul McCartney & Wings	June 5, 1976

Source: *Music Data Research*

ROD THE MOD

Three of Rod Stewart's singles held the top spot for an amazing six weeks or longer. He is one of the few acts to chart in Canada in three different decades: the 1970s, 1980s, and 1990s.

Chart Toppers

❦ TOP 10 ARTISTS OR GROUPS WITH THE MOST CANADIAN NO. 1 SINGLES

(Artist or group/No. 1 singles)

① Madonna, 16 **②** Elton John, 9 **③** Phil Collins, 6 **④** = Paula Abdul, 5; = Mariah Carey, 5; = Michael Jackson, 5; = Stevie Wonder, 5 **⑧** = Bryan Adams, 4; = Blondie, 4; = Janet Jackson, 4; = Paul McCartney & Wings, 4; = Milli Vanilli, 4

Source: *Music Data Research*

TOP 10 ★
SINGLES WITH THE MOST WEEKS AT NO. 1 IN THE US*

SINGLE/ARTIST OR GROUP/YEAR	WEEKS AT NO. 1
1 *One Sweet Day*, Mariah Carey & Boyz II Men, 1995	16
2 = *I Will Always Love You*, Whitney Houston, 1992	14
= *I'll Make Love to You*, Boyz II Men, 1994	14
= *Macarena (Bayside Boys Mix)*, Los Del Rio, 1995	14
= *Candle in the Wind (1997)/ Something about the Way You Look Tonight*, Elton John, 1997	14
6 = *End of the Road*, Boyz II Men, 1992	13
= *The Boy Is Mine*, Brandy & Monica, 1998	13
8 = *Don't Be Cruel/Hound Dog*, Elvis Presley, 1956	11
= *I Swear*, All-4-One, 1994	11
= *Un-break My Heart*, Toni Braxton, 1996	11
= *Independent Women Part 1*, Destiny's Child, 2000	11

* Based on Billboard charts

HOUSTON LIFTS OFF

Whitney Houston's long-staying debut No. 1 album, Whitney Houston, *spent 17 weeks at the top and sold an estimated one million copies in Canada.*

♣ TOP 10 CANADIAN ARTISTS WITH THE MOST WEEKS AT NO. 1

(Artist or group/weeks at No. 1)

1. Bryan Adams, 27 2. Celine Dion, 14
3. = Corey Hart, 9; = Shania Twain, 9;
= Los Del Mar, 9 6. = Tom Cochrane, 6;
= Hampton the Hampster, 6
8. SoulDecision, 5 9. = Northern Lights, 4;
= Alanis Morissette, 4;
= Boomtang Boys, 4

Source: *Music Data Research*

Way out in front, Bryan Adams has twice as many hits with weeks at No. 1 than the No. 2 contender, Celine Dion.

TOP 10 ♣

YOUNGEST ARTISTS TO HAVE A NO. 1 SINGLE IN CANADA*

ARTIST/TITLE/YEAR	AGE# YRS	MTHS
1. Britney Spears, ...Baby One More Time, 1998	16	11
2. Monica (with Brandy), The Boy Is Mine, 1998	17	7
3. Shaun Cassidy, Da Doo Ron Ron, 1977	17	10
4. Debbie Gibson, Foolish Beat, 1988	17	11
5. Christina Aguilera, Genie in a Bottle, 1999	18	8
6. Brandy (with Monica), The Boy Is Mine, 1998	19	3
7. Andy Gibb, I Just Want To Be Your Everything, 1977	19	6
8. Mariah Carey, Vision of Love, 1990	20	5
9. Bobby Brown, On Our Own, 1989	20	6
10. Kylie Minogue, The Locomotion, 1988	20	7

* To January 1, 2001

During first week of debut No. 1 Canadian single

Source: *Music Data Research*

The hit song ...Baby One More Time introduced Britney Spears to the world and also made her a music superstar.

TOP 10 ♣

SINGLES WITH THE MOST WEEKS AT NO. 1 IN CANADA*

SINGLE/ARTIST OR GROUP/YEAR	WEEKS
1. Candle in the Wind (1997)/ Something about the Way You Look Tonight, Elton John, 1997	45
2. Goodbye, Spice Girls, 1998	15
3. I'll Be Missing You, Puff Daddy & Faith Evans, 1997	13
4. = You Light Up My Life, Debby Boone, 1977	12
= Pop Muzik, M, 1979	12
= Faith, George Michael, 1987	12
= (Everything I Do) I Do It for You, Bryan Adams, 1991	12
= Said I Loved You...But I Lied, Michael Bolton, 1993	12
= The Power of Love, Celine Dion, 1994	12
= Fantasy, Mariah Carey, 1995	12

* Based on the official Canadian charts
Source: *Music Data Research*

TOP 10 ♣

BIGGEST JUMPS TO NO. 1 ON THE CANADIAN SINGLES CHART*

ALBUM/ARTIST/YEAR	PLACE BEFORE NO. 1
1. The Animal Song, Savage Garden, 1999	49
2. Star Wars Theme, Meco, 1978	41
3. I Want You, Savage Garden, 1997	29
4. Secret, Madonna, 1994	27
5. = Short People, Randy Newman, 1978	26
= Don't Tell Me, Madonna, 2001	26
7. The Hamsterdance Song, Hampton the Hampster, 2000	19
8. Staying Alive, Bee Gees, 1978	18
9. Thank U, Alanis Morissette, 1998	15
10. = Opposites Attract, Paula Abdul, 1990	12
= (Everything I Do) I Do It for You, Bryan Adams, 1991	12

* From within the Top 50

TOP 10 ★

ALBUMS WITH THE MOST CONSECUTIVE WEEKS AT NO. 1 IN THE UK

ALBUM/ARTIST OR GROUP	WEEKS AT NO. 1
1. South Pacific, Soundtrack	70
2. Please Please Me, The Beatles	30
3. Sgt. Pepper's Lonely Hearts Club Band, The Beatles	23
4. = With The Beatles, The Beatles	21
= A Hard Day's Night, The Beatles/Soundtrack	21
6. South Pacific, Soundtrack	19
7. = The Sound of Music, Soundtrack	18
= Saturday Night Fever, Soundtrack	18
9. Blue Hawaii, Elvis Presley/Soundtrack	17
10. Summer Holiday, Cliff Richard and The Shadows	14

Source: *The Popular Music Database*

TOP 10 ♣

ALBUMS WITH MOST WEEKS AT NO. 1 IN CANADA

ALBUM/ARTIST OR GROUP/YEAR	WEEKS AT NO. 1
1. Synchronicity, The Police, 1983	23
2. Jagged Little Pill, Alanis Morissette, 1996	20
3. Brothers In Arms, Dire Straits, 1985	18
4. = Whitney Houston, Whitney Houston, 1986	17
= Unplugged, Eric Clapton, 1992	17
6. The Raw and the Cooked, Fine Young Cannibals, 1989	16
7. = I Do Not Want What I Haven't Got, Sinead O'Connor, 1990	14
= True Blue, Madonna, 1986	14
= The Joshua Tree, U2, 1987	14
= Dirty Dancing, Soundtrack, 1987	14
= Born In the USA, Bruce Springsteen, 1984	14

Source: *Music Data Research*

Did You Know? Canadian-born Paul Anka wrote Diana at the age of 14 and released it aged 16. He became the first Canadian soloist to sell more than 1 million.

Hit Singles of the Decades

TOP 10 🍁
SINGLES OF THE 1960s IN CANADA

SINGLE/ARTIST OR GROUP	YEAR
1 *Get Back/Don't Let Me Down*, The Beatles	1969
2 *Lady Willpower*, Gary Puckett and the Union Gap	1968
3 *Wichita Lineman*, Glen Campbell	1968
4 *Something/Come Together*, The Beatles	1969
5 *Hey Jude/Revolution*, The Beatles	1968
6 *Shakin' All Over*, Guess Who	1965
7 *Aquarius/Let the Sunshine in*, Fifth Dimension	1969
8 *Sugar Sugar*, The Archies	1969
9 *Spinning Wheel*, Blood Sweat & Tears	1969
10 *A Little Bit Me/Girl I Knew Somewhere*, The Monkees	1967

The 1960s are recalled as the decade in which British music invaded Canada. The Beatles capture three of the Top 10 positions. The top Canadian single, *Shakin' All Over* by Winnipeg's Guess Who, places sixth for the decade.

TOP 10 🍁
SINGLES OF THE 1970s IN CANADA

SINGLE/ARTIST OR GROUP	YEAR
1 *YMCA*, Village People	1979
2 *Le Freak*, Chic	1978
3 *Heart of Glass*, Blondie	1979
4 *You Light Up My Life*, Debby Boone	1977
5 *Stayin' Alive*, Bee Gees	1978
6 *Born to Be Alive*, Patrick Hernandez	1979
7 *Boogie Oogie Oogie*, A Taste of Honey	1978
8 *Star Wars Theme/Cantina Band*, Meco	1977
9 *Grease*, Frankie Valli	1978
10 *Night Fever*, Bee Gees	1978

Source: *Music Data Research*

TOP 10 🍁
SINGLES OF THE 1980s IN CANADA

SINGLE/ARTIST OR GROUP	YEAR
1 *I Just Called to Say I Love You*, Stevie Wonder	1984
2 *Tears Are not Enough*, Northern Lights	1985
3 *We Are the World*, USA for Africa	1985
4 *Flashdance...What a Feeling*, Irene Cara	1983
5 *Live is Life*, Opus	1986
6 *Billie Jean*, Michael Jackson	1983
7 *Karma Chameleon*, Culture Club	1984
8 *Girls Just Want to Have Fun*, Cyndi Lauper	1984
9 *I Love Rock 'n' Roll*, Joan Jett and The Blackhearts	1982
10 *Funkytown*, Lipps Inc.	1980

Canada's top-selling single of the 1980s was a recording featured on the *Woman in Red* soundtrack. *I Just Called to Say I Love You* by Stevie Wonder was No. 1 for 11 weeks in Canada and is one of the longest-running No. 1's in chart history. Meanwhile, the No. 2 record included contributions from Canada's recording elite, raising money for African famine relief.

OUT OF PUFF

I'll Be Missing You, *by Sean Combs, aka Puff Daddy, was No. 1 in Canada for 13 weeks. It was written as a tribute to the late Notorious B.I.G.*

TOP 10 🍁
SINGLES OF EACH YEAR OF THE 1980s IN CANADA

YEAR	SINGLE/ARTIST OR GROUP
1980	*Rapper's Delight*, Sugarhill Gang
1981	*The Tide Is High*, Blondie
1982	*I Love Rock 'n' Roll*, Joan Jett and the Blackhearts
1983	*Total Eclipse of the Heart*, Bonnie Tyler
1984	*I Just Called to Say I Love You*, Stevie Wonder
1985	*Never Surrender*, Corey Hart
1986	*The Lady in Red*, Chris DeBurgh
1987	*Faith*, George Michael
1988	*Groovy Kind of Love*, Phil Collins
1989	*The Locomotion*, Kylie Minogue

Source: *Music Data Research*

TOP 10 🍁
SINGLES OF THE 1990s IN CANADA

SINGLE/ARTIST OR GROUP	YEAR
1 *Candle in the Wind (1997)/ Something about the Way You Look Tonight*, Elton John	1997
2 *Goodbye*, Spice Girls	1998
3 *(Everything I Do) I Do It for You*, Bryan Adams	1991
4 *I'll Be Missing You*, Puff Daddy and Faith Evans (featuring 112)	1997
5 *More than Words*, Extreme	1991
6 *Step by Step*, New Kids on the Block	1990
7 *Swing the Mood*, Jive Bunny and the Mastermixers	1990
8 *Vogue*, Madonna	1990
9 *Strokin'*, Clarence Carter	1990
10 *Broken*, Nine Inch Nails	1997

Source: *Music Data Research*

TOP 10 🍁
SINGLES OF EACH YEAR OF THE 1990s IN CANADA

YEAR	SINGLE/ARTIST OR GROUP
1990	*Vogue*, Madonna
1991	*More than Words*, Extreme
1992	*Beauty and the Beast*, Celine Dion and Peabo Bryson
1993	*That's the Way Love Goes*, Janet Jackson
1994	*The Power of Love*, Celine Dion
1995	*Always*, Bon Jovi
1996	*Stayin' Alive*, N-Trance
1997	*Candle in the Wind (1997)/ Something about the Way You Look Tonight*, Elton John
1998	*Candle in the Wind (1997)/ Something about the Way You Look Tonight*, Elton John
1999	*Last Kiss*, Pearl Jam

Source: *Music Data Research*

TOP 10 🍁
SINGLES OF THE 1990s IN CANADA (SOLO MALE)

SINGLE/ARTIST	YEAR
1 *Candle in the Wind (1997)/ Something about the Way You Look Tonight*, Elton John	1997
2 *(Everything I Do) I Do It for You*, Bryan Adams	1991
3 *Strokin'*, Clarence Carter	1990
4 *Black or White*, Michael Jackson	1991
5 *Life Is a Highway*, Tom Cochrane	1991
6 *U Can't Touch This*, M.C. Hammer	1990
7 *Let Your Backbone Slide*, Maestro Fresh-Wes	1990
8 *Can't Stop This Thing We Started*, Bryan Adams	1991
9 *Poison*, Alice Cooper	1990
10 *Said I Loved You...But I Lied*, Michael Bolton	1994

TOP 10 🍁
SINGLES OF THE 1990s IN CANADA (SOLO FEMALE)

SINGLE/ARTIST	YEAR
1 *Vogue*, Madonna	1990
2 *Opposites Attract*, Paula Abdul	1990
3 *Justify My Love*, Madonna	1991
4 *The Power of Love*, Celine Dion	1994
5 *Fantasy*, Mariah Carey	1995
6 *Secret*, Madonna	1994
7 *That's the Way Love Goes*, Janet Jackson	1993
8 *This Used to Be My Playground*, Madonna	1992
9 *All Around the World*, Lisa Stansfield	1990
10 *Rush Rush*, Paula Abdul	1991

CHER SUCCESS

Now into her fifth decade of chart successes, both in partnership with Sonny Bono and solo, Cher has also carved out an Oscar-winning film career.

What was the first Canadian single to hit No. 1 in the US? *see p.133 for the answer*   A *Heart of Gold*, by Neil Young
B *Sundown*, by Gordon Lightfoot
C *Diana*, by Paul Anka

Hit Albums of the Decades

TOP 10 ★
ALBUMS OF THE 1960s IN THE US

ALBUM/ARTIST OR GROUP	YEAR RELEASED
1 *West Side Story* (Soundtrack), Various	1961
2 *Blue Hawaii* (Soundtrack), Elvis Presley	1961
3 *The Sound of Music* (Soundtrack), Various	1965
4 *Sgt. Pepper's Lonely Hearts Club Band*, The Beatles	1967
5 *More of the Monkees*, The Monkees	1967
6 *Days of Wine and Roses*, Andy Williams	1963
7 *G.I. Blues*, Elvis Presley	1960
8 *The Button-Down Mind of Bob Newhart*, Bob Newhart	1960
9 *Whipped Cream and Other Delights*, Herb Alpert and the Tijuana Brass	1965
10 *A Hard Day's Night* (Soundtrack), The Beatles	1964

TOP 10 🍁
ALBUMS OF EACH YEAR OF THE 1970s IN CANADA

YEAR	ALBUM/ARTIST OR GROUP
1970	*Bridge Over Troubled Water*, Simon and Garfunkel
1971	*Tapestry*, Carole King
1972	*American Pie*, Don McLean
1973	*Dark Side of the Moon*, Pink Floyd
1974	*Band on the Run*, Paul McCartney & Wings
1975	*Captain Fantastic and the Brown Dirt Cowboy*, Elton John
1976	*Frampton Comes Alive!*, Peter Frampton
1977	*Rumours*, Fleetwood Mac
1978	*Saturday Night Fever*, Soundtrack
1979	*Breakfast in America*, Supertramp

TOP 10 🍁
ALBUMS OF EACH YEAR OF THE 1980s IN CANADA

YEAR	ALBUM/ARTIST OR GROUP
1980	*The Wall*, Pink Floyd
1981	*Double Fantasy*, John Lennon
1982	*Business as Usual*, Men at Work
1983	*Thriller*, Michael Jackson
1984	*Thriller*, Michael Jackson
1985	*Born in the USA*, Bruce Springsteen
1986	*Whitney Houston*, Whitney Houston
1987	*Slippery when Wet*, Bon Jovi
1988	*Kick*, INXS
1989	*The Raw and the Cooked*, Fine Young Cannibals

The death of John Lennon in December 1980 prompted his album *Double Fantasy* to advance to the No. 1 spot posthumously. It spawned two No. 1 hit singles in Canada, *(Just Like) Starting Over* and *Woman*, and went on to become the No. 1 album of 1981.

RICH REWARDS

Formerly a member of the Commodores, Lionel Richie began a successful solo career in the 1980s, with Can't Slow Down *selling one million copies in the Canada alone within a year of its release.*

TOP 10 🍁
ALBUMS OF THE 1970s IN CANADA

ALBUM/ARTIST OR GROUP	YEAR RELEASED
1 *Rumours*, Fleetwood Mac	1977
2 *Their Greatest Hits 1971–1975*, The Eagles	1976
3 *Led Zeppelin IV*, Led Zeppelin	1971
4 *Bat Out of Hell*, Meat Loaf	1978
5 *Breakfast in America*, Supertramp	1979
6 *Saturday Night Fever* (Soundtrack), Various	1978
7 *Grease* (Soundtrack), Various	1978
8 *Dark Side of the Moon*, Pink Floyd	1973
9 *Hotel California*, The Eagles	1977
10 *Crime of the Century*, Supertramp	1977

Source: *Music Data Research*

TOP 10 🍁
ALBUMS OF THE 1980s IN CANADA

ALBUM/ARTIST OR GROUP	YEAR
1 *Thriller*, Michael Jackson	1983
2 *The Wall*, Pink Floyd	1980
3 *Brothers in Arms*, Dire Straits	1985
4 *Whitney Houston*, Whitney Houston	1986
5 *True Blue*, Madonna	1986
6 *The Joshua Tree*, U2	1987
7 *Dirty Dancing* (Soundtrack), Various	1987
8 *Born in the USA*, Bruce Springsteen	1984
9 *Colour by Numbers*, Culture Club	1983
10 *Girl You Know It's True*, Milli Vanilli	1989

Michael Jackson's *Thriller* is not only the No. 1 album of the 1980s in Canada, but also of all-time. It sold an unprecedented two million units and is the only album in history to top the yearly charts twice (1983 and 1984).

TOP 10
ALBUMS OF EACH YEAR IN THE 1990s IN CANADA

YEAR	ALBUM/ARTIST OR GROUP
1990	*...But Seriously,* Phil Collins
1991	*To the Extreme,* Vanilla Ice
1992	*Waking Up the Neighbours,* Bryan Adams
1993	*Unplugged,* Eric Clapton
1994	*The Sign,* Ace of Base
1995	*No Need to Argue,* The Cranberries
1996	*Jagged Little Pill,* Alanis Morissette
1997	*Let's Talk about Love,* Celine Dion
1998	*Titanic* (Soundtrack), Various
1999	*Millennium,* Backstreet Boys

TOP 10
CANADIAN ALBUMS OF THE 1990s IN CANADA

	ALBUM/ARTIST	YEAR RELEASED
1	*Jagged Little Pill*, Alanis Morissette	1996
2	*The Woman in Me*, Shania Twain	1995
3	*Come on Over*, Shania Twain	1997
4	*The Colour of My Love*, Celine Dion	1994
5	*Mad Mad World*, Tom Cochrane	1991
6	*Waking Up The Neighbours*, Bryan Adams	1991
7	*Alannah Myles*, Alannah Myles	1990
8	*Surfacing*, Sarah McLachlan	1997
9	*Let's Talk about Love*, Celine Dion	1997
10	*Falling into You*, Celine Dion	1997

Source: *Music Data Research*

After a successful career as a teen pop diva in the early 1990s, Ottawa-born Alanis Morissette re-emerged in the mid-1990s as an alternative rocker with *Jagged Little Pill*. It stayed at No. 1 for 23 weeks and is the biggest album of the 1990s.

TWAIN MAKES HER MARK

After achieving her first chart success in 1993, Timmins-born country singer Shania Twain has rapidly become one of the best-selling female artists of all time.

Did You Know? Shania Twain was born Eilleen Regina Edwards. Her new name, adopted in 1990, comes from the Native American Chippewa (Ojibway) phrase for "I'm on my way."

Female Singers

TOP 10
SINGLES BY FEMALE GROUPS IN CANADA

	SINGLE/GROUP*	YEAR
1	*Goodbye*, Spice Girls	1998
2	*I Love Rock 'n' Roll*, Joan Jett & the Heartbreakers	1982
3	*Funkytown*, Lipps Inc.	1980
4	*Heart of Glass*, Blondie	1979
5	*Call Me*, Blondie	1980
6	*Release Me*, Wilson Phillips	1990
7	*Boogie Oogie Oogie*, A Taste of Honey	1978
8	*The Tide Is High*, Blondie	1981
9	*Walk Like an Egyptian*, Bangles	1987
10	*Take My Breath Away*, Berlin	1986

* *Includes groups led by a woman*

Source: *Music Data Research*

Deborah Harry, lead singer of Blondie, went on to pursue a solo career when the group disbanded in 1982.

GIRL POWER

In a relatively short period, the Spice Girls set new records for best-sellers and single and album chart entries on the Canadian charts.

TOP 10
FEMALE SINGERS WITH THE MOST TOP 40 HITS IN CANADA

	SINGER	TOP 10 HITS
1	Madonna	46
2	Janet Jackson	30
3	Whitney Houston	27
4	Mariah Carey	26
5	Celine Dion	24
6	Alanis Morissette	17
7	Tina Turner	16
8	Gloria Estefan	15
9	Olivia Newton-John	15
10	Donna Summer	14

Source: *Music Data Research*

Alanis Morissette's 17 chart hits include those during her successful career as an alternative rock act of the late 1990s, as well as those during her stint as a dance-pop diva of the early 1990s.

TOP 10
ALBUMS BY FEMALE GROUPS IN CANADA*

	ALBUM/GROUP	YEAR
1	*Spice*, Spice Girls	1998
2	*No Need to Argue*, Cranberries	1995
3	*Joyride*, Roxette	1991
4	*Wilson Phillips*, Wilson Phillips	1990
5	*Spiceworld*, Spice Girls	1997
6	*Aquarium*, Aqua	1997
7	*Fanmail*, TLC	1999
8	*Crazy Sexy Cool*, TLC	1995
9	*All Saints*, All Saints	1998
10	*Breakout*, Pointer Sisters	1984

* *Includes groups led by a woman*

Source: *Music Data Research*

As this Top 10 list exemplifies, the 1990s saw a huge surge in the popularity of all-girl groups, with sales eclipsing those of such predecessors as the Supremes and the Bangles.

TOP 10
FEMALE GROUPS IN CANADA*

	GROUP	NO. 1	TOP 10	TOP 40
1	=Exposé	–	2	9
	=Pointer Sisters	–	5	9
	=Spice Girls	1	7	9
4	=Bangles	1	2	7
	=Salt-n-Pepa	–	3	7
	=West End Girls	1	1	7
	=Wilson Phillips	1	6	7
8	Bananarama	1	2	5
9	TLC	–	2	4
10	All Saints	–	2	3

* *Ranked according to total number of Top 40 singles*

Source: *Music Data Research*

In the late 1990s, Britain's Spice Girls took over the top spot among female groups. More than a decade earlier, the American sister-group the Pointer Sisters, who rank in this Top 10 list at No. 2, were making strong chart appearances with hit singles such as *Jump (for My Love)*, *Neutron Dance*, and *He's So Shy*.

After Elvis Presley, who has achieved the most weeks at US No. 1?

see p.148 for the answer

A Madonna
B Celine Dion
C Mariah Carey

TOP 10

SINGLES BY FEMALE SINGERS IN CANADA*

	SINGLE/ARTIST	YEAR
1	*Flashdance...What a Feelin'*, Irene Cara	1983
2	*Girls Just Wanna Have Fun*, Cyndi Lauper	1984
3	*Mickey*, Toni Basil	1983
4	*Physical*, Olivia Newton-John	1981
5	*You Light Up My Life*, Debby Boone	1977
6	*Touch Me (I Want Your Body)*, Samantha Fox	1987
7	*Bette Davis Eyes*, Kim Carnes	1981
8	*Ring My Bell*, Anita Ward	1979
9	*Time After Time*, Cyndi Lauper	1984
10	*Vogue*, Madonna	1990

* *Excludes duets between female solo singers*

Source: *Music Data Research*

Irene Cara's *Flashdance...What a Feelin'* was one of two No. 1 hits from the 1983 *Flashdance* soundtrack. It spent six weeks at No. 1 on the *The Record's* singles chart and sold over 200,000 copies in Canada.

TOP 10

ALBUMS BY FEMALE SINGERS IN CANADA

	ALBUM/ARTIST	YEAR	ESTIMATED COPIES SOLD
1 =	*The Woman in Me*, Shania Twain	1995	2,000,000
=	*Jagged Little Pill*, Alanis Morissette	1996	2,000,000
=	*Come on Over*, Shania Twain	1997	2,000,000
4 =	*True Blue*, Madonna	1986	1,000,000
=	*Whitney Houston*, Whitney Houston	1986	1,000,000
=	*Alannah Myles*, Alannah Myles	1990	1,000,000
=	*I Do Not Want What I Haven't Got*, Sinead O'Connor	1990	1,000,000
=	*The Bodyguard*, Soundtrack	1992	1,000,000
=	*The Colour of My Love*, Celine Dion	1994	1,000,000
=	*Let's Talk About Love*, Celine Dion	1997	1,000,000

Source: *Music Data Research*

TOP 10

YOUNGEST FEMALE SINGERS TO HAVE A NO. 1 SINGLE IN CANADA

	SINGER/SINGLE/YEAR	YEARS	AGE MTHS
1	Britney Spears, *...Baby One More Time*, 1998	16	11
2	Monica, *The Boy Is Mine*, 1998	17	7
3	Debbie Gibson, *Foolish Beat*, 1988	17	11
4	Christina Aguilera, *Genie in a Bottle*, 1999	18	8
5	Brandy, *The Boy Is Mine*, 1998	19	3
6	Mariah Carey, *Vision of Love*, 1990	20	5
7	Kylie Minogue, *The Locomotion*, 1988	20	7
8	Samantha Fox, *Touch Me (I Want Your Body)*, 1987	20	10
9	Debbie Boone, *You Light Up My Life*, 1977	21	1
10	Anita Ward, *Ring My Bell*, 1979	21	7

Source: *Music Data Research*

CHRISTINA AGUILERA

Within a year of her professional debut, Christina Aguilera became one of only a handful of teenage girls to achieve a No. 1 single. She also sold over one million copies of her first album in Canada and won a Grammy award.

All-Time Greats

TOP 10

AEROSMITH SINGLES IN CANADA

SINGLE	YEAR
1 I Don't Want to Miss a Thing	1998
2 Crazy	1994
3 Amazing	1994
4 Janie's Got a Gun	1990
5 Love in an Elevator	1989
6 Cryin'	1993
7 Jaded	2001
8 Livin' on the Edge	1993
9 Blind Man	1995
10 Dream On	1976

Source: *Music Data Research*

Although Aerosmith is known to many as a legendary hard rock band of the 1970s, the Boston rockers enjoyed their biggest successes in the 1990s with No. 2 chart hits *I Don't Want to Miss a Thing* and *Crazy*. *Love in an Elevator*, which peaked on the charts at No. 4 in 1989, was the band's biggest hit during the 1980s.

PRINCE SINGLES IN CANADA

SINGLE	YEAR
1 When Doves Cry	1984
2 Batdance	1989
3 Cream*	1991
4 7	1993
5 Purple Rain	1984
6 Kiss	1986
7 Let's Go Crazy	1984
8 My Name Is Prince	1992
9 Little Red Corvette	1983
10 Thieves in the Temple	1990

* *Prince & the New Power Generation*

Source: *Music Data Research*

BRUCE SPRINGSTEEN SINGLES IN CANADA

SINGLE	YEAR
1 Dancing in the Dark	1984
2 My Hometown	1986
3 Hungry Heart	1984
4 Human Touch	1992
5 Streets of Philadelphia	1994
6 Brilliant Disguise	1987
7 I'm Goin' Down	1985
8 Born in the USA	1985
9 Cover Me	1984
10 I'm on Fire	1985

Source: *Music Data Research*

🍁 TOP 10 ACTS OF THE 1970s IN CANADA

1 Bee Gees **2** Donna Summer **3** Paul McCartney & Wings
4 Rod Stewart **5** ABBA **6** The Eagles **7** Barry Manilow **8** Elton John
9 Bay City Rollers **10** Captain & Tennille

Source: *Music Data Research*

PRINCE, CHARMING

In the early 1980s, Prince exploded onto the Canadian music scene with Little Red Corvette. *His first No. 1 single from his film* Purple Rain *spent two weeks at the top in 1984.*

TOP 10
JOHN LENNON SINGLES IN THE CANADA

	SINGLE	YEAR
1	*(Just Like) Starting Over*	1980
2	*Woman*	1981
3	*Imagine*	1971
4	*Whatever Gets You Through the Night*	1974
5	*Instant Karma*	1970
6	*Power to the People*	1971
7	*Watching the Wheels*	1981
8	*Give Peace a Chance*	1969
9	*Nobody Told Me*	1984
10	*Mind Games*	1973

Source: *Music Data Research*

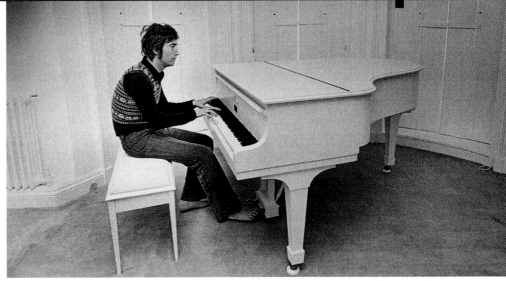

KEY PLAYER
The most charismatic of the Beatles, John Lennon achieved a run of hits before and after his 1980 murder, including the anthemic hit Imagine.

TOP 10
ANNE MURRAY SINGLES IN CANADA

	SINGLE	YEAR
1	*You Needed Me*	1978
2	*Danny's Song*	1973
3	*Love Song*	1974
4	*Cotton Jenny*	1972
5	*Snowbird*	1970
6	*Sing High, Sing Low*	1970
7	*You Won't See Me*	1974
8	*I Just Fall in Love Again*	1979
9	*Just One Look*	1974
10	*Talk It Over in the Morning*	1971

Source: *Music Data Research*

With a career spanning more than 30 years and album sales of over 40 million, Anne Murray is one of Canada's most revered recording artists. A museum that houses the superstar's various awards, photographs, and memorabilia opened in 1989 in her hometown of Springhill, Nova Scotia. Murray's biggest hit is the 1978 platinum single *You Needed Me,* a hit which culminated in a Grammy Award – the second of four.

TOP 10
ELTON JOHN SINGLES IN CANADA

	SINGLE	YEAR
1	*Candle in the Wind (1997)/ Something about the Way You Look Tonight*	1997
2	*Don't Go Breaking My Heart**	1976
3	*Nikita*	1986
4	*Island Girl*	1975
5	*Little Jeannie*	1980
6	*Sorry Seems to Be the Hardest Word*	1977
7	*Can You Feel the Love Tonight*	1994
8	*I Don't Wanna Go On With You Like That*	1988
9	*Pinball Wizard*	1975
10	*Believe*	1995

* *Elton John with Kiki Dee*
Source: *Music Data Research*

TOP 10
CANADIAN ARTISTS WITH THE MOST JUNO AWARDS

	ARTIST	AWARDS
1	Anne Murray	24
2	Celine Dion	18
3	Bryan Adams	17
4	Gordon Lightfoot	11
5	=Murray McLachlan	10
	=Tragically Hip	10
7	Alanis Morissette	9
8	=k.d. lang	8
	=Orchestre symphonique de Montreal	8
10	Bachman-Turner Overdrive	7

Source: *Canadian Academy of Recording Arts & Science*

The Juno Awards ceremony has been held annually since 1970; it was first telecast in 1975. The award was originally called the Juneau after Pierre Juneau, former chairperson of the CRTC, which had introduced Canadian content regulations in 1971. The spelling was later changed to Juno, after the highest goddess of the Roman pantheon.

♣ TOP 10 ACTS OF THE 1980s IN CANADA

1 Madonna **2** Phil Collins **3** Michael Jackson **4** Lionel Richie **5** Elton John **6** John Cougar Mellencamp **7** Prince **8** Daryl Hall & John Oates **9** Rod Stewart **10** George Michael
Source: *Music Data Research*

Did You Know? John Lennon's single *Imagine* was released in the US in 1971. Its UK release was delayed until 1975. It made No. 1 only after his death in 1980.

TOP 10 🍁
JANN ARDEN SINGLES IN CANADA

	SINGLE	YEAR
1	Insensitive	1995
2	Could I Be Your Girl	1994
3	Wonderdrug	1995
4	The Sound of...	1997
5	Looking for It	1996
6	Good Mother	1995
7	Wishing That	1998
8	I Know You	1998
9	Will You Remember Me?	1993
10	Unloved	1995

TOP 10 🍁
BARENAKED LADIES SINGLES IN CANADA

	SINGLE	YEAR
1	Jane	1994
2	It's All Been Done	1998
3	One Week	1998
4	Pinch Me	2000
5	Enid	1992
6	Alternative Girlfriend	1995
7	Too Little Too Late	2001
8	If I Had a $1,000,000	1993
9	Shoebox	1996
10	Brian Wilson	1993

THE 10 LATEST GRAMMY NEW ARTISTS OF THE YEAR
(Year/artist or group)

1 2000, Shelby Lynne
2 1999, Christina Aguilera **3** 1998, Lauryn Hill **4** 1997, Paula Cole
5 1996, LeeAnn Rimes **6** 1995, Hootie & The Blowfish **7** 1994, Sheryl Crow
8 1993, Toni Braxton **9** 1992, Arrested Development **10** 1991, Mark Cohn

🍁 TOP 10 BACKSTREET BOYS SINGLES IN CANADA
(Single/year)

1 *I Want It That Way,* 1999 **2** *Show Me the Meaning of Being Lonely,* 2000
3 *Everybody (Backstreet's Back),* 1997 **4** *Get Down (You're the One for Me),* 1996
5 *As Long As You Love Me,* 1997 **6** *Quit Playing Games (with My Heart),* 1997
7 *All I Have to Give,* 1998 **8** *Larger than Life,* 1999 **9** *Anywhere for You,* 1997
10 *We've Got It Goin' On,* 1997

TOP 10 🍁
BRITNEY SPEARS SINGLES IN CANADA

	SINGLE	YEAR
1	...Baby One More Time	1998
2	Oops!... I Did It Again	2000
3	(You Drive Me) Crazy	1999
4	Lucky	2000
5	Sometimes	1999
6	Stronger	2000
7	From the Bottom of My Broken Heart	2000
8	My Only Wish (This Year)	2001
9	Don't Let Me Be the Last to Know	2001
10	Born to Make You Happy	1999

Source: *Music Data Research*

TOP 10 🍁
'N SYNC SINGLES IN CANADA

	SINGLE	YEAR
1	Bye Bye Bye	2000
2	It's Gonna Be Me	2000
3	I Want You Back	1998
4	Tearin' Up My Heart	1998
5	This I Promise You	2000
6	(God Must Have Spent) A Little More Time on You	1999
7	I Drive Myself Crazy	1999
8	Music of My Heart	1999
9	I Believe in You	2001
10	Merry Christmas, Happy Holidays	1999

Source: *Music Data Research*

TOP 10 ⭐
LATEST GRAMMY POP VOCAL PERFORMANCES OF THE YEAR

MALE VOCALIST/SONG	YEAR	FEMALE VOCALIST/SONG
Sting, *She Walks This Earth (Soberana Rosa)*	2000	Macy Gray, *I Try*
Sting, *Brand New Day*	1999	Sarah McLachlan, *I Will Remember You*
Eric Clapton, *My Father's Eyes*	1998	Celine Dion, *My Heart Will Go On*
Elton John, *Candle in the Wind (1997)*	1997	Sarah McLachlan, *Building a Mystery*
Eric Clapton, *Change the World*	1996	Toni Braxton, *Un-Break My Heart*
Seal, *Kiss From a Rose*	1995	Annie Lennox, *No More "I Love You"s*
Elton John, *Can You Feel the Love Tonight*	1994	Sheryl Crow, *All I Wanna Do*
Sting, *If I Ever Lose My Faith in You*	1993	Whitney Houston, *I Will Always Love You*
Eric Clapton, *Tears in Heaven*	1992	k.d. lang, *Constant Craving*
Michael Bolton, *When a Man Loves a Woman*	1991	Bonnie Raitt, *Something to Talk About*

The first winner of this award was Perry Como in 1958, for his million-selling *Catch a Falling Star.* A separate award for female singers in this category was not introduced until 1976, when Carole King won for her single *Tapestry.*

What is the title of the top best-selling album in Canada?
see p.130 for the answer

A *Rumours,* by Fleetwood Mac
B *Thriller,* by Michael Jackson
C *The Woman in Me,* by Shania Twain

THE 10 🍁
LATEST JUNO AWARDS FOR BEST NEW GROUP

YEAR	GROUP
2001	Nickelback
2000	Sky
1999	Johnny Favourite Swing Orchestra
1998	Leahy
1997	The Killjoys
1996	The Philosopher Kings
1995	Moist
1994	The Waltons
1993	Skydiggers
1992	Infidels

Source: *CARAS*

The 1996 winner, The Philosopher Kings, is a Toronto pop-soul band whose hits include *Charms* in 1995 and *Cry* and *Hurts to Love You* in 1998. However, two of the members are best known for creating and supplying the voices for Prozzäk, a 1998 pop group consisting of two animated characters.

TOP 10 🍁
MADONNA SINGLES IN CANADA

	SINGLE	YEAR
1	*Vogue*	1990
2	*Justify My Love*	1990
3	*Secret*	1994
4	*Music*	2000
5	*Papa Don't Preach*	1986
6	*This Used to Be My Playground*	1992
7	*Live to Tell*	1986
8	*American Pie*	2000
9	*Like a Virgin*	1985
10	*Like a Prayer*	1989

MATERIAL GIRL

Madonna's hit singles span three decades. Her marriage in 2000 to British film director Guy Ritchie generated media frenzy, despite being an unusually private celebrity event.

TOP 10
RAP ALBUMS IN CANADA

	TITLE/ARTIST	YEAR
1	*The Marshall Mathers LP*, Eminem	2000
2	*Please Hammer Don't Hurt 'Em*, M.C. Hammer	1990
3	*To the Extreme*, Vanilla Ice	1990
4	*Very Necessary*, Salt-N-Pepa	1993
5	*Chronic 2001*, Dr. Dre	2000
6	*Totally Krossed Out*, Kris Kross	1992
7	*Harlem World*, Mase	1997
8	*No Way Out*, Puff Daddy and The Family	1997
9	*Unleash the Dragon*, Sisqo	2000
10	*Black Sunday*, Cypress Hill	1993

TOP 10
JAZZ ALBUMS IN THE US

	ALBUM/ARTIST OR GROUP	YEAR
1	*Time Out Featuring Take Five*, Dave Brubeck Quartet	1960
2	*Hello Dolly*, Louis Armstrong	1964
3	*Getz & Gilberto*, Stan Getz and Joao Gilberto	1964
4	*Sun Goddess*, Ramsey Lewis	1975
5	*Jazz Samba*, Stan Getz and Charlie Byrd	1962
6	*Bitches Brew*, Miles Davis	1970
7	*The In Crowd*, Ramsey Lewis Trio	1965
8	*Time Further Out*, Dave Brubeck Quartet	1961
9	*Mack The Knife – Ella In Berlin*, Ella Fitzgerald	1960
10	*Exodus To Jazz*, Eddie Harris	1961

Dave Brubeck's *Time Out* album spent 86 weeks in the American Top 40 between 1960 and 1962, an unprecedented achievement for a jazz album during that era and due, not least, to the huge popularity of the track featured in its full title, *Take Five*, which hit US No. 25 on the pop chart.

TOP 10
RAP SINGLES IN CANADA

	TITLE/ARTIST OR GROUP	YEAR
1	*Rapper's Delight*, Sugarhill Gang	1980
2	*I'll Be Missing You*, Puff Daddy & Faith Evans (featuring 112)	1997
3	*Push It*, Salt-N-Pepa	1988
4	*Let Your Backbone Slide*, Maestro Fresh-Wes	1990
5	*Wild Thing*, Tone Loc	1989
6	*U Can't Touch This*, M.C. Hammer	1990
7	*Bust a Move*, Young M.C.	1989
8	*Walk This Way*, Run D.M.C.	1986
9	*Insane in the Brain*, Cyprus Hill	1993
10	*I'll Be There For You/ You're All I Need (To Get By)*, Method Man featuring Mary J. Blige	1995

Source: *Music Data Research*

Sugarhill Gang's *Rapper Delight*, the biggest rap record ever in Canada, charted in the early 1980s, long before the heydays of rap – the 1990s. It sold over 200,000 copies, more than any other rap single in history, even though it spent only eight weeks at No. 1.

TOP 10
HEAVY-METAL ALBUMS IN CANADA

	TITLE/ARTIST/YEAR	SALES ($)
1 =	*Bat Out of Hell*, Meatloaf, 1978	2,000,000
=	*Led Zeppelin IV*, Led Zeppelin, 1971	2,000,000
3 =	*1984*, Van Halen, 1984	1,000,000
=	*Back in Black*, AC/DC, 1980	1,000,000
=	*The Best of Bon Jovi: Crossroads*, Bon Jovi, 1994	1,000,000
=	*Metallica*, Metallica, 1991	1,000,000
=	*Slippery When Wet*, Bon Jovi, 1987	1,000,000
8	*Hysteria*, Def Leppard, 1988	900,000
9 =	*Bat Out of Hell II*, Meatloaf, 1993	800,000
=	*Get a Grip*, Aerosmith, 1993	800,000

Source: *Music Data Research*

♣ TOP 10 COUNTRY ALBUMS IN CANADA

(Album/artist or group, year)

① *Come On Over*, Shania Twain, 1997 **②** *The Woman in Me*, Shania Twain, 1995 **③** *Kenny Roger's Greatest Hits*, Kenny Rogers, 1980 **④** *Anne Murray's Greatest Hits*, Anne Murray, 1980 **⑤** *John Denver's Greatest Hits*, John Denver, 1973 **⑥** *Once Upon a Christmas*, Kenny Rogers and Dolly Parton, 1984 **⑦** *Ropin' the Wind*, Garth Brooks, 1991 **⑧** *No Fences*, Garth Brooks, 1990 **⑨** *Wide Open Spaces*, Dixie Chicks, 1999 **⑩** *Greatest Hits Collection*, Alan Jackson, 1995   Source: *Music Data Research*

TOP 10 ★
REGGAE ALBUMS IN THE US, 2000

ALBUM/ARTIST OR GROUP

1 *Chant Down Babylon*, Bob Marley

2 *Art and Life*, Beenie Man

3 *Reggae Gold 2000*, Various Artists

4 *Stage One*, Sean Paul

5 *Reggae Party*, Various Artists

6 *Reggae Gold 1999*, Various Artists

7 *Scrolls of the Prophet –
The Best of Peter Tosh*, Peter Tosh

8 *Unchained Spirit*, Buju Banton

9 *1999 Biggest Ragga Dancehall
Anthems*, Various Artists

10 *More Fire*, Capleton

Source: Billboard

TOP 10 🍁
FRANCOPHONE ALBUMS IN CANADA

ALBUM/ARTIST OR GROUP	YEAR
1 *D'eux*, Celine Dion	1995
2 *Notre-Dame de Paris*, Various artists	1997
3 *Beau Dommage*, Beau Dommage	1994
4 *Harmonium*, L'Heptade	1991
5 *Helene*, Roch Voisine	1993
6 *Dion Chante Plamondon*, Celin Dion	1991
7 *En Catimini*, La Chicane	1999
8 *Grand Paleur Petit Faiseur*, Kevin Parent	1998
9 *Incognito*, Celine Dion	1991
10 *Rendez-vous doux*, Gerry Boulet	1991

TOP 10 🍁
COUNTRY SINGLES IN CANADA

SINGLE/ARTIST OR GROUP	YEAR
1 *Islands in the Stream*, Kenny Rogers and Dolly Parton	1983
2 *To All the Girls I've Loved Before*, Julio Iglesias and Willie Nelson	1984
3 *My Way*, Elvis Presley	1977
4 *You Needed Me*, Anne Murray	1978
5 *Queen of Hearts*, Juice Newton	1981
6 *Coward of the County*, Kenny Rogers	1980
7 *Lady*, Kenny Rogers	1980
8 *Angel of the Morning*, Juice Newton	1981
9 *Southern Nights*, Glen Campbell	1977
10 *Don't It Make My Brown Eyes Blue*, Crystal Gayle	1977

Source: *Music Data Research*

Duets take the top two spots in this list. *Islands in the Stream*, written by the Bee Gees, sold over 200,000 copies in Canada and spent nine weeks at No. 1 in 1983. Meanwhile, *To All the Girls I've Loved Before*, a No. 1 hit in 1984, paired Julio Iglesias, one of the world's greatest Latin easy-listening singers, with US country music legend Willie Nelson.

BON JOVI
Born John Francis Bongiovi, Jon Bon Jovi and his band Bon Jovi have won chart success and global acclaim since their first recordings in 1984, with Slippery When Wet *one of the best-selling albums of the 1980s.*

Gold, Platinum & Diamond Discs

TOP 10 🍁
ACTS WITH THE MOST GOLD SINGLES IN CANADA

	ARTIST	GOLD ALBUM AWARDS
1	Bee Gees	10
2	Donna Summer	9
3	Culture Club	7
4 =Bryan Adams		6
	=Cyndi Lauper	6
6 =David Bowie		5
	=Elton John	5
	=Kenny Rogers	5
	=Lionel Richie	5
	=John Cougar Mellencamp	5

Source: CRIA

The Canadian Recording Industry Association (CRIA) awards Gold certifications to those artists who have sold 50,000 units. Platinum Awards represent sales of 100,000 units, and Diamond Awards represent sales of 1 million.

TOP 10 ★
FEMALE ARTISTS WITH THE MOST GOLD ALBUMS IN THE US

	ARTIST	GOLD ALBUM AWARDS
1	Barbra Streisand	41
2	Reba McEntire	20
3	Linda Ronstadt	16
4	Olivia Newton-John	15
5	Madonna	14
6 =Aretha Franklin		13
	=Anne Murray	13
8 =Dolly Parton		12
	=Gloria Estefan	12
	=Tanya Tucker	12
	=Amy Grant	12

Source: RIAA

TOP 10 🍁
FEMALE ARTISTS WITH THE MOST PLATINUM AND MULTI-PLATINUM ALBUMS IN CANADA

	ARTIST	PLATINUM AND MULTI-PLATINUM ALBUM AWARDS
1	Celine Dion	23
2 =Anne Murray		17
	=Mariah Carey	17
4	Whitney Houston	16
5 =Pat Benatar		16
6 =Barbra Streisand		14
7 =Olivia Newton-John		13
8 =Cyndi Lauper		10
9 =Tina Turner		9
	=Madonna	9

Source: CRIA

MARIAH CAREY

Mariah Carey has sold over 100 million albums since 1990, and her singles success ranks her second only to Elvis Presley for weeks at US No. 1.

TOP 10 🍁
ACTS WITH THE MOST PLATINUM AND MULTI-PLATINUM ALBUMS IN CANADA

	ARTIST	PLATINUM AND MULTI-PLATINUM ALBUM AWARDS
1	U2	33
2	Kenny Rogers	32
3	Billy Joel	25
4	Celine Dion	23
5 =Pink Floyd		20
	=Van Halen	20
	=Dire Straits	20
	=John Cougar Mellencamp	20
	=Bruce Springsteen	20
10	Bee Gees	18

Source: CRIA

TOP 10 🍁
MALE ARTISTS WITH THE MOST PLATINUM AND MULTI-PLATINUM ALBUMS IN CANADA

	ARTIST	PLATINUM AND MULTI-PLATINUM ALBUM AWARDS
1	Kenny Rogers	32
2	Billy Joel	25
3 =John Cougar Mellencamp		20
	=Bruce Springsteen	20
5 =Bob Seger		17
	=Bryan Adams	17
7	Elton John	16
8	Michael Jackson	15
9	Neil Diamond	12
10	Corey Hart	11

Source: CRIA

TWO OF U2

Formed in Ireland in 1976, supergroup U2 has enjoyed two decades of chart hits and sell-out international tours. The band still retains its original lineup.

TOP 10 ★
ACTS WITH THE MOST PLATINUM AND MULTI-PLATINUM ALBUMS IN THE US

ARTIST	PLATINUM AND MULTI-PLATINUM ALBUM AWARDS
1 The Beatles	118
2 =Led Zeppelin	97
=Garth Brooks	97
4 Elvis Presley	75
5 Billy Joel	74
6 Pink Floyd	66
7 The Eagles	63
8 Elton John	58
9 Barbra Streisand	55
10 Aerosmith	53

Source: *RIAA*

TOP 10 ★
ARTISTS WITH THE MOST PLATINUM AND MULTI-PLATINUM ALBUMS IN THE UK

ARTIST	PLATINUM AND MULTI-PLATINUM ALBUM AWARDS
1 Michael Jackson	38
=Madonna	38
=Simply Red	38
4 Queen	33
5 Phil Collins	31
6 Oasis	28
7 Dire Straits	27
8 U2	25
9 =Fleetwood Mac	23
=George Michael	23

Source: *BPI*

THE 10 🍁
FIRST DIAMOND ALBUMS IN CANADA

	ALBUM/ARTIST	DATE
1	*Rumours*, Fleetwood Mac	May 1978
2	*Saturday Night Fever*, Soundtrack,	June 1978
3	*Grease*, Soundtrack	Nov 1978
4	*Bat Out of Hell*, Meat Loaf	Mar 1979
5	*Breakfast in America*, Supertramp	Oct 1979
6	*Crime of the Century*, Supertramp	Nov 1979
7	*Dark Side of the Moon*, Pink Floyd	Aug 1980
8	*Kenny Rogers' Greatest Hits*, Kenny Rogers	May 1981
9	*Led Zeppelin IV*, Led Zeppelin	Dec 1982
10	*Thriller*, Michael Jackson	Nov 1983

Source: *CRIA*

Which speciality cable channel has the most subscribers?
see p.184 for the answer

A TSN – The Sports Network
B CBC Newsworld
C YTV (Youth Television)

Classical & Opera

TOP 10 CITIES WITH THE MOST OPERAS

(City/performances)*

❶ **Vienna**, Austria, 32 ❷ **Berlin**, Germany, 21 ❸ **Prague**, Czech Republic, 20 ❹ **Paris**, France, 16 ❺ **Hamburg**, Germany, 13 ❻ = **London**, UK, 12; = **Zurich**, Switzerland, 12 ❽ = **New York**, US, 11; = **Munich**, Germany, 11 ❿ **Hanover**, Germany, 10

* Sample during a 12-month period

TOP 10 ★
LONGEST OPERAS PERFORMED AT THE METROPOLITAN OPERA HOUSE*

OPERA/COMPOSER	RUNNING TIME* HR:MIN
1 *Götterdämmerung*, Richard Wagner	4:27
2 *Die Meistersinger von Nürnberg*, Richard Wagner	4:21
3 *Parsifal*, Richard Wagner	4:17
4 =*Les Troyens*, Hector Berlioz	4:02
=*Siegfried*, Richard Wagner	4:02
6 *Tristan und Isolde*, Richard Wagner	4:00
7 *Die Walküre*, Richard Wagner	3:41
8 *Don Carlo*, Giuseppe Verdi	3:33
9 *Semiramide*, Gioachino Rossini	3:30
10 *Lohengrin*, Richard Wagner	3:28

* In current repertory

 # Excluding intervals

Source: *Metropolitan Opera House*

ANDREA BOCELLI

Despite his blindness, Italian opera singer Andrea Bocelli has achieved remarkable success both in performance and through his internationally best-selling albums.

TOP 10 ★
MOST PROLIFIC CLASSICAL COMPOSERS

COMPOSER	HOURS OF MUSIC
1 Joseph Haydn (1732–1809, Austrian)	340
2 George Handel (1685–1759, German-English)	303
3 Wolfgang Amadeus Mozart (1756–91, Austrian)	202
4 Johann Sebastian Bach (1685–1750, German)	175
5 Franz Schubert (1797–1828, German)	134
6 Ludwig van Beethoven (1770–1827, German)	120
7 Henry Purcell (1659–95, English)	116
8 Giuseppe Verdi (1813–1901, Italian)	87
9 Anton Dvorák (1841–1904, Czech)	79
10 =Franz Liszt (1811–86, Hungarian)	76
=Peter Tchaikovsky (1840–93, Russian)	76

This list is based on a survey conducted by *Classical Music* magazine, which ranked classical composers by the total number of hours of music each composed. If the length of the composer's working life is brought into the calculation, Schubert wins: his 134 hours were composed in a career of 18 years, giving an average of 7 hours 27 minutes per annum.

TOP 10 🍁
CLASSICAL ALBUMS IN CANADA

ALBUM/PERFORMER(S)	YEAR
1 *Romanza*, Andrea Bocelli	1997
2 *Sogno*, Andrea Bocelli	1999
3 *Three Tenors 1994*, José Carreras, Placido Domingo, Luciano Pavarotti	1994
4 *Sacred Arias*, Andrea Bocelli	1999
5 *Voice of an Angel*, Charlotte Church	1999
6 *Pavarotti & Friends 2*, Luciano Pavarotti	1995
7 *Perhaps Love*, Placido Domingo	1981
8 *Luciano Pavarotti & Friends*, Luciano Pavarotti	1993
9 *Bach: The Goldberg Variations*, Glen Gould	1982
10 *Switch-On Back*, Walter Carlos	1969

Source: *Music Data Research*

THE 10 🍁
LATEST WINNERS OF THE "BEST CLASSICAL ALBUM: SOLO OR CHAMBER ENSEMBLE" JUNO AWARD

YEAR	SOLOIST/INSTRUMENT	COMPOSER/TITLE
2001	James Ehnes, violin	Bach, *The Six Sonatas and Partitas for Solo Violin*
2000	St. Lawrence String Quartet	Schumann, *String Quartets*
1999	Angela Hewitt, piano	Bach, *Well-Tempered Clavier – Book 1*
1998	Marc-André Hamelin, piano	*Marc-André Hamelin Plays Franz Liszt*
1997	Marc-André Hamelin, piano	Scriabin, *The Complete Piano Sonatas*
1996	Marc-André Hamelin, piano	Alkan, *Grande Sonate/Sonatine/Le Festin d'Esope*
1995	Erica Goodman, harp	*Erica Goodman Plays Canadian Harp Music*
1994	Louis Lortie, piano	Beethoven, *Piano Sonatas, Opus 10, Nos. 1–3*
1993	Louis Lortie, piano	Beethoven, *Piano Sonatas*
1992	Louis Lortie, piano	Liszt, *Années de Pelerinage*

Source: *Canadian Academy of Recording Arts and Sciences*

TOP 10 ★
LARGEST OPERA THEATERS

	THEATER	LOCATION	CAPACITY*
1	Arena di Verona#	Verona, Italy	16,663
2	Municipal Opera Theater#	St. Louis, US	11,745
3	Teatro alla Scala	Milan, Italy	3,600
4	Civic Opera House	Chicago, US	3,563
5	=The Metropolitan	New York, US	3,500
	=Teatro San Carlo	Naples, Italy	3,500
7	Music Hall	Cincinnati, US	3,417
8	=Teatro Massimo	Palermo, Italy	3,200
	=Hummingbird Centre	Toronto, Canada	3,200
10	Halle aux Grains	Toulouse, France	3,000

* *For indoor venues seating capacity only is given, although capacity is often larger when standing capacity is included*

Open-air venue

Although there are many more venues in the world where opera is regularly performed, the above list is limited to those venues whose principal performances are opera.

CLASSIC CONDUCTOR
Leonard Bernstein's posthumous Grammy Award for Candide *was one of the 16 Grammys he won, including a Lifetime Achievement Award.*

THE 10 🍁
LATEST WINNERS OF THE "BEST CLASSICAL ALBUM: LARGE ENSEMBLE" JUNO AWARD

YEAR	COMPOSER/WORK	CONDUCTOR*/ORCHESTRA
2001	Sibelius, *Lemminkäinen Suite – Night Ride and Sunrise*	Jukka-Pekka Saraste, Toronto Symphony Orchestra
2000	Respighi, *La Boutique Fantasque*	Orchestre Symphonique de Montreal
1999	Handel, *Music for the Royal Fireworks*	Jeanne Lamon, Tafelmusik
1998	Mozart, *Horn Concertos*	Mario Bernardi, CBC Vancouver Orchestra
1997	*Ginastera/Villa-Lobos/Evangelista*	I Musici de Montreal
1996	Shostakovich, *Symphonies Nos. 5 and 9*	Charles Dutoit, Orchestre Symphonique de Montreal
1995	Bach, *Brandenburg Concertos Nos. 1–6*	Jeanne Lamon, Tafelmusik
1994	Handel, *Concerti Grossi, Opus 3, Nos. 1–6*	Jeanne Lamon, Tafelmusik
1993	Handel, *Excerpts from Floridante*	Jeanne Lamon, Tafelmusik
1992	Debussy, *Pelléas et Mélisande*	Charles Dutoit, Orchestre Symphonique de Montreal

* *Or musical director*

Source: *Canadian Academy of Recording Arts and Sciences*

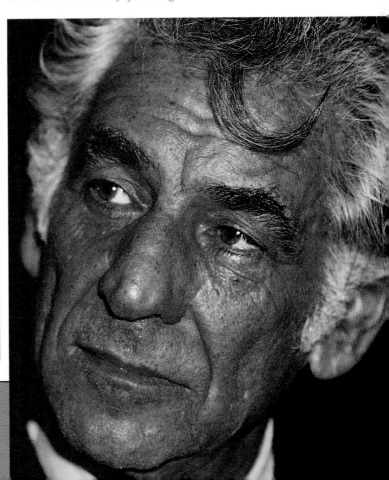

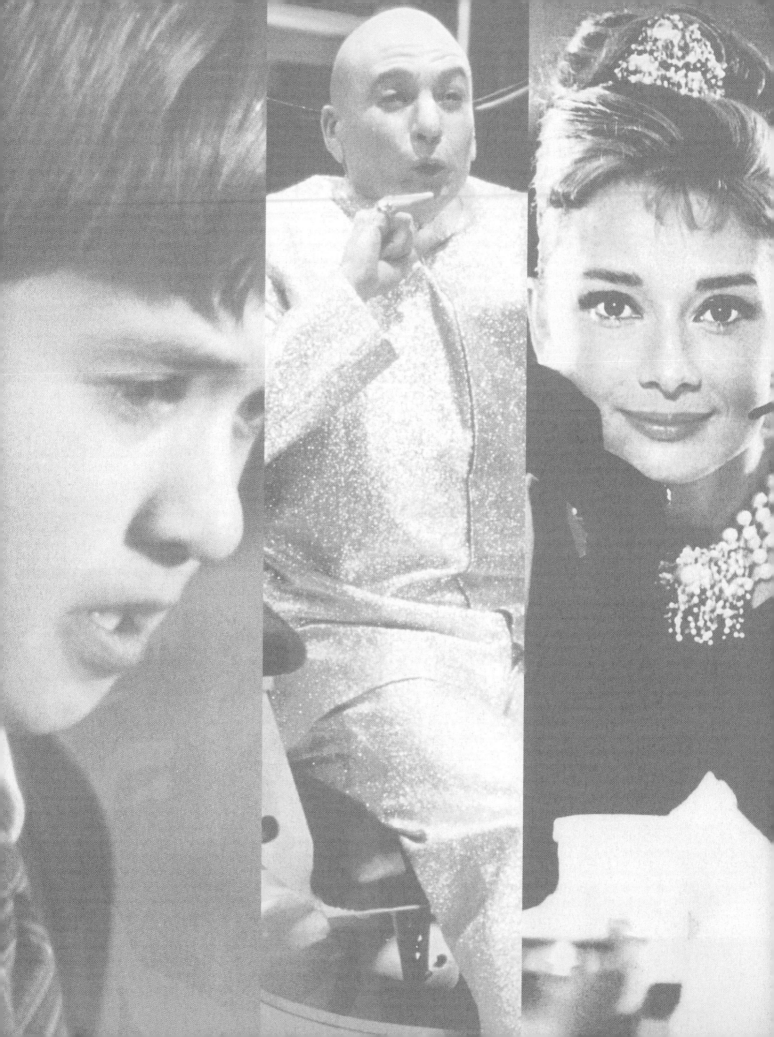

STAGE & SCREEN

MUCH ADO ABOUT SOMETHING

Much Ado About Nothing, starring Emma Thompson and Kenneth Branagh (who also directed it), achieved both critical and commercial success.

THE 10
LATEST DORA AWARDS FOR OUTSTANDING MUSICAL PRODUCTION

YEAR	MUSICAL
2000	*Cabaret*
1999	*Norma*
1998	*Oedipus Rex*
1997	*Ragtime*
1996	*A Little Night Magic*
1995	*Tommy*
1994	*Crazy for You*
1993	*Kiss of the Spiderwoman*
1992	*Closer than Ever*
1991	*Hush*

The Dora Mavor Moore Awards, established in 1981, honor outstanding achievements in Toronto theater and dance. These juried annual awards are presented to winners in a total of 29 categories. They are named after Dora Mavor Moore (1888–1979), a Scottish-born actor and director who was influential in early Canadian professional theater.

THE 10
LATEST DORA AWARDS FOR OUTSTANDING PRODUCTION OF A PLAY

YEAR	PLAY
2000	*Endgame*
1999	*The Drawer Boy*
1998	*Patience*
1997	*The Three Lives of Lucie Cabrol*
1996	*The Seven Streams of the River Ota*
1995	*Molly Wood*
1994	*Homeward Bound*
1993	*Whale*
1992	*Three Sisters*
1991	*Lilies*

TOP 10
FILMS OF SHAKESPEARE PLAYS

	FILM	YEAR
1	*William Shakespeare's Romeo + Juliet*	1996
2	*Romeo and Juliet*	1968
3	*Much Ado About Nothing*	1993
4	*Hamlet*	1990
5	*Henry V*	1989
6	*Hamlet*	1996
7	*Richard III*	1995
8	*Othello*	1995
9	*The Taming of the Shrew*	1967
10	*Hamlet*	1948

The romantic appeal of *Romeo and Juliet* has ensured its leading positions on this list.

THE 10
FIRST PLAYS WRITTEN BY SHAKESPEARE

	PLAY	YEAR WRITTEN (APPROX.)
1	*Titus Andronicus*	1588–90
2	*Love's Labour's Lost*	1590
3	*Henry VI, Parts I–III*	1590–91
4 =	*The Comedy of Errors*	1591
=	*Richard III*	1591
=	*Romeo and Juliet*	1591
7	*The Two Gentlemen of Verona*	1592–93
8	*A Midsummer Night's Dream*	1593–94
9	*Richard II*	1594
10	*King John*	1595

Only scant records remain of the early performances of Shakespeare's plays, and only half of the plays appeared in print in his lifetime.

THE 10 LATEST TONY AWARDS FOR BEST MUSICAL
(Year/play)

❶ 2000 *Contact* ❷ 1999 *Fosse* ❸ 1998 *The Lion King* ❹ 1997 *Titanic* ❺ 1996 *Rent* ❻ 1995 *Sunset Boulevard* ❼ 1994 *Passion* ❽ 1993 *Kiss of the Spider Woman* ❾ 1992 *Crazy for You* ❿ 1991 *The Will Rogers Follies*

THE 10 ★
LATEST TONY AWARDS FOR AN ACTOR*

YEAR	ACTOR/PLAY
2000	Stephen Dillane, *The Real Thing*
1999	Brian Dennehy, *Death of a Salesman*
1998	Anthony LaPaglia, *A View From the Bridge*
1997	Christopher Plummer, *Barrymore*
1996	George Grizzard, *A Delicate Balance*
1995	Ralph Fiennes, *Hamlet*
1994	Stephen Spinella, *Angels in America Part II: Perestroika*
1993	Ron Leibman, *Angels in America Part I: Millennium Approaches*
1992	Judd Hirsch, *Conversations with My Father*
1991	Nigel Hawthorne, *Shadowlands*

In a play

The Tony Awards, established in 1947 by the American Theater Wing, honor outstanding Broadway plays and musicals, actors and actresses, music, costume, and other contributions. The awards are named after Antoinette Perry (1888–1946), a Broadway actor who helped set up the Stage Door Canteen during World War II.

THE 10 ★
LATEST TONY AWARDS FOR AN ACTRESS*

YEAR	ACTRESS/PLAY
2000	Jennifer Ehle, *The Real Thing*
1999	Judi Dench, *Amy's View*
1998	Marie Mullen, *The Beauty Queen of Leenane*
1997	Janet McTeer, *A Doll's House*
1996	Zoë Caldwell, *Master Class*
1995	Cherry Jones, *The Heiress*
1994	Diana Rigg, *Medea*
1993	Madeline Kahn, *The Sisters Rosensweig*
1992	Glenn Close, *Death and the Maiden*
1991	Mercedes Ruehl, *Lost in Yonkers*

In a play

TOP 10 ★
LONGEST-RUNNING SHOWS ON BROADWAY

	SHOW	PERFORMANCES*
1	*Cats*, 1982–2000	7,485
2	*A Chorus Line*, 1975–90	6,137
3	*Oh! Calcutta!*, 1976–89	5,962
4	*Les Misérables*, 1987–	5,698#
5	*The Phantom of the Opera*, 1988–	5,398#
6	*Miss Saigon*, 1991–2001	4,095
7	*42nd Street*, 1980–89	3,486
8	*Grease*, 1972–80	3,388
9	*Fiddler on the Roof*, 1964–72	3,242
10	*Life with Father*, 1939–47	3,224

* As of January 1, 2001

Still running

Source: *The League of American Theaters and Producers*

Cats, which finally closed on September 10, 2000, became the longest-running Broadway show of all time on June 19, 1997, when it notched up its 6,138th performance. *Life with Father*, the earliest show to be listed here and the only non-musical, was a roaring success from the moment it opened. Its popularity had not been predicted, and after the lead parts were refused by major actors and actresses, the author Howard Lindsay and his wife, Dorothy Stickney, decided to play the roles themselves. They continued to do so, amid rave reviews, for the next five years.

TOP 10 ★
LONGEST-RUNNING THRILLERS OF ALL TIME ON BROADWAY

	THRILLER	PERFORMANCES
1	*Deathtrap*, 1978–82	1,793
2	*Arsenic and Old Lace*, 1941–44	1,444
3	*Angel Street*, 1941–1944	1,295
4	*Sleuth*, 1970–73	1,222
5	*Dracula*, 1977–80	925
6	*Witness for the Prosecution*, 1954–56	644
7	*Dial M for Murder*, 1952–54	552
8	*Sherlock Holmes*, 1975–76	479
9	*An Inspector Calls*, 1994–95	454
10	*Ten Little Indians*, 1944–45	424

Source: Theatre World

OUT OF THEIR MISERY

Les Misérables has achieved the dual feat of being one of the longest-running musicals both in London and on Broadway.

Film Hits

TOP 10

FILMS SHOWN AT THE MOST CINEMAS IN THE US

	FILM	OPENING WEEKEND	CINEMAS
1	Mission: Impossible II	May 24, 2000	3,653
2	Scream 3	Feb 4, 2000	3,467
3	The Perfect Storm	June 30, 2000	3,407
4	Wild Wild West	June 30, 1999	3,342
5	Book of Shadows: Blair Witch 2	Oct 27, 2000	3,317
6	Austin Powers: The Spy Who Shagged Me	June 11, 1999	3,312
7	Godzilla	May 20, 1998	3,310
8	Battlefield Earth	May 12, 2000	3,307
9	Lost in Space	Apr 3, 1998	3,306
10	The Lost World: Jurassic Park	May 23, 1997	3,281

TOP 10 — FILMS BY ATTENDANCE

	FILM	YEAR	ATTENDANCE
1	Gone With the Wind	1939	208,100,000
2	Star Wars	1977	198,600,000
3	The Sound of Music	1965	170,600,000
4	E.T.: The Extra-Terrestrial	1982	151,600,000
5	The Ten Commandments	1956	132,800,000
6	The Jungle Book	1967	126,300,000
7	Titanic	1997	124,300,000
8	Jaws	1975	123,300,000
9	Doctor Zhivago	1965	122,700,000
10	101 Dalmatians	1961	119,600,000

This list is based on the actual number of people buying tickets at the US box office. Because it takes account of the large numbers of tickets sold to children and other discounted sales, it differs both from lists that present total box office receipts and those that are adjusted for inflation.

TOP 10 — FILM SERIES OF ALL TIME

	FILM SERIES	DATES
1	Star Wars / The Empire Strikes Back / Return of the Jedi / Episode I – The Phantom Menace	1977–99
2	Jurassic Park / The Lost World: Jurassic Park	1993–97
3	Batman / Batman Returns / Batman Forever / Batman & Robin	1989–97
4	Raiders of the Lost Ark / Indiana Jones and the Temple of Doom / Indiana Jones and the Last Crusade	1981–89
5	Mission: Impossible / Mission: Impossible 2	1996–2000
6	Star Trek: The Motion Picture / II / III / IV / V / VI / Generations / First Contact / Insurrection	1979–98
7	Back to the Future / II / III	1985–90
8	Lethal Weapon / 2 / 3 / 4	1987–98
9	Toy Story / Toy Story 2	1995–99
10	Home Alone / 2: Lost in NY	1990–92

TOP 10 — HIGHEST-GROSSING FILMS OF ALL TIME

	FILM	YEAR	CANADA & US	GROSS INCOME (US$) WORLD TOTAL
1	Titanic	1997	600,800,000	1,835,400,000
2	Star Wars: Episode I – The Phantom Menace	1999	431,100,000	922,600,000
3	Jurassic Park	1993	357,100,000	920,100,000
4	Independence Day	1996	306,200,000	811,200,000
5	Star Wars	1977	461,000,000	798,000,000
6	The Lion King	1994	312,900,000	771,900,000
7	E.T.: The Extra-Terrestrial	1982	399,800,000	704,800,000
8	Forrest Gump	1994	329,700,000	679,700,000
9	The Sixth Sense	1999	293,500,000	660,700,000
10	The Lost World: Jurassic Park	1997	229,100,000	614,400,000

THE 10 — LATEST GOLDEN REEL AWARD WINNERS*

YEAR	FILM	DOMESTIC BOX OFFICE ($)
2000	The Art of War	4,500,000
1999	Les Boys II	5,500,000
1998	Les Boys	6,800,000
1997	Air Bud	over 1,600,000
1996	Crash	over 1,230,000
1995	Johnny Mnemonic	over 3,000,000
1994	Louis 19, le roi des ondes	1,800,000
1993	La Florida	1,640,000
1992	Black Robe	2,850,000
1991	Ding et dong, le film	2,350,000

* Given by the Academy of Canadian Cinema & Television (ACC&T) to the Canadian movie earning the most revenue at the box office

Source: ACC&T

TITANIC RISES

All-time highest grossing film Titanic has earned almost twice as much at the global box office as its closest rival, Star Wars: Episode I.

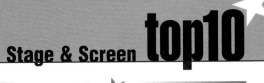

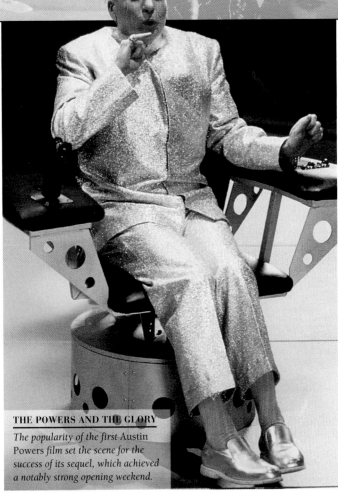

THE POWERS AND THE GLORY

The popularity of the first Austin Powers film set the scene for the success of its sequel, which achieved a notably strong opening weekend.

TOP 10 ⭐

OPENING WEEKENDS IN THE US

	FILM	RELEASE DATE	OPENING WEEKEND GROSS INCOME (US$)
1	The Lost World: Jurassic Park	May 23, 1997	72,132,785
2	Star Wars: Episode I – The Phantom Menace	May 21, 1999	64,820,970
3	Mission: Impossible II	May 24, 2000	57,845,297
4	Toy Story 2	Nov 24, 1999	57,388,839
5	Austin Powers: The Spy Who Shagged Me	June 11, 1999	54,917,604
6	X-Men	July 14, 2000	54,471,475
7	Batman Forever	June 16, 1995	52,784,433
8	Men in Black	July 2, 1997	51,068,455
9	Independence Day	July 3, 1996	50,228,264
10	Jurassic Park	June 11, 1993	47,059,560

A high-earning opening weekend (generally three days, Friday to Sunday, but sometimes a four-day holiday weekend) in the US is usually a pointer to the ongoing success of a film, but does not guarantee it.

TOP 10 🍁

HIGHEST-GROSSING CANADIAN FILMS WORLDWIDE*

	FILM	YEAR	GROSS INCOME (US$)
1	Porky's	1981	109,000,000
2	The Art of War	2000	32,000,000
3	Air Bud	1997	25,300,000
4	The Care Bears Movie	1985	23,000,000
5	The Red Violin	1999	15,000,000
6	Meatballs	1979	10,000,000
7	Dead Ringers	1996	9,130,000
8	The Sweet Hereafter	1997	8,150,000
9 =	Porky's II: The Next Day	1982	6,000,000
=	Les Boys	1997	6,000,000

* *Based on figures published in* Variety   *Source:* Take One

TOP 10 ⭐

FILMS OF 2000

	FILM	GROSS INCOME (US$) CANADA & US	WORLD TOTAL
1	How the Grinch Stole Christmas	260,000,000	340,300,000
2	Cast Away	216,900,000	346,600,000
3	Mission: Impossible II	215,400,000	545,400,000
4	Gladiator	186,700,000	470,700,000
5	The Perfect Storm	182,600,000	325,800,000
6	What Women Want	177,800,000	215,800,000
7	Meet the Parents	165,200,000	277,200,000
8	X-Men	157,300,000	294,300,000
9	Scary Movie	157,000,000	277,000,000
10	What Lies Beneath	155,400,000	275,500,000

GLAD TO SEE YOU

One of the most successful films of 2000, Gladiator echoes the epics of the past, a genre that many believed had been consigned to movie history.

Films of the Decades

FILMS OF THE 1930s

1	Gone With the Wind*	1939
2	Snow White and the Seven Dwarfs	1937
3	The Wizard of Oz	1939
4	The Woman in Red	1935
5	King Kong	1933
6	San Francisco	1936
7 =	Hell's Angels	1930
=	Lost Horizon	1937
=	Mr. Smith Goes to Washington	1939
10	Maytime	1937

* Winner of "Best Picture" Academy Award

Gone With the Wind and Snow White and the Seven Dwarfs have generated more income than any other prewar film. If the income from Gone With the Wind is adjusted to allow for inflation in the period since its release, it could also be regarded as the most successful film ever, earning some US$885 million in the US alone.

FILMS OF THE 1940s

1	Bambi	1942
2	Pinocchio	1940
3	Fantasia	1940
4	Cinderella	1949
5	Song of the South	1946
6	The Best Years of Our Lives*	1946
7	The Bells of St. Mary's	1945
8	Duel in the Sun	1946
9	Mom and Dad	1948
10	Samson and Delilah	1949

* Winner of "Best Picture" Academy Award

With the top four films of the decade classic Disney cartoons, the 1940s may be regarded as the "golden age" of the animated film. This colorful genre was especially appealing during and after the drabness of the war years.

MONKEY BUSINESS

In an iconic scene from King Kong, one of the 1930s' highest-earning films, the giant ape fights off his attackers while perched atop the newly opened Empire State Building.

FILMS OF THE 1950s

1	Lady and the Tramp	1955
2	Peter Pan	1953
3	Ben-Hur*	1959
4	The Ten Commandments	1956
5	Sleeping Beauty	1959
6	Around the World in 80 Days*	1956
7 =	The Greatest Show on Earth*	1952
=	The Robe	1953
9	The Bridge on the River Kwai*	1957
10	Peyton Place	1957

* Winner of "Best Picture" Academy Award

While the popularity of animated films continued, the 1950s was outstanding as the decade of the "big" picture (in cast and scale).

TOP 10 FILMS OF THE 1960s

❶ 101 Dalmatians, 1961 ❷ The Jungle Book, 1967 ❸ The Sound of Music*, 1965 ❹ Thunderball, 1965 ❺ Goldfinger, 1964 ❻ Doctor Zhivago, 1965 ❼ You Only Live Twice, 1967 ❽ The Graduate, 1968 ❾ Mary Poppins, 1964 ❿ Butch Cassidy and the Sundance Kid, 1969

* Winner of "Best Picture" Academy Award

TOP 10 ★
FILMS OF THE LAST 10 YEARS

1	Titanic*	1997
2	Star Wars: Episode I – The Phantom Menace	1999
3	Jurassic Park	1993
4	Independence Day	1996
5	The Lion King	1994
6	Forrest Gump*	1994
7	The Sixth Sense	1999
8	The Lost World: Jurassic Park	1997
9	Men in Black	1997
10	Armageddon	1998

Winner of "Best Picture" Academy Award

BRINGING THE HOUSE DOWN

The White House sustains a direct hit from an invading spacecraft in a scene from Independence Day, *one of the top films of the last 10 years.*

TOP 10 ★
FILMS OF THE 1970s

1	Star Wars	1977/97*
2	Jaws	1975
3	Close Encounters of the Third Kind	1977/80*
4	The Exorcist	1973/98*
5	Moonraker	1979
6	The Spy Who Loved Me	1977
7	The Sting #	1973
8	Grease	1978
9	The Godfather #	1972
10	Saturday Night Fever	1977

* *Date of re-release*

\# *Winner of "Best Picture" Academy Award*

In the 1970s the arrival of two prodigies, Steven Spielberg and George Lucas, set the scene for the high adventure blockbusters whose domination has continued ever since.

JAWS OF DEATH

After holding the record as the world's highest earning film, Jaws *was overtaken before the decade was out by* Star Wars.

TOP 10 FILMS OF THE 1980s

1 *E.T.: The Extra-Terrestrial*, 1982 **2** *Indiana Jones and the Last Crusade*, 1989 **3** *Batman*, 1989 **4** *Rain Man*, 1988 **5** *Return of the Jedi*, 1983 **6** *Raiders of the Lost Ark*, 1981 **7** *The Empire Strikes Back*, 1980 **8** *Who Framed Roger Rabbit?*, 1988 **9** *Back to the Future*, 1985 **10** *Top Gun*, 1986

Did You Know? In *Independence Day*, the American flag left on the Moon in 1969 by *Apollo 11* astronauts is seen standing proudly on the surface. In reality, the flag fell over when Neil Armstrong and "Buzz" Aldrin blasted off from the surface.

Film Genres

TOP 10 ★ WESTERNS

1	Dances With Wolves	1990
2	Wild Wild West	1999
3	Maverick	1994
4	Unforgiven	1992
5	Butch Cassidy and the Sundance Kid	1969
6	Jeremiah Johnson	1972
7	How the West Was Won	1962
8	Young Guns	1988
9	Young Guns II	1990
10	Pale Rider	1985

TOP 10 ★ GHOST FILMS

1	The Sixth Sense	1999
2	Ghost	1990
3	Ghostbusters	1984
4	Casper	1995
5	What Lies Beneath	2000
6	Ghostbusters II	1989
7	Sleepy Hollow	1999
8	The Haunting	1999
9	Beetlejuice	1988
10	The Nightmare Before Christmas	1993

TOP 10 ★ WEDDING FILMS

1	My Best Friend's Wedding	1997
2	Runaway Bride	1999
3	Four Weddings and a Funeral	1994
4	The Wedding Singer	1998
5	Father of the Bride	1991
6	Father of the Bride Part II	1995
7	Muriel's Wedding	1994
8	The Princess Bride	1987
9	Betsy's Wedding	1990
10	A Wedding	1978

TOP 10 ★ HORROR FILMS

1	Jurassic Park	1993
2	The Sixth Sense	1999
3	The Lost World: Jurassic Park	1997
4	Jaws	1975
5	The Mummy	1999
6	Godzilla	1998
7	The Exorcist	1973
8	Scary Movie	2000
9	The Blair Witch Project	1999
10	Interview With the Vampire	1994

TOP 10 ★ JAMES BOND FILMS

	FILM/YEAR	BOND ACTOR
1	The World Is Not Enough, 1999	Pierce Brosnan
2	GoldenEye, 1995	Pierce Brosnan
3	Tomorrow Never Dies, 1997	Pierce Brosnan
4	Moonraker, 1979	Roger Moore
5	For Your Eyes Only, 1981	Roger Moore
6	The Living Daylights, 1987	Timothy Dalton
7	The Spy Who Loved Me, 1977	Roger Moore
8	Octopussy, 1983	Roger Moore
9	Licence to Kill, 1990	Timothy Dalton
10	A View to a Kill, 1985	Roger Moore

TOP 10 ★ FILMS FEATURING DINOSAURS

1	Jurassic Park	1993
2	The Lost World: Jurassic Park	1997
3	Godzilla	1998
4	Dinosaur*	2000
5	Mission to Mars	2000
6	Fantasia*	1940
7	T-Rex: Back to the Cretaceous	1998
8	The Flintstones in Viva Rock Vegas	2000
9	The Land Before Time*	1988
10	Super Mario Bros.	1993

* Animated; others live-action with mechanical or computer-generated sequences

BLOCKBUSTERS
Ghostbusters starred Bill Murray alongside Dan Aykroyd and Harold Ramis, both of whom also cowrote the first film and its sequel.

FUTURE PERFECT

Schoolkid Marty McFly (Michael J. Fox) and scientist Dr. Emmett "Doc" L. Brown (Christopher Lloyd) test the Doc's time machine DeLorean.

TOP 10 ★
TIME TRAVEL FILMS

1	Terminator II: Judgment Day	1991
2	Back to the Future	1985
3	Austin Powers: The Spy Who Shagged Me	2000
4	Back to the Future III	1990
5	Back to the Future II	1989
6	Twelve Monkeys	1995
7	Timecop	1994
8	The Terminator	1984
9	Austin Powers: International Man of Mystery	1997
10	Pleasantville	1998

JAMES BOND

In 1952, at his Jamaica house Goldeneye, former Royal Navy intelligence officer-turned-journalist Ian Fleming (1908–64) was working on a spy story and searching for a suitable name for his hero, when his eye fell on a book, *Field Guide of Birds of the West Indies* by American ornithologist James Bond (1900–89). As Fleming later commented, "It struck me that this name, brief, unromantic, and yet very masculine, was just what I needed", and thus an internationally popular fictitious character and, later, a huge cinema industry, was born. The fictional James Bond's first appearance in print was in *Casino Royale*, published in Britain in 1953 and in the US a year later.

TOP 10 MAFIA FILMS

1 *The Untouchables*, 1987 2 *Analyze This*, 1999
3 *The Godfather, Part III*, 1990 4 *The Godfather*, 1972
5 *L.A. Confidential*, 1997 6 *Donnie Brasco*, 1997
7 *The Client*, 1994 8 *The Godfather, Part II*, 1974
9 *The Firm*, 1993 10 *The Whole Nine Yards*, 2000

TOP 10 ★
COP FILMS

1	The Fugitive	1993
2	Die Hard: With a Vengeance	1995
3	Basic Instinct	1992
4	Se7en	1995
5	Lethal Weapon 3	1993
6	Beverly Hills Cop	1984
7	Beverly Hills Cop II	1987
8	Lethal Weapon 4	1998
9	Speed	1994
10	Die Hard 2	1990

Although films in which one of the central characters is a policeman have never been among the most successful films of all time, many have earned respectable amounts at the box office. Both within and outside the Top 10, they are divided between those with a comic slant, such as the two *Beverly Hills Cop* films, and darker police thrillers, such as *Basic Instinct*. Films featuring FBI and CIA agents have been excluded from the reckoning, hence eliminating blockbusters such as *Mission: Impossible* and *The Silence of the Lambs*.

TOP 10 ★
COMEDY FILMS

1	Forrest Gump	1994
2	Home Alone	1990
3	Ghost	1990
4	Pretty Woman	1990
5	Mrs. Doubtfire	1993
6	There's Something About Mary	1998
7	Flintstones	1995
8	Notting Hill	1999
9	Who Framed Roger Rabbit?	1988
10	How the Grinch Stole Christmas	1999

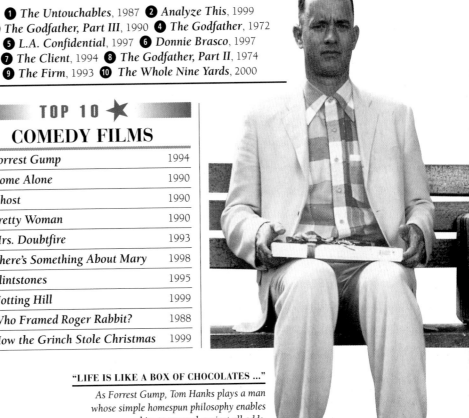

"LIFE IS LIKE A BOX OF CHOCOLATES ..."

As Forrest Gump, Tom Hanks plays a man whose simple homespun philosophy enables him to succeed against all odds.

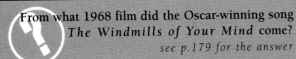

From what 1968 film did the Oscar-winning song *The Windmills of Your Mind* come?
see p.179 for the answer

A *The Graduate*
B *Funny Girl*
C *The Thomas Crown Affair*

Oscar-Winning Films

FILMS NOMINATED FOR THE MOST OSCARS

FILM/YEAR	AWARDS	NOMINATIONS
1 = *All About Eve*, 1950	6	14
= *Titanic*, 1997	11	14
3 = *Gone With the Wind*, 1939	8*	13
= *From Here to Eternity*, 1953	8	13
= *Shakespeare in Love*, 1998	7	13
= *Mary Poppins*, 1964	5	13
= *Who's Afraid of Virginia Woolf?*, 1966	5	13
= *Forrest Gump*, 1994	6	13
9 = *Mrs. Miniver*, 1942	6	12
= *The Song of Bernadette*, 1943	4	12
= *Johnny Belinda*, 1948	1	12
= *A Streetcar Named Desire*, 1951	4	12
= *On the Waterfront*, 1954	8	12
= *Ben-Hur*, 1959	11	12
= *Becket*, 1964	1	12
= *My Fair Lady*, 1964	8	12
= *Reds*, 1981	3	12
= *Dances With Wolves*, 1990	7	12
= *Schindler's List*, 1993	7	12
= *The English Patient*, 1996	9	12
= *Gladiator*, 2000	5	12

* *Plus two special awards*

While *Johnny Belinda* and *Becket* at least had the consolation of winning once out of their 12 nominations each, both *The Turning Point* (1977) and *The Color Purple* (1985) suffered the ignominy of receiving 11 nominations without a single win.

FILMS TO WIN THE MOST OSCARS

FILM/YEAR	NOMINATIONS	AWARDS
1 = *Ben-Hur*, 1959	12	11
= *Titanic*, 1997	14	11
3 *West Side Story*, 1961	11	10
4 = *Gigi*, 1958	9	9
= *The Last Emperor*, 1987	9	9
= *The English Patient*, 1996	12	9
7 = *Gone With the Wind*, 1939	13	8*
= *From Here to Eternity*, 1953	13	8
= *On the Waterfront*, 1954	12	8
= *My Fair Lady*, 1964	12	8
= *Cabaret*, 1972	10	8
= *Gandhi*, 1982	11	8
= *Amadeus*, 1984	11	8

* *Plus two special awards*

FIRST "BEST PICTURE" OSCAR-WINNING FILMS

YEAR	FILM
1927/28	*Wings*
1928/29	*Broadway Melody*
1930	*All Quiet on the Western Front*
1931	*Cimarron*
1932	*Grand Hotel*
1933	*Cavalcade*
1934	*It Happened One Night**
1935	*Mutiny on the Bounty*
1936	*The Great Ziegfeld*
1937	*The Life of Emile Zola*

* *Winner of Oscars for "Best Director," "Best Actor," "Best Actress," and "Best Screenplay"*

The first Academy Awards, popularly known as Oscars, were presented at a ceremony at the Hollywood Roosevelt Hotel on May 16, 1929, and were for films released in the period 1927–28. *Wings*, the first film to be honored as "Best Picture," was silent. A second ceremony, held at the Ambassador Hotel on October 31 of the same year, was for films released in 1928–29, and was won by *Broadway Melody*.

HIGHEST-EARNING "BEST PICTURE" OSCAR WINNERS

	FILM	YEAR
1	*Titanic*	1997
2	*Forrest Gump*	1994
3	*Gladiator*	2000
4	*Dances With Wolves*	1990
5	*Rain Man*	1988
6	*Schindler's List*	1993
7	*Shakespeare in Love*	1998
8	*The English Patient*	1996
9	*American Beauty*	1999
10	*Braveheart*	1995

Winning the Academy Award for "Best Picture" is no guarantee of box-office success: the award is given for a picture released the previous year, and by the time the Oscar ceremony takes place, the film-going public has already effectively decided on the winning picture's fate. Receiving the Oscar may enhance a successful picture's continuing earnings, but it is generally too late to revive a film that may already have been judged mediocre.

"BEST PICTURE" OSCAR WINNERS OF THE 1950s

YEAR	FILM
1950	*All About Eve*
1951	*An American in Paris*
1952	*The Greatest Show on Earth*
1953	*From Here to Eternity*
1954	*On the Waterfront*
1955	*Marty*
1956	*Around the World in 80 Days*
1957	*The Bridge on the River Kwai*
1958	*Gigi*
1959	*Ben-Hur*

The first winning film of the 1950s, *All About Eve*, received the most Oscar nominations (14), while the last, *Ben-Hur*, won the most (11).

SWORD PLAY

Michelle Yeoh stars in Crouching Tiger, Hidden Dragon, which crowned its international success and host of awards with the "Best Foreign Language Film" Oscar.

THE 10 ⭐

LATEST "BEST FOREIGN LANGUAGE FILM" OSCAR WINNERS

YEAR	ENGLISH TITLE/LANGUAGE
2000	*Crouching Tiger, Hidden Dragon,* Mandarin
1999	*All About My Mother,* Spanish
1998	*Life is Beautiful,* Italian
1997	*Character,* Dutch/English/ German/French
1996	*Kolya,* Czech/Russian
1995	*Antonia's Line,* Dutch
1994	*Burnt by the Sun,* Russian
1993	*The Age of Beauty,* Spanish
1992	*Indochina,* French/Vietnamese
1991	*Mediterraneo,* Italian

THE 10 ⭐
"BEST PICTURE" OSCAR WINNERS OF THE 1960s

YEAR	FILM
1960	*The Apartment*
1961	*West Side Story*
1962	*Lawrence of Arabia*
1963	*Tom Jones*
1964	*My Fair Lady*
1965	*The Sound of Music*
1966	*A Man for All Seasons*
1967	*In the Heat of the Night*
1968	*Oliver!*
1969	*Midnight Cowboy*

The 1960 winner, *The Apartment*, was the last black-and-white winner until *Schindler's List*, which was released in 1993.

THE 10 "BEST PICTURE" OSCAR WINNERS OF THE 1970s

(Year/film)

1 1970 *Patton* **2** 1971 *The French Connection* **3** 1972 *The Godfather* **4** 1973 *The Sting* **5** 1974 *The Godfather Part III* **6** 1975 *One Flew Over the Cuckoo's Nest* **7** 1976 *Rocky* **8** 1977 *Annie Hall* **9** 1978 *The Deer Hunter* **10** 1979 *Kramer vs. Kramer*

THE 10 ⭐
"BEST PICTURE" OSCAR WINNERS OF THE 1980s

YEAR	FILM
1980	*Ordinary People*
1981	*Chariots of Fire*
1982	*Gandhi*
1983	*Terms of Endearment*
1984	*Amadeus*
1985	*Out of Africa*
1986	*Platoon*
1987	*The Last Emperor*
1988	*Rain Man*
1989	*Driving Miss Daisy*

THE 10 ⭐
LATEST "BEST PICTURE" OSCAR WINNERS

YEAR	FILM
2000	*Gladiator*
1999	*American Beauty*
1998	*Shakespeare in Love*
1997	*Titanic*
1996	*The English Patient*
1995	*Braveheart*
1994	*Forrest Gump*
1993	*Schindler's List*
1992	*Unforgiven*
1991	*The Silence of the Lambs*

Which actor supplied the voice of Mushu in the animated film *Mulan*?
see p.169 for the answer
A Bruce Willis
B Eddie Murphy
C Jim Carrey

Oscar-Winning Stars

YOUNGEST OSCAR-WINNING ACTORS AND ACTRESSES

	ACTOR OR ACTRESS	AWARD/FILM (WHERE SPECIFIED)	YEAR	AGE*
1	Shirley Temple	Special Award – outstanding contribution during 1934	1934	6
2	Margaret O'Brien	Special Award (*Meet Me in St. Louis*)	1944	8
3	Vincent Winter	Special Award (*The Little Kidnappers*)	1954	8
4	Ivan Jandl	Special Award (*The Search*)	1948	9
5	Jon Whiteley	Special Award (*The Little Kidnappers*)	1954	10
6	Tatum O'Neal	"Best Supporting Actress" (*Paper Moon*)	1973	10
7	Anna Paquin	"Best Supporting Actress" (*The Piano*)	1993	11
8	Claude Jarman, Jr.	Special Award (*The Yearling*)	1946	12
9	Bobby Driscoll	Special Award (*The Window*)	1949	13
10	Hayley Mills	Special Award (*Pollyanna*)	1960	13

* At the time of the Award ceremony; those of apparently identical age have been ranked according to their precise age in days at the time of the ceremony

The Academy Awards ceremony usually takes place at the end of March in the year following that in which the film was released in the US, so the winners are generally at least a year older when they receive their Oscars than when they acted in their award-winning films.

THE 10 "BEST ACTRESS" OSCAR WINNERS OF THE 1970s

(Year/actress/film)

1 1970 Glenda Jackson, *Women in Love* **2** 1971 Jane Fonda, *Klute*
3 1972 Liza Minnelli, *Cabaret* **4** 1973 Glenda Jackson, *A Touch of Class*
5 1974 Ellen Burstyn, *Alice Doesn't Live Here Any More* **6** 1975 Louise Fletcher, *One Flew Over the Cuckoo's Nest**# **7** 1976 Faye Dunaway, *Network* **8** 1977 Diane Keaton, *Annie Hall**
9 1978 Jane Fonda, *Coming Home* **10** 1979 Sally Field, *Norma Rae*

* Winner of "Best Picture" Oscar
 # Winner of "Best Director," "Best Actor," and "Best Screenplay" Oscars

OSCAR

Founded on May 4, 1927, the Hollywood-based Academy of Motion Picture Arts and Sciences proposed improving the image of the film industry by issuing "awards for merit or distinction" in various categories. The award itself, a statuette designed by Cedric Gibbons, was modeled by a young artist, George Stanley. The gold-plated naked male figure holds a sword and stands on a reel of film. It was simply called "the statuette" up until 1931, when Academy librarian Mrs. Margaret Herrick said, "It looks like my Uncle Oscar!" – and the name stuck until this day.

WHO WAS · WHO WAS · WHO WAS · WHO WAS ?

"BEST ACTOR" OSCAR WINNERS OF THE 1970s

YEAR	ACTOR/FILM
1970	George C. Scott, *Patton**
1971	Gene Hackman, *The French Connection**
1972	Marlon Brando, *The Godfather**
1973	Jack Lemmon, *Save the Tiger*
1974	Art Carney, *Harry and Tonto*
1975	Jack Nicholson, *One Flew Over the Cuckoo's Nest**#
1976	Peter Finch, *Network*
1977	Richard Dreyfuss, *The Goodbye Girl*
1978	John Voight, *Coming Home*
1979	Dustin Hoffman, *Kramer vs. Kramer**

* Winner of "Best Picture" Oscar

 # Winner of "Best Director," "Best Actress," and "Best Screenplay" Oscars

FIRST CUCKOO

Winner of five Oscars, One Flew Over the Cuckoo's Nest *established the movie careers of both its stars, actor Jack Nicholson and producer Michael Douglas.*

THE 10 ★
"BEST ACTOR" OSCAR WINNERS OF THE 1980s

YEAR	ACTOR/FILM
1980	Robert De Niro, *Raging Bull*
1981	Henry Fonda, *On Golden Pond**
1982	Ben Kingsley, *Gandhi*#
1983	Robert Duvall, *Tender Mercies*
1984	F. Murray Abraham, *Amadeus*#
1985	William Hurt, *Kiss of the Spider Woman*
1986	Paul Newman, *The Color of Money*
1987	Michael Douglas, *Wall Street*
1988	Dustin Hoffman, *Rain Man*#
1989	Daniel Day-Lewis, *My Left Foot*

* *Winner of "Best Actress" Oscar*

Winner of "Best Picture" Oscar

THE 10 ★
"BEST ACTRESS" OSCAR WINNERS OF THE 1980s

YEAR	ACTRESS/FILM
1980	Sissy Spacek, *Coal Miner's Daughter*
1981	Katharine Hepburn, *On Golden Pond**
1982	Meryl Streep, *Sophie's Choice*
1983	Shirley MacLaine, *Terms of Endearment*#
1984	Sally Field, *Places in the Heart*
1985	Geraldine Page, *The Trip to Bountiful*
1986	Marlee Matlin, *Children of a Lesser God*
1987	Cher, *Moonstruck*
1988	Jodie Foster, *The Accused*
1989	Jessica Tandy, *Driving Miss Daisy*#

* *Winner of "Best Actor" Oscar*

Winner of "Best Picture" Oscar

FARGO

Frances McDormand's performance as policewoman Marge Gunderson in Fargo, directed by her husband Joel Cohen, gained her the 1996 "Best Actress" Oscar.

THE 10 ★
LATEST "BEST ACTOR" OSCAR WINNERS

YEAR	ACTOR/FILM
2000	Russell Crowe, *Gladiator*
1999	Kevin Spacey, *American Beauty**
1998	Roberto Benigni, *La vita é bella* (*Life Is Beautiful*)
1997	Jack Nicholson, *As Good as It Gets*#
1996	Geoffrey Rush, *Shine*
1995	Nicolas Cage, *Leaving Las Vegas*
1994	Tom Hanks, *Forrest Gump**
1993	Tom Hanks, *Philadelphia*
1992	Al Pacino, *Scent of a Woman*
1991	Anthony Hopkins, *The Silence of the Lambs**#

* *Winner of "Best Picture" Oscar*

Winner of "Best Actress" Oscar

Tom Hanks shares the honor of two consecutive wins with Spencer Tracy (1937: *Captains Courageous* and 1938: *Boys Town*). Only four other actors have won twice: Marlon Brando (1954; 1972), Gary Cooper (1941; 1952), Dustin Hoffman (1979; 1988), and Jack Nicholson (1975; 1997).

THE 10 ★
LATEST "BEST ACTRESS" OSCAR WINNERS

YEAR	ACTRESS/FILM
2000	Julia Roberts, *Erin Brockovich*
1999	Hilary Swank, *Boys Don't Cry*
1998	Gwyneth Paltrow, *Shakespeare in Love**
1997	Helen Hunt, *As Good as It Gets*#
1996	Frances McDormand, *Fargo*
1995	Susan Sarandon, *Dead Man Walking*
1994	Jessica Lange, *Blue Sky*
1993	Holly Hunter, *The Piano*
1992	Emma Thompson, *Howard's End*
1991	Jodie Foster, *The Silence of the Lambs**#

* *Winner of "Best Picture" Oscar*

Winner of "Best Actor" Oscar

And the Winner Is . . .

THE 10 ★
LATEST WINNERS OF THE CANNES PALME D'OR FOR "BEST FILM"

YEAR	FILM/COUNTRY
2000	*Dancer in the Dark*, Denmark
1999	*Rosetta*, France
1998	*Eternity and a Day*, Greece
1997	*The Eel*, Japan/ *The Taste of Cherries*, Iran
1996	*Secrets and Lies*, UK
1995	*Underground*, Yugoslavia
1994	*Pulp Fiction*, US
1993	*Farewell My Concubine*, China/ *The Piano*, Australia
1992	*Best Intentions*, Denmark
1991	*Barton Fink*, US

In its early years, there was no single "Best Film" award at the Cannes Film Festival, several films being honored jointly. A "Grand Prize," first awarded in 1949, has been known since 1955 as the "Palme d'Or."

THE 10 ★
LATEST ENGLISH-LANGUAGE FILMS TO WIN THE CANNES PALME D'OR

	FILM/DIRECTOR/COUNTRY	YEAR
1	*Secrets and Lies*, Mike Leigh, UK	1996
2	*Pulp Fiction*, Quentin Tarantino, US	1994
3	*The Piano**, Jane Campion, Australia	1993
4	*Barton Fink*, Joel Coen, US	1991
5	*Wild at Heart*, David Lynch, US	1990
6	*sex, lies, and videotape*, Steven Soderbergh, US	1989
7	*The Mission*, Roland Joffé, UK	1986
8	*Paris, Texas*, Wim Wenders, US	1984
9	*Missing*#, Constantin Costa-Gavras, US	1982
10	*All that Jazz*+, Bob Fosse, US	1980

* *Shared with* Farewell My Concubine *(Chen Kaige, China)*

\# *Shared with* Yol *(Serif Goren, Turkey)*

\+ *Shared with* Kagemusha *(Akira Kurosawa, Japan)*

THE 10 🍁
LATEST WINNERS OF THE "BEST MOTION PICTURE" GENIE AWARD

YEAR*	FILM
2000	*Maelström*
1999	*Sunshine*
1998	*The Red Violin*
1997	*The Sweet Hereafter*
1996	*Lilies – Les Feluettes*
1996	*Le Confessionnal*
1994	*Exotica*
1993	*Thirty-Two Short Films about Glenn Gould*
1992	*Naked Lunch*
1991	*Black Robe*

* *Two awards were given in 1996 and none in 1995 due to broadcast changes.*

THE 10 🍁
LATEST WINNERS OF THE "ACHIEVEMENT IN DIRECTION" GENIE AWARD

YEAR*	DIRECTOR/FILM
2000	Denis Villeneuve, *Maelström*
1999	Jeremy Podeswa, *The Five Senses*
1998	François Girard, *The Red Violin*
1997	Atom Egoyan, *The Sweet Hereafter*
1996	David Cronenberg, *Crash*
1996	Robert Lepage, *Le Confessionnal*
1994	Atom Egoyan, *Exotica*
1993	François Girard, *Thirty-Two Short Films about Glenn Gould*
1992	David Cronenberg, *Naked Lunch*
1991	Bruce Beresford, *Black Robe*

* *Two awards were given in 1996 and none in 1995 due to broadcast changes.*   Source: ACC&T

SONG AND DANCE

Winner of the 2000 Palme d'Or, Dancer in the Dark *also won the "Best Actress" award for Icelandic singer Björk. She had previously appeared in* Juniper Tree *(1987) and in a cameo role in* Prêt-à-Porter *(1994).*

THE 10 ★
LATEST WINNERS OF THE BAFTA "BEST FILM" AWARD

YEAR	FILM/COUNTRY
2000	*Gladiator*, US
1999	*American Beauty*, US
1998	*Shakespeare in Love*, US
1997	*The Full Monty*, UK
1996	*The English Patient*, UK
1995	*Sense and Sensibility*, UK
1994	*Four Weddings and a Funeral*, UK
1993	*Schindler's List*, US
1992	*Howards End*, UK
1991	*The Commitments*, US/UK

The British Academy of Film and Television Arts (BAFTA), founded in 1946, holds annual award ceremonies in four areas: film, television, children's film and tv, and interactive media. The winner of the BAFTA "Best Picture" (film) often corresponds with the Oscar equivalent.

THE 10 🍁
LATEST WINNERS OF THE "BEST PERFORMANCE BY AN ACTOR IN A LEADING ROLE" GENIE AWARD

YEAR*	ACTOR/FILM
2000	Tony Nardi, *My Father's Angel*
1999	Bob Hoskins, *Felicia's Journey*
1998	Roshan Seth, *Such a Long Journey*
1997	Ian Holm, *The Sweet Hereafter*
1996	William Hutt, *Long Day's Journey into Night*
1996	David La Haye, *L'Enfant d'Eau*
1994	Maury Chaykin, *Whale Music*
1993	Tom McCamus, *I Love a Man in Uniform*
1992	Tony Nardi, *La Sarrasine*
1991	Rémy Girard, *Amoureaux Fou*

* Two awards were given in 1996 and none in 1995 due to broadcast changes.   Source: ACC&T

THE 10 ★
LATEST WINNERS OF THE BAFTA "BEST ACTRESS" AWARD

YEAR	ACTRESS/FILM/COUNTRY
2000	Julia Roberts, *Erin Brockovich*, US
1999	Annette Bening, *American Beauty*, US
1998	Cate Blanchette, *Elizabeth*, UK
1997	Judi Dench, *Mrs. Brown*, UK
1996	Brenda Blethyn, *Secrets and Lies*, UK
1995	Emma Thompson, *Sense and Sensibility*, UK
1994	Susan Sarandon, *The Client*, US
1993	Holly Hunter, *The Piano*, Australia
1992	Emma Thompson, *Howard's End*, UK
1991	Jodie Foster, *The Silence of the Lambs*, US

THE 10 🍁
LATEST WINNERS OF THE "BEST PERFORMANCE BY AN ACTRESS IN A LEADING ROLE" GENIE AWARD

YEAR*	ACTRESS/FILM
2000	Marie-Josée Croze, *Maelström*
1999	Sylvie Moreau, *Post Mortem*
1998	Sandra Oh, *Last Night*
1997	Molly Parker, *Kissed*
1996	Martha Henry, *Long Day's Journey into Night*
1996	Helena Bonham Carter, *Margaret's Museum*
1994	Sandra Oh, *Double Happiness*
1993	Sheila McCarthy, *The Lotus Eaters*
1992	Janet Wright, *Bordertown Café*
1991	Pascale Montpetit, *H*

* Two awards were given in 1996 and none in 1995 due to broadcast changes.   Source: ACC&T

ERIN BROCKOVICH

Julia Roberts's BAFTA and Golden Globe Award for her eponymous role in Erin Brockovich foreshadowed her "Best Actress" Oscar.

Which author won the 2000 Governor General's Award for English Fiction?
see p110 for the answer

A Carol Shields
B Michael Ondaatje
C Margaret Atwood

Leading Men

TOP 10
JIM CARREY FILMS

1	Batman Forever	1995
2	The Mask	1994
3	How the Grinch Stole Christmas	2000
4	Liar Liar	1997
5	The Truman Show	1998
6	Dumb and Dumber	1994
7	Ace Ventura: When Nature Calls	1995
8	Me, Myself & Irene	2000
9	The Cable Guy	1996
10	Ace Ventura: Pet Detective	1994

TOP 10
NICOLAS CAGE FILMS

1	The Rock	1996
2	Face/Off	1997
3	Gone in Sixty Seconds	2000
4	Con Air	1997
5	City of Angels	1998
6	Snake Eyes	1998
7	8MM	1999
8	Moonstruck	1987
9	Leaving Las Vegas	1995
10	Peggy Sue Got Married	1986

RATTLING THE CAGE

Nicolas Cage stars as FBI biochemist Dr. Stanley Goodspeed in the 1996 film The Rock, which is his highest-earning film to date.

TOP 10
PIERCE BROSNAN FILMS

1	Mrs. Doubtfire	1993
2	The World Is Not Enough	1999
3	GoldenEye	1995
4	Tomorrow Never Dies	1997
5	Dante's Peak	1997
6	The Thomas Crown Affair	1999
7	Mars Attacks!	1996
8	The Mirror Has Two Faces	1996
9	The Lawnmower Man	1992
10	Love Affair	1994

Pierce Brosnan, now best known as James Bond, provided the voice of King Arthur in the animated film *Quest for Camelot* (1998). If included, it would be ranked ninth.

PIERCING LOOK

Irish-born Pierce Brosnan took over the role of James Bond with GoldenEye. This, along with Tomorrow Never Dies and The World Is Not Enough, are the highest earning of all the Bond movies.

TOP 10
TOM CRUISE FILMS

1	Mission: Impossible 2	2000
2	Mission: Impossible	1996
3	Rain Man	1988
4	Top Gun	1986
5	Jerry Maguire	1996
6	The Firm	1993
7	A Few Good Men	1992
8	Interview With the Vampire	1994
9	Days of Thunder	1990
10	Eyes Wide Shut	1999

TOP 10
KEVIN SPACEY FILMS

1	American Beauty	1999
2	Se7en	1995
3	Outbreak	1995
4	A Time to Kill	1996
5	L.A. Confidential	1997
6	The Negotiator	1998
7	The Usual Suspects	1995
8	Pay it Forward	2000
9	See No Evil, Hear No Evil	1989
10	Heartburn	1986

Kevin Spacey provided the voice of Hopper in the animated film *A Bug's Life* (1998). If included, this would be his No. 1 film.

TOP 10 ★
US$100 MILLION FILM ACTORS

	ACTOR*	FILMS#	TOTAL (US$)+
1	Harrison Ford	16	5,090,800,000
2	Samuel L. Jackson	10	3,426,000,000
3	Bruce Willis	13	3,420,100,000
4	Tom Cruise	10	3,055,300,000
5	James Earl Jones	9	3,001,200,000
6	Robin Williams	11	2,749,800,000
7	Mel Gibson	14	2,595,700,000
8	Tommy Lee Jones	11	2,405,800,000
9	Eddie Murphy	10	2,366,000,000
10	Leonardo DiCaprio	4	2,293,500,000

* *Appeared in or provided voice in film*

\# *Earning over US$100 million worldwide as of the end of 2000*

\+ *Of all US$100-million-plus films*

TOP 10 ★
BRAD PITT FILMS

1	*Se7en*	1995
2	*Interview With the Vampire*	1994
3	*Sleepers*	1996
4	*Legends of the Fall*	1994
5	*Twelve Monkeys*	1995
6	*The Devil's Own*	1997
7	*Meet Joe Black*	1998
8	*Seven Years in Tibet*	1997
9	*Fight Club*	1999
10	*Thelma & Louise*	1991

PITT STOPPER

Brad (William Bradley) Pitt plays Detective David Mills in Se7en, his most successful film to date. Pitt appeared in more than twenty films during the 1990s.

TOP 10 EDDIE MURPHY FILMS

❶ *Beverly Hills Cop*, 1984 ❷ *Beverly Hills Cop II*, 1987 ❸ *Doctor Dolittle*, 1998
❹ *Coming to America*, 1988 ❺ *The Nutty Professor*, 1996
❻ *Nutty Professor II: The Klumps*, 2000 ❼ *Another 48 Hrs.*, 1990
❽ *The Golden Child*, 1986 ❾ *Boomerang*, 1992 ❿ *Harlem Nights**, 1989

* Also director

Eddie Murphy also provided the voice of Mushu in the animated film *Mulan* (1998), which, if included, would rank second in his Top 10.

TOP 10 ★
SAMUEL L. JACKSON FILMS

1	*Star Wars: Episode I – The Phantom Menace*	1999
2	*Jurassic Park*	1993
3	*Die Hard: With a Vengeance*	1995
4	*Coming to America*	1988
5	*Pulp Fiction*	1994
6	*Patriot Games*	1992
7	*Deep Blue Sea*	1999
8	*A Time to Kill*	1996
9	*Unbreakable*	2000
10	*Sea of Love*	1989

TOP 10 ★
JOHN CUSACK FILMS

1	*Con Air*	1997
2	*The Thin Red Line*	1998
3	*Stand by Me*	1986
4	*Broadcast News*	1987
5	*Being John Malkovich*	1999
6	*High Fidelity*	2000
7	*City Hall*	1996
8	*Grosse Pointe Blank*	1997
9	*Midnight in the Garden of Good and Evil*	1997
10	*The Player*	1992

John Cusack supplied the voice of Dimitri in the animated film *Anastasia* (1997). Were it included here, it would rank in second place.

TOP 10 ★
BRUCE WILLIS FILMS

1	*The Sixth Sense*	1999
2	*Armageddon*	1998
3	*Die Hard: With a Vengeance*	1995
4	*The Fifth Element*	1997
5	*Die Hard 2*	1990
6	*Pulp Fiction*	1994
7	*Twelve Monkeys*	1995
8	*The Jackal*	1997
9	*Death Becomes Her*	1992
10	*Die Hard*	1988

Look Who's Talking (1989), in which typically tough-guy Willis took the role of a baby, is discounted here because the role consisted only of Willis's dubbed voice.

♦ TOP 10 KEANU REEVES FILMS

❶ *The Matrix*, 1999 ❷ *Speed*, 1994
❸ *Dracula*, 1992 ❹ *The Devil's Advocate*, 1997 ❺ *Parenthood*, 1989
❻ *A Walk in the Clouds*, 1995 ❼ *Chain Reaction*, 1996 ❽ *Johnny Mnemonic*, 1995
❾ *The Replacements*, 2000
❿ *Point Break*, 1991

Did You Know? The first actor to receive a movie contract was prizefighter James John Corbett. In August 1894, he signed with the Kinetoscope Exhibition Company to appear in a film of a six-round fight against Pete Courtney.

Leading Ladies

RYAN'S DAUGHTER

Born Margaret Mary Emily Anne Hyra, Meg Ryan took her mother's maiden name before her film debut in 1981. She has gone on to enjoy huge success in a range of romantic comedies.

TOP 10 ★
MICHELLE PFEIFFER FILMS

1	Batman Returns	1992
2	What Lies Beneath	2000
3	Dangerous Minds	1995
4	Wolf	1994
5	Up Close and Personal	1996
6	One Fine Day	1996
7	The Witches of Eastwick	1987
8	The Story of Us	1999
9	Tequila Sunrise	1988
10	Scarface	1983

Michelle Pfeiffer also provided the voice of Tzipporah in the animated film *The Prince of Egypt* (1998). If included in her Top 10, this would feature in third place.

CATWOMAN

Batman Returns is Michelle Pfeiffer's most successful film to date, but half the films in her Top 10 have earned a healthy US$100 million-plus.

TOP 10 ★
MEG RYAN FILMS

1	Top Gun	1986
2	You've Got Mail	1998
3	Sleepless in Seattle	1993
4	City of Angels	1998
5	French Kiss	1995
6	Courage under Fire	1996
7	When Harry Met Sally	1989
8	Addicted to Love	1997
9	When a Man Loves a Woman	1994
10	Hanging Up	2000

Meg Ryan provided the voice of Anastasia in the 1997 film of that title. If included, it would appear in ninth place.

TOP 10 ★
BETTE MIDLER FILMS

1	The First Wives Club	1996
2	What Women Want	2000
3	Get Shorty	1995
4	Ruthless People	1986
5	Down and Out in Beverly Hills	1986
6	Beaches*	1988
7	Outrageous Fortune	1987
8	The Rose	1979
9	Big Business	1988
10	Hocus Pocus	1993

* Also producer

Bette Midler's role in *Get Shorty* is no more than a cameo. If this were excluded, *Hawaii* (1966) would join the list in 10th place.

TOP 10
JUDI DENCH FILMS

❶ *The World is Not Enough*, 1999 ❷ *GoldenEye*, 1995 ❸ *Tomorrow Never Dies*, 1997 ❹ *Shakespeare in Love*, 1998 ❺ *Tea with Mussolini*, 1999 ❻ *A Room with a View*, 1986 ❼ *Mrs. Brown*, 1997 ❽ *Henry V*, 1989 ❾ *Chocolat*, 2000 ❿ *Hamlet*, 1996

TOP 10 ★
MINNIE DRIVER FILMS

1	GoldenEye	1995
2	Good Will Hunting	1997
3	Sleepers	1996
4	Circle of Friends	1995
5	Return to Me	2000
6	Grosse Pointe Blank	1997
7	Hard Rain	1998
8	An Ideal Husband	1999
9	Big Night	1996
10	The Governess	1998

Minnie Driver has also had three successful voice-only roles: Jane Porter in *Tarzan* (1999), Lady Eboshi in *Mononoke Hime* (1997), and Brooke Shields in *South Park: Bigger, Longer and Uncut* (1999).

PRETTY WOMAN

Julia Roberts, shown here in My Best Friend's Wedding, *became the first Hollywood actress to be paid US$10 million (for her role in the 1996 film* Mary Reilly*).*

TOP 10 ★

JULIA ROBERTS FILMS

1	*Pretty Woman**	1990
2	*Notting Hill*	1999
3	*Hook*	1991
4	*My Best Friend's Wedding*	1997
5	*Runaway Bride*	1999
6	*Erin Brockovich#*	2000
7	*The Pelican Brief*	1993
8	*Sleeping with the Enemy*	1991
9	*Stepmom*	1998
10	*Conspiracy Theory*	1997

* *Academy Award nomination for "Best Actress"*

Winner of "Best Actress" Oscar

TOP 10 ★

US$100 MILLION FILM ACTRESSES

	ACTRESS*	FILMS#	TOTAL (US$)+
1	Julia Roberts	10	2,602,300,000
2	Carrie Fisher	4	2,047,700,000
3	Whoopi Goldberg	7	2,027,200,000
4	Glenn Close	6	1,777,700,000
5	Demi Moore	6	1,672,200,000
6	Bonnie Hunt	5	1,577,800,000
7	Drew Barrymore	5	1,561,800,000
8	Rene Russo	7	1,524,900,000
9	Annie Potts	4	1,351,600,000
10	Minnie Driver	5	1,337,400,000

* *Appeared in or provided voice in film*

Earning over US$100 million worldwide to end of 2000

+ *Of all US$100-million-plus films*

Among well-known high-earning stars, this list contains several surprising names of less familiar or prolific artists who have appeared in or provided voices for some of the most successful films of all time. One such is Annie Potts, who appeared in both *Ghostbusters* films and supplied the voice of Bo Peep for both *Toy Story* films.

TOP 10 ★

SHARON STONE FILMS

1	*Basic Instinct*	1992
2	*Total Recall*	1990
3	*The Specialist*	1995
4	*Last Action Hero*	1993
5	*Sliver*	1993
6	*Casino**	1995
7	*Sphere*	1998
8	*Diabolique*	1996
9	*Police Academy 4: Citizens on Patrol*	1987
10	*Gloria*	1999

* *Academy Award nomination for "Best Actress"*

Sharon Stone's first film role was a fleeting appearance in Woody Allen's *Stardust Memories* (1980), where she appears credited only as "Pretty girl on train."

TOP 10 ★

DREW BARRYMORE FILMS

1	*E.T.: The Extra-Terrestrial*	1982
2	*Batman Forever*	1995
3	*Charlie's Angels*	2000
4	*Scream*	1996
5	*The Wedding Singer*	1998
6	*Never Been Kissed*	1999
7	*Ever After*	1998
8	*Wayne's World 2*	1993
9	*Everyone Says I Love You*	1996
10	*Boys on the Side*	1995

Drew Barrymore also provided the voice of Akima in the animated *Titan A.E.* (2000), which would be in 10th place in her Top 10 if included.

TOP 10 ★

GWYNETH PALTROW FILMS

1	*Se7en*	1995
2	*Hook*	1991
3	*Shakespeare in Love**	1998
4	*A Perfect Murder*	1998
5	*The Talented Mr. Ripley*	1999
6	*Sliding Doors*	1998
7	*Great Expectations*	1998
8	*Malice*	1993
9	*Emma*	1996
10	*Bounce*	2000

* *Winner of "Best Actress" Oscar*

TOP 10 UMA THURMAN FILMS

❶ *Batman & Robin*, 1997
❷ *Pulp Fiction*, 1994 ❸ *The Truth About Cats and Dogs*, 1996 ❹ *The Avengers*, 1998 ❺ *Dangerous Liaisons*, 1988
❻ *Final Analysis*, 1992 ❼ *Beautiful Girls*, 1996 ❽ *Les Misérables*, 1998
❾ *Johnny Be Good*, 1988
❿ *Gattaca*, 1997

Did You Know? One of the most prolific actresses in movie history was Bess Flowers (1898–1984). In the period from 1923 to 1964, she appeared, often uncredited, in at least 371 films.

The Directors & Writers

FILMS DIRECTED BY ACTORS

FILM/YEAR	DIRECTOR
1 *Pretty Woman*, 1990	Garry Marshall
2 *Dances With Wolves*, 1990	Kevin Costner
3 *The Bodyguard*, 1992	Kevin Costner
4 *How the Grinch Stole Christmas*, 2000	Ron Howard
5 *Apollo 13*, 1995	Ron Howard
6 *Ransom*, 1996	Ron Howard
7 *Rocky IV*, 1985	Sylvester Stallone
8 *Doctor Dolittle*, 1998	Betty Thomas
9 *Runaway Bride*, 1999	Garry Marshall
10 *Waterworld*, 1995	Kevin Costner

FILMS DIRECTED BY WOMEN

FILM/YEAR	DIRECTOR
1 *Look Who's Talking*, 1989	Amy Heckerling
2 *Doctor Dolittle*, 1998	Betty Thomas
3 *Sleepless in Seattle*, 1993	Nora Ephron
4 *What Women Want*, 2000	Nancy Meyers
5 *The Birdcage*, 1996	Elaine May
6 *You've Got Mail*, 1998	Nora Ephron
7 *Wayne's World*, 1992	Penelope Spheeris
8 *Big*, 1988	Penny Marshall
9 *Michael*, 1996	Nora Ephron
10 *A League of Their Own*, 1992	Penny Marshall

DIRECTORS, 2000

DIRECTOR*	FILM(S)#
1 Ron Howard	*How the Grinch Stole Christmas*
2 John Woo	*Mission: Impossible 2*
3 Robert Zemeckis	*What Lies Beneath, Cast Away*
4 Ridley Scott	*Gladiator*
5 Wolfgang Petersen	*The Perfect Storm*
6 Jay Roach	*Meet the Parents*
7 Bryan Singer	*X-Men*
8 Keenan Ivory Wayans	*Scary Movie*
9 Eric Leighton, Ralph Zondag	*Dinosaur*
10 Steven Soderbergh	*Erin Brockovich, The Limey*

* *Including codirectors*

Ranking based on total domestic (US) gross of all films released in 2000

WOOING THE AUDIENCES

Mission: Impossible 2 *director John Woo moved from Hong Kong to Hollywood to become a thriller specialist. He was the first Asian director to make a mainstream Hollywood film,* Hard Target, *in 1993.*

FILMS DIRECTED BY RON HOWARD

1	*How the Grinch Stole Christmas*	2000
2	*Apollo 13*	1995
3	*Ransom*	1996
4	*Backdraft*	1991
5	*Parenthood*	1989
6	*Cocoon*	1985
7	*Splash*	1984
8	*Far and Away*	1992
9	*Willow*	1988
10	*The Paper*	1994

FILMS DIRECTED BY NORMAN JEWISON

FILM	YEAR
1 *Moonstruck*	1987*
2 *Fiddler on the Roof*	1971*
3 *The Hurricane*	1999
4 *Best Friends*	1982
5 *Other People's Money*	1991
6 *...And Justice for All*	1979
7 *Jesus Christ Superstar*	1973
8 *Agnes of God*	1985
9 *A Soldier's Story*	1984
10 *In the Heat of the Night*	1967*

* *Academy Award nomination for "Best Director"*

TOP 10 FILMS DIRECTED BY STANLEY KUBRICK

❶ *Eyes Wide Shut*, 1999 ❷ *The Shining*, 1980 ❸ *2001: A Space Odyssey*, 1968 ❹ *Full Metal Jacket*, 1987 ❺ *A Clockwork Orange*, 1971 ❻ *Spartacus*, 1960 ❼ *Barry Lyndon*, 1975 ❽ *Dr. Strangelove*, 1964 ❾ *Lolita*, 1962 ❿ *Paths of Glory*, 1957

TOP 10 SCREENPLAYS BY STEPHEN KING

1 *The Green Mile*, 1999 **2** *The Shining*, 1980 **3** *Misery*, 1990 **4** *The Shawshank Redemption*, 1994 **5** *Pet Sematary*, 1989 **6** *Stand by Me*, 1986 **7** *Dolores Claiborne*, 1995 **8** *The Running Man*, 1987 **9** *Carrie*, 1976 **10** *Sleepwalkers*, 1992

TOP 10 ⭐

FILMS BASED ON CLASSIC ENGLISH NOVELS

FILM/YEAR	NOVELIST/PUBLISHED
1 *Bram Stoker's Dracula*, 1992	Bram Stoker, 1897
2 *Sense and Sensibility*, 1995	Jane Austen, 1811
3 *Mary Shelley's Frankenstein*, 1994	Mary Shelley, 1818
4 *Emma*, 1996	Jane Austen, 1816
5 *The Age of Innocence*, 1993	Edith Wharton, 1920
6 *A Passage to India*, 1984	E.M. Forster, 1924
7 *Howard's End*, 1992	E.M. Forster, 1910
8 *A Room with a View*, 1986	E.M. Forster, 1908
9 *The Portrait of a Lady*, 1996	Henry James, 1881
10 *The Wings of the Dove*, 1997	Henry James, 1902

This Top 10 excludes films inspired by novels but not following the text and storyline.

🍁 TOP 10 FILMS DIRECTED BY IVAN REITMAN

1 *Ghostbusters*, 1984 **2** *Twins*, 1988 **3** *Ghostbusters II*, 1989 **4** *Kindergarten Cop*, 1990 **5** *Six Days Seven Nights*, 1998 **6** *Junior*, 1994 **7** *Stripes*, 1981 **8** *Dave*, 1993 **9** *Legal Eagles*, 1986 **10** *Father's Day*, 1997

TOP 10 ⭐

WRITERS, 2000

WRITER*	FILM(S)#
1 William Goldman	Mission: Impossible 2, Hollow Man
2 Ed Solomon	X-Men, Charlie's Angels
3 Zak Penn	Nutty Professor II: The Klumps, Charlie's Angels
4 John Logan	Gladiator, Any Given Sunday
5 Jeffrey Price, Peter S. Seaman, Dr. Seuss	How the Grinch Stole Christmas
6 Brannon Braga, David Marconi, Ronald D. Moore, Michael Tolkin, Robert Towne	Mission: Impossible 2
7 David H. Franzoni, William Nicholson	Gladiator
8 Bo Goldman, Sebastian Junger, William D. Wittliff	The Perfect Storm
9 Joss Whedon	X-Men, Titan A.E.
10 Susannah Grant	Erin Brockovich, 28 Days, Center Stage

* *Including writing teams*

Ranking based on total domestic (US) gross of all films by these writers released in 2000

MILES AHEAD

The Green Mile is by far the highest-earning film based on a Stephen King story. To date, some 40 film adaptations of his work have been released.

THE 10 🍁

LATEST FILMS DIRECTED BY DAVID CRONENBERG

FILM	YEAR
1 *Spider*	2002
2 *eXistenZ*	1999
3 *Crash*	1996
4 *M. Butterfly*	1993
5 *Naked Lunch*	1991
6 *Dead Ringers*	1988
7 *The Fly**	1986
8 *The Dead Zone*	1983
9 *Videodrome*	1983
10 *Scanners*	1981

* *To date, The Fly has grossed the most revenue worldwide of all Cronenberg's films – US$37.6 million.*

Toronto-born David Cronenberg is known as the "King of venereal horror." He is also a writer, actor, editor, producer, cinematographer, and director of television programs.

The Studios

TOP 10 NEW LINE FILMS

❶ *Se7en*, 1995 ❷ *The Mask*, 1994 ❸ *Austin Powers: The Spy Who Shagged Me*, 1999
❹ *Dumb and Dumber*, 1994 ❺ *Rush Hour*, 1998 ❻ *Teenage Mutant Ninja Turtles*, 1990
❼ *Lost in Space*, 1998 ❽ *Blade*, 1998 ❾ *Mortal Kombat*, 1995
❿ *The Wedding Singer*, 1998

TOP 10 ★ PARAMOUNT FILMS

1	Titanic*	1997
2	Forrest Gump	1994
3	Mission: Impossible 2	2000
4	Ghost	1990
5	Indiana Jones and the Last Crusade	1989
6	Mission: Impossible	1996
7	Grease	1978
8	Raiders of the Lost Ark	1981
9	Deep Impact	1998
10	Top Gun	1986

* Coproduction with Fox, which had overseas rights

TOP 10 ★ MCA/UNIVERSAL FILMS

1	Jurassic Park	1993
2	E.T.: The Extra-Terrestrial	1982
3	The Lost World: Jurassic Park	1997
4	Jaws	1975
5	The Mummy	1999
6	The Flintstones	1994
7	Notting Hill	1999
8	Back to the Future	1985
9	How the Grinch Stole Christmas	2000
10	Apollo 13	1995

TOP 10 MIRAMAX FILMS

❶ *Shakespeare in Love*, 1998 ❷ *Scary Movie*, 2000 ❸ *The English Patient*, 1996
❹ *Good Will Hunting*, 1997 ❺ *Life is Beautiful (La Vita è Bella)*, 1998
❻ *Pulp Fiction*, 1994 ❼ *Scream*, 1996 ❽ *Scream 2*, 1997 ❾ *Scream 3*, 2000
❿ *The Talented Mr. Ripley*, 1999

TOP 10 ★ DREAMWORKS FILMS

1	Saving Private Ryan*	1998
2	Gladiator*	2000
3	Deep Impact*	1998
4	American Beauty	1999
5	What Lies Beneath*	2000
6	The Prince of Egypt	1998
7	The Haunting	1990
8	Chicken Run	2000
9	Antz	1998
10	Mouse Hunt	1997

* Coproduction with another studio

TOP 10 ★ WARNER BROS. FILMS

1	Twister	1996
2	The Matrix	1999
3	Batman	1989
4	The Bodyguard	1992
5	Robin Hood: Prince of Thieves	1991
6	The Fugitive	1993
7	Batman Forever	1995
8	The Perfect Storm	2000
9	Lethal Weapon 3	1992
10	The Exorcist	1973

It was the coming of sound that launched the newly formed Warner Bros. into its important place in cinema history with *The Jazz Singer* (1927), its best-known early sound production. The Depression years were not easy for the company, but in the 1940s it produced a number of films that received acclaim from both critics and the public. Meanwhile, it came to be acknowledged as one of the major forces in the field of animation with its *Bugs Bunny* and

STORMING AHEAD

Each of the top four films produced by Warner Bros. has earned more than US$400 million at the world box office, while earnings from Twister approach half a billion dollars.

174

TOP 10 TWENTIETH CENTURY-FOX FILMS

1 *Titanic**, 1997 **2** *Star Wars: Episode I – The Phantom Menace*, 1999 **3** *Independence Day*, 1996 **4** *Star Wars*, 1977 **5** *The Empire Strikes Back*, 1980 **6** *Home Alone*, 1990 **7** *Return of the Jedi*, 1983 **8** *Mrs. Doubtfire*, 1993 **9** *True Lies*, 1994 **10** *Die Hard: With a Vengeance*, 1995

* *Coproduced with Paramount; Twentieth Century-Fox controlled overseas rights*

TOP 10 ★ WALT DISNEY/ BUENA VISTA FILMS

1	The Lion King	1994
2	The Sixth Sense	1999
3	Armageddon	1998
4	Toy Story 2	1999
5	Aladdin	1992
6	Pretty Woman	1990
7	Tarzan	1999
8	A Bug's Life	1998
9	Toy Story	1995
10	Beauty and the Beast	1991

TOP 10 ★ STUDIOS WITH THE MOST "BEST PICTURE" OSCARS

	STUDIO	AWARDS
1	United Artists	13
2	Columbia	12
3	Paramount	11
4	MGM	9
5	Twentieth Century-Fox	7
6	Warner Bros.	6
7	Universal	5
8	Orion	4
9	=DreamWorks	2
	=Miramax	2
	=RKO	2

TOP 10 ★ SONY (COLUMBIA/ TRI-STAR) FILMS

1	Men in Black	1997
2	Terminator 2: Judgment Day	1991
3	Godzilla	1998
4	Basic Instinct	1992
5	Close Encounters of the Third Kind	1977/80
6	As Good as It Gets	1997
7	Air Force One	1997
8	Hook	1991
9	Rambo: First Blood Part II	1985
10	Look Who's Talking	1989

Founded in 1924 by Harry Cohn and his brother Jack, Columbia was built up into a studio to rival the established giants MGM and Paramount. In 1934, Frank Capra's *It Happened One Night*, starring Clark Gable and Claudette Colbert, swept the board, unprecedentedly winning "Best Picture," "Best Director," "Best Actor," and "Best Actress" Oscars. In subsequent years, films such as *Lost Horizon* (1937) and *The Jolson Story* (1946) consolidated Columbia's commercial success.

SENSE OF ACHIEVEMENT
Disney's *The Lion King* remains its most successful film so far, but *The Sixth Sense* comes an honorable second, with world earnings of nearly US$700 million.

TOP 10 ★ STUDIOS, 2000

	STUDIO	EARNINGS (US$)*	MARKET SHARE (%)
1	Buena Vista	1,174,000,000	15.78
2	Universal	1,053,600,000	14.16
3	Warner Bros.	903,400,000	12.14
4	DreamWorks	789,800,000	10.62
5	Paramount	781,000,000	10.50
6	Sony	688,200,000	9.25
7	Twentieth Century-Fox	659,300,000	8.86
8	New Line	372,500,000	5.01
9	Dimension	322,500,000	4.44
10	Miramax	128,400,000	1.73

* *Domestic (US) box office gross in 2000*

Total US box office gross for 2000 was estimated as US$7,439,400,655, of which the Top 10 studios earned US$6,872,700,000, or 92 percent.

Did You Know? Although United Artists has won the most "Best Picture" Oscars, MGM has received the most wins in all categories, with a total of 190.

Film Out-Takes

MOST EXPENSIVE ITEMS OF FILM MEMORABILIA EVER SOLD AT AUCTION

	ITEM/SALE	PRICE (US$)
1	Judy Garland's ruby slippers from *The Wizard of Oz*, Christie's, New York, May 26, 2000	666,000
2	Clark Gable's Oscar for *It Happened One Night*, Christie's, Los Angeles, Dec 15, 1996	607,500
3	Vivien Leigh's Oscar for *Gone With the Wind*, Sotheby's, New York, Dec 15, 1993	562,500
4	Poster for *The Mummy*, 1932, Sotheby's, New York, Mar 1, 1997	453,500
5	James Bond's Aston Martin DB5 from *Goldfinger*, Sotheby's, New York, June 28, 1986	275,000
6	Clark Gable's personal script for *Gone With the Wind*, Christie's, Los Angeles, Dec 15, 1996	244,500
7	"Rosebud" sled from *Citizen Kane*, Christie's, Los Angeles, Dec 15, 1996	233,500
8	Herman J. Mankiewicz's scripts for *Citizen Kane* and *The American*, Christie's, New York, June 21, 1989	231,000
9	Mel Gibson's broadsword from *Braveheart*, Sotheby's, New York, Mar 6, 2001	170,000
10	Judy Garland's ruby slippers from *The Wizard of Oz*, Christie's, New York, June 21, 1988	165,000

FILMS WITH THE MOST EXTRAS

	FILM/COUNTRY/YEAR	EXTRAS
1	*Gandhi*, UK, 1982	300,000
2	*Kolberg*, Germany, 1945	187,000
3	*Monster Wang-magwi*, South Korea, 1967	157,000
4	*War and Peace*, USSR, 1967	120,000
5	*Ilya Muromets*, USSR, 1956	106,000
6	*Tonko*, Japan, 1988	100,000
7	*The War of Independence*, Romania, 1912	80,000
8	*Around the World in 80 Days*, US, 1956	68,894
9	=*Dny Zrady*, Czechoslovakia, 1972	60,000
	=*Intolerance*, US, 1916	60,000

COUNTRIES WITH THE BIGGEST INCREASES IN MOVIE VISITS

	COUNTRY	TOTAL ATTENDANCE 1998	1999	INCREASE
1	Mexico	104,000,000	120,000,000	16,000,000
2	Australia	80,000,000	88,000,000	8,000,000
3	Poland	19,900,000	26,620,000	6,720,000
4	UK	136,500,000	140,260,000	3,760,000
5	Finland	6,320,000	7,040,000	720,000
6	New Zealand	16,270,000	16,760,000	490,000
7	Germany	148,880,000	149,000,000	120,000
8	Sweden	15,890,000	15,980,000	90,000
9	Iceland	1,510,000	1,570,000	60,000
10	Spain	112,140,000	131,350,000	19,210

Source: Screen Digest

TOP 10 MOST PROLIFIC FILM-PRODUCING COUNTRIES

(Country/films produced, 1999)

❶ India, 764 ❷ US, 628 ❸ Japan, 270 ❹ Philippines, 220 ❺ France, 181 ❻ Hong Kong, 146 ❼ Italy, 108 ❽ Spain, 97 ❾ UK, 92 ❿ China, 85

Source: Screen Digest

JUDY'S RUBY SLIPPERS

One of several pairs made for her most famous role, the ruby slippers worn by Judy Garland in The Wizard of Oz top the list of expensive film memorabilia.

TOP 10 ★
COUNTRIES IN WHICH THE TOP FILM TAKES THE LARGEST SHARE OF THE BOX OFFICE

	COUNTRY	TOP FILM'S PERCENTAGE OF BOX OFFICE, 1998
1	Poland	24.2
2	Japan	18.3
3	Denmark	16.9
4	Sweden	16.5
5	Czech Republic	15.5
6	Norway	14.7
7	Argentina	14.1
8	France	12.2
9 =	Germany	12.1
=	UK	12.1

Source: Screen Digest

TOP 10 ★
MOVIE-GOING COUNTRIES

	COUNTRY	TOTAL ATTENDANCE, 1999
1	India	2,860,000,000
2	US	1,465,200,000
3	Indonesia	222,200,000
4	France	155,500,000
5	Germany	149,000,000
6	Japan	144,760,000
7	UK	140,260,000
8	Spain	131,350,000
9	China	121,000,000
10	Mexico	120,000,000

Source: Screen Digest

Countries such as the former Soviet Union and China have long reported massive movie attendance figures – the latter once claiming a figure of over 20 billion. However, such inflated statistics include local screenings of propaganda films in mobile movie theaters as well as the commercial feature films on which this list is based. Ranked on a per capita basis, Iceland edges ahead of the US with 5.71 annual movie visits per person compared with the US's 5.45, while India drops out of the Top 10 with 2.99.

TOP 10 ★
COUNTRIES WITH THE MOST MOVIE THEATERS

	COUNTRY	MOVIE SCREENS
1	China	65,000
2	US	37,185
3	India	12,900
4	France	5,000
5	Germany	4,651
6	Spain	3,343
7	UK	2,825
8	Italy	2,740
9	Canada	2,685
10	Indonesia	2,100

Source: Screen Digest

TOP 10 ★
COUNTRIES WITH THE MOST BOX OFFICE REVENUE

	COUNTRY	BOX OFFICE REVENUE, 1999 (US$)
1	US	7,490,000,000
2	UK	1,037,800,000
3	France	891,100,000
4	Germany	860,900,000
5	Italy	566,700,000
6	Spain	528,200,000
7	Canada	399,000,000
8	Switzerland	135,100,000
9	Belgium	113,700,000
10	Netherlands	111,400,000

Source: Screen Digest

TOP 10 ★
FILM-RELEASING COUNTRIES

	COUNTRY*	NEW RELEASES, 1999
1	Japan	568
2	Spain	505
3	Belgium	500
4	France#	448
5	US	442
6	Taiwan#	441
7	Hong Kong	439
8	Italy	423
9	UK	387
10	South Korea	370

*No reliable figures available for India
1998 figure

Source: Screen Digest

TOP 10 ★
COUNTRIES SPENDING THE MOST ON FILM PRODUCTION

	COUNTRY	INVESTMENT, 1999 (US$)
1	US	8,699,000,000
2	Japan	1,053,160,000
3	UK	817,850,000
4	France	732,580,000
5	Bulgaria	544,020,000
6	Germany	380,450,000
7	Canada	225,950,000
8	Italy	171,100,000
9	Spain	168,460,000
10	Argentina	133,330,000

Source: Screen Digest

TOP 10 COUNTRIES WITH THE BIGGEST INCREASE IN FILM PRODUCTION

(Country/percentage increase in production, 1989–98)

❶ Ireland, 400.0 ❷ Luxembourg, 200.0 ❸ UK, 117.5 ❹ Iceland, 100.0
❺ New Zealand, 75.0 ❻ Australia, 72.7 ❼ Norway, 55.6 ❽ Venezuela, 42.9
❾ France, 33.6 ❿ = Austria, 33.3; = Brazil, 33.3

Source: Screen Digest

Did You Know? The longest nonstop film screening ran for 250 hours in Montreal, Canada, from midnight on Thursday, June 11 to dawn on Monday, June 22, 1992. Only one person sat through all of the 136 films that were shown.

Film Music

MUSICAL FILMS

FILM	YEAR
1 *Grease*	1978
2 *Saturday Night Fever*	1977
3 *The Sound of Music*	1965
4 *Evita*	1996
5 *The Rocky Horror Picture Show*	1975
6 *Staying Alive*	1983
7 *American Graffiti*	1973
8 *Mary Poppins*	1964
9 *Flashdance*	1983
10 *Fantasia 2000*	2000

POP MUSIC FILMS

FILM	YEAR
1 *Spice World*	1997
2 *Purple Rain*	1984
3 *The Blues Brothers*	1980
4 *La Bamba*	1987
5 *What's Love Got to Do With It?*	1993
6 *The Doors*	1991
7 *Blues Brothers 2000*	1998
8 *The Wall*	1982
9 *The Commitments*	1991
10 *Sgt. Pepper's Lonely Hearts Club Band*	1978

JAMES BOND FILM THEMES IN CANADA

THEME/ARTIST OR GROUP	YEAR
1 *A View to a Kill*, Duran Duran	1985
2 *Live and Let Die*, Paul McCartney & Wings	1973
3 *Nobody Does It Better* (from *The Spy Who Loved Me*), Carly Simon	1977
4 *Goldfinger*, Shirley Bassey	1965
5 *Goldfinger*, John Barry	1965
6 *For Your Eyes Only*, Sheena Easton	1981
7 *Thunderball*, Tom Jones	1966
8 *All Time High* (from *Octopussy*), Rita Coolidge	1983
9 *You Only Live Twice*, Nancy Sinatra	1967
10 *Diamonds Are Forever*, Shirley Bassey	1972

Source: *Music Data Research*

Not all the James Bond themes have been major hits, especially not those from the later movies.

🍁 TOP 10 SOUNDTRACK ALBUMS IN CANADA

(Album/year)

❶ *Saturday Night Fever*, 1978 ❷ *Grease*, 1978 ❸ *Dirty Dancing*, 1987
❹ *Titanic*, 1998 ❺ *The Bodyguard*, 1992 ❻ *Armageddon*, 1998
❼ *Dangerous Minds*, 1995 ❽ *Forrest Gump*, 1994 ❾ *Cocktail*, 1988
❿ *The Lion King*, 1994   Source: *Music Data Research*

"BEST SONG" OSCAR-WINNING SINGLES IN CANADA

SINGLE/ARTIST OR GROUP	YEAR
1 *I Just Called to Say I Love You*, Stevie Wonder	1984
2 *Flashdance... What a Feeling*, Irene Cara	1983
3 *You Light up My Life*, Debby Boone	1977
4 *Say You, Say Me*, Lionel Richie	1986
5 *Evergreen*, Barbra Streisand	1977
6 *Take My Breath Away*, Berlin	1986
7 *The Way We Were*, Barbra Streisand	1974
8 *Up Where We Belong*, Joe Cocker and Jennifer Warnes	1982
9 *(I've Had) The Time of My Life*, Bill Medley and J. Warnes	1987
10 *Beauty and the Beast*, Celine Dion and Peabo Bryson	1992

Source: *Music Data Research*

ON AND ON

Featured in the world's most successful film, Titanic, Celine Dion's My Heart Will Go On became one of the best-selling Oscar-winning singles of all time worldwide.

BREAKFAST AT TIFFANY'S

Sung by Audrey Hepburn in the film Breakfast at Tiffany's, *Oscar-winning song* Moon River *became a chart hit for Andy Williams in the US and for Danny Williams in the UK.*

THE 10 ★
LATEST "BEST SONG" OSCAR WINNERS

YEAR	SONG/FILM
2000	*Things Have Changed,* Wonder Boys
1999	*You'll Be in My Heart,* Tarzan
1998	*When You Believe,* The Prince of Egypt
1997	*My Heart Will Go On,* Titanic
1996	*You Must Love Me,* Evita
1995	*Colors of the Wind,* Pocahontas
1994	*Can You Feel the Love Tonight,* The Lion King
1993	*Streets of Philadelphia,* Philadelphia
1992	*Whole New World,* Aladdin
1991	*Beauty and the Beast,* Beauty and the Beast

TOP 10 ★
"BEST SONG" OSCAR WINNERS OF THE 1980s

YEAR	SONG/FILM
1980	*Fame,* Fame
1981	*Up Where We Belong,* An Officer and a Gentleman
1982	*Arthur's Theme (Best That You Can Do),* Arthur
1983	*Flashdance,* Flashdance
1984	*I Just Called to Say I Love You,* The Woman in Red
1985	*Say You, Say Me,* White Nights
1986	*Take My Breath Away,* Top Gun
1987	*(I've Had) The Time of My Life,* Dirty Dancing
1988	*Let the River Run,* Working Girl
1989	*Under the Sea,* The Little Mermaid

TOP 10 ★
"BEST SONG" OSCAR WINNERS OF THE 1970s

YEAR	SONG/FILM
1970	*For All We Know,* Lovers and Other Strangers
1971	*Theme from Shaft,* Shaft
1972	*The Morning After,* The Poseidon Adventure
1973	*The Way We Were,* The Way We Were
1974	*We May Never Love Like This Again,* The Towering Inferno
1975	*I'm Easy,* Nashville
1976	*Evergreen,* A Star Is Born
1977	*You Light up My Life,* You Light up My Life
1978	*Last Dance,* Thank God It's Friday
1979	*It Goes Like It Goes,* Norma Rae

TOP 10 ★
"BEST SONG" OSCAR WINNERS OF THE 1960s

YEAR	SONG/FILM
1960	*Never on Sunday,* Never on Sunday
1961	*Moon River,* Breakfast at Tiffany's
1962	*Days of Wine and Roses,* Days of Wine and Roses
1963	*Call Me Irresponsible,* Papa's Delicate Condition
1964	*Chim Chim Cheree,* Mary Poppins
1965	*The Shadow of Your Smile,* The Sandpiper
1966	*Born Free,* Born Free
1967	*Talk to the Animals,* Dr. Doolittle
1968	*The Windmills of Your Mind,* The Thomas Crown Affair
1969	*Raindrops Keep Falling on My Head,* Butch Cassidy and the Sundance Kid

Did You Know? First-ever "Best Song" Oscar winner *The Continental,* from the 1934 film *The Gay Divorcee,* entered the charts 42 years later when it was released by Maureen McGovern.

Animated Action

TOP 10 ★
ANIMATED FILMS

	TITLE	YEAR
1	The Lion King	1994
2	Toy Story 2	1999
3	Aladdin	1992
4	Tarzan	1999
5	A Bug's Life	1998
6	Toy Story	1995
7	Beauty and the Beast	1991
8	Who Framed Roger Rabbit*	1988
9	Pocahontas	1995
10	The Hunchback of Notre Dame	1996

* Part animation, part live action

The 1990s provided 9 of the 10 most successful animated films of all time, ejecting a number of their high-earning predecessors from this Top 10. Animated films stand out among the moneymakers of each decade: Snow White was the second highest earning film of the 1930s (after Gone With the Wind), Bambi, Fantasia, Cinderella, and, through additional earnings from its rerelease, Pinocchio were the four most successful films of the 1940s.

THE 10 ★
FIRST BUGS BUNNY CARTOONS

	TITLE	RELEASED
1	Porky's Hare Hunt	Apr 30, 1938
2	Hare-um Scare-um	Aug 12, 1939
3	Elmer's Candid Camera	Mar 2, 1940
4	A Wild Hare	July 27, 1940
5	Elmer's Pet Rabbit	Jan 4, 1941
6	Tortoise Beats Hare	Mar 15, 1941
7	Hiawatha's Rabbit Hunt	June 7, 1941
8	The Heckling Hare	July 5, 1941
9	All This and Rabbit Stew	Sep 13, 1941
10	Wabbit Twouble	Dec 20, 1941

Bugs Bunny's debut was as a costar alongside Porky Pig in Porky's Hare Hunt, but he was not named until the release of Elmer's Pet Rabbit. A Wild Hare was the first in which he said the line to become his trademark: "Eh, what's up, Doc?" Actor Mel Blanc (1908-89) was the voice behind Bugs Bunny, and that of other well-known Warner Bros. cartoon characters, such as Daffy Duck and Elmer Fudd.

THE 10 ★
FIRST FULL-LENGTH SIMPSONS EPISODES

	EPISODE	FIRST SCREENED
1	Simpsons Roasting on an Open Fire	Dec 17, 1989
2	Bart the Genius	Jan 14, 1990
3	Homer's Odyssey	Jan 21, 1990
4	There's No Disgrace Like Homer	Jan 28, 1990
5	Bart the General	Feb 4, 1990
6	Moaning Lisa	Feb 11, 1990
7	The Call of the Simpsons	Feb 18, 1990
8	The Telltale Head	Feb 25, 1990
9	Life in the Fast Lane	Mar 18, 1990
10	Homer's Night Out	Mar 25, 1990

Matt Groening's enormously successful animated series originally appeared in 1987 as short episodes screened on the Tracey Ullman Show.

THE 10 ★
FIRST DISNEY ANIMATED FEATURES

	TITLE	YEAR
1	Snow White and the Seven Dwarfs	1937
2	Pinocchio	1940
3	Fantasia	1940
4	Dumbo	1941
5	Bambi	1942
6	Victory Through Air Power	1943
7	The Three Caballeros	1945
8	Make Mine Music	1946
9	Fun and Fancy Free	1947
10	Melody Time	1948

Excluding part-animated films such as Song of the South and Mary Poppins, and films made specially for television serialization, Disney had made a total of 42 full-length animated feature films by the end of 2000.

SMALL SOLDIERS, BIG SUCCESS

Part animation, part live action films are comparatively rare, but Small Soldiers stands out as the highest earner of the last year of the 20th century.

TOP 10 ★
PART ANIMATION/PART LIVE ACTION FILMS

	TITLE	YEAR		TITLE	YEAR
1	Who Framed Roger Rabbit	1988	6	Small Soldiers	1999
2	Casper	1995	7	Song of the South	2000
3	Space Jam	1996	8	Fantasia 2000	1946
4	9 to 5	1980	9	James and the Giant Peach	1996
5	Mary Poppins	1964	10	Pete's Dragon	1977

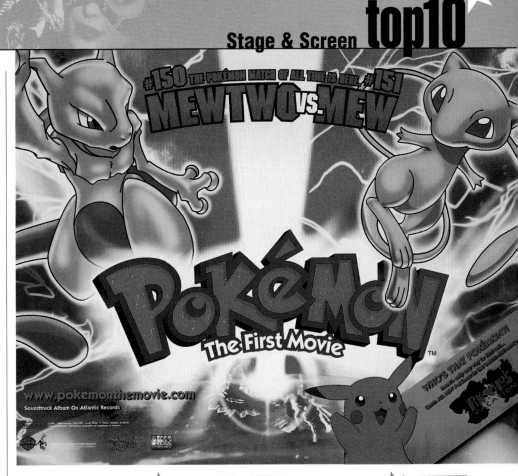

MONSTER MOVIE

Riding high on 1999's pre-eminent marketing phenomenon, Pokémon the First Movie earned over US$150 million worldwide.

TOP 10 ★
NON-DISNEY ANIMATED FEATURE FILMS

	TITLE	YEAR
1	*The Prince of Egypt*	1998
2	*Chicken Run*	2000
3	*Antz*	1998
4	*Pokémon the First Movie: Mewtwo Strikes Back*	1999
5	*Pocket Monsters Revelation Lugia*	1999
6	*The Rugrats Movie*	1998
7	*South Park: Bigger, Longer and Uncut*	1999
8	*The Land Before Time*	1988
9	*Pokémon: The Movie 2000*	2000
10	*An American Tail*	1986

Such was the success of *Pocket Monsters Revelation Lugia* in Japan that it earned a place in this list even before being released internationally.

THE 10 🍁
LATEST GENIE AWARD-WINNING BEST ANIMATED SHORTS

	TITLE	YEAR
1	*Village of Idiots*	2000
2	*When the Day Breaks*	1999
3	*Bingo*	1998
4	*The Old Lady and the Pigeons*	1997
5	*Pearl's Diner*	1993
6	*Strings*	1992
7	*Juke Bar*	1990
8	*The Cat Came Back*	1989
9	*Get a Job*	1987
10	*The Big Snit*	1986

* Genie Awards, presented by the Academy of Canadian Cinema and Television, were not given in this category each year.

THE 10 ★
FIRST OSCAR-WINNING ANIMATED FILMS*

	FILM	YEAR
1	*Flowers and Trees*	1931/32
2	*The Three Little Pigs*	1932/33
3	*The Tortoise and the Hare*	1934
4	*Three Orphan Kittens*	1935
5	*The Country Cousin*	1936
6	*The Old Mill*	1937
7	*Ferdinand the Bull*	1938
8	*The Ugly Duckling*	1939
9	*The Milky Way*	1940
10	*Lend a Paw*	1941

* In the category "Short Subjects (Cartoons)"

With the exception of *The Milky Way*, which was directed by Rudolf Ising, all were directed by Walt Disney. Oscars were awarded in the category "Short Subjects (Cartoons)" until 1971, when it was altered to "Short Subjects (Animated Films)"; in 1974 it changed again, to "Short Films (Animated)."

THE 10 ★
LATEST OSCAR-WINNING ANIMATED FILMS*

YEAR	FILM/DIRECTOR/COUNTRY
2000	*Father and Daughter*, Michel Dudok de Wit, Netherlands/UK
1999	*The Old Man and the Sea*, Aleksandr Petrov, US
1998	*Bunny*, Chris Wedge, US
1997	*Geri's Game*, Jan Pinkava, US
1996	*Quest*, Tyron Montgomery, UK
1995	*A Close Shave*, Nick Park, UK
1994	*Bob's Birthday*, David Fine and Alison Snowden, Canada/UK
1993	*The Wrong Trousers*, Nick Park, UK
1992	*Mona Lisa Descending a Staircase*, Joan C. Gratz, US
1991	*Manipulation*, Daniel Greaves, UK

* In the category "Best Animated Short Film"

What is the name of the character played by Michael J. Fox in the *Back to the Future* films?
see p.161 for the answer

A Minty Maclean
B Marty McFly
C Mickey McQueen

On the Radio

US STATES WITH THE MOST NATIONAL PUBLIC RADIO MEMBER STATIONS

STATE	NPR STATIONS
1 New York	42
2 California	35
3 Michigan	31
4 Ohio	25
5 Wisconsin	22
6 Alaska	21
7 Texas	19
8 =Colorado	17
=Florida	17
=North Carolina	17
=Wyoming	17

Source: National Public Radio

RADIO FORMATS IN THE US BY NUMBER OF STATIONS

FORMAT	STATIONS
1 Country	2,320
2 News/Talk	1,695
3 Adult contemporary	784
4 Oldies	771
5 Religion (teaching and variety)	703
6 Adult standards	602
7 Spanish	600
8 Contemporary Christian	529
9 CHR (Top 40)	439
10 Variety	436

Source: M Street

RADIO-OWNING COUNTRIES

COUNTRY	RADIO SETS PER 1,000 POPULATION*
1 US	2,116
2 Finland	1,498
3 UK	1,443
4 Gibraltar	1,429
5 Guam	1,400
6 Australia	1,391
7 Denmark	1,145
8 Canada	1,067
9 Monaco	1,039
10 New Zealand	997

* In latest year for which data available

Source: UNESCO

RADIO FORMATS IN CANADA

FORMAT	PERCENTAGE OF LISTENING TIME*
1 Adult contemporary	23.0
2 Country	12.0
3 Gold/oldies/rock	11.9
4 Contemporary	11.2
5 Talk	11.1
6 Canadian Broadcasting Corporation (CBC)	9.7
7 Other	7.1
8 Album-oriented rock	6.0
9 US stations	3.4
10 Easy listening	2.5

* Ages 12 and older, fall 1999

Source: Statistics Canada

Sports captured just 0.1 percent of listening time.

MOST POPULAR CBC RADIO ONE SHOWS

SHOW	NUMBER OF LISTENERS*
1 World Report	722,000
2 Local Monday–Friday Morning Show (6–9 am)	585,000
3 The House	443,000
4 Basic Black	399,000
5 World at Six	351,000
6 This Morning with Shelagh Rogers	350,000
7 Canada at Five	348,000
8 =Local Saturday Morning Show (6–9 am)	339,000
=Quirks and Quarks	339,000
10 The Sunday Edition	324,000

* Based on BBM Bureau of Measurement fall 2000 figures

Source: CBC Research

World Report is broadcast on both CBC Radio One and CBC Radio Two three times a day, Monday to Saturday, and twice on Sunday mornings.

MOST POPULAR CBC RADIO TWO SHOWS

SHOW	NUMBER OF LISTENERS*
1 Vinyl Cafe	143,000
2 World Report	141,000
3 Canada at Five	132,000
4 Disc Drive	126,000
5 Take Five	116,000
6 I Hear Music	115,000
7 Music & Company	107,000
8 Sound Advice	106,000
9 Choral Concert	105,000
10 World at Six	92,000

* Based on BBM fall 2000 figures

Source: CBC Research

These figures represent the number of listeners during an average quarter hour, thereby allowing for varying program lengths. However, time slots, such as prime time, will effect audience size.

TOP 10 TIMES OF DAY FOR IN-CAR RADIO

(Time of day)

1. 7:00–7:15 am 2. 7:15–7:30 am 3. 5:00–5:15 pm 4. 5:15–5:30 pm 5. 6:45–7:00 am
6. 7:45–8:00 am 7. 5:30–5:45 pm 8. 6:45–7:00 am 9. 4:15–4:30 pm 10. 8:00–8:15 am

Source: Research Director, 1999 PD Profile®

THE 10
FIRST ENGLISH PROGRAMS BROADCAST ON CBC*

	PROGRAM	TIME
1	G.R. Markowsky and His Chateau Laurier Concert Trio	5:30 pm
2	Closing stock quotations (TSE)	5:45 pm
3	The Hitmakers, variety presentation with Percy Faith's orchestra	6:00 pm
4	Overseas program, rebroadcast of BBC Empire transmission	6:30 pm
5	At the Organ, popular organ recital by Ernest Dainty	7:00 pm
6	Les Cavaliers de LeSalle, novelty orchestra direction by Arthur Vander Haegue	7:15 pm
7	Adventure, tales of adventure in far-off lands	7:30 pm
8	Au Rhythme de la Rhumba	7:45 pm
9	Fanfare, orchestra and soloists	8:00 pm
10	Bob Chester and orchestra	8:30 pm

* Broadcast on the first official day of the CBC, November 2, 1936. Separate programming was broadcast to Quebec and eastern Canada simultaneously   Source: CBC Radio Archives

TOP 10
LONGEST RUNNING PROGRAMS ON NATIONAL PUBLIC RADIO

	PROGRAM	FIRST BROADCAST
1	All Things Considered	1971
2	Weekend All Things Considered	1974
3	Fresh Air with Terry Gross	1977
4	Marian McPartland's Piano Jazz	1978
5	Morning Edition	1979
6	Weekend Edition/ Saturday with Scott Simon	1985
7	Performance Today	1987
8	Weekend Edition/ Sunday with Liane Hansen	1987
9	Car Talk	1987
10	Talk of the Nation	1991

TOP 10
MOST-LISTENED TO RADIO STATIONS IN CANADA

	STATION	FORMAT	CITY	WEEKLY CIRCULATION*
1	CKOI-FM	Grands succes contemporains	Montreal, QC	1,197,200
2	CHUM-FM	Adult contemporary	Toronto, ON	1,107,200
3	CHFI-FM	Adult contemporary	Toronto, ON	1,066,600
4	CISS-FM	Contemporary hit radio	Toronto, ON	923,200
5	CKFM-FM	Adult rock	Toronto, ON	896,200
6	CFTR	All news	Toronto, ON	843,600
7	CILQ-FM	Rock/Talk	Toronto, ON	838,700
8	CBLA-FM	News/Talk	Toronto, ON	758,900
9	CFRB	News/Talk	Toronto, ON	756,300
10	CITE-FM	Adulte contemporain	Montreal, QC	735,100

* Total number of listeners age 12 and older tuning to a station during an average week

Source: RadioWorks Inc., a division of Hennessy & Bray Communications; based on fall 2000 BBM figures

As demographics across the country change, so do Canadian radio listening preferences. Many radio stations have been forced to change their formats to attract audiences. In Toronto, 44-year-old 1050 CHUM-AM, which started out playing Top 40 music in 1958, switched to soft rock in 1986, and in 2001 completely revised its format to become TEAM 1050, an all-sports station.

THE 10
PROVINCES WITH THE MOST HOURS OF RADIO LISTENING PER WEEK

	PROVINCE	AVERAGE HOURS (FALL 1999)
1	Prince Edward Island	22.1
2	Quebec*	21.3
3	Alberta	21.0
4	=Ontario	20.7
	=New Brunswick	20.7
6	Saskatchewan	20.4
7	=Manitoba	19.8
	=Nova Scotia	19.8
9	Newfoundland	19.1
10	British Columbia	18.4

* Includes anglophones, francophones, respondents not stating language spoken at home, and those for whom that language is other than English or French. Anglophones as a group reported 23.3 hours per week of radio listening, francophones 21.3.

Source: Statistics Canada

TOP 10
LATEST NAB HALL OF FAME INDUCTEES

YEAR	INDUCTEE
2001	Bruce Morrow, radio personality
2000	Tom Joyner, radio personality
1999	Wolfman Jack, radio personality
1998	Rush Limbaugh, radio personality
1997	Wally Phillips, radio personality
1996	Don Imus, radio personality
1995	Gary Owens, radio personality
1994	Harry Caray, radio sportscaster
1993	Grand Ole Opry, radio program
1992	Larry King, radio personality

Since 1977, the National Association of Broadcasters' Hall of Fame has been honoring radio personalities and programs that have earned a place in US broadcasting history. Among its earlier inductees were Orson Welles and Bing Crosby, while two US presidents have also been included: Herbert Hoover in 1977 and former radio sportscaster Ronald Reagan in 1981.

Top TV

TV REVENUE-EARNING COMPANIES

COMPANY/COUNTRY	TV REVENUE IN 1999 (US$)
1 Time Warner, US	18,802,000,000
2 Viacom, US	7,663,600,000
3 Walt Disney, US	7,512,000,000
4 GE/NBC, US	5,790,000,000
5 NHK, Japan	5,275,700,000
6 CBS, US	4,915,000,000
7 AT&T, US	4,871,000,000
8 News Corporation, Australia	4,004,700,000
9 Cablevision, US	3,943,000,000
10 DirecTV, US	3,785,000,000

Source: Television Business International

TOP 10 🍁

REGULAR PROGRAMS ON CANADIAN TELEVISION, 1999–2000

PROGRAM*	NETWORK	VIEWERS
1 Who Wants to Be a Millionaire? (Mon)	CTV	2,904,000
2 Who Wants to Be a Millionaire? (Fri)	CTV	2,441,000
3 Who Wants to Be a Millionaire? (Thu)	CTV	2,295,000
4 Who Wants to Be a Millionaire? (Wed)	CTV	2,271,000
5 Who Wants to Be a Millionaire? (Tue)	CTV	2,169,000
6 ER	CTV	1,825,000
7 Who Wants to Be a Millionaire? (Sun)	CTV	1,664,000
8 Law and Order: SVU	CTV	1,512,000
9 Ally McBeal	CTV	1,415,000
10 Law and Order	CTV	1,405,000

* On English-language networks; three or more telecasts from August 30, 1999, to August 27, 2000

Source: Nielsen Media Research

Popular Canadian programs *Royal Canadian Air Farce* (CBC) and *Hockey Night in Canada* (CBC) rank No. 12 and No. 16, respectively.

TOP 10 ★

TELEVISION-WATCHING COUNTRIES*

COUNTRY	AVERAGE DAILY VIEWING TIME HRS	MINS
1 US	3	58
2 Greece	3	39
3 =Italy	3	36
=UK	3	36
5 Spain	3	31
6 =Canada	3	14
=Ireland	3	14
8 Germany	3	8
9 France	3	7
10 Belgium	2	57

* In Western Europe and North America

Source: Screen Digest

A survey of TV-viewing habits in Western Europe and North America shows that the number of channels, including new digital channels, is proliferating at a much faster rate than the time spent actually watching them, thus creating, in the jargon of the industry, "audience fragmentation."

TOP 10 🍁

SPECIALTY CABLE CHANNELS IN CANADA

CHANNEL	RESIDENTIAL SUBSCRIBERS*
1 CBC Newsworld	9,043,109
2 YTV (Youth Television)	8,455,847
3 TSN – The Sports Network	8,269,951
4 RDI (Réseau de l'Information)	8,094,223
5 CMT (Country Music Television) Canada	7,788,406
6 The Weather Network	7,590,545
7 CTV Sports Net	7,470,109
8 Vision	7,422,530
9 CTV News Net	7,341,536
10 TLC – The Learning Channel	7,119,479

* As at January 2001

Source: MediaSTATS

TOP 10 ★

MOST-WATCHED PROGRAMS ON PBS TELEVISION

PROGRAM	BROADCAST	AVERAGE AUDIENCE
1 The Civil War	Sep 1990	8,800,000
2 Life On Earth	Jan 1982	7,900,000
3 The Living Planet: A Portrait of the Earth	Feb 1985	7,800,000
4 The American Experience: The Kennedys	Sep 1992	7,000,000
5 Nature: Kingdom of the Ice Bear	Feb 1986	6,900,000
6 Cosmos	Sep 1980	6,500,000
7 =Planet Earth	Jan 1986	6,300,000
=Lewis & Clark: The Journey of the Corps of Discovery	Nov 1997	6,300,000
9 The Scarlet Letter	Sep 1979	5,700,000
10 Baseball	Sep 1994	5,500,000

Source: PBS

TOP 10 ★

MOST-WATCHED TALK PROGRAMS ON US TELEVISION, 1999–2000

PROGRAM	VIEWERS
1 Oprah Winfrey Show	6,265,000
2 Jerry Springer	4,180,000
3 Live! With Regis and Kelly	3,657,000
4 Maury Povich Show	3,520,000
5 Montel Williams Show	3,303,000
6 Sally Jessy Raphael	3,161,000
7 Ricki Lake	2,701,000
8 The View	2,583,000
9 Jenny Jones Show	2,362,000
10 Change of Heart	2,181,000

Source: Nielsen Media Research

TOP 10

MOST-WATCHED SPECIALS ON CANADIAN TV, 1999–2000*

SPECIAL	NETWORK	VIEWERS
1 Academy Awards	CTV	5,344,000
2 Academy Awards Pre-Show	CTV	3,685,000
3 Grammy Awards	CTV	3,076,000
4 Golden Globe Awards	CTV	2,967,000
5 Anne of Green Gables 3	CBC	2,248,000
6 Emmy Awards	CTV	2,191,000
7 American Music Awards	CTV	2,072,000
8 People's Choice Awards	CTV	1,761,000
9 Celine Dion Special	CTV	1,631,000
10 How the Grinch Stole Christmas	CBC	1,534,000

* English-language networks, from August 30, 1999, to August 27, 2000

Source: Nielsen Media Research

TOP 10

MOST-WATCHED CHILDREN'S PROGRAMS ON US TELEVISION, 1999–2000*

PROGRAM	DATE	VIEWERS
1 Pokémon	Mar 18, 2000	3,625,000
2 Batman Beyond	Feb 5, 2000	2,561,000
3 Disney's 1 Saturday Morning	Sep 25, 2000	2,522,000
4 Catlin's Way (movie)	Mar 11, 2000	2,458,000
5 Rugrats on Vacation	Dec 10, 2000	2,424,000
6 Hang Time	Oct 2, 2000	2,407,000
7 Saved by the Bell	Oct 2, 1000	2,309,000
8 City Guys	Oct 2, 2000	2,289,000
9 Digimon: Digital Monsters	Mar 25, 2000	2,270,000
10 Tiny Toons Adventure	Jan 29, 2000	2,215,000

* Highest-rated telecast only listed   Source: Nielsen Media Research

TOP 10 CABLE TELEVISION COUNTRIES

(Country/subscribers)

❶ **US**, 67,011,180 ❷ **Germany**, 18,740,260 ❸ **Netherlands**, 6,227,472 ❹ **Russia**, 5,784,432 ❺ **Belgium**, 3,945,342 ❻ **Poland**, 3,830,788 ❼ **Romania**, 3,000,000 ❽ **UK**, 2,666,783 ❾ **France**, 2,478,630 ❿ **Switzerland**, 2,156,120

Source: The Phillips Group

TOP 10

NIELSEN'S TV AUDIENCES OF ALL TIME IN THE US

PROGRAM	DATE	TOTAL	HOUSEHOLDS VIEWING (%)
1 M*A*S*H Special	Feb 28, 1983	50,150,000	60.2
2 Dallas	Nov 21, 1980	41,470,000	53.3
3 Roots Pt. 8	Jan 30, 1977	36,380,000	51.1
4 Super Bowl XVI	Jan 24, 1982	40,020,000	49.1
5 Super Bowl XVII	Jan 30, 1983	40,480,000	48.6
6 XVII Winter Olympics	Feb 23, 1994	45,690,000	48.5
7 Super Bowl XX	Jan 26, 1986	41,490,000	48.3
8 Gone With the Wind Pt. 1	Nov 7, 1976	33,960,000	47.7
9 Gone With the Wind Pt. 2	Nov 8, 1976	33,750,000	47.4
10 Super Bowl XII	Jan 15, 1978	34,410,000	47.2

© 2000 Nielsen Media Research

Historically, as more households acquired television sets (there are currently 98 million "TV households" in the US), audiences generally increased. However, the rise in channel choice and the use of VCRs has somewhat checked this trend. Listing the Top 10 according to percentage of households viewing provides a clearer picture of who watches what.

TOP 10

FASTEST-GROWING CABLE AND SATELLITE TV COMPANIES

COMPANY/COUNTRY	CABLE AND SATELLITE SUBSCRIBERS 1998	1999	GROWTH %
1 BSkyB, UK	244,000	2,600,000	965.6
2 Premiere World, Germany	145,000	1,300,000	796.6
3 Cyfra Plus, Poland	60,000	295,000	391.7
4 Foxtel, Australia	40,000	131,800	229.5
5 Wizja TV, Poland	94,000	300,000	219.1
6 Canal Digitaal (Flemish), Belgium	11,900	25,400	113.4
7 Bell ExpressVu, Canada	180,000	370,000	105.6
8 Tele+, Italy	502,300	962,000	91.5
9 Star Choice, Canada	175,000	320,000	82.9
10 Echostar (DISH), US	1,940,000	3,410,000	75.8

Source: Screen Digest

The arrival of digital broadcasting and attractive incentives offered by many service providers has attracted large numbers of first-time subscribers.

TV Awards

LATEST WINNERS OF THE GEMINI CANADA AWARD

YEAR	PROGRAM
2000	Unwanted Soldiers
1999	Loyalties
1998	=The Rez: They Call Her Tanya
	=The Road Taken
1997	The Mind of a Child
1996	Nuhoniyeh: Our Story
1995	For Angela
1994	Speak It! From the Heart of Black Nova Scotia
1993	It's About Time
1992	Drums

Source: Academy of Canadian Cinema and Television

The Canada Award honors excellence in mainstream television programming that best reflects the racial and cultural diversity of Canada.

LATEST WINNERS OF THE GEMINI AWARD FOR BEST TV MOVIE*

YEAR	MOVIE
2000	Dr. Lucille: The Lucille Teasdale Story
1999	Milgaard
1998	Hiroshima
1997	Net Worth
1995	Due South
1994	The Diviners
1993	Scales of Justice
1992	Journey Into Darkness: The Bruce Curtis Story
1990	Where the Spirit Lives
1989	The Squamish Five

* Gemini Awards were not given in this category each year

Source: Academy of Canadian Cinema and Television

LATEST WINNERS OF THE GEMINI AWARD FOR BEST COMEDY PROGRAM OR SERIES

YEAR	PROGRAM
2000	This Hour Has 22 Minutes
1999	Made in Canada
1998	This Hour Has 22 Minutes
1997	This Hour Has 22 Minutes
1996	This Hour Has 22 Minutes
1995	This Hour Has 22 Minutes
1993	The Kids in the Hall
1992	Codco
1990	Material World
1989	Codco

* Gemini Awards were not given in this category each year

Source: Academy of Canadian Cinema and Television

FEMALE PERFORMERS WHO HAVE WON THE MOST EMMYS

NAME	EMMYS
1 =Dinah Shore	8
=Mary Tyler Moore	8
3 =Carol Burnett	5
=Cloris Leachman	5
=Lily Tomlin	5
=Tracey Ullman	5
7 =Candice Bergen	4
=Tyne Daly	4
=Valerie Harper	4
=Helen Hunt	4
=Michael Learned	4
=Rhea Perlman	4

PROGRAMS WITH THE MOST DAYTIME TV EMMY AWARDS*

PROGRAM	NOMINATIONS	WINS
1 The Young and the Restless	244	77
2 Sesame Street	205	76
3 Sixty Minutes	144	58
4 Guiding Light	176	54
5 All My Children	268	50
6 General Hospital	181	43
7 The Oprah Winfrey Show	75	34
8 The Price is Right	92	29
9 One Life to Live	110	27
10 The Bold and the Beautiful	74	26

* Up to and including 1999/2000 awards

MALE PERFORMERS WHO HAVE WON THE MOST EMMYS

NAME	EMMYS
1 Ed Asner	7
2 Art Carney	6
3 =Alan Alda	5
=Dick Van Dyke	5
=Peter Falk	5
=Hal Holbrook	5
=Don Knotts	5
=Carroll O'Connor	5
=Laurence Olivier	5
10 =Dennis Franz	4
=Harvey Korman	4
=John Larroquette	4

The actual Emmy (adapted from "immy," the nickname for the image orthicon television camera) is a 2 kg (4 lb 12 oz) metal statuette of a winged figure holding an atom.

THE 10 LATEST WINNERS OF THE EMMY AWARD FOR OUTSTANDING COMEDY SERIES

(Season ending/program)

1 2000 *Will and Grace* **2** 1999 *Ally McBeal* **3** 1998 *Frasier* **4** 1997 *Frasier* **5** 1996 *Frasier*
6 1995 *Frasier* **7** 1994 *Frasier* **8** 1993 *Seinfeld* **9** 1992 *Murphy Brown* **10** 1991 *Cheers*

THE 10 ★
LATEST WINNERS OF THE EMMY AWARD FOR OUTSTANDING LEAD ACTOR IN A DRAMA SERIES

SEASON ENDING	ACTOR/SERIES
2000	James Gandolfini, *The Sopranos*
1999	Dennis Franz, *NYPD Blue*
1998	Andre Braugher, *Homicide: Life on the Street*
1997	Dennis Franz, *NYPD Blue*
1996	Dennis Franz, *NYPD Blue*
1995	Mandy Patinkin, *Chicago Hope*
1994	Dennis Franz, *NYPD Blue*
1993	Tom Skerritt, *Picket Fences*
1992	Christopher Lloyd, *Avonlea*
1991	James Earl Jones, *Gabriel's Fire*

TOP 10 🍁
LATEST WINNERS OF THE GEMINI AWARD FOR BEST DRAMATIC SERIES

YEAR*	PROGRAM
2000	*DaVinci's Inquest*
1999	*DaVinci's Inquest*
1998	*Traders*
1997	*Due South*
1996	*Due South*
1995	*Due South*
1994	*E.N.G.*
1993	*E.N.G.*
1992	*E.N.G.*
1990	*E.N.G.*

* No award in 1991

THE 10 ★
LATEST WINNERS OF THE EMMY AWARD FOR OUTSTANDING LEAD ACTRESS IN A DRAMA SERIES

SEASON ENDING*	ACTRESS/SERIES
2000	Sela Ward, *Once and Again*
1999	Edie Falco, *The Sopranos*
1998	Christine Lahti, *Chicago Hope*
1997	Gillian Anderson, *The X-Files*
1995	Kathy Baker, *Picket Fences*
1994	Sela Ward, *Sisters*
1993	Kathy Baker, *Picket Fences*
1992	Dana Delaney, *China Beach*
1991	Patricia Wettig, *thirtysomething*
1990	Patricia Wettig, *thirtysomething*

* No award in 1996

THE 10 ★
LATEST WINNERS OF THE EMMY AWARD FOR OUTSTANDING DRAMA

SEASON ENDING	PROGRAM
2000	*The West Wing*
1999	*The Practice*
1998	*The Practice*
1997	*Law & Order*
1996	*ER*
1995	*NYPD Blue*
1994	*Picket Fences*
1993	*Picket Fences*
1992	*Northern Exposure*
1991	*L.A. Law*

THE 10 ★
LATEST WINNERS OF THE EMMY AWARD FOR OUTSTANDING LEAD ACTOR IN A COMEDY SERIES

SEASON ENDING	ACTOR/SERIES
2000	Michael J. Fox, *Spin City*
1999	John Lithgow, *3rd Rock from the Sun*
1998	Kelsey Grammer, *Frasier*
1997	John Lithgow, *3rd Rock from the Sun*
1996	John Lithgow, *3rd Rock from the Sun*
1995	Kelsey Grammer, *Frasier*
1994	Kelsey Grammer, *Frasier*
1993	Ted Danson, *Cheers*
1992	Craig T. Nelson, *Coach*
1991	Burt Reynolds, *Evening Shade*

THE 10 ★
LATEST WINNERS OF THE EMMY AWARD FOR OUTSTANDING LEAD ACTRESS IN A COMEDY SERIES

SEASON ENDING	ACTRESS/PROGRAM
2000	Patricia Heaton, *Everybody Loves Raymond*
1999	Helen Hunt, *Mad About You*
1998	Helen Hunt, *Mad About You*
1997	Helen Hunt, *Mad About You*
1996	Helen Hunt, *Mad About You*
1995	Candice Bergen, *Murphy Brown*
1994	Candice Bergen, *Murphy Brown*
1993	Roseanne, *Roseanne*
1992	Candice Bergen, *Murphy Brown*
1991	Kirstie Alley, *Cheers*

Helen Hunt's record four-year run of wins followed a three-year interval from 1993–5 when she was nominated for the Emmy in this category but failed to win it.

Top Videos

COUNTRIES WITH THE MOST VCRS

COUNTRY	VIDEO-OWNING HOUSEHOLDS
1 US	91,602,000
2 Japan	38,982,000
3 Germany	31,425,000
4 China	23,956,000
5 Brazil	21,330,000
6 UK	21,306,000
7 France	18,903,000
8 Russia	14,555,000
9 Italy	12,706,000
10 South Korea	11,616,000

Source: Screen Digest

TOP 10 ★

BEST-SELLING VIDEOS IN THE US*

TITLE/LABEL/RELEASE DATE	SALES (US$)
1 *Titanic*, Paramount, Sep 9, 1998	30,000,000
2 *The Lion King*, Buena Vista/Disney, Mar 3, 1995	27,500,000
3 *Snow White*, Buena Vista/Disney, Oct 28, 1994	27,000,000
4 *Aladdin*, Buena Vista/Disney, Oct 1, 1993	25,000,000
5 *Independence Day*, Fox Video, Nov 19, 1996	21,955,000
6 *Jurassic Park*, MCA/Universal, Oct 4, 1994	21,500,000
7 *Toy Story*, Buena Vista/Disney, Oct 29, 1996	21,000,000
8 *Beauty and the Beast*, Buena Vista/Disney, Oct 30, 1992	20,000,000
9 =*Pocahontas*, Buena Vista/Disney, Feb 26, 1996	18,000,000
=*Men in Black*, Columbia TriStar, Nov 25, 1997	18,000,000

* Since 1992

Source: Video Store

TOP 10 ★

BEST-SELLING MUSIC VIDEOS OF 2000 IN THE US

TITLE/ARTIST OR GROUP

1 *Time Out with Britney Spears*, Britney Spears
2 *S&M*, Metallica
3 *Listener Supported*, Dave Matthews Band
4 *A Farewell Celebration*, Cathedrals
5 *Hell Freezes Over*, Eagles
6 *Come on Over: Video Collection*, Shania Twain
7 *Welcome to Our Neighborhood*, Slipknot
8 *Death Row Uncut*, 2 Pac/Snoop Doggy Dogg
9 *'N the Mix With 'N Sync,* 'N Sync
10 *Baller Blockin'*, Cash Money Millionaires

Source: *VideoScan*

THE 10 🍁

FIRST MUSIC VIDEOS TO AIR ON MUCHMUSIC

TITLE/ARTIST OR GROUP

1 *Snappy Songs*, Eubi Black and Noble Sissle
2 *The Enemy Within*, Rush
3 *Let's Go Crazy*, Prince
4 *Relax*, Frankie Goes to Hollywood
5 *Love Is Love*, Culture Club
6 *Karma Chameleon (live)*, Culture Club
7 *Flesh for Fantasy*, Billy Idol
8 *Dancing in the Dark*, Bruce Springsteen
9 *Lights Out*, Peter Wolf
10 *Are We Ourselves*, The Fixx

Source: *MuchMusic*

Canada's national music channel, MuchMusic, debuted on August 31, 1984, when it aired *Snappy Songs*, by Eubi Blake and Noble Sissle – the first song ever to be set to a video.

TOP 10 🍁

HORROR FAVORITE/CLASSIC VIDEO RENTALS IN CANADA

TITLE/YEAR/LABEL

1 *The Blair Witch Project*, 1999, Universal Studios
2 *Scream*, 1996, Universal Studios
3 *Halloween*, 1978, Warner
4 *Bram Stoker's Dracula*, 1992, Columbia TriStar
5 *Nightmare on Elm Street*, 1984, Universal Studios
6 *Sleepy Hollow*, 1999, Paramount
7 *The Exorcist*, 1973, Warner
8 *The Howling*, 1981, Warner
9 *Night of the Living Dead*, 1968, Columbia TriStar
10 *Jaws*, 1975, Universal Studios

Source: *Rogers Video*

Two of the videos on this Top 10 are also among the top five sellers at Halloween. *Sleepy Hollow* (special edition) ranks as the No. 1 adult video at that time of year, while *Bram Stoker's Dracula* places at No. 5.

TOP 10 ★

BEST-SELLING VIDEOS OF THE LAST DECADE IN THE US*

YEAR	TITLE/LABEL
2000	*The Matrix*, Warner
1999	*Austin Powers: International Man of Mystery*, New Line/Warner
1998	*Titanic*, Paramount/20th Century-Fox
1997	*Men in Black*, Columbia
1996	*Babe*, Universal Studios
1995	*The Lion King*, Buena Vista/Disney
1994	*Aladdin*, Buena Vista/Disney
1993	*Beauty and the Beast*, Buena Vista/Disney
1992	*Fantasia*, Walt Disney
1991	*Pretty Woman*, Touchstone

* By year

Did You Know? DVD sales are expected to soon overtake those of VHS tapes. In 1999, 3 percent of Canadian households had a DVD player. In just one year, this number more than tripled, to 10 percent.

THE NUMBER ONE...

The Matrix was the fastest-selling DVD in 2000 in the US, as well as the best-selling video of the last decade in that country.

TOP 10 ★

DVD SALES IN THE US, 2000

TITLE/LABEL

1	*The Matrix*, Warner
2	*The Sixth Sense*, Hollywood Pictures/Buena Vista
3	*The Green Mile*, Warner
4	*American Pie*, Universal Studios
5	*Austin Powers: The Spy Who Shagged Me*, New Line/Warner
6	*Toy Story/Toy Story 2: 2-Pack*, Walt Disney/Buena Vista
7	*Braveheart*, Paramount
8	*The Patriot*, Columbia TriStar
9	*Independence Day*, Fox Video
10	*Saving Private Ryan*, DreamWorks

Source: *VideoScan*

DVD was launched in the US in March 1997. In that year, total sales of DVD players was 315,136. This increased in 1998 to 1,089,261, and in 1999 to 4,019,389, as traditional videotape recordings became progressively eclipsed by DVD.

TOP 10 ★

MOVIE RENTALS ON VIDEO, 2000

TITLE/LABEL

1	*American Pie*, Universal Studios
2	*The Matrix*, Warner
3	*American Beauty*, DreamWorks
4 =	*Fight Club*, Fox Video
=	*Magnolia*, New Line/Warner
6	*Girl, Interrupted*, Columbia TriStar
7	*Notting Hill*, Universal Studios
8	*Erin Brockovic*, Universal Studios
9	*Austin Powers: The Spy Who Shagged Me*, New Line/Warner
10	*Double Jeopardy*, Paramount

Source: *VideoScan*

COMMERCE & INDUSTRY

Wealth of Nations

POOREST COUNTRIES

COUNTRY	1998 GDP PER CAPITA (US$)
1 Ethiopia	100
2 Dem. Rep. of Congo	110
3 = Burundi	140
= Sierra Leone	140
5 Guinea-Bissau	160
6 Niger	190
7 = Eritrea	200
= Malawi	200
9 = Mozambique	210
= Nepal	210
= Tanzania	210

Source: *World Bank*, World Development Indicators

COUNTRIES WITH THE HIGHEST ANNUAL PER CAPITA EXPENDITURE

COUNTRY	EXPENDITURE PER CAPITA (US$)
1 Switzerland	26,060
2 Japan	24,670
3 US	18,840
4 Denmark	17,730
5 Germany	16,850
6 Norway	16,570
7 Belgium	16,550
8 Austria	16,020
9 Iceland	15,850
10 France	15,810
Canada	11,460

Average per capita expenditure varies enormously from country to country, from the levels encountered in the Top 10 to those in the low hundreds of dollars, or less. In Western industrial economies, the proportion of expenditure that is devoted to food is often about 20 percent, but this rises to 50 and even as much as 70 percent in less developed countries. Depending on levels of taxation, the more disposable expenditure that is not allocated to such essential items, the more may be spent on consumer goods, on education, and on leisure activities.

RICHEST COUNTRIES

COUNTRY	1998 GDP PER CAPITA (US$)
1 Liechtenstein	50,000*
2 Luxembourg	43,570
3 Switzerland	40,080
4 Norway	34,330
5 Denmark	33,260
6 Japan	32,380
7 Singapore	30,060
8 US	29,340
9 Iceland	28,010
10 Austria	26,850
Canada	20,020

* *World Bank estimate for the purpose of ranking*
Source: *World Bank*, World Development Indicators
GDP (gross domestic product) is the total value of all the goods and services provided annually within a country. Gross national product, or GNP, also includes income from overseas. Dividing GDP by the country's population produces the GDP per capita, often used as a measure of how "rich" a country is.

COUNTRIES WITH THE FASTEST SHRINKING INCOME PER CAPITA

COUNTRY	AVERAGE ANNUAL GROWTH IN GNP PER CAPITA 1997–98 (%)
1 Guinea Bissau	-30.4
2 Indonesia	-18.0
3 United Arab Emirates	-10.6
4 Moldova	-9.2
5 Thailand	-8.6
6 Romania	-8.1
7 Malaysia	-8.0
8 South Korea	-7.5
9 Eritrea	-6.7
10 Russia	-6.4

Source: *World Bank*, World Development Indicators 2000

FASTEST GROWING ECONOMIES

COUNTRY	AVERAGE ANNUAL GROWTH IN GNP PER CAPITA, 1997–98 (%)
1 Angola	16.3
2 Tajikstan	13.3
3 Belarus	10.8
4 Mozambique	9.7
5 Azerbaijan	8.9
6 Republic of Congo	8.4
7 Ireland	7.4
8 Chile	7.2
9 Rwanda	7.1
10 Albania	6.8
Canada	2.0

Source: *World Bank*, World Development Indicators 2000

COUNTRIES WITH THE LOWEST ANNUAL PER CAPITA EXPENDITURE

COUNTRY	ANNUAL EXPENDITURE PER CAPITA (US$)
1 Somalia	17
2 Mozambique	57
3 Ethiopia	87
4 Malawi	109
5 Laos	140
6 Tanzania	150
7 = Bangladesh	170
= Bhutan	170
= Chad	170
= Eritrea	170
= Nepal	170

It is hard for those brought up in Western consumer cultures to comprehend the poverty of the countries appearing in this Top – or Bottom – 10, where the total average annual expenditure of an individual would barely cover the cost of a few meals in the West. Such economies inevitably rely on a greater degree of self-sufficiency in food production.

THE 10 ★ COUNTRIES MOST IN DEBT

COUNTRY	TOTAL EXTERNAL DEBT (US$)
1 Brazil	232,004,000,000
2 Russia	183,601,000,000
3 Mexico	159,959,000,000
4 China	154,599,000,000
5 Indonesia	150,875,000,000
6 Argentina	144,050,000,000
7 South Korea	139,097,000,000
8 Turkey	102,074,000,000
9 India	98,232,000,000
10 Thailand	86,172,000,000

Source: *World Bank*, World Development Indicators 2000

TOP 10 🍁 COINS AND NOTES IN CIRCULATION IN CANADA

DENOMINATION	UNITS IN CIRCULATION*
1 Penny	18,796,182,001
2 Dime	3,489,052,010
3 Quarter	2,477,271,000
4 Nickel	2,347,666,005
5 $1 coin# (Loonie)	780,864,000
6 $20 bill	473,888,000
7 $2 coin	422,481,000
8 $5 bill	148,260,000
9 $100 bill	145,415,000
10 $10 bill	90,078,000

* Coins as of December 1999; notes as of December 2000

In 1987, the $1 bill was replaced by a circulation coin bearing the loon design, known as the "Loonie." No $1 circulation coins have been minted since 1997 because of an ongoing 75-million surplus resulting from the appearance of the $2 coin in 1996.

Source: *Royal Canadian Mint and Bank of Canada*

TOP 10 ★ COUNTRIES WITH THE MOST CURRENCY IN CIRCULATION 100 YEARS AGO

COUNTRY	TOTAL CURRENCY IN CIRCULATION (US$)
1 France	2,126,400,000
2 US	2,092,800,000
3 Germany	1,142,400,000
4 India	921,600,000
5 Russia	844,800,000
6 UK	782,400,000
7 China	720,000,000
8 Austria	494,400,000
9 Italy	432,000,000
10 Spain	350,400,000

TOP 10 ★ AID DONORS

COUNTRY	ANNUAL CONTRIBUTION (US$)
1 Japan	9,358,000,000
2 US	6,878,000,000
3 France	6,307,000,000
4 Germany	5,857,000,000
5 UK	3,433,000,000
6 Netherlands	2,947,000,000
7 Canada	2,045,000,000
8 Sweden	1,731,000,000
9 Denmark	1,637,000,000
10 Norway	1,306,000,000

TOP 10 AID RECIPIENTS

(Country/annual amount received in US$)

❶ China, 2,040,000,000 ❷ Egypt, 1,947,000,000 ❸ India, 1,678,000,000 ❹ Israel, 1,191,000,000 ❺ Bangladesh, 1,009,000,000 ❻ Vietnam, 997,000,000 ❼ Mozambique, 963,000,000; = Tanzania, 963,000,000 ❾ Bosnia, 863,000,000 ❿ Uganda, 840,000,000

TOP 10 🍁 EXPORT MARKETS FOR GOODS FROM CANADA*

COUNTRY	VALUE ($)
1 US	358,946,000,000
2 Japan	9,008,000,000
3 UK	5,727,000,000
4 China#	3,709,000,000
5 Germany	3,108,000,000
6 South Korea	2,233,000,000
7 Mexico	2,040,000,000
8 Belgium	2,001,000,000
9 France+	1,889,000,000
10 Italy★	1,741,000,000

* Total exports, all industries, 2000

Including Mongolia

+ Including Monaco and Andorra

★ Including Vatican City State

Source: *Industry Canada. Reproduced with the permission of the Minister of Public Works and Government Services Canada, 2001*

TOP 10 🍁 GOODS EXPORTED FROM CANADA*

TYPE OF GOODS	EXPORT VALUE ($MILLION)
1 Motor vehicles, spark ignition#	42,557
2 Natural gas in gaseous state	20,136
3 Crude petroleum oils	19,389
4 Trucks, spark ignition	12,513
5 Lumber	11,538
6 Motor vehicles, spark ignition+	8,748
7 Newsprint	6,999
8 Chemical woodpulp	6,672
9 Preparations of non-crude petroleum oils	5,692
10 Other motor vehicle parts	5,656

* Total exports for 2000

Cylinder capacity more than 3000cc

+ Cylinder capacity 1500–3000cc

Source: *Industry Canada*

Did You Know? Inflation in Hungary in June 1946 reached such a record level that the prewar gold pengő coin was valued at 130 million trillion paper pengős, and notes with a face value of 1,000 trillion pengős were printed.

Workers of the World

COUNTRIES WITH THE MOST WORKERS

COUNTRY	WORKERS*
1 China	743,000,000
2 India	431,000,000
3 US	138,000,000
4 Indonesia	98,000,000
5 Russia	78,000,000
6 Brazil	76,000,000
7 Japan	68,000,000
8 Bangladesh	64,000,000
9 Pakistan	49,000,000
10 Nigeria	48,000,000

* Based on people aged 15–64 who are currently employed; unpaid groups are not included

Source: *World Bank*, World Development Indicators 2000

COUNTRIES WITH THE HIGHEST PROPORTION OF CHILD WORKERS

COUNTRY	PERCENTAGE OF CHILDREN WORKING*
1 Mali	52
2 Burundi	49
3 Burkina Faso	47
4 =Niger	44
=Uganda	44
6 Nepal	43
7 Ethiopia	42
8 Rwanda	41
9 Kenya	40
10 Tanzania	38

* Aged 10–14 years

Source: *World Bank*, World Development Indicators 2000

COUNTRIES WITH THE HIGHEST PROPORTION OF WORKERS IN SERVICE INDUSTRIES*

COUNTRY	LABOR FORCE PERCENTAGE
1 Puerto Rico	77.0
2 =Argentina	76.5
=Jordan	76.5
4 Canada	74.5
5 =Australia	74.0
=US	74.0
7 =Ecuador	73.5
=Netherlands	73.5
9 =Peru	73.0
=Norway	73.0

* Service industries include wholesale and retail trade, restaurants, and hotels; transportation, storage, and communications; financing, insurance, real estate, and business services; and community, social, and personal services.

Source: *World Bank*, World Development Indicators 2000

♣ TOP 10 DISAPPEARING JOBS IN CANADA*

❶ Typist (on typewriter)
❷ Typesetter/Compositor ❸ Watch and clock repairer ❹ Statistical clerk
❺ Fisher ❻ = Bank teller/cashier;
= Telephone operator; = Tool and die maker ❾ = Farmer;
= Locomotive operator

* Based on approximate percentage decline, 2000–10
Source: Canada's Best Careers Guide 2000

HARD LABOR

India's huge workforce relies on traditional manual labor, but the country is increasingly becoming a major center for computer technology.

TOP 10 EMPLOYERS IN CANADA
(Company/employees, 2001)

1 Loblaw Cos., 108,000 **2** Laidlaw Inc., 100,000
3 Onex Corp., 83,000 **4** BCE Inc., 75,000
5 Nortel Networks Corp., 74,500 **6** Hudson's Bay Co., 70,000
7 Magna International Inc., 59,000 **8** Bombardier Inc., 56,000
9 Royal Bank of Canada, 51,891 **10** Brascan Corp., 50,200

TOP 10
GROWTH CAREERS IN CANADA

OCCUPATION	PERCENTAGE*
1 In-home nurse	81
2 Nurse practitioner	73
3 =Physician/Surgeon	64
=Teacher, special education	64
5 Pharmacist	62
6 =Programmer/Analyst	61
=Psychiatrist/Psychologist	61
=Radiology technician	61
9 =Registered nurse	59
=Physiotherapist	59

* Ranked by projected percentage growth between 2000 and 2010
Source: Canada's Best Careers Guide 2000

TOP 10
LABOR UNIONS IN CANADA

UNION	MEMBERS
1 Canadian Union of Public Employees	486,656
2 National Union of Public and General Employees	325,000
3 National Automobile, Aerospace, Transportation, and General Workers Union of Canada (CAW–Canada)	245,000
4 United Food and Commercial Workers' Union of Canada	220,000
5 United Steel Workers	187,000
6 =Public Service Alliance of Canada	150,000
=Communications, Energy and Paperworkers Union of Canada	150,000
8 =Teamsters Canada	95,000
=Federation des affaires sociales inc.	95,000
10 Service Employees International Union	80,000

FACTORY MADE
Despite the growth of the service sector, manufacturing remains a vital component of most developed economies, providing employment for countless workers in factories around the world.

TOP 10
BEST PAID JOBS IN CANADA*

JOB	AVERAGE ANNUAL SALARY ($)
1 Doctor	113,800
2 Dentist	104,600
3 Aircraft pilot	88,900
4 Lawyer	85,900
5 Community and hospital pharmacist	71,800
6 Chiropractor	69,097
7 Geologist	66,100
8 Real estate agent	64,200
9 Veterinarian	62,900
10 Civil engineer	61,600

* Full-time jobs, January 2001
Source: www.jobscanada.com
According to *Earnings of Men and Women* by Statistics Canada, full-time working women earned an average of 72.5% of the income earned by men in 1997. The higher the level of education, the smaller the earning gap.

TOP 10 COUNTRIES WITH THE HIGHEST PROPORTION OF FARMERS
(Country/percentage in agriculture, 1999)

1 Bhutan, 93.8 **2** Nepal, 93.1 **3** Burkina Faso, 92.2
4 Rwanda, 90.5 **5** Burundi, 90.4 **6** Niger, 88.1 **7** Guinea
Bissau, 83.1 **8** Ethiopia, 82.8 **9** Mali, 81.5 **10** Uganda, 79.5
Source: *Food and Agriculture Organization of the United Nations*
This is based on a study of the number of people who depend on agriculture for their livelihood as a proportion of the total population of the country.

Which is the only South American country to appear among the world's Top 10 gold producers?
see p.204 for the answer
A Brazil
B Bolivia
C Peru

Company Matters

BANKS (BY ASSETS)

	BANK/COUNTRY	ASSETS (US$)
1	**Deutsche Bank**, Germany	841,796,920,000
2	**Bank of Tokyo-Mitsubishi**, Japan	729,249,650,000
3	**BNP Parabas**, France	700,232,030,000
4	**Bank of America Corp.**, US	632,574,000,000
5	**UBS**, Switzerland	613,198,370,000
6	**Fuji Bank**, Japan	567,899,800,000
7	**HSBC Holdings**, UK	567,793,290,000
8	**Sumitomo Bank**, Japan	524,227,780,000
9	**Dai-Ichi Kangyo Bank**, Japan	506,980,440,000
10	**HypoVereinsbank**, Germany	504,412,630,000

Source: Fortune Global 500

BANKS (BY REVENUE)

	BANK/COUNTRY	REVENUE (US$)
1	**J.P. Morgan Chase**, US	60,065,000,000
2	**Deutsche Bank**, Germany	58,585,150,000
3	**Bank of America Corp.**, US	57,757,000,000
4	**Crédit Suisse**, Switzerland	49,361,980,000
5	**Fortis**, Belgium	43,660,190,000
6	**BNP Parabas**, France	40,098,550,000
7	**HSBC Holdings**, UK	39,348,150,000
8	**ABN AMRO Holdings**, Netherlands	38,820,670,000
9	**Crédit Agricole**, France	32,923,500,000
10	**Bank of Tokyo-Mitsubishi**, Japan	32,624,000,000

Source: Fortune Global 500

INTERNATIONAL INDUSTRIAL COMPANIES

	COMPANY/SECTOR/LOCATION	ANNUAL SALES (US$)
1	**Exxon Mobil**, Oil, gas, fuel, US	210,392,000,000
2	**Wal-Mart Stores, Inc.**, Retailing, US	193,295,000,000
3	**General Motors Corp.**, Transport, US	184,632,000,000
4	**Ford Motor Co.**, Transport, US	180,598,000,000
5	**Daimler Chrysler**, Transport, Germany	159,986,000,000
6	**General Electric**, Electronics, electrical equipment, US	129,853,000,000
7	**Mitsui and Co. Ltd.**, Trading, Japan	118,555,000,000
8	**Mitsubishi Corp.**, Trading, Japan	117,766,000,000
9	**Toyota Motor**, Transport, Japan	115,671,000,000
10	**Itochu Corp.**, Trading, Japan	109,069,000,000

Source: Fortune Global 500

Fortune magazine's authoritative Global 500 list contains 500 companies, each with annual sales in excess of US$9.7 billion. All those in the Top 100 achieve sales of more than US$32.7 billion. However, only those in the Top 10 (plus one other – the Royal Dutch/Shell Group) make the stratospheric US$100-billion-plus league.

AS LONG AS IT'S BLACK...

Long the world's best-selling car, the Model T Ford established the company's place among the foremost global manufacturers.

TOP 10 🍁
BANKS IN CANADA

	BANK	ASSETS ($MILLIONS)*
1	Royal Bank of Canada	290,656.1
2	CIBC	267,701.6
3	Toronto Dominion Bank	264,817.9
4	Scotiabank	253,170.8
5	Bank of Montreal	233,395.9
6	National Bank of Canada	75,827.0
7	HSBC Bank Canada	28,100.0#
8	Laurentian Bank of Canada	14,741.3
9	Alberta Treasury Branches	11,500.0+
10	Deutsche Bank Canada	7,876.3*

As of October 31, 2000, unless otherwise noted

As of June 30, 2000

+ As of December 31, 2000

* 1999; latest available figure

TOP 10 🍁
LIFE AND HEALTH INSURERS IN CANADA*

	COMPANY	LOCATION
1	Great-West Life Assurance Co.	Winnipeg, MB
2	Clarica Life Insurance Co.	Waterloo, ON
3	Manulife Financial Corp.	Toronto, ON
4	Sun Life Financial Services of Canada Inc.	Toronto, ON
5	Canada Life Financial Corp.	Toronto, ON
6	Transamerica Life Insurance Co. of Canada	Toronto, ON
7	Standard Life	Montreal, QC
8	Maritime Life Assurance	Halifax, NS
9	Industrial-Alliance Life Insurance Co.	Sillery, QC
10	Desjardins-Laurentian Group	Lévis, QC

Based on 1999 net premiums written in Canada. Except for Nos. 2 and 4, includes subsidiaries and affiliated companies of life insurers and non-life insurers, and mergers and acquisitions as of January 1, 2000

Source: *Canadian Life & Health Insurance Association*

TOP 10 ★
US COMPANIES MAKING THE GREATEST PROFIT PER SECOND

	COMPANY	PROFIT PER SECOND (US$)
1	Exxon Mobil	561
2	Citigroup	428
3	General Electric	403
4	Verizon Communications	374
5	Intel Corp.	334
6	Microsoft	298
7	Philip Morris	269
8	IBM	256
9	SBC Communications	252
10	Bank of America Corporation	238

TOP 10 ★
CORPORATIONS IN THE US

	CORPORATION	REVENUE* (US$)
1	Exxon Mobil	210,392,000,000
2	Wal-Mart Stores	193,295,000,000
3	General Motors	184,632,000,000
4	Ford Motor Company	180,598,000,000
5	General Electric	129,853,000,000
6	Citigroup	111,826,000,000
7	Enron	100,789,000,000
8	IBM	88,396,000,000
9	AT&T	65,981,000,000
10	Verizon Communications	64,707,000,000

* In latest year

Source: Fortune Global 500

Despite their involvement in new technologies, many of the companies listed here date back to the late 19th century: AT&T – originally the American Telephone and Telegraph Company – dates from 1885, while General Electric was established in 1892, when the Edison General Electric Company and Thomson Houston Company were merged. Even parts of computer giant IBM have their roots back in the 1880s.

TOP 10 🍁
OLDEST COMPANIES IN CANADA*

	COMPANY	FOUNDED
1	Hudson's Bay Company	1670
2	Molson Breweries Limited	1786
3	=Dow Brewery	1790
	=Steel Company of Canada	1790
5	Ogilvie Flour Mills Company	1801
6	Halifax Insurance Company	1809
7	Price Company Limited	1816
8	Bank of Montreal	1817
9	John Labatt Limited	1828
10	Moirs Limited	1830

* Listed under their latest name

Source: Early Canadian Companies, *Toronto Public Library*, 1967

Canada boasts over 200 companies now more than 100 years old. Some, particularly many of those in Quebec and the Atlantic provinces, were established as early as the 1700s. Although they might also qualify for this Top 10 list, published information on them is not complete.

TOP 10 🍁
PRICE GAINS ON THE TORONTO STOCK EXCHANGE

	COMPANY/CLOSE PRICE ($)	NET CHANGE 2000
1	E-L Financial Corp. (250.00)	110.00
2	Janna Systems Inc. (74.00)	60.50
3	Research in Motion (120.50)	53.80
4	Ballard Power Systems (94.50)	53.75
5	NPS Allelix Inc. (68.75)	50.30
6	Angiotech Pharmaceuticals Inc. (68.90)	48.80
7	Potash Corp. of Saskatchewan (117.30)	48.30
8	Crown Life Insurance (121.00)	44.00
9	Northstar Energy Corp. (91.70)	42.10
10	Dreco Energy Services (59.50)	36.50

Source: *Toronto Stock Exchange*

Did You Know? The world's biggest car makers General Motors became the first company in the world to assemble 100 million vehicles when, on March 16, 1966, an Oldsmobile Toronado rolled off the production line.

Advertising & Brands

TOP 10

GLOBAL MARKETERS

	COMPANY/BASE	MEDIA SPENDING, 1998 (US$)
1	Procter & Gamble Company, US	4,747,600,000
2	Unilever, Netherlands/UK	3,428,500,000
3	General Motors Corporation, US	3,193,500,000
4	Ford Motor Company, US	2,229,500,000
5	Philip Morris Companies, US	1,980,300,000
6	DaimlerChrysler, Germany/US	1,922,200,000
7	Nestlé, Switzerland	1,833,000,000
8	Toyota Motor Corporation, Japan	1,692,400,000
9	Sony Corporation, Japan	1,337,700,000
10	Coca-Cola Company, US	1,327,300,000

Source: *Competitive Media Reporting/ACNielsen MMS/Advertising Age*

TOP 10

ADVERTISERS BY CATEGORY IN THE US

	CATEGORY	TOTAL AD SPENDING IN 1999 (US$)
1	Automotive, access and equipment	10,454,795,800
2	Retail	8,501,141,700
3	Media and advertising	4,978,059,100
4	Financial	3,965,350,100
5	Drugs and proprietary remedies	3,903,115,600
6	Telecommunications	3,344,281,600
7	Automotiver dealers and services	3,311,770,500
8	Restaurants	3,111,872,400
9	Public transportation, hotels, and resorts	2,800,402,900
10	Department stores	2,641,114,800

Source: *Competitive Media Reporting/ Publishers Information Bureau*

TOP 10

ADVERTISERS ON THE WEB

	WEBSITE	IMPRESSIONS*
1	TRUSTe	504,182,490
2	Microsoft	370,575,192
3	Yahoo!	228,032,781
4	America Online	128,433,841
5	AllAdvantage	120,408,883
6	Amazon	110,318,224
7	eBay	95,391,668
8	Casino On Net	90,831,841
9	Next Card	71,844,247
10	Barnes and Noble	67,581,608

* *Number of times the advertising banner has been loaded within a browser, week ending July 23, 2000*

TOP 10

CORPORATE ADVERTISERS IN CANADA

	ADVERTISER	TOTAL AD SPENDING IN 1999 (US$)
1	General Motors Corp.	82,881,000
2	Sears, Roebuck & Co.	76,069,000
3	BCE	67,239,000
4	Government of Canada	65,243,000
5	Proctor & Gamble Co.	54,895,000
6	Rogers Communications	47,111,000
7	Hudson's Bay Co.	45,826,000
8	Viacom	41,085,000
9	Ford Motor Co.	40,941,000
10	Interbrew	40,566,000

Source: *ACNielsen*

Reprinted with permission from the Nov 2000 issue of Ad Age Global
© *Crain Communications Inc. 2000*

BIG MAC

Global fast food company McDonald's is ranked second only to Coca-Cola as the world's most valuable food and beverage brand.

Crowd cheers! Coke nears!
Game goes better refreshed.
Coca-Cola, never too sweet,
gives that special zing...refreshes best.

things go **better with Coke** Drink Coca-Cola

THE REAL THING

Best-selling, most advertised, and most valuable are only three of the many superlatives applied to Coca-Cola's top international status.

TOP 10 ★
MOST VALUABLE GLOBAL BRANDS

	BRAND*	INDUSTRY	BRAND VALUE (US$)
1	Coca-Cola	Beverages	72,537,000,000
2	Microsoft-Windows	Technology	70,197,000,000
3	IBM	Technology	53,184,000,000
4	Intel	Technology	39,049,000,000
5	Nokia, Finland	Technology	38,528,000,000
6	General Electric	Diversified	38,128,000,000
7	Ford	Automobiles	36,368,000,000
8	Disney	Leisure	33,553,000,000
9	McDonald's	Food retail	27,859,000,000
10	AT&T	Telecommunications	25,548,000,000

* *All US-owned unless otherwise stated*

Source: *Interbrand*

Brand consultant Interbrand uses a method of estimating value that takes account of the profitability of individual brands within a business (rather than the companies that own them), as well as such factors as their potential for growth. Well over half of the 75 most valuable global brands surveyed by Interbrand are US-owned, with Europe accounting for another 30 percent.

TOP 10 ★
BEST-SELLING GLOBAL BRANDS*

	BRAND/COUNTRY	INDUSTRY	SALES, 1999 (US$)
1	Ford, US	Automobiles	121,603,000,000
2	General Electric, US	Diversified	105,840,000,000
3	Shell, UK	Oil	105,366,000,000
4	Toyota, Japan	Automobiles	100,704,000,000
5	IBM, US	Technology	87,548,000,000
6	Mercedes, Germany	Automobiles	65,249,000,000
7	AT&T, US	Telecommunications	62,391,000,000
8	Honda, Japan	Automobiles	60,902,000,000
9	Panasonic, Japan	Electronics	60,314,000,000
10	BP, UK	Oil	56,464,000,000

* *By value of sales*

Source: *Interbrand*

Most of the companies appearing in this list have in common not only their impressive size and status but also a long history. Ford, Mercedes, and Shell, for example, date back over 100 years.

TOP 10 ★
MOST VALUABLE FOOD AND BEVERAGE BRANDS

	BRAND*	INDUSTRY	BRAND VALUE (US$)
1	Coca-Cola	Food/beverages	72,537,000,000
2	McDonald's	Food retail	27,859,000,000
3	Marlboro	Tobacco	22,111,000,000
4	Nescafé, Switzerland	Beverages	13,681,000,000
5	Heinz	Food/beverages	11,742,000,000
6	Budweiser	Alcohol	10,685,000,000
7	Kelloggs	Food/beverages	7,357,000,000
8	Pepsi-Cola	Beverages	6,637,000,000
9	Wrigley's	Food	4,324,000,000
10	Bacardi	Alcohol	3,187,000,000

* *All US-owned unless otherwise stated*

Source: *Interbrand*

Nearly half of these companies (McDonald's, Heinz, Kelloggs, Wrigley's, and Bacardi) are eponymous, deriving their names from those of their founders.

Retail Therapy

LARGEST SHOPPING MALLS IN CANADA

MALL/LOCATION	GROSS LEASABLE AREA (SQ FT)	GROSS LEASABLE AREA (SQ M)
1 West Edmonton Mall, Edmonton, AB	3,800,000	353,020
2 Toronto Eaton Centre, Toronto, ON	1,639,039	152,267
3 Yorkdale Shopping Centre, Toronto, ON	1,559,000	144,831
4 =Square One Shopping Centre, Mississauga, ON	1,400,000	130,060
=Vaughan Mills, Vaughan, ON	1,400,000	130,060
6 Kanata Centrum, Kanata, ON	1,300,000	120,770
7 Le Carrefour Laval, Laval, QC	1,242,665	115,444
8 Les Galeries D'Anjou, Ville D'Anjou, QC	1,233,130	114,558
9 Place Laurier Shopping Centre, Sainte-Foy, QC	1,205,123	111,956
10 Pen Centre, St. Catharines, ON	1,200,000	111,480

Source: *International Council of Shopping Centers*

Gross leasable area is defined here as "the total floor area designated for tenant occupancy" and includes space occupied by anchor stores.

TOP 10 ★

COMPLAINTS TO CONSUMER AGENCIES IN THE US

CATEGORY	% OF AGENCIES REPORTING MAJOR COMPLAINTS IN 1999
1 Home improvement	82
2 Auto sales	75
3 Household goods	66
4 Auto repair	64
5 Credit/lending	57
6 Utilities	34
7 Mail order	27
8 =Collections	16
=Landlord/tenant	16
10 Leisure/travel	14

Source: *The National Association of Consumer Agency Administrators*

TOP 10 🍁

FOOD STORES IN CANADA

COMPANY	REVENUES, 1999 ($)
1 Loblaw Cos.	18,783,000,000
2 Empire Co.	6,377,651,000
3 Sobeys*	6,231,800,000
4 Canada Safeway	4,942,300,000
5 Métro	3,995,500,000
6 The Great Atlantic & Pacific Co. of Canada	2,844,466,000
7 Alimentation Couche-Tard	917,068,000
8 Calgary Co-operative Association	594,428,000
9 Scotsburn Co-operative Services	183,083,000
10 Les Supermarchés G.P.	150,000,000

* *Not included in the FP 500 list*

Source: FP 500, National Post Business magazine, June 2000

SHOPPING SPREE

Despite the growth of online retailing, traditional shopping continues to be an activity enjoyed by many, and is both a yardstick and a mainstay of Western economies.

TOP 10
CANADIAN RETAIL WEBSITES VISITED BY CANADIANS AT HOME

	WEBSITE	UNIQUE VISITORS, DEC 2000	% REACH
1	sears.ca	1,102,000	8.7
2	futureshop.ca	954,000	7.5
3	chapters.ca	833,000	6.5
4	canadiantire.ca	713,000	5.6
5	columbiahouse canada.com	510,000	4.0
6	hbc.com	393,000	3.1
7	ticketmaster.ca	316,000	2.5
8	hmv.com	311,000	2.4
9	archambault.ca	222,000	1.7
10	indigo.ca	196,000	1.5

Source: *Media Metrix Canada,* Total Canada at Home, *December 2000*

About 6.3 million Canadians – almost half of the country's population – visited the website of a Canadian retailer in December 2000. On a list for the same month of most-visited retail sites, which would include US-based websites, those of Sears, Chapters, and Future Shop would all place – at No. 2, No. 3, and No. 4, respectively.

TOP 10
MERCHANDISERS IN CANADA

	COMPANY	REVENUES, 1999 ($)
1	Hudson's Bay Co.	7,295,751,000
2	Sears Canada	6,131,180,000
3	Canadian Tire Corp.	4,728,259,000
4	Costco Canada	3,087,962,000
5	Liquor Control Board of Ontario	2,349,832,000
6	Future Shop	1,960,274,000
7	The Katz Group	1,500,000,000
8	Société des alcools du Québec	1,255,905,000
9	Dylex	1,081,767,000
10	Hartco Enterprises	850,279,000

Source: *FP 500, National Post Business magazine, June 2000*

TOP 10
WORLD RETAIL SECTORS

	SECTOR	COMPANIES*
1	Supermarket	108
2	Specialty	94
3	Department	62
4	Hypermarket	53
5 =	Convenience	40
=	Discount	40
7	Mail order	22
8	Restaurant	21
9	Drug	16
10	DIY	15

* *Of those listed in Stores' Top 200 Global Retailers; stores can operate in more than one area*

Source: *Stores*

TOP 10
TYPES OF RETAILERS IN CANADA

	INDUSTRY	RETAIL SALES, 2000 ($)
1	Motor vehicle and recreational vehicle dealers	73,326,756,000
2	Supermarkets and grocery stores	56,654,691,000
3	General merchandise stores	31,301,416,000
4	Gasoline service stations	22,170,827,000
5	Durable and semi-durable goods	16,216,097,000
6	Automotive parts, accessories, and services	15,665,898,000
7	Household furnishings, furniture, and appliance stores	15,132,772,000
8	Clothing and shoe stores	15,115,501,000
9	Drug and patent medicine stores	13,612,306,000
10	Food stores other than supermarkets and grocery	4,523,895,000

Source: *Statistics Canada*

TOP 10
FASTEST-GROWING RETAIL SECTORS IN THE US

	RETAIL SECTOR*	PERCENTAGE SALES INCREASE#
1	Gasoline	20.1
2	Meat, fish, and seafood	13.4
3	Radio, television, and electronics	13.2
4	Sporting goods and bicycles	12.3
5	Books	9.7
6	Drug and proprietary stores	9.2
7 =	Liquor stores	8.0
=	Restaurants, lunchrooms, and cafeterias	8.0
9	Retail bakery products	7.9
10	Floor coverings	7.5
	Total retail sales	7.9

* *Excluding general categories*

2000 compared with 1999

Source: *US Census Bureau*

TOP 10
CANADIAN CITIES WITH THE MOST RETAIL SALES

	CITY*	RETAIL SALES, 1999
1	Toronto	33,992,014,030
2	Montreal	24,923,781,250
3	Vancouver	16,986,262,940
4	Edmonton	8,625,950,130
5	Calgary	8,355,285,950
6	Ottawa-Hull	7,658,017,830
7	Quebec	5,295,818,800
8	Winnipeg	5,234,676,490
9	Hamilton	4,804,709,520
10	London	3,515,730,700

* *Figures reflect the retail sales in census metropolitan areas (CMAs)*

Source: *CARD, Media Information Network*

Which food items do Canadians consume most?
see p.219 for the answer
A Fresh vegetables
B Meats
C Sugar and syrup

That's Rich

RICHEST RULERS

RULER/COUNTRY	ASSETS ($)
1 King Fahd Bin Abdulaziz **Alsaud**, Saudi Arabia	45,000,000,000
2 Sheikh Zayed Bin Sultan al Nahyan, UAE (Abu Dhabi)	34,000,000,000
3 Amir Jaber Al-Ahmed Al Jaber Al-Sabah, Kuwait	27,000,000,000
4 Sultan Hassanal Bolkiah, Brunei	24,000,000,000
5 Sheikh Maktoum Bin Rashid Al Maktoum, UAE (Dubai)	18,000,000,000
6 President Saddam Hussein, Iraq	10,500,000,000
7 Amir Hamad Bin Khalifa Al Thani, Qatar	7,500,000,000
8 Queen Beatrix, Netherlands	5,250,000,000
9 Bashar Al-Assad*, Syria	3,450,000,000
10 Queen Elizabeth II, UK	675,000,000

* Estimated wealth of his father, President Hafez Al-Assad

Based on data published in Forbes magazine

HIGHEST-EARNING ACTORS

ACTOR	2000 INCOME ($)
1 Bruce Willis	105,000,000
2 Tom Cruise	64,800,000
3 Eddie Murphy	59,250,000
4 Mel Gibson	47,700,000
5 Nicolas Cage	42,600,000
6 Keanu Reeves	38,250,000
7 Brad Pitt	35,700,000
8 Julia Roberts	28,350,000
9 Ben Affleck	27,450,000
10 Robin Williams	25,650,000

Used by permission of Forbes magazine

Actors with the audience magnetism of Bruce Willis and Tom Cruise can today routinely command US$20 million or more per film.

RICHEST PEOPLE

NAME/COUNTRY	NET WORTH ($ BILLIONS)
1 S. Robson Walton*, US	100.7
2 William H. Gates III, US	83.4
3 Lawrence Joseph Ellison, US	64.5
4 King Fahd, Saudi Arabia	44.2
5 Warren Edward Buffett, US	38.8
6 Paul Gardner Allen, US	37.8
7 Sheikh Zayed, Abu Dhabi	34.0
8 Forrest Mars Jr., US	31.1
9 = Theo and Karl Albrecht and family, Germany	29.6
= Prince Alwaleed, Saudi Arabia	29.6
= Barbara Cox, Anthony and Anne Cox Chambers, US	29.6

* Other members of the Walton family have equal wealth

Based on data published in The Sunday Times, April 2001

RICHEST CANADIANS*

NAME/ INDUSTRY SECTOR	NET WORTH ($ BILLIONS)
1 Kenneth Thomson, Publishing, information distribution, oil	23.6
2 Irving Brothers, Petroleum, forest products, shipbuilding, media	8.7
3 Bombardier Family, Aerospace, manufacturing	8.5
4 Galen Weston, Retail, real estate	7.6
5 Gururaj (Desh) Deshpande, Optical network components	7.1
6 Charles Bronfman, Alcohol, entertainment	6.9
7 Lede Brothers, Fiber optics, construction	6.4
8 Edward (Ted) Rogers Jr., Media/communications	4.2
9 Terry Matthews, Internet	3.8
10 Barry Sherman, Pharmaceuticals	3.6

* As of April 2001

Source: Canadian Business, The Sunday Times

CLOSING ON GATES

The fortune of Oracle software magnate Larry Ellison has risen sharply, making him the third richest person, not far behind Microsoft's Bill Gates.

COUNTRIES WITH THE MOST DOLLAR BILLIONAIRES

COUNTRY	$ BILLIONAIRES*
1 US	55
2 Japan	43
3 Germany	42
4 = Canada	15
= UK	15
4 = France	14
= Switzerland	14
8 = China (Hong Kong)	13
= Mexico	13
10 = Brazil	9
= India	9

* Individuals/families with a net worth of US$1 billion or more

Source: Forbes

TOP 10 ★
MOST EXPENSIVE SINGLE PRECIOUS STONES EVER SOLD AT AUCTION*

STONE/SALE	PRICE (US$)
1 *The Patino*, cushion-cut Burmese ruby of 32.08 carats, Chaumet (from the Patiño collection), Sotheby's, New York, Oct 26, 1989	4,620,000
2 Cushion-cut Burmese ruby of 27.37 carats, Sotheby's, Geneva, May 17, 1995	4,036,250 (SF4,843,500)
3 Cushion-cut Burmese ruby of 15.97 carats, Sotheby's, New York, Oct 18, 1988	3,630,000
4 Oval-cut Burmese ruby of 16.51 carats, Sotheby's, Geneva, May 26, 1993	3,036,896 (SF4,403,500)
5 *The Rockefeller Sapphire*, step-cut Burmese sapphire of 62.02 carats, Sotheby's, St. Moritz, Feb 20, 1988	2,828,571 (SF3,960,000)
6 Cushion-cut Burmese ruby of 16.20 carats, Christie's, New York, Oct 23, 1990	2,750,000
7 Jadeite cabochon ring, 1.3 x 0.74 x 0.58 in (33.08 x 18.78 x 14.83 mm), Christie's, Hong Kong, Nov 1, 1999	2,405,000 (HK$18,500,000)
8 Cushion-cut sapphire of 337.66 carats in a diamond pendant, Christie's, Geneva, May 16, 1991	2,340,000 (SF3,300,000)
9 Rectangular step-cut emerald of 19.77 carats, Cartier (from the Duchess of Windsor collection), Sotheby's, Geneva, Apr 2, 1987	2,126,667 (SF3,190,000)
10 Cushion-cut Burmese ruby of 12.10 carats, Christie's, Geneva, Nov 19, 1992	2,000,000 (SF2,860,000)

* Excluding diamonds

TOP 10 ★
COUNTRIES MAKING GOLD JEWELRY

COUNTRY	GOLD USED IN 1999 TONNES
1 India	644.0
2 Italy	511.0
3 US	178.2
4 China	166.0
5 Saudi Arabia and Yemen	149.2
6 Indonesia	126.0
7 Turkey	115.0
8 Egypt	114.3
9 Malaysia	68.0
10 Taiwan	63.0
Canada	24.2

Source: *Gold Fields Mineral Services Ltd., Gold Survey 2000*

TOP 10 ★
GOLD MANUFACTURERS

COUNTRY	GOLD USED IN FABRICATION, 1999 TONNES
1 India	685.2
2 Italy	522.8
3 US	323.1
4 China	181.5
5 Japan	158.7
6 Saudi Arabia and Yemen	149.2
7 Turkey	139.3
8 Indonesia	126.0
9 Egypt	114.3
10 South Korea	93.5
Canada	49.2

Source: *Gold Fields Mineral Services Ltd., Gold Survey 2000*

TOP 10 ★
PIECES OF JEWELRY AUCTIONED BY CHRISTIE'S

JEWELRY/SALE	PRICE (US$)
1 **Single strand jadeite necklace of 27 beads**, 0.59 to 0.62 in (15.09 to 15.84 mm), Christie's, Hong Kong, Nov 6, 1997	9,394,566 (HK$72,620,000)
2 ***The Begum Blue*** (from the collection of Princess Salimah Aga Khan), Christie's, Geneva, Nov 13, 1995 (SF8,803,500) *Fancy, deep blue, heart-shaped diamond of 13.78 carats and a heart-shaped diamond of 16.03 carats, D color, internally flawless*	7,790,000
3 ***The Mouna Diamond***, Christie's, Geneva, May 15, 1996 *Fancy intense yellow diamond brooch of 102.07 carats by Cartier, 1953*	3,237,868 (SF3,743,500)
4 ***The Allnat***, Christie's, Geneva, Nov 16, 1998 *Fancy, intense yellow cushion-shaped diamond pendant of 112.53 carats (VS1), mounted by Bulgari*	3,043,496 (SF4,403,500)
5 ***The Harcourt Emeralds***, Christie's, London, June 21, 1989 (£1,870,000) *Necklace set with diamonds and 13 emeralds weighing 16.219 carats*	2,879,800
6 **Single strand jadeite and diamond lavalière of 29 jadeite beads**, 0.19 to 0.64 in (4.78 to 16.22 mm), Christie's, Hong Kong, Nov 1, 1999	2,862,600 (HK$22,020,000)
7 ***The Indore Pears***, Christie's, Geneva, Nov 12, 1987	2,686,200 (SF3,630,000)
8 **A diamond necklace suspending a 17.57 carats heart-shaped diamond, with matching diamond ear-pendants**, Christie's, Geneva, Nov 15, 1995	2,643,500 (SF2,643,500)
9 **Jadeite bangle**, Christie's, Hong Kong, Nov 1, 1999	2,576,600 (HK$19,820,000)
10 **Jadeite ring**, 1.30 x 0.74 x 0.58 in (33.08 x 18.78 x 14.83 mm), Christie's, Hong Kong, Nov 1, 1999	2,405,000 (HK$18,500,000)

WORTH ITS WEIGHT IN GOLD

International trade in gold is customarily carried out with either 1-kg (32.15-troy ounce) or 12.5-kg (400-troy ounce) gold bars.

Natural Resources

TOP 10 ★
MOST PRODUCED NON-FUEL MINERALS

	MINERAL	1998 PRODUCTION (TONNES)
1	Iron ore*	1,020,000,000
2	Bauxite	122,000,000
3	Clay, kaolin	115,000,000
4	Aluminium	22,100,000
5	Manganese ore	18,700,000
6	Chromite	12,700,000
7	Copper	12,200,000
8	Clay, bentonite	9,330,000
9	Feldspar	8,080,000
10	Zinc	7,540,000

*From which iron and steel are produced

Source: U.S. Geological Survey, Minerals Yearbook

TOP 10 ★
SALT PRODUCERS

	COUNTRY	1998 PRODUCTION (TONNES)*
1	US	41,300,000
2	China	30,800,000
3	Germany	15,700,000
4	Canada	13,300,000
5	India	9,500,000
6	Australia	8,900,000
7	Mexico	8,400,000
8	France	7,000,000
9	UK	6,600,000
10	Brazil	6,500,000
	World	186,000,000

*Includes salt in brine

Source: The Salt Institute

TOP 10 ★
DIAMOND PRODUCERS, BY VALUE

	COUNTRY	1999 VALUE (US$)
1	Botswana	1,600,000,000
2	Russia	1,500,000,000
3	South Africa	900,000,000
4	Dem. Rep. of Congo	700,000,000
5	Angola	500,000,000
6 =	Australia	400,000,000
=	Canada	400,000,000
=	Namibia	400,000,000
9 =	Guinea	100,000,000
=	Sierra Leone	100,000,000

Source: De Beers

TOP 10 ★
GOLD PRODUCERS

	COUNTRY	1999 PRODUCTION (TONNES)
1	South Africa	449.5
2	US	341.9
3	Australia	302.8
4	Canada	157.9
5	China	156.3
6	Indonesia	154.5
7	Russia	138.2
8	Peru	127.4
9	Uzbekistan	85.7
10	Ghana	78.2

Source: Gold Fields Mineral Services Ltd

World-dominating gold producer South Africa saw its output fall yet again for the seventh consecutive year. Australia's output also fell in 1999, after having increased dramatically over recent years: the country's record annual production had stood at 119 tonnes since 1903, but in 1988 it rocketed to 152 tonnes, a total it doubled in 1998. During the 1990s, several other countries increased their mine output dramatically, most notably Indonesia and Peru, each of which escalated production by a factor of almost nine, while Papua-New Guinea's production falls only just outside the Top 10.

TOP 10 ★
SILVER PRODUCERS

	COUNTRY	1998 PRODUCTION (TONNES)
1	Mexico	2,686
2	US	2,060
3	Peru	1,934
4	Australia	1,469
5	China	1,400
6	Chile	1,340
7	Canada	1,179
8	Poland	1,000
9	Kazakhstan	470
10	Bolivia	380
	World	16,400

Source: U.S. Geological Survey, Minerals Yearbook

TOP 10 ★
IRON PRODUCERS

	COUNTRY	1999 PRODUCTION (TONNES)*
1	China	125,390,000
2	Japan	74,520,000
3	US	46,300,000
4	Russia	40,033,000
5	Germany	27,931,000
6	Brazil	25,060,000
7	South Korea	23,329,000
8	Ukraine	21,937,000
9	India	20,139,000
10	France	13,854,000
	Canada	8,783,000

*Pig iron

Source: U.S. Geological Survey, Minerals Yearbook

TOP 10 ALUMINUM PRODUCERS
(Country/1999 production in tonnes)

❶ US, 3,779,000 ❷ Russia, 3,146,000 ❸ China, 2,450,000 ❹ Canada, 2,390,000
❺ Australia, 1,718,000 ❻ Brazil, 1,250,000 ❼ Norway, 1,034,000
❽ South Africa, 687,000 ❾ Germany, 600,000 ❿ Venezuela, 570,000
World 23,100,000
Source: U.S. Geological Survey, Minerals Yearbook

Did You Know? Estimates indicate that if current production levels are maintained, US oil reserves will be exhausted in 2009, while those of the Middle East will last until 2086.

TOP 10 ★
COAL PRODUCERS

COUNTRY	1999 PRODUCTION TONNES OIL EQUIVALENT*
1 US	580,500,000
2 China	512,100,000
3 Australia	149,800,000
4 India	144,100,000
5 South Africa	116,700,000
6 Russia	112,600,000
7 Poland	73,100,000
8 Germany	59,600,000
9 Ukraine	42,300,000
10 Indonesia	40,300,000
Canada	39,300,000

* Commercial solid fuels only, i.e. bituminous coal and anthracite (hard coal), lignite, and brown (sub-bituminous) coal

Source: BP Amoco Statistical Review of World Energy 2000

TOP 10 ★
NATURAL GAS PRODUCERS

COUNTRY	1999 PRODUCTION TONNES OIL EQUIVALENT*
1 Russia	495,900,000
2 US	486,400,000
3 Canada	146,100,000
4 UK	89,700,000
5 Algeria	74,000,000
6 Indonesia	59,800,000
7 Netherlands	54,100,000
8 Uzbekistan	46,700,000
9 Norway	45,900,000
10 Saudi Arabia	41,600,000

* The amount of oil that would be required to produce the same energy output

Source: BP Amoco Statistical Review of World Energy 2000

TOP 10 ★
OIL PRODUCERS

COUNTRY	1999 PRODUCTION (TONNES)
1 Saudi Arabia	411,800,000
2 US	354,700,000
3 Russia	304,800,000
4 Iran	175,200,000
5 Mexico	166,100,000
6 Venezuela	160,500,000
7 China	159,300,000
8 Norway	149,100,000
9 UK	137,100,000
10 Iraq	125,500,000
Canada	120,500,000

Source: BP Amoco Statistical Review of World Energy 2000

While most leading countries have increased their oil production, Russia has fallen from the No. 1 slot in the global ranking it occupied 10 years ago.

TOP 10 ★
COUNTRIES WITH THE GREATEST COAL RESERVES

COUNTRY	RESERVES AT END OF 1999 (TONNES)
1 US	246,643,000,000
2 Russia	157,010,000,000
3 China	114,500,000,000
4 Australia	90,400,000,000
5 India	74,733,000,000
6 Germany	67,000,000,000
7 South Africa	55,333,000,000
8 Ukraine	34,356,000,000
9 Kazakhstan	34,000,000,000
10 Poland	14,309,000,000
Canada	8,623,000,000

Source: BP Amoco Statistical Review of World Energy 2000

Coal reserves are quantities of coal that can be recovered from known deposits, based on existing engineering and economic conditions, which, of course, may change over time.

TOP 10 ★
COUNTRIES WITH THE GREATEST NATURAL GAS RESERVES

COUNTRY	RESERVES 1999 TRILLION FT³	TRILLION M³
1 Russia	1,700.0	48.14
2 Iran	812.3	23.00
3 Qatar	300.0	8.49
4 United Arab Emirates	212.0	6.00
5 Saudi Arabia	204.5	5.79
6 US	164.0	4.65
7 Algeria	159.7	4.52
8 Venezuela	142.5	4.04
9 Nigeria	124.0	3.51
10 Iraq	109.8	3.11
Canada	63.9	1.81

Source: BP Amoco Statistical Review of World Energy 2000

Total world reserves in 1999 were put at 146.43 trillion cubic meters (5,171.8 trillion cubic feet), more than double the 1979 estimate.

TOP 10 ★
COUNTRIES WITH THE GREATEST CRUDE OIL RESERVES

COUNTRY	RESERVES AT END OF 1999 (TONNES)
1 Saudi Arabia	36,000,000,000
2 Iraq	15,100,000,000
3 Kuwait	13,300,000,000
4 United Arab Emirates	12,600,000,000
5 Iran	12,300,000,000
6 Venezuela	10,500,000,000
7 Russia	6,700,000,000
8 Mexico	4,100,000,000
9 Libya	3,900,000,000
10 US	3,500,000,000
Canada	800,000,000

Source: BP Amoco Statistical Review of World Energy 2000

The discovery of new oil means that total world reserves at the end of 1999 stood at 140.4 billion tonnes, 63 percent more than the 1979 estimate.

Background image: **COPPER, NICKEL, AND IRON ORES**

Energy & Environment

NUCLEAR ELECTRICITY-PRODUCING COUNTRIES

	COUNTRY	1999 PRODUCTION (KW/HR)
1	US	728,200,000,000
2	France	375,100,000,000
3	Japan	308,700,000,000
4	Germany	161,000,000,000
5	Russia	110,900,000,000
6	South Korea	97,900,000,000
7	UK	91,500,000,000
8	Canada	69,800,000,000
9	Ukraine	67,300,000,000
10	Sweden	66,600,000,000
	World	2,395,900,000,000

Source: *Energy Information Administration*

PAPER-RECYLING COUNTRIES

	COUNTRY	1999 RECYCLING (TONNES)
1	US	41,167,828
2	Japan	14,841,000
3	China	12,014,000
4	Germany	10,292,000
5	France	5,000,000
6	South Korea	3,869,000
7	UK	3,675,000
8	Italy	3,628,800
9	Netherlands	2,417,000
10	Canada	1,478,000
	World	115,331,303

Source: *Food and Agriqulture Organization of the United Nations*

WATT

James Watt (1736–1819) is remembered as the inventor of the modern steam engine, and the man after whom the unit of power is named. He introduced great improvements to the steam engine invented by Thomas Newcomen, patented many other inventions, and undertook experiments relating to power, introducing the concept of "horsepower." The use of the term "watt" was proposed in 1882, and is equivalent to an amp multiplied by a volt (each named after other electrical pioneers, André Marie Ampère and Allessandro Volta), or one joule per second. It is most commonly used as a measure of the intensity of light-bulbs, and in terms of electrical consumption in kilowatt/hours.

WHO WAS · WHO WAS · WHO WAS · WHO WAS ?

TOP 10 COUNTRIES WITH THE MOST RELIANCE ON NUCLEAR POWER

(Country/nuclear electricity as percentage of total electricity)

1 France, 75.00 **2** Lithuania, 73.11 **3** Belgium, 57.74 **4** Bulgaria, 47.12
5 Slovak Republic, 47.02 **6** Sweden, 46.80 **7** Ukraine, 43.77 **8** South Korea, 42.84
9 Hungary, 38.30 **10** Slovenia, 37.18

Source: *International Atomic Energy Agency*

ALTERNATIVE POWER-CONSUMING COUNTRIES*

	COUNTRY	1999 CONSUMPTION (KW/HR)
1	US	83,000,000,000
2	Japan	24,700,000,000
3	Germany	15,000,000,000
4	Brazil	9,900,000,000
5	Finland	9,500,000,000
6	Philippines	8,300,000,000
7	UK	8,200,000,000
8	Canada	7,500,000,000
9	Italy	7,000,000,000
10	Mexico	5,300,000,000
	World	227,400,000,000

* *Includes geothermal, solar, wind, wood, and waste electric power*

Source: *Energy Information Administration*

NUCLEAR REACTOR

Opened in 1985–86, Pacific Gas and Electric's Diablo Canyon Nuclear Power Station in California is one of the US's 104 nuclear reactors.

TOP 10 ★
CARBON DIOXIDE-EMITTING COUNTRIES

	COUNTRY	CO₂ EMISSIONS PER HEAD, 1997 (TONNES OF CARBON)
1	Qatar	18.19
2	United Arab Emirates	9.40
3	Kuwait	7.88
4	Guam	7.04
5	Bahrain	6.95
6	Singapore	6.39
7	US	5.48
8	Luxembourg	5.16
9	Brunei	4.79
10	Australia	4.71
	Canada	4.42

Source: *Gregg Marland and Tom Boden (Oak Ridge National Laboratory), and Bob Andres (University of North Dakota)*

CO₂ emissions derive from three principal sources: fossil fuel burning, cement manufacturing, and gas flaring. Since World War II, increasing industrialization in many countries has resulted in huge increases in carbon dioxide output, a trend that most are now actively attempting to reverse. The US remains the worst offender in total, with 1,500 million tonnes released in 1997.

TOP 10 ★
DEFORESTING COUNTRIES

	COUNTRY	AVERAGE ANNUAL FOREST LOSS, 1990-95 SQ MILES	SQ KM
1	Brazil	9,863	25,544
2	Indonesia	4,187	10,844
3	Dem. Rep. of Congo	2,857	7,400
4	Bolivia	2,245	5,814
5	Mexico	1,961	5,080
6	Venezuela	1,944	5,034
7	Malaysia	1,545	4,002
8	Myanmar (Burma)	1,496	3,874
9	Sudan	1,361	3,526
10	Thailand	1,271	3,294

Source: *Food and Agriculture Organization of the United Nations*

Some 47,740 sq km (18,433 sq miles) of tropical forest was lost in South America each year between 1990 and 1995, plus a further 37,480 sq km (14,471 sq miles) in Africa, and 33,280 sq km (12,849 sq miles) in Asia. The total global loss during that five-year period was 563,460 sq km (217,553 sq miles), an area equivalent to twice the size of the UK. However, while Brazil tops the list of countries with the highest amount of forest loss, the rate of deforestation is only 0.5 percent.

POWER TO THE PEOPLE

In the 20th century, the creation of national grids for the transmission of electricity brought power to even the most remote communities.

TOP 10 ★
ENERGY-CONSUMING COUNTRIES

	COUNTRY	OIL	GAS	1999 ENERGY CONSUMPTION* COAL	NUCLEAR	HEP#	TOTAL
1	US	882.8	555.3	543.3	197.7	25.8	2,204.9
2	China	200.0	19.3	511.0	4.1	18.2	752.6
3	Russia	126.2	327.3	109.3	31.2	13.8	607.8
4	Japan	258.8	67.1	91.5	82.0	8.0	507.4
5	Germany	132.4	72.1	80.6	43.8	2.0	330.9
6	India	94.8	21.4	150.0	3.3	6.9	276.4
7	France	96.4	33.9	14.1	101.5	6.6	252.4
8	Canada	83.0	64.3	31.9	19.0	29.6	227.8
9	UK	78.7	82.5	35.8	24.8	0.6	222.4
10	South Korea	99.9	16.9	38.1	26.6	0.5	182.0
	World	3,462.4	2,063.9	2,129.5	650.8	226.8	8,533.6

* *Millions of tonnes of oil equivalent* # *Hydroelectric power*

Source: BP Amoco Statistical Review of World Energy 2000

TOP 10 ★
ELECTRICITY-CONSUMING COUNTRIES

	COUNTRY	1999 CONSUMPTION (KW/HR)
1	US	3,254,900,000,000
2	China	1,084,100,000,000
3	Japan	947,000,000,000
4	Russia	728,200,000,000
5	Canada	497,500,000,000
6	Germany	495,200,000,000
7	India	424,000,000,000
8	France	398,800,000,000
9	Brazil	353,700,000,000
10	UK	333,000,000,000
	World	12,832,700,000,000

Source: *Energy Information Administration*

Did You Know? While other countries have steadily increased their energy consumption, in the 15 years from 1984 to 1999 India more than doubled its requirements.

Science & Invention

FIRST TRADEMARKS ISSUED IN CANADA

ISSUED TO/DATE		PRODUCT
1	D. Crawford & Co., July 29, 1865	Soap
2	J.D. King & Co., June 12, 1866	Cigars
3	Northrup & Russell, July 17, 1868	Washing machines
4	W.H. Bilton, July 18, 1868	Soda and ginger ale
5	Alfred Savage & Son, July 18, 1868	Soap
6	Damon & Baker, July 18, 1868	Unknown
7	T. Graham & Son, July 18, 1868	Cure-all "medicine"
8	C.P. Reid & Co., July 20, 1868	Cigars
9	Buchanan, Leckie & Co., July 30, 1868	Brandy put up in bottles
10	Buchanan, Leckie & Co., July 30, 1868	Brandy put up in casks

Source: *Canadian Intellectual Property Office*

A trademark is a letter, word, symbol, or design used by a business to identify itself and distinguish it from competitors. Canada's first trademarks act, the *Trade-mark & Design Act*, was enacted in 1864. The country's oldest registered trademark, Imperial soap, is still in use and now belongs to UL Canada.

COUNTRIES TO REGISTER THE MOST TRADEMARKS

COUNTRY	TRADEMARKS REGISTERED (1998)
1 Japan	132,066
2 US	129,871
3 China	98,961
4 Argentina	61,671
5 Spain	59,810
6 Germany	57,919
7 UK	48,600
8 Italy	46,707
9 Benelux	32,093
10 Mexico	28,362
Canada	18,486

Source: *World Intellectual Property Organization*

FIRST PATENTEES IN CANADA

PATENTEE/PATENT	DATE
1 Noah Cushing, Washing and fulling machine	June 8, 1824
2 Isaac Jones Barnard, Improved machine for cutting nails	July 21, 1824
3 James George, Improvement of the construction of wooden railroads	Dec 13, 1824
4 Robert Dalkin, Improvement of the drum-cylinder and double drum-cylinder	Nov 30, 1825
5 =Justin Jacob, Lever engine	Oct 31, 1826
=Charles Laurier, Instrument for ascertaining the number of revolutions of carriage wheels and millstones	Oct 31, 1826
=Noah Cushing, Threshing and winnowing machine	Oct 31, 1826
8 Robert Hoyle, Improved machine for dressing flax or hemp	Oct 3, 1829
9 William John Spence, Machine for distributing ink over printing types	Dec 19, 1829
10 Philip Schoolcraft, Machine for cutting timber into sidings, clapboards, shingles, laths, etc.	May 15, 1830

Source: *Patents of Canada from 1824 to 1849, Patent Office in Canada*

The Canadian General Electric Co., which received its first patent in 1894, owns the most patents of any company in Canada: 7,612.

COUNTRIES TO REGISTER THE MOST PATENTS

COUNTRY	PATENTS REGISTERED (1998)
1 US	147,520
2 Japan	141,448
3 Germany	51,685
4 France	46,213
5 UK	43,181
6 Italy	38,988
7 Russia	23,368
8 Netherlands	22,411
9 Spain	20,128
10 Sweden	18,482
Canada	9,572

Source: *World Intellectual Property Organization*

A patent is an exclusive licence to manufacture and exploit a unique product or process for a fixed period. The figures refer to the number of patents actually granted during 1998 – which, in most instances, represents only a fraction of the patents applied for.

FIRST CANADIAN INVENTIONS, INNOVATIONS, AND INVENTORS*

INVENTION/INVENTOR	YEAR
1 McIntosh apple, John McIntosh	1796
2 =Royal William, Atlantic-crossing steamship, John Gordie and Samuel Cunard	1833
=Ship propeller, John Patch	1833
4 Washing machine, James Brown	1835
5 Newsprint, Charles Fenerty	1838
6 Atlantic steamship mail service, Samuel Cunard	1840
7 Compound steam engine, Benjamin Franklin Tibbetts	1842
8 Rust-resistant red fife wheat, David Fife	1843
9 Potato digger, William Watts	1845
10 Kerosene, Dr. Abraham Gesner	1846

* *As of 1796; earlier inventions are undateable*

Source: *Science Technology Centre, Carleton University*

TOP 10 🍁

FIRST INDUCTEES TO THE CANADIAN SCIENCE AND ENGINEERING HALL OF FAME

PERSON/ACHIEVEMENT

1 Sir William Logan (1798–1875)
Founder of the Geological Survey of Canada

2 Sir Sanford Fleming (1827–1915)
Inventor of standard time and architect of the transcontinental railway

3 Alexander Graham Bell (1847–1922)
Inventor of the telephone and expert in speech and hearing physiology and anatomy

4 Reginald Fessenden (1866–1932)
Pioneer in the development of radio; built the first power-generating station, at Niagara Falls

5 Maude Abbott (1869–1940)
Pathologist and renowned expert on congenital heart disease

6 Wallace Turnbull (1870–1954)
Inventor of the variable-pitch propeller

7 Frère Marie-Victorin (1885–1944)
Founder of the Botanical Institute, in Montreal, and discoverer of many plant varieties

8 Andrew G.L. MacNaughton (1887–1966)
Inventor of the cathode ray-detection finder and new aerial mapping techniques

9 Margaret Newton (1887–1971)
Plant pathologist and developer of techniques to combat wheat rust

10 Sir Frederick Banting (1891–1941)
Co-discoverer of insulin; nobel laureate

Source: *Canada Science and Technology Museum*
The Canadian Science and Engineering Hall of Fame was established in 1991 at the Canada Science and Technology Museum in Ottawa.

🍁 TOP 10 PROVINCES GRANTED PATENTS

(Province/number of patents 1999–2000)

❶ **Ontario**, 1163 ❷ **Quebec**, 601
❸ **Alberta**, 323 ❹ **British Columbia**, 209
❺ **Saskatchewan**, 66 ❻ **Manitoba**, 58
❼ **New Brunswick**, 25 ❽ **Nova Scotia**, 17
❾ **Newfoundland**, 10 ❿ **Prince Edward Island**, 4 *Canada, 2,476*

Source: *Canadian Intellectual Property Office*

TOP 10 ⭐

COUNTRIES FOR RESEARCH AND DEVELOPMENT EXPENDITURE

COUNTRY	R&D EXPENDITURE AS PERCENTAGE OF GNP*
1 Sweden	3.76
2 South Korea	2.82
3 Japan	2.80
4 Finland	2.78
5 US	2.63
6 Switzerland	2.60
7 Germany	2.41
8 Israel	2.35
9 France	2.25
10 Italy	2.21
Canada	1.66

* *In latest year for which statistics available*

Source: *World Bank*, World Development Indicators 2000

TOP 10 ⭐

COUNTRIES FOR SCIENTIFIC AND TECHNICAL JOURNAL ARTICLES

COUNTRY	AVERAGE NUMBER PUBLISHED PER ANNUM (1995–97)
1 US	173,233
2 Japan	43,655
3 UK	39,670
4 Germany	35,294
5 France	26,455
6 Canada	20,989
7 Russia	17,589
8 Italy	16,256
9 Australia	11,830
10 Netherlands	10,914
World total	515,708

Source: *US National Science Foundation*

TOP 10 ⭐

COUNTRIES FOR RESEARCH AND DEVELOPMENT SCIENTISTS AND ENGINEERS

COUNTRY	R&D SCIENTISTS AND ENGINEERS PER MILLION*
1 Japan	4,909
2 Sweden	3,826
3 US	3,676
4 Norway	3,664
5 Russia	3,587
6 Australia	3,357
7 Denmark	3,259
8 Switzerland	3,006
9 Germany	2,831
10 Finland	2,799
Canada	2,719

* *In latest year for which statistics available*

Source: *World Bank*, World Development Indicators 2000

TOP 10 ⭐

COUNTRIES FOR HIGH-TECHNOLOGY EXPORTS

COUNTRY	HIGH-TECHNOLOGY EXPORTS (US$)*
1 US	170,681,000,000
2 Japan	94,777,000,000
3 UK	64,461,000,000
4 Germany	63,698,000,000
5 Singapore	54,783,000,000
6 France	54,183,000,000
7 Netherlands	35,377,000,000
8 Malaysia	31,419,000,000
9 South Korea	30,582,000,000
10 Ireland	23,944,000,000
Canada	21,736,000,000

* *In latest year for which statistics available*

Source: *World Bank*, World Development Indicators 2000

Did You Know? In 1976, the millionth Canadian patent was delivered to Canadian chemistry professor James E. Guillet and British researcher Dr. Harvey G. Troth for their discovery of a plastic that turns to dust when continually exposed to sunlight.

The inexorable rise of the cellular mobile phone is one of the most significant changes in world communications. Scandinavian countries have the world's highest ratio of phones to population.

TOP 10 ★
COUNTRIES WITH THE MOST TELEPHONES

COUNTRY	TOTAL TELEPHONE LINES	TELEPHONE LINES PER 100 INHABITANTS	COUNTRY	TOTAL TELEPHONE LINES	TELEPHONE LINES PER 100 INHABITANTS
1 Luxembourg	308,000	73.33	7 Iceland	183,000	65.36
2 Norway	3,155,000	71.19	8 Canada	19,630,000	63.67
3 US	193,862,000	70.98	9 Netherlands	9,878,000	62.60
4 Switzerland	5,023,000	70.11	10 Australia	11,609,000	61.04
5 Sweden	6,160,000	69.45			
6 Denmark	3,555,000	67.08			

Source: *Siemens AG*, International Telecom Statistics 2000

TOP 10 ★
COUNTRIES WITH THE HIGHEST RATIO OF CELLULAR MOBILE PHONE USERS

COUNTRY	SUBSCRIBERS	MOBILES PER 100 INHABITANTS
1 Finland	3,499,000	67.8
2 Norway	2,779,000	62.7
3 Sweden	5,234,000	59.0
4 Italy	30,068,000	52.2
5 Austria	4,147,000	51.3
6 Denmark	2,682,000	50.6
7 South Korea	23,493,000	49.9
8 Taiwan	10,835,000	49.4
9 Portugal	4,720,000	47.4
10 Switzerland	3,164,000	44.2
Canada	6,594,000	21.4

Source: *Siemens AG*, International Telecom Statistics 2000

TOP 10 ★
COUNTRIES MAKING THE MOST INTERNATIONAL PHONE CALLS

COUNTRY	MINUTES PER HEAD	TOTAL MINUTES OUTGOING CALLS PER ANNUM
1 US	102.7	28,363,000,000
2 UK	101.9	6,066,000,000
3 Germany	89.9	7,385,000,000
4 Canada	174.1	5,310,000,000
5 France	74.9	4,386,000,000
6 Italy	54.0	3,100,000,000
7 Switzerland	335.9	2,400,000,000
8 Netherlands	135.7	2,150,000,000
9 Japan	15.5	1,957,000,000
10 China	1.5	1,950,000,000

Source: *International Telecommunication Union*

THE FIRST TRANSPACIFIC TELEGRAPH CABLE

In 1858, the first transatlantic cable was laid, and following this, the idea of a transpacific cable between Canada and Australia was proposed in 1887. It was not until 1902, however, that the dream became a reality. In that year, a specially built ship, the *Colonia*, laid an undersea cable from Bamfield, on Vancouver Island, Canada, to the Fanning, Fiji, and Norfolk islands. From here it branched to Brisbane, Australia, and Doubtless Bay on the north island of New Zealand. Despite the technical difficulties of laying some 12,875 km (8,000 miles) of cable, often at great depths, the project was completed on schedule. On October 31, Canadian engineer Sir Sandford Fleming sent the first telegram from Canada to Australia, and the whole system was opened on December 8, remaining in service until 1964.

• YEARS AGO • YEARS AGO • 100 • YEARS AGO • YEARS AGO •

END OF THE LINE

In many countries, the recent expansion of mobile phone networks has resulted in a decline in the popularity of public telephones.

TOP 10 ★
LETTER-POSTING COUNTRIES

	COUNTRY	AVERAGE NO. OF LETTER POST ITEMS POSTED PER INHABITANT*
1	Vatican City	5,740.0
2	US	734.4
3	Sweden	502.8
4	France	442.8
5	Finland	396.5
6	Austria	371.6
7	Belgium	344.1
8	Norway	338.0
9	Luxembourg	336.1
10	Denmark	334.7

* In 1999 or latest year for which data available
Source: *Universal Postal Union*

The Vatican's population (which is variable, but seldom exceeds 750) is small. This statistical anomaly results in part from the large numbers of official missives dispatched via the Holy See's post office and its 32 postboxes, but mainly because Rome's inhabitants have discovered that mail posted in the Vatican City and bearing Vatican stamps is treated as priority.

TOP 10 ★
COUNTRIES WITH THE MOST POST OFFICES

	COUNTRY	POST OFFICES*
1	India	153,021
2	China	112,204
3	Russia	43,900
4	US	38,159
5	Japan	24,678
6	Indonesia	20,139
7	UK	18,760
8	Canada	18,607
9	France	17,038
10	Turkey	16,984

* In latest year for which data available
Source: *Universal Postal Union*

There are some 770,000 post offices around the world, 365,400 of which are in Asia and the Pacific countries. These range from major city offices offering a broad range of services to small establishments providing only basic facilities, such as the sale of postage stamps. The average number of inhabitants served by each also varies considerably, from fewer than 2,000 in Canada and Switzerland to as many as 225,000 in Burundi. The world average is 7,558.

TOP 10 COUNTRIES RECEIVING THE MOST LETTERS FROM ABROAD

(Country/items of mail handled, 1999)*

❶ Germany, 702,000,000　❷ India, 561,640,000
❸ UK, 535,812,069　❹ France, 476,000,000
❺ US, 474,347,500　❻ Saudi Arabia, 340,105,000
❼ Netherlands, 299,000,000　❽ Japan, 289,593,000
❾ Algeria, 217,600,000　❿ Italy, 217,446,823

* Or latest year in which data available
Source: *Universal Postal Union*

TOP 10 COUNTRIES SENDING THE MOST LETTERS ABROAD

(Country/items of mail handled, 1999)*

❶ UK, 986,786,244　❷ US, 904,600,000　❸ France, 576,200,000
❹ Germany, 402,600,000　❺ Saudi Arabia, 347,696,000　❻ Finland, 306,300,000　❼ Russia, 221,800,000　❽ Algeria, 201,000,000
❾ Belgium, 193,793,831　❿ India, 177,300,000

* In latest year for which data available
Source: *Universal Postal Union*

INDIAN STAMPS

India has more post offices and more postal workers than any other country in the world. Their system handles over 16 billion letters and 285 million packages a year.

Which Canadian film has earned the most money worldwide?
see p.157 for the answer

A *Porky's*
B *The Red Violin*
C *Air Bud*

The World Wide Web

ONLINE LANGUAGES

	LANGUAGE	INTERNET ACCESS*
1	English	230,000,000
2	Chinese	160,000,000
3	Spanish	60,000,000
4	Japanese	58,000,000
5	German	46,000,000
6	Korean	35,000,000
7	Portuguese	32,000,000
8	French	30,000,000
9	Italian	23,000,000
10	Russian	15,000,000
	World total	774,000,000

* *Online population estimate for 2003*

Source: *Global Reach*

BUSIEST INTERNET SITES

	SITE	HITS*
1	yahoo.com	65,910,000
2	aol.com	53,373,000
3	msn.com	47,330,000
4	microsoft.com	39,905,000
5	passport.com	37,807,000
6	geocities.com	36,294,000
7	AOLProprietary.aol	32,879,000
8	amazon.com	28,534,000
9	lycos.com	25,898,000
10	ebay.com	25,031,000

* *Number of accesses during December 2000*

Source: *PC Data Online*

INTERNET DOMAINS

	DOMAIN	COUNTRY	REGISTRATIONS
1	.com	US/International	21,151,560
2	.net	International	3,986,781
3	.org	International	2,503,682
4	.co.uk	UK	2,317,009
5	.de	Germany	1,032,618
6	.nl	Netherlands	544,594
7	.it	Italy	404,893
8	.co.kr	South Korea	332,801
9	.com.ar	Argentina	301,394
10	.org.uk	UK	154,838
	World total		34,995,298

ITEMS MOST PURCHASED ONLINE IN CANADA

	ITEM	PERCENTAGE*
1	Computers and computer related products	68
2	Books	54
3	CDs, recorded music	40
4	Clothing and accessories (women's)	29
5	=Electronic products (small)	20
	=Magazines	20
7	Hotel reservations	19
8	Air travel reservations	17
9	Videos, filmed entertainment	16
10	Clothing and accessories (men's)	14

* *Percentage of purchasers who have bought item online one or more times*

Source: *Ernst & Young*, Global Online Retailing, 2000

E-SHOPPING

The ability to locate and purchase both new and used books online has been heralded as among the most popular of the internet's many benefits.

TOP 10 ★
COUNTRIES WITH THE HIGHEST DENSITY OF INTERNET HOSTS

	COUNTRY	INTERNET HOSTS PER 1,000 PEOPLE
1	Finland	108.00
2	US	88.90
3	Iceland	78.70
4	Norway	71.80
5	Canada	53.50
6	New Zealand	49.70
7	Australia	42.70
8	Sweden	35.10
9	Netherlands	34.60
10	Switzerland	27.90

Source: *United Nations*, Human Development Report, 1999

An internet host is a computer system connected to the internet – either a single terminal directly connected or a computer that allows multiple users to access network services through it. The ratio of hosts to population is a crude measure of how "wired" a country is.

TOP 10 ★
COMPUTER COMPANIES

	COMPANY/COUNTRY	ANNUAL SALES (US$)*
1	IBM, US	88,396,000,000
2	Hewlett-Packard, US	48,782,000,000
3	Fujitsu, Japan	47,196,000,000
4	Compaq Computer, US	42,383,000,000
5	Dell Computer, US	31,888,000,000
6	Canon, Japan	23,062,000,000
7	Xerox, US	18,632,000,000
8	Sun Microsystems, US	15,721,000,000
9	Ricoh, Japan	12,997,000,000
10	Gateway, US	9,601,000,000

* In latest year for which figures available
Source: Fortune 500/Fortune *Global 500*

TOP 10 ★
COUNTRIES WITH THE MOST INTERNET USERS

	COUNTRY	PERCENTAGE OF POPULATION	INTERNET USERS*		COUNTRY	PERCENTAGE OF POPULATION	INTERNET USERS*
1	US	54.7	153,840,000	7	Italy	23.4	13,420,000
2	Japan	30.5	38,640,000	8	Canada	42.6	13,280,000
3	Germany	24.4	20,100,000	9	Brazil	5.8	9,840,000
4	UK	33.9	19,940,000	10	Russia	6.3	9,200,000
5	China	1.3	16,900,000		World total	6.7	407,100,000
6	South Korea	35.0	16,400,000				

* Estimates for weekly usage as of end of 2000
Source: *Computer Industry Almanac, Inc.*

TOP 10 ★
COUNTRIES WITH THE MOST COMPUTERS

	COUNTRY	PERCENTAGE OF WORLD TOTAL	COMPUTERS
1	US	28.32	164,100,000
2	Japan	8.62	49,900,000
3	Germany	5.28	30,600,000
4	UK	4.49	26,000,000
5	France	3.77	21,800,000
6	Italy	3.02	17,500,000
7	Canada	2.76	16,000,000
8	China	2.75	15,900,000
9 =	Australia	1.82	10,600,000
=	South Korea	1.82	10,600,000

Source: *Computer Industry Almanac, Inc.*

Computer industry estimates put the number of computers in the world at 98 million in 1990, 222 million in 1995, and 579 million in 2000 – a sixfold increase over the decade – with the Top 10 countries owning over 62 percent of the total.

TOP 10 ★
USES OF THE INTERNET IN CANADA

	PURPOSE OF USE	% INTERNET USERS*
1	E-mail	91.7
2	Other specific information#	85.1
3	General browsing	84.7
4	Medical/health information	54.2
5	Government information	44.1
6	Playing games	42.7
7	Formal education/training	32.0
8	Electronic banking	27.7
9	Obtaining/saving music	27.1
10	Chat groups	26.2

* Regular home-use households, 1999
# Other than medical/health or government information
Source: *Statistics Canada*

Other common uses of the internet identified in the poll were listening to the radio (17.5%) and purchasing goods and services (19.0%).

COMPUTER POWER FIRST DEMONSTRATED

Automatic programming of computers is credited to Grace Hopper, an employee of US manufacturers Remington-Rand. In 1951, her company had created the Univac I (UNIVersal Automatic Computer), an expensive and gigantic machine weighing some 32 tonnes (35 tons). It was slow (its clock speed was 2.25 MHz, while 500 MHz or more is now commonplace), and it required the operator to write programs on punch cards and then transfer them onto magnetic tape. Despite these drawbacks, the Univac I proved its accuracy when it was used by the CBS television network to correctly predict a landslide victory for Eisenhower in the 1952 US election. In 1954, General Electric purchased a Univac, thus becoming the first commercial organization to use a computer.

• YEARS AGO • YEARS AGO • YEARS AGO • **50**

Did You Know? In 1943, Thomas Watson, chairman of IBM, stated "I think there is a world market for maybe five computers." Six years later, *Popular Mechanics* magazine predicted that "Computers in the future may weigh no more than 1.5 tons."

Hazards at Home & Work

THE 10

MOST DANGEROUS INDUSTRIES IN CANADA

INDUSTRY	NUMBER OF FATALITIES, 1999
1 Manufacturing	189
2 Construction	164
3 Transportation and storage	108
4 Mining, quarrying, and oil wells	74
5 Government services	39
6 Logging and forestry	38
7 Communications and other utilities	27
8 Wholesale trade	26
9 Retail trade	24
10 Business services	17

Source: *Association of Workers' Compensation Boards of Canada,* Work Injuries and Diseases: Canada, 1997–1999

A death occurring in the workplace is recorded statistically during the year when the claim was accepted by a Compensation Board, not the year when the accident causing death occurred.

DANGER ON DECK

Exposure to extreme weather conditions and other hazards places fishing among the world's most dangerous industries.

THE 10 MOST COMMON CAUSES OF ACCIDENTAL DEATH IN THE US

(Type of accident/total deaths, 1997)

❶ **Motor vehicle**, 42,340 ❷ **Fall**, 11,858 ❸ **Poisoning**, 10,163 ❹ **Suffocation**, 4,420 ❺ **Drowning and submersion**, 4,051 ❻ **Adverse event-related** (medical care and drugs), 3,291 ❼ **Residential fire and flames**, 3,146 ❽ **Firearm**, 981 ❾ **Striking by/against**, 974 ❿ **Cutting and piercing**, 104

Total unintentional and adverse event-related deaths, 95,644

Source: *National Center for Injury Prevention and Control*

THE 10

CAUSES OF INJURIES AT WORK IN CANADA

EVENT	NUMBER OF TIME-LOSS INJURIES, 1999
1 Overexertion	88,158
2 Bodily reaction and exertion	53,000
3 Struck by object	42,209
4 Fall on same level	30,549
5 Struck against object	22,599
6 Fall to lower level	19,679
7 Caught in or compressed by equipment or objects	19,096
8 Repetitive motion	12,433
9 Rubbed or abraded by friction or pressure	10,381
10 Contact with extreme temperatures	6,525

Source: *Association of Workers' Compensation Boards of Canada*

THE 10

MOST COMMON PRODUCTS INVOLVED IN ACCIDENTS IN US HOMES

PRODUCT GROUP	ACCIDENTS, 1998
1 Sports activities and equipment	3,804,894
2 Home structures	2,682,576
3 Home furnishings and fixtures	2,151,528
4 Personal use items	382,646
5 Household containers	300,144
6 Home workshop tools, etc	290,313
7 Yard and garden equipment	239,482
8 Household appliances	158,050
9 Toys	147,994
10 Heating and air conditioning	122,251

Source: *US Consumer Product Safety Commission/NEISS (National Electronic Injury Surveillance System)*

A survey of injuries caused by some 15,000 products, based on a sample of 101 US hospitals during 1998, showed that their ERs were kept busy with patients suffering from injuries caused by these broad products groups and several others. Within the sports category, basketball stood out as the most likely to produce sports injuries (631,186 cases), followed by bicycles (597,284). In the home, stairs, ramps, landings, and floors were the most dangerous places, with a total of 1,975,074 injuries, while beds, mattresses, and pillows resulted in 456,559 accidents, clothing 152,276, and refrigerators and freezers 35,552. In the yard, fences were involved in a total of 124,202 cases, and lawnmowers in 676,421 cases.

THE 10 🍁
CHILDHOOD INJURIES IN CANADA*

INJURY EVENT	PERCENTAGE OF EMERGENCY ROOM VISITS, 1997
1 = Fracture	20
= Open wound	20
= Superficial injury	20
4 Sprain	13
5 Concussion/minor head injury	8
6 = Dislocation	3
= Foreign body	3
8 = Poisoning	2
= Burn	2
= Eye injury	2

* Aged 0–19 years

Source: Statistical Report on the Health of Canadians, *Health Canada, 1999*
© Minister of Public Works and Government Services Canada, 2001

THE 10 🍁
CAUSES OF FIRE IN CANADA

SOURCE OF IGNITION	NUMBER OF FIRES, 1997
1 Cooking equipment	5,829
2 Electrical distribution equipment	4,648
3 Heating equipment	3,858
4 Smoker's material or "open flame," unclassified	3,743
5 Smoker's material	3,448
6 Other electrical equipment	3,420
7 Exposure	2,813
8 Match, light (not used with smoking), lamp, candle, taper	2,659
9 Non-igniting object (e.g. lightning)	1,157
10 Cutting torch, welding equipment, varied torches	778

Source: *Canadian Council of Fire Marshals and Fire Commissioners*

DOMESTIC INFERNO

A combination of deliberate and accidental fires, many of which result from avoidable causes, contribute to losses of life and property.

THE 10 ★
MOST ACCIDENT-PRONE COUNTRIES

COUNTRIES	ACCIDENT DEATH RATE PER 100,000*
1 South Korea	120.2
2 Moldova	114.0
3 Russia	112.3
4 South Africa	99.4
5 Lithuania	95.0
6 Estonia	94.5
7 Latvia	94.1
8 Ukraine	89.0
9 Belarus	82.0
10 Slovenia	56.5

* Traffic accidents, accidental falls, and other accidents

Source: UN Demographic Yearbook

What gaseous phenomenon did safety lamp inventor Sir Humphrey Davy also discover?
see p.216 for the answer

A Hydrogen can be used in balloons
B The effects of laughing gas
C Inhaling helium makes human voices squeaky

DAVY

Regarded as Britain's foremost scientist, Sir Humphrey Davy (1778–1829) was knighted in 1812 in recognition of his many chemical discoveries, including six elements and the anesthetic effects of nitrous oxide ("laughing gas"). After a series of disastrous explosions in coal mines, Davy was called upon to devise a less risky method of illuminating mines. The 1815 miner's safety lamp that bears his name was his response: in it an oil lamp flame is surrounded by wire gauze, which absorbs the heat and prevents "firedamp" (a mixture of methane gas and air) from coming into contact with the flame.

WHO WAS • WHO WAS • WHO WAS • WHO WAS ?

THE 10 ★
WORST FIRES*

LOCATION/DATE/TYPE	ESTIMATED NO. KILLED
1 **Moscow**, Russia, 1570, City	200,000
2 **Constantinople**, Turkey, 1729, City	7,000
3 **London**, UK, July 11, 1212, London Bridge	3,000#
4 **Peshtigo**, Wisconsin, US, Oct 8, 1871, Forest	2,682
5 **Santiago**, Chile, Dec 8, 1863, Church of La Compañía	2,500
6 **Chungking**, China, Sep 2, 1949, Docks	1,700
7 **Hakodate**, Japan, Mar 22, 1934, City	1,500

LOCATION/DATE/TYPE	ESTIMATED NO. KILLED
8 **Constantinople**, Turkey, June 5, 1870, City	900
9 **Cloquet**, Minnesota, US, Oct 12, 1918, Forest	559
10 =**Lagunillas**, Venezuela, Nov 14, 1939, Oil refinery and city	over 500
=**Mandi Dabwali**, India, Dec 23, 1995, School tent	over 500

* *Excluding sports and entertainment venues, mining disasters, the results of military action, and fires associated with earthquakes*

\# *Burned, crushed, and drowned in ensuing panic; some chroniclers give the year as 1213*

THE 10 ★
WORST DISASTERS AT SPORTS VENUES

LOCATION/DATE/TYPE	NO. KILLED
1 **Hong Kong Jockey Club**, Hong Kong, Feb 26, 1918, Stand collapse and fire	604
2 **Lenin Stadium**, Moscow, USSR, Oct 20, 1982, Crush in soccer stadium	340
3 **Lima**, Peru, May 24, 1964, Riot in soccer stadium	320
4 **Sinceljo**, Colombia, Jan 20, 1980, Bullring stand collapse	222
5 **Hillsborough**, Sheffield, UK, Apr 15, 1989, Crush in soccer stadium	96
6 **Guatemala City**, Guatemala, Oct 16, 1996, Stampede in Mateo Flores National Stadium during World Cup soccer qualifying match, Guatemala v Costa Rica, with 127 injured	83
7 **Le Mans**, France, June 11, 1955, Racing car crash	82
8 **Katmandu**, Nepal, Mar 12, 1988 Stampede in soccer stadium	80
9 **Buenos Aires**, Argentina, May 23, 1968, Riot in soccer stadium	74
10 **Ibrox Park**, Glasgow, Scotland, Jan 2, 1971, Barrier collapse in soccer stadium	66

THE 10 ★
WORST MINING DISASTERS

LOCATION/DATE	NO. KILLED
1 **Honkeiko**, China, Apr 26, 1942	1,549
2 **Courrières**, France, Mar 10, 1906	1,060
3 **Omuta**, Japan, Nov 9, 1963	447
4 **Senghenydd**, UK, Oct 14, 1913	439
5 =**Hokkaido**, Japan, Dec 1, 1914	437
=**Coalbrook**, South Africa, Jan 21, 1960	437
7 **Wankie**, Rhodesia, June 6, 1972	427
8 **Tsinan**, China, May 13, 1935	400
9 **Dhanbad**, India, May 28, 1965	375
10 **Chasnala**, India, Dec 27, 1975	372

A mine disaster at the Fushun mines, Manchuria, on February 12, 1931, may have resulted in up to 3,000 deaths, but information was suppressed by the Chinese government. Soviet security was also responsible for obscuring details of an explosion at the East German Johanngeorgendstadt uranium mine on November 29, 1949, when as many as 3,700 may have died. The two worst disasters in the Top 10 both resulted from underground explosions, and the large numbers of deaths among mine workers resulted from that cause and from asphyxiation by poisonous gases. Among the most tragic disasters of the last century was the collapse of a slag heap at Aberfan, Wales, which killed 144, most of them children.

THE 10 ★
WORST FIRES AT THEATER AND ENTERTAINMENT VENUES*

LOCATION/DATE/TYPE	NO. KILLED
1 **Canton**, China, May 25, 1845, Theater	1,670
2 **Shanghai**, China, June 1871, Theater	900
3 **Vienna**, Austria, Dec 8, 1881, Ring Theater	640–850
4 **St. Petersburg**, Russia, Feb 14, 1836, Lehmann Circus	800
5 **Antoung**, China, Feb 13, 1937, Cinema	658
6 **Chicago**, IL, US, Dec 30, 1903, Iroquois Theater	602
7 **Boston**, MA, US, Nov 28, 1942, Cocoanut Grove Night Club	491
8 **Berditschoft**, Poland, Jan 13, 1883, Circus Ferroni	430
9 **Abadan**, Iran, Aug 20, 1978, Theater	422
10 **Niterói**, Brazil, Dec 17, 1961, Circus	323

* *19th and 20th centuries, excluding sports stadiums and race tracks*

TROUBLE IN STORE
Some 1,500 people were inside the Sampoong Department Store, Seoul, when it collapsed, leaving over a third of them dead and as many as 900 injured.

THE 10 ★
WORST EXPLOSIONS*

	LOCATION/DATE	TYPE	ESTIMATED NO. KILLED
1	**Rhodes**, Greece, 1856#	Lightning strike of gunpowder store	4,000
2	**St. Nazaiere**, Breschia, Italy, 1769#	Arsenal	over 3,000
3	**Salang Tunnel**, Afghanistan, Nov 3, 1982	Petrol tanker collision	over 2,000
4	**Lanchow**, China, Oct 26, 1935	Arsenal	2,000
5	**Halifax**, Canada, Dec 6, 1917	Ammunition ship *Mont Blanc*	1,963
6	**Hamont Station**, Belgium, Aug 3, 1918	Ammunition trains	1,750
7	**Memphis**, TN, US, Apr 27, 1865	*Sultana* boiler explosion	1,547
8=	**Archangel**, Russia, Feb 20, 1917	Munitions ship	1,500
=	**Ft. Smederovo**, Yugoslavia, June 9, 1941	Ammunition dump	1,500
10	**Bombay**, India, Apr 14, 1944	Ammunition ship *Fort Stikine*	1,376

* *Excluding mining disasters, terrorist and military bombs, and natural explosions, such as volcanoes* # *Precise date unknown*

THE 10 ★
WORST COMMERCIAL AND INDUSTRIAL DISASTERS*

	LOCATION/DATE	TYPE	NO. KILLED
1	**Bhopal**, India, Dec 3, 1984	Methylisocyante gas escape at Union Carbide plant	up to 3,000
2	**Seoul**, S. Korea, June 29, 1995	Collapse of Sampoong Department Store	640
3	**Oppau**, Germany, Sep 21, 1921	Chemical plant explosion	561
4	**Mexico City**, Mexico, Nov 20, 1984	Explosion at a PEMEX liquified petroleum gas plant	540
5	**Brussels**, Belgium, May 22, 1967	Fire in L'Innovation department store	322
6	**Novosibirsk**, USSR, Apr 1979 (precise date unknown)	Anthrax infection following accident at biological and chemical warfare plant	up to 300
7	**Guadalajara**, Mexico, Apr 22, 1992	Explosions caused by gas leak into sewers	230
8	**São Paulo**, Brazil, Feb 1, 1974	Fire in Joelma bank and office building	227
9	**Oakdale**, Pennsylvania, US, May 18, 1918	Chemical plant explosion	193
10	**Bangkok**, Thailand, 10 May 1993	Fire at a 4-story doll factory	187

* *Including industrial sites, factories, offices, and stores; excluding military, mining, marine, and other transport disasters, and mass poisonings*

Which chocolate brand in Canada has the largest share of the market?
see p.221 for the answer

A Coffee Crisp
B Oh Henry!
C Mars

Food for Thought

TOP 10 ★
FROZEN FOOD CONSUMERS

ANNUAL CONSUMPTION PER CAPITA

COUNTRY	LB	OZ	KG
1 Norway	78	8	35.6
2 Denmark	71	10	32.5
3 UK	68	2	30.9
4 Israel	63	8	28.8
5 Czech Republic	46	15	21.3
6 Sweden	44	12	20.3
7 Ireland	41	11	18.9
8 Belgium	39	4	17.8
9 Finland	36	10	16.6
10 US	35	15	16.3

Source: Euromonitor

TOP 10 ★
POTATO CHIP CONSUMERS

ANNUAL CONSUMPTION PER CAPITA

COUNTRY	LB	OZ	KG
1 =UK	6	13	3.1
=US	6	13	3.1
3 =Ireland	5	15	2.7
=New Zealand	5	15	2.7
5 Norway	5	12	2.6
6 Portugal	5	5	2.4
7 Netherlands	5	1	2.3
8 Australia	4	7	2.0
9 =Israel	3	8	1.6
=Sweden	3	8	1.6

Source: Euromonitor

BIRDSEYE

In 1915, while conducting a survey for the US Government in Labrador, Brooklyn-born Clarence "Bob" Birdseye (1886–1956) experimented with the Inuit method of preserving food in the winter by freezing it in barrels. After returning to the US in 1917, he became interested in the possibility of preserving food commercially by the same method. He opened General Seafoods in Gloucester, MA, and began preserving fish by rapid freezing. Birdseye became a millionaire in 1929 when he sold the company for US$22 million. He then devoted his life to inventing.

WHO WAS · WHO WAS · WHO WAS · WHO WAS

TOP 10 ★
BAKED BEAN CONSUMERS

ANNUAL CONSUMPTION PER CAPITA

COUNTRY	LB	OZ	KG
1 UK	11	11	5.3
2 Ireland	11	4	5.1
3 Mexico	9	4	4.2
4 New Zealand	4	14	2.2
5 =Australia	4	0	1.8
=France	4	0	1.8
7 Switzerland	3	5	1.5
8 Saudi Arabia	3	1	1.4
9 =Canada	2	14	1.3
=US	2	14	1.3

Source: Euromonitor

TOP 10 ★
BREAD CONSUMERS

ANNUAL CONSUMPTION PER CAPITA

COUNTRY	LB	OZ	KG
1 Slovak Republic	286	6	129.9
2 Turkey	285	15	129.7
3 Bulgaria	285	12	129.6
4 Saudi Arabia	247	2	112.1
5 Egypt	234	2	106.2
6 Romania	211	14	96.1
7 Chile	176	13	80.2
8 Poland	175	1	79.4
9 =Denmark	164	11	74.7
=Hungary	164	11	74.7
Canada	32	3	14.6

Source: Euromonitor

TOP 10 ★
MEAT CONSUMERS

ANNUAL CONSUMPTION PER CAPITA

COUNTRY	LB	OZ	KG
1 US	270	1	122.5
2 Cyprus	250	7	113.6
3 New Zealand	242	11	110.1
4 Australia	238	8	108.2
5 Spain	236	9	107.3
6 Austria	231	0	104.8
7 Denmark	227	8	103.2
8 Netherlands	223	9	101.4
9 Bahamas	222	7	100.9
10 France	219	9	99.6
Canada	207	7	94.1

Figures from the Meat and Livestock Commission show a huge range of meat consumption in countries around the world, ranging from the No. 1 meat consumer, the US, at 122.5 kg (270 lb 1 oz) per person per year, to very poor countries such as India, where meat consumption may be as little as 4.6 kg (10 lb 2 oz) per person per year. In general, meat is an expensive food and in poor countries is saved for special occasions, so the richer the country, the more likely it is to have a high meat consumption. In recent years, however, health scares relating to meat, and the rise in the number of vegetarians, have contributed to deliberate declines in consumption.

TOP 10 HOTTEST CHILLIES

(Chilli*/Scoville units#)

❶ Datil, Habanero, Scotch Bonnet, 100,000–350,000 ❷ Chiltepin, Santaka, Thai, 50,000–100,000 ❸ Aji, Cayenne, Piquin, Tabasco, 30,000–50,000 ❹ de Arbol, 15,000–30,000 ❺ Serrano, Yellow Wax, 5,000–15,000 ❻ Chipotle, Jalapeno, Mirasol, 2,500–5,000 ❼ Cascabel, Sandia, Rocotillo, 1,500–2,500 ❽ Ancho, Espanola, Pasilla, Poblano, 1,000–1,500 ❾ Anaheim, New Mexico, 500–1,000 ❿ Cherry, Peperoncini, 100–500

* Examples – there are others in most categories   # One part of capsaicin (the principal substance that determines how "hot" a chilli is) per million equals 15,000 Scoville units

TOP 10 ★
SPICE CONSUMERS

COUNTRY	ANNUAL CONSUMPTION PER CAPITA		
	LB	OZ	KG
1 United Arab Emirates	13	1	6.3
2 Hungary	13	0	5.9
3 Jamaica	9	14	4.5
4 Brunei	9	0	4.1
5 =Slovenia	8	3	3.7
=Sri Lanka	8	3	3.7
7 Seychelles	7	4	3.3
8 Cape Verdi	6	13	3.1
9 Kuwait	6	10	3.0
10 Bermuda	6	3	2.8
Canada	1	5	0.6
World	1	12	0.8

Source: *Food and Agriculture Organization of the United Nations*

This list inevitably features those countries where spices play an important part in national cuisine. India just fails to find a place in the list, its per capita consumption being estimated at 2 kg (4 lb 6 oz).

TOP 10 ★
VEGETABLE CONSUMERS

COUNTRY	ANNUAL CONSUMPTION PER CAPITA		
	LB	OZ	KG
1 Lebanon	766	1	347.9
2 United Arab Emirates	599	0	271.9
3 Greece	579	0	262.8
4 Israel	495	0	224.7
5 Libya	491	0	222.8
6 Turkey	471	1	213.9
7 South Korea	457	0	207.5
8 Kuwait	432	5	196.1
9 Iran	416	4	188.8
10 Portugal	410	0	186.2
Canada	262	9	119.1
World	208	0	94.6

Source: *Food and Agriculture Organization of the United Nations*

TOP 10 🍁
MAJOR FOOD ITEMS CONSUMED IN CANADA BY WEIGHT*

PRODUCT	ANNUAL CONSUMPTION PER CAPITA		
	LB	OZ	KG
1 Fresh vegetables	323	0	146.5
2 Cereal products	201	5	91.4
3 Fresh fruit	142	0	64.4
4 Meats#	137	3	62.3
5 Sugar and syrup	85	8	38.9
6 Poultry	73	2	33.2
7 Oils and fats	70	8	32.1
8 Dairy products	56	2	25.5
9 Eggs	22	7	10.3
10 Legumes and nuts	22	0	10.0

* Available for consumption (includes losses in stores, restaurants, and the home), rather than actual quantities consumed

Includes beef, pork, veal, mutton, lamb, and offal

Source: Food Consumption in Canada, *Statistics Canada, 1999*

TOP 10 ★
POTATO CONSUMERS

COUNTRY	ANNUAL CONSUMPTION PER CAPITA		
	LB	OZ	KG
1 Belarus	411	0	168.5
2 Ukraine	303	9	137.7
3 Latvia	301	9	136.8
4 Poland	296	1	134.3
5 Lithuania	289	14	131.5
6 Ireland	286	3	129.8
7 Portugal	280	1	127.4
8 Russia	272	2	123.4
9 Croatia	251	2	113.9
10 Malawi	250	0	113.4
Canada	123	10	56.1
World	66	0	30.0

Source: *Food and Agriculture Organization of the United Nations*

The potato has long been a staple part of the national diet for the countries at the top of the list.

TOP 10 ★
BUTTER CONSUMERS

COUNTRY	ANNUAL CONSUMPTION PER CAPITA		
	LB	OZ	KG
1 New Zealand	20	15	9.5
2 France	19	13	9.0
3 Estonia	17	5	8.0
4 Germany	15	6	7.0
5 Switzerland	13	10	6.2
6 =Belgium–Luxembourg	12	12	5.8
=Fiji Islands	12	12	5.8
8 Iceland	12	9	5.7
9 Belarus	12	2	5.5
10 Macedonia	11	0	5.0
Canada	5	0	2.7
World	2	6	1.1

Source: *Food and Agriculture Organization of the United Nations*

TOP 10 ★
FISH CONSUMERS

COUNTRY	ANNUAL CONSUMPTION PER CAPITA*		
	LB	OZ	KG
1 Maldives	353	2	160.2
2 Iceland	202	2	91.7
3 Kiribati	170	3	77.2
4 Japan	159	2	72.2
5 Seychelles	142	13	64.8
6 Portugal	129	7	58.7
7 Norway	120	6	54.6
8 Malaysia	119	4	54.1
9 French Polynesia	114	3	51.8
10 South Korea	113	12	51.6
Canada	53	5	24.2
World	44	14	20.4

* Combines sea and freshwater fish totals

Source: *Food and Agriculture Organization of the United Nations*

The majority of the fish consumed in the world comes from the sea, the average annual consumption of freshwater fish being 4.4 kg (9 lb 11 oz). The largest consumers are Norwegians, who each consume 11.8 kg (26 lb) per annum.

Did You Know? The cultivation of potatoes was banned in Scotland in 1728 because they were considered an "unholy nightshade" and were not mentioned in the Bible.

Sweet Dreams

TOP 10 ★ SUGAR PRODUCERS

	COUNTRY	TOTAL ANNUAL SUGAR PRODUCTION (TONNES)*
1	India	18,935,000
2	Brazil	14,500,000
3	China	8,379,000
4	US	7,937,000
5	Australia	5,778,000
6	Thailand	5,630,000
7	Mexico	4,984,000
8	France	4,380,000
9	Cuba	4,134,000
10	Germany	4,100,000
	Canada	138,000
	World	128,810,000

* Raw centrifugal sugar

Source: *Food and Agriculture Organization of the United Nations*

TOP 10 ★ CHEWING GUM CONSUMERS

		ANNUAL CONSUMPTION PER CAPITA		
	COUNTRY	LB	OZ	KG
1	Denmark	2	10	1.2
2	Norway	2	3	1.0
3 =	Switzerland	1	9	0.7
=	US	1	9	0.7
5 =	Israel	1	5	0.6
=	Spain	1	5	0.6
7 =	Argentina	1	2	0.5
=	France	1	2	0.5
=	Germany	1	2	0.5
10 =	Canada	0	14	0.4
=	Ireland	0	14	0.4
=	Japan	0	14	0.4
=	Mexico	0	14	0.4
=	Morocco	0	14	0.4
=	UK	0	14	0.4

Source: *Euromonitor*

Worldwide chewing gum consumption in 1999 was estimated at 761,293.3 tonnes.

TOP 10 ★ SUGAR CONSUMERS

		ANNUAL CONSUMPTION PER CAPITA*		
	COUNTRY	LB	OZ	KG
1	Belize	136	10	62.0
2	Cape Verde	130	8	59.2
3	Cuba	130	1	59.0
4	Ecuador	121	4	55.0
5	Barbados	115	11	52.2
6 =	Brazil	113	8	51.5
=	Trinidad and Tobago	113	8	51.5
8	Iceland	111	8	50.6
9	Macedonia	111	1	50.4
10	Swaziland	108	14	49.4
	Canada	7	6	32.4
	World	41	14	19.0

* Refined equivalent

Source: *Food and Agriculture Organization of the United Nations*

Each citizen of Belize, the current world leader in the sweet-tooth stakes, would appear to consume more than 1 kg (2.2 lb) of sugar every week.

TOP 10 ★ SWEETENER CONSUMERS*

		ANNUAL CONSUMPTION PER CAPITA		
	COUNTRY	LB	OZ	KG
1	US	88	6	40.1
2	South Korea	30	13	14.0
3	Brunei	26	14	12.2
4	Bermuda	25	9	11.6
5 =	Hungary	25	2	11.4
=	Iceland	25	2	11.4
7	Japan	23	5	10.6
8	Bahamas	18	11	8.5
9	Canada	18	4	8.3
10	Estonia	14	15	6.8
	World	6	2	2.8

* Excluding sugar

Source: *Food and Agriculture Organization of the United Nations*

TOP 10 ★ FRUIT CONSUMERS

		ANNUAL CONSUMPTION PER CAPITA		
	COUNTRY	LB	OZ	KG
1	Dominica	885	9	401.7
2	Belize	709	0	321.8
3	Lebanon	532	14	241.7
4	Uganda	522	11	237.1
5	Saint Lucia	486	12	220.8
6	São Tomé and Principe	478	6	217.0
7	Rwanda	477	8	216.6
8	Bermuda	456	13	207.2
9	Papua New Guinea	451	1	204.6
10	Bahamas	425	8	193.0
	Canada	272	4	123.5
	World	125	10	57.0

Source: *Food and Agriculture Organization of the United Nations*

World fruit consumption varies from those in the list – where some people devour more than five times their own body weight every year – to Eritrea, with just 1.4 kg (3 lb) per capita.

TOP 10 ★ HONEY CONSUMERS

		ANNUAL CONSUMPTION PER CAPITA		
	COUNTRY	LB	OZ	KG
1	Central African Republic	6	10	3.0
2	Turkmenistan	5	1	2.3
3	Angola	3	15	1.8
4 =	Greece	3	8	1.6
=	New Zealand	3	8	1.6
6	Switzerland	3	1	1.4
7 =	Germany	2	10	1.2
=	Ukraine	2	10	1.2
9 =	Austria	2	0	1.1
=	Canada	2	0	1.1
=	Slovenia	2	0	1.1
	World	0	7	0.2

Source: *Food and Agriculture Organization of the United Nations*

TOP 10 CANDY COMPANIES IN CANADA*

1. Cadbury Chocolate Canada　2. Nestlé Canada　3. Hershey Chocolate Canada
4. Adams Brands　5. Wrigley Canada　6. Effem Foods　7. Trebor Allan
8. Beta Brands　9. Ferrero Canada　10. Kerr Foods

Based on $ sales volume of confectionery market
Source: *Euromonitor*

TOP 10 CHEWING GUM BRANDS IN CANADA*

BRAND	1999 MARKET SHARE (%)
1 Dentyne	15.0
2 Extra	14.1
3 Trident	13.0
4 Clorets	12.5
5 Excel	11.4
6 Freedent	10.4
7 = Doublemint	2.5
= Spearmint	2.5
9 Hubba Bubba	2.2
10 Bubblicious	2.0

Based on $ sales volume of gum market
Source: *Euromonitor*

TOP 10 CHOCOLATE CONSUMERS

	COUNTRY	ANNUAL CONSUMPTION PER CAPITA		
		LB	OZ	KG
1	Switzerland	26	0	11.8
2	UK	21	10	9.8
3	Belgium	18	12	8.5
4	Ireland	17	3	7.8
5	Norway	17	0	7.7
6	Germany	16	1	7.3
7	Austria	13	14	6.3
8	Australia	12	13	5.8
9	US	12	9	5.7
10	Sweden	10	9	4.8

Source: *Euromonitor*

TOP 10 CHOCOLATE BRANDS IN CANADA*

BRAND	1999 MARKET SHARE (%)
1 Oh Henry!	3.4
2 Mars	3.2
3 Hershey's Milk Chocolate	3.1
4 M&M's	2.9
5 Coffee Crisp	2.8
6 = Kinder Surprise	2.7
= KitKat	2.7
= Smarties	2.7
9 Caramilk	2.4
10 Reese's Peanut Butter Cups	2.1

Based on $ sales volume of chocolate market
Source: *Euromonitor*

TOP 10 COCOA CONSUMERS

COUNTRY	TOTAL COCOA CONSUMPTION TONNES
1 US	656,200
2 Germany	284,500
3 UK	212,200
4 France	186,000
5 Japan	131,900
6 Brazil	124,600
7 Italy	97,200
8 Russia	95,600
9 Spain	67,600
10 Canada	63,500
World	2,767,300

Cocoa is the principal ingredient of chocolate, and its consumption is therefore closely linked to the production of chocolate in each consuming country. Like coffee, the consumption of chocolate tends to occur mainly in the Western world and in more affluent countries. Europe has the highest intake of the world's regions, with a total cocoa consumption of 1,381,600 tonnes; the Americas are next with 1,021,300 (over half of which is accounted for by the US); Asia and Oceania 303,400; and lastly, Africa, where 61,000 tonnes are consumed.

TOP 10 ICE CREAM CONSUMERS

	COUNTRY	ANNUAL CONSUMPTION PER CAPITA	
		PINTS	LITERS
1	Australia	29.2	16.6
2	Italy	25.0	14.2
3	US	24.5	13.9
4	New Zealand	23.2	13.2
5	Sweden	21.5	12.2
6	Ireland	18.1	10.3
7	Norway	16.2	9.2
8	Canada	16.0	9.1
9	Israel	15.8	9.0
10	Finland	15.5	8.8

Source: *Euromonitor*

TOP 10 DATE CONSUMERS

	COUNTRY	ANNUAL CONSUMPTION PER CAPITA		
		LB	OZ	KG
1	United Arab Emirates	77	10	35.2
2	Saudi Arabia	67	11	30.7
3	Iraq	36	13	16.7
4	Libya	31	5	14.2
5	Algeria	26	12	12.1
6	Iran	25	12	11.7
7	Egypt	25	2	11.4
8	= Sudan	12	2	5.5
	= Tunisia	12	2	5.5
10	Kuwait	10	6	4.7
	Canada	0	7	0.2

Source: *Food and Agriculture Organization of the United Nations*

Did You Know? Chocolate was consumed mostly as a drink until 1879, when Swiss manufacturer Rudolphe Lindt added cocoa butter, and Daniel Peter pioneered the first milk chocolate bar.

221

Alcoholic & Soft Drinks

ALCOHOL-CONSUMING COUNTRIES

COUNTRY	CONSUMPTION PER CAPITA, 1999 (100 PERCENT ALCOHOL) PINTS	LITERS
1 Luxembourg	21.5	12.2
2 Ireland	20.4	11.6
3 Portugal	19.4	11.0
4 France	18.8	10.7
5 Germany	18.7	10.6
6 Czech Republic	18.5	10.5
7 Romania	18.1	10.3
8 Spain	17.4	9.9
9 Hungary	17.1	9.7
10 Denmark	16.7	9.5
Canada	10.9	6.2

Source: *Productschap voor Gedistilleerde Dranken*

After heading this list for many years – and with an annual consumption that peaked at 17.7 liters (31.2 pints) per head in 1961 – France was overtaken by Luxembourg, which is acknowledged as the world's leading alcohol consumer. While Western European countries have the highest average consumption of alcohol in the world – 8.0 liters (14.1 pints) per person per annum, compared to a world average of 3.8 liters (6.7 pints) – the trend is toward lower drinking levels. Average consumption in Western Europe fell by 5.9 percent between 1990 and 1999.

SCHWEPPES

German-born Jean Jacob Schweppe (1740–1821), an amateur scientist, moved to Geneva, Switzerland, where he became interested in the manufacture of artificial mineral waters. He moved to London in 1792 and began producing his own brand of soda water, forming Schweppe & Co. (later Schweppes Ltd.). By the 1870s, the company was also producing ginger ale and "Indian Tonic Water." Tonic water was made by adding quinine to sweetened soda water after the style of the British in India, who drank it as a malaria antidote. So began the gin and tonic fashion.

TOP 10 COUNTRIES WITH THE BIGGEST INCREASE IN BEER PRODUCTION

(Country/percentage increase, 1980–98)

① China, 2,783 ② Argentina, 435 ③ South Africa, 208 ④ Brazil, 207 ⑤ Turkey, 116 ⑥ Mexico, 105 ⑦ Chile, 94 ⑧ Portugal, 91 ⑨ Poland, 81 ⑩ Finland, 66 Canada, 6

Source: *Productschap voor Gedistilleerde Dranken*

BEER-DRINKING COUNTRIES

COUNTRY	CONSUMPTION PER CAPITA, 1999 PINTS	LITERS
1 Ireland	272.2	154.7
2 Germany	224.3	127.5
3 Luxembourg	191.8	109.0
4 Austria	191.6	108.9
5 Denmark	179.3	101.9
6 UK	174.2	99.0
7 Belgium	171.5	97.5
8 Australia	160.4	91.2
9 Slovak Republic	155.0	88.1
10 US	148.5	84.4

Source: *Productschap voor Gedistilleerde Dranken*

WINE-PRODUCING COUNTRIES

COUNTRY	PRODUCTION, 1998 PINTS	LITERS
1 Italy	9,535,749,556	5,418,800,000
2 France	9,268,795,026	5,267,100,000
3 Spain	5,335,571,096	3,032,000,000
4 US	3,291,266,036	1,870,300,000
5 Argentina	2,230,134,977	1,267,300,000
6 Germany	1,900,533,240	1,080,000,000
7 South Africa	1,435,078,572	815,500,000
8 Australia	1,304,856,850	741,500,000
9 Chile	963,464,767	547,500,000
10 Romania	880,228,451	500,200,000

Source: *Productschap voor Gedistilleerde Dranken*

BEER-PRODUCING COUNTRIES

COUNTRY	PRODUCTION, 1998 PINTS	LITERS
1 US	41,829,328,810	23,770,000,000
2 China	30,443,726,900	17,300,000,000
3 Germany	19,656,441,010	11,170,000,000
4 Brazil	14,352,545,470	8,156,000,000
5 Japan	12,633,090,810	7,178,900,000
6 UK	9,969,352,696	5,665,200,000
7 Mexico	9,618,281,972	5,465,700,000
8 Russia	5,724,476,509	3,253,000,000
9 South Africa	4,511,830,717	2,563,900,000
10 Spain	4,397,798,722	2,499,100,000

Source: *Productschap voor Gedistilleerde Dranken*

WINE-DRINKING COUNTRIES

COUNTRY	CONSUMPTION PER CAPITA, 1999 PINTS	LITERS
1 Luxembourg	107.3	61.0
2 France	100.7	57.2
3 Portugal	91.0	51.7
4 Italy	90.6	51.5
5 Switzerland	76.7	43.6
6 Argentina	62.6	35.6
7 Greece	61.9	35.2
8 Spain	59.3	33.7
9 Uruguay	56.3	32.0
10 Austria	54.4	30.9
Canada	15.7	8.9

Source: *Productschap voor Gedistilleerde Dranken*

TOP 10 ★
COLA-DRINKING COUNTRIES

| COUNTRY | CONSUMPTION PER CAPITA, 1998 | |
	PINTS	LITERS
1 Mexico	172.3	97.9
2 United Arab Emirates	167.4	95.1
3 Bermuda	157.7	89.6
4 US	150.1	85.3
5 St. Lucia	136.0	77.3
6 Bahrain	135.0	76.7
7 Dominica	134.8	76.6
8 Belize	129.7	73.7
9 Luxembourg	118.1	67.1
10 Granada	117.7	66.9

Source: *Euromonitor*

TOP 10 ★
SPARKLING WINE-DRINKING COUNTRIES

| COUNTRY | CONSUMPTION PER CAPITA, 1999 | |
	PINTS	LITERS
1 France	7.6	4.3
2 Germany	6.9	3.9
3 =Hungary	3.7	2.1
=New Zealand	3.7	2.1
5 Australia	2.8	1.6
6 Czech Republic	2.5	1.4
7 Belgium	2.3	1.3
8 =Italy	2.1	1.2
=Poland	2.1	1.2
10 =Portugal	1.8	1.0
=Romania	1.8	1.0

Source: *Euromonitor*

TOP 10 COUNTRIES WITH THE BIGGEST INCREASE IN ALCOHOL CONSUMPTION
(Country/percentage increase, 1970–99)

1 Brazil, 466.8 2 Paraguay, 275.0 3 Turkey, 177.8 4 Colombia, 166.6
5 Cyprus, 114.8 6 Ireland, 97.0 7 Venezuela, 96.8 8 Finland, 70.7
9 Greece, 69.6 10 Cuba, 69.3 *Canada, 2.3*

Source: *Productschap voor Gedistilleerde Dranken*

TOP 10 ★
COFFEE-DRINKING COUNTRIES

| COUNTRY | ANNUAL CONSUMPTION PER HEAD | | | |
	LB	OZ	KG	CUPS*
1 Finland	25	1	11.37	1,706
2 Norway	23	4	10.56	1,584
3 Denmark	22	4	10.09	1,514
4 Sweden	19	3	8.70	1,305
5 Austria	18	1	8.19	1,229
6 Germany	16	11	7.58	1,137
7 Switzerland	16	0	7.26	1,089
8 Netherlands	13	10	6.19	929
9 France	12	3	5.52	828
10 Belgium and Luxembourg	11	12	5.33	800

* Based on 150 cups per 1 kg (2 lb 3 oz)

Source: *International Coffee Organization*

TOP 10 ★
CHAMPAGNE-IMPORTING COUNTRIES

COUNTRY	BOTTLES IMPORTED, 2000
1 UK	20,433,640
2 US	19,268,837
3 Germany	14,235,737
4 Italy	8,239,536
5 Belgium	7,320,681
6 Switzerland	6,518,658
7 Japan	3,174,914
8 Netherlands	2,122,547
9 Spain	2,035,983
10 Australia	1,434,895

Source: *Comité Interprofessionnel du Vin de Champagne (CIVC)*

TOP 10 ★
SOFT DRINK-DRINKING COUNTRIES

| COUNTRY | ANNUAL CONSUMPTION PER CAPITA* | |
	PINTS	LITERS
1 US	385	219
2 Mexico	265	151
3 Iceland	246	140
4 Malta	236	134
5 Norway	222	126
6 Canada	215	122
7 Australia	211	120
8 Israel	195	111
9 Chile	194	110
10 Ireland	192	109

* *Carbonated only*

Source: *Zenith International*

As one might expect, affluent Western countries feature prominently in this list and, despite the spread of so-called "Coca-Cola culture," former Eastern Bloc and Third World countries rank very low – some African nations recording consumption figures of less than 1 liter (1.76 pints) per annum.

TOP 10 🍁
PROVINCES AND TERRITORIES WITH THE HIGHEST BEER CONSUMPTION, 2000

PROVINCE OR TERRITORY	LITERS PER CAPITA
1 Yukon Territory	110.34
2 Quebec	75.70
3 Newfoundland	71.33
4 Alberta	69.61
5 New Brunswick	64.56
6 Nova Scotia	63.51
7 Ontario	63.19
8 British Columbia	61.27
9 Prince Edward Island	60.41
10 Manitoba	60.06

Source: *Brewers Association of Canada*

Did You Know? Champagne was invented by blind Benedictine monk Dom Pierre Pérignon (1639–1715), cellar master of the Abbey of Hautvilliers, France.

ON THE MOVE

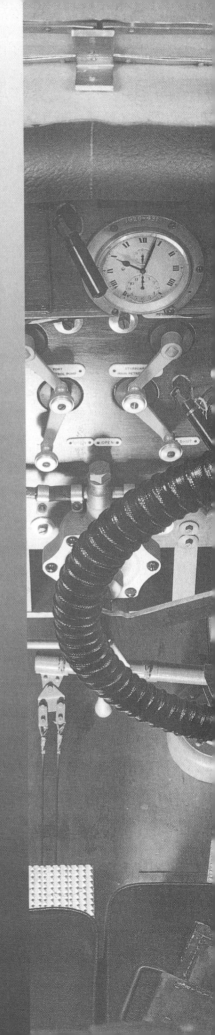

Speed Records

THE 10 ★

FIRST AMERICAN HOLDERS OF THE LAND SPEED RECORD

	DRIVER*/CAR/LOCATION	DATE	MPH	KM/H
1	William Vanderbilt, Mors, Albis, France	Aug 5, 1902	76.08	122.44
2	Henry Ford#, Ford Arrow, Lake St. Clair, US	Jan 12, 1904	91.37	147.05
3	Fred Marriott#, Stanley Rocket, Daytona Beach, US	Jan 23, 1906	121.57	195.65
4	Barney Oldfield#, Benz, Daytona Beach, US	Mar 16, 1910	131.27	211.26
5	Bob Burman#, Benz, Daytona Beach, US	Apr 23, 1911	141.37	227.51
6	Ralph de Palma#, Packard, Daytona Beach, US	Feb 17, 1919	149.87	241.19
7	Tommy Milton#, Duesenberg, Daytona Beach, US	Apr 27, 1920	156.03	251.11
8	Ray Keech, White Triplex, Daytona Beach, US	Apr 22, 1928	207.55	334.02
9	Craig Breedlove#, Spirit of America, Bonneville Salt Flats, Utah, US	Aug 5, 1963	407.45	655.73
10	Tom Green, Wingfoot Express, Bonneville Salt Flats, Utah, US	Oct 2, 1964	413.20	664.98

* Excluding those who subsequently broke their own records

\# Record not recognized in Europe

THE 10 ★

LATEST HOLDERS OF THE MOTORCYCLE SPEED RECORD

	RIDER/MOTORCYCLE	YEAR	MPH	KM/H
1	Dave Campos, Twin 1,491cc Ruxton Harley-Davidson Easyriders	1990	322.15	518.45
2	Donald A. Vesco, Twin 1,016cc Kawasaki Lightning Bolt	1978	318.60	512.73
3	Donald A. Vesco, 1,496cc Yamaha Silver Bird	1975	302.93	487.50
4	Calvin Rayborn, 1,480cc Harley-Davidson	1970	264.96	426.40
5	Calvin Rayborn, 1,480cc Harley-Davidson	1970	254.99	410.37
6	Donald A. Vesco, 700cc Yamaha	1970	251.82	405.25
7	Robert Leppan, 1,298cc Triumph	1966	245.62	395.27
8	William A. Johnson, 667cc Triumph	1962	224.57	361.40
9	Wilhelm Herz, 499cc NSU	1956	210.08	338.08
10	Russell Wright, 998cc Vincent HRD	1955	184.95	297.64

All the records listed here were achieved at the Bonneville Salt Flats, Utah, US, with the exception of No. 10 (Christchurch, New Zealand). Nos. 1 and 2 had two engines and were stretched to 6.4 m (21 ft) and 7 m (23 ft) respectively.

COOL RUNNER

In 1904 Henry Ford set the land speed record – although it was actually achieved on ice – on the frozen Lake St. Clair, near Detroit. A former employee of Thomas Edison, Ford (standing) had established the Ford Motor Company the previous year.

TOP 10 ★

LATEST HOLDERS OF THE LAND SPEED RECORD

	DRIVER/CAR	DATE	MPH	KM/H
1	Andy Green, Thrust SSC*	Oct 15, 1997	763.04	1,227.99
2	Richard Noble, Thrust 2*	Oct 4, 1983	633.47	1,013.47
3	Gary Gabelich, The Blue Flame	Oct 23, 1970	622.41	995.85
4	Craig Breedlove, Spirit of America – Sonic 1	Nov 15, 1965	600.60	960.96
5	Art Arfons, Green Monster	Nov 7, 1965	576.55	922.48
6	Craig Breedlove, Spirit of America – Sonic 1	Nov 2, 1965	555.48	888.76
7	Art Arfons, Green Monster	Oct 27, 1964	536.71	858.73
8	Craig Breedlove, Spirit of America	Oct 15, 1964	526.28	842.04
9	Craig Breedlove, Spirit of America	Oct 13, 1964	468.72	749.95
10	Art Arfons, Green Monster	Oct 5, 1964	434.02	694.43

* Achieved at Black Rock Desert, Nevada, US; all other speeds were achieved at Bonneville Salt Flats, Utah, US

FERRARI

Enzo Ferrari (1898–1988) attended his first motor race at the age of 10, vowing to become a race car driver. He achieved his ambition while working for a carmaker, later becoming part of the Alfa Romeo team and starting his own firm in 1929. Ferrari retired from driving and began producing his first race cars in 1940, and his first Grand Prix cars in the late 1940s. For over half a century, Ferraris have been among the most desirable – as well as the most expensive – of all cars, while the company's Formula One cars lead the constructors' table for the most wins.

TOP 10 ★
FASTEST PRODUCTION MOTORCYCLES

	MAKE/MODEL	MPH	KM/H
1	Suzuki GSX1300R Hayabusa	192	309
2=	Honda CBR1100XX Blackbird	181	291
=	Honda RC45(m)	181	291
4=	Harris Yamaha YZR500	180	289
=	Kawasaki ZZR1100 D7	180	289
6	Bimota YB10 Biposto	176	283
7	Suzuki GSX-R1100WP (d)	174	280
8	Suzuki GSX-R750-WV	173	279
9=	Bimota Furano	173	278
=	Kawasaki ZZR1100 C1	173	278

TOP 10 ★
FASTEST PRODUCTION CARS

	MODEL*/ COUNTRY OF MANUFACTURE	MPH	KM/H[#]
1	McLaren F1, UK	240	386
2	Lamborghini Diablo 6.0, Italy	208	335
3	Lister Storm, UK	201	323
4	Marcos Mantara LM 600 Coupe/Cabriolet, UK	200	322
5	Ferrari 550 Maranello, Italy	199	320
6	Renault Espace Privilege/Initiale 3.0 Auto, France	194	312
7=	Ascari Escosse, Italy	>190	>305
=	Pagani Zonda, Italy	>190	>305
9=	Callaway C12, US	190	305
=	Porsche 911 Turbo, Germany	190	305

* *Fastest of each manufacturer*

[#] *May vary according to specification modifications to meet national legal requirements*

Source: Auto Express/Top Gear Magazine

It is believed that it would be virtually impossible to build a road car capable of more than 402 km/h (250 mph), but these supercars come closest to that limit. The list includes the fastest example of each marque, but excludes "limited edition" cars.

TOP 10 ★
PRODUCTION CARS WITH THE FASTEST 0–60MPH TIMES

	MODEL*/ COUNTRY OF MANUFACTURE	SECONDS TAKEN[#]
1	Renault Espace F1, France	2.8
2	McLaren F1, UK	3.2
3	Caterham Seven Superlight R500, UK	3.4
4=	Marcos Mantara LM600 Coupe/Cabriolet, UK	3.6
=	Westfield FW400, UK	3.6
6	Lamborghini Diablo 6.0, Italy	3.9
7	Ascari Escosse, Italy	4.1
8=	AC Cobra Superblower, UK	4.2
=	Callaway C12, US	4.2
=	TVR Tuscan Speed Six 4.0, UK	4.2

* *Fastest of each manufacturer*

[#] *May vary according to specification modifications to meet national legal requirements*

Source: Auto Express/Top Gear Magazine

SUPERCAR

Racing technology applied to a road car in the McLaren F1 set new records for speed and acceleration. It was also at one time the highest-priced production car ever built.

Cars & Road Transport

DISTRIBUTION OF PUBLIC ROADS IN CANADA*

	PROVINCE	LENGTH PER 1,000 PERSONS	TWO-LANE KM#
1	Saskatchewan	199.08	201,903
2	Alberta	66.22	181,437
3	Ontario	15.31	167,891
4	Quebec	16.55	119,878
5	Manitoba	77.78	87,868
6	British Columbia	17.37	65,728
7	Nova Scotia	28.02	25,992
8	New Brunswick	29.11	21,884
9	Newfoundland	23.03	13,081
10	Prince Edward Island	42.19	5,687
	Canada total	30.73	901,904

* As at 1995 (per capita ratios as at August 1999)

\# Two-lane equivalent kilometers

Source: Transport Canada

COUNTRIES WITH THE LONGEST ROAD NETWORKS

	COUNTRY	LENGTH* MILES	KM
1	US	3,944,605	6,348,227
2	India	2,062,731	3,319,644
3	Brazil	1,230,315	1,980,000
4	China	751,859	1,210,000
5	Japan	715,948	1,152,207
6	Russia	589,060	948,000
7	Australia	557,312	913,000
8	Canada	560,416	901,904
9	France	554,884	893,000
10	Germany	407,706	656,140

* Both paved and unpaved roads

The proportion of paved roads varies considerably: India's total includes 1,517,077 km (942,668 miles) paved, while only 184,140 km (114,419 miles) of Brazil's and 271,300 km (168,578 miles) of China's total are paved.

FIRST COUNTRIES TO MAKE SEAT BELTS COMPULSORY

	COUNTRY	INTRODUCED
1	Czechoslovakia	Jan 1969
2	Ivory Coast	Jan 1970
3	Japan	Dec 1971
4	Australia	Jan 1972
5 =	Brazil	June 1972
=	New Zealand	June 1972
7	Puerto Rico	Jan 1974
8	Spain	Oct 1974
9	Sweden	Jan 1975
10 =	Belgium	June 1975
=	Luxembourg	June 1975
=	Netherlands	June 1975

Seat belts were not designed for use in private cars until the 1950s. Ford was the first manufacturer in Europe to fit anchorage-points; belts were first fitted as standard in Swedish Volvos from 1959.

MOTOR VEHICLE-OWNING COUNTRIES

	COUNTRY	CARS	COMMERCIAL VEHICLES	TOTAL
1	US	134,981,000	65,465,000	200,446,000
2	Japan	44,680,000	22,173,463	66,853,463
3	Germany	40,499,442	3,061,874	43,561,316
4	Italy	30,000,000	2,806,500	32,806,500
5	France	25,100,000	5,195,000	30,295,000
6	UK	24,306,781	3,635,176	27,941,957
7	Russia	13,638,600	9,856,000	23,494,600
8	Spain	14,212,259	3,071,621	17,283,880
9	Canada	13,182,996	3,484,616	16,667,612
10	Brazil	12,000,000	3,160,689	15,160,689

Source: American Automobile Manufacturers Association

FRENCH JAM

France has one of the world's highest ratios of cars to people and can claim a record traffic jam of 176 km (190 miles), which occurred between Paris and Lyons on Feb 16, 1980.

A CAR IS BORN

Japan's car production, which places increasing reliance on advanced robotic technology, closely rivals that of world leader the US.

TOP 10 ★
COUNTRIES PRODUCING THE MOST MOTOR VEHICLES

	COUNTRY	CARS	COMMERCIAL VEHICLES	TOTAL (1999)
1	US	5,554,390	6,451,689	12,006,079
2	Japan	8,055,736	1,994,029	10,049,792
3	Germany	5,348,115	378,673	5,726,788
4	France	2,603,021	351,139	2,954,160
5	Spain	2,216,571	609,492	2,826,063
6	Canada	1,122,287	1,050,375	2,172,662
7	UK	1,748,277	232,793	1,981,070
8	South Korea	1,625,125	329,369	1,954,494
9	Italy	1,402,382	290,355	1,692,737
10	China	507,103	1,120,726	1,627,829

Source: Ward's Motor Vehicle Facts and Figures

TOP 10 ★
BEST-SELLING CARS OF ALL TIME

	MANUFACTURER/MODEL	YEARS IN PRODUCTION	ESTIMATED NO. MADE*
1	Toyota Corolla	1966–	23,000,000
2	Volkswagen Beetle	1937–#	21,500,000
3	Volkswagen Golf	1974–	over 20,000,000
4	Lada Riva	1972–97	19,000,000
5	Ford Model T	1908–27	16,536,075
6	Honda Civic	1972–	14,000,000
7	Nissan Sunny/Pulsar	1966–94	13,571,100
8	Ford Escort/Orion	1967–84	12,000,000
9	Honda Accord	1976–	11,500,000
10	Volkswagen Passat	1973–	10,435,700

* To January 1, 2001

Still produced in Mexico

Estimates of manufacturers' output of their best-selling models vary from the vague to the unusually precise 16,536,075 of the Model T Ford, with 15,007,033 produced in the US and the rest in Canada and the UK between 1908 and 1927.

THE CAR IN FRONT ...

The Toyota Motor Company was started in 1937, in Koromo, Japan, by Kiichiro Toyoda. Its Corolla model became the world's best-selling car.

TOP 10 🍁
BEST-SELLING VEHICLES IN CANADA

	MODEL	SALES, 2000
1	Dodge Caravan	87,737
2=	Chevrolet Silverado	77,054
=	GMC Sierra	77,054
4	Ford F-series	76,025
5	Honda Civic	60,407
6	GM Minivan family*	55,485
7	Ford Windstar	49,636
8	Ford Focus	48,598
9	Chevrolet Cavalier	45,984
10	Pontiac Sunfire	41,098

* Includes Chevrolet Venture, Pontiac Montana, and Oldsmobile Silhouette

Source: *Canadian Auto World*

COR 163

Road Accidents

AGE GROUPS MOST VULNERABLE TO ROAD FATALITIES AND INJURIES IN CANADA

	AGE GROUP	1999 DEATHS	1999 NO. INJURIES
1	25–34	473	42,772
2	35–44	416	39,150
3	15–19	410	29,321
4	20–24	358	28,860
5	45–54	344	27,137
6	65+	530	16,188
7	55–64	247	14,647
8	5–14	128	14,143
9	Not stated	12	6,698
10	0–4	51	3,359

Source: *Transport Canada*

❧ THE 10 WORST YEARS FOR MOTOR VEHICLE COLLISIONS IN CANADA *

(Year/no. collisions)

1 1987, 196,806 **2** 1988, 193,605
3 1989, 192,428 **4** 1986, 186,992
5 1980, 184,302 **6** 1981, 183,643
7 1985, 183,423 **8** 1990, 181,960
9 1979, 178,832 **10** 1991, 173,921

* *Collisions causing injury or death, since 1945*

Source: *Transport Canada*

MOST COMMON CAUSES OF FATAL CRASHES IN THE US

	CAUSE	FATALITIES (1999)
1	Failure to keep in proper lane, or running off road	16,904
2	Driving too fast for conditions, or in excess of posted speed limit	11,100
3	Failure to yield right of way	5,076
4	Inattention (talking, eating, etc.)	3,908
5	Operating vehicle in erratic, reckless, careless, or negligent manner	2,985
6	Failure to obey traffic signs, signals, or officer	2,817
7	Swerving due to wind or slippery surface, or avoiding vehicle, object, non-driver in road, etc.	1,986
8	Drowsiness, sleep, fatigue, illness, or blackout	1,808
9	Overcorrecting/oversteering	1,793
10	Making improper turn	1,323

Source: *National Highway Traffic Safety Administration*

In this list – which remains astonishingly consistent from year to year – other causes include obscured vision (1,310 fatalities) and driving on the wrong side of the road (1,256), with a further 20,552 fatalities being reported with no cause listed and 601 as "unknown." The total number of drivers involved is 56,352, with the sum of the numbers and percentages being greater because in some cases more than one factor resulted in the fatal accident.

SPEED LIMIT

Excess speed is a major cause of accidents the world over. Speed limits, increasing surveillance by speed cameras, and rigorous enforcement attempt to reduce the toll that speeding drivers take on lives.

MOST ACCIDENT-PRONE CAR COLORS

	COLOR	ACCIDENTS PER 10,000 CARS OF EACH COLOR
1	Black	179
2	White	160
3	Red	157
4	Blue	149
5	Gray	147
6	Gold	145
7	Silver	142
8	Beige	137
9	Green	134
10=	Brown	133
=	Yellow	133

Research figures appeared to refute the notion that white cars were safest because they were the easiest to see, especially at night. These statistics were immediately disputed by some car manufacturers, insurance companies, and psychologists, who pointed out that the type of vehicle and age and experience of drivers were equally salient factors. In the light of these comments, until further surveys are conducted it would be misleading to consider any color "safer" than another.

PROVINCES WITH THE MOST MOTOR VEHICLE FATALITIES

	PROVINCE OR TERRITORY	CASUALTY RATE *
1	Yukon	6.3
2	Northwest Territories	4.3
3	Saskatchewan	2.6
4	New Brunswick	2.2
5	Prince Edward Island	2.1
6	Quebec	1.9
7=	Nova Scotia	1.7
=	Manitoba	1.7
=	British Columbia	1.7
10	Alberta	1.6

* *1999; per 10,000 vehicles registered*

Source: *Transport Canada*

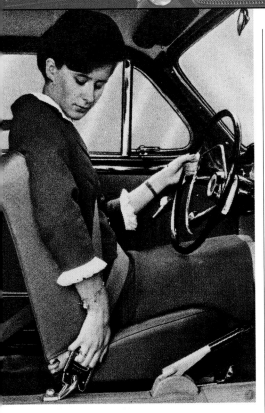

BELTING UP

Seat belts were first fitted as standard equipment in Swedish Volvos in 1959 and became compulsory in most countries from the 1970s onward.

THE 10 ★
COUNTRIES WITH THE HIGHEST NUMBER OF ROAD DEATHS

	COUNTRY	TOTAL DEATHS*
1	US	41,471
2	Thailand	15,176
3	Japan	10,805
4	South Korea	10,416
5	France	8,918
6	Germany	7,792
7	Poland	7,080
8	Brazil	6,759
9	Turkey	6,416
10	Italy	6,326
	Canada	2,934

* In latest year for which figures available

THE 10 ★
COUNTRIES WITH THE MOST DEATHS BY CAR ACCIDENTS

	COUNTRY	DEATH RATE PER 100,000 POPULATION
1	South Korea	38.4
2	Latvia	27.7
3	Greece	24.2
4 =	Portugal	22.5
=	Venezuela	22.5
6 =	El Salvador	20.3
=	Kuwait	20.3
8	Lithuania	19.7
9	Russia	19.5
10	Cuba	18.3
	Canada	10.5

Source: *United Nations*

Not all countries report accurate motor vehicle accident statistics, but among those that do, the Top 10 represents a group of countries in which visitors clearly need to take special care on the road.

THE 10 ★
MOST COMMON COLLISIONS IN THE US

	OBJECT/EVENT	COLLISIONS (1999)
1	Another vehicle, at an angle	1,948,000
2	Another vehicle, rear end	1,859,000
3	Another vehicle, sideswipe	514,000
4	Parked motor vehicle	329,000
5	Animal	267,000
6	Culvert/curb/ditch	197,000
7	Pole or post	180,000
8	Shrubbery/tree	126,000
9	Rollover	124,000
10	Another vehicle, head on	109,000

Source: *National Highway Traffic Safety Administration*

Out of a total of 6,279,000 crashes recorded in 1999 (omitting those described as "other" or "unknown"), the next most common event is a collision with a guard rail, with 91,000 cases.

THE 10 ★
WORST MOTOR VEHICLE AND ROAD DISASTERS

LOCATION/DATE/INCIDENT	NO. KILLED
1 Afghanistan, Nov 3, 1982 *Following a collision with a Soviet army truck, a gasoline tanker exploded in the 2.7-km (1.7-mile) Salang Tunnel. Some authorities have put the death toll from the explosion, fire, and fumes as high as 3,000.*	over 2,000
2 Colombia, Aug 7, 1956 *Seven army ammunition trucks exploded at night in the center of Cali, destroying eight city blocks, including a barracks where 500 soldiers were sleeping.*	1,200
3 Thailand, Feb 15, 1990 *A dynamite truck exploded.*	over 150
4 Nigeria, Nov 4, 2000 *A gasoline tanker collided with a line of parked cars on the Ile-Ife-Ibadan Expressway, exploding and burning many to death. Some 96 bodies were recovered, but some estimates put the final toll as high as 200.*	150
5 Nepal, Nov 23, 1974 *Hindu pilgrims were killed when a suspension bridge over the River Mahahali collapsed.*	148
6 Egypt, Aug 9, 1973 *A bus drove into an irrigation canal.*	127
7 Togo, Dec 6, 1965 *Two trucks collided with dancers during a festival at Sotouboua.*	over 125
8 Spain, July 11, 1978 *A liquid gas tanker exploded in a camping site at San Carlos de la Rapita.*	over 120
9 South Korea, Apr 28, 1995 *An underground explosion destroyed vehicles and caused about 100 cars and buses to plunge into the pit it created.*	110
10 = The Gambia, Nov 12, 1992 *After brake failure, a bus ferrying passengers to a dock plunged into a river.*	c.100
= Kenya, early Dec 1992 *A bus carrying 112 skidded, hit a bridge, and plunged into a river.*	c.100

The worst-ever car racing accident occurred on June 13, 1955, at Le Mans, France, when, in attempting to avoid other cars, French driver Pierre Levegh's Mercedes-Benz 300 SLR went out of control, hit a wall, and exploded in midair, showering wreckage into the crowd and thereby killing a total of 82 people.

 Which company is the second oldest in Canada, after the Hudson's Bay Company?
see p.197 for the answer
A Bank of Montreal
B Molson Breweries Limited
C Halifax Insurance Company

Rail Transport

WORST RAIL DISASTERS

LOCATION/DATE/INCIDENT	NO. KILLED

1 Bagmati River, India, June 6, 1981   c.800
The carriages of a train traveling from Samastipur to Banmukhi in Bihar plunged off a bridge over the River Bagmati near Mansi when the driver braked, apparently to avoid hitting a sacred cow. Although the official death toll was said to have been 268, many authorities have claimed that the train was so massively overcrowded that the actual figure was in excess of 800.

2 Chelyabinsk, Russia, June 3, 1989   up to 800
Two passenger trains, laden with vacationers heading to and from Black Sea resorts, were destroyed when liquid gas from a nearby pipeline exploded.

3 Guadalajara, Mexico, Jan 18, 1915   over 600
A train derailed on a steep incline, but political strife in the country meant that full details of the disaster were suppressed.

4 Modane, France, Dec 12, 1917   573
A troop-carrying train ran out of control and was derailed. It has been claimed that the train was overloaded and that as many as 1,000 may have died.

5 Balvano, Italy, Mar 2, 1944   521
A heavily laden train stalled in the Armi Tunnel, and many passengers were asphyxiated. Like the disaster at Torre (No. 6), wartime secrecy prevented full details from being published.

6 Torre, Spain, Jan 3, 1944   over 500
A double collision and fire in a tunnel resulted in many deaths – some have put the total as high as 800.

7 Awash, Ethiopia, Jan 13, 1985   428
A derailment hurled a train laden with some 1,000 passengers into a ravine.

8 Cireau, Romania, Jan 7, 1917   374
An overcrowded passenger train crashed into a military train and was derailed.

9 Quipungo, Angola, May 31, 1993   355
A train was derailed by UNITA guerrilla action.

10 Sangi, Pakistan, Jan 4, 1990   306
A train was diverted onto the wrong line, resulting in a fatal collision.

Figures for rail accidents are often extremely imprecise, especially during wartime, and half of these disasters occurred during the two world wars.

FIRST COUNTRIES WITH RAILWAYS

	COUNTRY	FIRST RAILWAY ESTABLISHED
1	UK	Sep 27, 1825
2	France	Nov 7, 1829
3	US	May 24, 1830
4	Ireland	Dec 17, 1834
5	Belgium	May 5, 1835
6	Germany	Dec 7, 1835
7	Canada	July 21, 1836
8	Russia	Oct 30, 1837
9	Austria	Jan 6, 1838
10	Netherlands	Sep 24, 1839

Although there were earlier horse-drawn railways, the Stockton & Darlington Railway inaugurated the world's first steam service. In their early years some of those listed here offered only limited services over short distances, but their opening dates mark the generally accepted beginning of each country's steam railway system. By 1850, railways had also begun operating in Italy, Hungary, Denmark, and Spain.

LONGEST UNDERGROUND RAILWAY NETWORKS

	CITY/COUNTRY	OPENED	STATIONS	TOTAL TRACK LENGTH MILES	KM
1	**London**, UK	1863	267	244	392
2	**New York**, US	1904	468	231	371
3	**Moscow**, Russia	1935	150	163	262
4	**Paris**, France*	1900	297	125	201
5	**Copenhagen**, Denmark#	1934	79	119	192
6	**Seoul**, South Korea	1974	114	113	183
7	**Mexico City**, Mexico	1969	154	112	178
8	**Chicago**, US	1943	145	108	173
9	**Tokyo**, Japan+	1927	150	107	172
10	**Berlin**, Germany	1902	135	89	143

* Metro + RER   # Only partly underground   + Through-running extensions raise total to 683 km (391 miles), with 502 stations

Source: Tony Pattison, Centre for Environmental Initiatives Researcher

GOING UNDERGROUND

Now over 100 years old, the Paris Metro – with its distinctive Art Deco entrances – is among the world's longest and most used underground railway systems.

RAILROAD

Although the US still has the longest rail network in the world, US rail mileage has declined considerably since its 1916 peak of 408,773 km (254,000 miles).

TOP 10 ★
LONGEST RAIL NETWORKS

	LOCATION	TOTAL RAIL LENGTH MILES	KM
1	US	149,129	240,000
2	Russia	93,205	150,000
3	China	40,793	65,650
4	India	39,093	62,915
5	Germany	25,368	40,826
6	Argentina	23,815	38,326
7	Canada	22,440	36,114
8	Australia	21,014	33,819
9	France	19,846	31,939
10	Mexico	19,292	31,048

The total of all world networks is today considered to be 1,201,337 km (746,476 miles). Of this, 239,430 km (148,775 miles) are narrow gauge and some 190,000 to 195,000 km (118,061 to 121,167 miles) are electrified.

TOP 10 ★
FASTEST RAIL JOURNEYS*

	JOURNEY	COUNTRY	TRAIN	DISTANCE MILES	KM	SPEED MPH	KM/H
1	Hiroshima–Kokura	Japan	Nozomi 500	119.3	192.0	162.7	261.8
2	Massy–St. Pierre des Corps	France	7 TGV	128.5	206.9	157.4	253.3
3	Brussels–Paris	International	Thalys 9342	194.7	313.4	140.7	226.5
4	Madrid–Seville	Spain	5 AVE	292.4	470.5	129.9	209.1
5	Karlsruhe–Mannheim	Germany	2 trains	44.1	71.0	120.4	193.8
6	London–York	UK	1 IC225	188.5	303.4	112.0	180.2
7	Skövde–Södertälje	Sweden	3 X2000	172.1	277.0	106.4	171.3
8	Piacenza–Parma	Italy	ES 9325	35.4	57.0	106.2	171.0
9	North Philadelphia–Newark Penn	US	1 NE Direct	76.0	122.4	95.0	153.0
10	Salo–Karjaa	Finland	S220 132	33.0	53.1	94.3	151.7

* *Fastest journey for each country; all those in the Top 10 have other similarly or equally fast services*

Source: Railway Gazette International

Japan is not only the leader for scheduled train journeys: its MLX01 maglev train holds the world speed record for an experimental vehicle, traveling at over 550 km/h (341.7 mph). At the other end of the scale, Albania has achieved a 47 percent increase from 34.2 km/h (21.3 mph) to 50.5 km/h (31.3 mph).

Did You Know? Before they were adopted nationally, the American Railway Association introduced Standard Time Zones in 1883 to overcome the timetable confusion resulting from some 100 different local times.

TOP 10 ★

LONGEST CRUISE SHIPS

SHIP/COUNTRY/YEAR BUILT	FT	LENGTH IN	M
1 *Norway* (former *France*), France, 1961	1,035	2	315.53
2 =*Voyager of the Seas*, Finland, 1999	1,020	9	311.12
=*Explorer of the Seas*, Finland, 2000	1,020	9	311.12
4 *Disney Magic*, Italy, 1998	964	8	294.06
5 =*Disney Wonder*, Italy, 1999	964	7	294.00
=*Millennium*, France, 2000	964	7	294.00
7 *Queen Elizabeth 2*, UK, 1969	963	0	293.53
8 *Costa Atlantica*, Finland, 2000	957	0	291.70
9 *Grand Princess*, Italy, 1998	949	10	289.51
10 *Enchantment of the Seas*, Finland, 1997	917	4	279.60

Source: *Lloyd's Register, MIPG/PPMS*

For comparison, the *Great Eastern* (launched in 1858) measured 211 m (692 ft) long. The *Titanic*, which sank dramatically on its maiden voyage in 1912, was 269 m (882 ft) long and, until the influx of new vessels in 1998, would have ranked 8th in this Top 10. Former entrant in this list the *Queen Mary* (311 m/1,019 ft) is now a floating museum in Long Beach, California.

PORT OF CALL

Its substantial and well-protected harbor has contributed to Singapore's becoming the most important commercial center in Southeast Asia.

TOP 10 BUSIEST PORTS*

(Port/location)

❶ Singapore ❷ Hong Kong, China
❸ Kaohsiung, Taiwan ❹ Rotterdam, Netherlands ❺ Pusan, South Korea
❻ Long Beach, US ❼ Hamburg, Germany
❽ Antwerp, Belgium
❾ Los Angeles, US ❿ Shanghai, China

* *Ports handling the most TEUs (Twenty-foot Equivalent Units)*
Source: *International Association of Ports & Harbors*

TOP 10 🍁

BUSIEST PORTS IN CANADA

PORT	1998 TONNAGE*
1 Vancouver	70,720
2 Sept-Îles/Pointe-Noire	24,575
3 Montreal/Contrecoeur	20,998
4 Port-Cartier	19,276
5 Saint John	18,496
6 Quebec/Lévis	15,570
7 Port Hawkesbury	14,397
8 Halifax	13,478
9 Hamilton	12,296
10 Nanticoke	11,720

* *Tonnage of cargo loaded and unloaded, both domestic and international, thousands of tonnes*
Source: *Statistics Canada*

Significant declines in shipments of coal and wheat to Far East markets due to the Asian economic crisis decreased the amount of freight tonnage at the port of Prince Rupert in British Columbia by almost one-third, bumping the port from the No. 10 position it held in 1997.

THE *UNITED STATES* GAINS THE BLUE RIBAND

From the 19th century onward, ocean liners vied for the prize for the fastest transatlantic crossing by a passenger ship. The record, popularly known as the "Blue Riband," and the Hales Trophy, awarded since 1935, go to the vessel with the fastest crossing, which is based on average speed rather than shortest time because the route lengths vary. In 1838 the record stood at 7.3 knots over an 18-day voyage. This was steadily improved upon until, in 1938, the *Queen Mary* established the westbound record crossing at a speed of 30.99 knots. It took until July 15, 1952, for the *United States* to establish a new record of 3 days 10 hours 40 minutes at an average speed of 34.51 knots. A new eastbound record of 2 days 20 hours 9 minutes (41.28 knots) was set in 1998, but the *United States'* westbound record has remained unbeaten for half a century.

50 YEARS AGO

THE 10 ★
WORST MARINE DISASTERS

LOCATION/DATE/INCIDENT	APPROX. NO. KILLED
1 Off Gdansk, Poland, January 30, 1945	up to 7,800

The German liner Wilhelm Gustloff, laden with refugees, was torpedoed by a Soviet submarine, S-13. The precise death toll remains uncertain but is in the range of 5,348 to 7,800.

| **2 Off Cape Rixhöft** (Rozeewie), Poland, April 16, 1945 | 6,800 |

A German ship, Goya, carrying evacuees from Gdansk, was torpedoed in the Baltic.

| **3 Off Yingkow**, China, December 3, 1948 | over 6,000 |

The boilers of an unidentified Chinese troopship carrying Nationalist soldiers from Manchuria exploded, detonating ammunition.

| **4 Lübeck**, Germany, May 3, 1945 | 5,000 |

The German ship Cap Arcona, carrying concentration camp survivors, was bombed and sunk by British aircraft.

| **5 Off St. Nazaire**, France, June 17, 1940 | 3,050 |

The British troop ship Lancastria sank.

| **6 Off Stolpmünde** (Ustka), Poland, February 9, 1945 | 3,000 |

German war-wounded and refugees were lost when the Steuben was torpedoed by the same Russian submarine that had sunk the Wilhelm Gustloff.

LOCATION/DATE/INCIDENT	APPROX. NO. KILLED
7 Tabias Strait, Philippines, December 20, 1987	up to 3,000

The ferry Dona Paz was struck by oil tanker MV Victor.

| **8 Woosung**, China, December 3, 1948 | over 2,750 |

The overloaded steamship Kiangya, carrying refugees, struck a Japanese mine.

| **9 Lübeck**, Germany, May 3, 1945 | 2,750 |

The refugee ship Thielbeck sank during the British bombardment of Lübeck harbor in the closing weeks of World War II.

| **10 South Atlantic**, September 12, 1942 | 2,279 |

The British passenger vessel Laconia, carrying Italian prisoners-of-war, was sunk by German U-boat U-156.

Recent reassessments of the death tolls in some of the World War II marine disasters mean that the most famous marine disaster of all, the *Titanic*, the British liner that struck an iceberg in the North Atlantic and sank on April 15, 1912, with the loss of 1,517 lives, no longer ranks in this list. However, the *Titanic* tragedy remains one of the worst ever peacetime disasters, along with such notable incidents as that involving the *General Slocum*, an excursion liner that caught fire in the port of New York on June 15, 1904, with the loss of 1,021 lives.

THE 10 ★
WORST OIL TANKER SPILLS

TANKER/LOCATION/DATE	APPROX. SPILLAGE (TONNES)
1 Atlantic Empress and **Aegean Captain**, Trinidad, July 19, 1979	269,549
2 Castillio de Bellver, Cape Town, South Africa, Aug 6, 1983	251,097
3 Olympic Bravery, Ushant, France, Jan 24, 1976	246,051
4 Amoco Cadiz, Finistère, France, Mar 16, 1978	219,748
5 Odyssey, Atlantic, off Canada, Nov 10, 1988	137,862
6 Haven, off Genoa, Italy, Apr 11, 1991	134,344
7 Torrey Canyon, Scilly Isles, UK, Mar 18, 1967	122,189
8 Sea Star, Gulf of Oman, Dec 19, 1972	121,229
9 Irenes Serenade, Pilos, Greece, Feb 23, 1980	117,071
10 Texaco Denmark, North Sea, off Belgium, Dec 7, 1971	100,758

Source: *Environmental Technology Center/Oil Spill Intelligence Report*

ENVIRONMENTAL DISASTER
The 1979 collision of the Atlantic Empress *and the* Aegean Captain *off Trinidad resulted in the worst oil spill of all time.*

Kenneth Thomson is the richest Canadian. Who is the fourth richest?
see p.202 for the answer
A Galen Weston
B Charles Bronfman
C Edward (Ted) Rogers Jr.
235

Air Records

FIRST TRANSATLANTIC FLIGHTS

AIRCRAFT/CREW/COUNTRY	CROSSING	DATE*
1 US Navy/Curtiss flying boat *NC-4*, Lt.-Cdr. Albert Cushing Read and crew of five, US	Trepassy Harbor, Newfoundland to Lisbon, Portugal	May 16–27, 1919
2 Twin Rolls-Royce-engined converted Vickers Vimy bomber#, Capt. John Alcock and Lt. Arthur Whitten Brown, UK	St. John's, Newfoundland to Galway, Ireland	June 14–15, 1919
3 British airship *R-34*+, Maj. George Herbert Scott and crew of 30, UK	East Fortune, Scotland to Roosevelt Field, New York	July 2–6, 1919
4 Fairey IIID seaplane *Santa Cruz*, Adm. Gago Coutinho and Cdr. Sacadura Cabral, Portugal	Lisbon, Portugal to Recife, Brazil	Mar 30–June 5, 1922
5 Two Douglas seaplanes, *Chicago* and *New Orleans*, Lt. Lowell H. Smith and Leslie P. Arnold/Erik Nelson and John Harding, US	Orkneys, Scotland to Labrador, Canada	Aug 2–31, 1924
6 Renamed German-built *ZR 3* airship *Los Angeles*, Dr. Hugo Eckener with 31 passengers and crew, Germany	Friedrichshafen, Germany to Lakehurst, New Jersey	Oct 12–15, 1924
7 Dornier Wal twin-engined flying boat *Plus Ultra*, Capt. Julio Ruiz de Alda and crew, Spain	Huelva, Spain to Recife, Brazil	Jan 22–Feb 10 1926
8 Savoia-Marchetti S.55 flying boat *Santa Maria*, Francesco Marquis de Pinedo, Capt. Carlo del Prete, and Lt. Vitale Zacchetti, Italy	Cagliari, Sardinia to Recife, Brazil	Feb 8–24, 1927
9 Dornier Wal flying boat, Sarmento de Beires and Jorge de Castilho, Portugal	Lisbon, Portugal to Natal, Brazil	Mar 16–17, 1927
10 Savoia-Marchetti flying boat, João De Barros and crew, Brazil	Genoa, Italy to Natal, Brazil	Apr 28–May 14, 1927

* *All dates refer to the actual Atlantic legs of the journeys; some started earlier and ended beyond their first transatlantic landfalls*

\# *First nonstop flight*

+ *First east–west flight*

ATLANTIC FLIER

Alcock and Brown made the first nonstop Atlantic crossing in 16 hours 28 minutes in a converted Vickers Vimy bomber.

FIRST PEOPLE TO FLY IN HEAVIER-THAN-AIR AIRCRAFT

PILOT/NATIONALITY/AIRCRAFT	DATE
1 Orville Wright, US, *Wright Flyer I*	Dec 17, 1903
2 Wilbur Wright, US, *Wright Flyer I*	Dec 17, 1903
3 Alberto Santos-Dumont, Brazil, *No. 14-bis*	Oct 23, 1906
4 Charles Voisin, France, *Voisin-Delagrange I*	Mar 30, 1907
5 Henri Farman, UK, later France, *Voisin-Farman I-bis*	Oct 7, 1907
6 Léon Delagrange, France, *Voisin-Delagrange I*	Nov 5, 1907
7 Robert Esnault-Pelterie, France, *REP No. 1*	Nov 16, 1907
8 Charles W. Furnas*, US, *Wright Flyer III*	May 14, 1908
9 Louis Blériot, France *Blériot VIII*	June 29, 1908
10 Glenn Hammond Curtiss, US, *AEA June Bug*	July 4, 1908

* *As a passenger in a plane piloted by Wilbur Wright, Furnas was the first airplane passenger in the US.*

FIRST ROCKET AND JET AIRCRAFT

AIRCRAFT/COUNTRY	FIRST FLIGHT
1 Heinkel He 176*, Germany	June 20, 1939
2 Heinkel He 178, Germany	Aug 27, 1939
3 DFS 194*, Germany	Aug 1940#
4 Caproni-Campini N-1, Italy	Aug 28, 1940
5 Heinkel He 280V-1, Germany	Apr 2, 1941
6 Gloster E.28/39, UK	May 15, 1941
7 Messerschmitt Me 163 Komet*, Germany	Aug 13, 1941
8 Messerschmitt Me 262V-3, Germany	July 18, 1942
9 Bell XP-59A Airacomet, US	Oct 1, 1942
10 Gloster Meteor F Mk 1, UK	Mar 5, 1943

* *Rocket-powered* # *Precise date unknown*

ROCKET PILOT
X-15 pilot Joseph A. Walker held the world record seven times in 1960–62, before finally losing the mantle to William J. Knight.

FIRST FLIGHTS OF MORE THAN ONE HOUR

	PILOT	HR:MIN:SEC	DATE
1	Orville Wright	1:02:15	Sep 9, 1908
2	Orville Wright	1:05:52	Sep 10, 1908
3	Orville Wright	1:10:00	Sep 11, 1908
4	Orville Wright	1:15:20	Sep 12, 1908
5	Wilbur Wright	1:31:25	Sep 21, 1908
6	Wilbur Wright	1:07:24	Sep 28, 1908
7	Wilbur Wright*	1:04:26	Oct 6, 1908
8	Wilbur Wright	1:09:45	Oct 10, 1908
9	Wilbur Wright	1:54:53	Dec 18, 1908
10	Wilbur Wright	2:20:23	Dec 31, 1908

* First ever flight of more than one hour with a passenger (M. A. Fordyce)

FASTEST X-15 FLIGHTS

	PILOT/DATE	MACH*	FLIGHT MPH	KM/H
1	William J. Knight, Oct 3, 1967	6.70	4,520	7,274
2	William J. Knight, Nov 18, 1966	6.33	4,261	6,857
3	Joseph A. Walker, June 27, 1962	5.92	4,105	6,606
4	Robert M. White, Nov 9, 1961	6.04	4,094	6,589
5	Robert A. Rushworth, Dec 5, 1963	6.06	4,018	6,466
6	Neil A. Armstrong, July 26, 1962	5.74	3,989	6,420
7	John B. McKay, June 22, 1965	5.64	3,938	6,388
8	Robert A. Rushworth, July 18, 1963	5.63	3,925	6,317
9	Joseph A. Walker, June 25, 1963	5.51	3,911	6,294
10	William H. Dan, Oct 4, 1967	5.53	3,910	6,293

* Mach no. varies with altitude – the list is ranked on actual speed

Although achieved more than 33 years ago, the speeds attained by the rocket-powered X-15 and X-15A-2 aircraft are the greatest ever attained by piloted vehicles in the Earth's atmosphere.

BIGGEST AIRSHIPS EVER BUILT

	AIRSHIP	COUNTRY	YEAR	VOLUME CU FT	CU M	LENGTH FT	M
1 =	Hindenburg	Germany	1936	7,062,934	200,000	804	245
=	Graf Zeppelin II	Germany	1938	7,062,934	200,000	804	245
3 =	Akron	US	1931	6,500,000	184,060	785	239
=	Macon	US	1933	6,500,000	184,060	785	239
5	R101	UK	1930	5,500,000	155,744	777	237
6	Graf Zeppelin	Germany	1928	3,708,040	105,000	776	237
7	L72	Germany	1920	2,419,055	68,500	743	226
8	R100	UK	1929	5,500,000	155,744	709	216
9	R38	UK*	1921	2,724,000	77,136	699	213
10 =	L70	Germany	1918	2,418,700	62,200	694	212
=	L71	Germany	1918	2,418,700	62,200	694	212

* UK-built, but sold to US Navy

THE FIRST JET AIRLINER

The jet airliner began life only 50 years ago, with the launch on May 3, 1952, of the scheduled BOAC de Havilland Comet service between London and Johannesburg, a distance of 10,821 km (6,724 miles) flown in stages with a journey time of 23 hours 34 minutes. The 36-seat aircraft *Yoke Peter* inaugurated the route, following exhaustive tests on freight-only flights to destinations such as Beirut, New Delhi, Jakarta, and Singapore. By August 1952, a weekly Comet service to Colombo, Ceylon (Sri Lanka), had also been established. Soon after, several crashes involving Comets cast doubts over the safety of passenger jets, but these were overcome as the world's airline routes became established.

50 YEARS AGO · YEARS AGO · YEARS AGO ·

Did You Know? Following a feud with the Smithsonian Institution in Washington, DC, the Wright Brothers' *Flyer*, the first aircraft to fly, was kept in the Science Museum, London, from 1928 until 1948.

237

Air Transport

THE 10 ★
WORST AIRSHIP DISASTERS

LOCATION/DATE/INCIDENT	NO. KILLED
1 Off the New Jersey coast, US, Apr 4, 1933 *US navy airship Akron crashed into the sea in a storm,* *leaving only three survivors.*	73
2 Over the Mediterranean, Dec 21, 1923 *French airship Dixmude is assumed to have been struck by lightning,* *and broke up and crashed into the sea.*	52
3 Near Beauvais, France, Oct 5, 1930 *British airship R101 crashed into a hillside leaving 48 dead,* *with two dying later, and six survivors.*	50
4 Off the coast near Hull, UK, Aug 24, 1921 *Airship R38 broke in two on a training and test flight.*	44
5 Lakehurst, New Jersey, US, May 6, 1937 *German Zeppelin Hindenburg caught fire when mooring.*	36
6 Hampton Roads, Virginia, US, Feb 21, 1922 *Roma, an Italian airship bought by the US army, crashed,* *killing all but 11 men on board.*	34
7 Berlin, Germany, Oct 17, 1913 *German airship LZ18 crashed after engine failure during* *a test flight at Berlin-Johannisthal.*	28
8 Baltic Sea, Mar 30, 1917 *German airship SL9 was struck by lightning on a flight from* *Seerappen to Seddin, and crashed into the sea.*	23
9 Mouth of the River Elbe, Germany, Sep 3, 1915 *German airship L10 was struck by lightning and plunged into the sea.*	19
10=Off Heligoland, Sep 9, 1913 *German navy airship L1 crashed into the sea, leaving six survivors.*	14
=Caldwell, Ohio, US, Sep 3, 1925 *US dirigible Shenandoah broke up in a storm, scattering sections* *over many miles of the Ohio countryside.*	14

Fatalities occurred from the earliest days of airships: the *Pax* crashed in
Paris on May 12, 1902, killing its Brazilian inventor and pilot Augusto
Severo and his assistant, and on October 13 of the same year Ottokar de
Bradsky and his mechanic were killed in an airship crash, also in Paris.

TOP 10 AIRLINERS IN SERVICE
(Aircraft/no. in service)

① Boeing B-737-300, 1,076 **② Boeing B-757-200**, 913
③ Airbus A-320, 839 **④ Boeing B-727-200**, 771 **⑤ Boeing**
B-737-200, 752 **⑥ Boeing B-767-300**, 560 **⑦ Boeing B-747-400**,
524 **⑧ Boeing B-737-400**, 460 **⑨ Raytheon Beech 1900**, 408
⑩ Saab 340, 407

Source: Air Transport Intelligence at www.rati.com

THE 10 ★
WORST AIR DISASTERS

LOCATION/DATE/INCIDENT	NO. KILLED
1 Tenerife, Canary Islands, Mar 27, 1977 *Two Boeing 747s (Pan Am and KLM, carrying 364 passengers and 16 crew and* *230 passengers and 11 crew respectively) collided and caught fire on the runway* *of Los Rodeos airport after the pilots received incorrect control-tower instructions.*	583
2 Mt. Ogura, Japan, Aug 12, 1985 *A JAL Boeing 747 on an internal flight from Tokyo to Osaka crashed, killing* *all but four on board in the worst-ever disaster involving a single aircraft.*	520
3 Charkhi Dadri, India, Nov 12, 1996 *Soon after taking off from New Delhi's Indira Gandhi International Airport,* *a Saudi Airways Boeing 747 collided with a Kazakh Airlines Ilyushin IL-76* *cargo aircraft on its descent and exploded, killing all 312 on the Boeing* *and 37 on the Ilyushin, in the world's worst midair crash.*	349
4 Paris, France, Mar 3, 1974 *A Turkish Airlines DC-10 crashed at Ermenonville, north of Paris, just* *after takeoff for London, with many English rugby fans among the dead.*	346
5 Off the Irish coast, June 23, 1985 *An Air India Boeing 747 on a flight from Vancouver to Delhi exploded* *in midair, perhaps as a result of a terrorist bomb.*	329
6 Riyadh, Saudi Arabia, Aug 19, 1980 *A Saudia (Saudi Arabian) Airlines Lockheed Tristar caught fire* *during an emergency landing.*	301
7 Kinshasa, Zaïre, Jan 8, 1996 *A Zaïrean Antonov-32 cargo plane crashed shortly after takeoff,* *killing shoppers in a city center market.*	298
8 Off the Iranian coast, July 3, 1988 *An Iran Air A300 airbus was shot down in error by a missile* *fired by the USS Vincennes.*	290
9 Chicago, US, May 25, 1979 *The worst air disaster in the US occurred when an engine fell off an* *American Airlines DC-10 as it took off from Chicago O'Hare airport and the* *plane plunged out of control, killing all 271 on board and two on the ground.*	273
10 Lockerbie, Scotland, Dec 21, 1988 *Pan Am Flight 103 from London Heathrow to New York exploded in* *mid air as a result of a terrorist bomb, killing 243 passengers,* *16 crew, and 11 on the ground, in the UK's worst-ever air disaster.*	270

FIERY FINALE

Astonishingly, 61 of the 97 people on board the Hindenburg
survived its explosion, but the awesome images of the
catastrophe heralded the end of the airship era.

FLYING HIGH

First flown in 1982, and now costing upward of US$70 million each, the Boeing B-757-200 has a maximum range of 7,240 km (4,520 miles) and is extensively used on both short- and long-haul routes.

TOP 10 ★
BUSIEST INTERNATIONAL AIRPORTS

AIRPORT/LOCATION	INTERNATIONAL PASSENGERS PER ANNUM
1 **London Heathrow**, London, UK	50,612,000
2 **Frankfurt**, Frankfurt, Germany	32,333,000
3 **Charles de Gaulle**, Paris, France	31,549,000
4 **Schiphol**, Amsterdam, Netherlands	30,832,000
5 **Hong Kong**, Hong Kong, China	28,316,000
6 **London Gatwick**, Gatwick, UK	24,385,000
7 **Singapore International**, Singapore	23,799,000
8 **New Tokyo International (Narita)**, Tokyo, Japan	22,941,000
9 **J.F. Kennedy International**, New York, US	17,378,000
10 **Zurich**, Zurich, Switzerland	16,747,000

Source: *International Civil Aviation Organization*

TOP 10 AIRLINES WITH THE MOST AIRCRAFT
(Airline/country/fleet size)*

1 **American Airlines**, 714 2 **United Airlines**, 603 3 **Delta Airlines**, 600
4 **Northwest Airlines**, 424 5 **US Airways**, 384 6 **Continental Airlines**, 364
7 **Southwest Airlines**, 327 8 **British Airways**, UK, 268
9 **American Eagle Airlines**, 245 10 **Lufthansa German Airlines**, Germany, 233

* All from the US unless otherwise stated
Source: Airline Business/*Air Transport Intelligence at www.rati.com*

TOP 10 ★
AIRLINES CARRYING THE MOST PASSENGERS

AIRLINE/COUNTRY	PASSENGERS, 1999
1 **Delta Airlines**, US	105,500,000
2 **United Airlines**, US	87,100,000
3 **American Airlines**, US	84,700,000
4 **US Airways**, US	58,800,000
5 **Southwest Airlines**, US	57,700,000
6 **Northwest Airlines**, US	56,100,000
7 **Continental Airlines**, US	45,500,000
8 **All Nippon Airways**, Japan	42,700,000
9 **Air France**, France	39,800,000
10 **Lufthansa**, Germany	38,900,000

Source: Airline Business/*Air Transport Intelligence at www.rati.com*

BOEING

The name of William Edward Boeing (1881–1956) is known the world over from the aircraft made by his company – the world's largest. Detroit-born Boeing made a fortune in the timber industry and, having become passionate about aviation, set up an aircraft manufacturing company in 1916. The firm prospered and, in 1927, set up an airline, Boeing Air Transport. Boeing retired from the business in 1934, when US Government antitrust legislation made it illegal for a company to build aircraft and operate an airline. The airline was sold off and became United – one of the world's largest – while the Boeing Company continued to supply the world's airlines with its aircraft.

 Pierre-Luc Gagnon, of Canada, a world-class athlete, competes using what? *see p.262 for the answer* A A snowboard B A skateboard C A mountain bike

World Tourism

TOURIST DESTINATIONS IN ASIA AND THE PACIFIC

	COUNTRY	TOTAL VISITORS (2000)
1	China	31,236,000
2	Hong Kong	13,059,000
3	Malaysia	10,000,000
4	Thailand	9,574,000
5	Singapore	7,003,000
6	Macau	6,682,000
7	South Korea	5,336,000
8	Indonesia	5,012,000
9	Australia	4,882,000
10	Japan	4,758,000

Source: *World Tourism Organization*

TOURIST DESTINATIONS IN THE AMERICAS

	COUNTRY	TOTAL VISITORS (2000)
1	US	52,690,000
2	Canada	20,423,000
3	Mexico	20,000,000
4	Brazil	5,190,000
5	Puerto Rico	3,094,000
6	Argentina	2,988,000
7	Dominican Republic	2,977,000
8	Uruguay	1,968,000
9	Chile	1,719,000
10	Cuba	1,700,000

Source: *World Tourism Organization*

DESTINATIONS FOR CANADIAN TOURISTS

	DESTINATION COUNTRY	VISITORS (1999)
1	US	14,116,000
2	UK	816,000
3	Mexico	608,000
4	France	408,000
5	Cuba	350,000
6	Germany	228,000
7	Italy	192,000
8	Netherlands	154,000
9	Dominican Republic	153,000
10	Hong Kong	115,000

Source: *Statistics Canada*

TOURIST DESTINATIONS IN EUROPE

	COUNTRY	TOTAL VISITORS (2000)		COUNTRY	TOTAL VISITORS (2000)
1	France	74,500,000	6	Germany	18,916,000
2	Spain	48,500,000	7	Poland	18,183,000
3	Italy	41,182,000	8	Austria	17,818,000
4	UK	24,900,000	9	Hungary	15,571,000
5	Russia	22,783,000	10	Greece	12,500,000

Source: *World Tourism Organization*

BUSIEST CANADA/US BORDER CROSSINGS

	LAND BORDER	NO. OF INBOUND TRAVELERS*
1	Ambassador Bridge, Windsor, ON	11,079,453
2	Detroit and Canada Tunnel, Windsor, ON	8,410,910
3	Peace Bridge, Fort Erie, ON	7,004,965
4	Rainbow Bridge, Niagara Falls, ON	5,780,627
5	Douglas, BC	5,718,872
6	Sarnia, ON	5,237,112
7	Queenston-Lewiston Bridge, Queenston, ON	4,375,091
8	Pacific Highway, BC	3,370,660
9	Sault Ste. Marie, ON	3,181,434
10	Cornwall, ON	2,196,197

* From April 1, 1999, to March 31, 2000

Source: *Canada Customs and Revenue Agency*

IT JUST KEEPS ROLLING ALONG

In operation since 1914, the Rutschbanen in Copenhagen's Tivoli Gardens is Europe's oldest working roller coaster. The oldest American one predates this by 12 years.

TOP 10 ★
WORLDWIDE AMUSEMENT AND THEME PARKS, 2000

PARK/LOCATION	ATTENDANCE (000s)
1 Tokyo Disneyland, Tokyo, Japan	16,507
2 The Magic Kingdom at Walt Disney World, Lake Buena Vista, Florida, US	15,400
3 Disneyland, Anaheim, California, US	13,900
4 Disneyland Paris, Marne-La-Vallée, France	12,000
5 Epcot at Walt Disney World	10,600
6 Everland, Kyonggi-Do, South Korea	9,153
7 Disney–MGM Studios at Walt Disney World	8,900
8 Disney's Animal Kingdom at Walt Disney World	8,300
9 Universal Studios Florida, Orlando, Florida, US	8,100
10 Lotte World, Seoul, South Korea	7,200

Source: *Amusement Business*

TOP 10 ★
OLDEST AMUSEMENT PARKS

PARK/LOCATION	YEAR FOUNDED
1 Bakken, Klampenborg, Denmark	1583
2 The Prater, Vienna, Austria	1766
3 Blackgang Chine Cliff Top Theme Park, Ventnor, Isle of Wight, UK	1842
4 Tivoli Gardens, Copenhagen, Denmark	1843
5 Lake Compounce Amusement Park, Bristol, Connecticut, US	1846
6 Hanayashiki, Tokyo, Japan	1853
7 Grand Pier, Teignmouth, UK	1865
8 Blackpool Central Pier, Blackpool, UK	1868
9 Cedar Point, Sandusky, Ohio, US	1870
10 Clacton Pier, Clacton, UK	1871

TOP 10 ★
OLDEST ROLLER COASTERS*

ROLLER COASTER/LOCATION	YEAR FOUNDED
1 Leap-the-Dips, Lakemont Park, Altoona, Pennsylvania, US	1902
2 Scenic Railway, Luna Park, Melbourne, Australia	1912
3 Rutschbanen, Tivoli, Copenhagen, Denmark	1914
4 Jack Rabbit, Clementon Amusement Park, Clementon, New Jersey, US	1919
5 = Jack Rabbit, Sea Breeze Park, Rochester, New York, US	1920
= Scenic Railway, Dreamland, Margate, UK	1920
7 = Jack Rabbit, Kennywood, West Mifflin, Pennsylvania, US	1921
= Roller Coaster, Lagoon, Farmington, Utah, US	1921
9 = Big Dipper, Blackpool Pleasure Beach, Blackpool, UK	1923
= Thunderhawk, Dorney Park, Allentown, Pennsylvania, US	1923
= Zippin Pippin, Libertyland, Memphis, Tennessee, US	1923

* In operation at same location since founded

Leap-the-Dips at Lakemont Park, Altoona, Pennsylvania, the world's oldest roller coaster, went out of operation in 1985 but was restored and reopened in 1999.

TOP 10 ★
FASTEST ROLLER COASTERS

ROLLER COASTER/ LOCATION/YEAR OPENED	SPEED MPH	KM/H
1 = Superman The Escape, Six Flags Magic Mountain, Valencia, California, 1997	100	161
= Tower of Terror, Dreamworld, Gold Coast, Australia, 1997	100	161
3 Millennium Force, Cedar Point, Sandusky, Ohio, 2000	92	148
4 = Goliath, Six Flags Magic Mountain, Valencia, California, 2000	85	137
= Titan, Six Flags Over Texas, Arlington, Texas, 2001*	85	137
6 = Desperado, Buffalo Bill's Resort and Casino, Primm, Nevada, 1994	80	129
= HyperSonic XLC, Paramount's Kings Dominion, Doswell, Virginia, 2001*	80	129
= Nitro, Six Flags Great Adventure, Jackson, New Jersey, 2001*	80	129
= Phantom's Revenge, Kennywood Park, West Mifflin, Pennsylvania, 2001*	80	129
= Superman The Ride of Steel, Six Flags, Darien Lake, New York, 2000	80	129

* Under construction at time of going to press

THE OLDEST ROLLER COASTER

The first simple roller coasters were built in 1884 at Coney Island, New York, by Lemarcus Adna Thompson, but the world's oldest surviving example is Leap-the-Dips at Lakemont Park, Altoona, Pennsylvania. Invented and built in 1902 by the Edward Joy Morris Company to a design Morris had patented in 1894, it is small and slow by modern standards, measuring only 443 m (1,452 ft) in length and standing 12 m (41 ft) at its highest point, with a maximum speed of 16 km/h (10 mph). A figure-of-eight design, it operates on a principle known as side friction. As one of the few remaining examples of this type, it was placed in the US National Register of Historical Places in 1991, attaining National Landmark status in 1996. Leap-the-Dips was recently restored and reopened in advance of its 100th anniversary.

100 YEARS AGO · YEARS AGO · YEARS AGO ·

Did You Know? The world's oldest surviving Ferris wheel, dating from 1895, is in Asbury Park, New Jersey, US. Europe's oldest has stood in the Prater, Vienna, Austria, since 1897.

THE SPORTING WORLD

Summer Olympics

MOST SUCCESSFUL COUNTRIES AT ONE SUMMER OLYMPICS

COUNTRY	VENUE	YEAR	GOLD	SILVER	BRONZE	TOTAL
1 US	St. Louis	1904	80	86	72	238
2 USSR	Moscow	1980	80	69	46	195
3 US	Los Angeles	1984	83	61	30	174
4 Great Britain	London	1908	56	50	39	145
5 USSR	Seoul	1988	55	31	46	132
6 East Germany	Moscow	1980	47	37	42	126
7 USSR	Montreal	1976	49	41	35	125
8 EUN*	Barcelona	1992	45	38	29	112
9 US	Barcelona	1992	37	34	37	108
10 US	Mexico City	1968	45	28	34	107

Unified Team representing the Commonwealth of Independent States (former Soviet republics), formed in 1991

OLYMPIC MEDAL-WINNING COUNTRIES THAT HAVE NEVER WON A GOLD MEDAL

COUNTRY	SILVER	BRONZE	TOTAL
1 Mongolia	5	9	14
2 Chinese Taipei	4	6	10
3 =Chile	6	3	9
=Philippines	2	7	9
5 Georgia	0	8	8
6 =Latvia	5	2	7
=Slovenia	2	5	7
8 Puerto Rico	1	5	6
9 =Ghana	1	3	4
=Israel	1	3	4
=Lebanon	2	2	4
=Moldovia	2	2	4
=Namibia	4	0	4
=Nigeria	1	3	4

SUMMER OLYMPICS ATTENDED BY THE MOST COMPETITORS, 1896–2000

LOCATION	YEAR	COUNTRIES REPRESENTED	COMPETITORS
1 Atlanta	1996	197	10,310
2 Sydney	2000	199	10,000*
3 Barcelona	1992	169	9,364
4 Seoul	1988	159	8,465
5 Munich	1972	121	7,123
6 Los Angeles	1984	140	6,797
7 Montreal	1976	92	6,028
8 Mexico City	1968	112	5,530
9 Rome	1960	83	5,346
10 Moscow	1980	80	5,217

Estimated

OLYMPIAN OPENING

Widely regarded as one of the most successful Olympics of modern times, the 2000 Sydney Games were launched by the arrival of the Olympic flame borne by 400-m champion Cathy Freeman.

OAR INSPIRING
British rower Steve Redgrave, here with team members Matthew Pinsent, Tim Foster, and James Cracknell, won his fifth consecutive gold at the 2000 Olympics.

TOP 10 🍁
SPORTS WITH THE MOST OLYMPICS MEDALS FOR CANADA

SPORT	GOLD	SILVER	BRONZE	TOTAL
1 Athletics	13	14	23	50
2 Swimming	7	13	19	39
3 Rowing	8	12	12	32
4 Speed skating	6	10	11	27
5 Figure skating	2	7	9	18
6 Boxing	3	7	7	17
7 Canoeing	3	8	5	16
8 Hockey	6	5	2	13
9 Wrestling	1	5	5	11
10 Alpine skiing	4	1	5	10

Source: *Canadian Olympic Association*

TOP 10 ⭐
COUNTRIES WITH THE MOST SUMMER OLYMPICS MEDALS, 1896–2000

COUNTRY	GOLD	SILVER	BRONZE	TOTAL
1 US	872	659	581	2,112
2 USSR*	485	395	354	1,234
3 Great Britain	188	245	232	665
4 France	189	195	217	601
5 Germany#	165	198	210	573
6 Italy	179	144	155	478
7 Sweden	138	157	176	471
8 Hungary	150	134	158	442
9 East Germany	153	130	127	410
10 Australia	103	110	139	352

* *Includes Unified Team of 1992; excludes Russia since then*

\# *Not including West/East Germany 1968–88*

TOP 10 ⭐
MEDAL WINNERS IN A SUMMER OLYMPICS CAREER

WINNER	COUNTRY	SPORT	YEARS	GOLD	SILVER	BRONZE	TOTAL
1 Larissa Latynina	USSR	Gymnastics	1956–64	9	5	4	18
2 Nikolay Andrianov	USSR	Gymnastics	1972–80	7	5	3	15
3 =Edoardo Mangiarotti	Italy	Fencing	1936–60	6	5	2	13
=Takashi Ono	Japan	Gymnastics	1952–64	5	4	4	13
=Boris Shakhlin	USSR	Gymnastics	1956–64	7	4	2	13
6 =Sawao Kato	Japan	Gymnastics	1968–76	8	3	1	12
=Paavo Nurmi	Finland	Athletics	1920–28	9	3	0	12
8 =Viktor Chukarin	USSR	Gymnastics	1952–56	7	3	1	11
=Vera Cáslavská	Czechoslovakia	Gymnastics	1964–68	7	4	0	11
=Carl Osburn	US	Shooting	1912–24	5	4	2	11
=Mark Spitz	US	Swimming	1968–72	9	1	1	11
=Matt Biondi	US	Swimming	1984–92	8	2	1	11

Larissa Latynina won six medals at each of three Games between 1956 and 1964. The only discipline at which she did not win a medal was on the beam in 1956, when she came fourth. The only Winter Games competitor who would be eligible for this list is Björn Dählie of Norway, who won a total of 12 medals (8 gold and 4 silver) for Nordic Skiing in the Olympics of 1992–98.

TOP 10 COUNTRIES AT THE SYDNEY OLYMPICS WITH THE HIGHEST RATIO OF MEDALS
(Country/medals per million population)

① Bahamas, 6.80 **②** Barbados, 3.76 **③** Iceland, 3.65 **④** Australia, 3.09
⑤ Jamaica, 2.72 **⑥** Cuba, 2.61 **⑦** Norway, 2.26 **⑧** Estonia, 2.07
⑨ Hungary, 1.68 **⑩** Belarus, 1.66

Canada, 0.46   Source: *eCountries*

The Bahamas, with a population of 294,000, tops this list of Olympic medal winners with one silver and one gold won by their female sprinters. Barbados came 2nd, having won just one bronze in the men's 100 m.

What sport was introduced in the 1998 Winter Olympics?
see p.247 for the answer
A Snowmobile racing
B Women's ski-jumping
C Snowboarding

TOP 10 ★

COMPETITOR-ATTENDED WINTER OLYMPICS

	HOST CITY	COUNTRY	YEAR	COMPETITORS
1	Nagano	Japan	1998	2,177
2	Albertville	France	1992	1,801
3	Lillehammer	Norway	1994	1,736
4	Calgary	Canada	1988	1,425
5	Sarajevo	Yugoslavia	1984	1,274
6	Grenoble	France	1968	1,158
7	Innsbruck	Austria	1976	1,123
8	Innsbruck	Austria	1964	1,091
9	Lake Placid	US	1980	1,072
10	Sapporo	Japan	1972	1,006

The first Winter Games at Chamonix, France, in 1924 were attended by 258 competitors representing 16 countries. Subsequent Games have seen both the numbers of competitors and countries generally increase: a total of 72 countries took part at the XVIII Games at Nagano.

TOP 10 ★

WINTER OLYMPIC MEDAL-WINNING COUNTRIES, 1908–98

	COUNTRY	GOLD	SILVER	BRONZE	TOTAL
1	Norway	83	87	69	239
2	Soviet Union*	87	63	67	217
3	US	59	59	41	159
4	Austria	39	52	53	144
5	Finland	38	49	48	135
6	Germany#	46	38	32	116
7	East Germany	39	36	35	110
8	Sweden	39	28	35	102
9	Switzerland	29	32	32	93
10	Canada	25	25	29	79

* Includes United Team of 1992; excludes Russia since then

Not including East/West Germany 1968–88

Figure skating was first featured at the 1908 Summer Olympics held in London, and ice hockey as part of the 1920 Summer Olympics in Antwerp.

FINNISH FIRST

At the 1998 Nagano Games, Finland added two gold, four silver, and six bronze medals to its tally, with Jani Soininen winning gold in the ski jumping event.

Canada's Jeremy Wotherspoon, the world's fastest speed skater, can cover 500 m in how many seconds?
see p.276 for the answer

A 34.63
B 35.21
C 37.18

TOP 10 ★
INDIVIDUAL GOLD MEDALLISTS AT THE WINTER OLYMPICS

	MEDALLIST/COUNTRY/SPORT	GOLD MEDALS
1	Bjørn Dählie, Nor, Nordic skiing	8
2 =	Lydia Skoblikova, USSR, Speed skating	6
=	Lyubov Yegorova, EUN*/Rus, Nordic skiing	6
4 =	Bonnie Blair, US, Speed skating	5
=	Eric Heiden, US, Speed skating	5
=	Larissa Lazurtina, EUN*/Rus, Nordic skiing	5
=	Clas Thunberg, Nor, Speed skating	5
8 =	Ivar Ballangrud, Nor, Speed skating	4
=	Yevgeni Grishin, USSR, Speed skating	4
=	Sixten Jernberg, Swe, Nordic skiing	4
=	Johan-Olav Koss, Nor, Speed skating	4
=	Galina Kulakova, USSR, Nordic skiing	4
=	Chun Lee-kyung, Kor, Short track speed skating	4
=	Matti Nykänen, Fin, Ski jumping	4
=	Nikolai Simyatov, USSR, Nordic skiing	4
=	Raisa Smetanina, USSR, Nordic skiing	4
=	Alexander Tikhonov, USSR, Biathlon	4

* EUN = Unified Team (Commonwealth of Independent States 1992)

TOP 10 ★
WINTER OLYMPIC MEDAL-WINNING COUNTRIES, 1908–98 (MEN'S EVENTS) *

	COUNTRY	GOLD	SILVER	BRONZE	TOTAL
1	Norway	76	79	56	211
2	Soviet Union#	52	35	35	122
3	Finland	29	38	35	102
4	Austria	26	33	37	96
5	Sweden	32	23	31	86
6	US	33	32	20	85
7	Switzerland	19	24	25	68
8	East Germany	24	19	23	66
9	Germany+	27	14	15	56
10	Italy	17	22	15	54

* In figure skating, men's singles and pairs have been counted together

\# Includes Unified Team of 1992; excludes Russia since then

\+ Not including East/West Germany 1968–88

The only person to win gold medals at both the Summer and Winter Games is Eddie Eagan of the US. After winning the 1920 light-heavyweight boxing title, he then went on to win a gold medal as a member of the American four-man bobsled team in 1932.

SNOW FALL

Seen here in an uncharacteristic pose, Nordic skier Bjørn Dählie has won a record eight gold medals at three Winter Olympics, 1992–98.

ON BOARD

Introduced at the 1998 Games, the snowboarding halfpipe event was won by Nicola Thost, adding to the tally of German medal winners.

TOP 10 ★
WINTER OLYMPIC MEDAL-WINNING COUNTRIES, 1908–98 (WOMEN'S EVENTS) *

	COUNTRY	GOLD	SILVER	BRONZE	TOTAL
1	Soviet Union#	35	28	32	95
2	US	26	27	21	74
3	Germany+	19	24	17	60
4	Austria	13	19	16	48
5	East Germany	15	17	12	44
6	Finland	9	11	13	33
7 =	Canada	11	9	8	28
=	Norway	7	8	13	28
9	Switzerland	10	8	7	25
10	Italy	7	8	9	24

* In figure skating, women's singles and ice dance have been counted together

\# Includes Unified Team of 1992; excludes Russia since then

\+ Not including East/West Germany 1968–88

Football Feats

TOP 10 ★
NFL PLAYERS WITH THE MOST CAREER POINTS

	PLAYER	POINTS
1	Gary Anderson*	2,059
2	George Blanda	2,002
3	Morten Andersen*	1,934
4	Norm Johnson	1,736
5	Nick Lowery	1,711
6	Jan Stenerud	1,699
7	Eddie Murray*	1,591
8	Al Del Greco*	1,568
9	Pat Leahy	1,470
10	Jim Turner	1,439

* Still active 2000 season   Source: NFL

TOP 10 ★
WINNING MARGINS IN THE SUPER BOWL

	GAME*	YEAR	MARGIN
1	San Francisco 49ers v. Denver Broncos	1990	45
2	Chicago Bears v. New England	1986	36
3	Dallas Cowboys v. Buffalo Bills	1993	35
4	Washington Redskins v. Denver Broncos	1988	32
5	Los Angeles Raiders v. Washington Redskins	1984	29
6	Baltimore Ravens v. New York Giants	2001	27
7	Green Bay Packers v. Kansas City Chiefs	1967	25
8	San Francisco 49ers v. San Diego Chargers	1995	23
9	San Francisco 49ers v. Miami Dolphins	1985	22
10	Dallas Cowboys v. Miami Dolphins	1972	21

* Winners listed first

Source: National Football League

TOP 10 🍁
CFL PLAYERS WITH THE MOST CAREER POINTS

	PLAYER	POINTS
1	Lui Passaglia	3,985
2	Mark McLoughlin	2,517
3	Paul Osbaldiston	2,510
4	Dave Ridgway	2,374
5	Dave Cutler	2,237
6	Trevor Kennerd	1,840
7	Bernie Ruoff	1,772
8	Terry Baker	1,760
9	Trow Westwood	1,648
10	Lance Chomyc	1,498

Source: Canadian Football League

TOP 10 ★
POINT SCORERS IN AN NFL SEASON

	PLAYER/TEAM	YEAR	POINTS
1	Paul Hornung, Green Bay Packers	1960	176
2	Gary Anderson, Minnesota Vikings	1998	164
3	Mark Moseley, Washington Redskins	1983	161
4	Marshall Faulk, St. Louis Rams	2000	160
5	Gino Cappelletti, Boston Patriots	1964	155*
6	Emmitt Smith, Dallas Cowboys	1995	150
7	Chip Lohmiller, Washington Redskins	1991	149
8	Gino Cappelletti, Boston Patriots	1961	147
9	Paul Hornung, Green Bay Packers	1961	146
10=	Jim Turner, New York Jets	1968	145
=	John Kasay, Carolina Panthers	1996	145
=	Mike Vanderjagt, Indianapolis Colts	1999	145

* Including a two-point conversion   Source: NFL

TOP 10 🍁
WINNING MARGINS IN THE GREY CUP

	GAME*	YEAR	MARGIN
1	Queen's University v. Regina Roughriders	1923	54
2	Hamilton Tigers v. Toronto Parkdale	1913	42
3	Winnipeg Blue Bombers v. Edmonton Eskimos	1990	39
4	Edmonton Eskimos v. Hamilton Tiger-Cats	1980	38
5=	Montreal Alouettes v. Edmonton Eskimos	1977	35
=	Toronto Argonauts v. Winnipeg Blue Bombers	1945	35
7=	Hamilton Tigers v. Regina Roughriders	1928	30
=	Winnipeg Blue Bombers v. Hamilton Tiger-Cats	1984	30
9	Hamilton Tiger-Cats v. Saskatchewan Roughriders	1957	25
10=	Toronto Argonauts v. Edmonton Eskimos	1997	24
=	Hamilton Tiger-Cats v. Edmonton Eskimos	1986	24

* Winners listed first   Source: CFL

TOP 10 🍁
PLAYERS WITH THE MOST PASSING YARDS IN A CFL CAREER

	PLAYER	PASSING YARDS
1	Damon Allen	50,789
2	Ron Lancaster	50,535
3	Matt Dunigan	43,857
4	Doug Flutie	41,355
5	Tracy Ham	40,534
6	Tom Clements	39,041
7	Kent Austin	36,030
8	Dieter Brock	34,830
9	Danny McManus	33,532
10	Tom Burgess	30,308

Source: Canadian Football League

Did You Know? Until improvements in the rules and equipment were introduced, American college football was one of the most dangerous of all team sports, the 1905 season resulting in 18 deaths and 159 other serious injuries.

TOP 10 ⭐
HEAVIEST PLAYERS IN THE NFL

PLAYER/TEAM	WEIGHT LB	KG
1 Aaron Gibson, Detroit Lions	380	172
2 Willie Jones, Kansas City Chiefs	372	169
3 L.J. Shelton, Arizona Cardinals	360	163
4 David Dixon, Minnesota Vikings	358	162
5 Anthony Clement, Arizona Cardinals	351	159
6 =Derrick Fletcher, Washington Redskins	350	159
=Stockar McDougle, Detroit Lions	350	159
8 Tra Thomas, Philadelphia Eagles	349	158
9 Yusuf Scott, Arizona Cardinals	348	158
10 =Jon Clark, Arizona Cardinals	346	157
=Korey Stringer, Minnesota Vikings	346	157

Source: *National Football League*

TOP 10 ⭐
MOST SUCCESSFUL TEAMS

TEAM	SUPER BOWL GAMES WINS	LOSSES	PTS*
1 Dallas Cowboys	5	3	13
2 San Francisco 49ers	5	0	10
3 Pittsburgh Steelers	4	1	9
4 Washington Redskins	3	2	8
5 Denver Broncos	2	4	8
6 =Green Bay Packers	3	1	7
=Oakland/ Los Angeles Raiders	3	1	7
8 Miami Dolphins	2	3	7
9 New York Giants	2	1	5
10 =Buffalo Bills	0	4	4
=Minnesota Vikings	0	4	4

* Based on two points for a Super Bowl win, and one for runner-up; wins take precedence over runners-up in determining ranking

Source: *National Football League*

TOP 10 ⭐
LARGEST NFL STADIUMS

STADIUM/HOME TEAM	CAPACITY
1 Pontiac Silverdome, Detroit Lions	80,311
2 FedEx Field, Washington Redskins	80,116
3 Giants Stadium, New York Giants/Jets	79,469
4 Arrowhead Stadium, Kansas City Chiefs	79,409
5 Ralph Wilson Stadium, Buffalo Bills	75,339
6 Pro Player Stadium, Miami Dolphins	75,192
7 Sun Devil Stadium, Arizona Cardinals	73,273
8 Ericsson Stadium, Carolina Panthers	73,250
9 Cleveland Browns Stadium, Cleveland Browns	73,200
10 Alltel Stadium, Jacksonville Jaguars	73,000

Source: *National Football League*

TOP 10 ⭐
LONGEST CAREERS OF NFL PLAYERS*

PLAYER/TEAM	YEARS
1 =Gary Anderson, Minnesota Vikings	19
=Morten Andersen, Atlanta Falcons	19
=Eddie Murray, Washington Redskins	19
4 =Darrell Green, Washington Redskins	18
=Trey Junkin, Arizona Cardinals	18
=Bruce Matthews, Tennessee Titans	18
7 =Irving Fryar, Washington Redskins	17
=Al Del Greco, Tennessee Titans	17
=Mike Horan, St. Louis Rams	17
=Warren Moon, Kansas City Chiefs	17

* Current players   Source: *NFL*

TOP 10 MOST SUCCESSFUL COACHES IN AN NFL CAREER
(Coach/games won)

1 Don Shula, 347   **2** George Halas, 324   **3** Tom Landry, 270   **4** Curly Lambeau, 229   **5** Chuck Noll, 209   **6** Chuck Knox, 193   **7** Dan Reeves*, 179   **8** Paul Brown, 170   **9** Bud Grant, 168   **10** Marv Levy, 154

* Still active 2000 season   Source: *National Football League*

THE FIRST ROSE BOWL

The Valley Hunt Club in Pasadena, California, first staged its Tournament of Roses in 1890. A celebration of California's mild winter weather, it grew in popularity and, following the event's famed parade, it was decided to stage a college football game. At the first-ever Rose Tournament game, held on New Year's Day 1902 at Tournament Park, the University of Michigan beat Stanford University with a score of 49–0 before a crowd of 8,000. So great was the defeat that the organizers decided not to stage the event again, the following year replacing it with a Roman-style chariot race. It was not until 1916 that football returned to the festivities, but as the crowd outgrew the seating capacity at Tournament Park, a new 57,000-seat stadium was constructed; the first game was held there on January 1, 1923. The stadium and the annual game played there were named the "Rose Bowl" by Harlan "Dusty" Hall, the Rose Tournament's press agent.

100 YEARS AGO

LATEST CANADIAN PRESS ATHLETES OF THE YEAR

MEN

YEAR	ATHLETE	SPORT
2000	Mike Weir	Golf
Century*	Wayne Gretsky	Hockey
1998	Larry Walker	Baseball
1997	Jacques Villeneuve	Auto racing
1996	Donovan Bailey	Track
1995	Jacques Villeneuve	Auto racing
1994	Elvis Stojko	Figure skating
1993	Mario Lemieux	Hockey
1992	Mark Tewksbury	Swimming
1991	Kurt Browning	Figure skating

WOMEN

YEAR	ATHLETE	SPORT
2000	Lorie Kane	Golf
Century*	Nancy Greene	Skiing
1998	Lorie Kane	Golf
1997	Lorie Kane	Golf
1996	Alison Sydor	Cycling
1995	Susan Auch	Speed skating
1994	Myriam Bédard	Biathlon
1993	Kate Pace	Skiing
1992	Silken Laumann	Rowing
1991	Silken Laumann	Rowing

* No Athlete of the Year was awarded in 1999. Instead, Wayne Gretsky and Nancy Greene were each voted Athlete of the Century.

Source: Canadian Press/Broadcast News

THE 10 LATEST WINNERS OF THE JESSE OWENS INTERNATIONAL TROPHY

(Year/athlete/sport)

❶ 2001 Marion Jones, athletics ❷ 2000 Lance Armstrong, cycling ❸ 1999 Marion Jones, athletics ❹ 1998 Haile Gebrselassie, athletics ❺ 1997 Michael Johnson, athletics ❻ 1996 Michael Johnson, athletics ❼ 1995 Johann Olav Koss, speed skating ❽ 1994 Wang Junxia, athletics ❾ 1993 Vitaly Scherbo, gymnastics ❿ 1992 Mike Powell, athletics

The Jesse Owens International Trophy has been presented by the International Amateur Athletic Association since 1981. It is named in honor of American athlete Jesse Owens (1913–80).

FASTEST TIMES IN THE BOSTON MARATHON

MEN

	RUNNER/COUNTRY	YEAR	HR:MIN:SEC
1	Cosmas Ndeti, Kenya	1994	2:07:15
2	Andres Espinosa, Mexico	1994	2:07:19
3	Moses Tanui, Kenya	1998	2:07:34
4	Joseph Chebet, Kenya	1998	2:07:37
5	Rob de Castella, Aus.	1986	2:07:51
6	Gert Thys, S. Africa	1998	2:07:52
7	Jackson Kipngok, Kenya	1994	2:08:08
8	Hwant Young-Cho, Korea	1984	2:08:09
9	Ibrahim Hussein, Kenya	1992	2:08:14
10	Gelindo Bordin, Italy	1980	2:08:19

Source: Boston Athletic Association

WOMEN

	RUNNER/COUNTRY	YEAR	HR:MIN:SEC
1	Uta Pippig, Germany	1994	2:21:45
2	Joan Benoit, US	1983	2:22:43
3	Fatuma Roba, Ethiopia	1998	2:23:21
4	Fatuma Roba	1999	2:23:25
5	Valentina Yegorova, Russia	1994	2:23:33
6	Olga Markova, CIS	1992	2:23:43
7	Wanda Panfil, Poland	1991	2:24:18
8	Rosa Mota, Portugal	1988	2:24:30
9	Ingrid Kristiansen, Norway	1989	2:24:33
10	Ingrid Kristiansen	1986	2:24:55

FASTEST MILES EVER RUN

	ATHLETE/COUNTRY	YEAR	TIME
1	Hicham El Guerrouj, Morocco	1999	3:43.13
2	Noah Ngeny, Kenya	1999	3:43.40
3	Novreddine Morceli, Algeria	1993	3:44.39
4	Hicham El Guerrouj	1998	3:44.60
5	Hicham El Guerrouj	1997	3:44.90
6	Novreddine Morceli	1995	3:45.19
7	Hicham El Guerrouj	1997	3:45.64
8	Hicham El Guerrouj	2000	3:45.96
9	Hicham El Guerrouj	2000	3:46.24
10	Steve Cram, UK	1985	3:46.32

The current world record is almost 13 percent faster than Roger Bannister's breakthrough first sub-four-minute mile of 1954, and over 20 percent faster than the unofficial record set by British runner Walter Chinnery in 1868.

HIGHEST POLE VAULTS*

	ATHLETE/COUNTRY	YEAR	HEIGHT METERS
1	Sergei Bubka, Ukraine#	1993	6.15
2	Maxim Tarasov, Russia	1999	6.05
3 =	Okkert Brits, South Africa	1995	6.03
=	Jeff Hartwig, US	2000	6.03
5	Rodion Gataullin, USSR#	1989	6.02
6	Igor Trandenkov, Russia	1996	6.01
7 =	Jeane Galfione, France	1999	6.00
=	Tim Lobinger, Germany	1997	6.00
=	Dmitri Markov, Belarus	1998	6.00
10	Lawrence Johnson, US	1996	5.98

* Highest by each athlete only

\# Indoor

One of Canada's first stars in pole vaulting was Victor Pickard, who competed in the 1924 and 1928 Olympic Games and 1930 Commonwealth Games. Sylvanus Apps, who later became an NHL player, won a gold medal in the 1934 Commonwealth Games.

TOP 10 ★
FASTEST WOMEN EVER*

ATHLETE/COUNTRY	YEAR	SECONDS
1 Florence Griffith Joyner, US	1988	10.49
2 Marion Jones, US	1998	10.65
3 Christine Arron, France	1998	10.73
4 Merlene Ottey, Jamaica	1996	10.74
5 Evelyn Ashford, US	1984	10.76
6 Irina Privalova, Russia	1994	10.77
7 Dawn Sowell, US	1989	10.78
8 Inger Miller, US	1999	10.79
9 Marlies Göhr, East Germany	1983	10.81
10=Gail Devers, US	1992	10.82
=Gwen Torrence, US	1994	10.82

* Based on fastest time for the 100 meters

TOP 10 ★
FASTEST MEN EVER*

ATHLETE/COUNTRY	YEAR	SECONDS
1 Maurice Greene, US	1999	9.79
2 =Donovan Bailey, Canada	1996	9.84
=Bruny Surin, Canada	1999	9.84
4 Leroy Burrell, US	1994	9.85
5 =Ato Boldon, Trinidad	1998	9.86
=Frank Fredericks, Namibia	1996	9.86
=Carl Lewis, US	1991	9.86
8 =Linford Christie, UK	1993	9.87
=Obadele Thompson, Barbados	1998	9.87
10 Dennis Mitchell, US	1991	9.91

* Based on fastest time for the 100 meters

Many would argue that Michael Johnson (US) should be in this category with his remarkable 200-meter record of 19.32 seconds (equivalent to a 100-meter time of 9.66 seconds), but his best 100-meter time is only 10.09 seconds.

KEEPING UP WITH THE JONES

Marion Jones' personal best of 10.65 seconds for the 100 meters makes her the fastest living female athlete. The record-holder at 10.49 was Florence Griffith Joyner, who died in 1998.

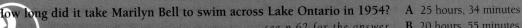

How long did it take Marilyn Bell to swim across Lake Ontario in 1954?

see p.62 for the answer

A 25 hours, 34 minutes
B 20 hours, 55 minutes
C 18 hours, 17 minutes

251

Basketball Bests

DIVISION 1 NCAA TEAMS

COLLEGE	DIVISION 1 WINS
1 Kentucky	1,787
2 North Carolina	1,778
3 Kansas	1,732
4 Duke	1,635
5 St. John's	1,610
6 Temple	1,563
7 Syracuse	1,546
8 Pennsylvania	1,505
9 Indiana	1,493
10 Oregon State	1,485

Source: *NCAA*

NCAA basketball was launched on March 17, 1939. Ironically, James Naismith, basketball's inventor, died on November 28 of the same year.

POINT SCORERS IN AN NBA CAREER

PLAYER	TOTAL POINTS*
1 Kareem Abdul-Jabbar	38,387
2 Karl Malone#	32,919
3 Wilt Chamberlain	31,419
4 Michael Jordan	29,277
5 Moses Malone	27,409
6 Elvin Hayes	27,313
7 Oscar Robertson	26,710
8 Dominique Wilkins	26,668
9 Hakeem Olajuwon#	26,511
10 John Havlicek	25,395

* Regular season games only
\# Still active at end of 2000–01 season
Source: *NBA*

COACHES IN THE NBA

COACH	GAMES WON*
1 Lenny Wilkens#	1,226
2 Pat Riley#	1,049
3 Don Nelson#	979
4 Bill Fitch	944
5 Red Auerbach	938
6 Dick Motta	935
7 Jack Ramsay	864
8 Cotton Fitzsimmons	832
9 =Gene Shue	784
=Jerry Sloan#	784

* Regular season games only
\# Still active at end of 2000–01 season
Source: *NBA*

Lenny Wilkens reached his 1,000th win on March 1, 1996, when the Atlanta Hawks beat the Cleveland Cavaliers 74–68 at The Omni. Pat Riley, as coach of the LA Lakers, the New York Knicks, and the Miami Heat, acquired the best percentage record, with 1,049 wins from 1,515 games, representing a 0.692 percent success rate.

TOP 10 COACHES IN THE NCAA

(Coach/wins)

❶ Dean Smith, 879 ❷ Adolph Rupp, 876 ❸ Jim Phelan*, 816 ❹ Henry Iba, 767 ❺ Bob Knight*, 764 ❻ Lefty Driesell*, 762 ❼ = Jerry Tarkanian*, 759; = Ed Diddle, 759 ❾ Phog Allen, 746 ❿ Lou Henson*, 740

* Still active at end of 2000–01 season   Source: *NCAA*

BIGGEST ARENAS IN THE NBA

ARENA/LOCATION	HOME TEAM	CAPACITY
1 **The Palace of Auburn Hills**, Auburn Hills, Michigan	Detroit Pistons	22,076
2 **United Center**, Chicago, Illinois	Chicago Bulls	21,711
3 **MCI Center**, Washington, DC	Washington Wizards	20,674
4 **Gund Arena**, Cleveland, Ohio	Cleveland Cavaliers	20,562
5 **Alamodome**, San Antonio, Texas	San Antonio Spurs	20,557
6 **First Union Center**, Philadelphia, Pennsylvania	Philadelphia 76ers	20,444
7 **Charlotte Coliseum**, Charlotte, North Carolina	Charlotte Hornets	20,085
8 **Continental Airlines Arena**, East Rutherford, New Jersey	New Jersey Nets	20,049
9 **The Rose Garden**, Portland, Oregon	Portland Trailblazers	19,980
10 **Delta Center**, Salt Lake City, Utah	Utah Jazz	19,911

The smallest arena is the 15,200-capacity Miami Arena, home of the Miami Heat. The largest-ever NBA stadium was the Louisiana Superdome, completed in May 1995 at a cost of $173 million, and used by Utah Jazz from then until 1979; the stadium was capable of holding crowds of up to 47,284.
Source: *NBA*

PLAYERS WITH THE HIGHEST POINTS AVERAGES

PLAYER	POINTS SCORED	POINTS AVERAGE
1 Michael Jordan	29,277	31.5
2 Wilt Chamberlain	31,419	30.1
3 Shaquille O'Neal*	16,812	27.7
4 Elgin Baylor	23,149	27.4
5 Jerry West	25,192	27.0
6 Bob Pettit	20,880	26.4
7 George Gervin	20,708	26.2
8 Karl Malone*	32,919	25.9
9 Oscar Robertson	26,710	25.7
10 Dominique Wilkins	26,668	24.8

* Still active at end of 2000–01 season
Source: *NBA*

Which arena is the largest in the National Hockey League?
see p.271 for the answer
A Air Canada Centre, Toronto
B United Center, Chicago
C Molson Centre, Montreal

top10 ★

TOP 10 TEAMS WITH THE MOST NCAA CHAMPIONSHIP WINS

(College/wins)

❶ UCLA, 11 ❷ Kentucky, 7 ❸ Indiana, 5 ❹ = North Carolina, 3; = Duke, 3 ❻ = Cincinnati, 2; = Kansas, 2; = Louisville, 2; = Michigan State, 2; = North Carolina State, 2; = Oklahoma A & M*, 2; = San Francisco, 2

* Now known as Oklahoma State

TOP 10 ★
POINTS SCORED IN THE WNBA

PLAYER/GAME	DATE	PTS
1 **Cynthia Cooper**, Houston v Sacramento	July 25, 1997	44
2 **Cynthia Cooper**, Houston v Utah	Aug 16, 1999	42
3 **Cynthia Cooper**, Houston v Charlotte	Aug 11, 1997	39
4 **Jennifer Gillom**, Phoenix v Cleveland	Aug 10, 1998	36
5 =**Cynthia Cooper**, Houston v Los Angeles	Aug 1, 1997	34
=**Cynthia Cooper**, Houston v Phoenix	Aug 7, 1997	34
=**Ruthie Bolton-Holifield**, Sacramento v Utah	Aug 8, 1997	34
=**Ruthie Bolton-Holifield**, Sacramento v Cleveland	Aug 12, 1997	34
=**Cynthia Cooper**, Houston v Sacramento	July 3, 1998	34
=**Cynthia Cooper**, Houston v Detroit	Aug 7, 1998	34

Source: WNBA

TOP 10 ★
FREE THROW PERCENTAGES

	PLAYER	ATTEMPTS	MADE	PERCENTAGE
1	Mark Price	2,362	2,135	90.4
2	Rick Barry	4,243	3,818	90.0
3	Calvin Murphy	3,864	3,445	89.2
4	Scott Skiles	1,741	1,548	88.9
5	Larry Bird	4,471	3,960	88.6
6	Reggie Miller*	6,038	5,338	88.4
7	Bill Sharman	3,559	3,143	88.3
8	Ricky Pierce	3,871	3,389	87.5
9	Kiki Vandeweghe	3,997	3,484	87.2
10	Jeff Malone	3,383	2,947	87.1

* Still active at end of 2000–01 season
Source: NBA

TOP 10 PLAYERS WITH THE MOST CAREER ASSISTS

(Player/assists)

❶ John Stockton*, 14,501 ❷ Magic Johnson, 10,141 ❸ Oscar Robertson, 9,887 ❹ Mark Jackson*, 9,235 ❺ Isiah Thomas, 9,061 ❻ Maurice Cheeks, 7,392 ❼ Lenny Wilkens, 7,211 ❽ Rod Strickland*, 7,026 ❾ Bob Cousy, 6,995 ❿ Guy Rodgers, 6,917

* Still active at end of 2000–01 season
Source: NBA

MAGIC TOUCH
Magic (Earvin) Johnson turned professional in 1979, becoming one of the NBA's most legendary players.

TOP 10 ★
PLAYERS TO HAVE PLAYED MOST GAMES IN THE NBA AND ABA

	PLAYER	GAMES PLAYED*
1	Robert Parish	1,611
2	Kareem Abdul-Jabbar	1,560
3	Moses Malone	1,455
4	Buck Williams	1,348
5	John Stockton#	1,339
6	Artis Gilmore	1,329
7	Elvin Hayes	1,303
8	Caldwell Jones	1,299
9	Sam Perkins#	1,286
10	Karl Malone#	1,273

* Regular season only
 # Still active at end of 2000–01 season
Source: NBA

253

Combat Sports

BOXING CHAMPIONS WITH THE MOST CONSECUTIVE SUCCESSFUL DEFENSES*

FIGHTER/DIVISION/REIGN YEARS	DEFENSES
1 Joe Louis#, Heavyweight, 1937–49	25
2 Ricardo Lopez, Strawweight (WBC), 1990–	22
3 =Henry Armstrong#, Welterweight, 1938–40	19
=Eusebio Pedroza, Featherweight (WBA), 1978–85	19
=Khaosai Galaxy, Junior bantamweight (WBA), 1984–91	19
6 =Wilfredo Gomez, Junior featherweight (WBC), 1977–83	17
=Myung Woo Yuh, Junior flyweight (WBA), 1985–91	17
8 Orlando Canizales, Bantamweight (IBF), 1988–94	16
9 =Bob Foster#, Light heavyweight, 1968–74	14
=Carlos Monzon#, Middleweight, 1970–77	14
=Miguel Canto, Flyweight (WBC), 1975–79	14

* One champion per division listed

Undisputed champion

BOXERS WITH THE MOST KNOCKOUTS IN A CAREER

BOXER/COUNTRY*	CAREER	KNOCKOUTS
1 Archie Moore	1936–63	129
2 Young Stribling	1921–63	126
3 Billy Bird	1920–48	125
4 Sam Langford, Canada	1902–26	116
5 George Odwell	1930–45	114
6 Sugar Ray Robinson	1940–65	110
7 Sandy Saddler	1944–65	103
8 Henry Armstrong	1931–45	100
9 Jimmy Wilde, UK	1911–23	99
10 Len Wickwar	1928–47	93

* All from the US unless otherwise stated

Although this is the most generally accepted Top 10, boxing historians disagree considerably on this subject. Some, for example, include exhibition matches as well as the professional bouts on which this list is based. As the dates suggest, careers of this length, and the numbers of contests implied by knockout figures in the hundreds, are things of the past.

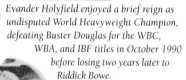

HEAVYWEIGHT CHAMP

Evander Holyfield enjoyed a brief reign as undisputed World Heavyweight Champion, defeating Buster Douglas for the WBC, WBA, and IBF titles in October 1990 before losing two years later to Riddick Bowe.

BOXERS WHO HAVE FOUGHT THE MOST BOUTS*

BOXER/COUNTRY#	YEARS	BOUTS
1 Len Wickwar	1928–47	466
2 Wildcat Monte	1923–37	406
3 Jack Britton	1904–30	357
4 Johnny Dundee, Italy	1910–32	340
5 Billy Bird	1920–48	318
6 George Marsden	1928–46	311
7 Duke Tramel	1922–36	305
8 Maxie Rosenbloom	1923–39	300
9 Harry Greb	1913–26	299
10 Sam Langford, Canada	1902–26	298

* Excluding exhibition bouts

All from the US unless otherwise stated

LATEST UNDISPUTED WORLD HEAVYWEIGHT CHAMPIONS

YEAR	FIGHTER/COUNTRY*
1999	Lennox Lewis, UK
1992	Riddick Bowe
1990	Evander Holyfield
1990	James Buster Douglas
1987	Mike Tyson
1978	Leon Spinks
1974	Muhammed Ali
1973	George Foreman
1970	Joe Frazier
1964	Cassius Clay

* All from the US unless otherwise stated

"Undisputed" champions are those who are recognized by the four main governing bodies: the World Boxing Council (WBC), World Boxing Association (WBA), International Boxing Federation (IBF), and World Boxing Organization (WBO).

JUDO CHAMPIONS
Brazil gained two silver medals for judo at the 2000 Olympics, one of them won by Tiago Camilo, seen here defeating Gil Offer of Israel in the Lightweight class.

TOP 10 ★
OLYMPIC FREESTYLE WRESTLING COUNTRIES

	COUNTRY	MEDALS			
		GOLD	SILVER	BRONZE	TOTAL
1	US	44	35	24	103
2	USSR*	31	17	15	63
3 =	Bulgaria	7	17	9	33
=	Japan	16	9	8	33
=	Turkey	16	11	6	33
6 =	Iran	5	9	12	26
=	Sweden	8	10	8	26
8	Finland	8	7	10	25
9	Korea	4	7	8	19
10	Great Britain	3	4	10	17
	Canada	1	5	5	11

* Includes United Team of 1992; excludes Russia since then

Freestyle wrestling was introduced in the 1904 Olympic Games.

TOP 10 ★
OLYMPIC GRECO-ROMAN WRESTLING COUNTRIES

	COUNTRY	MEDALS			
		GOLD	SILVER	BRONZE	TOTAL
1	USSR*	37	19	13	69
2	Finland	19	21	19	59
3	Sweden	20	16	19	55
4	Hungary	15	10	11	36
5	Bulgaria	9	14	7	30
6	Romania	6	8	13	27
7	Germany#	4	13	8	25
8	Poland	5	8	6	19
9 =	Italy	5	4	9	18
=	Turkey	11	4	3	18

* Includes United Team of 1992; excludes Russia since then

 # Not including West/East Germany 1968–88

The principal difference between freestyle and Greco-Roman wrestling is that in the latter competitors may not seize their opponents below the hips or grip using their legs. Canada has never won an Olympic medal in this sport.

TOP 10 ★
OLYMPIC JUDO COUNTRIES

	COUNTRY	MEDALS			
		GOLD	SILVER	BRONZE	TOTAL
1	Japan	23	12	13	48
2	France	10	5	17	32
3	Korea	7	10	13	30
4	USSR*	7	5	15	27
5	Cuba	5	7	8	20
6	Great Britain	–	7	9	16
7	Netherlands	4	–	7	11
8 =	Brazil	2	3	5	10
=	China	4	1	5	10
=	Germany#	1	1	8	10
=	Italy	2	3	5	10
	Canada	–	2	2	4

* Includes Unified Team of 1992; excludes Russia since then

 # Not including West/East Germany 1968–88

Men's judo debuted at the 1964 Tokyo Olympics, women's judo at the 1992 Barcelona Games.

TOP 10 ★
OLYMPIC FENCING COUNTRIES

	COUNTRY	MEDALS			
		GOLD	SILVER	BRONZE	TOTAL
1	France	39	38	33	110
2	Italy	40	36	26	102
3	Hungary	33	20	26	79
4	USSR*	19	17	18	54
5	Germany#	6	8	9	23
6	Poland	4	8	8	20
7	US	2	6	11	19
8	West Germany	7	8	1	16
9	Belgium	5	3	5	13
10	Romania	3	3	6	12

* Includes Unified Team of 1992; excludes Russia since then

 # Not including West/East Germany 1968–88

Fencing was introduced at the first modern Olympics in 1896. Hungarian competitor Aladár Gerevich (1910–91) achieved the unique feat of winning seven gold medals at six consecutive Games, spanning the 28 years from 1932 to 1960.

THE 10 WRESTLING WEIGHT DIVISIONS
(Weight/limit in lb/kg)

❶ **Heavyweight plus**, over 220/over 100 ❷ **Heavyweight**, 220/100
❸ **Light-heavyweight**, 198/90 ❹ **Middleweight**, 181/82 ❺ **Welterweight**, 163/74
❻ **Lightweight**, 150/68 ❼ **Featherweight**, 137/62 ❽ **Bantamweight**, 126/57
❾ **Flyweight**, 115/52 ❿ **Light-flyweight**, 106/48

Did You Know? Italian-born Angelo Parsi won four Olympic medals in judo for two different countries, competing for Great Britain in 1972, when he won a bronze, and for France in 1980 and 1984, winning a gold and two silvers.

Baseball Teams

NEWEST MAJOR LEAGUE TEAMS

TEAM	AL/NL*	1ST SEASON
1 = Arizona Diamondbacks	NL	1998
= Tampa Bay Devil Rays	AL	1998
3 = Colorado Rockies	NL	1993
= Florida Marlins	NL	1993
5 = Seattle Mariners	AL	1977
= Toronto Blue Jays	AL	1977
7 = Kansas City Royals	AL	1969
= Montreal Expos	NL	1969
= Seattle Pilots/ Milwaukee Brewers	AL	1969
10 = Houston Astros	NL	1962
= New York Mets	NL	1962

* AL = American League; NL = National League

Source: *Major League Baseball*

AVERAGE ATTENDANCES

TEAM	AVERAGE ATTENDANCE (2000)
1 Cleveland Indians	42,671
2 St. Louis Cardinals	41,036
3 San Francisco Giants	40,973
4 Colorado Rockies	40,898
5 Baltimore Orioles	40,428
6 New York Yankees	40,346
7 Atlanta Braves	39,930
8 Seattle Mariners	38,868
9 Houston Astros	37,757
10 Los Angeles Dodgers	37,088

Source: *Major League Baseball*

BIGGEST SINGLE GAME WINS IN THE WORLD SERIES

TEAMS*/GAME	DATE	SCORE
1 New York Yankees v New York Giants (Game 2)	Oct 2, 1936	18–4
2 New York Yankees v Pittsburgh Pirates (Game 2)	Oct 6, 1960	16–3
3 = New York Yankees v New York Giants (Game 5)	Oct 9, 1951	13–1
= New York Yankees v Pittsburgh Pirates (Game 6)	Oct 12, 1960	12–0
= Detroit Tigers v St. Louis Cardinals (Game 6)	Oct 9, 1968	13–1
= New York Yankees v Milwaukee Brewers (Game 6)	Oct 19, 1982	13–1
7 = New York Yankees v Philadelphia Athletics (Game 6)	Oct 26, 1911	13–2
= St. Louis Cardinals v Detroit Tigers (Game 7)	Oct 9, 1934	11–0
= Chicago White Sox v Los Angeles Dodgers (Game 1)	Oct 1, 1959	11–0
= Kansas City Royals v St. Louis Cardinals (Game 7)	Oct 27, 1985	11–0
= Atlanta Braves v New York Yankees (Game 1)	Oct 20, 1996	12–1

* Winners listed first

Source: *Major League Baseball*

TOTAL ATTENDANCES OF EACH YEAR IN THE PAST DECADE

YEAR	ATTENDANCE
2000	71,755,353
1999	70,139,380
1998	70,372,221
1997	63,196,222
1996	60,097,381
1995	50,469,236*
1994	50,010,016*
1993	70,256,459
1992	55,872,271
1991	56,813,760

* Strike/lockout year

Source: *Major League Baseball*

LATEST WINNERS OF THE WORLD SERIES

YEAR*	WINNER/LEAGUE LOSER/LEAGUE	SCORE
2000	New York (AL) New York (NL)	4–1
1999	New York (AL) Atlanta (NL)	4–0
1998	New York (AL) San Diego (NL)	4–0
1997	Florida (NL) Cleveland (AL)	4–3
1996	New York (AL) Atlanta (NL)	4–2
1995	Atlanta (NL) Cleveland (AL)	4–2
1993	Toronto (AL) Philadelphia (NL)	4–2
1992	Toronto (AL) Atlanta (NL)	4–2
1991	Minnesota (AL) Atlanta (NL)	4–2
1990	Cincinnati (NL) Oakland (AL)	4–0

* The 1994 event was canceled due to a players' strike

AL = American League NL = National League

Source: *Major League Baseball*

THE 10 MAJOR LEAGUE PLAYERS' SALARIES OF THE LAST DECADE

(Year/average salary in US$)

1 2000 1,995,025 2 1999 1,720,050 3 1998 1,441,406 4 1997 1,383,578
5 1996 1,176,967 6 1995 1,071,029 7 1994 1,188,679 8 1993 1,120,254
9 1992 1,084,408 10 1991 891,188

Source: *Associated Press*

TOP 10 ★
TEAMS WITH THE MOST WORLD SERIES WINS

	TEAM*	WINS
1	New York Yankees	26
2=	Philadelphia/Kansas City/Oakland Athletics	9
=	St. Louis Cardinals	9
4	Brooklyn/Los Angeles Dodgers	6
5=	Boston Red Sox	5
=	Cincinnati Reds	5
=	New York/San Francisco Giants	5
=	Pittsburgh Pirates	5
9	Detroit Tigers	4
10=	Boston/Milwaukee/Atlanta Braves	3
=	St. Louis/Baltimore Orioles	3
=	Washington Senators/Minnesota Twins	3

* Teams separated by / indicate changes of franchise and are regarded as the same team for Major League record purposes

Source: *Major League Baseball*

Major League baseball started in the US with the formation of the National League in 1876. The rival American League was started in 1901, and two years later Pittsburgh, champion of the National League, invited American League champion Boston to take part in a best-of-nine games series to establish the "real" champion. Boston won 5–3. The following year the National League champion, New York, refused to play Boston, and there was no World Series. However, it was resumed in 1905 and has been held every year since, except in 1994 when a players' strike curtailed the season. It has been a best-of-seven games series since 1905, with the exception of 1919–21 when it reverted to a nine-game series.

TOP 10 ★
BASEBALL TEAM PAYROLLS

	TEAM	AVERAGE 2000 SALARY (US$)	TOTAL 2000 PAYROLL (US$)
1	New York Yankees	3,190,974	92,538,260
2	Los Angeles Dodgers	3,263,862	88,124,286
3	Atlanta Braves	2,817,928	84,537,836
4	Baltimore Orioles	2,808,532	81,447,435
5	Arizona Diamondbacks	2,893,851	81,027,833
6	New York Mets	3,180,391	79,509,776
7	Boston Red Sox	2,598,011	77,940,333
8	Cleveland Indians	2,918,495	75,880,871
9	Texas Rangers	2,722,920	70,795,921
10	Tampa Bay Devil Rays	2,024,682	62,765,129

Source: *Associated Press*

TOP 10 ★
LARGEST MAJOR LEAGUE BALLPARKS*

	STADIUM	HOME TEAM	CAPACITY
1	Qualcomm Stadium	San Diego Padres	66,307
2	Veterans Stadium	Philadelphia Phillies	62,411
3	Dodger Stadium	Los Angeles Dodgers	56,000
4	Shea Stadium	New York Mets	55,775
5	Yankee Stadium	New York Yankees	55,070
6	Cinergy Field	Cincinnati Reds	52,953
7	SkyDome	Toronto Blue Jays	50,516
8	Coors Field	Colorado Rockies	50,249
9	Turner Field	Atlanta Braves	50,062
10	Busch Stadium	St. Louis Cardinals	49,738

* By capacity

Source: *Major League Baseball*

Stadium capacities vary constantly, some being adjusted according to the event: Veterans Stadium, for example, holds fewer spectators for baseball games than it does for football games.

TOP 10 ★
OLDEST STADIUMS IN MAJOR LEAGUE BASEBALL

	STADIUM	HOME CLUB	FIRST GAME
1	Fenway Park	Boston Red Sox	Apr 20, 1912
2	Wrigley Field	Chicago Cubs	Apr 23, 1914
3	Yankee Stadium	New York Yankees	Apr 18, 1923
4	Dodger Stadium	Los Angeles Dodgers	Apr 10, 1962
5	Shea Stadium	New York Mets	Apr 17, 1964
6	Edison International Field of Anaheim*	Anaheim Angels	Apr 19, 1966
7	Busch Stadium	St. Louis Cardinals	May 12, 1966
8	Qualcomm Stadium#	San Diego Padres	Apr 5, 1968
9	Network Associates Coliseum+	Oakland Athletics	Apr 17, 1968
10	Cinergy Field	Cincinnati Reds	June 30, 1970

* Formerly known as Anaheim Stadium

Formerly known as Jack Murphy Stadium

+ Formerly known as Oakland-Alameda County Coliseum

Source: *Major League Baseball*

Having outgrown its former Huntington Avenue ballpark, the Boston Red Sox moved to Fenway Park. Their inaugural game, when they defeated the New York Highlanders before a crowd of 27,000, was sadly overshadowed by the sinking of the *Titanic*, which occurred in the same week.

Where is John Lennon's Rolls-Royce Phantom V located?
see p.125 for the answer
A Royal British Columbia Museum, Victoria, BC
B Smithsonian Institute, Washington, DC
C Abbey Road Museum, London, UK

Baseball Stars

FIRST PITCHERS TO THROW PERFECT GAMES

PLAYER/MATCH		DATE
1	Lee Richmond, Worcester v Cleveland	June 12, 1880
2	Monte Ward, Providence v Buffalo	June 17, 1880
3	Cy Young, Boston v Philadelphia	May 5, 1904
4	Addie Joss, Cleveland v Chicago	Oct 2, 1908
5	Charlie Robertson, Chicago v Detroit	Apr 30, 1922
6	Don Larsen*, New York v Brooklyn	Oct 8, 1956
7	Jim Bunning, Philadelphia v New York	June 21, 1964
8	Sandy Koufax, Los Angeles v Chicago	Sep 9, 1965
9	Catfish Hunter, Oakland v Minnesota	May 8, 1968
10	Len Barker, Cleveland v Toronto	May 15, 1981

* Larsen's perfect game was, uniquely, in the World Series.

TOP 10 ★

PLAYERS MOST AT-BAT IN A CAREER

PLAYER		AT-BAT
1	Pete Rose	14,053
2	Hank Aaron	12,364
3	Carl Yastrzemski	11,988
4	Ty Cobb	11,429
5	Eddie Murray	11,336
6	Cal Ripken, Jr.	11,074
7	Robin Yount	11,008
8	Dave Winfield	11,003
9	Stan Musial	10,972
10	Willie Mays	10,881

Source: *Major League Baseball*

TOP 10 ★

PLAYERS WHO PLAYED THE MOST GAMES IN A CAREER

PLAYER		GAMES
1	Pete Rose	3,562
2	Carl Yastrzemski	3,308
3	Hank Aaron	3,298
4	Ty Cobb	3,034
5=	Eddie Murray	3,026
=	Stan Musial	3,026
7	Willie Mays	2,992
8	Dave Winfield	2,973
9	Rusty Staub	2,951
10	Brooks Robinson	2,896

Source: *Major League Baseball*

TOP 10 ★

PLAYERS WITH THE MOST CAREER STRIKEOUTS

PLAYER		STRIKEOUTS
1	Nolan Ryan	5,714
2	Steve Carlton	4,136
3	Bert Blyleven	3,701
4	Tom Seaver	3,640
5	Don Sutton	3,574
6	Gaylord Perry	3,534
7	Walter Johnson	3,508
8	Roger Clemens*	3,504
9	Phil Niekro	3,342
10	Ferguson Jenkins	3,192

* Still active 2000 season

Source: *Major League Baseball*

Nolan Ryan was known as the "Babe Ruth of strikeout pitchers," pitching faster (a record 162.5 km/h [101 mph]) and longer (27 seasons – 1966 and 1968–93) than any previous player. As well as his 5,714 strikeouts, including 383 in one season, he walked 2,795 batters and allowed the fewest hits (6.55) per nine innings.

TOP 10 ★

PITCHERS WITH THE MOST CAREER WINS

PLAYER		WINS
1	Cy Young	511
2	Walter Johnson	417
3=	Grover Alexander	373
=	Christy Mathewson	373
5	Warren Spahn	363
6=	Pud Galvin	361
=	Kid Nichols	361
8	Tim Keefe	344
9	Steve Carlton	329
10=	John Clarkson	326
=	Eddie Plank	326

Source: *Major League Baseball*

TOP 10 ★

PLAYERS WITH THE HIGHEST CAREER BATTING AVERAGES

PLAYER		AT-BAT	HITS	AVERAGE*
1	Ty Cobb	11,434	4,189	.366
2	Rogers Hornsby	8,173	2,930	.358
3	Joe Jackson	4,981	1,772	.356
4	Ed Delahanty	7,505	2,597	.346
5	Tris Speaker	10,195	3,514	.345
6=	Billy Hamilton	6,268	2,158	.344
=	Ted Williams	7,706	2,654	.344
8=	Dan Brouthers	6,711	2,296	.342
=	Harry Heilmann	7,787	2,660	.342
=	Babe Ruth	8,399	2,873	.342

* Calculated by dividing the number of hits by the number of times a batter was "at bat"

Source: *Major League Baseball*

Second only to the legendary Ty Cobb, Rogers Hornsby stands as the best second-hitting baseman of all time, with an average of over .400 in a five-year period. Baseball's greatest right-handed hitter, slugging 20-plus homers on seven occasions, he achieved a career average of .358.

THE 10 ★
FIRST PLAYERS TO HIT FOUR HOME RUNS IN ONE GAME

	PLAYER	CLUB	DATE
1	Bobby Lowe	Boston	May 30, 1884
2	Ed Delahanty	Philadelphia	July 13, 1896
3	Lou Gehrig	New York	June 3, 1932
4	Chuck Klein	Philadelphia	July 10, 1936
5	Pat Seerey	Chicago	July 18, 1948
6	Gil Hodges	Brooklyn	Aug 31, 1950
7	Joe Adcock	Milwaukee	July 31, 1954
8	Rocky Colavito	Cleveland	June 10, 1959
9	Willie Mays	San Francisco	Apr 30, 1961
10	Mike Schmidt	Philadelphia	Apr 17, 1976

The only other players to score four homers in one game are Bob Horner, who did so for Atlanta on July 6, 1986, and Mark Whitten, for St. Louis, on September 7, 1993.

TOP 10 ★
PLAYERS WITH THE MOST HOME RUNS IN A CAREER

	PLAYER	HOME RUNS
1	Hank Aaron	755
2	Babe Ruth	714
3	Willie Mays	660
4	Frank Robinson	586
5	Harmon Killebrew	573
6	Reggie Jackson	563
7	Mark McGwire	554
8	Mike Schmidt	548
9	Mickey Mantle	536
10	Jimmie Foxx	534

Source: *Major League Baseball*

George Herman "Babe" Ruth set a home run record in 1919 by hitting 29, breaking it the next season by hitting 54. His career total of 714 came from 8,399 "at bats," which represents an average of 8.5 percent. The next man in the averages, Harmon Killebrew, averages at 7.0 percent.

TOP 10 ★
PLAYERS WITH MOST CONSECUTIVE GAMES PLAYED

	PLAYER	GAMES
1	Cal Ripken, Jr.	2,600
2	Lou Gehrig	2,130
3	Everett Scott	1,307
4	Steve Garvey	1,207
5	Billy Williams	1,117
6	Joe Sewell	1,103
7	Stan Musial	895
8	Eddie Yost	829
9	Gus Suhr	822
10	Nellie Fox	798

Source: *Major League Baseball*

Cal Ripken took himself out of the starting line-up on September 21, 1998, in a game between the Orioles and the Yankees, having played in every game since May 30, 1982.

TOP 10 ★
PLAYERS WITH THE MOST RUNS IN A CAREER

	PLAYER	RUNS*
1	Ty Cobb	2,245
2	Rickey Henderson#	2,178
3 =	Hank Aaron	2,174
=	Babe Ruth	2,174
5	Pete Rose	2,165
6	Willie Mays	2,062
7	Stan Musial	1,949
8	Lou Gehrig	1,888
9	Tris Speaker	1,881
10	Mel Ott	1,859

* *Regular season only, excluding World Series*
\# *Still active in 2000 season*
Source: *Major League Baseball*

The still unbroken record of Tyrus Raymond "Ty" Cobb (1886–1961) was achieved in a career with Detroit and Philadelphia, 1905–28.

TOP 10 ★
BASEBALL PLAYERS WITH THE BIGGEST CONTRACTS

	PLAYER/CLUB	PERIOD OF CONTRACT	TOTAL (US$)
1	Alex Rodriguex, Texas Rangers	2001–10	252,000,000
2	Manny Ramirez, Boston Red Sox	2001–08	160,000,000
3	Mike Hampton, Colorado Rockies	2001–08	121,000,000
4	Ken Griffey, Jr., Cincinnati Reds	2000–08	116,500,000
5	Kevin Brown, Los Angeles Dodgers	1999–2005	105,000,000
6	Mike Piazza, New York Mets	1999–2005	91,000,000
7	Chipper Jones, Atlanta Braves	2001–06	90,000,000
8	Mike Mussina, New York Yankees	2001–06	88,500,000
9	Bernie Williams, New York Yankees	1999–2005	87,500,000
10	Shawn Green, Los Angeles Dodgers	2000–05	84,000,000

Source: *Major League Baseball*

TOP 10 ★
LOWEST EARNED RUN AVERAGES IN A CAREER

	PLAYER	ERA
1	Ed Walsh	1.82
2	Addie Joss	1.89
3	"Three Finger" Brown	2.06
4	John Ward	2.10
5	Christy Mathewson	2.13
6	Rube Waddell	2.16
7	Walter Johnson	2.17
8	Orval Overall	2.23
9	Tommy Bond	2.25
10	Ed Reulbach	2.28

Source: *Major League Baseball*

In proportion to its population, which province or territory has the highest number of motor vehicle fatalities?
see p.230 for the answer

A Manitoba
B Quebec
C Yukon

International Soccer

TOP 10 ★
MOST WATCHED WORLD CUP FINALS

	HOST NATION	YEAR	MATCHES	SPECTATORS	AVERAGE
1	US	1994	52	3,587,538	68,991
2	Brazil	1950	22	1,337,000	60,773
3	Mexico	1970	32	1,673,975	52,312
4	England	1966	32	1,614,677	50,459
5	Italy	1990	52	2,515,168	48,369
6	West Germany	1974	38	1,774,022	46,685
7	France	1998	64	2,775,400	43,366
8	Argentina	1978	38	1,610,215	42,374
9	Mexico	1986	52	2,184,522	42,010
10	Switzerland	1954	26	943,000	36,269

Since the World Cup's launch in 1930, a total of 24,814,267 people have watched the 580 final stage matches, at an average of 42,783 per game. The worst attended finals were in Italy in 1934, when the 17 matches were watched by 395,000, at an average of 23,235 per game.

TOP 10 ★
COUNTRIES IN THE WORLD CUP

	COUNTRY	WIN	R/U	3RD	4TH	TOTAL PTS*
1	Brazil	4	2	2	1	27
2	Germany/ West Germany	3	3	2	1	26
3	Italy	3	2	1	1	21
4	Argentina	2	2	–	–	14
5	Uruguay	2	–	–	2	10
6	France	1	–	2	1	9
7	Sweden	–	1	2	1	8
8	Holland	–	2	–	1	7
9 =	Czechoslovakia	–	2	–	–	6
=	Hungary	–	2	–	–	6

Based on 4 points for winning the tournament, 3 points for runner-up, 2 points for 3rd place, and 1 point for 4th; up to and including the 1998 World Cup

THE 10 ★
LEAST SUCCESSFUL WORLD CUP COUNTRIES

	COUNTRY	TOURNAMENTS	PLAYED	MATCHES WON
1	South Korea	5	14	0
2 =	El Salvador	2	6	0
=	Bolivia	3	6	0
4	Republic of Ireland	1	5	0
5	Egypt	2	4	0
6 =	Canada	1	3	0
=	Greece	1	3	0
=	Haiti	1	3	0
=	Iraq	1	3	0
=	Japan	1	3	0
=	New Zealand	1	3	0
=	South Africa	1	3	0
=	United Arab Emirates	1	3	0
=	Zaïre	1	3	0

FRANCE WINS WORLD CUP

Host nation France celebrates its win against Brazil in the 1998 World Cup, one of only seven different victorious countries since the first Cup in 1930.

TOP 10 ★
HIGHEST-SCORING WORLD CUP FINALS

	YEAR	GAMES	GOALS	AVERAGE PER GAME		YEAR	GAMES	GOALS	AVERAGE PER GAME
1	1954	26	140	5.38	6	1958	35	126	3.60
2	1938	18	84	4.66	7	1970	32	95	2.96
3	1934	17	70	4.11	8	1982	52	146	2.81
4	1950	22	88	4.00	9 =	1962	32	89	2.78
5	1930	18	70	3.88	=	1966	32	89	2.78

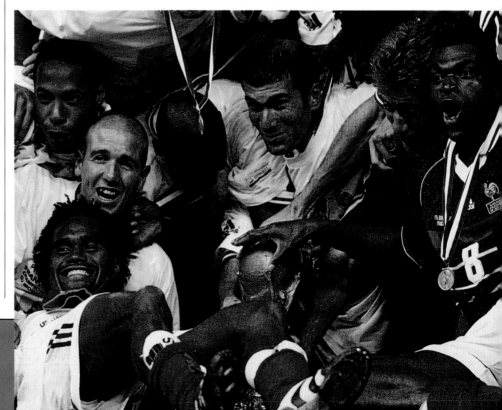

TOP 10 ★
GOALSCORERS
IN FULL INTERNATIONALS

	PLAYER	COUNTRY	YEARS	GOALS
1	Ferenc Puskás	Hungary/Spain	1945–56	83
2	Pelé	Brazil	1957–91	77
3	Sándor Kocsis	Hungary	1947–56	75
4	Hossam Hassan*	Egypt	1985–2000	73
5	Gerd Müller	West Germany	1966–74	68
6	Imre Schlosser	Hungary	1906–27	60
7	Kazuyoshi Miura*	Japan	1990–2000	55
8 =	Gabriel Batistuta*	Argentina	1991–2000	54
=	Ali Daei*	Iran	1993–2000	54
10	Joachim Streich	East Germany	1969–84	53

* *Active in 2001*

TOP 10 RICHEST SOCCER TEAMS
(Team/country/income in US$)

❶ **Manchester United**, England, 178,500,000 ❷ **Bayern Munich**, Germany, 134,400,000 ❸ **Real Madrid**, Spain, 122,500,000 ❹ **Chelsea**, England, 95,200,000 ❺ **Juventus**, Italy, 94,200,000 ❻ **Barcelona**, Spain, 89,700,000 ❼ **Milan**, Italy, 87,100,000 ❽ **Lazio**, Italy, 80,500,000 ❾ **Internazionale**, Italy, 79,000,000 ❿ **Arsenal**, England, 78,200,000

TOP 10 ★
MOST EXPENSIVE TRANSFER FEES

	PLAYER	FROM	TO	YEAR	FEE (US$)
1	Luis Figo	Barcelona	Real Madrid	2000	56,514,000
2	Christian Vieri	Lazio	Inter Milan	1999	54,737,000
3	Hernan Crespi	Parma	Lazio	2000	52,133,000
4	Denilson	Sao Paulo	Real Betis	1998	40,157,000
5	Nicolas Anelka	Arsenal	Real Madrid	1999	39,443,000
6	Marcio Amoruso	Udinese	Parma	1999	36,545,000
7	Marc Overmars	Arsenal	Barcelona	2000	36,508,000
8	Gabriel Batistuta	Fiorentina	Roma	2000	32,857,000
9	Nicolas Anelka	Real Madrid	Paris St. Germain	2000	32,127,000
10	Rivaldo	Deportivo	Barcelona	1997	30,125,000

In August 1996, former Portland University goalkeeper Kasey Keller became the most expensive American to play in the English Football League when he was transferred from Millwall to Leicester City for US$1.4 million (£900,000).

RAVELLI'S REIGN
Swedish goalkeeper Thomas Ravelli's record number of appearances for his country was unchallenged until Germany's Lothar Matthäus played his 143rd game in February 2000.

TOP 10 ★
MOST CAPPED
INTERNATIONAL PLAYERS

	PLAYER	COUNTRY	YEARS	CAPS
1	Lothar Matthäus*	West Germany/Germany	1980–2000	150
2 =	Claudio Suarez*	Mexico	1992–2000	147
=	Hossam Hassan*	Egypt	1985–2000	147
4	Thomas Ravelli	Sweden	1981–1997	143
5 =	Majed Abdullah	Saudi Arabia	1978–1994	140
=	Mohamed Al-Deayea*	Saudi Arabia	1990–2000	140
7	Cobi Jones*	US	1992–2000	134
8	Marcelo Balboa*	US	1988–2000	128
9 =	Mohammed Al-Khilaiwi*	South Korea	1992–2000	127
=	Peter Schmeichel*	Denmark	1987–2000	127

* *Active in 2001*

TOP 10 EUROPEAN TEAMS WITH
THE MOST DOMESTIC LEAGUE
TITLES
(Team/country/titles)

❶ **Glasgow Rangers**, Scotland, 49 ❷ **Linfield**, Northern Ireland, 43 ❸ **Glasgow Celtic**, Scotland, 36 ❹ **Rapid Vienna**, Austria, 31* ❺ **Benfica**, Portugal, 30 ❻ **Olympiakos**, Greece, 29 ❼ **CSKA Sofia**, Bulgaria, 28 ❽ = **Ajax**, Holland, 27; = **Real Madrid**, Spain, 27 ❿ = **Ferencvaros**, Hungary, 26; = **Jeunesse Esch**, Luxembourg, 26

* Rapid Vienna also won one German League title, in 1941

In what sport has Canada won the most Olympic medals?
see p.245 for the answer

A Hockey
B Athletics
C Swimming

Free Wheelers

STREET SKATEBOARDERS

	SKATEBOARDER/COUNTRY*	POINTS#
1	Carlos de Andrade, Brazil	490
2	Kerry Getz	470
3 =	Kyle Berard	445
=	Eric Koston	445
5	Chris Senn	440
6	Pat Channita	406
7	Rick McCrank, Canada	377
8	Ryan Johnson	340
9	Chad Fernandez	320
10	Andy Macdonald	310

* All from the US unless otherwise stated

\# Based on skateboarder's best four US events and best two from Europe/Brazil in the World Cup Skateboarding Tour

These skateboarders are ranked by World Cup Skateboarding (WCS), the organization recognized worldwide as the sanctioning body for skateboarding. The World Cup Skateboarding Tour has been held since 1994 and already includes 18 events in nine countries. Despite its name, street skateboarders rarely skate on the actual street itself, but prefer curbs, benches, handrails, and other elements of urban landscapes.

VERT. SKATEBOARDERS

	SKATEBOARDER/COUNTRY	POINTS*
1	Bob Burnquist, Brazil	600
2	Andy Macdonald, US	570
3	Pierre-Luc Gagnon, Canada	535
4	Rune Glifberg, Denmark	480
5	Sandro Dias, Brazil	425
6	Lincoln Ueda, Brazil	410
7	Anthony Furlong, US	370
8	Max Schaaf, US	350
9	Buster Halterman, US	325
10	Cristiano Mateus, Brazil	320

* Based on skateboarder's best four US events and best two from Europe/Brazil in the World Cup Skateboarding Tour

Vert. skateboarding is skateboarding on the vertical rather than the horizontal plane, which usually involves skateboarding on ramps and other vertical structures specifically designed for skateboarding. Skateboarding first became popular with surfers as a means of keeping in shape when there were no waves to surf, but over the past 40 years the sport has gained worldwide recognition in its own right, with a world ranking system since 1995.

DOWNHILL RIDERS IN THE UCI MOUNTAIN BIKE WORLD CUP, 2000 (MEN)

	RIDER/COUNTRY	POINTS*
1	Nicolas Vouilloz, France	1,256
2	Steve Peat, Great Britain	1,184
3	David Vazquez, Spain	1,166
4	Mickael Pascal, France	966
5	Cedric Gracia, France	944
6	Gerwin Peters, Netherlands	942
7	Bas De Bever, Netherlands	919
8	Eric Carter, US	895
9	Fabien Barel, France	890
10	Oscar Saiz, Spain	854

* Total points scored over a series of eight competitions

DOWNHILL RIDERS IN THE UCI MOUNTAIN BIKE WORLD CUP, 2000 (WOMEN)

	RIDER/COUNTRY	POINTS*
1	Anne Caroline Chausson, France	1,340
2	Missy Giove, US	1,203
3	Katja Repo, Finland	1,117
4	Sari Jorgensen, Switzerland	952
5	Leigh Donovan, US	935
6	Sabrina Jonnier, France	934
7	Marla Streb, US	905
8	Nolvenn Le Caer, France	897
9	Tara Llanes, US	895
10	Sarah Stieger, Switzerland	891

* Total points scored over a series of eight competitions

FINNISH THIRD

Born in Helsinki, Finland, in 1973, Katja Repo has competed in professional cycling events since 1993, and finished third in the 2000 World Cup.

INTERNATIONAL ROLLER HOCKEY COUNTRIES, 2000

	COUNTRY	POINTS*
1	Argentina	2,615
2	Spain	2,585
3	Portugal	2,560
4	Italy	2,485
5	Brazil	2,235
6	France	2,210
7	Switzerland	2,160
8	Angola	2,025
9	Chile	1,980
10	Germany	1,955

* *Ranked by the ELO system, which employs a statistical formula to calculate the probability of winning future games based on the results so far attained*

LONGEST TOURS DE FRANCE

	WINNER/ COUNTRY/YEAR	STAGES	DISTANCE MILES	KM
1	Lucien Buysse, Belgium, 1926	17	3,570	5,745
2	Firmin Lambot, Belgium, 1919	15	3,455	5,560
3	Gustave Garrigou, France, 1911	15	3,445	5,544
4	Philippe Thys, Belgium, 1920	15	3,419	5,503
5	Léon Scieur, Belgium, 1921	15	3,408	5,484
6	Ottavio Bottecchia, Italy, 1925	18	3,374	5,430
7	Ottavio Bottecchia, 1924	15	3,372	5,427
8	Philippe Thys, 1914	15	3,364	5,414
9	Philippe Thys, 1913	15	3,347	5,387
10	Henri Pélissier, France, 1923	15	3,347	5,386

US IN TOUR DE FRANCE

After triumphing over illness, Lance Armstrong won the 2000 Tour de France, thereby elevating the US to fifth place among nationalities competing in the world's most prestigious cycle race.

OLYMPIC CYCLING COUNTRIES

	COUNTRY	GOLD	MEDALS SILVER	BRONZE	TOTAL
1	France	37	21	23	81
2	Italy	34	15	7	56
3	Great Britain	10	22	18	50
4	US	12	14	17	43
5	Germany*	11	13	12	36
6	Netherlands	13	15	7	35
7	Australia	7	13	11	31
8	=Belgium	6	8	10	24
	=Soviet Union#	11	4	9	24
10	Denmark	6	7	8	21

* *Not including West/East Germany 1968–88*

Includes United Team of 1992; excludes Russia since then

COUNTRIES WITH THE MOST TOUR DE FRANCE WINNERS

	COUNTRY	WINNERS
1	France	36
2	Belgium	18
3	Italy	9
4	Spain	8
5	US	5
6	Luxembourg	4
7=	Netherlands	2
	=Switzerland	2
9=	Denmark	1
	=Germany	1
	=Ireland	1

The Tour de France is the toughest, longest, and most popular cycling race in the world.

TOP 10 OLDEST CLASSIC CYCLING RACES

(Race/first held)

❶ Bordeaux–Paris, 1891 ❷ Liège Bastogne–Liège, 1892 ❸ Paris–Brussels, 1893 ❹ Paris–Roubaix, 1896 ❺ Tour de France, 1903 ❻ Tour of Lombardy, 1905 ❼ Giro d'Italia (Tour of Italy), 1906 ❽ Milan–San Remo, 1907 ❾ Tour of Flanders, 1913 ❿ Grand Prix des Nations, 1932

Did You Know? The first cycle race in the US was held over a 4.8-km (3-mile) course in Beacon Park, Boston, MA, on May 24, 1878. It was won by C.A. Parker in a time of 12 minutes 27 seconds.

LAST DRIVERS KILLED DURING THE INDIANAPOLIS 500

	DRIVER	YEAR
1	Swede Savage	1973
2	=Eddie Sachs	1964
	=Dave MacDonald	1964
4	Pat O'Connor	1958
5	Bill Vukovich, Sr.	1955
6	Carl Scarborough	1953
7	Shorty Cantlon	1947
8	Floyd Roberts	1939
9	Clay Weatherly	1935
10	=Mark Billman	1933
	=Lester Spangler	1933

Since the death of Harry Martin during practice for the first ever Indianapolis 500 in 1911, the race has claimed the lives of 38 drivers: 14 of them during the race and 24 in practice or while qualifying. The race has also been the scene of a number of dramatic multiple-vehicle collisions.

MONEY-WINNERS AT THE INDIANAPOLIS 500

	FINISHING DRIVER	POSITION	TOTAL PRIZES (2000) US$
1	Juan Montoya	1	1,235,690
2	Buddy Lazier	2	567,100
3	Eliseo Salazar	3	468,900
4	Greg Ray	33	388,700
5	Eddie Cheever, Jr.	5	360,000
6	Jeff Ward	4	355,000
7	Scott Goodyear	9	347,800
8	Scott Sharp	10	312,000
9	Stephan Gregoire	8	305,900
10	Mark Dismore	11	293,500
	Total prize money for all drivers		9,436,505

Source: *Indianapolis Motor Speedway*

Drivers are ranked here according to their winnings, which vary according to such designations as first using a particular brand of tire.

FASTEST WINNING SPEEDS OF THE DAYTONA 500

	DRIVER*/CAR/YEAR	SPEED MPH	KM/H
1	Buddy Baker, Oldsmobile, 1980	177.602	285.823
2	Bill Elliott, Ford, 1987	176.263	283.668
3	Dale Earnhardt#, Chevrolet, 1998	172.712	277.953
4	Bill Elliott, Ford, 1985	172.265	277.234
5	Dale Earnhardt, Chevrolet, 1998	172.071	276.921
6	Richard Petty, Buick, 1981	169.651	273.027
7	Derrike Cope, Chevrolet, 1990	165.761	266.766
8	Michael Waltrip, Chevrolet, 2001	161.783	260.364
9	Jeff Gordon, Chevrolet, 1999	161.551	259.991
10	A.J. Foyt, Jr., Mercury, 1972	161.550	259.990

* All drivers from the US

Killed on final turn of last lap of 2001 Daytona 500

Source: *NASCAR*

FASTEST WINNING SPEEDS OF THE INDIANAPOLIS 500

	DRIVER/COUNTRY*	CAR	YEAR	SPEED MPH	KM/H
1	Arie Luyendyk, Netherlands	Lola-Chevrolet	1990	185.984	299.307
2	Rick Mears	Chevrolet-Lumina	1991	176.457	283.980
3	Bobby Rahal	March-Cosworth	1986	170.722	274.750
4	Emerson Fittipaldi, Brazil	Penske-Chevrolet	1989	167.581	269.695
5	Rick Mears	March-Cosworth	1984	163.612	263.308
6	Mark Donohue	McLaren-Offenhauser	1972	162.962	262.619
7	Al Unser	March-Cosworth	1987	162.175	260.995
8	Tom Sneva	March-Cosworth	1983	162.117	260.902
9	Gordon Johncock	Wildcat-Cosworth	1982	162.029	260.760
10	Al Unser	Lola-Cosworth	1978	161.363	259.689

* All from the US unless otherwise stated

Source: *Indianapolis Motor Speedway*

The first Indianapolis 500, known affectionately as the "Indy," was held on May 30, 1911. Ray Harroun won, driving a six-cylinder Marmon Wasp at an average speed of 120.04 km/h (74.59 mph). The race takes place over 200 laps of the 4-km (2.5-mile) Indianapolis Raceway. Over the years, the speed has steadily increased: Harroun's race took 6 hours 42 minutes 6 seconds, while Arie Luyendyk's record-breaking win was achieved in just 2 hours 18 minutes 18.248 seconds. The track record, set by Emerson Fittipaldi in the 1990 qualifying competition, is 362.587 km/h (225.301 mph).

HARLEY AND DAVIDSON

In Milwaukee, Wisconsin, in 1901, childhood friends William Harley (1880–1943) and Arthur Davidson (1881–1950) began their first motorcycle-building experiments, based on a bicycle with an engine they had built themselves. Davidson's two brothers joined the firm, which steadily increased production and introduced such innovations as the twist-grip throttle (1909). The Harley-Davidson soon became sufficiently established that 20,000 were supplied to the US army in World War I, and 90,000 in World War II. The firm remains the oldest-established and one of the largest motorcycle companies in the world.

TOP 10 ★
NASCAR MONEY WINNERS OF ALL TIME*

	DRIVER	TOTAL PRIZES (US$)
1	Dale Earnhardt	38,262,514
2	Jeff Gordon	29,570,670
3	Rusty Wallace	23,269,214
4	Mark Martin	23,126,188
5	Bill Elliott	23,005,860
6	Terry Labonte	22,632,033
7	Dale Jarrett	22,116,791
8	Darrell Waltrip	19,256,474
9	Ricky Rudd	18,970,391
10	Geoffrey Bodine	14,689,188

* To December 6, 2000

Source: NASCAR

TOP 10 ★
CART MONEY WINNERS OF ALL TIME

	DRIVER	TOTAL PRIZES* (US$)
1	Al Unser, Jr.	18,342,156
2	Michael Andretti	16,841,369
3	Bobby Rahal	16,344,008
4	Emerson Fittipaldi	14,293,625
5	Mario Andretti	11,552,154
6	Rick Mears	11,050,807
7	Jimmy Vasser	9,809,994
8	Danny Sullivan	8,884,126
9	Paul Tracy	8,011,570
10	Arie Luyendyk	7,732,188

* As at December 2000

Source: Championship Auto Racing Teams

TOP 10 ★
MOTORBIKE RIDERS WITH THE MOST SUPERBIKE WORLD CHAMPIONSHIP WINS

	RIDER/COUNTRY	WINS
1	Carl Fogarty, UK	56
2	Doug Polen, US	27
3	Raymand Roche, France	23
4	Troy Corser, Australia	19
5=	Colin Edwards, US	15
=	John Kocinski, US	15
7=	Pier Francesco Chili, Italy	14
=	Scott Russell, US	14
9	Giancarlo Falappa, Italy	12
10	Aalon Slight, New Zealand	11

TOP 10 ★
DRIVERS WITH THE MOST WINSTON CUP WINS

	DRIVER	YEARS	VICTORIES
1	Richard Petty	1958–92	200
2	David Pearson	1960–86	105
3=	Bobby Allison	1975–88	84
=	Darrell Waltrip*	1975–92	84
5	Cale Yarborough	1957–88	83
6	Dale Earnhardt*	1979–2000	76
7	Lee Petty	1949–64	54
8	Rusty Wallace*	1986–2000	53
9	Jeff Gordon*	1994–2000	52
10=	Ned Jarrett	1953–66	50
=	Junior Johnson	1953–66	50

* Still driving at end of 2000 season

Source: NASCAR

The Winston Cup is a season-long series of races organized by the National Association of Stock Car Auto Racing (NASCAR). Races take place over enclosed circuits such as Daytona speedway. The series started in 1949 as the Grand National series but changed its name to the Winston Cup in 1970 when sponsored by the R.J. Reynolds tobacco company, manufacturers of Winston cigarettes.

THE 10 ★
ALL-TIME CHAMPIONSHIP CAR VICTORY LEADERS WITH MOST RACE WINS

	DRIVER	YEARS	WINS
1	A.J. Foyt, Jr.	1960–81	67
2	Mario Andretti	1965–93	52
3	Michael Andretti	1986–2000	40
4	Al Unser	1965–87	39
5	Bobby Unser	1966–81	35
6	Al Unser, Jr.	1984–95	31
7	Rick Mears	1978–91	29
8	Johnny Rutherford	1965–86	27
9	Rodger Ward	1953–66	26
10	Gordon Johncock	1965–83	25

Source: Championship Auto Racing Teams

Seventeen-year race driving veteran Michael Andretti is the only leader on this Top 10 list currently driving on the CART circuit. Until his switch to Formula 1 racing, Colombian Juan Montoya seemed the most likely to next make the list. With seven wins during the 1999 season, he became the youngest series champion ever.

THE 10 ★
LATEST WORLD CHAMPION ENDURANCE MOTORBIKE RIDERS

YEAR	RIDER(S)/COUNTRY	BIKE
2000	Peter Linden, Sweden/ Warwick Nowland, UK	Suzuki
1999	Terry Rymer, UK/ Jéhan d'Orgeix, France	Suzuki
1998	Doug Polen, US/ Christian Lavielle, France	Honda
1997	Peter Goddard, Australia/ Doug Polen, US	Suzuki
1996	Brian Morrison, UK	Kawasaki
1995	Stephene Mertens, Belgium/ Jean Michel Mattioli, France	Honda
1994	Adrien Morillas, France	Kawasaki
1993	Doug Toland, US	Kawasaki
1992	Terry Rymer, UK/ Carl Fogarty, UK	Kawasaki
1991	Alex Vieira, Portugal	Kawasaki

The World Endurance Championship consists of four 24-hour races, at Le Mans (France), Spa Francorchamps (Belgium), Oschersleben (Germany), and Bol d'Or (France), and two 8-hour races at Estoril (Portugal) and Suzuka (Japan).

Canadians Donovan Bailey and Bruny Surin are the second fastest in the world at what?
see p.251 for the answer

A Bobsledding
B Running 100 meters
C Lawn-mower racing

Golfing Greats

YOUNGEST WINNERS OF THE BRITISH OPEN

	PLAYER/COUNTRY	AGE YRS	AGE MTHS
1	Tom Morris, Jr., UK	17	5
2	Willie Auchterlonie, UK	21	1
3	Severiano Ballesteros, Spain	22	3
4	John H. Taylor, UK	23	3
5	Gary Player, South Africa	23	8
6	Bobby Jones, US	24	3
7	Tiger Woods, US	24	6
8	Peter Thomson, Australia	24	11
9 =	Arthur Havers, UK	25	0
=	Tony Jacklin, UK	25	0

The dates of birth for Tom Kidd and Jack Simpson, the 1873 and 1884 winners, have never been established. Hugh Kirkaldy, the 1891 winner, was born in 1865 and could have been either 25 or 26 when he won the title, but his exact date of birth, too, has never been confirmed.

AMERICAN PLAYERS WITH THE MOST WINS IN THE RYDER CUP

	PLAYER	WINS
1	Arnold Palmer	22
2 =	Billy Casper	20
=	Lanny Wadkins	20
4 =	Jack Nicklaus	17
=	Lee Trevino	17
6	Tom Kite	15
7	Gene Littler	14
8	Hale Irwin	13
9 =	Sam Snead	10
=	Tom Watson	10

The Ryder Cup was launched in 1927 by Samuel Ryder (1858–1936), a British merchant who made his fortune selling penny seed packets. The tournament is international in scope: two teams, one from the US and one from Europe, compete for the cup. Except for a break during World War II, it has been held once every two years.

LOWEST WINNING SCORES IN THE US MASTERS

	PLAYER*	YEAR	SCORE
1	Tiger Woods	1997	270
2 =	Jack Nicklaus	1965	271
=	Raymond Floyd	1976	271
4 =	Ben Hogan	1953	274
=	Ben Crenshaw	1995	274
6 =	Severiano Ballesteros, Spain	1980	275
=	Fred Couples	1992	275
8 =	Arnold Palmer	1964	276
=	Jack Nicklaus	1975	276
=	Tom Watson	1977	276
=	Nick Faldo, UK	1996	276

All from the US unless otherwise stated

The US Masters, the brainchild of American amateur golfer Robert Tyre "Bobby" Jones, is the only major played on the same course each year, at Augusta, Georgia. The course was built on the site of an old nursery, and the abundance of flowers, shrubs, and plants is a reminder of its former days, with each of the 18 holes named after the plants growing adjacent to it.

WINNERS OF WOMEN'S MAJORS

	PLAYER*	TITLES
1	Patty Berg	16
2 =	Louise Suggs	13
=	Mickey Wright	13
4	Babe Zaharias	12
5 =	Julie Inkster	8
=	Betsy Rawls	8
7	JoAnne Carner	7
8 =	Pat Bradley	6
=	Glenna Collett Vare	6
=	Betsy King	6
=	Patty Sheehan	6
=	Kathy Whitworth	6

All from the US

BEST OF THE REST

Swedish golfer Annika Sorenstam (b. 1970) won more LPGA tournaments (18) than any other player in the 1990s, and is the highest earning non-American woman golfer of all time.

CAREER EARNINGS BY WOMEN GOLFERS

	PLAYER*/YEARS	WINNINGS# (US$)
1	Betsy King, 1977–2000	6,828,688
2	Annika Sorenstam, Sweden, 1992–2000	6,200,596
3	Karrie Webb, Australia, 1995–2000	6,162,895
4	Julie Inkster, 1983–2000	6,057,400
5	Beth Daniel, 1979–2000	6,022,461
6	Dottie Pepper, 1987–2000	5,882,131
7	Pat Bradley, 1974–2000	5,743,605
8	Patty Sheehan, 1980–2000	5,500,983
9	Meg Mallon, 1987–2000	5,466,338
10	Nancy Lopez, 1977–2000	5,297,955

All from the US unless otherwise stated
As of November 20, 2000

❦ THE 10 LATEST WINNERS OF THE CPGA MEN'S CHAMPIONSHIP

(Year/winner)

1 2000, Chad Wright **2** 1999, Scott Petersen **3** 1998, Tim Clark **4** 1997, Guy Hill **5** 1996, Ashley Chinner **6** 1995, Trevor Dodds **7** 1994, Stuart Hendley **8** 1993, Steve Stricker **9** 1992, Kip Byrne **10** 1991, Tom Harding

Source: *Canadian Professional Golfers' Association*

❦ THE 10 LATEST WINNERS OF THE CPGA WOMEN'S CHAMPIONSHIP

(Year/winner)

1 2000, Nancy Harvey **2** 1999, Lorie Kane **3** 1998, Lorie Kane **4** 1997, Lorie Kane **5** 1996, Lorie Kane **6** 1995, Nancy Harvey **7** 1994, Nancy Harvey **8** 1993, Lanie Cahill **9** 1992, Terrie Brecher **10** 1991, Jackie Twamley

Source: *Canadian Professional Golfers' Association*

TOP 10 MONEY-WINNING GOLFERS, 2000

(Player*/winnings in 2000#, US$)

1 Tiger Woods, 9,501,387 **2** Phil Mickelson, 4,791,743 **3** Ernie Els, South Africa, 3,855,829 **4** Hal Sutton, 3,061,444 **5** Lee Westwood, UK, 2,966,066 **6** Vijay Singh, Fiji, 2,702,858 **7** Darren Clarke, UK, 2,671,040 **8** Mike Weir, 2,547,829 **9** Jesper Parnevik, Sweden, 2,499,079 **10** David Duval, 2,471,244

* All from the US unless otherwise stated
 # As of December 18, 2000

This list is based on winnings on the world's five top tours: US PGA Tour, European PGA Tour, PGA Tour of Japan, Australasian PGA Tour, and FNB Tour of South Africa.

TOP 10 ★

PLAYERS TO WIN THE MOST MAJORS IN A CAREER

	PLAYER*	BRITISH OPEN	US OPEN	US MASTERS	PGA	TOTAL
1	Jack Nicklaus	3	4	6	5	18
2	Walter Hagen	4	2	0	5	11
3 =	Ben Hogan	1	4	2	2	9
=	Gary Player, South Africa	3	1	3	2	9
5	Tom Watson	5	1	2	0	8
6 =	Bobby Jones	3	4	0	0	7
=	Arnold Palmer	2	1	4	0	7
=	Gene Sarazen	1	2	1	3	7
=	Sam Snead	1	0	3	3	7
=	Harry Vardon, UK	6	1	0	0	7

* All from the US unless otherwise stated

GOOD AS GOLD

In a career spanning over 30 years, Jack Nicklaus, nicknamed the Golden Bear, won more majors than any other player in golfing history.

Horse Racing

LATEST HORSES TO WIN THE QUEEN'S PLATE*

YEAR	HORSE/JOCKEY	TIME MIN:SEC#	YEAR	HORSE/JOCKEY	TIME MIN:SEC#
2000	Scatter the Gold, *Todd Kabel*	2:05.2	1994	Basqueian, *Jack Laron*	2:03.2
1999	Woodcarver, *Mickey Walls*	2:03.0	1993	Peteski, *Craig Perret*	2:04.1
1998	Archers Bay, *Kent Desormeaux*	2:02.1	1992	Alydeed, *Craig Perret*	2:04.3
1997	Awesome Again, *A.E. Smith*	2:04.1	1991	Dance Smartly, *Pal Day*	2:03.2
1996	Victor Cooley, *Emile Ramsammy*	2:03.4			
1995	Regal Discovery, *Todd Kabel*	2:03.4			

* Held at Toronto's Woodbine Racetrack
\# Fractions of a second are in fifths
Source: *Ontario Jockey Club*

TOP 10 ⭐

MONEY-WINNING HORSES, 2000

	HORSE	WINNINGS (US$)
1	Dubai Millennium	3,600,000
2	Tiznow	3,445,950
3	Fantastic Light	3,238,998
4	T.M. Opera O	2,278,332
5	Fusaichi Pegasus	1,987,800
6	Spain	1,979,500
7	Captain Steve	1,882,276
8	Behrens	1,764,500
9	Lemon Drop Kid	1,673,900
10	Giant's Causeway	1,600,593

Source: *National Thoroughbred Racing Association*

TOP 10 ⭐

MONEY-WINNING HORSES

	HORSE	WINS	WINNINGS (US$)
1	Cigar	19	9,999,815
2	Skip Away	18	9,616,360
3	Hokuto Vega	16	8,337,603
4	Silver Charm	12	6,944,369
5	Alysheba	11	6,679,242
6	John Henry	39	6,597,947
7	Singspiel	9	5,950,217
8	Sakura Laurel	9	5,763,926
9	Best Pal	18	5,668,245
10	Taiki Blizzard	6	5,544,484

Source: *National Thoroughbred Racing Association*

TOP 10 ⭐

FASTEST WINNING TIMES OF THE KENTUCKY DERBY

	HORSE	YEAR	TIME MIN:SEC
1	Secretariat	1973	1:59.2
2	Northern Dancer	1964	2:00.0
3	Spend a Buck	1985	2:00.2
4	Decidedly	1962	2:00.4
5	Proud Clarion	1967	2:00.6
6	Grindstone	1996	2:01.0
7	=Lucky Debonair	1965	2:01.2
	=Affirmed	1978	2:01.2
	=Thunder Gulch	1995	2:01.2
	=Fusaichi Pegasus	2000	2:01.2

Source: *The Jockey Club*

The Kentucky Derby is held on the first Saturday in May at Churchill Downs, Louisville, Kentucky. The course was established in 1874 by Colonel Lewis Clark. The first leg of the Triple Crown, it was first raced in 1875 over a distance of 1 mile 4 furlongs, but after 1896 was reduced to 1 mile 2 furlongs. It is said that the hat, known in England as a "bowler," manufactured in the US by James H. Knapp of South Norwalk, Connecticut, became popular attire at the first Kentucky Derbys, thereby acquiring the name "derby."

DERBY

The man who gave his name to horse races in the UK, US, and elsewhere was Edward Stanley, 12th Earl of Derby (1752–1834). Derby offered a prize for a race for three-year-old fillies, which was named after The Oaks, the house he lived in near the Epsom racecourse in Surrey, UK, and in 1780, he introduced a race for three-year-old fillies or colts, which was named the Derby. Further Derbies followed – the Hong Kong Derby was first run in 1873, and the Kentucky Derby followed shortly after, in 1875 – while the name came to be used in a more general way to describe other types of sporting events.

TOP 10 🍁

JOCKEYS AT WOODBINE IN 2000

	JOCKEY	WINS*	EARNINGS ($)
1	Patrick Husbands	178	8,123,227
2	Todd Kabel	120	6,789,652
3	David Clark	117	5,548,126
4	Emile Ramsammy	106	5,101,329
5	Constant Montpellier	91	4,372,735
6	Gary Boulanger	78	4,095,997
7	Robert C. Landry	71	4,527,308
8	James McKnight	68	2,797,340
9	Raymond B. Sabourin	63	2,566,529
10	Na Somsanith	55	2,795,291

* Ranked by first place wins at Toronto's Woodbine Racetrack
Source: *Ontario Jockey Club*

TOP 10 ⭐

MONEY-WINNING NORTH AMERICAN JOCKEYS

	JOCKEY	EARNINGS (US$)
1	Chris McCarron	247,335,327
2	Pat Day	241,500,532
3	Laffit Pincay Jr.	215,819,671
4	Jerry Bailey	199,325,433
5	Gary Stevens	190,344,329
6	Eddie Delahoussaye	182,028,673
7	Angel Cordero Jr.	164,561,227
8	Jose Santos	132,564,875
9	Jorge Velasquez	125,534,962
10	Bill Shoemaker	123,375,524

Source: *NTRA Communications*

TOP 10 ★

JOCKEYS IN THE BREEDERS' CUP

	JOCKEY	YEARS	WINS
1	Pat Day	1984–99	11
2	Jerry Bailey	1991–2000	9
3=	Chris McCarron	1985–2000	8
=	Mike Smith	1992–97	8
=	Gary Stevens	1990–2000	8
6=	Eddie Delahoussaye	1984–93	7
=	Laffit Pincay Jr.	1985–93	7
8=	Jose Santos	1986–97	6
=	Pat Valenzuela	1986–92	6
10	Corey Nakatani	1996–99	5

Source: *The Breeders Cup*

Held at a different venue each year, the Breeders' Cup is an end-of-season gathering, with seven races run during the day, and the season's best thoroughbreds competing in each category. Staged in October or November, the cup has US$10 million prize money on offer. Of that, $3 million goes to the winner of the day's senior race, the Classic. Churchill Downs is the most-used venue, with five Breeders' Cups since the first in 1984.

TOP 10 ★

LATEST TRIPLE CROWN-WINNING HORSES*

	HORSE	YEAR
1	Affirmed	1978
2	Seattle Slew	1977
3	Secretariat	1973
4	Citation	1948
5	Assault	1946
6	Count Fleet	1943
7	Whirlaway	1941
8	War Admiral	1937
9	Omaha	1935
10	Gallant Fox	1930

* Horses that have won the Kentucky Derby, the Preakness, and Belmont Stakes in the same season

Since 1875, only 11 horses have won all three races in one season.

TOP 10 🍁

CANADIAN-BRED MONEY-WINNING HORSES IN A HARNESS-RACING CAREER

	TROTTERS				PACERS	
	HORSE	WINNINGS ($)		WINNINGS ($)		HORSE
1	Grades Singing	2,190,872	1	1,763,740		Apache's Fame
2	Glory's Comet	2,048,445	2	1,397,540		Odie's Fame
3	Goodtimes	1,981,345	3	1,226,789		D.M. Dilinger
4	No Sex Please	1,884,392	4	1,005,566		Tricky Tooshie
5	Yankee Paco	1,486,197	5	973,382		She's a Great Lady
6	Impeccable Image	1,283,668	6	932,251		Nines Wild
7	Hanko Angus	1,024,183	7	931,253		Duke of Abby
8	Earl	984,318	8	907,974		Northern Luck
9	Elegant Image	955,368	9	897,929		Survivor Gold
10	Armbro Marshall	947,288	10	859,822		Boomer Drummond

Source: *Standardbred Canada*

Harness-racing horses pull a jockey on a two-wheeled "sulky" (introduced in 1829) around an oval track. Unlike thoroughbred racehorses, standardbred harness-racing horses are trained to trot and pace, but do not gallop. A trotter is a horse whose diagonally opposite legs move forward together, while a pacer's legs are extended laterally and with a swinging motion. Pacers usually travel faster than trotters. The lineage of the modern standardbred can be traced back to a stallion named Messenger, a thoroughbred brought to the US from England in 1788 and then bred to pure thoroughbred and mixed breed mares. The offspring of Hambletonian, great-grandson of Messenger, are considered to be the first standardbreds, so called because of the requirement that such horses be able to reach a certain speed for the standard distance of one mile. Armstrong Bros., based in Ontario, has annually been one of the top breeding farms in North America. Horses with the prefix "Armbro" have won numerous major stakes races.

THE 10 ★

JOCKEYS IN THE US TRIPLE CROWN RACES

	JOCKEY	KENTUCKY	PREAKNESS	BELMONT	TOTAL
1	Eddie Arcaro	5	6	6	17
2	Bill Shoemaker	4	2	5	11
3=	Pat Day	1	5	3	9
=	Bill Hartack	5	3	1	9
=	Earle Sande	3	1	5	9
6	Jimmy McLaughlin	1	1	6	8
7=	Angel Cordero Jr.	3	2	1	6
=	Chas Kurtsinger	2	2	2	6
=	Gary Stevens	3	1	2	6
=	Ron Turcotte	2	2	2	6

The US Triple Crown consists of the Kentucky Derby, Preakness Stakes (held at Pimlico, Maryland, since 1873), and Belmont Stakes (held at Belmont, New York, since 1867). The only jockey to complete the Triple Crown twice is Eddie Arcaro on Whirlaway in 1941 and on Citation in 1948.

Did You Know? The first horse race trotting course in the US was established at Jamaica, New York. A horse called Screwdriver won the inaugural race there on May 16, 1825.

Hockey Highlights

BEST-PAID PLAYERS IN THE NHL, 2000–01

PLAYER	TEAM	SALARY (US$)
1 =Peter Forsberg	Colorado Avalanche	10,000,000
=Paul Kariya	Anaheim Mighty Ducks	10,000,000
3 Jaromir Jagr	Pittsburgh Penguins	9,482,708
4 Pavel Bure	Florida Panthers	9,000,000
5 Keith Tkachuk	Phoenix Coyotes	8,300,000
6 =Teemu Selanne	Anaheim Mighty Ducks	8,000,000
=Steve Yzerman	Detroit Red Wings	8,000,000
8 Joe Sakic	Colorado Avalanche	7,900,000
9 Brian Leetch	New York Rangers	7,680,000
10 =Dominik Hasek	Buffalo Sabres	7,500,000
=Patrick Roy	Colorado Avalanche	7,500,000
=Mats Sundin	Toronto Maple Leafs	7,500,000

Source: *National Hockey League Players Association*

TOP 10 ★

GOALIES WITH THE BEST SAVES PERCENTAGES IN THE NHL, 2000–01

PLAYER/TEAM	GAMES PLAYED	TOTAL SAVES	SAVES %
1 =Corey Hirsch, Washington Capitals	1	8	100.0
=Jason Labarbera, New York Rangers	1	2	100.0
3 Marty Turco, Dallas Stars	26	492	92.5
4 Mike Dunham, Nashville Predators	48	1,274	92.3
5 Sean Burke, Phoenix Coyotes	62	1,628	92.2
6 =Roman Cechmanek, Philadelphia Flyers	59	1,349	92.1
=Dominik Hasek, Buffalo Sabres	67	1,589	92.1
8 =Emmanuel Fernandez, Minnesota Wild	42	1,055	92.0
=Manny Legace, Detroit Red Wings	39	836	92.0
=Roberto Luongo, Florida Panthers	47	1,226	92.0

Source: *National Hockey League Players Association*

TOP 10 TEAM SALARIES IN THE NHL, 2000–01

(Team/salary, US$)

1 New York Rangers, 60,732,037 **2** Detroit Red Wings, 55,807,500 **3** Dallas Stars, 55,342,200 **4** Colorado Avalanche, 51,061,076 **5** Philadelphia Flyers, 41,924,500 **6** Anaheim Mighty Ducks, 41,847,500 **7** Florida Panthers, 41,742,500 **8** Toronto Maple Leafs, 41,096,273 **9** Washington Capitals, 40,165,000 **10** St. Louis Blues, 38,840,833

Source: *National Hockey League Players Association*

TOP 10 ★

GOAL SCORERS IN AN NHL SEASON

PLAYER/TEAM	SEASON	GOALS
1 Wayne Gretzky, Edmonton Oilers	1981–82	92
2 Wayne Gretzky, Edmonton Oilers	1983–84	87
3 Brett Hull, St. Louis Blues	1990–91	86
4 Mario Lemieux, Pittsburgh Penguins	1988–89	85
5 =Phil Esposito, Boston Bruins	1970–71	76
=Alexander Mogilny, Buffalo Sabres	1992–93	76
=Teemu Selanne, Winnipeg Jets	1992–93	76
8 Wayne Gretzky, Edmonton Oilers	1984–85	73
9 Brett Hull, St. Louis Blues	1989–90	72
10 =Wayne Gretzky, Edmonton Oilers	1982–83	71
=Jari Kurri, Edmonton Oilers	1984–85	71

TOP 10 🍁

SEASONS BY WAYNE GRETZKY

SEASON	GOALS	ASSISTS	POINTS
1 1985–86	52	163	215
2 1981–82	92	120	212
3 1984–85	73	135	208
4 1983–84	87	118	205
5 1982–83	71	125	196
6 1986–87	62	121	183
7 1988–89	54	114	168
8 1980–81	55	109	164
9 1990–91	41	122	163
10 1987–88	40	109	149

Canadian Wayne Gretzky, who retired in 1999 after 20 seasons in the NHL, is considered the greatest ice hockey player of all time. He gained more records than any player in history, including the most goals, assists, and points.

GOALIES
IN AN NHL CAREER*

	PLAYER	SEASONS	GAMES WON
1	Patrick Roy#	17	484
2	Terry Sawchuk	21	447
3	Jacques Plante	18	434
4	Tony Esposito	16	423
5	Glenn Hall	18	407
5	Grant Fuhr#	19	403
7	Mike Vernon#	18	383
8	Andy Moog	18	372
9	Rogie Vachon	16	355
10	Tom Barrasso#	17	353

* *Regular season only*

\# *Still active at end of 2000–01 season*

TEAMS
WITH THE MOST
STANLEY CUP WINS

	TEAM	WINS
1	Montreal Canadiens	23
2	Toronto Maple Leafs	13
3	Detroit Red Wings	9
4 =	Boston Bruins	5
=	Edmonton Oilers	5
6 =	New York Islanders	4
=	New York Rangers	4
=	Ottawa Senators	4
9	Chicago Black Hawks	3
10 =	Montreal Maroons	2
=	Philadelphia Flyers	2
=	Pittsburgh Penguins	2

During his time as Governor General of Canada from 1888 to 1893, Sir Frederick Arthur Stanley (Lord Stanley of Preston and 16th Earl of Derby) became interested in what is called hockey in the US, and ice hockey elsewhere, and in 1893 presented a trophy to be contested by the best amateur teams in Canada. The first trophy went to the Montreal Amateur Athletic Association, who won it without a challenge from any other team.

WINNERS
OF THE HART TROPHY

	PLAYER	YEARS	WINS
1	Wayne Gretzky	1980–89	9
2	Gordie Howe	1952–63	6
3	Eddie Shore	1933–38	4
4 =	Bobby Clarke	1973–76	3
=	Mario Lemieux	1988–96	3
=	Howie Morenz	1928–32	3
=	Bobby Orr	1970–72	3
8 =	Jean Beliveau	1956–64	2
=	Bill Cowley	1941–43	2
=	Phil Esposito	1969–74	2
=	Dominic Hasek	1997–98	2
=	Bobby Hull	1965–66	2
=	Guy Lafleur	1977–78	2
=	Mark Messier	1990–92	2
=	Stan Mikita	1967–68	2
=	Nels Stewart	1926–30	2

Source: *National Hockey League*

GOAL SCORERS
IN 2000–01

	PLAYER/TEAM	GOALS
1	Pavel Bure, Florida Panthers	59
2	Joe Sakic, Colorado Avalanche	54
3	Jaromir Jagr, Pittsburgh Penguins	52
4	Peter Bondra, Washington Capitals	45
5	Alexei Kovalev, Pittsburgh Penguins	44
6	Alexander Mogilny, New Jersey Devils	43
7 =	Milan Hejduk, Colorado Avalanche	41
=	Markus Naslund, Vancouver Canucks	41
=	Jeff O'Neill, Carolina Hurricanes	41
10 =	Patrik Elias, New Jersey Devils	40
=	Bill Guerin, Boston Bruins	40
=	Alexei Yashin, Ottawa Senators	40
=	Scott Young, St. Louis Blues	40

Source: *National Hockey League*

GOAL SCORERS
IN AN NHL CAREER*

	PLAYER	SEASONS	GOALS
1	Wayne Gretzky	20	894
2	Gordie Howe	26	801
3	Marcel Dionne	18	731
4	Phil Esposito	18	717
5	Mike Gartner	19	708
6	Mark Messier#	22	651
7	Mario Lemieux#	13	648
8	Bobby Hull	16	610
9	Dino Ciccarelli	19	608
10	Jari Kurri	17	601

* *Regular season only*

\# *Still active at end of 2000–01 season*

BIGGEST NHL ARENAS

	STADIUM/LOCATION/ HOME TEAM	CAPACITY
1	Molson Centre, Montreal, Montreal Canadiens	21,631
2	United Center, Chicago, Chicago Blackhawks	21,500
3 =	Air Canada Centre, Toronto, Toronto Maple Leafs	21,000
=	Dallas, Dallas, Dallas North Stars	21,000
5	Canadian Airlines Saddledrome, Calgary, Calgary Flames	20,035
6 =	MCI Center, Washington, Washington Capitals	20,000
=	Nashville Arena, Nashville, Nashville Predators	20,000
=	Philips Arena, Atlanta, Atlanta Thrashers	20,000
=	Raleigh Entertainment & Sports Arena, Raleigh, Carolina Hurricanes	20,000
=	Staples Center, Los Angeles, Los Angeles Kings	20,000

Which player in the Canadian Football League has the most passing yards in a CFL career?
see p.248 for the answer

A Matt Dunigan
B Ron Lancaster
C Damon Allen

271

What a Racquet

WINNERS OF THE TABLE TENNIS WORLD CHAMPIONSHIP

	COUNTRY	MEN'S	WOMEN'S	TOTAL
1	China	13	13	26
2	Japan	7	8	15
3	Hungary	12	–	12
4	Czechoslovakia	6	3	9
5	Romania	–	5	5
6	Sweden	4	–	4
7=	England	1	2	3
=	US	1	2	3
9	Germany	–	2	2
10=	Austria	1	–	1
=	North Korea	–	1	1
=	South Korea	–	1	1
=	USSR	–	1	1

Originally a European event, table tennis was later extended to a world championship. This Top 10 takes account of men's wins since 1926 and women's since 1934. Winning men's teams receive the Swaythling Cup, and women the Marcel Corbillon Cup. The championship has been held biennially since 1959.

WINNERS OF WOMEN'S GRAND SLAM SINGLES TITLES

	PLAYER/COUNTRY	A	F	W	US	TOTAL
1	Margaret Court (née Smith), Aus	11	5	3	5	24
2	Steffi Graf, Ger	4	5	7	5	21
3	Helen Wills-Moody, US	0	4	8	7	19
4=	Chris Evert-Lloyd, US	2	7	3	6	18
=	Martina Navratilova, Cze/US	3	2	9	4	18
6=	Billie Jean King (née Moffitt), US	1	1	6	4	12
=	Suzanne Lenglen, Fra	0	6	6	0	12
8=	Maureen Connolly, US	1	2	3	3	9
=	Monica Seles, Yug/US	4	3	0	2	9
10	Molla Mallory (née Bjurstedt), US	0	0	0	8	8

A – Australian Open; F – French Open; W – Wimbledon; US – US Open

WINNERS OF INDIVIDUAL OLYMPIC TENNIS MEDALS

	PLAYER/COUNTRY/YEARS	GOLD	TOTAL
1	Max Decugis, France, 1900–20	4	6
2	Kitty McKane, GB, 1920–24	1	5
3=	Reginald Doherty, GB, 1900–08	3	4
=	Gunnar Setterwall, Sweden, 1908–12	0	4
5=	Charles Dixon, GB, 1908–12	0	3
=	Mary Joe Fernandez, US, 1992–96	2	3
=	Suzanne Lenglen, France, 1920	2	3
=	Harold Mahony, Ireland, 1900	0	3
=	Jana Novotna, Czech Republic, 1988–96	0	3
=	Vince Richards, US, 1924	2	3
=	Josiah Ritchie, GB, 1908	1	3
=	Arantxa Sanchez-Vicario, Spain, 1992–96	0	3
=	Charles Winslow, South Africa, 1912–20	2	3

TOP 10 MALE TENNIS PLAYERS*

(Player/country/weeks at No. 1)

❶ Pete Sampras, US, 276 **❷ Ivan Lendl**, Czechoslovakia, 270 **❸ Jimmy Connors**, US, 268 **❹ John McEnroe**, US, 170 **❺ Bjorn Borg**, Sweden, 109 **❻ Stefan Edberg**, Sweden, 72 **❼ Jim Courier**, US, 58 **❽ Andre Agassi**, US, 51 **❾ Ilie Nastase**, Romania, 40 **❿ Mats Wilander**, Sweden, 20

* Based on weeks at No. 1 in ATP rankings (1973–2000)

BRILLIANT CAREER

In 1995, Andre Agassi was the 12th player to be ranked world No. 1. In 1999, he became only the fifth male player to complete a Grand Slam.

THE 10 ⭐
LATEST WINNERS OF THE SQUASH WORLD OPEN (FEMALE)

YEAR*	PLAYER/COUNTRY
1999	Cassandra Campion, England
1998	Sarah Fitz-Gerald, Australia
1997	Sarah Fitz-Gerald
1996	Sarah Fitz-Gerald
1995	Michelle Martin, Australia
1994	Michelle Martin
1993	Michelle Martin
1992	Susan Devoy, New Zealand
1991	Susan Devoy
1990	Martine le Moignan, Guernsey

* No championship in 2000

Source: *Women's International Squash Players Assoc.*

THE 10 ⭐
LATEST WINNERS OF THE SQUASH WORLD OPEN (MALE)

YEAR*	PLAYER/COUNTRY
1999	Peter Nichol, Scotland
1998	Jonathon Power, Canada
1997	Rodney Eyles, Australia
1996	Jansher Khan, Pakistan
1995	Jansher Khan
1994	Jansher Khan
1993	Jansher Khan
1992	Jansher Khan
1991	Rodney Martin, Australia
1990	Jansher Khan

* No championship in 2000

Source: *Professional Squash Association*

TOP 10 ⭐
PLAYERS WITH THE MOST BADMINTON WORLD TITLES

	PLAYER/COUNTRY	MALE/FEMALE	TITLES
1	Park Joo-bong, South Korea	M	5
2 =	Han Aiping, China	F	3
=	Li Lingwei, China	F	3
=	Guan Weizhan, China	F	3
=	Lin Ying, China	F	3
6 =	Tian Bingyi, China	M	2
=	Christian Hadinata, Indonesia	M	2
=	Lene Köppen, Denmark	F	2
=	Kim Moon-soo, South Korea	M	2
=	Chung Myung-hee, South Korea	F	2
=	Nora Perry, England	F	2
=	Yang Yang, China	M	2
=	Li Yongbo, China	M	2

TOP 10 ⭐
DAVIS CUP-WINNING TEAMS

	COUNTRY	WINS
1	US	31
2	Australia	21
3	France	8
4	Sweden	7
5	Australasia	6
6	British Isles	5
7	Great Britain	4
8	West Germany	2
9 =	Czechoslovakia	1
=	Germany	1
=	Italy	1
=	South Africa	1

The UK has been represented by the British Isles from 1900 to 1921, England from 1922 to 1928, and Great Britain since 1929. The combined Australia/New Zealand team took part as Australasia between 1905 and 1922. Australia first entered a separate team in 1923 and New Zealand in 1924. South Africa's sole win was gained when, for political reasons, India refused to meet them in the 1974 final.

TOP 10 ⭐
CAREER MONEY-WINNING WOMEN TENNIS PLAYERS

	PLAYER/COUNTRY	WINNINGS (US$)*
1	Steffi Graf, Germany	21,895,277
2	Martina Navratilova, US	20,396,399
3	Arantxa Sanchez-Vicario, Spain	15,747,252
4	Martina Hingis, Switzerland	15,080,325
5	Monica Seles, US	12,891,708
6	Lindsay Davenport, US	11,934,628
7	Jana Novotna, Czech Republic	11,249,134
8	Conchita Martinez, Spain	9,335,263
9	Chris Evert-Lloyd, US	8,896,195
10	Gabriela Sabatini, Argentina	8,785,850

* To end of 2000 season

GOLDEN GIRL

In 1995 the first player ever to win all four Grand Slam titles four times each, Steffi Graf is also the sport's highest-earning female player of all time.

Water Sports

POWERING AHEAD
American powerboat racer Bill Seebold retired in 1997 after 46 years in the sport, during which he won 912 races and some 60 championships.

TOP 10 ★
POWERBOAT DRIVERS WITH THE MOST RACE WINS

	DRIVER	COUNTRY	WINS
1	Bill Seebold	US	912
2	Jimbo McConnell	US	217
3	Chip Hanuer	US	203
4	Steve Curtis	UK	185
5	Mikeal Frode	Sweden	152
6	Neil Holmes	UK	147
7	Peter Bloomfield	UK	126
8	Renato Molinari	Italy	113
9	Cees Van der Valden	Netherlands	98
10	Bill Muncey	US	96

Source: *Raceboat International*

TOP 10 ★
US COLLEGES IN THE INTERCOLLEGIATE ROWING ASSOCIATION REGATTA*

	COLLEGE	WINNING YEARS (FIRST/LAST)	WINS
1	Cornell	1896–1982	24
2	Navy	1921–84	13
3	California	1928–2000	12
4	Washington	1923–97	11
5	Pennsylvania	1898–1989	9
6 =	Wisconsin	1951–90	7
=	Brown	1979–95	7
8	Syracuse	1904–78	6
9	Columbia	1895–1929	4
10	Princeton	1985–98	3

* Men's varsity eight-oared shells event

Source: *Intercollegiate Rowing Association Regatta*

The Intercollegiate Rowing Association Regatta, a contest between northeastern universities, has been held since 1895.

TOP 10 ★
WINNERS OF THE MOST SURFING WORLD CHAMPIONSHIPS

	SURFER/COUNTRY	WINS
1	Kelly Slater, US	6
2	Mark Richards, Australia	4
3	Tom Curren, US	3
4 =	Tom Carroll, Australia	2
=	Damien Hardman, Australia	2
6 =	Wayne Bartholemew, Australia	1
=	Derek Ho, US	1
=	Barton Lynch, Australia	1
=	Martin Potter, UK	1
=	Shaun Tomson, South Africa	1
=	Peter Townend, Australia	1
=	Mark Occhilupo, Australia	1
=	Sunny Garcia, US	1

TOP 10 ★
WATERSKIERS WITH THE MOST WORLD CUP WINS

	WATERSKIER/COUNTRY	MALE/FEMALE	SLALOM	JUMP	TOTAL
1	Andy Mapple, UK	M	29	-	29
2	Emma Sheers, Australia	F	2	15	17
3	Jaret Llewellyn, Canada	M	-	16	16
4	Toni Neville, Australia	F	4	7	11
5	Wade Cox, US	M	10	-	10
6 =	Bruce Neville, Australia	M	-	9	9
=	Kristi Overton-Johnson (née Overton), US	F	9	-	9
8	Freddy Krueger, US	M	-	8	8
9	Scot Ellis, US	M	-	7	7
10 =	Susi Graham, Canada	F	6	-	6
=	Carl Roberge, US	M	1	5	6

Waterskiing was invented in 1922 by 18-year-old Ralph W. Samuelson of Lake City, Minnesota, US, using two 2.4-m (8-ft) planks and 30 m (100 ft) of sash cord. It grew in popularity, and the first international governing body, the World Water Ski Union, was established in 1946 in Geneva, Switzerland. Its successor, the International Water Ski Federation, organized the Water Ski World Cup, which by 2000 had expanded to include the Moomba World Cup, the US Masters, the US Open, the French Masters, the Recetto World Cup, the Austrian Masters, the Italian Masters, and the British Masters.

274

What sort of vehicles are used in the Iditarod Race?
see p.277 for the answer
A   Dog sleds
B   Hovercraft
C   Land yachts

TOP 10 ★
OLYMPIC ROWING COUNTRIES

| COUNTRY | GOLD | MEDALS | | TOTAL |
		SILVER	BRONZE	
1 US	29	29	21	79
2 =East Germany	33	7	8	48
=Germany*	21	13	14	48
4 Great Britain	21	16	7	44
5 USSR#	12	20	11	43
6 Italy	14	13	10	37
7 =Canada	8	12	13	33
=France	6	14	13	33
9 Romania	15	10	7	32
10 Australia	7	8	10	25

* *Not including West/East Germany 1968–88*

Includes Unified Team of 1992; excludes Russia since then

TOP 10 ★
FASTEST MEN'S 100-M FREESTYLE TIMES IN THE SUMMER OLYMPICS

SWIMMER/COUNTRY	YEAR	TIME (SECONDS)
1 Pieter van den Hoogenband, Netherlands	2000	47.84
2 Pieter van den Hoogenband	2000	48.30
3 Matt Biondi, US	1988	48.63
4 Pieter van den Hoogenband	2000	48.64
5 Alexander Popov, Russia	2000	48.69
6 Gary Hall Jr., US	2000	48.73
7 =Alexander Popov	1996	48.74
=Michael Klim, US	2000	48.74
9 Michael Klim	2000	48.80
10 Gary Hall Jr.	1996	48.81

Gary Hall Jr., who makes two appearances in this list, in two Olympics, is a member of a family of swimmers. His grandfather Charles Keating was an All-America swimmer at the University of Cincinnati, his uncle was a member of the 1976 US Olympics team, and his father, Gary Hall Sr., won silver medals at the 1968 and 1972 Olympics and a bronze in 1976.

TOP 10 ★
OLYMPIC SWIMMING COUNTRIES

| COUNTRY | GOLD | MEDALS* | | TOTAL |
		SILVER	BRONZE	
1 US	192	138	104	434
2 Australia	45	46	51	142
3 East Germany	38	32	22	92
4 USSR#	18	24	27	69
5 Germany+	12	23	30	65
6 Great Britain	14	22	26	62
7 Hungary	24	20	16	60
8 Japan	15	20	14	49
9 Netherlands	14	14	16	44
10 Canada	7	13	19	39

* *Excluding diving, water polo, and synchronized swimming*

Includes Unified Team of 1992; excludes Russia since then

+ *Not including West/East Germany 1968–88*

WATER BOY

At the 2000 Sydney Olympics, Australia's teenage swimming sensation, Ian Thorpe, added three gold and two silver medals to his country's impressive tally.

SWISS ROLL

The bobsled event has been part of the Winter Olympics since 1924. Switzerland has won more medals than any other country.

TOP 10 ★
MEN'S WORLD AND OLYMPIC FIGURE SKATING TITLES

	SKATER/COUNTRY	YEARS	TITLES
1	Ulrich Salchow, Sweden	1901–11	11
2	Karl Schäfer, Austria	1930–36	9
3	Richard Button, US	1948–52	7
4	Gillis Grafstrom, Sweden	1920–29	6
5 =	Hayes Alan Jenkins, US	1953–56	5
=	Scott Hamilton, US	1981–84	5
7 =	Willy Bockl, Austria	1925–28	4
=	David Jenkins, US	1957–60	4
=	Ondrej Nepela, Czechoslovakia	1971–73	4
=	Kurt Browning, Canada	1989–93	4

TOP 10 OLYMPIC BOBSLEDDING COUNTRIES
(Country/medals)

1 Switzerland, 26 **2** US, 14 **3** East Germany, 13 **4** = Germany*, 11; = Italy, 11
6 West Germany, 6 **7** Great Britain, 4 **8** = Austria, 3; = Soviet Union#, 3
10 = Canada, 2; = Belgium, 2

* Not including East/West Germany 1968–88   # Includes United Team of 1992; excludes Russia since then

TOP 10 ★
SKIERS IN THE 2000/01 ALPINE WORLD CUP (FEMALE)

	SKIER/COUNTRY	OVERALL POINTS*
1	Martina Ertl, Germany	346
2	Janica Kostelic, Croatia	239
3	Michaela Dorfmeister, Austria	186
4	Sonja Nef, Switzerland	166
5	Anja Paerson, Sweden	165
6	Regine Cavagnoud, France	144
7	Christel Saioni, France	135
8	Brigitte Obermoser, Austria	131
9	Andrine Flemmen, Norway	109
10	Karen Putzer, Italy	101

* Awarded for performances in slalom, giant slalom, super giant, downhill, and combination disciplines; as at November 30, 2000

Source: *International Ski Federation*

TOP 10 ★
SKIERS IN THE 2000/01 ALPINE WORLD CUP (MALE)

	SKIER/COUNTRY	OVERALL POINTS*
1	Hermann Maier, Austria	276
2	Lasse Kjus, Norway	246
3	Stephan Eberharter, Austria	240
4	Michael Gruenigen, Switzerland	168
5	Heinz Schilchegger, Austria	152
6	Andreas Schifferer, Austria	140
7	Fredrik Nyberg, Sweden	135
8	Kjetil Andre Aamodt, Norway	131
9	Josef Strobl, Austria	114
10	Didier Cuche, Switzerland	101

* Awarded for performances in slalom, giant slalom, super giant, downhill, and combination disciplines; as at November 30, 2000

Source: *International Ski Federation*

TOP 10 ★
FASTEST MALE SPEED SKATERS*

	SKATER/COUNTRY/DATE	TIME IN SECONDS FOR 500 M
1	Jeremy Wotherspoon, Canada, Jan 29, 2000	34.63
2	Michael Ireland, Canada, Mar 18, 2000	34.66
3	Hiroyasu Shimizu, Japan, Feb 20, 1999	34.79
4	Jan Bos, Netherlands, Feb 21, 1999	34.87
5	Minetaka Sasabuchi, Japan, Jan 29, 2000	35.08
6 =	Toyoki Takeda, Japan, Jan 29, 2000	35.10
=	Syoji Kato, Japan, Mar 18, 2000	35.10
8	Junichi Inoue, Japan, Mar 19, 2000	35.13
9	Patrick Bouchard, Canada, Jan 29, 2000	35.18
10	Sylvain Bouchard, Canada, Mar 28, 1998	35.21

* 500 m; all speeds attained at Calgary

Source: *International Skating Union*

Did You Know? British ski enthusiast Sir Arnold Lunn (1888–1974), credited with introducing the slalom event in 1923, was knighted in 1953 "for services to skiing."

TOP 10 ★
WOMEN'S WORLD AND OLYMPIC FIGURE SKATING TITLES

	SKATER/COUNTRY	YEARS	TITLES
1	Sonja Henie, Norway	1927–36	13*
2 =	Carol Heiss, US	1956–60	6
=	Herma Plank-Szabo, Austria	1922–26	6#
=	Katarina Witt, East Germany	1984–88	6
5 =	Sjoukje Dijkstra, Holland	1962–64	4
=	Peggy Fleming, US	1966–68	4
=	Lily Kronberger, Hungary	1908–11	4
=	Michelle Kwan, US	1996–2001	4
8 =	Tenley Albright, US	1953–56	3
=	Meray Horvath, Hungary	1912–14	3
=	Anett Potzsch, East Germany	1978–80	3
=	Beatrix Schuba, Austria	1971–72	3
=	Barbara Ann Scott, Canada	1947–48	3
=	Madge Syers, GB	1906–08	3
=	Kristi Yamaguchi, US	1991–92	3

* *Irina Rodnina (USSR) also won 13 titles, but in pairs competitions, 1969–80.*

\# *Plus three further titles in pairs competitions*

TOP 10 ★
OLYMPIC FIGURE-SKATING COUNTRIES

	COUNTRY	GOLD	SILVER	BRONZE	TOTAL
1	US	12	13	14	39
2	Soviet Union*	13	10	6	29
3	Austria	7	9	4	20
4	Canada	2	7	9	18
5	GB	5	3	7	15
6	France	2	2	7	11
7 =	Sweden	5	3	2	10
=	East Germany	3	3	4	10
9	Germany#	4	4	1	9
10 =	Hungary	0	2	4	6
=	Norway	3	2	1	6

* *Includes United Team of 1992; excludes Russia since then*

\# *Not including East/West Germany 1968–88*

Figure skating was part of the Summer Olympics in 1908 and 1920, becoming part of the Winter program in 1924.

TOP 10 ★
FASTEST WINNING TIMES OF THE IDITAROD DOG SLED RACE

	WINNER	YEAR	DAY	TIME HR	TIME MIN	TIME SEC
1	Doug Swingley	2000	9	0	58	6
2	Doug Swingley	1995	9	2	42	19
3	Jeff King	1996	9	5	43	19
4	Jeff King	1998	9	5	52	26
5	Martin Buser	1997	9	8	30	45
6	Doug Swingley	1999	9	14	31	7
7	Doug Swingley	2001	9	19	55	50
8	Martin Buser	1994	10	13	2	39
9	Jeff King	1993	10	15	38	15
10	Martin Buser	1992	10	19	17	15

Source: *Iditarod Trail Committee*

The race, held annually since 1973, is named after a deserted mining village along the route. It commemorates an emergency operation in 1925 to get medical supplies to Nome (the race's finish point) after a diphtheria epidemic.

TOP DOUG

Doug Swingley from Simms, Montana, is one of only two non-Alaskans (the other is Martin Buser) to win the grueling 1,864-km (1,158-mile) Anchorage-to-Nome Iditarod dog sled race.

Sporting Miscellany

FASTEST WINNING TIMES FOR THE HAWAII IRONMAN

	WINNER/COUNTRY	YEAR	TIME HR:MIN:SEC
1	Luc Van Lierde, Belgium	1996	8:04:08
2	Mark Allen, US	1993	8:07:45
3	Mark Allen	1992	8:09:08
4	Mark Allen	1989	8:09:16
5	Luc Van Lierde	1999	8:17:17
6	Mark Allen	1991	8:18:32
7	Greg Welch, Australia	1994	8:20:27
8	Mark Allen	1995	8:20:34
9	Peter Reid, Canada	2000	8:21:01
10	Peter Reid	1998	8:24:20

This is perhaps one of the most grueling of all sporting contests, in which competitors engage in a 3.86-km (2.4-mile) swim, followed by a 180-km (112-mile) cycle race, ending with a full marathon (42.195 km/26 miles 385 yards). The first Hawaii Ironman was held at Waikiki Beach in 1978, but since 1981 it has been at Kailua-Kona.

THE 10 LATEST COUNTRIES TO WIN THE WORLD CURLING CHAMPIONSHIPS

(Year/women's/men's)

❶ 2001, Canada, Sweden ❷ 2000, Canada, Canada
❸ 1999, Sweden, Scotland ❹ 1998, Sweden, Canada ❺ 1997, Canada, Sweden
❻ 1996, Canada, Canada ❼ 1995, Sweden, Canada ❽ 1994, Canada, Canada
❾ 1993, Canada, Canada ❿ 1992, Sweden, Switzerland

Curling is a quintessentially Canadian sport. By one estimate, more than 90 percent of the world's curlers are Canadian, and Canadian teams continue to dominate world championships.

UNIVERSITY SPORTS IN CANADA*

	SPORT	UNIVERSITY TEAMS, 2000–01 MEN	WOMEN
1	Basketball	40	39
2	Soccer	37	39
3	=Cross country	32	33
	=Swimming	32	31
5	Hockey	31	26
6	Track and field	28	29
7	Volleyball	26	35
8	Football/Rugby#	24	27
9	Wrestling	17	16
10	Field hockey	–	17

* Based on participation in Canadian Interuniversity Athletic Union (CIAU) sports, ranked by men's university teams

In Canada, university football teams consist of male players only, university rugby teams of female players

Source: CIAU

The 1999–2000 CIAU champions were the Alberta Golden Bears/Pandas, with a total of nine medals.

PHYSICAL RECREATION ACTIVITIES IN CANADA

	ACTIVITY	PERCENT OF POPULATION* (1999) MEN	WOMEN
1	Exercise walking	75	87
2	Gardening, yard work	74	67
3	Swimming	56	53
4	Social dancing	45	48
5	Home exercise	44	46
6	Bicycling	51	39
7	Weight training	35	24
8	Bowling	28	26
9	Golf	36	16
10	Jogging, running	29	21

* Age 18+, participated at least once within the last 12 months; ranked by men's results

Source: 1999 Physical Activity Monitor, Canadian Fitness and Lifestyle Research Institute

ALL-AROUND CHAMPION COWBOYS

	COWBOY	YEARS	WINS
1	Ty Murray	1989–98	7
2	=Tom Ferguson	1974–79	6
	=Larry Mahan	1966–73	6
4	Jim Shoulders	1949–59	5
5	=Joe Beaver	1995–2000	3
	=Lewis Feild	1985–87	3
	=Dean Oliver	1963–65	3
8	= Everett Bowman	1935–37	2
	=Louis Brooks	1943–44	2
	=Clay Carr	1930–33	2
	=Bill Linderman	1950–53	2
	=Phil Lyne	1971–72	2
	=Gerald Roberts	1942–48	2
	=Casey Tibbs	1951–55	2
	=Harry Tompkins	1952–60	2

ROUGH RIDE

Recognized as the "ultimate cowboy championship," the title of PRCA World Champion All-Around Cowboy is the most prestigious title in professional rodeo.

TOP 10 ⭐

HIGHEST-EARNING SPORTSMEN

	SPORTSMAN	SPORT/TEAM	2000 INCOME (US$)
1	Michael Schumacher, Germany	Motor racing, Ferrari	59,000,000
2	Tiger Woods, US	Golf	53,000,000
3	Mike Tyson, US	Boxing	48,000,000
4	Michael Jordan, US	Basketball, Chicago Bulls	37,000,000
5	Dale Earnhardt*, US	Stock car racing	26,500,000
6	Grant Hill, US	Basketball, Detroit Pistons	26,000,000
7	Shaquille O'Neal, US	Basketball, LA Lakers	24,000,000
8 =	Oscar De La Hoya, US	Boxing	23,000,000
=	Lennox Lewis, UK	Boxing	23,000,000
10	Kevin Garnett, US	Basketball, Minnesota Timberwolves	21,000,000

* Killed February 18, 2001, during Daytona 500

Used by permission of Forbes *magazine*

TOP 10 ⭐

MOST WATCHED SPORTING EVENTS ON US TELEVISION

	EVENT	DATE	RATING
1	Super Bowl XVI	Jan 24, 1982	49.1
2	Super Bowl XVII	Jan 30, 1983	48.6
3	XVII Winter Olympics	Feb 23, 1994	48.5
4	Super Bowl XX	Jan 26, 1986	48.3
5	Super Bowl XII	Jan 15, 1978	47.2
6	Super Bowl XIII	Jan 21, 1979	47.1
7 =	Super Bowl XVIII	Jan 22, 1984	46.4
=	Super Bowl XIX	Jan 20, 1985	46.4
9	Super Bowl XIV	Jan 20, 1980	46.3
10	Super Bowl XXX	Jan 28, 1996	46.0

Source: *Nielsen Media Research*

TOP 10 AUSTRALIAN FOOTBALL LEAGUE TEAMS

(Team/Grand Final wins)

① = Carlton Blues, 16; = Essendon Bombers, 16
③ Collingwood Magpies, 14 **④** Melbourne Demons, 12
⑤ Richmond Tigers, 10 **⑥** Hawthorn Hawks, 9
⑦ Fitzroy Lions, 8 **⑧** Geelong Cats, 6 **⑨** Kangaroos (North Melbourne), 4 **⑩** South Melbourne, 3

AUSTRALIAN RULES
The Victorian Football League was formed in 1896, changing its name in 1990 to the Australian Football League.

Did You Know? The first ever rodeo organized as a competition was held at Prescott, Arizona, on July 4, 1888. It was won by Juan Leivas, who won a silver trophy and the title "Best Cowboy."

Index

Acknowledgments

UK research assistants:
Laurence Hill, Manuela Mackenzie

Special US research:
Dafydd Rees with help from Bonnie Fantasia, Linda Rees, and Christiaan Rees

Thanks to the individuals, organizations, and publications listed below that kindly supplied information to enable me to prepare many of the lists.

Caroline Ash, Javier Beltram, Richard Braddish, Pete Compton, Kaylee Coxall, Luke Crampton, Sidney S. Culbert, François Curiel, Philip Eden, Steve Fielding, Christopher Forbes, Russell E. Gough, Monica Grady, Stan Greenberg, Heidi Gyani, Duncan Hislop, Andreas Hörstemeier, Tony Hutson, Alan Jeffreys, Larry Kilman, Robert Lamb, Jo LaVerde, Dr Benjamin Lucas, Chris Mead, Ian Morrison, William Nicholson, William O'Hara, Tony Pattison, Adrian Room, Leslie Roskind, Bill Rudman, Jacob Schwartz, Robert Senior, Lisa E. Smith, Mitchell Symons, Thomas Tranter, Lucy T. Verma, Tony Waltham

Academy of Canadian Cinema and Television (Gemini and Genie Awards), Academy of Motion Picture Arts and Sciences, ACNielsen MMS, adherents.com, *Advertising Age, Airline Business,* Air Transport Intelligence, American Forests, American Institute of Stress, American Society of Composers, Authors, and Publishers, Amnesty International, *Amusement Business, Art Newspaper,* Art Sales Index, Associated Press, Association of Tennis Professionals (ATP), Association of Workers' Compensation Boards of Canada, Audit Bureau of Circulations, Australian Department of Immigration and Multicultural Affairs, Australian Football League (AFL), *Auto Express,* Bank of Canada, Beverage Marketing Corporation, *Billboard,* Booker Prize, Boston Athletics Association, *BP Amoco Statistical Review of World Energy 2000,* BPI, Breeders Cup, Brewers Association of Canada, British Cave Research Association, British Columbia Register of Big Trees, British Columbia Vital Statistics Agency, British Home Office, British Library, British Museum (Natural History), Bureau of Federal Prisons, Business Ethics, Canada Customs and Revenue Agency, Canada Science and Technology Museum, Canadian Academy of Recording Arts & Science (Juno Awards), Canadian Association of Research Libraries, *Canadian Auto World,* Canadian Bankers Association, *Canadian Business,* Canadian Cat Association, Canadian Centre for Justice Statistics, Canadian Council of Fire Marshals and Fire Commissioners, Canadian Fitness and Lifestyle Research Institute, Canadian Football League (CFL), Canadian Forest Service – Science Branch, Canadian Intellectual Property Office, Canadian Interuniversity Athletic Union (CIAU), Canadian Kennel Club, Canadian Life & Health Insurance Association, Canadian Newspaper Association, Canadian Olympic Association, Canadian Press, Canadian Professional Golfers' Association (CPGA), Canadian Real Estate Association, Canadian Recording Industry Association, Canadian Space Agency, Canadian Toy Testing Council, Cannes Film Festival, Carbon Dioxide Information Analysis Center, CARD – Media Information Network, Cat Fancier's Association, CBC Radio Archives, CBC Research, Center for Disease Control, Central Intelligence Agency, Central Statistics Office/An Priomh-Oifig Staidrimh, Ireland, Centre for Education Statistics, *Chainstore Age,* Championship Auto Racing Teams (CART), Christian

Research, Christie's, Citizenship and Immigration Canada, CIVC, *Classical Music,* Columbia University (Pulitzer Prizes), Competitive Media Reporting, Computer Industry Almanac, Council of Administrators of Large Urban Public Libraries, Country Music Association, Crain Communications, Davis Cup, Death Penalty Information Center, De Beers, Deloitte & Touche, Duncan's American Radio, *The Economist, Editor & Publisher Year Book,* Electoral Reform Society, Energy Information Administration, Environmental Technology Center, Ernst & Young, Euromonitor, Eurotoys, *FBI Uniform Crime Reports, Financial Times,* Fleetwood-Owen, *Flight International,* Food and Agriculture Organization of the United Nations, *Forbes, Fortune,* Genealogical Association of the Royal Nova Scotia Historical Society, Geographical Names Board of Canada, Geographical Survey of Canada, Geomatics Canada, Global Reach, *Globe and Mail,* Gold Fields Mineral Services, Goose Lane Editions, *The Handbook of Private Schools,* Harley Medical Group, Hasbro Canada, Hawaii Ironman, Health Canada, Historic Sites and Monuments Board of Canada, Honda UK, House of Commons Reference Library, Iditarod Trail Committee, IMS Health Canada, Indianapolis Motor Speedway, Industry Canada, Institute for Family Enterprise, Bryant College, Institute of Island Studies, Interbrand, Intercollegiate Rowing Association, International Amateur Athletic Association, International Association of Ports and Harbors, International Atomic Energy Agency, International Civil Aviation Organization, International Cocoa Organization, International Coffee Organization, International Commission on Large Dams, International Council of Shopping Centers, International Federation of Red Cross and Red Cross Societies, International Game Fish Association, International Skating Union, International Ski Federation, International Table Tennis Federation, International Telecommunication Union, International Union for the Conservation of Nature, *International Water Power and Dam Construction,* International Water Ski Federation, Inter-Parliamentary Union, JobsCanada, Jockey Club, League of American Theaters and Producers, Lloyds Register of Shipping/MIPG/ PPMS, Magazine Publishers of America, Major League Baseball, Mazda UK, Meat and Livestock Commission, Media Metrix Canada, MediaSTATS, Metropolitan Museum of Art, Metropolitan Opera House, New York, Modern Language Association of America, Montreal Museum of Fine Arts, MuchMusic, MRIB, *M Street,* Music Data Research (Canada), NASA, National Academy of Popular Music, National Academy of Recording Arts and Sciences (NARAS), National Academy of Television Arts and Sciences (Emmy Awards), National Association of Broadcasters, National Association of College Bookstores, National Association of Consumer Agency Administration, National Association of Stock Car Auto Racing (NASCAR), National Basketball Association (NBA), National Book Foundation, National Center for Education Statistics, National Center for Health Statistics, National Center for Injury Prevention and Control, National Collegiate Athletic Association (NCAA), National Fire Protection Association, National Football League (NFL), National Gallery, Washington, DC, National Highway Traffic Safety Administration, National Hockey League (NHL), National Hockey League Players Association, National Hurricane Center, *National Post,* National Public Radio (NPR), National Retail Federation, National Thoroughbred Racing Association, National Wildlife Research Centre – Canadian Wildlife Service, Natural Resources Canada, New South Wales Registry of Births, Deaths and Marriages, Niagara Falls

Museum, Nielsen Media Research, Nobel Foundation, NPD, Office for National Statistics, UK, Ontario Institute for Studies in Education Library, Ontario Jockey Club, Oxford University Press, Parks Canada, PC Data Online, Pet Industry Joint Advisory Council, Phillips Group, Phobics Society, Popular Music Database, Public Library Association, Produktschap voor Gedistilleerde Dranken, Professional Golfers' Association (PGA), Professional Rodeo Cowboys Association (PRCA), Professional Squash Association, Public Broadcasting System (PBS), Publishers Information Bureau, *Publishers Weekly, Raceboat International,* RadioWorks Inc., a division of Hennessy & Bray Communications, *Railway Gazette International,* Recording Industry Association of America (RIAA), Research Director, 1999 PD Profile®, Rogers Video, Royal Aeronautical Society, Royal Canadian Mint, Ryder Cup, Salt Institute, Scott Polar Research Institute, *Screen Digest,* showbizdata, Siemens AG, W.H. Smith, Solo Swims of Ontario, Sotheby's, *Spaceflight,* Sports Business Research Network, *Sports Illustrated,* Standardbred Canada, Stanford Institute for the Quantitative Study of Society, *Statistical Abstract of the United States,* Statistics Canada, Stephen Leacock Associates, Stockholm International Peace Research Institute, *Stores, Sunday Times, Supermarket News, Take One, Television Business International, Theatre World, Time, Top Gear,* Toronto Public Library, Toronto Stock Exchange, Toronto Theatre Alliance (Dora Mavor Moore Awards), Tour de France, Tourism Industries, International Trade Administration, Toyota UK, Transport Canada, UCI Mountain Bike World Cup, UNESCO, UNICEF, United Nations, Universal Postal Union, US Agency for International Development, US Bureau of Economic Analysis, US Bureau of Engraving and Printing, US Bureau of Labor Statistics, US Census Bureau, US Committee for Refugees, US Consumer Product Safety Commission, US Department of Agriculture/Economic Research Service, US Department of Agriculture Forest Service, US Department of Justice, US Department of Transportation, US Geological Survey, US Immigration and Naturalization Service, US National Park Service, US National Science Foundation, *Variety,* Vehicle Information Centre of Canada, VH1, VideoScan, *Video Store,* Volkswagen UK, Ward's Automotive, Warwick Publishing, *Wavelength,* Westbridge Publications, Westminster Kennel Club, Women's International Squash Players Association, Women's National Basketball Association (WNBA), World Association of Newspapers, World Bank, World Cup Skateboarding, World Health Organization, World Intellectual Property Organization, World Motorbike Endurance Championship, World Resources Institute, World Science Fiction Society, World Superbike Championship, World Tourism Organization, Zenith International

Index
Patrica Coward

DK Picture Librarians
Melanie Simmonds

Packager's acknowledgments:
Cooling Brown would like to thank Carolyn MacKenzie for proof reading and Peter Cooling for technical support.

International Book Productions would like to thank John Adams, Sharada Boucher-Sharma, Ken Farr, Richard Herd, Nanda Lwin of Music Data Research (Canada), Gerry Rogers, Ann Therriault, and the librarians at the Toronto Reference Library.

Picture Credits

The publisher would like to thank the following for their kind permission to reproduce their photographs:

(Abbreviations key: t=top, b=bottom, r=right, l=left, c=centre)

Advertising Archives: 199tl.

AKG London: Marion Kalter 121; Tony Vaccaro 122tl.

Allsport: 279; Andrew Redington 266tr; Ben Radford 243l, 260; Clive Brunskill 242l, 245, 273; David Cannon 242c, 267; Doug Pensinger 242r, 263tr; Gary M Prior 246l; Jamie Squire 244; Michael Steele 262bl; Mike Powell 243r, 247bl, 251; Nathan Silow 247tr; Nick Wilson 275; Scott Barbour 255; Shaun Botterill 261, 276tl; Simon Bruty 5bc, 254; Stephen Dunn 253; Stu Forster 272; Tom Herbert 268–269.

Apple Computer: 212.

Aviation Images: Mark Wagner 239.

Bite Communications Ltd: 202tr.

The Booker Prize for Fiction: 99r, 111.

Breitling SA: 46c, 63b.

Capital Pictures: Phil Loftus 145.

China Photo Library: 96b.

Christie's Images Ltd: 99l, 108bl, 118tr, 119br, 123br, 176bl.

Bruce Coleman Ltd: Jeff Foott 34bl.

Corbis: 73tr; Bettmann 158br, 226; Bob Rowan/Progressive Image 195tr, 206bl; C Moore 93r; Daniel Lane 79l, 88tl; Earl Kowall 30r, 44l, 97br; Jack Fields 3, 77br; James Marshall 8l, 18l; Jay Dickman 215t; Jean-Pierre Lescourret 224l, 228; Jim Richardson 26bl; Kevin Fleming 45tl; Michael S Yamashita 155br, 229tl; Natalie Fobes 214bl; Paul A Souders 207tr; Peter Turnley 72l; Phililp James Corwin 71; Richard T Nowitz 22t; Robert Holmes 104tl; Sheldan Collins 103t, 194bl; Stephen Frink 35br; Trisha Rafferty/Eye Ubiquitous 198; Wayne Lawler/Ecoscene 21t.

Brian Cosgrove: 9r, 24–25.

Eyewire: 210l.

Gables: 52bl.

Galaxy Picture Library: D Roddy/LPI 13tl; Gordan Garradd 10tr.

Gettyimages Stone: Antonia Reeve 102tl; Ron Sherman 98l, 105br; Will and Deni McIntyre 19tc; Yann Layma 78l, 85t.

Ronald Grant Archive: 181tr; ©1992 Warner Bros/DC Comics 170br; ©1998 Warner Bros/Brian Hamill 170tl; ©1998 Universal/Dreamworks, photo Bruce Talamon 180bl; ©1996 20th Century Fox 158–159; ©1985 Amblin/Universal 161tl; ©2000 Chan Kam Chuen/Columbia/Sony 163; ©1996 Hollywood Pictures/Buena Vista 168tr; ©2000 Jaap Buitendijk/DreamWorks/Universal 153r, 157br; ©1999 K Wright/New Line 152c, 157tl; ©1997 Keith Hamshire/Eon Productions, photo Keith Hamshire 168bl; ©1961 Paramount 152r, 179; ©1999 Warner Bros, photo Jason Boland 189; ©1999 Ralph Nelson/Castle Rock/Warner Bros 153l, 173; ©1998 Ron Phillips/Hollywood Pictures 152l, 175tr;

©1975 United Artists/Fantasy Films 164; ©1997 Wallace Merie/20th Century Fox/Paramount 156bl; ©1996 Warner Bros/Universal/Amblin 174; ©1996 Working Title/Polygram 165.

Hulton Getty: 60tr.

Kobal Collection: ©1975 Universal (UIP) 159br; ©1989 Columbia 160bl; ©1993 Sam Goldwyn/Renaissance Films/BBC 154; ©1995 New Line Cinema/Entertainment Film 169tr; ©1997 Columbia Tristar 171; ©2000 Arte France/Blind Spot/Dinovi 166; ©2000Bob Marshak/Universal 167; ©1994 Paramount UIP 161br.

London Features International: Jen Lowery 2.

Mclaren Cars Limited (www.mclarencars.com): 227.

The Museum of the Moving Image: 177.

NASA: 10bl, 16; Finley Holiday Films 11t.

Nordfoto: Liselotte Sabroe 240.

Panos Pictures: Caroline Penn 104br.

Amit Pashricha: 211br.

PetExcellence: 277br.

Photodisc: 3, 47l, 51tr, 77l, 192; 218–219, 220–221, 256–257, 258–259.

Popperfoto: 238bl; Reuter 217l.

Redferns: 132tr; Amanda Edwards 147; David Redfern 130br, 138bl; Ebet Roberts 134; Fin Costello 126c, 133br; Graham Salter 150; Harry Herd 131tl; JM International 136tr, 140; Michel Linssen 178; Mick Hutson 5c, 126l, 127r, 139r, 141, 148bl; Nicky J Sims 146; Paul Bergen 126r, 127l, 137r, 142, 149t; Richie Asron 151; Tom Hanley 143tr.

Rex Features: Bill Zygmant 125.

Science Photo Library: 48l; Frank Zullo 12bl; GJLP 49br; Hank Morgan 48tr; Hans-Ulrich Osterwalder 28tl; Laguna Design 27tr; Peter Thorne, Johnson Matthey 203br.

Bill Seebold's Bud Light Racing Team: Rick Stoff 274.

Frank Spooner Pictures: G Mingasson-Liaison 278; Regan/Liaison 172.

Steiff Teddy Bears: Paul & Rosemary Volpp 98l, 114.

Still Pictures: Fritz Polking 33cr.

Swift Imagery, Swift Media: 107.

Sygma: Corbis 235br.

Kim Taylor: 41br.

Topham Picturepoint: 57tc; Associated Press 237tl; Max Nash/SEF 56b; Tony Arruza 29t; Young Joon 65tr.

Toyota (GB) PLC: 229br.

Jerry Young: 37tr.

All other images © Dorling Kindersley.
For further information see: www.dkimages.com